Rabbinic

Reference Bible

The Connection between Tanach and Tradition™

Volume III: Leviticus

cover photo: JeremyWhat/Shutterstock.com
Printed in the United States of America

First printing, 2018

ISBN: 978-1-945091-80-3

Library of Congress Control Number: 2018945513

Set in New Times Roman, Papyrus, and Cambria

Ordering information: Special discounts are available on quantity purchases by
bookstores, corporations, associations, and others. For details, contact the publisher at:

  sales@braughlerbooks.com
  or at 937-58-BOOKS

For questions or comments about this book, please write to:

  info@braughlerbooks.com

Braughler™
Books
braughlerbooks.com

Introduction

In my Torah studies, I look to our Rabbis and sages to understand how we've historically interpreted Scripture. My desire for truth led me to make investments in Philip Blackman's *Mishnayot*, Ramchal's *Derech Hashem*, Midrash Rabbah, *Artscroll*'s *Schottenstein Bavli* and *Yerushalmi* [which is still in production at the time of this publication], *Midrash Tanchuma, Kitzur Shulchan Aruch, Mishneh Torah*, Ramban's Commentary on the Torah, the *Tosefta, Ein Yaakov,* and *Sefer haZohar*, in addition to many other books. In spite of having a library with shelves circling the walls of my office, I found I was not utilizing these books to their fullest. I read them, but found I was incapable of effectively and fully remembering where Tanach passages were referenced. I wanted to use the reference works during my Parashah studies, but I found it impossible to know what pages in these works would provide insight into the Biblical passages I was reading. Therefore, I searched for a reference work [a *Mafteach*, a key, if you will] that would tell me where a verse is discussed in the Rabbinic writings. This search was fruitless. This is when I encountered a hole in *The Connection between Tanach and Tradition*™.

In early 2012, I began creating a reference work I hope will serve our community. The intent is to provide a quick connection between a Biblical passage to the Talmud, the Midrash, or many of the other fascinating and authoritative works by the Rabbis of old. My goal in this compilation is to serve both as a reference work and a daily-use Bible.

The *Jewish Publication Society*'s books and publications have always been impressive. I am glad they upgraded the English of their current Tanach. The public domain-version from 1917, while superior to anything else at the time, was written using King James English. I took that version and changed Middle-English words to more modern usages. Next, I used a public-domain version of the Hebrew text. I positioned the half-million or so references from over 100 reference works and placed them as footnotes at the bottom of each page of the *Rabbinic Reference Bible*.

I wanted to use traditional Jewish texts – ones generally considered authoritative, those of the utmost importance. In my search for these traditional texts, I made every attempt to include all Taanaic and Amoraic text I could locate – the limitations of this was availability, affordability, and my knowledge of the text. This includes the Dead Sea Scroll [Qumran] documents and fragments, *Kitzur Shulchan Aruch*, the Massorah notes, Josephus, Philo, and *Pesikta Rabbati*, among many others.

I began my work by taking my mother's Bible and copying the few reference notes in the center column. I soon discovered this to be a very arduous task. Thus, I searched the Internet and found a website that contained a downloadable document linking verses across the Bible[1]. I made every attempt to show the textual differences between the

---

[1]*The Open Bible — Bible Cross-Reference Data* found at the following URL: http://www.openbible.info/labs/cross-references/cross-reference-data.zip. References from the Christian

Masoretic Text and the DSS Biblical books[2] and the Septuagint[3], because these differences can illumine and provide insight into the differing Biblical autographs. I have also included variants found in the Mesorah[4]. Please refer to *Rabbinic Reference Bible Volume One: Genesis* for the complete bibliography of sources from which non-Biblical sources references came.

Further Comments:

The author and editors would never purport to be perfect, and if only one percent of all the references contained in these volumes are mistakes, that would mean there are more than 6,000 errors. Therefore, our staff would like to ask a favor, our esteemed reader. If you find a missing reference, a spelling error, a grammatical error, or an incorrect reference, please send a correction to the email address below. We will verify the error, correct the mistake, and your name will appear in subsequent printings under a *Special Thanks*. While we cannot make any claims beyond what is stated here, we greatly appreciate anything you do to assist in making this a treasured reference work, B"H.

RabRef@mail.com

Bible that differ from the Jewish Tanach were changed to match the Jewish Tanach. This Reference Data is held by http://openbible.info under a CC-Attribution License, ©2001.

[2] Abegg Jr, Martin & Peter Flint & Eugene Ulrich — *The Dead Sea Scrolls Bible; The Oldest Known Bible Translated for the First Time into English*. New York, NY, Harper Collins Publishers, Inc., ©1999.

[3] Brenton, Sir Lancelot C. L. — *The Septuagint with Apocrypha: Greek and English*. Chicago, IL, Hendrickson Publishers, Inc., ©1851, 1986, 1987, 1990, 1992, 1995, 1997.

[4] Ginsburg L.L.D., Christian D — *Introduction to the Massoretico-Critical Edition of the Hebrew Bible with a Prolegomenon by Harry M Orlinsky; The Masoretic Text: A Critical Evaluation*. New York, NY; Ktav Publishing House Inc., ©1897, 1966.

Table of Contents

Introduction...3
Table of Contents..5
Tractates of Mishnah, Talmuds, and Tosefta..7
    Tractates of Mishnah, Talmuds, and Tosefta...9
    A Brief Introduction to the Tractates 10
    A Brief Introduction to Mishneh Torah 20
    The List of Generations from Moshe Rabbeinu to R'Ashi.......................26
Vayikra...28
    Vayikra..28-53
        [Leviticus 1:1 – 5:26]
    Tzav...54-71
        [Leviticus 6:1 – 8:36
    Shemini 72-89
        [Leviticus 9:1 – 11:47]
    Tazria 90-102
        [Leviticus 12:1 – 13:59]
    Metzora 104-120
        [Leviticus 14:1 – 15:33]
    Acharei Mot 122-139
        [Leviticus 16:1 – 18:30]
    Kedoshim..140-155
        [Leviticus 19:1 – 20:27]
    Emor..156-181
        [Leviticus 21:1 – 24:23]
    Behar Sinai...182-192
        [Leviticus 25:1 – 26:2]
    Bechukkotai 194-208
        [Leviticus 26:3 – 27:34]

Bereshit [12 parashiyot]

Bereshit	Chayyei Sarah	Vayeshev
Noach	Toledot	Mikketz
Lech Lecha	Vayetze	Vayigash
Vayera	Vayishlach	Vayechi

Shemot [11 parashiyot]

Shemot	Yitro	Tetzaveh
Vaera	Mishpatim	Ki Tisa
Bo	Terumah	Vayakhel
Beshallach		Pekudei

Vayikra [10 parashiyot]

Vayikra	Tazria	Emor
Tzav	Metzora	Behar
Shemini	Acharei Mot	Bechukkotai
	Kedoshim	

Bamidbar [10 parashiyot]

Bamidbar	Shelach Lecha	Pinchas
Naso	Korach	Mattot
Beha'alotcha	Chukkat	Massei
	Balak	

Devarim [11 parashiyot]

Devarim	Shoftim	Nitzavim
Vaetchanan	Ki Tetze	Vayelech
Ekev	Ki Tavo	Haazinu
Re'eh		Vezot Habracha

Tractates of Mishnah, Talmuds, and Tosefta

Tractate	Chapters Mishnah	Pages Yerushalmi	Pages Bavli	Chapters Tosefta
Seder Zeraim [11 thus]				
Berachot	9	68	64	6
Peah	8	37	—	4
Demai	7	34	—	8
Kilayim	9	44	—	5
Sheviit	10	31	—	8
Terumot	11	59	—	10
Maaserot	5	26	—	3
Maaser Sheni	5	33	—	5
Challah	4	28	—	2
Orlah	3	20	—	1
Bikkurim	4	13	—	2
Seder Moed [12 thus]				
Shabbat	24	92	157	17
Eruvin	10	65	105	8
Pesachim	10	71	121	10 [Pisha]
Shekalim	8	33	—	3
Yoma	8	42	88	4 [Kippurim]
Succah	5	26	56	4
Beitzah	5	22	40	4 [Yom Tov]
Rosh Hashanah	4	22	35	2
Taanis	4	26	31	3 [Taaniyot]
Megillah	4	34	32	3
Moed Katan	3	19	29	2 [Moed]
Chagigah	3	22	27	3
Seder Nashim [7 thus]				
Yevamot	16	85	122	14
Ketubot	13	72	72	12
Nedarim	11	40	40	7
Nazir	9	47	47	6 [Nezirus]
Sotah	9	47	47	15
Gittin	9	54	90	7
Kiddushin	4	48	82	5

Tractate	Chapters Mishnah	Pages Yerushalmi	Pages Bavli	Chapters Tosefta
Massechta Ketannos [15 thus]				
Avos de R'Nasan	—	—	41	—
Sopherim	—	—	21	—
Semachot	—	—	14	—
Kallah	—	—	8	—
Kallah Rabbati	10	—	—	—
Derek Eretz Rabbah	—	—	11	—
Derek Eretz Zuta	—	—	10	—
Perek Hashalom	—	—	1	—
Gerim	4	—	—	—
Kutim	2	—	—	—
Abadim	3	—	—	—
Sefer Torah	5	—	—	—
Tefillin	1	—	—	—
Tzitzit	1	—	—	—
Mezuzah	2	—	—	—
Seder Nezikin [10 thus]				
Bava Kamma	10	44	119	11
Bava Metzia	10	37	119	11
Bava Batra	10	34	176	11
Sanhedrin	11	57	113	14
Makkot	3	9	24	5
Shevuot	8	44	49	6
Eduyot	8	—	—	3
Avodah Zarah	5	37	76	8
Avos	6	—	—	—
Horayot	3	19	14	2
Seder Kodashim [11 thus]				
Zevachim	14	—	120	13
Menachot	13	—	110	13
Chullin	12	—	142	10 [Shechitat Chullin]
Bechorot	9	—	61	7
Arachin	9	—	34	5
Temurah	7	—	34	4
Kereitot	6	—	28	4
Meilah	6	—	22	3
Tamid	7	—	8	—
Middot	5	—	—	—
Kinnim	3	—	—	—

	Chapters	Pages	Pages	Chapters
Tractate	**Mishnah**	**Yerushalmi**	**Bavli**	**Tosefta**
Seder Naharot [12 thus]				
Kelim	30	—	—	—
Kelim Bava Kamma				7
Kelim Bava Metzia				11
Kelim Bava Batra				7
Ohalot	18	—	—	18 [Achilot]
Negaim	14	—	—	9
Parah	12	—	—	12
Taharot	10	—	—	11
Mikvaot	10	—	—	7
Niddah	10	13	73	9
Machshirin	6	—	—	3
Zavim	5	—	—	5
Tevul Yom	4	—	—	2
Yadayim	4	—	—	2
Uktzin	3	—	—	3

A Brief Introduction to the Tractates

Abadim, *Slaves*, is a minor tractate with three chapters. Since slavery in Israel was never a demeaning institution of chattel who suffered under the indiscriminate machinations of a ruthless master, this tractate provides laws for the ethical treatment of slaves and their integration into the social structure of Israel or the return to their homeland.

Achilot; see *Ohalot*; title of the tractate in Tosefta

Arachin, *Assessments*, has nine chapters in the Mishnah, 34 pages in Bavli, and five chapters in Tosefta. The tractate uses Leviticus 25:25-34 27:10-27 to place a value on items, real estate, personal items, bodily valuations, values for religious injunctions. It ends with a discussion on the Yovel and the redemption of real estate.

Avodah Kochavim, see *Avodah Zara.*

Avodah Zarah, *Idolatry*, also called *Avodah Kochavim*, has five chapters in the Mishnah, 37 pages in Bavli, 76 pages in Bavli, and eight chapters in Tosefta. It provides laws on business dealings with idolaters, the use of images or a part of an image, use of baths or places of worship frequented by idolaters, destroying idols, wine and the idolater, Jews employed in the wine business owned by an idolater, eating or drinking with an idolater, and the prohibitions of wine used in libations.

Avos de Rabbi Natan, the *Fathers According to R'Natan*, is a minor tractate with forty-one chapters. It is a gemara on Tractate *Avos* of the Mishnah. When reading the mishnayos of R'Natan, one can see this work is based a very early [non-redacted] version of *Avos*. It also excludes the sixth chapter now found in *Avos*. The tractate may be dated as early as the middle of the 1st-Century CE. Some versions of Talmud Bavli, like the *Vilna-Romm* edition, place this at the end of *Seder Nezikin*; there it is the first of seven tractates of later or noncanonical origin.

Avot, *Ethics of our Fathers* or *Pirkei Avos*, has five chapters in the Mishnah, but in a later redaction, it was increased to six chapters to accommodate the tradition of reading a chapter a week between Pesach and Shavuos. The sixth chapter is often called *Perek of the Acquisition of Torah, or The Baraisa of Rabbi Meir*. The closest we have to a gemara on Avot is the minor tractate called *Avos de Rabbi Natan*, which is a 41-chapter work on the first five chapters of *Avot*. The version of *Avot* used in the *ARN* is slightly different than the version we now hold, showing that redactive improvements continued until about the time of Rambam. This tractate is a collection of rules and proverbs from about 60 sages who lived between 300 BCE and 200 CE.

Baraisa of Rabbi Meir, see *Avos de Rabbi Natan*

Bava Batra, the *Last Gate*, has 10 chapters in the Mishnah, 34 pages in Bavli, 176 pages in Bavli, 11 chapters in Tosefta. The tractate uses Numbers 27:7-11 to discuss land owned jointly by partners, establishing ownership rights, the laws of commerce, succession via heredity, and legislation for deeds and documents.

Bava Kamma, the *First Gate*, has 10 chapters in the Mishnah, 44 pages in Bavli, 119 pages in Bavli, and 11 chapters in Tosefta. The tractate uses Exodus 21:28-27 22:1-6 to discuss damages and injuries.

Bava Metzia, the *Middle Gate*, has 10 chapters in the Mishnah, 37 pages in Bavli, 119 pages in Bavli, 11 chapters in Tosefta. The tractate uses Exodus 22:6-12 22:24-26, Leviticus 25:14 25:35-37, and Deuteronomy 22:1-4 to discuss found property, buying and selling, trust, lending and renting, hiring, and business partnerships.

Bechorot, *Firstborn*, has nine chapters in the Mishnah, 61 pages in Bavli, and seven chapters in Tosefta. The tractate refers to Exodus 8:12-13 13:2 13:12, Numbers 18:15-18, and Deuteronomy 15:19-20. The tractate provides laws about the firstborn, both of man and animal. [Bechorim is used in reference to humans, while Bechorot is mostly used in reference to animals.]

Beitzah, *Egg*, has five chapters in the Mishnah, 22 pages in Yerushalmi, 40 pages in Bavli, and four chapters in Tosefta [where it is called Yom Tov]. While *Beitzah* means *egg*, it refers to Yom Tov, and it clarifies labors that are prohibited and permitted on holidays. Refer to Exodus 12:16 20:10 and Leviticus 23:3 23:7-8 23:21 23:25 23:35-36; Deuteronomy 5:14

Berachot, *Blessings*, has nine chapters in Mishnah, 68 pages in Yerushalmi, 64 pages in Bavli, and six chapters in Tosefta. This tractate details liturgical rules. Chapters 1 through 3 discuss the Shema; Chapters 4 and 5 discuss the Amidah [Shemoneh Esrei]; Chapters 6 and 7 detail birchat hamazon, Havdalah, and various brachos; Chapter 8 discusses mealtime laws; Chapter 9 contains various nonfood brachos.

Bikkurim, *Firstfruits*, has four chapters in Mishnah, 13 pages in Yerushalmi, and two chapters in Tosefta. The last tractate of *Seder Zeraim* discusses the first fruits that are brought to the Temple. It also details the hermaphrodite or those born of unknown sexual or uncertain sexual [physical] orientation [i.e., the hermaphrodite or androgyne]. Please see Exodus 23:19 and Deuteronomy 26:1-11 for the basis of tractate *Bikkurim*.

Chagigah, *Festival Offerings*, has three chapters in the Mishnah, 22 pages in Yerushalmi, 27 pages in Bavli, and three chapters in Tosefta. Using Exodus 23:14-17 34:18-24, Leviticus 23:37, Numbers 10:10, and Deuteronomy 16:16-17, this tractate describes the laws of the private freewill korbanot [like a shelamim] on Pesach, Shavuos, and Succus. It is also referred in II Chronicles 30:22 35:10-18.

Challah, *Dough*, has four chapters in Mishnah, 28 pages in Yerushalmi, and two chapters in Tosefta. Challah, the dough set aside for the priests, is discussed in Challah. It details the minimum measure, when the obligation takes effect, the tevel prohibition, and its consumption. See Numbers 15:17-21 for the basis of this tractate.

Chullin, *Profane Things*, has 12 chapters in the Mishnah, 142 pages in Bavli, and 10 chapters in Tosefta. It provides laws regarding dietary laws and slaughtering, defining prohibited sacrifices, killing an animal and its offspring on the same day, consuming meat and dairy together, uncleanness from carcasses and creeping things, and setting free the mother bird.

Demai, the *Uncertain Tithe*, has seven chapters in Mishnah, 34 pages in Yerushalmi, and eight chapters in Tosefta. Demai discusses doubtful tithing and its possible purchase. The tractate is based upon Leviticus 22:15, and suggests that produce purchased from amei haaretz [even those who are generally observant] need to be tithed [by the purchaser] prior to consuming or benefitting from the produce.

Derech Eretz Rabbah, is a minor tractate with eleven chapters. It contains ethical and moral teachings, encouraging the reader toward good manners and correct behavior. Some versions of Talmud Bavli place this at the end of *Seder Nezikin*, where it is the fifth of seven tractates of later or noncanonical origin.

Derech Eretz Zutah, is a minor tractate with ten chapters. It contains ethical and moral teachings in the short, disconnected proverbs in the style of *Pirkei Avos*. Some versions of Talmud Bavli place this at the end of *Seder Nezikin*, where it is the sixth of seven tractates of later or noncanonical origin.

Eduyot, *Testimonies*, has eight chapters in the Mishnah, 9 pages in Bavli, and three pages in Bavli. This is a collection of apparently random laws that are discussed elsewhere. It includes laws of niddah, challah, mikvah, customs of the Mikdash and Yerushalayim, purity, zeraim, kiddushin, Rosh Chodesh, the leap year, and the future mission of the navi.

Eivel Rabbati, see *Semachot*

Eruvin, *Combinations*, has 10 chapters in the Mishnah, 65 pages in Yerushalmi, 105 pages in Bavli, and eight chapters in Tosefta. This deals with the extension of Shabbat boundaries. Please refer to Exodus 16:29. The four domains are reshus hayachid, reshus harabim, karmelis, and makom petur.

Ethics of our Fathers, see *Avos*

Gerim, is a minor tractate with four chapters. This is the tractate on *Proselytes*. It provides rules for receiving Gerim, and application of circumcision, Torah, and sacrifice. Further, rules on the greater Jewish community's treatment of the ger toshav. Finally, it ends with a midrash for the proselyte, to explain how there are regarded by God for following after Avraham Avinu.

Gittin, *Divorces*, has nine chapters in the Mishnah, 54 pages in Yerushalmi, 90 pages in Bavli, and seven chapters in Tosefta. This tractate provides information on the laws of divorce as afforded by Deuteronomy 24:1-5. The tractate provides laws on what makes a get legal, witness authentication, how is must be drawn up, cancellation, and laws regarding dowry, alimony, and debt. The essential phrase, "You are free to marry any man," is an essential part of the get.

Great Mourning, see *Semachot*

Horayot, decisions, has three chapters in the Mishnah, 19 pages in Yerushalmi, 14 pages in Bavli, and two chapters in Tosefta. This tractate uses Leviticus 4:1-5:26. The tractate provides laws on how to handle erroneous legal decisions from the Sanhedrin or the Kohen Gadol. The congregational chattat offering and the special korban for the Nasi are discussed. Lastly, the priority for assigning the Aliyah in Torah Service are discussed.

Kallah Rabbati, is a minor tractate with ten chapters. Eliyahu Zuta claims the tractate came out of Beis Rava in Mehuza in the 3rd-Century CE, but an equally strong argument says the author was Rava, a talmid of Yedudai Gaon in the 8th-Century CE. The tractate contains commentary of tractate *Kallah*, information emulating Massechta *Derech Eretz* and the *Perek on the Acquisition of the Torah*, the *Baraisa of R'Meir* which is appended to *Pirkei Avos*. The tractate ends with comments on *The Chapters of Ben Azai*.

Kallah, the Tractate of the *Bride*, is a minor tractate of baraisos with one chapter. It deals with moral purity, chastity, betrothal, and marriage. The tractate is said to have been written by Yedudai Gaon of Babylonia sometime in the 8th-Century CE., but it also is said to have been written by R'Eliezer b'Hyrkanos in the 1st- and 2nd-Centruy CE. Some versions of Talmud Bavli place this at the end of *Seder Nezikin*, where it is the fourth of seven tractates of later or noncanonical origin.

Keilim Bava Batra seven chapters in Tosefta. The tractate deals with issues of tumah.

Keilim Bava Kamma seven chapters in Tosefta. It deals with issues of tumah.

Keilim Bava Metzia 11 chapters in Tosefta. This tractate deals with issues of tumah.

Keilim, *Vessels*, has 30 chapters in the Mishnah. Using Leviticus 11:33-35, this tractate details garments and utensils and the effect ritual impurity has on them. The tractate provides laws detailing the primary source of tumah, the levels of tumah and taharah.

The tractate provides information on the effects of tumah on utensils, earthen vessels, ovens, fireplaces, metal utensils, nonmetal vessels, wooden and leather vessels, marine-animal skins, sealskin, beds, farming implements, carpenter tools, saws, looms, tables, seats and other furniture, riding equipment, footwear, bags, skins [for wine or water], and glass utensils

Kereitot, *Excisions*, has six chapters in the Mishnah, 28 pages in Bavli, and four chapters in Tosefta. The tractate provides the laws regarding punishments that require being cut off from the community. It provides a list of sins that are punished by karet. It provides laws about the offerings of women after childbirth, miscarriage, or flux. Laws pertaining to various sexual sins and other forbidden acts and their associative asham or korban chattat are discussed.

Ketubot, *Marriage Pacts*, has 13 chapters in the Mishnah, 72 pages in Yerushalmi, 112 pages in Bavli, and 12 chapters in Tosefta. This tractate provides laws regarding marriage contracts and dowries, grounds for annulment, issues of women's property, conjugal obligations, penalties for seduction. It also details the superiority of Israel to other lands, and Jerusalem's superiority to other Israeli cities and towns.

Kiddushin, *Betrothal*, has four chapters in the Mishnah, 48 pages in Yerushalmi, 82 pages in Bavli, and five chapters in Tosefta. This tractate speaks on how a man acquires a wife, and how marriages by proxy are handled.

Kilayim, *Mixing*, has nine chapters in Mishnah, 44 pages in Yerushalmi, and five chapters in Tosefta. Kilayim deals with prohibited mixing of animal breeds [Kilei Mehamah], clothing [Kilei Begadim], and plantings [Kilei Zeraim], and grapes [Kilei HaKerem]. It also discusses the important limitations of Kilayim. This tractate is based upon Leviticus 19:19 and Deuteronomy 22:9-11.

Kinnim, *Bird Nests*, has three chapters in the Mishnah and four pages in Bavli. This tractate provides laws for the sacrifices of birds, and the offerings of the poor; it refers specifically to Leviticus 1:14 1:57 12:8 15:14 15:29 and numbers 6:9.

Kippurim, see *Yoma*; title of the tractate in Tosefta

Kodashim, the *Order of Moral and Ethical Teachings*, is the fifth order of the Mishnah. It includes the Temple procedure, the daily morning service, dietary laws, and the devotion afforded to holy objects. It contains eleven tractates: *Zevachim, Menachot, Chullin, Bechorot, Arachin, Temurah, Kereitot, Meilah, Tamid, Middot*, and *Kinnim*.

Kutim, *Samaritans*, is a minor tractate with two chapters. The tractate discusses the Samaritans and whether they should be considered members of the community of the Jews. While the tractate provides a mostly favorable view of Samaritans, it eventually poskins they are gentiles and forbids intermarrying with them. It concludes in a positive manner, however, by claiming they may one day be accepted into the community of Israel.

Maaser Sheni, *Second Tithe*, has five chapters in Mishnah, 33 pages in Bavli, and five chapters in Tosefta. This references the second tithe and its specific timing [the first, second, fourth, and fifth years]. The verses referenced in Tractate *Maaser Sheni* are Leviticus 27:30-31, Deuteronomy 12:17 14:22-29 26:12.

Maaserot, *Tithes*, has five chapters in Mishnah, 26 pages in Yerushalmi, and three chapters in Tosefta. This details the tithes that must be given to the Leviim. Additionally, law regarding produce that is exempt from tevel are discussed. This tractate is based upon Leviticus 2:30-33 and Numbers 18:21-26.

Machshirin, *Preparations*, has six chapters in the Mishnah and three chapters in Tosefta. Leviticus 11:34 and 38 are the basis of this tractate and its discussion about fluids that will render seeds and fruit unclean. Most noted are the seven fluids that impart uncleanness.

Makkot, *Stripes*, has three chapters in the Mishnah, 9 pages in Yerushalmi, 24 pages in Bavli, and five chapters in Tosefta. This deals with the 59 crimes that are punished by stripes, the city of refuge, and the false witness. It uses Numbers 35:10-32 and Deuteronomy 19:1-13 19:16-19 as its base texts.

Massechta Ketannos, or the *Minor Tractates of the Talmud*, is a collection of as many as fifteen units of small gemarot or Mishnayot, that are deemed too small for inclusion. Ramban in *Torat Adam* mentions seven and Eliachim Carmoly printed them under the title *Septem Libri Talmudici Parvi Hiersolymitani*, which was edited by Raphael Kirchheim in 1851. All fifteen are printed in English for the first time by Rev. Dr. Abraham Cohen MA Ph.D. DHL under the title *The Minor Tractates of the Talmud* in 1965 by *Soncino Press*. The tractates include *Avot de Rabbi Natan, Sopherim, Semachot, Kallah, Kallah Rabbati, Derech Eretz Rabbati, Derech Eretz Zutah, Perek Hashalom, Gerim, Kutim, Abadim, Sefer Torah, Tefillin, Tzitzit,* and *Mezuzah*

Megillah, *Scroll*, has four chapters in the Mishnah, 34 pages in Yerushalmi, 32 pages in Bavli, and three chapters in Tosefta. This provides information on why we read *Sefer Rut* on Purim. It also provides for the readings of the Torah on the Four Shabbatot, on Rosh Chodesh, and on Yamim Tovim. It also speaks of the minyan, the recitation of the Shema, and the Birchat Kohanim.

Meilah, *Trespass*, has six chapters in the Mishnah, 22 pages in Bavli, and three chapters in Tosefta. This tractate details the laws regarding misappropriation of holy items. It uses Exodus 29:38-42, Leviticus 5:16-16, and Numbers 28:2-8 as its basis. It also deals with the violation of sacred things, and the exact moment an item becomes holy or sanctified is discussed.

Menachot, *Meal Offerings*, [the plural of *Minchah*] has 13 chapters in the Mishnah, 110 pages in Bavli, and 13 chapters in Tosefta. The tractate uses Leviticus 2:1-16 as its basis. The topics are: intent, validity, consecration of the mizbeach and Shulchan and menorah, defining a handful, preparation of the Shavuos loaves, minchah exceptions, and distribution to the Kohanim.

Mezuzah, *Doorpost*, a minor tractate with two chapters. It provides laws on the permissible material used to make the scroll, the size of the four margins, and the qualifying language that can be used for the writing. It lists the buildings and room upon which a mezuzah should not be affixed. This is the tractate that defines the placement on the right-hand doorpost and defines how it shall be affixed. Since this command is obligatory in Eretz Israel and in the Diaspora, the length of time between the need of a mezuzah and its affixing is defined.

Middot, *Measurements*, has five chapters in the Mishnah and four pages in Bavli. It provides dimensions and descriptions of the Temple and its courts, and it provides laws for the Priestly guards. It discusses the night watches at the Temple. The dimensions of the Temple and mizbeach, and the general architecture of the Temple Complex are provided.

Mikvaot, *Ritual Immersion Baths*, has 10 chapters in the Mishnah and 7 chapters in Tosefta. The tractate discusses ritual baths and reservoirs and the properties that make them permissible, water and uncleanness.

Moed Katan, *Minor or Half Festival*, has three chapters in the Mishnah, 19 pages in Bavli, 29 pages in Bavli, and two chapters in Tosefta [where it is simply called

Moed]. The minor festival days, and Chol HaMoed [the intervening days] of Pesach and Sukkot are detailed in Tractate *Moed Katan*.

Moed, see *Moed Katan*; title of the tractate in Tosefta

Moed, the *Order of the Holidays* and their significant historic importance, is the second order of the Mishnah. It contains twelve tractates: *Shabbat, Eruvin, Pesachim, Shekalim, Yoma, Sukkah, Beitzah, Rosh Hashanah, Taanit, Megillah, Moed Katan*, and *Chagigah*.

Nashim, the *Order of Family Purity*, is the third order of the Mishnah. It contains seven tractates: *Yevamot, Ketubot, Nedarim, Nazir, Sotah, Gittin*, and *Kiddushin*.

Nazir has nine chapters in the Mishnah, 47 pages in Yerushalmi, 66 pages in Bavli, and six chapters in Tosefta. Based upon Numbers 6:2-21, this tractate defines the laws regarding The Vow. It deals with time restriction of Nezirus, how Nezirus works in the Diaspora, and tumat met and the nazir or Kohen Gadol. It ends with a discussion of the Prophet Shmuel's Nezirus.

Nedarim, *Vows*, has 11 chapters in the Mishnah, 40 pages in Yerushalmi, 91 pages in Bavli, and seven chapters in Tosefta. The laws revolving vows as provided in Numbers 30:3-16 are discussed in *Nedarim*. It deals with synonyms for vows, expressions that are not to be deemed as vows, distinction between a vow and an oath, invalid vows and false oaths, what is forbidden when one makes a vow, and canceling a wife's or daughter's vow.

Negaim, *Plague*, has 14 chapters in the Mishnah and 9 chapters in Tosefta. It uses Leviticus 13:1-14:57. It discusses topics related to "leprosy," infections on clothing and in dwellings.

Nezikin, the *Order of Civil and Criminal Law*, is the fourth order of the Mishnah. Its ten tractates include *Bava Kamma, Bava Metzia, Bava Batra, Sanhedrin, Makkot, Shevuot, Eduyot, Avodah Zarah, Avot*, and *Horayot*.

Nezirus, see *Nazir*; title of the tractate in Tosefta

Niddah, *Menstruant*, has 10 chapters in the Mishnah, 13 pages in Yerushalmi, 73 chapters in Tosefta, and nine chapters in Tosefta. The tractate uses Leviticus 12:2-8 15:19-31 to discuss women and their menstrual cycle, as well as conditions that may emulate niddah.

Ohalot, *Tents*, has 18 chapters in the Mishnah and 18 chapters in Tosefta. This tractate provides the laws of a dead body's effect on houses and tents, doorways, fields, and baskets. It uses Numbers 19:14-16 19:22.

Orlah, *Uncircumcised*, has three chapters in Mishnah, 20 pages in Yerushalmi, and one chapter in Tosefta. It discusses the prohibited fruit from [uncircumcised] trees in their first four years. While Orlah generally means foreskin or uncircumcised membrum, it is used here to represent that which is rejected or unclean. Orlah requires one to first define a tree, for non-trees are exempt from Orlah. Therefore, one must refer to b.Berachos 40a for the definition of a tree. See Leviticus 19:23-25 for the basis of this tractate.

Parah, *Red Heifer*, has 12 chapters in the Mishnah and 12 chapters in Tosefta. Using Numbers 19:1-22, this tractate details the rituals surrounding the Parah Adumah [the red heifer] and her ashes. The laws within discuss the age of the heifer, the presence of nonred hair, the slaughtering, burning, the vessels permitted, mingling the ashes, the permitted sources of water, and the use of the hyssop.

Peah, *Corner*, has eight chapters in Mishnah, 37 pages in Yerushalmi, and four chapters in Tosefta. This tractate discusses Peyos [corners of the field, Leviticus 19:9-10 and

23:22], Leket [gleanings, Leviticus 19:9-10], Shichchah [forgotten produce, Deuteronomy 24:19], Peret and Oleilos [fallen and unripe clusters of grapes, Leviticus 19:10, Deuteronomy 24:21], Maaaser Ani [the tithe dedicated to the poor, Deuteronomy 14:28-29], and the Tithing cycle [Deuteronomy 26:12]. All this for the poor, the widow, the orphan, and the resident non-Jew.

Perek Hashalom, *Chapter on Peace*, is a minor tractate with one chapter. It provides a grim description of the sad state of affairs preceding the appearance of Moshiach, whose arrival will bring abiding peace to the world. Some versions of Talmud Bavli place this at the end of *Seder Nezikin*, where it is the seventh of seven tractates of later or noncanonical origin. In the *Vilna Talmud*, this tractate is the eleventh chapter of *Derech Eretz Zutah*.

Perek of the Acquisition of Torah, see *Avos*

Pesachim, *Passovers*, has 10 chapters in the Mishnah, 71 pages in Yerushalmi, 121 pages in Bavli, and 10 chapters in Tosefta [where it is called Pisha]. This tractate provides a basic Pesach Seder [it is in chronological order], the laws of Chag Matzos, and the Korban Pesach. It includes the law related to the prohibition of chametz [consumption, benefit, and possession], the command to eliminate chametz, the mitzvah of matzah, and the command to recount the story of our exodus from Egypt.

Pirkei Avos, see *Avos*

Pisha, see *Pesachim*; title of the tractate in Tosefta

Rosh Hashanah, *New Year*, has four chapters in the Mishnah, 22 pages in Bavli, 35 pages in Bavli, and two chapters in Tosefta. The tractate on the New Year. It refers to Leviticus 23:24-25 and Numbers 29:1. It gives an account of the inauguration of the New Month by the Nasi and the Av Beis Din of the Sanhedrin, the form and use of the shofar, the witnesses and announcement, and the Rosh Hashanah service.

Sanhedrin, *Courts*, has 11 chapters in the Mishnah, 57 pages in Bavli, 113 pages in Bavli, 14 chapters in Tosefta. This is the tractate that outlines the Sanhedrin [courts of three, 23, or 71 judges], the rights of the Kohen Gadol, the rights of the King in regard to judging. It discusses lawsuits, objections in court, examining witnesses, ruling members of the court or its proceedings as ineligible to participate, and the application of punishment for capital crimes.

Sefer Torah, the *Tractate on the Torah Scroll*, is a minor tractate with five chapters, and contains similarities with the first five chapters of *Sopherim*. It describes the material one must use to write a Sefer Torah and the languages permitted. It provides some of the differences between the LXX and the MT, and provides information on sheets, columns, and open and closed parashiyot of the Sefer Torah. It legislates the number of spaces required between letters, words, parashiyot, columns, and books, blanks spaces, the size of top and bottom margins, sewing and mending, and the disposal of unusable pages. The last chapter details what to do when the Name of God is written on someone's body, and how to properly dispose of sacred writings.

Semachot, is a minor tractate with fourteen chapters, is called the *Tractate of Joy*. One must understand this is a euphemistic title since it contains baraisos of mourning for the dead. This collection, originally called *Eivel Rabbati*, or *Great Mourning*, was compiled by R'Eliezer b'Tzadok in the 1st-Century CE. It was redacted in the 2nd-Century in Babylon by R'Chiyya. Some versions of Talmud Bavli place this at the end of *Seder Nezikin*, where it is the third of seven tractates of later or noncanonical origin.

Shabbat, *Sabbath*, has 24 chapters in the Mishnah, 92 pages in Yerushalmi, 157 pages in Bavli, and 17 chapters in Tosefta. The tractate deals with labors that are prohibited on Shabbos. Using Exodus 20:8-10 as a starting point, the tractate uses dozens of additional passages to determine the 39 categories [Avos] of prohibited labor. From the Avos, additional tolados [derivative labors] can be extrapolated.

Shechitat Chullin, see *Chullin*; title of the tractate in Tosefta

Shekalim, *Half-Shekel Temple Tax*, has eight chapters in the Mishnah, 33 pages in Yerushalmi, and three chapters in Tosefta. See Exodus 30:11-16 for the basis of the half-shekel Temple tax. This half-shekel "kippah" tax was paid annually when the Temple stood. This tax was used to pay for the Temple offerings; it also was used to pay the wages of scholars who taught the Kohanim how to perform the Avodah. Every Jew, whether in Eretz Israel or in the Diaspora, was required to pay this tax; this also afforded him the ability to be included in atonement the sacrifice provided.

Sheviit, *Sabbatical Year*, has 10 chapters in the Mishnah, 31 pages in Yerushalmi, and eight chapters in Tosefta. This tractate discusses the Sabbatical year and the dissolution of personal debts. This law became the obligatory fourteen years after our arrival in the land under Joshua, since the Text says the main conquest took seven years to complete. Another thought says it began on the seventh year of the conquest since Torah states the marker by which we use to determine the cycle is *when you enter the land*. The Shmittah was not observed during the 490-year monarchy, since a galut of 70 years was decreed against us. The tractate is based upon Exodus 23:10-11, Leviticus 25:1-8, Leviticus 25:20-22, and Deuteronomy 15:1-11.

Shevuot, *Oaths*, has eight chapters in the Mishnah, 44 pages in Yerushalmi, 49 pages in Bavli, and six chapters in Tosefta. It refers to Exodus 22:6-10 and Leviticus 5:4-5 5:21-22. The tractate classifies oaths and provides penalties for violating them. Laws regarding deposits is provided. *Shevuot* also discusses defilement, leprosy, and how to handle one who enters the Temple in a state of impurity.

Sopherim, is a minor tractate with twenty-one chapters. This details the laws and regulations for the scribe. This tractate details the material and the personal piety required to copy Torah scrolls and other documents used for religious purpose. The tractate is said to date to the middle of the 8th-Century CE. Some versions of Talmud Bavli place this at the end of *Seder Nezikin*, where it is the second of seven tractates of later, noncanonical origin.

Sotah, *Suspected Wife*, has nine chapters in the Mishnah, 47 pages in Yerushalmi, 49 pages in Bavli, and 15 chapters in Tosefta. While this command may never have been used, Tractate Sotah nonetheless defines the laws of the wife suspected of adultery. It is based upon Numbers 5:11-31. The tractate defines how a husband must warn his wife, how she must be brought to the Sanhedrin, preparation of the bitter waters, and what to expect when she drinks the water. It also deals with the priest's speech prior to war, the heifer whose neck is broken, prophesies of the Messianic era, and various laws on holiness and piety.

Sukkah, *Tent*, has five chapters in the Mishnah, 26 pages in Yerushalmi, 56 pages in Bavli, and four chapters in Tosefta. His tractate delineates the laws of Chag Succus or Sukkot. The tractate is based upon Leviticus 23:33-36 23:42, Numbers 29:12-39, and Deuteronomy 16:13-17. The tractate provides rules for constructing a sukkah, sleeping and eating, the lulav and esrog, the water libation service, sounding the shofar, the sacrifices of Succus, and the Kohen divisions and how the sacrifices and showbread are shared.

Taanit, *Fasting*, has four chapters in the Mishnah, 26 pages in Yerushalmi, 31 pages in Bavli, and three chapters in Tosefta [where it is called *Taaniyot*]. This tractate provides information on the minor public fast days. Also included are rules for prayers and fasting for rain, continuation of hostilities or floods, and information on the 17ᵗʰ of Tammuz, the 9ᵗʰ of Av, and Yom Kippur.

Taaniyot, see *Taanit*; title of the tractate in Tosefta

Taharot, Purifications, has 10 chapters in the Mishnah and 11 chapters in Tosefta. While the title is rather euphemistic, as it should be called *Tumos*. It details with lesser impurities that last only until sunset as well as uncleanness of the Leviim. The tractate refers to Leviticus 11:24-28.

Taharot, the *Order of Cleanliness*, is the sixth order of the Mishnah. Its name is more euphemistic than accurate since *Order Taharot* really deals with issues of uncleanness. Its twelve tractates include *Keilim, Ohalot, Negaim, Parah, Taharot, Mikvaot, Niddah, Machshirin, Zavim, Tevul Yom, Yadayim,* and *Uktzin*.

Tamid, *Twice-Daily Sacrifice*, has seven chapters in the Mishnah and nine pages in Bavli. It refers to Exodus 29:38-42 and Numbers 28:20-8 for the laws regarding the Tamid. The daily and the Shabbat morning Synagogue service is designed to be a remembrance of the Tamid. The tractate provides information on the Kohanim watches, removal of ash from the mizbeach, cleansing the mizbeach, arrangement of wood on the altar, drawings lots for duty, when in the morning the Tamid is performed, the daily morning prayer in the Temple, the Birchat Kohanim, and the Tehillim sung on various weekdays.

Tefillin, *Phylacteries*, is a minor tractate with one chapter. It details the materials and language permitted to write the scroll encased in the tefillin. It is forbidden to treat tefillin with disrespect. It provides laws on the placement of the Rosh tefillin above the eyes and the Yad tefillin on the arm. The tractate finally discusses when tefillin can be worn and when they cannot be worn, and why the command, along with tzitziyos and mezzuzos, is so important.

Temurah, *Substitution*, has seven chapters in the Mishnah, 34 pages in Bavli, and four chapters in Tosefta. The tractate defines the laws when one wants to exchange a dedicated item for another. Like Arachin, it refers to Leviticus 27:10-27. The tractate defines who can make substitution and what items are permitted to be exchanged. It provides laws for water used in Mikvaot, water for sprinkling. It makes a distinction between communal and individual korbanot, and the contrast between the bechorot and the tenth to pass under the rod.

Terumot, *Heave Offerings*, has 11 chapters in the Mishnah, 59 pages in Yerushalmi, and 10 chapters in Tosefta. The tractate provides information on which produce is subject to terumah, establishing produce as tevel, the required measure, how it is separated, the blessing of terumah, and its consumption. This tractate is based upon Leviticus 22:4-7 22:14, Numbers 18:8 18:12 18:24 18:26, and Deuteronomy 14:22 18:4.

Tevul Yom, *Immersed During the Day*, has four chapters in the Mishnah and two chapters in Tosefta. This tractate provides the laws for one who has performed the mikveh but is now waiting for sunset to be rendered fully taharah.

Tractate of Joy, see *Semachot*

Tumot, see *Taharot* [the tractate, not the order]

Tzitzit, *Fringes*, is a minor tractate with one chapter. The tractate discusses one whom and what garments are subject to the requirement of tzitzit. Herein, the discussion on whether the absence of blue or white disqualifies the tzitzit. Chillazon is herein declared to be the only blue that qualifies as kosher for tzitzit.

Uktzin*, Stalks*, has three chapters in the Mishnah and three chapters in Tosefta. The tractate deals with the laws on how fruit, stalks, and their shells are protected from uncleanness, are susceptible in tumah, or how they convey uncleanness.

Yadayim*, Hands*, has four chapters in the Mishnah and two chapters in Tosefta. This tractate provides the laws regarding uncleanness of hands and their purification.

Yevamot*, Sister Wives*, has 16 chapters in the Mishnah, 85 pages in Yerushalmi, 122 pages in Bavli, and 14 chapters in Tosefta. This tractate uses Leviticus 18:18 and Deuteronomy 25:5-10 to discuss Levirate marriage, chalitzah, the right of refusal, remarriage, and issues of reporting death.

Yom Tov, see *Beitzah*; title of the tractate in Tosefta

Yoma*, The Day*, has eight chapters in the Mishnah, 42 pages in Yerushalmi, 88 pages in Bavli, and four chapters in Tosefta [where it is called *Kippurim*]. The tractate provides information on the Yom Kippur from start to completion, its laws, the korbanot associated with the Tom Tov [the two inner chattat, the three outer chattat, and various olos]. The tractate refers to Leviticus 16:3-34 23:26-32 and Numbers 29:7-11.

Zavim*, One with a Discharge*, has four chapters in the Mishnah and five chapters in Tosefta. This tractate and Leviticus 15:2-18 provide laws regarding the sufferer of inexplicable emissions, which some attribute to gonorrhea and other STDs. The laws specify the number of clean days requires and the cleansing process to be considered taharah.

Zeraim, the *Order of Seeds*, is the first order of the Mishnah. Its eleven tractates include *Berachot, Peah, Demai, Kilayim, Sheviit, Terumot, Maaserot, Maaser Sheni, Challah, Orlah*, and *Bikkurim*.

Zevachim*, Sacrifices*, has 14 chapters in the Mishnah, 120 pages in Bavli, and 13 chapters in Tosefta. This tractate refers to Leviticus 1:1-4:35. Topics discussed include: the intent required for korbanot, invalidation of a korban, sprinkling of blood, where and how different animals are sacrificed, the ramp, the vessels, how holiness of the mizbeach is communicated, cleansing garments and utensils, offences at the altar, sacrificing outside the temple.

A Brief Introduction to Mishneh Torah

The commandments of Hashem [as given by the hand of Moshe Rebbeinu] are not as easy to apply to our lives as we would first expect or desire. Since the commandments were given to the Jewish people through Moshe, the complexities and particulars of obedience were determined in antiquity by the sages of Israel. Like it or not, Moshe told us, *You shall not do as we are doing here today, each doing whatever is right in his own eyes; because[5] you have not come to the rest and to the inheritance, which Hashem your God is giving you[6]*. This means, we do not have the right to create a different way to perform the command of mezuzah or tefillin, or even to determine a new way to write the Torah of Moshe. New challenges and circumstances that arise through human intervention must be handled in a way that does not contradict the sages of old[7].

In order to make it easier to sail the Sea of Talmud, Rambam took the Mishnayos and the baraisos found in Shas and arranged them into categories[8]. With it, one can get an excellent foundation in Taryag Torah, the 613 Commands of Moshe.

Shemoneh Perakim — Rambam's commentary on m.Avos. Chapter One: The soul and its powers; Chapter Two: Nature of the soul's power; Chapter Three: Spiritual illness; Chapter Four: Healing the spiritually sick; Chapter Five: Directing power to one goal; Chapter Six: The difference between the righteous and one who overcomes desire; Chapter Seven: The veils and how they operate; Chapter Eight: Human nature.

Pirkei Avot — Containing the Commentary of the Ramban in five chapters.

Pirkei Avos Chapter Six — Containing the Commentary of the Ramban.

Introduction to Perek Chelek — Ramban's introduction to b.Sanhedrin Chapter Ten, containing the Thirteen principles of Faith.

R'Chaninia b'Akashya said... — Ramban's commentary on m.Makkos 3:16, which is the last mishnah of the tractate.

Ramban's Introduction to Mishnah Torah — Ramban divides the mishnayos into fourteen books.

Positive Commandments — Ramban's 248 positive mitzvot are listed in Volume IV of *Rabbinic Reference Bible.*

Negative Commandments — Ramban's 365 negative mitzvot are listed in Volume IV of *Rabbinic Reference Bible.*

Sefer Rishon: Hamada - The Book of Knowledge — This contains all the commands related to the foundations of the faith, from which all observance stems.

1. **Hilchot Yesodei haTorah** — *The Foundations of the Torah* contain six positive and four negative commands in ten chapters.
2. **Hilchot De'ot** — *The Laws of Personal Development* contain five positive and six negative commandments in seven chapters.

---

[5] i.e., *this is why*
[6] Deuteronomy 12:8-9
[7] i.e., how do internal-combustion or electric vehicles, household furnaces, electric lights, or laser and infrared door motion sensors fit into a Shomer Shabbos lifestyle.
[8] This section relies heavily on the 31-volume work of R'Moshe ben Maimon [aka Rambam, Maimonides] as translated by R'Eliyahu Touger *Mishneh Torah*, *Moznaim Publishing Corporation*, Jerusalem, Israel ©1994.

3. **Hilchot Talmud Torah** — *The Laws of Torah Study* contain two positive commandments in seven chapters.

4. **Hilchot Avodat Kochavim v'Chokkoteichem** — *The Laws Against Worshipping the Stars and the Statues of the Idolaters* contain two positive and 49 negative commands in 12 chapters.

5. **Hilchot Teshuvah** — *The Laws of Return* contains one positive command in 10 chapters.

Sefer Sheni: Sefer Ahavah - The Book of the Love of G-d — This includes all the commands related to loving and remembering God. At the end of this sefer, Ramban includes *Seder Tefilos Kol Hashanah*, which can be translated as *Order of Prayers for the Whole Year*. It is an interesting study for one to compare the modern order of service to Ramban's order.

1. **Hilchot Kriat Shema** — *The Laws of Reciting Shema* contains one positive commandment in four chapters.

2. **Hilchot Tefilah u'Birkat Kohanim** — T*he Laws of Prayer and the Blessing of the Priests* contain two positive commands in 15 chapters. This is often shortened to *Hilchot Tefilah. The Laws of the Priestly Blessing* [*Hilchot Nesiat Kapayim*] begins on Chapter 14.

3. **Hilchot Tefillin u'Mezuzah v'Sefer Torah** — *The Laws of Tefillin, Mezuzah, and Torah Scrolls* contain five positive commandments in 10 chapters. *Hilchot Mezuzah* begins on Chapter 5 and *Hilchot Sefer Torah* begins on Chapter 7.

4. **Hilchot Tzitzit** — *The Laws of Tzitzit* contains one positive commandment in three chapters.

5. **Hilchot Berachot** — *The Laws of Blessing* contains one positive commandment in 11 chapters.

6. **Hilchot Milah** — *The Laws of Circumcision* contains one positive commandment in three chapters.

Sefer Shelishi: Sefer Zemanim - The Book of Seasons — This contains all the commands related to moadim, specified times, and holidays.

1. **Hilchot Shabbat** — *The Laws of Sabbath* contain two positive and three negative commands in 30 chapters.

2. **Hilchot Eruvin** — *The Laws of Boundaries* contain eight chapters, discussing one or two positive Rabbinic commandments, depending upon one's perspective. The focus of the first five chapters is on the establishment of boundaries, *eruvim*, around courtyards for the purpose of carrying on Shabbat and Yamim Tovim. The remaining three chapters offers the extension of Shabbat walking distances through *eruv t'chumim*. Since the name *eruv* is used in both mitzvot, some view these as one mitzvot, yet they appear to be different.

3. **Hilchot Shevitat Asor** — *The Laws of Refraining on the Tenth* contain two positive and two negative commands in three chapters. This relates to the rest required on Yom Kippur, the Tenth of Tishrei.

4. **Hilchot** Shevitat Yom Tov — *The Laws of Refraining on Holidays* contain six positive and six negative commandments in eight chapters.

5. **Hilchot Chametz u'Matzah** — *The Laws of Leavening and Unleavened Bread* contain three positive and five negative commandments in eight chapters. Ramban ends the section with his basic text of the Haggadah.

6. **Hilchot Shofar, Sukkah, v'Lulav** — *The Laws of Shofar, Sukkah, and Lulav* contain three positive commands in eight chapters. *Hilchot Shofar* begins in

Chapter One. *Hilchot Sukkah* begins in Chapter Four. *Hilchot Lulav* begins in Chapter Seven.

7. **Hilchot Shekalim** — *The Laws of the Half Shekel* contains one positive commandment in four chapters. This is in relation to the one-yearly half-shekel tax for Temple upkeep. This is included in *Sefer Zemanim* because the half-shekel is collected during the month of Adar.

8. **Hilchot Kiddush HaChodesh** — *The Laws of Renewing the Month* contains one positive commandment in 19 chapters.

9. **Hilchot Taaniyot** — *The Laws of Fasting* contains one positive command in five chapters.

10. **Hilchot Megillah v'Chanukkah** — *The Laws of Reading the Megillah and of Hanukkah* contains two rabbinic positive commandments in four chapters.

Sefer Revii: Sefer Nashim - The Book of Women — This includes all the mitzvot involving intimate relations.

1. **Hilchot Ishut** — *The Laws of Marriage* detail two positive and two negative commandments in 25 chapters.

2. **Hilchot Gerushin** — *The Laws of Divorce* contains one positive and one negative command in 13 chapters. The Mizbeach cries when a couple divorces [b.Gittin 90b].

3. **Hilchot Yibbum v'Chalitzah** — *The Laws of Yibum* [Marrying One's Childless Brother] *and Chalitzah* [Freeing the Widow From the Obligation] contain two positive and one negative commandment in eight chapters. During Ramban's time, the Ashkenazi communities no longer practiced yibbum.

4. **Hilchot Naarah Betulah** — *The Laws of the Young Maiden* contain three positive and two negative commandments in three chapters.

5. **Hilchot Sotah** — *The Laws of the Woman Who Deviates* contains one positive and two negative commands in four chapters. This mitzvah requires the Temple.

Sefer Chamishi: Sefer Kedushah - The Book of Holiness — All the commands God uses to sanctify and separate us from the nations, specifically related to forbidden relations and forbidden foods are included herein.

1. **Hilchot Issurei Biah** — *The Laws of Forbidden Sexual Relations* contains one positive and 36 negative commandments in 22 chapters.

2. **Hilchot Ma'achalot Assurot** — *The Laws of Forbidden Foods* contain four positive and 24 negative commandments in 17 chapters.

3. **Hilchot Shechitah** — *The Laws of Ritual Slaughtering* contain three positive and two negative commands in 14 chapters.

Sefer Shishi: Sefer Hafla'ah - The Book of Promises — This includes the command regarding oaths and vows [nedarim]. This is also called *The Book of Utterances.*

1. **Hilchot Shevuot** — *The Laws of Oaths* contain one positive and four negative commandments in 12 chapters.

2. **Hilchot Nedarim** — *The Laws of Vows* include two positive and one negative commandments in 13 chapters.

3. **Hilchot Nazirut** — *The Laws of the Nazirite Vow* contain two positive and eight negative commands in 10 chapters.

4. **Hilchot Arachim v'Charamim** — *The Laws of Endowment and Cherem* contain five positive and two negative commandments in eight chapters. *Hilchot Arachim*

are found in chapters One through Five. *Hilchot Charamim* is found in Chapters Six and Seven.

Sefer Shevii: Sefer Zeraim - The Book of Seeds — This includes all the commandments related to Eretz Israel, which includes tithing, Shmittah, and Yovel. This is also called *The Book of Agriculture.*

5. **Hilchot Kilayim** — *The Laws of forbidden Mixtures* contain five negative commandments in ten chapters.

6. **Hilchot Matnot Aniyim** — *The Laws of Gifts to the Poor* contain seven positive and six negative commands in ten chapters

7. **Hilchot Terumot** — *The Laws of the 24 Gifts* contain two positive and six negative commandments in 15 chapters.

8. **Hilchot Maaserot** — *The Laws of Tithing* contain one positive command in 14 chapters

9. **Hilchot Maaser Sheni v'Nata Revai** — Th*e Laws of the Second Tithe and the Fourth-Year Produce* contain three positive and six negative commandments in 11 chapters. *Hilchot Maaser Sheni* are in Chapters One through eight. *Hilchot Nata Revai* are detailed in Chapters Nine through 11.

10. **Hilchot Bikkurim Im Shear Matnos Kehunah Shebagevulin** — *The Laws of Choice Fruits and Gifts to Kohanim in Outlying Regions* contain eight positive and one negative commandments in 12 chapters.

11. **Hilchot Shemitah v'Yovel** — *The Laws of the Sabbatical Year and the Year of Jubilee* contain nine positive and 13 negative commandments in 13 chapters. *Hilchot Shemitah* are found in Chapters One through Nine. *Hilchot Yovel* run from Chapter 10 through 13.

Sefer Shemini: Sefer HaAvodah - The Book of Service — This book details all the mitzvot related to the Temple construction and its communal service.

1. **Hilchot Beit haBechirah** — *The Laws of His Choice House* contain three positive and three negative commands in eight chapters.

2. **Hilchot Klei Hamikdash v'Haovdim Bo** — *The Laws of the Temple Utensils and Those Who Serve Here* contain six positive and eight negative commandments in 10 chapters. The Anointing Oil is detailed in Chapters One; Incense The Ketoret in Chapter Two. The Levi are contained in Chapter Three. The Kohen are detailed in Chapter Four. The Kohen Gadol in Chapter Five. The Ivri are detailed in Chapter Six. The 15 officers are detailed in Chapter Seven. The Bigdei Kehuna are detailed in Chapter Eight. The head plate is detailed in Chapter Nine. The order of the Bigdei Kehuna is detailed in Chapter 10.

3. **Hilchot Biat Hamikdash** — *The Laws of Entering the Temple* contains two positive and 13 negative commands in nine chapters.

4. **Hilchot Issurei Mizbeach** — *The Laws of Korban Forbidden to be Offered on the Altar* contains four positive and ten negative commands in seven chapters.

5. **Hilchot Maaseh Hakorbanot** — *The Laws of the Procedures of Sacrifice* contain 10 positive and 13 negative commandments in 19 chapters.

6. **Hilchot Temidim u'Musafim** — *The Laws of Continual and Additional Offerings* contain 18 positive and one negative commands in 10 chapters.

7. **Hilchot Pesulei Hamukdashim** — T*he Laws of Consecrated items that Become Disqualified* contain two positive and six negative commands in 19 chapters.

8. **Hilchot Avodat Yom haKippurim** — *The Laws of the Service of Yom Kippur* spend five chapters explaining one mitzvah, which is actually located in the first perek of Acharei Mot, the sixth parshah of Leviticus.

9. **Hilchot Meilah** — *The Laws of Misappropriated Items of Kedushah* contain one positive and two negative commandments in eight chapters.

Sefer Teshiit: Sefer Korbanot - The Book of Sacrifices — Included herein are all the commands regarding the korbanot brought by the individual.

1. **Hilchot Korban Pesach** — *The Laws of the Passover Offering* contain four positive and 12 negative commandments in 10 chapters.

2. **Hilchot Chagigah** — *The Laws of the Festival Offering* contain four positive and two negative commands in three chapters.

3. **Hilchot Bechorot** — *The Laws of the Firstborn Offering* contain two positive and three negative commands in eight chapters.

4. **Hilchot Shegagot** — *The Laws of Offerings for Unintentional Transgressions* contain five positive commandments in 15 chapters.

5. **Hilchot Mechusrei Kapparah** — *The Laws of Offerings Brought By Those with Incomplete Atonement* contain four positive commandments in five chapters.

6. **Hilchot Temurah** — *The Laws of Transferring Kedushah from One Korban Animal to Another* contain one positive and two negative commandments in four chapters.

Sefer Asiri: Sefer Taharah - The Book of Ritual Purity — This book contains all the command related to issues of tahor [purity] and tamei [contamination].

1. **Hilchot Tumat Meit** — *The Laws of Impurity Communicated by a Human Corpse* contain one positive commandment in 25 chapters.

2. **Hilchot Parah Adumah** — *The Laws of the Red Heifer* contain two positive commandments in 15 chapters.

3. **Hilchot Tumat Tzaraat** — *The Laws of Impurity Communicated by a Metzorah* contain six positive and two negative commands in 16 chapters.

4. **Hilchot Metamei Mishkav u'Moshav** — T*he Laws of Imparting Impurity to Places One Sits and Lies* contain four positive commandments in 13 chapters.

5. **Hilchot Shear Avot haTumah** — *The Laws of Primary Sources of Impurity* contain three positive commandments in 20 chapters.

6. **Hilchot Tumat Ochalin** — *The Laws of Impurity Contracted by Food* contain one positive command in 16 chapters.

7. **Hilchot Keilim** — *The Laws of Impurity Contracted by Vessels* contain three positive commandments in 28 chapters.

8. **Hilchot Mikvaot** — *The Laws of Ritual Baths* contain one positive command in 11 chapters.

Sefer Echad-Esrei: Sefer Nezikim - The Book of Injuries — This includes all the commands regulating the relations between a person and his neighbor, specifically relating to personal injury or property damage. This is also called *The Book of Damages*.

1. **Hilchot Nizkei Mammon** — *The Laws of Property Damage* contain four positive commandments in 14 chapters.

2. **Hilchot Geneivah** — *The Laws of the Thief* contain two positive and five negative commandments in nine chapters.

3. **Hilchot Gezelah v'Avedah** — *The Laws of Theft and Lost Property* contain two positive and five negative commands in 18 chapters.

4. **Hilchot Chovel u'Mazik** — *The Laws of Personal Injury* contains one positive commandment in eight chapters.
5. **Hilchot Rotzeach u'Shmirat Nefesh** — *The Laws of Murder and Sanctity of Human Life* contain seven positive and 10 negative commands in 13 chapters.

Sefer Shenaim-Esrai: Sefer Kinyan - The Book of Acquisition — This book details all the command related to acquisition and the sale of product.
1. **Hilchot Mechirah** — *The Laws of Selling* contain one positive and four negative commands in 30 chapters.
2. **Hilchot Zechiyah u'Matanah** — *The Laws of Acquisition and Gifts* contains no specific mitzvot, but communicates basic business ethics in 12 chapters.
3. **Hilchot Shechenim** — *The Laws of Relationships with Neighbors* contains no specific mitzvot, but communicates basic relationship ethics in 14 chapters.
4. **Hilchot Sheluchin v'Shutafin** — *The Laws of Mediators and Associates* contains no specific mitzvot, but communicates basic business ethics in 10 chapters.
5. **Hilchot Avadim** — *The Laws of Servants* contain five positive and eight negative commandments in nine chapters.

Sefer Shelosh-Esrai: Sefer Mishpatim - The Book of Judgments — This includes all the commands regulating the relations between a person and his neighbor, not related to personal injury or property damage.
1. **Hilchot Sechirut** — T*he Laws of Rentals and Relationships between Employers and Employees* contain three positive and four negative commandments in 13 chapters.
2. **Hilchot Sheilah u'Fikadon** — *The Laws of Borrowing and Caring for Items of Another* contain two positive commandments in eight chapters.
3. **Hilchot Malveh v'Loveh** — *The Laws of Lenders and Borrowers* contain four positive and eight negative commandments in 27 chapters.
4. **Hilchot Toen v'Nitan** — *The Laws of Plaintiffs and Defendants* contains one positive commandment in 16 chapters.
5. **Hilchot Nachalot** — *The Laws of Inheritance* contain one positive commandment in 11 chapters.

Sefer Arbaa-Esrai: Sefer Shoftim - The Book of Judges — Included herein are all the commands entrusted to the Sanhedrin and the king.
1. **Hilchot Sanhedrin v'haAnashin haMesurim Lahem** — *The Laws of Courts and Penalties* contain 10 positive and 20 negative commandments in 26 chapters.
2. **Hilchot Edut** — *The Laws of the Witness* contain three positive and five negative commandments in 22 chapters.
3. **Hilchot Mamrim** — *The Laws of the Rebel* contain three positive and six negative commands in seven chapters.
4. **Hilchot Evel** — *The Laws of Mourning* contain one positive and three negative commandments in 14 chapters.
5. **Hilchot Melachim u'Milchamotechem** — *The Laws of Kings and Their Wars* contain 10 positive and 13 negative commands in 12 chapters.

The List of Generations from Moshe Rabbeinu to R'Ashi

Moshe received the Torah from Sinai [from the mouth of Hashem] *and passed in down to Joshua, and Joshua to the Elders, and the Elders to the Prophets, and the prophets pass it down to the Anshei Knesset Hagedolah. They* [the men of the Great Assembly] *said three things: Weigh your judgments carefully, establish many disciples, and make a protective fence for the Torah*[9]. [m.Avos 1:1]

Ramban took this verse and expanded it to include the 40 generations of sages from Moshe to R'Ashi [b. 352, d. 427 CE], who was the first editor of Bavli, the Babylonian Talmud[10].

1. Moshe Rabbeinu received the tradition from the Almighty at Sinai[11].
2. Joshua received the tradition from Moshe Rabbeinu[12].
3. Pinchas received the tradition from Joshua.
4. Eli received the tradition from Pinchas[13].
5. Samuel received the tradition from Eli.
6. David received the tradition from Samuel.
7. Achiah of Shiloh[14] received the tradition from David.
8. Elijah received the tradition from Achiah of Shiloh.
9. Elisha received the tradition from Elijah.
10. Yehoyada the Kohen received the tradition from Elisha.
11. Zechariah received the tradition from Yehoyada the Kohen.
12. Hoshea received the tradition from Zechariah.
13. Amos received the tradition from Hoshea.
14. Isaiah received the tradition from Amos.
15. Michah received the tradition from Isaiah.
16. Joel received the tradition from Michah.
17. Nachum received the tradition from Joel.
18. Habakkuk received the tradition from Nachum.
19. Zephaniah received the tradition from Habakkuk.
20. Jeremiah received the tradition from Zephaniah.
21. Baruch b'Neriyah received the tradition from Jeremiah.
22. Ezra received the tradition from Baruch b'Neriyah.
23. Shimon the Just received the tradition from Ezra and the Anshei Knesset Hagedolah, which included such luminaries as Haggai, Zechariah, Malachi,

---

[9] M.Avos 1:1
[10] The final redactor was Ravina II, R'Ashi's student, who finished the work in 475 CE.
[11] As indicated by Exodus 24:12 and Deuteronomy 31:26
[12] As indicated in Deuteronomy 13:1. In addition to Joshua, the Seventy elders, Elazar, and Pichas were also recipients.
[13] This makes Pinchas of extreme age by this point, which is in line with the Bris Shalom in Numbers 25. Pinchas's first appearance is in Exodus 6:25 and his last in Judges 20:28. Tradition tells us he exits from the narrative with the arrival of Eli the High Priest and Judge of Israel, only to reappear much later as Elijah from 1 Kings 17:1 through 2 Kings 2:11. With God's help, a timeline for post-Torah events will appear in the first volume of the Neviim.
[14] See b.Bava Basra 121b for an explantion of Achiah's extremely long life.

Daniel, Hananiah, Mishael, Azariah, Nehemiah b'Chachaliah, Mordechai, Zerubbabel, among others – a total of 120 men of renown].

24. Antigonos of Socho received the tradition from Shimon the Just. He served as Kohen Gadol after Ezra and was the last of the Anshei Knesset Hagedolah.

25. Yose b'Yoezer of Tzreidah and Yosef b'Yochanan of Jerusalem received the tradition from Antigonos of Socho.

26. Yehoshua b'Perachiah and Nittai of Arbel received the tradition from Yose b'Yoezer of Tzreidah and Yosef b'Yochanan of Jerusalem.

27. Yehudah b'Tabbai and Shimon b'Shatach received the tradition from Yehoshua b'Perachiah and Nittai of Arbel.

28. Shemaiah and Avtalion, who were righteous converts, received the tradition from Yehudah b'Tabbai and Shimon b'Shatach.

29. Hillel and Shammai received the tradition from Shemaiah and Avtalion.

30. Rabban Yochanan b'Zakkai [15] and R'Shimon received the Tradition from R'Shimon's father, Hillel, and Shammai.

31. Rabban Gamliel the elder received the tradition from his father Rabban Shimon b'Hillel.

32. Rabban Shimon received the tradition from his father Rabban Gamliel the elder.

33. Rabban Gamliel received the tradition from his father Rabban Shimon.

34. R'Shimon received the tradition from his father Rabban Gamliel.

35. Rabbeinu Hakadosh R'Yehudah haNasi b'Rabban Shimon[16] received the tradition from his father R'Shimon b'Shamua and Rabban Shimon.

36. R'Yochanan[17], Rav, and Shmuel received the tradition from Rabbeinu Hakadosh.

37. R'Huna[18] received the tradition from R'Yochanan[19], Rav[20], and Shmuel[21].

38. Rabbah[22] received the tradition from R'Huna and R'Yehudah.

39. Rava received the tradition from Rabbah and R'Nachman

40. R'Ashi[23] received the tradition from Rava, and he began the redaction of the Talmud Bavli.

---

[15] Rabban Yochanan b'Zakkai had five students after the incident of the 24,000: R'Eliezar the great, R'Yehoshua, R'Yose the priest, R'Shimon b'Natenel and R'Elazar b'Arach. R'Akiva b'Yosef was a student of R'Eliezar the great. Yosef, R'Akiva's father, was a righteous convert. R'Akiva's fellow talmidim included R'Tarfon [the teacher of R'Yosse of Galil], R'Shimon b'Elazar, and R'Yochanan b'Nuri. R'Yishmael and R'Meir [a son of righteous converts] sat under R'Akiva. R'Meir also received from R'Yishmael. Fellow talmidim of R'Meir include R'Chananiah R'Elazar b'Shamua, b'Teradion, R'Nechamiah, R'Shimon, R'Yehudah, R'Yose, R'Yochanan the cobbler, and Shimon b'Azzai.
[16] R'Yehudah haNasi compiled the Mishnah. His students included Shimon and Gamliel his sons, bar Kapra, R'Chanina b'Chama, R'Chiyya [who compiled the *Tosefta*], R'Effess, R'Hoshaya, Rav, R'Yannai, R'Yochanan, and Shemuel.
[17] Fellow talmidim of R'Yochanan included R'Ami, R'Assi, R'Avin, Rabbah bar bar Channah, R'Dimi.
[18] Fellow talmidim of R'Huna included R'Kahana, R'Nachman, and R'Yehudah
[19] R'Yochanan, who later became a student of R'Yannai, compiled *Talmud Yerushalmi*, but the final text was redacted by R'Mannah and R'Yose ben R'Bun about 100 years after R'Yochanan's death.
[20] Rav, also a student of R'Yannai, compiled the *Sifra* and *Sifre*
[21] Shemuel was also a student of R'Chanina b'Chama
[22] A fellow talmid of Rabbah was R'Yosef. They, in turn, taught Abbaya and Ravva.
[23] A fellow talmid of R'Ashi was Ravva; thye, in turn taught Mar bar R'Ashi

Vayikra

Vayikra[1] – Chapter 1

וַיִּקְרָא[2] אֶל־מֹשֶׁה וַיְדַבֵּר יְהֹוָה אֵלָיו
מֵאֹהֶל מוֹעֵד לֵאמֹר

1[3] And the LORD called to Moses[4], and spoke to him out of the tent of meeting, saying:

דַּבֵּר אֶל־בְּנֵי יִשְׂרָאֵל וְאָמַרְתָּ אֲלֵהֶם
אָדָם כִּי־יַקְרִיב מִכֶּם קָרְבָּן לַיהֹוָה מִן־
הַבְּהֵמָה מִן־הַבָּקָר וּמִן־הַצֹּאן תַּקְרִיבוּ
אֶת־קָרְבַּנְכֶם

2[5] Speak to the children of Israel, and say to them: When any man among you brings *an offering*[6] to the LORD, you shall bring your offering of the cattle: of the *herd*[7] or of the flock.

---

[1] Vayikra aliyot: [1] Leviticus 1:1–13, [2] Leviticus 1:14–2:6, [3] Leviticus 2:7–16, [4] Leviticus 3:1–17, [5] Leviticus 4:1–26, [6] Leviticus 4:27–5:10, [7] Leviticus 5:11–26, Genesis.R 3:5; Leviticus is separated into 10 yearly Parashiyot or 25 triennial Sedarim

[2] Traditional Small א in וַיִּקְרָא

[3] Leviticus 1:1 - 3 Enoch 24:8, b.Eruvin [Rashi] 2a, b.Sanhedrin 101a, b.Sotah [Rashi] 37b, b.Yoma 4b, Chibbur Yafeh 17 {78b}, Ecclesiastes.R 6:9, Ein Yaakov Sanhedrin:101a, Ein Yaakov Yoma:4b, Exodus 19:3 24:1-2 24:12 1:22 5:42 9:7 15:32 40:34-35, Exodus.R 19:3 46:3, Genesis.R 52:5, Jastrow 294b 1419a, John 1:17, Leviticus.R 1:1 1:10, Mas.Kallah Rabbati 8:9, Mekilta de R'Ishmael Pisha 1:5, Midrash Psalms 103:18, Midrash Tanchuma Behaalotcha 6, Midrash Tanchuma Vayikra 1-4 8, mt.Hilchot Maaseh haKorbanot 5:6, Numbers 8:29, Numbers.R 2:10 14:19 14:21 15:8, Pesikta Rabbati 5:4, Sifre Devarim Ekev 41, Song of Songs.R 2:13, Tanna Devei Eliyahu 6, z.Acharei Mot 1 56a, z.Balak 288 291, z.Metzora 53b 22, z.Miketz 194b 36, z.Toldot 138a 29, z.Trumah 138a 139b 216 243 564, z.Vaetchanan 92, z.Vayechi 520 611 612 239a, z.Vayelech 33, z.Vayera 140 102b, z.Vayikra 2b 4b 16 26 28 42 47 50
Leviticus 1:1-3 - Liber Antiquitatum Biblicarum 14:1
Leviticus 1:1-7 - 4QLevc
Leviticus 1:1-13 - Minchah [Shabbat Monday Thursday Torah reading - Parashah Vayikra]

[4] LXX adds *again*

[5] Leviticus 1:2 - 1 Chronicles 16:29, b.Arachin [Tosefot] 2b, b.Avodah Zara [Rashi] 22b 46a, b.Avodah Zara [Tosefot] 6a, b.Bava Kamma 40b, b.Bechorot [Rashi] 19a 57a, b.Bechorot 41a, b.Beitzah [Rashi] 8a, b.Chagigah 16b, b.Chullin [Rashi] 40a, b.Chullin [Tosefot] 115a, b.Chullin 5a 13b, b.Eruvin 69a 96b, b.Kiddushin 36a, b.Menachot [Rashi] 5b 61b 93b, b.Menachot [Tosefot] 22b, b.Menachot 80a 91a 93, b.Nazir 35a, b.Nedarim [Ran] 3a, b.Nedarim 10b, b.Niddah 41a, b.Rosh Hashanah 33a, Genesis 4:3 4:5, b.Succah 30a, b.Sanhedrin [Tosefot] 14a, b.Shekalim 4a, b.Temurah 28ab, b.Temurah [Rashi] 2a 29a, b.Zevachim [Rashi] 8b 9a 71a, b.Zevachim [Tosefot] 4b, b.Zevachim 34a 85b, Ecclesiastes.R 2:11, Ein Yaakov Chullin 5a, Ephesians 5:2, Exodus.R 17:1, Genesis.R 1:13, Jastrow 685b, Guide for the Perplexed 3:32, Leviticus 22:18-19, Mekilta de R'Ishmael Nezikin 1:4, Leviticus.R 1:1 2:1 2:4 2:6 2:9, Midrash Tanchuma Bechukkotai 5 6, Midrash Tanchuma Tazria 9, Midrash Tanchuma Tzav 1, Midrash Tanchuma Vayikra 3 7 8, mt.Hilchot Issurei Mizbeiach 5:6, mt.Hilchot Shegagot 3:7, Romans 12:1 12:6, Numbers.R 20:5, Sifre Devarim Haazinu Hashamayim 306, Sifre Devarim Nitzavim 306, Tanna Devei Eliyahu 6, y.Pesachim 9:5, y.Shekalim 1:4, y.Yevamot 11:2, z.Mishpatim 108a 260, z.Tzav 6, z.Pekudei 239a 355, z.Shmini 98, z.Tazria 48a 106, z.Vayechi 239b 619 621 797, z.Vayikra 5a 5b 8b 28 50 62 69, z.Yitro 405, z.Emor 185, z.Lech Lecha 299 303, z.Pinchas 419, z.Safra Det'zniuta 50

[6] LXX *gifts*

[7] LXX *oxen*

אִם־עֹלָ֤ה קָרְבָּנוֹ֙ מִן־הַבָּקָ֔ר זָכָ֥ר תָּמִ֖ים 3[1]
יַקְרִיבֶ֑נּוּ אֶל־פֶּ֜תַח אֹ֤הֶל מוֹעֵד֙ יַקְרִ֣יב
אֹת֔וֹ לִרְצֹנ֖וֹ לִפְנֵ֥י יְהוָֽה

וְסָמַ֣ךְ יָד֔וֹ עַ֖ל רֹ֣אשׁ הָעֹלָ֑ה וְנִרְצָ֥ה ל֖וֹ 4[3]
לְכַפֵּ֥ר עָלָֽיו

וְשָׁחַ֛ט אֶת־בֶּ֥ן הַבָּקָ֖ר לִפְנֵ֣י יְהוָ֑ה 5[4]
וְ֠הִקְרִיבוּ בְּנֵי֩ אַהֲרֹ֨ן הַכֹּהֲנִים֙ אֶת־הַדָּ֔ם
וְזָרְק֨וּ אֶת־הַדָּ֤ם עַל־הַמִּזְבֵּ֙חַ֙ סָבִ֔יב
אֲשֶׁר־פֶּ֖תַח אֹ֥הֶל מוֹעֵֽד

3[1] If his offering is a [2]burnt offering of the herd, he shall offer a male without blemish; he shall bring it to the door of the tent of meeting, so he may be accepted before the LORD.

4[3] And he shall press his hand on the head of the burnt offering; and it shall be accepted for him to make atonement for him.

5[4] And *he*[5] shall kill the bullock before the LORD; Aaron's sons, the priests, shall present the blood, and dash the blood around the altar that is at the door of the tent of meeting.

---

[1] Leviticus 1:3 - 1 Peter 1:18-19, 2 Corinthians 8:12 9:7, b.Arachin 2a 21a, b.Bava Kamma [Tosefot] 67a, b.Bava Kamma 66b 67b, b.Bechorot 41b 42a, b.Chagigah 16b, b.Chullin [Rashi] 5b 14b, b.Chullin [Tosefot] 23a, b.Kereitot 7a, b.Kiddushin 50a, b.Menachot [Rashi] 93b, b.Menachot 3a 5b 6a 10a 91a 104b, b.Nazir [Rashi] 25a, b.Rosh Hashanah 6a, b.Sanhedrin [Rashi] 47a, b.Yevamot 16a, b.Zevachim [Tosefot] 32a, b.Zevachim 34a 119b, Commandment #475, Deuteronomy 12:5-6 12:13-14 12:27 15:21 17:1, Ephesians 2:18 5:27, Exodus 12:5 24:5 5:4 5:18 5:42 8:6 11:5 11:21 11:29 12:3 14:1, Ezekiel 20:40, Genesis 8:20 22:2 22:8 22:13, Hebrews 7:26 9:14 10:8-10, Isaiah 1:11, Jastrow 1492b, John 1:36 10:7 10:9, Leviticus 3:1 4:23 6:9-13 7:16 8:18 8:21 16:7 17:4 17:9 22:19-24, Leviticus.R 7:1 7:1 8:3-4, Luke 1:35, m.Arachin 5:6, m.Zevachim 14:10, Malachi 1:14, mt.Hilchot Maaseh haKorbanot 14:16, Numbers 23:3 23:10-11 23:19 23:23-24 23:27 23:30 29:8-11 5:13, Philo De Specialibus Legibus I 199, Psalms 40:9 14:3, Tanya Igeret Hateshuvah §2, y.Sanhedrin 7:3, z.Noach 70a, z.Vayechi 246a 759, Zechariah 13:7, z.Noach 230, z.Vayikra 70 72 117
[2] LXX adds *whole-*
[3] Leviticus 1:4 - 1 John 2:2, 2 Chronicles 29:23-24, 2 Corinthians 5:20-21, b.Arachin [Tosefot] 2a, b.Beitzah [Rashi] 8a, b.Chagigah 16b, b.Chullin 2b, b.Eruvin 96b, b.Megillah 8a 25ab, b.Menachot 19a 93b, b.Menachot [Rashi] 22b 61b, b.Pesachim [Rashi] 7b, b.Pesachim [Tosefot] 61a, b.Pesachim 62a 66b, b.Sanhedrin [Rashi] 13b, b.Temurah [Rashi] 2a, b.Yoma [Tosefot] 36a, b.Zevachim [Rashi] 5b 39b, b.Yoma 5a 16a, b.Zevachim [Tosefot] 10a, b.Zevachim 52 6a 32a 33a 119b, Daniel 9:24, Exodus 5:10 5:15 5:19, Hebrews 10:4, Isaiah 53:4-6 8:7, Jastrow 368b 1000a 1493a, Leviticus 3:2 3:8 3:13 4:4 4:15 4:20 4:24 4:26 4:29 4:31 4:35 5:6 6:7 8:14 8:22 9:7 16:21 16:24 22:21 22:27, m.Chagigah 2:2, m.Menachot 9:8, Mekilta de R'Ishmael Bahodesh 10:54, Midrash Psalms 4:9 94:2 118:16 134:4, Midrash Tanchuma Bamidbar 12, Midrash Tanchuma Yitro 16, mt.Hilchot Maaseh haKorbanot 3:7 3:13, Numbers 8:12 15:25 15:28 1:13, Numbers.R 2:5, Philippians 4:18, Romans 3:25 5:11 12:1, Sifre Devarim Vaetchanan 32, Song of Songs.R 6:14, Tanya Igeret Hateshuvah §02, y.Berachot 1:1, y.Kiddushin 2:1
[4] Leviticus 1:5 - 1 Peter 1:2, 2 Chronicles 29:22-24 11:11, b.Berachot 31b, b.Chagigah 11a, b.Chullin [Rashi] 2b 10b 27b, b.Chullin [Tosefot] 2a 30b 133a, b.Chullin 13a 14a 21b 16a, b.Eruvin 57a, b.Kiddushin [Rashi] 36b 57b, b.Kiddushin 36a, b.Megillah 20b, b.Menachot [Rashi] 5a 6b 7b 13b 93b, b.Menachot [Tosefot] 9a 22b 61a, b.Menachot 10a 19a 11a, b.Pesachim [Rashi] 7b 94b, b.Sheviit 16a, b.Yoma 25b 16a, b.Zevachim [Rashi] 24b 43a 62b 115b, b.Zevachim [Tosefot] 16a 36b 48ab 58a, b.Zevachim 4a 13a 32a-33a 47a 51b 53b 56b 57a 81ab 99a 119b, Ein Yaakov Berachot 31b, Exodus 24:6-8 5:16, Ezekiel 12:25, Hebrews 10:11 12:24, Isaiah 4:15, Jastrow 971a 1309a 1415a 1546b, Leviticus 1:11 1:15 3:2 3:8 3:13 16:15, Leviticus.R 2:11 7:1, m.Megillah 2:5, m.Zevachim 14:10 4:4 5:4, Micah 6:6, Midrash Psalms 4:9 134:4, Midrash Tanchuma Tzav 14, mt.Hilchot Beit Habechirah 2:13, mt.Hilchot Biat haMikdash 9:6, mt.Hilchot Maaseh haKorbanot 5:1, Numbers 18:17, Pesikta Rabbati 2:6, Sifre Devarim Reeh 126, t.Demai 2:7, t.Zevachim 1:8, y.Berachot 1:1, z.Naso 124a 61
[5] LXX *they*

וְהִפְשִׁיט אֶת־הָעֹלָה וְנִתַּח אֹתָהּ לִנְתָחֶיהָ	6[1]	And *he*[2] shall flay the [3]burnt offering *and cut it into its pieces*[4].
וְנָתְנוּ בְּנֵי אַהֲרֹן הַכֹּהֵן אֵשׁ עַל־הַמִּזְבֵּחַ וְעָרְכוּ עֵצִים עַל־הָאֵשׁ	7[5]	And the sons of Aaron the priest shall put fire on the altar, and lay wood in order on the fire.
וְעָרְכוּ בְּנֵי אַהֲרֹן הַכֹּהֲנִים אֵת הַנְּתָחִים אֶת־הָרֹאשׁ וְאֶת־הַפָּדֶר עַל־הָעֵצִים אֲשֶׁר עַל־הָאֵשׁ אֲשֶׁר עַל־הַמִּזְבֵּחַ	8[6]	And Aaron's sons, the priests, shall lay the pieces, and the head, and the suet, in order on the wood that is on the fire which is on the altar;
וְקִרְבּוֹ וּכְרָעָיו יִרְחַץ בַּמָּיִם וְהִקְטִיר הַכֹּהֵן אֶת־הַכֹּל הַמִּזְבֵּחָה עֹלָה אִשֵּׁה רֵיחַ־נִיחוֹחַ לַיהוָה	9[7]	But he shall wash its innards and its legs with water; and the priest shall make it all smoke on the altar for a burnt offering, *an offering made by fire*[8], of a sweet savor to the LORD.
וְאִם־מִן־הַצֹּאן קָרְבָּנוֹ מִן־הַכְּשָׂבִים אוֹ מִן־הָעִזִּים לְעֹלָה זָכָר תָּמִים יַקְרִיבֶנּוּ	10[9]	And if his offering is from the flock, whether of the sheep or of the goats, for a [10]burnt offering, he shall offer a male without blemish.

[1] Leviticus 1:6 - b.Chullin 11a 16a, b.Ketubot [Rashi] 65b, b.Kiddushin [Tosefot] 66b, b.Menachot [Rashi] 35a, b.Yoma [Rashi] 67b, b.Zevachim [Rashi] 50a 115b, b.Zevachim 85a 103b, Genesis 3:21, Guide for the Perplexed 3:46, Jastrow 363a 943b, Leviticus 7:8, Midrash Psalms 27:6, mt.Hilchot Maaseh haKorbanot 6:9
Leviticus 1:6-17 - Shacharit Korbanot-Parshat Haolah [burnt offering]
[2] LXX *they*
[3] LXX adds *whole-*
[4] LXX *they shall divide it by its limbs*
[5] Leviticus 1:7 - 1 Chronicles 21:26, 2 Chronicles 7:1, b.Eruvin 63a, b.Menachot [Rashi] 89b, b.Menachot [Tosefot] 80a, b.Tamid [Pirush] 25b 29a 33a, b.Yoma 21b 24b 26b 45a 53a, b.Zevachim 18a, Ein Yaakov Eruvin, Gates of Repentance 3.116, Genesis 22:9, Jastrow 1117a, Leviticus 6:12-13 9:24-10:1, Leviticus.R 7:1 8:3, Malachi 1:10, Midrash Tanchuma Vayikra 5, mt.Hilchot Temidim Umusafim 2:1-2, Nehemiah 13:31, y.Yoma 2:1
[6] Leviticus 1:8 - 1 Kings 18:23 18:33, b.Bechorot 43b, b.Chullin [Rashi] 80a, b.Chullin [Tosefot] 27b, b.Makkot [Rashi] 14b, b.Menachot [Rashi] 8b 21b, b.Menachot 22a 26b 16a, b.Yoma 16a, b.Zevachim [Rashi] 28a 43a, b.Zevachim 18a 50a 62b 85b, Exodus 29:17-18, Leviticus 1:12 8:18-21 9:13-14, Leviticus.R 7:1 8:3, mt.Hilchot Biat haMikdash 9:1, y.Yoma 2:4
[7] Leviticus 1:9 - 2 Corinthians 2:15, Avot de R'Natan 4, b.Chullin [Rashi] 16a, b.Chullin 80a, b.Menachot 11a, b.Sheviit 15a, b.Zevachim [Rashi] 46b 50a, b.Zevachim 2b 50a 86a 119b, Derech Hashem Part I 4§07, Ein Yaakov Menachot 110a, Ein Yaakov Shevuot 15a, Ephesians 5:2, Exodus 5:18 5:25, Ezekiel 20:28 20:41, Genesis 8:21, Jeremiah 4:14, Leviticus 1:13 1:17 3:11 8:21 9:14, Leviticus.R 2:12, m.Menachot 13:11, m.Zevachim 9:5, Matthew 23:25-28, mt.Hilchot Maaseh haKorbanot 6:1, Numbers 15:8-10, Philippians 4:18, Philo Legum Allegoriae III 143, Psalms 51:7 66:15, Sifre Devarim Reeh 78, Tanna Devei Eliyahu 6, Zechariah 13:7, z.Vayikra 98
[8] LXX *a sacrifice*
[9] Leviticus 1:10 - b.Bechorot 41a 42a, b.Chullin [Tosefot] 23a, b.Kereitot [Rashi] 22b, b.Menachot [Rashi] 83b, b.Menachot 3a 91a 105a, b.Nazir 35a, b.Shekalim 6b, b.Zevachim [Tosefot] 5a, b.Zevachim 34a 48a, Exodus 12:5, Genesis 4:4 8:20, Isaiah 53:6-7, John 1:29, Leviticus 1:2-3 4:23 22:19, Leviticus.R 7:1, Liber Antiquitatum Biblicarum 13:2, Malachi 1:14, Mekhilta de R'Shimon bar Yochai Shirata 34:2, Mekilta de R'Ishmael Pisha 4:13, y.Shekalim 2:4
[10] LXX adds *whole-*

וְשָׁחַ֨ט אֹת֜וֹ עַ֣ל יֶ֧רֶךְ הַמִּזְבֵּ֛חַ צָפֹ֖נָה לִפְנֵ֣י יְהוָ֑ה וְזָרְק֡וּ בְּנֵי֩ אַהֲרֹ֨ן הַכֹּהֲנִ֧ים אֶת־דָּמ֛וֹ עַל־הַמִּזְבֵּ֖חַ סָבִֽיב **11**[1]

וְנִתַּ֤ח אֹתוֹ֙ לִנְתָחָ֔יו וְאֶת־רֹאשׁ֖וֹ וְאֶת־פִּדְר֑וֹ וְעָרַךְ֙ הַכֹּהֵ֔ן אֹתָ֕ם עַל־הָעֵצִים֙ אֲשֶׁ֣ר עַל־הָאֵ֔שׁ אֲשֶׁ֖ר עַל־הַמִּזְבֵּֽחַ **12**[4]

וְהַקֶּ֥רֶב וְהַכְּרָעַ֖יִם יִרְחַ֣ץ בַּמָּ֑יִם וְהִקְרִ֨יב הַכֹּהֵ֤ן אֶת־הַכֹּל֙ וְהִקְטִ֤יר הַמִּזְבֵּ֔חָה עֹלָ֣ה ה֗וּא אִשֵּׁ֛ה רֵ֥יחַ נִיחֹ֖חַ לַֽיהוָֽה **13**[6]

וְאִ֧ם מִן־הָע֛וֹף עֹלָ֥ה קָרְבָּנ֖וֹ לַֽיהוָ֑ה וְהִקְרִ֣יב מִן־הַתֹּרִ֗ים א֛וֹ מִן־בְּנֵ֥י הַיּוֹנָ֖ה אֶת־קָרְבָּנֽוֹ **14**[8]

וְהִקְרִיב֤וֹ הַכֹּהֵן֙ אֶל־הַמִּזְבֵּ֔חַ וּמָלַק֙ אֶת־ **15**[9]

11[1] *And he*[2] shall kill it on the side of the altar northward before the LORD; and Aaron's sons, the priests, shall dash *its*[3] blood around the altar.

12[4] And *he*[5] shall cut it into its pieces; and the priest shall lay them, with its head and its suet, in order on the wood that is on the fire, which is on the altar.

13[6] And he shall wash the innards and the legs with water; and the priest shall offer it all, and make it smoke on the altar; it is a burnt offering, *an offering made by fire*[7], of a sweet savor to the LORD.

14[8] And if his offering to the LORD is a burnt offering of fowls, then he shall bring his offering of turtle doves, or of young pigeons.

15[9] And the priest shall bring it to the altar, and *pinch*[1] off its head, and make it

---

[1] Leviticus 1:11 - b.Kereitot [Rashi] 22b, b.Kiddushin [Rashi] 36b, b.Menachot [Rashi] 3a 8b 19a 55b, b.Menachot [Tosefot] 5a 19b, b.Menachot 10b 56a, b.Pesachim 64b, b.Succah [Rashi] 49a, b.Tamid [Pirush] 30b, b.Yoma [Rashi] 36a, b.Yoma 37a, b.Zevachim [Rashi] 20a 26a 63a, b.Zevachim 48ab 58a 59a 62b 119b, Exodus 16:22, Exodus.R 36:1, Ezekiel 8:5, Jastrow 921b 1295b 1297b, Korbanot, Leviticus 1:5 1:7-9 6:25 7:2 9:12-14, Leviticus.R 2:11, m.Zevachim 14:10, Maamodot [every day], Midrash Psalms 48:2 83:2, Midrash Tanchuma Vayishlach 6, mt.Hilchot Beit Habechirah 1:17 5:16, mt.Hilchot Maaseh haKorbanot 5:3, mt.Hilchot Pesulei haMikdashim 1:8 1:16, Numbers.R 1:3, pap4QLXXLevb, Parshat Hatamid [daily offering], Pesikta Rabbati 41:2, Shacharit, Tanna Devei Eliyahu 6
Leviticus 1:11-17 - 4QLevb
[2] LXX *And he shall lay his hand on its head; and they*
[3] 4QLevb *the*
[4] Leviticus 1:12 - b.Chullin 16a, b.Menachot [Rashi] 21b, b.Tamid 29b, b.Yoma 25b 16a, b.Zevachim [Rashi] 11a, Midrash Tanchuma Bechukkotai 4, mt.Hilchot Maaseh haKorbanot 6:4, Pesikta Rabbati 48:3, Sifre Devarim Reeh 78, t.Zevachim 4:2, y.Yoma 2:4
[5] LXX *they*
[6] Leviticus 1:13 - b.Chullin [Tosefot] 22a, b.Eruvin 104a, b.Menachot [Tosefot] 19b, b.Pesachim 65b, b.Tamid [Pirush] 30a 31b, b.Yoma 16a, b.Zevachim 4a 12b 14b 22a 24b 35a, Leviticus 1:9, Leviticus.R 2:12, Midrash Psalms 114:6, mt.Hilchot Maaseh haKorbanot 6:6, Numbers.R 3:8, Pesikta Rabbati 13:6, Philo Legum Allegoriae III 144, Sifre Devarim Reeh 78, Tanna Devei Eliyahu 6, Tanya Igeret Hateshuvah §02, z.Noach 70a 230 233
[7] LXX *a sacrifice*
[8] Leviticus 1:14 - 2 Corinthians 8:12, b.Avodah Zara [Tosefot] 5b, b.Bava Metzia [Tosefot] 111b, b.Chullin [Rashi] 61b, b.Chullin [Tosefot] 23a, b.Chullin 22ab, b.Kereitot 9a, b.Menachot [Rashi] 58a, b.Menachot 105a, b.Sheviit 12b, b.Zevachim [Rashi] 80a, b.Zevachim [Tosefot] 35b 68b 85b, b.Zevachim 65a, Exodus.R 17:1, Genesis 15:9, Hebrews 7:26, Jastrow 1155a, Leviticus 5:7 12:8, Leviticus.R 8:3 8:3 8:4, Luke 2:24, m.Menachot 13:6, m.Zevachim 4:4, Matthew 11:29, Midrash Tanchuma Vayikra 8, mt.Hilchot Issurei Mizbeiach 3:2, Pesikta Rabbati 48:2, z.Pekudei 239a, z.Pekudei 356, z.Pinchas 532, z.Tzav 7
[9] Leviticus 1:15 - 1 John 2:27, b.Bechorot 42a, b.Chullin [Rashi] 20ab, b.Chullin 21a-22a, b.Kereitot 9a, b.Kiddushin [Rashi] 36b, b.Kiddushin 36a, b.Kinnim [Pirush] 22a, b.Meilah [Rashi] 9a, b.Menachot [Rashi] 2b, b.Menachot 2a, b.Tamid [Pirush] 28b, b.Yoma [Rashi] 24b, b.Zevachim [Rashi] 48b, b.Zevachim [Rashi] 68a, b.Zevachim [Tosefot] 26b 66b, b.Zevachim 65a 66a, Isaiah 53:4-5 5:10, Jastrow 329a, Leviticus 5:8-5:9, m.Kiddushin 1:8, m.Zevachim 4:4, Matthew 26:1-27, Psalms 22:2 22:22 69:2-22, t.Demai 2:7, y.Yoma 1:1

רֹאשׁוֹ וְהִקְטִיר הַמִּזְבֵּחָה וְנִמְצָה דָמוֹ
עַל קִיר הַמִּזְבֵּחַ

smoke on the altar; and its blood shall be drained out on the *side*[2] of the altar.

וְהֵסִיר אֶת־מֻרְאָתוֹ בְּנֹצָתָהּ וְהִשְׁלִיךְ
אֹתָהּ אֵצֶל הַמִּזְבֵּחַ קֵדְמָה אֶל־מְקוֹם
הַדָּשֶׁן

16[3] And he shall remove its crop with its feathers and cast it beside the altar on the east side, in the place of the ashes.

וְשִׁסַּע אֹתוֹ בִכְנָפָיו לֹא יַבְדִּיל וְהִקְטִיר
אֹתוֹ הַכֹּהֵן הַמִּזְבֵּחָה עַל־הָעֵצִים אֲשֶׁר
עַל־הָאֵשׁ עֹלָה הוּא אִשֵּׁה רֵיחַ נִיחֹחַ
לַיהוָה

17[4] And he shall rend it by its wings, *but*[5] shall not divide it; and the priest shall make it smoke on the altar, on the wood that is on the fire; it is a burnt offering, *an offering made by fire*[6], of *a*[7] sweet savor to the LORD.

Vayikra – Chapter 2

וְנֶפֶשׁ כִּי־תַקְרִיב קָרְבַּן מִנְחָה לַיהוָה
סֹלֶת יִהְיֶה קָרְבָּנוֹ וְיָצַק עָלֶיהָ שֶׁמֶן
וְנָתַן עָלֶיהָ לְבֹנָה

1[8] And when anyone brings a meal offering to the LORD, his offering shall be of fine flour; and he shall pour oil on it and put frankincense on it[9].

---

[1] LXX *wring*

[2] LXX *bottom*

[3] Leviticus 1:16 - 1 Peter 1:2, b.Chullin [Tosefot] 114a, b.Meilah 12a, b.Succah [Rashi] 48b, b.Yoma [Rashi] 21b, b.Zevachim [Rashi] 63a 64a, b.Zevachim [Tosefot] 46a, b.Zevachim 65a, Hebrews 13:11-13:14, Jastrow 370a 889b, Leviticus 4:12 6:10-11 16:27, Leviticus.R 3:4, Luke 1:35, m.Zevachim 4:4, mt.Hilchot Maaseh haKorbanot 6:21, y.Yoma 2:2

[4] Leviticus 1:17 - 1 Peter 1:19-1:21 3:18, b.Beitzah [Tosefot] 8a, b.Chullin [Rashi] 21b 123b, b.Chullin [Tosefot] 22a, b.Menachot [Rashi] 21b, b.Menachot 11a, b.Shabbat 18a, b.Sheviit 15a, b.Zevachim 65a-66a, Ein Yaakov Menachot:110a, Ein Yaakov Shevuot:15a, Genesis 8:21 15:10, Hebrews 10:6-12 13:15-16, Jastrow 140b 1565a, John 19:30, Leviticus 1:9-10 1:13 5:8, Leviticus.R 3:5, m.Menachot 13:11, m.Zevachim 4:4, Matthew 3:50, Psalms 16:10, Romans 4:25, z.Noach 70a

[5] 4QLevb *and*

[6] LXX *a sacrifice*

[7] 4QLevb *it is a burnt offering of a*

[8] Leviticus 2:1 - 1 John 2:20 2:27, b.Bava Batra [Rashbam] 81b, b.Chullin [Rashi] 132b, b.Menachot [Rashi] 5a 18a 19a 60b 105b 16a, b.Menachot [Tosefot] 75a, b.Menachot 9a 18b 20a 21b 25ab 51a 59ab 104b 106b 107a, b.Pesachim 36a, b.Shekalim 18b, b.Sotah [Rashi] 14a, b.Sotah 14b, b.Zevachim [Rashi] 63a, b.Zevachim 5b 76b 91b, Commandment #476, Ecclesiastes.R 4:5, Exodus 5:2, Guide for the Perplexed 3:46, Isaiah 18:20, Jastrow 530a 589a, Joel 1:9 2:14, John 6:35, Jude 1:20, Leviticus 2:4-8 2:15-16 6:14-18 6:20-23 7:10-12 9:17, Leviticus.R 3:1 3:4-5, Luke 1:9-10, m.Demai 1:3, m.Sotah 2:1, m.Kiddushin 1:8, m.Menachot 1:3 12:5, Malachi 1:11, Midrash Psalms 22:31, Midrash Tanchuma Vayikra 5, mt.Hilchot Beit Habechirah 6:13, mt.Hilchot Maaseh haKorbanot 12:4, Numbers 7:13 7:19 15:4-21, Pesikta Rabbati 29/30:1, Philo De Somniis II 71, Revelation 8:3, Sifre.z Numbers Shelah 15:4, t.Demai 2:7, z.Mishpatim 108a 260

Leviticus 2:1-3 - m.Yevamot 11:5, mt.Hilchot Beit HaBechirah 6:13, Parshat Minchas Soless [meal offering]

Leviticus 2:1-10 - m.Megillah 1:4

Leviticus 2:1-16 - 4QLevb

[9] 4QExod-Lev6 adds *it is a grain offering*; LXX adds *it is a sacrifice*

וְהֵבִיאָהּ אֶל־בְּנֵי אַהֲרֹן הַכֹּהֲנִים וְקָמַץ מִשָּׁם מְלֹא קֻמְצוֹ מִסָּלְתָּהּ וּמִשַּׁמְנָהּ עַל כָּל־לְבֹנָתָהּ וְהִקְטִיר הַכֹּהֵן אֶת־אַזְכָּרָתָהּ הַמִּזְבֵּחָה אִשֵּׁה רֵיחַ נִיחֹחַ לַיהוָה

2¹ And he shall bring it to Aaron's sons the priests; and he shall take from there his handful of the fine flour, and of its oil, together with all its frankincense; and the priest shall make its memorial part smoke on the altar, *an offering made by fire²*, of a sweet savor to the LORD.

וְהַנּוֹתֶרֶת מִן־הַמִּנְחָה לְאַהֲרֹן וּלְבָנָיו קֹדֶשׁ קָדָשִׁים מֵאִשֵּׁי יְהוָה

3³ But what is left of the meal offering shall be Aaron's and his sons'; it is a thing most holy of the offerings of the LORD *made by fire⁴*.

וְכִי תַקְרִב קָרְבַּן מִנְחָה מַאֲפֵה תַנּוּר סֹלֶת חַלּוֹת מַצֹּת בְּלוּלֹת בַּשֶּׁמֶן וּרְקִיקֵי מַצּוֹת מְשֻׁחִים בַּשָּׁמֶן

4⁵ And when *you bring⁶* a meal offering baked in the oven, it shall be unleavened cakes of fine flour mingled with oil, or unleavened wafers spread with oil.

וְאִם־מִנְחָה עַל־הַמַּחֲבַת קָרְבָּנֶךָ סֹלֶת בְּלוּלָה בַשֶּׁמֶן מַצָּה תִהְיֶה

5⁷ And if your offering is a meal offering baked on a griddle, it shall be of fine unleavened flour, mingled with oil.

---

¹ Leviticus 2:2 - Acts 10:4, b.Kiddushin 36a, b.Meilah [Rashi] 8b, b.Meilah 9a, b.Menachot [Rashi] 7b 8b 10b 21b 26b, b.Menachot 6b 8b 9b 11a 18b 19ab 23b 16a 11a, b.Pesachim [Rashi] 78a, b.Sheviit 15a, b.Sotah 14b, b.Yevamot [Rashi] 1a, b.Yoma [Rashi] 47a, b.Zevachim [Rashi] 11a, b.Zevachim 24b 63a, Ein Yaakov Menachot:110a, Esther.R 10:4, Exodus 6:16, Isaiah 18:3, Lamentations.R Petichata DChakimei:10, Leviticus 2:9 2:16 5:12 6:15 24:7, Leviticus.R 3:5, m.Kiddushin 1:8, m.Kilayim 17:10, m.Megillah 2:5, m.Zevachim 4:3 6:1, mt.Hilchot Beit Habechirah 6:13, mt.Hilchot Maaseh haKorbanot 13:12 13:14, Nehemiah 13:14 13:22, Numbers 5:18, Pesikta Rabbati 29/30:1, Ralbag SOS 1, t.Demai 2:7, y.Yoma 5:1
Leviticus 2:2-5 - Jubilees 6:3
² LXX *a sacrifice*
³ Leviticus 2:3 - 1 Samuel 2:28, b.Meilah [Rashi] 9a, b.Meilah 8b, b.Menachot [Rashi] 6b 7b 8a 9a 26b, b.Menachot 9b, b.Yoma 61a, Exodus 5:37, Exodus.R 37:3, Leviticus 2:10 6:16-17 6:26 7:9 10:12-13 21:22, Leviticus.R 3:6 10:3, m.Zevachim 14:3, mt.Hilchot Beit Habechirah 6:13, mt.Hilchot Pesulei haMikdashim 11:20, Numbers 18:9
Leviticus 2:3-5 - pap4QLXXLevb
⁴ Missing in LXX
⁵ Leviticus 2:4 - 1 Chronicles 23:28-29, 1 Corinthians 5:7-8, 1 Peter 2:1 2:22, b.Menachot [Rashi] 52b 59a 60b 78a, b.Menachot [Tosefot] 53a, b.Menachot 63ab 75a 76b 104b, b.Yevamot [Tosefot] 42a, b.Zevachim [Rashi] 50a, b.Zevachim [Tosefot] 96a, Exodus 12:8 16:31 5:2, Ezekiel 22:20, Hebrews 7:26, Isaiah 18:1 44:3-5 13:1, Jastrow 530a 1472b, John 3:34 12:27, Leviticus 1:11 6:17 7:12 10:12, m.Menachot 5:3, Matthew 2:38, mt.Hilchot Maaseh haKorbanot 12:4 13:8, Parshat Minchas Maafeh [baked offering], Psalms 22:15, Sifre Devarim Nitzavim 306, t.Demai 2:7, z.Korach 55
⁶ LXX *he brings*
⁷ Leviticus 2:5 - b.Bava Batra [Rashbam] 81b, b.Menachot [Rashi] 52b 60b 104b, b.Menachot [Tosefot] 18b, b.Menachot 53a 74b 75a, Jastrow 173a, Leviticus 6:21 7:9, Leviticus.R 3:7, m.Menachot 12:2 5:3, Midrash Tanchuma Acharei Mot 10, Midrash Tanchuma Vayikra 5, mt.Hilchot Maaseh haKorbanot 12:4, Tanna Devei Eliyahu 6
Leviticus 2:5-6 - Parshat Michvas [pan offering]
Leviticus 2:5-8 - m.Zevachim 14:3

פָּתוֹת אֹתָהּ֙ פִּתִּ֔ים וְיָצַקְתָּ֥ עָלֶ֖יהָ שָׁ֑מֶן מִנְחָ֖ה הִֽוא ‎6[1]

You shall break it in pieces and pour oil on it; it is a meal offering[2].

וְאִם־מִנְחַ֥ת מַרְחֶ֖שֶׁת קָרְבָּנֶ֑ךָ סֹ֥לֶת בַּשֶּׁ֖מֶן תֵּעָשֶֽׂה ‎7[3]

And if your offering is a meal offering from the stewing pan, it shall be made of fine flour with oil.

וְהֵבֵאתָ֣ אֶת־הַמִּנְחָ֗ה אֲשֶׁ֧ר יֵעָשֶׂ֛ה מֵאֵ֖לֶּה לַיהֹוָ֑ה וְהִקְרִיבָהּ֙ אֶל־הַכֹּהֵ֔ן וְהִגִּישָׁ֖הּ אֶל־הַמִּזְבֵּֽחַ ‎8[4]

And *you*[5] shall bring the meal offering that is made of these things to the LORD; and it shall be presented to the priest, and he shall bring it to the altar.

וְהֵרִ֨ים הַכֹּהֵ֜ן מִן־הַמִּנְחָה֙ אֶת־אַזְכָּ֣רָתָ֔הּ וְהִקְטִ֖יר הַמִּזְבֵּ֑חָה אִשֵּׁ֛ה רֵ֥יחַ נִיחֹ֖חַ לַיהֹוָֽה ‎9[6]

And the priest shall take off from the meal offering its memorial part, and shall make it smoke on the altar—*an offering made by fire*[7], of a sweet savor to the LORD.

וְהַנּוֹתֶ֙רֶת֙ מִן־הַמִּנְחָ֔ה לְאַהֲרֹ֖ן וּלְבָנָ֑יו קֹ֤דֶשׁ קׇֽדָשִׁים֙ מֵאִשֵּׁ֣י יְהֹוָֽה ‎10[8]

But whatever is left of the meal offering shall be Aaron's and his sons'; it is a thing most holy of the offerings of the LORD made by fire.

כׇּל־הַמִּנְחָ֗ה אֲשֶׁ֤ר תַּקְרִ֙יבוּ֙ לַֽיהֹוָ֔ה לֹ֥א ‎11[9]

No[10] meal offering, which you shall bring to the LORD, shall be made with

---

[1] Leviticus 2:6 - b.Berachot [Rashi] 37b, b.Chullin [Rashi] 9a 132b, b.Horayot [Tosefot] 4a, b.Menachot [Rashi] 18ab, b.Menachot 75ab, b.Pesachim [Rashi] 36a, b.Zevachim [Rashi] 112a, Jastrow 1171a 1250a, John 18:1-19, Leviticus 1:6, Mark 14:1-15, mt.Hilchot Maaseh haKorbanot 13:6 13:37, mt.Hilchot Pesulei haMikdashim 11:7, Psalms 22:2-22, y.Horayot 1:3, y.Nazir 5:1, y.Sotah 5:1

[2] LXX adds *to the LORD*

[3] Leviticus 2:7 - b.Menachot [Rashi] 60b 14b, b.Menachot 74b 75a, Leviticus 2:1-2:2 7:9, m.Menachot 12:2 5:3, Midrash Tanchuma Vayikra 5, mt.Hilchot Maaseh haKorbanot 12:4
Leviticus 2:7-8 - pap4QLXXLevb
Leviticus 2:7-13 - Parshat Marcheshes

[4] Leviticus 2:8 - b.Beitzah 7a, b.Menachot [Tosefot] 11b 57a, b.Menachot 8b 60ab 61a, b.Sotah 14b, b.Zevachim [Rashi] 63a, b.Zevachim 63a 64a 119b, Genesis.R 44:14, Leviticus.R 3:3, m.Megillah 2:5, m.Menachot 5:5, m.Zevachim 14:10, y.Sotah 3:1

[5] 4QLevb *he*

[6] Leviticus 2:9 - b.Meilah [Tosefot] 8b, b.Menachot [Rashi] 6b, b.Menachot8b 9b 61a, b.Zevachim [Rashi] 76b 19b, Ephesians 5:2, Exodus 5:18, Isaiah 5:10, Leviticus 2:2 6:15, m.Menachot 13:11, Philippians 2:17 4:18, Psalms 22:14-22:15, Romans 12:1 15:16, y.Sotah 3:1, Zechariah 13:7 13:9

[7] LXX *A burnt offering*

[8] Leviticus 2:10 - b.Shabbat 25a, b.Sotah 15a, Esther.R 3:6, Leviticus 2:3, t.Kippurim 1:5, y.Challah 3:5, y.Sotah 3:1, y.Yoma 1:1

[9] Leviticus 2:11 - 1 Corinthians 5:6-8, 1 Peter 4:2, Acts 14:22, b.Bava Batra [Rashbam] 79a, b.Bava Metzia [Tosefot] 115b, b.Bechorot 33b, b.Kereitot [Rashi] 6a, b.Menachot [Rashi] 22a 23b 58b, b.Menachot [Tosefot] 26b 48a, b.Menachot [Tosefot] 52b 60a, b.Menachot 55ab 56b 57ab 58a 16b, b.Nazir [Rashi] 36a, b.Pesachim [Rashi] 37a, b.Pesachim 43b, b.Shabbat 111a, b.Sheviit [Rashi] 15ab, b.Sheviit 12b, b.Sotah [Rashi] 23a, b.Yevamot [Rashi] 1a, b.Yoma [Rashi] 47b, b.Zevachim [Rashi] 76b 77a 11a, b.Zevachim 76b, Commandment #477, Exodus 12:19-20 23:18 10:25, Galatians 5:9, Guide for the Perplexed 3:46, Jastrow 685b, Leviticus 6:16-17, Luke 12:1 21:34, m.Menachot 5:2, Mark 8:15, Matthew 16:6 16:11-12, Midrash Tanchuma Pinchas 12, Midrash Tanchuma Vayikra 5, mt.Hilchot Chametz uMatzah 29:14, mt.Hilchot Issurei Mizbeiach 5:1, mt.Hilchot Klei haMikdash Vihaovdim Bo 2:8, mt.Hilchot Maaseh haKorbanot 12:15 12:18, mt.Hilchot Sanhedrin vHainshin Hameurim Lahem 19:4, Philo De Congressu Quaerendae Eruditionis Gratia 169, Proverbs 24:13 1:16 1:27, Shacharit Korbanot, t.Makkot 5:3, t.Menachot 6:8-9 7:14, y.Shabbat 7:2

[10] 4QLevb *every*

תַעֲשֶׂה חָמֵץ כִּי כָל־שְׂאֹר וְכָל־דְּבַ֫שׁ
לֹא־תַקְטִ֫ירוּ מִמֶּ֫נּוּ אִשֶּׁה לַיהֹוָה

leaven; for you shall make no leaven, nor any honey, smoke as an offering made by fire to the LORD.

קָרְבַּ֫ן רֵאשִׁ֫ית תַּקְרִ֫יבוּ אֹתָם לַיהֹוָה
וְאֶל־הַמִּזְבֵּ֫חַ לֹא־יַעֲל֫וּ לְרֵ֫יחַ נִיחֹ֫חַ

12[1] As an offering of firstfruits you may bring them to the LORD; but they shall not come up for a sweet savor on the altar.

וְכָל־קָרְבַּ֫ן מִנְחָתְךָ֙ בַּמֶּ֫לַח תִּמְלָ֔ח וְלֹא
תַשְׁבִּ֫ית מֶ֫לַח בְּרִ֫ית אֱלֹהֶ֫יךָ מֵעַ֫ל
מִנְחָתֶ֑ךָ עַל כָּל־קָרְבָּנְךָ֖ תַּקְרִ֫יב מֶֽלַח

13[2] And you shall season every meal offering with salt; you shall not omit the salt of the covenant of *your God*[3] to be lacking from your meal offering; with all your offerings you shall offer salt.

וְאִם־תַּקְרִ֫יב מִנְחַ֫ת בִּכּוּרִ֫ים לַיהֹוָה
אָבִ֫יב קָל֫וּי בָּאֵ֫שׁ גֶּ֫רֶשׂ כַּרְמֶ֫ל תַּקְרִ֔יב
אֵ֖ת מִנְחַ֫ת בִּכּוּרֶֽיךָ

14[4] And *if*[5] you bring a meal offering of firstfruits to the LORD, you shall bring for the meal offering of *your firstfruits corn in the ear parched with fire, even crushed grains of the fresh ear*[6].

וְנָתַתָּ֫ עָלֶ֫יהָ שֶׁ֫מֶן וְשַׂמְתָּ֫ עָלֶ֫יהָ לְבֹנָ֑ה
מִנְחָ֖ה הִֽוא

15[7] And you shall put oil on it, and lay frankincense on it; *it is a meal offering*[8].

וְהִקְטִ֫יר הַכֹּהֵ֫ן אֶת־אַזְכָּרָתָ֫הּ מִגִּרְשָׂהּ֙

16[9] The priest shall make the memorial part of it smoke, even of its crushed grains,

---

[1] Leviticus 2:12 - 1 Corinthians 15:20, 2 Chronicles 7:5, b.Menachot [Rashi] 5b 83b, b.Menachot 57b 58a 84b 16b, b.Sotah [Rashi] 23a, b.Yevamot [Rashi] 1a, b.Yoma 47b, b.Zevachim 76b 77a 87a, Deuteronomy 2:10, Exodus 22:29 23:10-11 23:19, Genesis 23:10-11 23:17, Leviticus 7:13 23:10, mt.Hilchot Issurei Mizbeiach 5:3 5:4, mt.Hilchot Maaseh haKorbanot 7:2, Numbers 15:20, Revelation 14:4, t.Makkot 5:2, t.Menachot 6:6, y.Shabbat 7:2

[2] Leviticus 2:13 - 2 Chronicles 13:5, b.Berachot 5a, b.Chullin [Rashi] 132b, b.Menachot [Rashi] 11a, b.Menachot [Tosefot] 19b, b.Menachot 20a 20b 21a 21b, b.Nedarim [Ran] 18b, b.Sotah 15a, b.Tamid [Pirush] 31b, b.Zevachim [Rashi] 64b 18a, Colossians 4:6, Commandment #478 #479, Ein Yaakov Berachot:5a, Ezekiel 19:24, Ezra 7:22, Guide for the Perplexed 3:46, Jastrow 162b 1519b, m.Nedarim 2:4, m.Zevachim 14:3 6:5, Mark 9:49-50, Matthew 5:13, Midrash Psalms 20:8, mt.Hilchot Beit HaBechirah 5:11 5:17, mt.Hilchot Berachot 7:3, mt.Hilchot Issurei Mizbeiach 5:11, mt.Hilchot Maaseh haKorbanot 2:1, mt.Hilchot Nedarim 2:7, mt.Hilchot Sanhedrin vHainshin Hameurim Lahem 19:4, mt.Hilchot Temidim Umusafim 9:11, Numbers 18:19, Numbers.R 9:23, Philo De Specialibus Legibus I 289, z.Vayechi 666
[3] LXX *the LORD*

[4] Leviticus 2:14 - 1 Corinthians 15:20, 2 Kings 4:42, b.Avodah Zara [Rashi] 19a, b.Bechorot [Tosefot] 12b, b.Kereitot [Rashi] 4b, b.Menachot [Rashi] 59a 60b, b.Menachot 64b 66ab 68b 71a 72a 83b 84a, b.Rosh Hashanah [Rashi] 3a, b.Sanhedrin [Rashi] 11b, b.Sheviit 12b, b.Sotah 14a, Deuteronomy 2:2, Esther.R 10:4, Genesis 4:3, Isaiah 53:2-10, Jastrow 530a 785b 1375b, Leviticus 22:29 23:10 23:14-17 23:20, m.Bava Metzia 4:8, m.Menachot 10:4, Malachi 1:11, Mekilta de R'Ishmael Bahodesh 11:55, Mekilta de R'Ishmael Kaspa 1:3, mt.Hilchot Beit Habechirah 1:13, Numbers 4:2, Numbers.R 11:1, Pesikta de R'Kahana 8.1, Pesikta Rabbati 18:1, Proverbs 3:9-10, Revelation 14:4, y.Challah 1:1, y.Shabbat 19:1, y.Sotah 2:1
[5] 4QLevb *when*

[6] LXX *new grains ground and roasted for the Lord; so shall you bring the sacrifice of the firstfruits*
[7] Leviticus 2:15 - b.Menachot 59a, b.Nedarim [Ran] 84b, Midrash Tanchuma Behaalotcha 1
[8] LXX *it is a sacrifice*
[9] Leviticus 2:16 - b.Bechorot [Tosefot] 14b, b.Menachot [Rashi] 60b, b.Menachot [Tosefot] 19b, b.Menachot 19a 16a, b.Sotah 14b 15a, Hebrews 5:7, Isaiah 11:2-4 13:1, Leviticus 2:1-2 2:4-7 2:9 2:12, Psalms 21:2, Romans 8:26-27

וּמִשַּׁמְנָהּ עַל כָּל־לְבֹנָתֶהּ אִשֶּׁה לַיהוָה

and of its oil, with all its frankincense; it is an offering made by fire to the LORD.

Vayikra – Chapter 3

וְאִם־זֶבַח שְׁלָמִים קָרְבָּנוֹ אִם מִן־הַבָּקָר הוּא מַקְרִיב אִם־זָכָר אִם־נְקֵבָה תָּמִים יַקְרִיבֶנּוּ לִפְנֵי יְהוָה

1[1] And if his offering is a sacrifice[2] of peace offerings: if he offers of the *herd*[3], whether male or female, he shall offer it without blemish before the LORD.

וְסָמַךְ יָדוֹ עַל־רֹאשׁ קָרְבָּנוֹ וּשְׁחָטוֹ פֶּתַח אֹהֶל מוֹעֵד וְזָרְקוּ בְּנֵי אַהֲרֹן הַכֹּהֲנִים אֶת־הַדָּם עַל־הַמִּזְבֵּחַ סָבִיב

2[4] And he shall press his hand on the head of his offering, and kill it at the door of the tent of meeting; and Aaron's sons the priests shall dash the blood around the altar[5].

וְהִקְרִיב מִזֶּבַח הַשְּׁלָמִים אִשֶּׁה לַיהוָה אֶת־הַחֵלֶב הַמְכַסֶּה אֶת־הַקֶּרֶב וְאֵת כָּל־הַחֵלֶב אֲשֶׁר עַל־הַקֶּרֶב

3[6] And *he*[7] shall present of the sacrifice of peace offerings an offering made by fire to the LORD: the fat that covers the innards, and all the fat on the innards,

וְאֵת שְׁתֵּי הַכְּלָיֹת וְאֶת־הַחֵלֶב אֲשֶׁר

4[8] and the two kidneys, and the fat on them, which is by the loins, and the

---

[1] Leviticus 3:1 - 1 Chronicles 21:26, 1 John 1:3, 4QLevb, Amos 5:22, b.Bechorot 15b 61a, b.Beitzah [Rashi] 20a, b.Chullin [Tosefot] 22b, b.Menachot [Rashi] 2b 83b 93ab, b.Menachot 58a, b.Pesachim [Rashi] 61a, b.Temurah [Rashi] 13b, b.Temurah [Rashi] 2a, b.Temurah [Tosefot] 31b, b.Temurah 14b 18a, b.Zevachim [Rashi] 1b, b.Zevachim [Tosefot] 8b, b.Zevachim 4b 99b, Colossians 1:20, Exodus 20:21 24:5 5:28, Ezekiel 21:15, Ezekiel the Tragedian 177, Hebrews 10:22, Judges 20:26 21:4, Leviticus 1:3 7:11-34 17:5 22:19-21, Malachi 1:8 1:14, Numbers 6:14 7:17, Pesikta Rabbati 29/30:1, Proverbs 7:14, Romans 5:1-2, y.Nazir 5:2, z.Vayikra 9b 134 178
Leviticus 3:1-16 - Parshat Shelamim [peace offering]
[2] 4QLevb adds *to the LORD*
[3] LXX *oxen*
[4] Leviticus 3:2 - 1 John 1:9-1:10, 2 Corinthians 5:21, Acts 2:36-38 3:15 3:26 4:10-12 4:26-28, b.Beitzah [Rashi] 20a, b.Eruvin 2a, b.Kiddushin 57b, b.Makkot 14b, b.Menachot [Rashi] 19a 61a 93, b.Menachot [Tosefot] 95a, b.Menachot 8a, b.Nazir 45a, b.Sheviit [Tosefot] 16b, b.Yoma 62b, b.Zevachim [Rashi] 26a 53b 61a, b.Zevachim [Tosefot] 9a 36b, b.Zevachim 55ab 62b 63a, Exodus 5:10, Isaiah 5:6, Leviticus 1:4-5 1:11 8:22 16:21-22, m.Beitzah 2:4, m.Kilayim 1:8, m.Megillah 2:5, mt.Hilchot Beit Habechirah 7:19 7:19, mt.Hilchot Maaseh haKorbanot 3:6 5:4 5:6, Numbers.R 10:21, Sifre Devarim Reeh 75, t.Zevachim 7:1, Zechariah 12:10
Leviticus 3:2-8 - 4QLeve
[5] LXX adds *of burnt-offerings*
[6] Leviticus 3:3 - b.Chullin [Rashi] 75a, b.Chullin 49ab, b.Pesachim 2b, Deuteronomy 6:6, Exodus 5:13 5:22, Ezekiel 12:26, Isaiah 6:10, Jastrow 784a, Leviticus 3:16 4:8-9 7:3-4, Leviticus.R 22:10, m.Menachot 2:1, Matthew 13:16 15:8, mt.Hilchot Maaseh haKorbanot 1:18, Numbers.R 13:2, Proverbs 23:26, Psalms 119:70, Romans 5:5 6:6, t.Shechitat Chullin 9:14 9:14
[7] LXX *they*
[8] Leviticus 3:4 - b.Chullin [Rashi] 75a, b.Chullin 93a, b.Horayot [Rashi] 7b, Exodus 5:13 5:22, Jastrow 654b 1623a, Leviticus 3:10 3:15 4:9 7:4 8:16 8:25 9:10 9:19, m.Menachot 2:1, pap4QLXXLevb, Sifre Devarim Reeh 75, z.Pinchas 362

עֲלֵהֶן אֲשֶׁר עַל־הַכְּסָלִים וְאֶת־הַיֹּתֶרֶת
עַל־הַכָּבֵד עַל־הַכְּלָיוֹת יְסִירֶנָּה
וְהִקְטִירוּ אֹתוֹ בְנֵי־אַהֲרֹן הַמִּזְבֵּחָה עַל־
הָעֹלָה אֲשֶׁר עַל־הָעֵצִים אֲשֶׁר עַל־
הָאֵשׁ אִשֵּׁה רֵיחַ נִיחֹחַ לַיהוָה

וְאִם־מִן־הַצֹּאן קָרְבָּנוֹ לְזֶבַח שְׁלָמִים
לַיהוָה זָכָר אוֹ נְקֵבָה תָּמִים יַקְרִיבֶנּוּ

אִם־כֶּשֶׂב הוּא־מַקְרִיב אֶת־קָרְבָּנוֹ
וְהִקְרִיב אֹתוֹ לִפְנֵי יְהוָה

וְסָמַךְ אֶת־יָדוֹ עַל־רֹאשׁ קָרְבָּנוֹ וְשָׁחַט
אֹתוֹ לִפְנֵי אֹהֶל מוֹעֵד וְזָרְקוּ בְּנֵי אַהֲרֹן
אֶת־דָּמוֹ עַל־הַמִּזְבֵּחַ סָבִיב
וְהִקְרִיב מִזֶּבַח הַשְּׁלָמִים אִשֶּׁה לַיהוָה
חֶלְבּוֹ הָאַלְיָה תְמִימָה לְעֻמַּת הֶעָצֶה
יְסִירֶנָּה וְאֶת־הַחֵלֶב הַמְכַסֶּה אֶת־הַקֶּרֶב
וְאֵת כָּל־הַחֵלֶב אֲשֶׁר עַל־הַקֶּרֶב

lobe *above*[1] the liver, which he shall remove with the kidneys.

5[2] And Aaron's sons shall make it smoke on the altar on the burnt offering, which is on the wood that is on the fire[3]; it is an offering made by fire, of a sweet savor to the LORD.

6[4] And if his offering for *a*[5] sacrifice of peace offerings to the LORD is of the flock, male or female, he shall offer it without blemish.

7[6] If he brings a lamb for his offering, then shall he present it before the LORD.

8[7] And he shall press his hand on the head of his offering, and kill it *before*[8] the tent of meeting; and Aaron's sons shall dash its blood around the altar.

9[9] And he shall present the sacrifice of peace offerings *an offering made by fire*[10] to the LORD: its fat, the entire fat tail, which he shall remove close to the rump bone; and the fat covering the innards, and all the fat on the innards,

---

[1] pap4QLXXLevb *from*
[2] Leviticus 3:5 - 1 Kings 9:4, 1 Peter 2:5, 1 Samuel 2:15-2:16, 2 Chronicles 11:14, b.Kiddushin 36a, b.Zevachim [Tosefot] 65a, Exodus 5:13 29:38-29:42, Ezekiel 20:7 20:15, Leviticus 1:9 4:31 4:35 6:12 7:29-7:34 9:9-9:10, Pesikta de R'Kahana 6.3, y.Pesachim 5:10
[3] LXX adds *upon the altar*
[4] Leviticus 3:6 - Acts 4:27, b.Arachin 2a, b.Bechorot 42a, b.Chullin [Tosefot] 22b, b.Menachot [Rashi] 61b 93b, b.Menachot 83b 92b 93, b.Shekalim 6b, b.Temurah [Rashi] 2a 18b, b.Zevachim 8b 9a, Ephesians 1:10 2:13-22, Galatians 3:28 4:4, Isaiah 12:7, Jastrow 1472b, Leviticus 1:2 1:10 3:1-17, Romans 12:1-12:2, t.Zevachim 11:1, Titus 2:11-12, y.Pesachim 5:2, y.Shekalim 2:4, z.Mishpatim 108a
[5] 4QLeve *the*
[6] Leviticus 3:7 - 1 Kings 9:2, b.Arachin 2a, b.Kereitot 28b, b.Menachot [Rashi] 93a, b.Menachot 83b 92b 93, b.Pesachim 57b 96b, b.Temurah 18b, b.Zevachim [Tosefot] 7b 49a, b.Zevachim 9a 37b, Ein Yaakov Pesachim:57b, Ephesians 5:2 5:12, Hebrews 9:14, Leviticus 3:1 17:8-9, Leviticus.R 7:1 8:3, pap4QLXXLevb
Leviticus 3:7-10 - Jubilees 21:7
[7] Leviticus 3:8 - 1 Peter 2:24, 2 Corinthians 5:19 5:21, b.Arachin 2a 2b, b.Kiddushin 57b, b.Menachot [Rashi] 61b 93, b.Menachot 92b 93 94a, b.Zevachim 55ab, Ephesians 2:18 3:12, Hebrews 10:19-22, Isaiah 5:6 53:11-53:12, Leviticus 1:5 1:11 3:2-5 3:13 4:4 4:15 4:24, m.Megillah1 2:5, Matthew 3:17, mt.Hilchot Beit Habechirah 6:7, mt.Hilchot Biat haMikdash 9:1, mt.Hilchot Maaseh haKorbanot 5:4, Sifre Devarim Reeh 75
Leviticus 3:8-14 - 4QLevb
[8] LXX *by the doors of*
[9] Leviticus 3:9 - b.Chullin 11a 114a, b.Menachot [Rashi] 83b, b.Pesachim [Rashi] 3b 84b 96b, b.Zevachim [Rashi] 9a 46b, b.Zevachim 28a, Exodus 5:22, Isaiah 5:10, Jastrow 585a 1102a 1208a 1677a, Leviticus 3:3-4 7:3 8:25 9:19, m.Zevachim 2:2-3, mt.Hilchot Maaseh haKorbanot 1:18, Proverbs 23:26
Leviticus 3:9-14 - pap4QLXXLevb
[10] LXX *burnt offering*

וְאֵת֙ שְׁתֵּ֣י הַכְּלָיֹ֔ת וְאֶת־הַחֵ֙לֶב֙ אֲשֶׁ֣ר 10[1]
עֲלֵהֶ֔ן אֲשֶׁ֖ר עַל־הַכְּסָלִ֑ים וְאֶת־הַיֹּתֶ֙רֶת֙
עַל־הַכָּבֵ֔ד עַל־הַכְּלָיֹ֖ת יְסִירֶֽנָּה

וְהִקְטִיר֥וֹ הַכֹּהֵ֖ן הַמִּזְבֵּ֑חָה לֶ֛חֶם אִשֶּׁ֖ה 11[2]
לַיהוָֽה

וְאִ֥ם עֵ֖ז קָרְבָּנ֑וֹ וְהִקְרִיב֖וֹ לִפְנֵ֥י יְהוָֽה 12[5]

וְסָמַ֤ךְ אֶת־יָדוֹ֙ עַל־רֹאשׁ֔וֹ וְשָׁחַ֣ט אֹת֔וֹ 13[6]
לִפְנֵ֖י אֹ֣הֶל מוֹעֵ֑ד וְ֠זָרְקוּ בְּנֵ֨י אַהֲרֹ֧ן אֶת־
דָּמ֛וֹ עַל־הַמִּזְבֵּ֖חַ סָבִֽיב

וְהִקְרִ֨יב מִמֶּ֜נּוּ קָרְבָּנ֗וֹ אִשֶּׁה֙ לַֽיהוָ֔ה אֶת־ 14[9]
הַחֵ֙לֶב֙ הַֽמְכַסֶּ֣ה אֶת־הַקֶּ֔רֶב וְאֵת֙ כָּל־
הַחֵ֔לֶב אֲשֶׁ֖ר עַל־הַקֶּֽרֶב

וְאֵת֙ שְׁתֵּ֣י הַכְּלָיֹ֔ת וְאֶת־הַחֵ֙לֶב֙ אֲשֶׁ֣ר 15[10]
עֲלֵהֶ֔ן אֲשֶׁ֖ר עַל־הַכְּסָלִ֑ים וְאֶת־הַיֹּתֶ֙רֶת֙
עַל־הַכָּבֵ֔ד עַל־הַכְּלָיֹ֖ת יְסִירֶֽנָּה

וְהִקְטִירָ֥ם הַכֹּהֵ֖ן הַמִּזְבֵּ֑חָה לֶ֤חֶם אִשֶּׁה֙ 16[13]
לְרֵ֣יחַ נִיחֹ֔חַ כָּל־חֵ֖לֶב לַיהוָֽה

10[1] and the two kidneys, and the fat on them, which is by the loins, and the lobe above the liver, which he shall remove with the kidneys.

11[2] And the priest shall *make it smoke*[3] on the altar; it is the food[4] of the offering made by fire to the LORD.

12[5] And if his offering is a goat, then he shall present it before the LORD.

13[6] And he shall lay his hand on its head, and kill it *before*[7] the tent of meeting; and the sons of Aaron shall *dash*[8] its blood around the altar.

14[9] And he shall present from his offering, even an offering made by fire to the LORD: the fat covering the innards, and all the fat is on the innards,

15[10] and the two kidneys, and the fat on them, which is *by the loins*[11], and the *lobe above*[12] the liver, which he shall remove with the kidneys.

16[13] And the priest shall make them smoke on the altar; it is the food of the offering made by fire, for a sweet savor; all the fat is the LORD's.

---

[1] Leviticus 3:10 - Jastrow 1208a, Leviticus 3:4, m.Zevachim 2:3, mt.Hilchot Maaseh haKorbanot 1:18

[2] Leviticus 3:11 - 1 Corinthians 10:21, b.Menachot 89b, b.Pesachim 64b, Ezekiel 20:7, Isaiah 53:4-10, Jubilees 21:9, Leviticus 3:5 3:16 21:6 21:8 21:17 21:21-22 22:25, m.Zevachim 2:3, Malachi 1:7 1:12, mt.Hilchot Temidim Umusafim 10:16, Numbers 4:2, Psalms 22:15, Revelation 3:20, Romans 8:32, y.Pesachim 5:10, z.Vayikra 190

[3] 4QLevb *burn*

[4] pap4QLevb adds *for a pleasing odor*

[5] Leviticus 3:12 - 2 Corinthians 5:21, b.Kereitot 28b, b.Menachot [Rashi] 93a, b.Menachot 83b, b.Pesachim 57b, b.Temurah [Rashi] 2a, b.Zevachim [Tosefot] 8b, b.Zevachim 9a, Ein Yaakov Pesachim 57b, Isaiah 5:2 5:6, Leviticus 1:2 1:6 1:10 3:1 3:7-17 9:3 9:15 10:16 22:19-27, Leviticus.R 8:4, Matthew 25:32-33, Philo De Sacrificiis Abelis et Cain 118, Romans 8:3

[6] Leviticus 3:13 - 1 Peter 1:2 2:24 3:18, 2 Corinthians 5:21, b.Arachin [Tosefot] 2a, b.Kiddushin 57b, b.Menachot [Tosefot] 93a, b.Zevachim [Rashi] 56a, b.Zevachim 55ab, Hebrews 12:24, Isaiah 4:15 5:6 53:11-12, Leviticus 3:1-5 3:8, Romans 5:6-11 5:15-21

[7] LXX *by the doors of*

[8] LXX *pour out*

[9] Leviticus 3:14 - b.Menachot [Tosefot] 93a, Jeremiah 20:18, Leviticus 3:3-5 3:9-11, Matthew 22:37 2:38, Proverbs 23:26, Psalms 22:15-16, Romans 12:1-2

[10] Leviticus 3:15 - m.Chagigah 1:2, z.Acharei Mot 65b

[11] LXX *upon the thighs*

[12] LXX *caul of*

[13] Leviticus 3:16 - 1 Samuel 2:15-16, 2 Chronicles 7:7, b.Chullin [Tosefot] 103a 115b, b.Chullin 114a, b.Kereitot 23b, b.Meilah 15a, b.Menachot [Rashi] 47b, b.Pesachim 64b, b.Sheviit [Rashi] 24b, b.Temurah 32b, b.Zevachim [Rashi] 83b, Exodus 5:13 5:22, Isaiah 5:10, Leviticus 3:3-5 3:9-11 3:14-15 4:8-19 4:26 4:31 7:23-25 8:25 9:24 17:6, Matthew 22:37, mt.Hilchot Issurei Mizbeiach 7:11, mt.Hilchot Maachalot Assurot 7:5, Pesikta Rabbati 5:4, Philo De Posteritate Caini 123, Siman 34:5, y.Pesachim 5:10
Leviticus 3:16-17 - 4QLeve

חֻקַּת עוֹלָם לְדֹרֹתֵיכֶם בְּכֹל מוֹשְׁבֹתֵיכֶם 17¹ It shall be a perpetual statute
כָּל־חֵלֶב וְכָל־דָּם לֹא תֹאכֵלוּ   throughout your generations in all your
                                             dwellings, that you shall eat neither fat
                                             nor blood.

Vayikra – Chapter 4²

וַיְדַבֵּר יְהוָה אֶל־מֹשֶׁה לֵּאמֹר 1³ And the LORD spoke to Moses,
                                       saying:

דַּבֵּר אֶל־בְּנֵי יִשְׂרָאֵל לֵאמֹר נֶפֶשׁ כִּי־ 2⁴ Speak to the children of Israel, saying:
תֶחֱטָא בִשְׁגָגָה מִכֹּל מִצְוֹת יְהוָה אֲשֶׁר   If anyone shall sin through error⁵, in
לֹא תֵעָשֶׂינָה וְעָשָׂה מֵאַחַת מֵהֵנָּה   any of the *things the LORD has
                                              commanded not to be done, and shall
                                              do any one of them*⁶:

אִם הַכֹּהֵן הַמָּשִׁיחַ יֶחֱטָא לְאַשְׁמַת הָעָם 3⁷ if the anointed priest shall sin so as to
וְהִקְרִיב עַל חַטָּאתוֹ אֲשֶׁר חָטָא פַּר בֶּן־   *bring guilt on the people*⁸, then let him
בָּקָר תָּמִים לַיהוָה לְחַטָּאת   offer for his sin he has sinned, a young
                                           bullock without blemish to the LORD
                                           for a sin offering.

---

¹ Leviticus 3:17 - 1 Samuel 14:32-34, 1 Timothy 4:4, Acts 15:20-21 15:29, b.Bava Batra 74b, b.Bechorot [Tosefot] 15a, b.Chullin [Rashi] 37a 103a, b.Chullin [Tosefot] 5b, b.Kereitot [Rashi] 22b, b.Kereitot 2a 4ab, b.Kiddushin [Rashi] 37b, b.Menachot [Tosefot] 56b 74b, b.Sheviit [Tosefot] 23a, b.Sotah [Rashi] 15a, Deuteronomy 12:16 12:23 15:23 8:14, Ephesians 1:7 5:26, Ezekiel 9:25 20:7 20:15, Genesis 9:4, Jastrow 464a, Leviticus 3:16 6:18 7:23 7:25-27 7:36 16:34 17:7 17:10-16 23:14, m.Keritot 3:1 5:1, m.Meilah 4:2, Mas.Semachot 3:10, Matthew 16:24 2:28, Midrash Psalms 2:15, mt.Hilchot Sanhedrin vHainshin Hameurim Lahem 16:5, mt.Hilchot Yesodei haTorah 9:1, Nehemiah 8:10, Numbers 19:21, Pesikta Rabbati 10:3, Philo De Specialibus Legibus IV 123, Song of Songs.R 7:7, y.Nazir 6:1
² Jastrow 360a, Tanya Igeret Hateshuvah §03
³ Leviticus 4:1 - z.Vayikra 13a, Midrash Tanchuma Vayikra 6
Leviticus 4:1-6 - 4QLeve
Leviticus 4:1-12 - m.Eduyot 8:6, m.Horayot 2:7
Leviticus 4:1-21 - m.Meilah 2:3, m.Zevachim 4:4
⁴ Leviticus 4:2 - 1 Samuel 14:27, 1 Timothy 1:13, b.Horayot [Tosefot] 4a, b.Kereitot [Rashi] 22b, b.Kereitot 3a 4a, b.Sanhedrin [Tosefot] 4a, b.Sanhedrin 62a, b.Shabbat 103ab, b.Sheviit [Rashi] 28b 91a, b.Sheviit 12b, b.Yoma 36b, b.Zevachim [Rashi] 16b, Deuteronomy 19:4, Ecclesiastes.R 3:19, Ein Yaakov Yoma:36b, Genesis 20:9, Hebrews 5:2 9:7, James 3:10, Jastrow 1212b, Leviticus 4:13 4:22 4:27 5:15-18, Leviticus.R 4:1 4:3, m.Megillah 1:9, m.Shabbat 1:1, Midrash Tanchuma Vayikra 6 7, Numbers 15:22-29, Psalms 19:13, Saadia Opinions 6:5, y.Horayot 2:2, y.Shabbat 7:1 12:3
Leviticus 4:2-12 - mt.Hilchot Shegagot 1:4, z.Vayikra 207 263
⁵ LXX adds *before the LORD*
⁶ LXX *commandments of the Lord concerning things which he ought not to do, and shall do some of them*
⁷ Leviticus 4:3 - 2 Corinthians 5:21, b.Chullin [Rashi] 114a, b.Horayot [Rashi] 10b, b.Horayot 6b 7ab 10a 12a, b.Ketubot 45a, b.Megillah 9b, b.Menachot 3a, b.Nazir [Rashi] 47b, b.Sanhedrin [Rashi] 61b, b.Nazir [Tosefot] 47a, Exodus 5:7 5:14 5:21 6:10, Ezekiel 19:19, Ezra 8:35, Guide for the Perplexed 3:46, Hebrews 5:3 7:27-28, Jastrow 580b 852a 838b, Leviticus 4:14 5:6 8:12 9:2 16:6 16:11 21:10-12, Leviticus.R 5:1 5:3, m.Horayot 2:1 2:6, m.Megillah 1:9, m.Sheviit 1:6, mt.Hilchot Klei haMikdash Vihaovdim Bo 4:14, mt.Hilchot Shegagot 12:1 15:1 15:6 15:10, Numbers 8:8, Romans 8:3, Saadia Opinions 8:9, y.Horayot 2:2, y.Megillah 1:10, y.Shabbat 7:1, z.Vayikra 17a 17b, z.Vayikra 286 294 312 389
Leviticus 4:3-4 - pap4QLXXLevb
Leviticus 4:3-9 - MaslLeva
⁸ LXX *cause the people to sin*

וְהֵבִיא אֶת־הַפָּר אֶל־פֶּתַח אֹהֶל מוֹעֵד
לִפְנֵי יְהוָה וְסָמַךְ אֶת־יָדוֹ עַל־רֹאשׁ
הַפָּר וְשָׁחַט אֶת־הַפָּר לִפְנֵי יְהוָה

4[1] And he shall *bring*[2] the bullock to the door of the tent of meeting before the LORD; and he shall press his hand upon the head[3] of the bullock, and kill the bullock before the LORD.

וְלָקַח הַכֹּהֵן הַמָּשִׁיחַ מִדַּם הַפָּר וְהֵבִיא
אֹתוֹ אֶל־אֹהֶל מוֹעֵד

5[4] And the anointed priest shall take of the blood of the bullock, and bring it to the tent of meeting.

וְטָבַל הַכֹּהֵן אֶת־אֶצְבָּעוֹ בַּדָּם וְהִזָּה
מִן־הַדָּם שֶׁבַע פְּעָמִים לִפְנֵי יְהוָה אֶת־
פְּנֵי פָּרֹכֶת הַקֹּדֶשׁ

6[5] And the priest shall dip his finger in the blood, and sprinkle of the blood seven times[6] before the LORD, *in front of the veil of the sanctuary*[7].

וְנָתַן הַכֹּהֵן מִן־הַדָּם עַל־קַרְנוֹת מִזְבַּח
קְטֹרֶת הַסַּמִּים לִפְנֵי יְהוָה אֲשֶׁר בְּאֹהֶל
מוֹעֵד וְאֵת כָּל־דַּם הַפָּר יִשְׁפֹּךְ אֶל־
יְסוֹד מִזְבַּח הָעֹלָה אֲשֶׁר־פֶּתַח אֹהֶל
מוֹעֵד

7[8] And the priest shall put of the blood[9] on the horns of the altar of *sweet*[10] incense before the LORD in the tent of meeting; and he shall pour out the remaining blood of the bullock at the base of the altar of *burnt offering*[11] at the *door*[12] of the tent of meeting.

וְאֶת־כָּל־חֵלֶב פַּר הַחַטָּאת יָרִים מִמֶּנּוּ
אֶת־הַחֵלֶב הַמְכַסֶּה עַל־הַקֶּרֶב וְאֵת
כָּל־הַחֵלֶב אֲשֶׁר עַל־הַקֶּרֶב

8[13] And he shall take off all the fat of the bullock of the sin offering, the fat that covers the inwards, and all the fat that is on the innards,

---

[1] Leviticus 4:4 - 1 Peter 3:18, b.Nazir [Tosefot] 47a, b.Shabbat 70a, b.Yevamot 9a, b.Zevachim [Rashi] 40a, b.Zevachim [Tosefot] 32a, Daniel 9:26, Exodus 29:10-11, Isaiah 5:6, Leviticus 1:3-4 16:21, m.Megillah 2:5, pap4QLXXLevb
[2] pap4QLXXLevb *lead in*
[3] pap4QLXXLevb adds *before the LORD*
[4] Leviticus 4:5 - 1 John 1:7, b.Arachin [Rashi] 102b 103b, b.Kiddushin 36b, b.Menachot [Rashi] 26b, b.Menachot [Tosefot] 34b, b.Yoma 48a, b.Zevachim [Rashi] 24a 52a, b.Zevachim 25ab 26a, Leviticus 4:16-4:17 16:14 16:19, m.Megillah 1:9, mt.Hilchot Biat haMikdash 5:17, Numbers 19:4, y.Horayot 2:4
[5] Leviticus 4:6 - b.Ketubot [Rashi] 5b, b.Menachot 7b 25ba, b.Zevachim [Rashi] 13b 14b 52a, b.Zevachim [Tosefot] 25a 40b, b.Zevachim 40ab 41b 93b, Jastrow 580b 1011a, Joshua 6:4 6:8, Leviticus 4:17 4:25 4:30 4:34 8:15 9:9 14:16 14:18 14:27 16:14 16:19 1:8 2:18 2:24 2:28, m.Megillah 2:5, mt.Hilchot Maaseh haKorbanot 5:15, Numbers 19:4, y.Taanit 2:1
Leviticus 4:6-8 - pap4QLXXLevb
[6] pap4QLXXLevb adds *with his finger*
[7] LXX *over against the holy veil*
[8] Leviticus 4:7 - b.Chullin [Rashi] 132a, b.Kinnim [Pirush] 22a, b.Menachot [Tosefot] 64b, b.Sanhedrin [Rashi] 4a, b.Sanhedrin [Rashi] 4b, b.Tamid [Pirush] 29a 30b, b.Yoma [Rashi] 25b, b.Yoma 48a 56b 58b 59a, b.Zevachim [Rashi] 10a 14b 53a 64b, b.Zevachim [Tosefot] 51b, b.Zevachim 25a 40ab 51a 52a 57a 58b 64a, Ephesians 2:13, Exodus 30:1-10, Hebrews 9:15 9:21, Jastrow 1616a, Leviticus 4:18 4:30 4:34 5:9 8:15 9:9 16:18, m.Yoma 5:6, mt.Hilchot Pesulei haMikdashim 2:3, Psalms 22:27, y.Yoma 5:6
[9] pap4QLXXLevb adds *of the bull*
[10] LXX *the compound*
[11] pap4QLXXLevb *offering*
[12] LXX plural
[13] Leviticus 4:8 - b.Chullin [Rashi] 114a, b.Sanhedrin [Tosefot] 3b, b.Yoma [Tosefot] 33a, b.Zevachim [Tosefot] 41b, Isaiah 5:10, John 12:27, Leviticus 3:3-5 3:9:11 3:14-16 4:19 4:26 4:31 4:35 7:3-5 16:25, mt.Hilchot Maaseh haKorbanot 7:1

וְאֵת֙ שְׁתֵּ֣י הַכְּלָיֹ֔ת וְאֶת־הַחֵ֙לֶב֙ אֲשֶׁ֣ר עֲלֵיהֶ֔ן אֲשֶׁ֖ר עַל־הַכְּסָלִ֑ים וְאֶת־הַיֹּתֶ֙רֶת֙ עַל־הַכָּבֵ֔ד עַל־הַכְּלָי֖וֹת יְסִירֶֽנָּה	9[1] and the two kidneys, and the fat on them, which is by the loins, and the *lobe above*[2] the liver, which he shall remove with the kidneys,
כַּאֲשֶׁ֣ר יוּרַ֔ם מִשּׁ֖וֹר זֶ֣בַח הַשְּׁלָמִ֑ים וְהִקְטִירָם֙ הַכֹּהֵ֔ן עַ֖ל מִזְבַּ֥ח הָעֹלָֽה	10[3] as it is taken off from the ox of the sacrifice of peace offerings; and the priest shall make them smoke on the altar of burnt offering.
וְאֶת־ע֤וֹר הַפָּר֙ וְאֶת־כָּל־בְּשָׂר֔וֹ עַל־רֹאשׁ֖וֹ וְעַל־כְּרָעָ֑יו וְקִרְבּ֖וֹ וּפִרְשֽׁוֹ	11[4] But the skin of the bullock, and all its flesh, with its head, and with its legs, and its inwards, and its dung,
וְהוֹצִ֣יא אֶת־כָּל־הַ֠פָּר אֶל־מִח֨וּץ לַֽמַּחֲנֶ֜ה אֶל־מָק֤וֹם טָהוֹר֙ אֶל־שֶׁ֣פֶךְ הַדֶּ֔שֶׁן וְשָׂרַ֥ף אֹת֛וֹ עַל־עֵצִ֖ים בָּאֵ֑שׁ עַל־שֶׁ֧פֶךְ הַדֶּ֛שֶׁן יִשָּׂרֵֽף	12[5] even the whole bullock he shall carry forth outside the camp to a clean place, where the ashes are poured out, and burn it on wood with fire; it shall be burned where the ashes are poured out.
וְאִ֥ם כָּל־עֲדַ֨ת יִשְׂרָאֵ֜ל יִשְׁגּ֗וּ וְנֶעְלַ֤ם דָּבָר֙ מֵעֵינֵ֣י הַקָּהָ֔ל וְעָשׂ֞וּ אַחַ֣ת מִכָּל־מִצְוֺ֧ת יְהוָ֛ה אֲשֶׁ֥ר לֹא־תֵעָשֶׂ֖ינָה וְאָשֵֽׁמוּ	13[6] And if the whole congregation of Israel shall *err*[7], the thing being hid from the eyes of the assembly, and they do anything the LORD has commanded not to be done, and are guilty:
וְנֽוֹדְעָה֙ הַֽחַטָּ֔את אֲשֶׁ֥ר חָטְא֖וּ עָלֶ֑יהָ וְהִקְרִ֨יבוּ הַקָּהָ֜ל פַּ֤ר בֶּן־בָּקָר֙ לְחַטָּ֔את וְהֵבִ֣יאוּ אֹת֔וֹ לִפְנֵ֖י אֹ֥הֶל מוֹעֵֽד	14[8] When the sin they have sinned becomes known, the assembly shall offer a young bullock for a sin offering, and bring *it*[9] before the tent of meeting.

[1] Leviticus 4:9 - b.Chullin [Rashi] 114a, b.Zevachim [Tosefot] 40b, b.Zevachim 41b, Leviticus 3:4, mt.Hilchot Maaseh haKorbanot 7:1

[2] LXX *caul that is on*

[3] Leviticus 4:10 - b.Chullin [Tosefot] 21a, b.Chullin 114a, b.Meilah [Tosefot] 15a, b.Zevachim [Tosefot] 40b 41b 45a, b.Zevachim 44b 49b, Midrash Tanchuma Bechukkotai 4, mt.Hilchot Maaseh haKorbanot 7:1
Leviticus 4:10-11 - pap4QLXXLevb

[4] Leviticus 4:11 - b.Yoma 67b 68a, b.Zevachim 50ab, Exodus 5:14, Hebrews 13:11-13, Leviticus 4:21 6:30 8:14-17 9:8-11 16:27, Numbers 19:5, Psalms 7:12

[5] Leviticus 4:12 - b.Pesachim [Rashi] 83a, b.Pesachim 75ab, b.Sanhedrin 42b, b.Yoma 50a 68ab, b.Zevachim [Rashi] 47ab 83a, b.Zevachim 35b 50a 105b 16a, Exodus 5:14, Guide for the Perplexed 3:46, Hebrews 13:11, Jastrow 564b 1316b 1617a, Leviticus 6:10-11 13:46 16:27, m.Parah 8:3, mt.Hilchot Maaseh haKorbanot 7:5, mt.Hilchot Temidim Umusafim 2:14, Numbers 5:3 15:35 19:3 19:5
Leviticus 4:12-14 - 4QLeve

[6] Leviticus 4:13 - 1 Corinthians 11:27, 1 Timothy 1:13, b.Horayot [Rashi] 7a 10b, b.Horayot 2ab 3b 4ab 5a 7b 8ab, b.Kereitot 26b, b.Menachot [Tosefot] 4a, b.Pesachim [Rashi] 93a, b.Sanhedrin [Rashi] 61b, b.Sanhedrin 87a, b.Yevamot 9a, b.Zevachim [Rashi] 41a, Commandment #480, Exodus.R 38:4, Ezra 10:19, Genesis.R 44:14, Guide for the Perplexed 3:41, Hebrews 10:26-29, Hosea 5:15, Joshua 7:11 7:24-26, Leviticus 4:1-4:2 5:2-5 5:17 6:4, Leviticus.R 5:3, m.Horayot 1:2-5 1:3 1:4 1:7 2:2-3 2:6, m.Sheviit 2:3, Midrash Tanchuma Behaalotcha 16, Midrash Tanchuma Vayikra 7, mt.Hilchot Shegagot 13:1 14:1, Numbers 15:24-29, Sifre.z Numbers Shelah 15:24, t.Horayot 1:8, y.Horayot 1:1 1:3 1:8 2:4, z.Vayikra 18b 20a 23a, z.Vayikra 315 334 349 387 389
Leviticus 4:13-21 - m.Eduyot 8:6

[7] LXX *trespass ignorantly*

[8] Leviticus 4:14 - b.Horayot 5a 8a, b.Kereitot 26ab, b.Yevamot 9a, Genesis.R 82:5, Leviticus 4:3 4:23 4:28, m.Parah 1:4, mt.Hilchot Shegagot 12:1 12:2 14:4, y.Horayot 1:8 2:4

[9] MT LXX masculine; 4QLevb feminine

וְסָמְכוּ זִקְנֵי הָעֵדָה אֶת־יְדֵיהֶם עַל־רֹאשׁ הַפָּר לִפְנֵי יְהוָה וְשָׁחַט אֶת־הַפָּר לִפְנֵי יְהוָה

15[1] And the elders of the congregation shall press their hands on the head of the bullock before the LORD; and the bullock shall be killed before the LORD.

וְהֵבִיא הַכֹּהֵן הַמָּשִׁיחַ מִדַּם הַפָּר אֶל־אֹהֶל מוֹעֵד

16[2] And the anointed priest shall bring of the blood of the bullock to the tent of meeting.

וְטָבַל הַכֹּהֵן אֶצְבָּעוֹ מִן־הַדָּם וְהִזָּה שֶׁבַע פְּעָמִים לִפְנֵי יְהוָה אֵת פְּנֵי הַפָּרֹכֶת

17[3] And the priest shall dip his finger in the blood, and sprinkle it seven times before the LORD, in front of the veil[4].

וּמִן־הַדָּם יִתֵּן עַל־קַרְנֹת הַמִּזְבֵּחַ אֲשֶׁר לִפְנֵי יְהוָה אֲשֶׁר בְּאֹהֶל מוֹעֵד וְאֵת כָּל־הַדָּם יִשְׁפֹּךְ אֶל־יְסוֹד מִזְבַּח הָעֹלָה אֲשֶׁר־פֶּתַח אֹהֶל מוֹעֵד

18[5] And *he*[6] shall put of the blood on the horns of the altar[7] before the LORD in the tent of meeting, and *he shall pour out all the remaining blood*[8] at the base of the altar of burnt offering at the door of the tent of meeting.

וְאֵת כָּל־חֶלְבּוֹ יָרִים מִמֶּנּוּ וְהִקְטִיר הַמִּזְבֵּחָה

19[9] *And he shall take off all its fat*[10], and make it smoke on the altar.

וְעָשָׂה לַפָּר כַּאֲשֶׁר עָשָׂה לְפַר הַחַטָּאת כֵּן יַעֲשֶׂה־לּוֹ וְכִפֶּר עֲלֵהֶם הַכֹּהֵן וְנִסְלַח לָהֶם

20[11] Thus, shall he do with the bullock; as he did with the bullock of the sin offering, so shall he do with this; and the priest shall make atonement for them, and *they shall be forgiven*[12].

---

[1] Leviticus 4:15 - b.Menachot [Rashi] 62b 93b, b.Menachot 92ab 93, b.Sanhedrin 3b 13b 14a, b.Sotah 44b, b.Yevamot 11b, Deuteronomy 21:3-21:9, Exodus 24:1 24:9, Jastrow 1000a, Leviticus 1:4 4:4 8:14 8:22 16:21, Leviticus.R 5:7, m.Megillah 2:5, m.Sanhedrin 1:3, mt.Hilchot Maaseh haKorbanot 3:10, Numbers 8:10 11:16 11:25, t.Menachot 10:14, y.Horayot 1:8, y.Sanhedrin 1:2, y.Sotah 9:1

[2] Leviticus 4:16 - Hebrews 9:12-9:14, Leviticus 4:5-4:12, Saadia Opinions 8:9

[3] Leviticus 4:17 - b.Zevachim [Rashi] 40a 41b, b.Zevachim [Tosefot] 39b, b.Zevachim [Tosefot] 40b, Leviticus 4:6-7, mt.Hilchot Avodat Yom haKippurim 5:23, mt.Hilchot Maaseh haKorbanot 5:10, mt.Hilchot Pesulei haMikdashim 2:3, y.Taanit 2:1

[4] LXX adds *of the sanctuary*

[5] Leviticus 4:18 - b.Menachot [Rashi] 61a, b.Sanhedrin [Tosefot] 3b, b.Sanhedrin 4a, b.Zevachim [Rashi] 40b 51a 111a, b.Zevachim [Tosefot] 39b, b.Zevachim 40a 62a, Guide for the Perplexed 3:46, Leviticus 4:7, mt.Hilchot Beit Habechirah 2:17 2:17
Leviticus 4:18-19 - pap4QLXXLevb

[6] LXX *the priest*

[7] LXX adds *of the incense of composition*

[8] Missing in LXX

[9] Leviticus 4:19 - b.Menachot 77b, b.Zevachim [Rashi] 41a, Hebrews 1:3 9:14, Leviticus 4:8-4:10 4:26 4:31 4:35 5:6 6:7 12:8 14:18, Numbers 15:25, Psalms 22:15

[10] LXX *And he shall take away all the fat from it*

[11] Leviticus 4:20 - 1 John 1:7 2:2, b.Chullin [Tosefot] 21a 114a, b.Menachot [Rashi] 27b, b.Menachot 16a, b.Sanhedrin [Rashi] 4b, b.Sanhedrin 42b, b.Temurah [Rashi] 15b, b.Zevachim [Rashi] 47b 49b 52b 105b, b.Zevachim [Tosefot] 38a 41b, b.Zevachim 39ab 40ab 41a, Daniel 9:24, Exodus 8:30, Galatians 3:13, Hebrews 1:3 2:17 9:14 10:10-10:12, Leviticus 1:4 4:26 5:6 6:7 12:8 14:18, Numbers 15:25 15:28, Revelation 1:5, Romans 5:11

[12] LXX *the trespass shall be forgiven them*

וְהוֹצִיא אֶת־הַפָּר אֶל־מִחוּץ לַמַּחֲנֶה וְשָׂרַף אֹתוֹ כַּאֲשֶׁר שָׂרַף אֵת הַפָּר הָרִאשׁוֹן חַטַּאת הַקָּהָל הוּא	21[1] And *he*[2] shall carry forth the bullock outside the camp and burn it as he burned the first bullock; it is the sin offering for the assembly.
אֲשֶׁר נָשִׂיא יֶחֱטָא וְעָשָׂה אַחַת מִכָּל־מִצְוֹת יְהוָה אֱלֹהָיו אֲשֶׁר לֹא־תֵעָשֶׂינָה בִּשְׁגָגָה וְאָשֵׁם	22[3] When a ruler sins, and errs through any one of all the things the LORD his God has commanded not to be done[4], and is guilty:
אוֹ־הוֹדַע אֵלָיו חַטָּאתוֹ אֲשֶׁר חָטָא בָּהּ וְהֵבִיא אֶת־קָרְבָּנוֹ שְׂעִיר עִזִּים זָכָר תָּמִים	23[5] If his sin, in which he has sinned, becomes known to him, he shall bring for his offering[6] a [7]goat, a male without blemish.
וְסָמַךְ יָדוֹ עַל־רֹאשׁ הַשָּׂעִיר וְשָׁחַט אֹתוֹ בִּמְקוֹם אֲשֶׁר־יִשְׁחַט אֶת־הָעֹלָה לִפְנֵי יְהוָה חַטָּאת הוּא	24[8] And he shall press his hand on the head of the *goat*[9], and [10]kill it in the place where they kill the [11]burnt offering before the LORD; it is a sin offering.
וְלָקַח הַכֹּהֵן מִדַּם הַחַטָּאת בְּאֶצְבָּעוֹ	25[12] And the priest shall take of the blood of

---

[1] Leviticus 4:21 - 1 Timothy 2:5-2:6, 2 Chronicles 29:21-29:24, 2 Corinthians 5:21, b.Horayot [Rashi] 5a, b.Horayot 13a, b.Sanhedrin 42b, b.Yoma 68a, b.Zevachim [Rashi] 4a 84ab, b.Zevachim [Tosefot] 8b 47b, b.Zevachim 105b, Ezra 8:35, Guide for the Perplexed 3:48, Jastrow 677a, Leviticus 4:11-4:12 16:15 16:21, m.Parah 8:3, Matthew 20:28, y.Taanit 2:1, y.Yoma 6:6

[2] LXX *they*

[3] Leviticus 4:22 - 2 Samuel 21:1-21:3 24:10-24:17, b.Arachin [Rashi] 96a, b.Chullin 5b, b.Horayot 8a 9a 10ab 11a, b.Kereitot 14b 26b, b.Menachot 3a, b.Sanhedrin [Rashi] 63a 65a, b.Yevamot 9a, b.Yoma 80a, Ein Yaakov Horayot:10a, Ein Yaakov Horayot:9a, Exodus 18:21, Guide for the Perplexed 3:46, Jastrow 1528a, Leviticus 4:2 4:13 4:27, m.Horayot 2:5 26-7 3:1, m.Yevamot 10:2, mt.Hilchot Shegagot 15:6 15:9 15:10, Numbers 16:2 7:13, Philo De Specialibus Legibus I 233, t.Bava Kamma 7:5, t.Shevuot 1:6, y.Horayot 3:2, z.Vayikra 23a, z.Vayikra 389 393

Leviticus 4:22-23 - mt.Hilchot Shegagot 15:1

Leviticus 4:22-26 - mt.Hilchot Shegagot 1:4

[4] LXX adds *unwillingly*

[5] Leviticus 4:23 - 2 Kings 22:10-22:13, b.Chullin [Rashi] 5b, b.Horayot [Rashi] 8b, b.Horayot 5a, b.Kereitot [Rashi] 4a 28b, b.Kereitot 7b 11b 19ab 26ab 27b, b.Ketubot 45a, b.Kiddushin [Tosefot] 65b, b.Menachot 3a, b.Nazir [Rashi] 57a, b.Nazir 27b, b.Pesachim [Rashi] 57b, b.Sanhedrin [Rashi] 62b 65a, b.Shabbat [Rashi] 72a, b.Sheviit 18b 19b, b.Sotah [Tosefot] 31b, Jastrow 564b 565a 1098b, Leviticus 4:3 4:14 4:28 5:4 9:3 23:19, mt.Hilchot Shegagot 2:3, Numbers 7:16 7:22 7:28 7:34 15:24 4:15 4:30 5:5 5:11 5:16 5:19, Pesikta Rabbati 5:5, Romans 8:3, Ruth.R 5:6, t.Kereitot 2:13, y.Horayot 1:1, y.Sheviit 2:4, y.Terumot 8:1, z.Tazria 133, z.Vayikra 393 401 405

Leviticus 4:23-28 - 4QLeve

[6] 4QLevc adds *for that which he has sinned*

[7] LXX adds *a kid of the*

[8] Leviticus 4:24 - b.Menachot [Rashi] 53a, b.Menachot [Tosefot] 61a 92a, b.Menachot 4a 55b 92b, b.Sanhedrin [Tosefot] 82b, b.Zevachim [Rashi] 14a, b.Zevachim [Tosefot] 52b 63b, b.Zevachim 5b 10b 11a 48ab, Exodus 5:38, Isaiah 5:6, Leviticus 1:5 1:11 3:2 3:8 3:13 4:3-4:35 6:25 7:2 16:15

Leviticus 4:24-26 - 11QpaleoLeva

[9] LXX *kid*

[10] LXX adds *they shall*

[11] LXX adds *whole*

[12] Leviticus 4:25 - b.Arachin [Rashi] 1a, b.Chullin [Rashi] 21b, b.Chullin [Tosefot] 114b, b.Chullin 5b, b.Menachot [Rashi] 10b 83a, b.Menachot 10a 19a 25ba, b.Pesachim 65a, b.Sanhedrin [Tosefot] 3b, b.Sanhedrin 4a, b.Yoma [Tosefot] 52b, b.Yoma 57b, b.Zevachim [Rashi] 11a 37a 38a 51a 53a 98a, b.Zevachim 34b 37b, Hebrews 2:10 9:22, Isaiah 16:21, Leviticus 4:7 4:18 4:30 4:34 8:10 8:15 9:9 16:18, mt.Hilchot Maaseh haKorbanot 5:7, Romans 3:24-3:26 8:3-8:4 10:4, y.Yoma 5:4

וְנָתַן עַל־קַרְנֹת מִזְבַּח הָעֹלָה וְאֶת־דָּמוֹ
יִשְׁפֹּךְ אֶל־יְסוֹד מִזְבַּח הָעֹלָה

the sin offering with his finger, and put it on the horns of the altar of [1]burnt offering, *and he shall pour out its remaining blood*[2] at the base of the altar of [3]burnt offering.

26[4] וְאֶת־כָּל־חֶלְבּוֹ יַקְטִיר הַמִּזְבֵּחָה כְּחֵלֶב
זֶבַח הַשְּׁלָמִים וְכִפֶּר עָלָיו הַכֹּהֵן
מֵחַטָּאתוֹ וְנִסְלַח לוֹ

And he shall make all its fat smoke on the altar, as the fat of the sacrifice of peace offerings; and the priest shall make atonement for him concerning his sin, and he shall be forgiven.

27[5] וְאִם־נֶפֶשׁ אַחַת תֶּחֱטָא בִשְׁגָגָה מֵעַם
הָאָרֶץ בַּעֲשֹׂתָהּ אַחַת מִמִּצְוֹת יְהוָה
אֲשֶׁר לֹא־תֵעָשֶׂינָה וְאָשֵׁם

And if any of the *common people*[6] sin through error, in doing any of the things the LORD has commanded not to be done, and is guilty:

28[7] אוֹ הוֹדַע אֵלָיו חַטָּאתוֹ אֲשֶׁר חָטָא
וְהֵבִיא קָרְבָּנוֹ שְׂעִירַת עִזִּים תְּמִימָה
נְקֵבָה עַל־חַטָּאתוֹ אֲשֶׁר חָטָא

If his sin, which he has sinned, becomes known to him, then he shall bring for his offering a [8]goat, a female without blemish, for his sin he has sinned.

29[9] וְסָמַךְ אֶת־יָדוֹ עַל רֹאשׁ הַחַטָּאת וְשָׁחַט
אֶת־הַחַטָּאת בִּמְקוֹם הָעֹלָה

And he shall press his hand upon the head of the sin offering, and [10]kill the sin offering in the place of the [11]burnt offering.

---

[1] LXX adds *whole*

[2] 11QpaleoLeva *and he shall pour out its blood*

[3] LXX adds *whole*

[4] Leviticus 4:26 - b.Megillah [Rashi] 20b, b.Menachot [Rashi] 27b, b.Sanhedrin 4b, b.Zevachim 38a, b.Zevachim [Tosefot] 8a 36b, Guide for the Perplexed 3:45, Leviticus 3:5 4:8-10 4:20 4:31 4:35 5:10 5:13 5:16 5:18 6:7 6:20-30, m.Parah 8:3, mt.Hilchot Pesulei haMikdashim 2:21 15:3, Numbers 15:28
Leviticus 4:26-28 - pap4QLXXLevb

[5] Leviticus 4:27 - b.Horayot [Rashi] 6b 7a 9b 10b, b.Horayot 2ab 8ab 11a, b.Kereitot 22b 25b 26b, b.Menachot [Tosefot] 4a, b.Shabbat 3a 69a 92b 93ab, b.Sheviit [Rashi] 5a, b.Yevamot 9a, b.Zevachim [Rashi] 8a 12b, b.Zevachim 48a, Exodus 12:49, Gates of Repentance 4.002, Genesis.R 44:14, Guide for the Perplexed 3:46, Leviticus 4:2 4:13, m.Niddah 2:2, Midrash Tanchuma Vayikra 7, mt.Hilchot Mechusrei Kapparah 4:2, mt.Hilchot Shegagot 1:2, mt.Hilchot Shabbat 1:15 13:5, Numbers 5:6 15:16 15:27 15:29, y.Horayot 1:1 2:5, y.Shabbat 1:1 10:5 13:6, y.Sheviit 2:4, y.Yevamot 4:15
Leviticus 4:27-28 - Commandment #481, mt.Hilchot Shegagot 11:1
Leviticus 4:27-30 - mt.Hilchot Chametz uMatzah 1:1, mt.Hilchot Teshuvah 1:1 1:1
Leviticus 4:27-31 - mt.Hilchot Shegagot 1:4, Parshat Chattat [sin offering]
Leviticus 4:27-35 - m.Horayot 1:1 1:4-5 3:1, m.Kelim 17:12, m.Sanhedrin 7:8, m.Yoma 8:2 8:8

[6] LXX MT *people of the land*

[7] Leviticus 4:28 - b.Bava Metzia [Rashi] 3b, b.Horayot 2a, b.Kereitot [Rashi] 18a 28a, b.Kereitot 19a 26ab 27b, b.Ketubot 45a, b.Menachot 3a, b.Nazir 27b 28a, b.Shabbat [Rashi] 72a, b.Shabbat 71b, b.Sheviit [Tosefot] 3b, b.Yevamot 87b, b.Zevachim [Rashi] 6a, Galatians 3:28 4:4-4:5, Genesis 3:15, Isaiah 7:14, Jastrow 564b 565a, Jeremiah 7:23, Leviticus 4:3 4:14 4:23 4:32 5:6, mt.Hilchot Pesulei haMikdashim 15:3, Romans 8:3, y.Horayot 1:1, y.Sheviit 1:2, y.Terumot 8:1

[8] LXX adds *a kid of the*

[9] Leviticus 4:29 - b.Menachot [Rashi] 56a, b.Menachot 55b, b.Zevachim [Tosefot] 47b 49b, b.Zevachim 11a 48ab 49a, Hebrews 10:4-10:14, Leviticus 1:4 4:4 4:15 4:24 4:33

[10] LXX adds *they shall*

[11] LXX adds *whole*

וְלָקַ֨ח הַכֹּהֵ֤ן מִדָּמָהּ֙ בְּאֶצְבָּע֔וֹ וְנָתַ֕ן עַל־ קַרְנֹ֖ת מִזְבַּ֣ח הָעֹלָ֑ה וְאֶת־כָּל־דָּמָ֣הּ יִשְׁפֹּ֔ךְ אֶל־יְס֖וֹד הַמִּזְבֵּֽחַ

30[1] And the priest shall take of its blood with his finger, and put it on the horns of the altar of [2]burnt offering, and he shall pour all its remaining blood at the base of the altar.

וְאֶת־כָּל־חֶלְבָּ֣הּ יָסִ֗יר כַּאֲשֶׁ֨ר הוּסַ֤ר חֵ֙לֶב֙ מֵעַ֣ל זֶ֣בַח הַשְּׁלָמִ֔ים וְהִקְטִ֤יר הַכֹּהֵן֙ הַמִּזְבֵּ֔חָה לְרֵ֥יחַ נִיחֹ֖חַ לַיהוָ֑ה וְכִפֶּ֥ר עָלָ֛יו הַכֹּהֵ֖ן וְנִסְלַ֥ח לֽוֹ

31[3] And he shall remove all its fat, as the fat is taken away from the sacrifice of peace offerings; and the priest shall make it smoke on the altar for a sweet savor to the LORD; and the priest shall make atonement for him, and he shall be forgiven.

וְאִם־כֶּ֥בֶשׂ יָבִ֛יא קָרְבָּנ֖וֹ לְחַטָּ֑את נְקֵבָ֥ה תְמִימָ֖ה יְבִיאֶֽנָּה

32[4] And if he brings a lamb as his offering for a sin offering, he shall bring a female without blemish.

וְסָמַ֤ךְ אֶת־יָדוֹ֙ עַ֣ל רֹ֣אשׁ הַֽחַטָּ֔את וְשָׁחַ֥ט אֹתָהּ֙ לְחַטָּ֔את בִּמְק֕וֹם אֲשֶׁ֥ר יִשְׁחַ֖ט אֶת־ הָעֹלָֽה

33[5] And he shall press his hand on the head of the sin offering, and [6]kill it *for a sin offering*[7] in the place where they kill the [8]burnt offering.

וְלָקַ֨ח הַכֹּהֵ֜ן מִדַּ֤ם הַֽחַטָּאת֙ בְּאֶצְבָּע֔וֹ וְנָתַ֕ן עַל־קַרְנֹ֖ת מִזְבַּ֣ח הָעֹלָ֑ה וְאֶת־כָּל־ דָּמָ֣הּ יִשְׁפֹּ֔ךְ אֶל־יְס֖וֹד הַמִּזְבֵּֽחַ

34[9] And the priest shall take of the blood of the sin offering with his finger, and put it on the horns of the altar of [10]burnt offering, and *all its remaining blood he shall pour out at the base of the altar*[11].

---

[1] Leviticus 4:30 - b.Menachot [Rashi] 26a, b.Menachot 56a, b.Niddah [Rashi] 40b, b.Sanhedrin 4a, b.Yoma 57b 59a, b.Zevachim [Rashi] 14a 37a 38a 51a, b.Zevachim [Tosefot] 11a, b.Zevachim 34b 37b 53a 62a 64a, Hebrews 2:10, Isaiah 18:21, Leviticus 4:7 4:25 4:34, mt.Hilchot Pesulei haMikdashim 2:21, pap4QLXXLevb, Pirkei de R'Eliezer 29, Romans 8:3-8:4 10:4, y.Yoma 5:4
[2] LXX adds *whole*
[3] Leviticus 4:31 - 1 John 1:7 4:9-4:10, 1 Peter 2:4-2:5, b.Menachot [Rashi] 27b, b.Sanhedrin 4b, b.Zevachim [Tosefot] 36b, b.Zevachim 38a, Ephesians 5:2, Exodus 5:18, Ezra 6:10, Gates of Repentance 4.002, Genesis 8:21, Hebrews 1:3 9:12 9:14-15 10:12 10:14, Isaiah 18:21 5:10, Job 18:8, Leviticus 1:9 1:13 1:17 3:3-5 3:9-11 3:14-16 4:8-10 4:19 4:26 4:35 8:21, Matthew 3:17, Philo De Somniis I 81, Psalms 40:7-8 51:17-18 69:31-32, Revelation 5:9
[4] Leviticus 4:32 - 1 Peter 1:18-20 2:22 2:24 3:18, b.Kereitot 27b 28ab, b.Ketubot 45a, b.Menachot 3a, b.Nazir 28a, b.Pesachim 57b, b.Temurah 15a, b.Zevachim 8a, Ein Yaakov Pesachim 57b, Ephesians 5:27, Exodus 12:3 12:5, Genesis.R 44:14, Hebrews 7:26 9:14, Isaiah 5:7, John 1:29 1:36, Leviticus 3:6-7 4:28 5:6, Leviticus.R 8:4, Luke 1:35, Revelation 5:6 5:8-9, y.Nazir 4:4, z.Tazria 133
[5] Leviticus 4:33 - b.Chullin [Tosefot] 31b, b.Menachot [Tosefot] 48b, b.Menachot 3b 4a, b.Zevachim [Rashi] 8a 10b 46b, b.Zevachim 3b 5a 7ab 9b, Leviticus 4:4 4:29-31, mt.Hilchot Pesulei haMikdashim 15:3, t.Zevachim 1:1, y.Pesachim 5:2
[6] LXX adds *they shall*
[7] Missing in LXX
[8] LXX adds *whole*
[9] Leviticus 4:34 - 1 Peter 1:18-1:20 2:24 3:18, 2 Corinthians 5:21, b.Bava Metzia [Tosefot] 61a, b.Menachot [Rashi] 56a, b.Sanhedrin [Rashi] 4a, b.Sotah [Rashi] 32b, b.Zevachim [Rashi] 37a 38a 47b 51a 98a, b.Zevachim 8a 24ab 37b 48ab, Hebrews 2:10 10:29, Isaiah 18:21, Jastrow 1561b, John 17:19, Leviticus 4:7 4:25 4:30, mt.Hilchot Beit Habechirah 2:17, One of 32 readings called Severin, Romans 8:1 8:3 10:4
[10] LXX adds *whole*
[11] lXX *he shall pour out all its blood by the bottom of the altar of whole burnt offering*

וְאֶת־כָּל־חֶלְבָּהּ יָסִיר כַּאֲשֶׁר יוּסַר
חֵלֶב־הַכֶּשֶׂב֙ מִזֶּ֣בַח הַשְּׁלָמִ֔ים וְהִקְטִ֨יר
הַכֹּהֵ֤ן אֹתָם֙ הַמִּזְבֵּ֔חָה עַ֖ל אִשֵּׁ֣י יְהוָ֑ה
וְכִפֶּ֨ר עָלָ֧יו הַכֹּהֵ֛ן עַל־חַטָּאת֥וֹ אֲשֶׁר־
חָטָ֖א וְנִסְלַ֥ח לֽוֹ

35[1] And he shall remove all its fat, as the fat of the lamb is taken away from the sacrifice of peace offerings; and the priest shall make them smoke on the altar, *on the offerings of the LORD made by fire*[2]; and the priest shall make atonement for him for the sin he is guilty, and he shall be forgiven.

Vayikra – Chapter 5

וְנֶ֣פֶשׁ כִּֽי־תֶחֱטָ֗א וְשָֽׁמְעָה֙ ק֣וֹל אָלָ֔ה
וְה֣וּא עֵ֔ד א֥וֹ רָאָ֖ה א֣וֹ יָדָ֑ע אִם־ל֥וֹא
יַגִּ֖יד וְנָשָׂ֥א עֲוֺנֽוֹ

1[3] And if anyone sins, in that he hears the voice of *solemn appeal*[4], he being a witness, whether he has seen or known, if he does not utter it, then he shall bear his iniquity;

א֣וֹ נֶ֗פֶשׁ אֲשֶׁ֣ר תִּגַּע֮ בְּכָל־דָּבָ֣ר טָמֵא֒ אוֹ
בְנִבְלַ֨ת חַיָּ֜ה טְמֵאָ֗ה א֤וֹ בְּנִבְלַת֙ בְּהֵמָ֣ה
טְמֵאָ֔ה א֖וֹ בְּנִבְלַ֣ת שֶׁ֑רֶץ טָמֵ֔א וְנֶעְלַ֖ם
מִמֶּ֑נּוּ וְה֥וּא טָמֵ֖א וְאָשֵֽׁם

2[5] *Or if anyone touches an unclean thing, whether the carcass of an unclean beast, or the carcass of unclean cattle, or the carcass of unclean swarming things, and is guilty, it being hidden from him that he is unclean*[6];

---

[1] Leviticus 4:35 - 1 John 1:7 2:2 4:9-10, 1 Peter 1:18-19 2:22 2:24 3:18, 2 Corinthians 5:21, b.Chullin [Tosefot] 31b, b.Menachot [Rashi] 27b, b.Sanhedrin 4b, b.Shabbat 71b, b.Zevachim [Tosefot] 8a 36b, b.Zevachim 38a, Colossians 1:14, Ephesians 1:6-1:7 5:2, Hebrews 1:3 4:14 7:26 9:14, Leviticus 1:1-6 4:20 4:26 4:30-31 5:6 5:10 5:13 6:7 9:7 12:8 14:18 14:53 16:1-34, Numbers 15:25, Revelation 1:5-6, Romans 3:24-26 4:25 5:6-11 5:15-21 8:1 8:3-4 10:4

[2] LXX *and the priest shall put it on the altar for a whole burnt offering to the Lord*

[3] Leviticus 5:1 - 1 Kings 8:31 22:16, 1 Peter 2:24, 2 Chronicles 18:15, b.Arachin 17b 18a, b.Bava Batra [Rashbam] 128a 168a, b.Bava Kamma 56a, b.Chullin [Rashi] 21a, b.Gittin 71a, b.Horayot [Rashi] 8b, b.Kereitot [Rashi] 10b, b.Kereitot [Tosefot] 4a, b.Kereitot 9a, b.Ketubot [Rashi] 18b, b.Menachot 4a, b.Niddah [Rashi] 49b, b.Sanhedrin [Rashi] 30b 44b, b.Sanhedrin 30a 37b, b.Shabbat [Rashi] 68b, b.Sheviit [Rashi] 13a 29b 30a 31ab, b.Sheviit [Tosefot] 2a, b.Sheviit 32a 33b 34a 35ab 36a, b.Sotah [Tosefot] 2b, b.Sotah 33a, b.Yoma 74a, b.Zevachim [Rashi] 8b, Commandment #240, Ein Yaakov Sanhedrin:37b, Exodus 22:11, Ezekiel 18:4 18:20, Isaiah 5:11, Jastrow 330b 428b 871b 939b, Judges 17:2, Leviticus 4:2 5:15 5:17 7:18 17:16 19:8 20:17, Leviticus.R 4:2 6:1 7:2, m.Horayot 25, m.Sanhedrin 4:5, m.Shekalim 4:2, m.Sheviit 3:8 4:1 4:13 4:9, Matthew 26:63, Mekhilta de R'Shimon bar Yochai Nezikin 73:1, Midrash Tanchuma Vayikra 7, mt.Hilchot Beit HaBechirah 2:13, mt.Hilchot Edut 1:1 9:12 14:2 17:1, mt.Hilchot Maaseh haKorbanot 14:8, mt.Hilchot Shevuot 9:2 9:7, Numbers 9:13, Numbers.R 9:35, Proverbs 5:24 6:9, Psalms 38:5, Saadia Opinions 5:1, Siman 181:11, t.Horayot 1:9, t.Shevuot 2:5-6 2:15 3:1 3:4-5 3:7-8, y.Sanhedrin 3:9 4:9, y.Sheviit 3:10 4:1-2 4:5-6 4:9-10 5:1-2, z.Vayikra 213
Leviticus 5:1-5 - mt.Hilchot Shegagot 10:5
Leviticus 5:1-6 - Parshat Olah Veyared [variable burnt offering]
Leviticus 5:1-13 - 4QLevc

[4] LXX *swearing*

[5] Leviticus 5:2 - 2 Corinthians 6:17, b.Chullin 70b 71a, b.Horayot [Rashi] 8b, b.Horayot 8b, b.Kereitot [Rashi] 10b, b.Kereitot 19a, b.Niddah 28b, b.Shabbat [Rashi] 2a, b.Sheviit [Rashi] 2a 14b 31b, b.Sheviit 4ab 5a 7a 18b 19a 24b, b.Yoma [Rashi] 41a, b.Zevachim [Rashi] 8b, Deuteronomy 14:8, Haggai 2:13, Isaiah 4:11, Leviticus 4:13 5:4 5:17 7:21 11:11 11:24-40, Leviticus.R 1:2 4:2, Luke 11:44, m.Nazir 7:4, m.Sheviit 2:5, mt.Hilchot Biat haMikdash 3:12, Numbers 19:11-16, Psalms 19:13, t.Shevuot 1:5 1:7-8, y.Horayot 1:1, y.Sheviit 1:2 2:4

[6] LXX *That soul which shall touch any unclean thing, or carcase, or that which is unclean being taken of beasts, or the dead bodies of abominable reptiles which are unclean, or carcases of unclean cattle*

Rabbinic Reference Bible

אוֹ כִי יִגַּע בְּטֻמְאַת אָדָם לְכֹל טֻמְאָתוֹ אֲשֶׁר יִטְמָא בָּהּ וְנֶעְלַם מִמֶּנּוּ וְהוּא יָדַע וְאָשֵׁם — 3[1]

אוֹ נֶפֶשׁ כִּי תִשָּׁבַע לְבַטֵּא בִשְׂפָתַיִם לְהָרַע אוֹ לְהֵיטִיב לְכֹל אֲשֶׁר יְבַטֵּא הָאָדָם בִּשְׁבֻעָה וְנֶעְלַם מִמֶּנּוּ וְהוּא־יָדַע וְאָשֵׁם לְאַחַת מֵאֵלֶּה — 4[2]

וְהָיָה כִי־יֶאְשַׁם לְאַחַת מֵאֵלֶּה וְהִתְוַדָּה אֲשֶׁר חָטָא עָלֶיהָ — 5[3]

וְהֵבִיא אֶת־אֲשָׁמוֹ לַיהוָה עַל חַטָּאתוֹ אֲשֶׁר חָטָא נְקֵבָה מִן־הַצֹּאן כִּשְׂבָּה אוֹ־שְׂעִירַת עִזִּים לְחַטָּאת וְכִפֶּר עָלָיו הַכֹּהֵן מֵחַטָּאתוֹ — 6[4]

or if he touches the uncleanness of man, whatever his uncleanness is or however he is unclean, and it is hid from him; and, when he becomes aware of it, is guilty;

Or if anyone swears clearly with his lips to do evil, or to do good, whatever it is that a man shall utter clearly with an oath, and it is hidden from him; and, when he knows of it, is guilty in one of these things;

And it shall be, when he discovers his guilt in one of these things, he shall confess that he has sinned;

And he shall bring his *guilt offering to the LORD*[5] for his sin, which he has sinned, a female from the flock, a lamb or a [6]goat, for a sin offering; and the priest shall make atonement for him as concerning his sin[7].

[1] Leviticus 5:3 - b.Kereitot 19a, b.Meilah [Rashi] 10b, b.Sheviit [Rashi] 31b, b.Sheviit [Tosefot] 34b, b.Sheviit 4a-5a 7ab 19b 24b, Jastrow 564b, Leviticus 12:1-8 15:1-33 22:4-6, Leviticus.R 3:6, m.Sheviit 2:5, mt.Hilchot Shegagot 11:1, Numbers 19:11-19:16, t.Shevuot 1:7 1:8, y.Horayot 1:1, y.Sheviit 1:2
[2] Leviticus 5:4 - 1 Samuel 1:11 14:24-28 24:21-22 1:22, 2 Kings 6:31, 2 Samuel 21:7, Acts 23:12, b.Bava Kamma 91b, b.Bava Metzia 36a, b.Horayot [Rashi] 8b, b.Makkot [Ramban] 22a, b.Nazir 62b, b.Nedarim 14a, b.Niddah [Rashi] 31b, b.Sheviit [Rashi] 2a 4b 19b 24a 28a 31b, b.Sheviit [Tosefot] 22a, b.Sheviit 20a 24b 25a-26b 16a 28b 34a 49b, b.Temurah [Rashi] 3b, Ecclesiastes 5:3-7, Ezekiel 17:18-19, Jastrow 815a 1441a 1472b, Joshua 2:14 9:15, Judges 9:19 11:31 21:7 21:18, Leviticus 27:2-34, Leviticus.R 4:2, m.Horayot 2:5, m.Sheviit 3:5 3:7, Mark 6:23, Mas.Kallah Rabbati 2:2, Matthew 14:7 14:9, Mekilta de R'Ishmael Bahodesh 7:2, Midrash Psalms 106:7, mt.Hilchot Shevuot 1:1 1:3 1:9 2:10 3:8, mt.Nizirut 2:18, Numbers 6:8 6:10, Philo De Somniis II 296, Psalms 132:2-5, t.Horayot 1:9, y.Nazir 5:1, y.Nedarim 2:2, y.Sheviit 1:2 3:5 3:10 6:6, y.Terumot 3:4, z.Vayikra 263
[3] Leviticus 5:5 - 1 John 1:8-1:10, b.Bava Metzia [Rashi] 3b, b.Horayot [Rashi] 8b, b.Horayot 8b 9a, b.Kereitot 12a, b.Sheviit [Rashi] 2a 13a 22a 31b, b.Sheviit 25b 32a 33b 34a, Daniel 9:4, Ezra 10:11-12, Gates of Repentance 1.040, Jeremiah 3:13, Job 9:27, Joshua 7:19, Leviticus 16:21 2:40, Leviticus.R 3:7, m.Megillah 1:5, mt.Hilchot Teshuvah 1:1, Numbers 5:7, Numbers.R 8:5, Philo De Mutatione Nominum 234, Philo De Specialibus Legibus IV 119, Proverbs 4:13, Psalms 32:5, Romans 10:10, y.Horayot 2:6, y.Sheviit 1:2
Leviticus 5:5-6 - Sifre.z Numbers Naso 5:4
[4] Leviticus 5:6 - b.Bava Metzia [Rashi] 3b 36a, b.Kereitot 27b, b.Kiddushin [Rashi] 55b, b.Menachot 101a, b.Nazir [Rashi] 28a, b.Shabbat [Rashi] 2a, b.Sheviit [Rashi] 2a, b.Zevachim 8a, b.Zevachim [Tosefot] 8b, Ezekiel 16:39 18:13, Leviticus 4:20 4:28 4:32 6:6 7:1-7 14:12-13 19:21-22, m.Keritot 1:2, mt.Hilchot Issurei Mizbeiach 6:5, Numbers 6:12, pap4QLXXLevb, z.Acharei Mot 122, z.Vayikra 193
Leviticus 5:6-11 - Jastrow 594a, m.Sheviit 1:2 3:1 8:6, mt.Hilchot Arachim Vacharamim 8:13
[5] LXX *transgressions against the LORD*
[6] LXX adds *kid of the*
[7] Pap4QLevb LXX adds *which he has sinned and it shall be forgiven to him*

וְאִם־לֹא תַגִּיעַ יָדוֹ דֵּי שֶׂה וְהֵבִיא אֶת־ אֲשָׁמוֹ אֲשֶׁר חָטָא שְׁתֵּי תֹרִים אוֹ־שְׁנֵי בְנֵי־יוֹנָה לַיהוָה אֶחָד לְחַטָּאת וְאֶחָד לְעֹלָה **7¹**

7¹ And if his means cannot suffice for a lamb, then he shall bring his penalty for that which he has sinned, two turtledoves, or two young pigeons, to the LORD: one for a sin offering, and the other for a burnt offering.

וְהֵבִיא אֹתָם אֶל־הַכֹּהֵן וְהִקְרִיב אֶת־ אֲשֶׁר לַחַטָּאת רִאשׁוֹנָה וּמָלַק אֶת־ רֹאשׁוֹ מִמּוּל עָרְפּוֹ וְלֹא יַבְדִּיל **8²**

8² And he shall bring them to the priest, who shall offer the one for the sin offering first, and pinch off its head *close by its*³ neck, but shall not divide it.

וְהִזָּה מִדַּם הַחַטָּאת עַל־קִיר הַמִּזְבֵּחַ וְהַנִּשְׁאָר בַּדָּם יִמָּצֵה אֶל־יְסוֹד הַמִּזְבֵּחַ חַטָּאת הוּא **9⁴**

9⁴ And he shall sprinkle of the blood of the sin offering on the side of the altar; and the rest of the blood shall be drained out at the base of the altar;⁵ it is a sin offering.

וְאֶת־הַשֵּׁנִי יַעֲשֶׂה עֹלָה כַּמִּשְׁפָּט וְכִפֶּר עָלָיו הַכֹּהֵן מֵחַטָּאתוֹ אֲשֶׁר־חָטָא וְנִסְלַח לוֹ **10⁶**

10⁶ And he shall prepare the second for a ⁷burnt offering, *according to the ordinance*⁸;⁹ and the priest shall make atonement for him concerning his sin that he has sinned, and he shall be forgiven.

---

¹ Leviticus 5:7 - 2 Corinthians 8:12, b.Chullin [Rashi] 22b, b.Horayot 9a, b.Ketubot [Tosefot] 5a, b.Kiddushin [Rashi] 14a, b.Menachot [Rashi] 2a, b.Menachot [Tosefot] 4b, b.Nazir [Tosefot] 24a, b.Sheviit [Rashi] 6b, b.Temurah [Rashi] 20a, Commandment #482, Ein Yaakov Horayot:9a, Hebrews 10:6-10, James 2:5-2:6, Leviticus 1:14-15 5:8-9 5:11 9:3 12:8 14:21-22 14:31 15:14-15 15:30 16:5, Leviticus.R 3:7, Luke 2:24, m.Keritot 1:2, Matthew 3:16 10:16, Numbers.R 8:1, t.Challah 2:7, t.Shevuot 1:6, Tanna Devei Eliyahu 6, z.Pinchas 229
Leviticus 5:7-10 - Leviticus.R 3:5
Leviticus 5:7-13 - m.Keritot 6:6
² Leviticus 5:8 - 1 Peter 3:18, b.Chullin [Rashi] 21ab, b.Chullin 19b 25ba 27b, b.Horayot 13a, b.Menachot [Tosefot] 49b, b.Nazir [Rashi] 45a, b.Pesachim 59a, b.Sotah [Rashi] 46b, b.Zevachim [Rashi] 64b, b.Zevachim 65ab 66a 80a, Commandment #483, Jastrow 742a, Leviticus 1:15 1:17, Leviticus.R 3:7, m.Kiddushin 1:8, m.Megillah 2:5, m.Nazir 6:7, m.Zevachim 6:4, mt.Hilchot Maaseh haKorbanot 7:6, mt.Hilchot Sanhedrin vHainshin Hameurim Lahem 19:4, Numbers.R 8:1, Romans 4:25, t.Demai 2:7, y.Sanhedrin 1:3, z.Tzav 69
Leviticus 5:8-10 - pap4QLXXLevb
³ LXX *from the*
⁴ Leviticus 5:9 - b.Chullin [Rashi] 22a, b.Kereitot [Rashi] 26b, b.Kiddushin [Rashi] 36b, b.Kinnim [Pirush] 22a, b.Meilah [Rashi] 9a, b.Meilah 8b, b.Menachot [Rashi] 2b 74b, b.Menachot [Tosefot] 3a 57b 61a, b.Pesachim [Rashi] 63b, b.Sanhedrin [Rashi] 4b, b.Yoma [Rashi] 24b, b.Zevachim [Rashi] 14b 52b 63b 64a 92b, b.Zevachim [Tosefot] 51b 65b, b.Zevachim 37a 52a 64b, Exodus 12:22-23, Hebrews 2:10 12:24, Isaiah 18:21, Jastrow 825b, Leviticus 1:5 1:15 4:7 4:18 4:25 4:30 4:34 7:2, t.Zevachim 1:1
⁵ pap4QLXXLevb adds *for*
⁶ Leviticus 5:10 - 1 John 2:2, b.Chullin 21ab, b.Kereitot 9a 27b, b.Menachot [Rashi] 101a, b.Menachot [Tosefot] 2a 10b, b.Pesachim 59a, b.Temurah [Tosefot] 15b, b.Zevachim [Tosefot] 24b, b.Zevachim 80a, Ephesians 5:2, James 5:15, Leviticus 1:14-1:17 4:20 4:26 4:31 4:35 5:6 5:13 5:16, mt.Pirkei Avot 4:5, Romans 5:11, z.Mishpatim 101b
⁷ LXX adds *whole*
⁸ LXX *as it is fit*
⁹ i.e., Leviticus 1:14-17

וְאִם־לֹא תַשִּׂיג יָדוֹ לִשְׁתֵּי תֹרִים אוֹ
לִשְׁנֵי בְנֵי־יוֹנָה וְהֵבִיא אֶת־קָרְבָּנוֹ
אֲשֶׁר חָטָא עֲשִׂירִת הָאֵפָה סֹלֶת
לְחַטָּאת לֹא־יָשִׂים עָלֶיהָ שֶׁמֶן וְלֹא־יִתֵּן
עָלֶיהָ לְבֹנָה כִּי חַטָּאת הִיא

11¹

But if his means suffice not for two turtledoves, or two young pigeons, then he shall bring his offering for that which he has sinned, the tenth part of an ephah of fine flour for a sin offering; he shall put no oil on it; neither shall he put any frankincense in it, for it is a sin offering.

וְהֱבִיאָהּ אֶל־הַכֹּהֵן וְקָמַץ הַכֹּהֵן מִמֶּנָּה
מְלוֹא קֻמְצוֹ אֶת־אַזְכָּרָתָהּ וְהִקְטִיר
הַמִּזְבֵּחָה עַל אִשֵּׁי יְהוָה חַטָּאת הִוא

12²

And he shall bring it to the priest, and the priest shall take his handful of it as its memorial part, and make it smoke on the altar, on the offerings of the LORD made by fire; it is a sin offering.

וְכִפֶּר עָלָיו הַכֹּהֵן עַל־חַטָּאתוֹ אֲשֶׁר־
חָטָא מֵאַחַת מֵאֵלֶּה וְנִסְלַח לוֹ וְהָיְתָה
לַכֹּהֵן כַּמִּנְחָה

13³

And the priest shall make atonement on his behalf for his sin that he has sinned in any of these things, and he shall be forgiven; and the remnant shall be the priest's, *as the meal offering⁴*.

וַיְדַבֵּר יְהוָה אֶל־מֹשֶׁה לֵּאמֹר

14⁵

And the LORD spoke to Moses, saying:

נֶפֶשׁ כִּי־תִמְעֹל מַעַל וְחָטְאָה בִּשְׁגָגָה

15⁶

If anyone commits a trespass, and sins

¹ Leviticus 5:11 - 2 Corinthians 5:21, b.Horayot 9a, b.Kereitot [Rashi] 7a, b.Kiddushin [Rashi] 53a, b.Menachot [Rashi] 2b 11a 49a 60b 63b, b.Menachot [Tosefot] 2a 61a, b.Menachot 2a 4ab 23a 59b 60a 18a, b.Sotah 15a, b.Zevachim [Rashi] 9b 30a 64a, b.Zevachim [Tosefot] 8b, b.Zevachim 63b, Commandment #484 #485, Ein Yaakov Horayot:9a, Exodus 16:18 16:36, Genesis.R 44:14, Guide for the Perplexed 3:46, Isaiah 53:2-53:10, Jastrow 799a, Leviticus 2:1-2 2:4-5 2:15-16 5:6 5:9 5:12, Leviticus.R 3:1, m.Demai 1:3, m.Keritot 1:2 6:8, m.Menachot 1:3 2:6 5:4, m.Zevachim 10:4, Midrash Tanchuma Ki Tissa 2, mt.Hilchot Maaseh haKorbanot 12:4 12:7, mt.Hilchot Pesulei haMikdashim 11:10, mt.Hilchot Sanhedrin vHainshin Hameurim Lahem 19:4, Numbers 5:15 7:13 7:19-89 15:4-9, Psalms 22:2-22 69:2-22, t.Shevuot 1:6
² Leviticus 5:12 - Acts 10:4, b.Menachot [Rashi] 9b 10b 60b, b.Menachot [Tosefot] 11b, b.Menachot 10a 16a, b.Zevachim 11a 24b, Ephesians 5:2, Leviticus 1:9 1:13 1:17 2:2 2:9 2:16 3:4 3:11 4:35 6:15, Mekhilta de R'Shimon bar Yochai Pisha 13:1, mt.Hilchot Pesulei haMikdashim 15:3, Numbers 5:26
³ Leviticus 5:13 - 1 Corinthians 9:13, 1 Samuel 2:28, b.Horayot 9a, b.Kereitot 27b, b.Menachot 73b 74a 101a, Hosea 4:8, Leviticus 2:3 2:10 4:20 4:26 4:31 5:6 7:6, Leviticus.R 3:1 3:4, t.Shevuot 3:4, y.Sotah 3:6
⁴ LXX *as an offering of fine flour*
⁵ Leviticus 5:14 - b.Nedarim 54a, m.Chagigah 1:8
⁶ Leviticus 5:15 - b.Arachin [Rashi] 5b, b.Arachin 20b, b.Bava Batra [Rashbam] 88b 123b, b.Chagigah [Rashi] 10b, b.Chagigah [Tosefot] 6a, b.Kereitot [Rashi] 22a 23b 26b, b.Kereitot 10b 18b 22b 16a, b.Ketubot [Rashi] 11a, b.Makkot [Riven] 21b, b.Meilah [Rashi] 2a 4b 11a 19b, b.Meilah [Tosefot] 3b 4a 6b 25ba, b.Meilah 15a 18ab 19a, b.Menachot [Rashi] 47b 48b 102a, b.Menachot [Tosefot] 62b, b.Nazir 24a, b.Pesachim [Rashi] 33a 66b, b.Pesachim 26a 32b, b.Sanhedrin [Rashi] 15a 84a, b.Sheviit [Rashi] 22a 24b 34a 36b, b.Succah 49b, b.Temurah [Rashi] 14a, b.Temurah 19b 22a 32b, b.Temurah 2b 3a, b.Yoma [Rashi] 20a, b.Zevachim [Rashi] 46a 83b 89b 84ab, b.Zevachim 45a 48a, Deuteronomy 12:5-12 12:26 15:19-20 26:1-15, Exodus 6:13, Ezra 10:19, Jastrow 815b 816b, Leviticus 4:2 5:1-2 5:16 5:18 6:6 7:1 7:6 10:17-18 22:1-16 24:5-9 26:2-8 26:12-13 26:17-18 26:23-27 27:9-33, Leviticus.R 4:2, m.Chagigah 1:8, m.Chullin 8:6, m.Eduyot 3:9 8:6, m.Kelim 17:9, m.Keritot 5:2, m.Kiddushin 2:8, m.Makkot 3:9, m.Shekalim 2:2 6:6, m.Terumah 4:1 7:2, m.Yoma 5:6, Mekhilta de R'Shimon bar Yochai Nezikin 74:3, Mesillat Yesharim 11:Traits-of-Nekuyut, mt.Hilchot Pesulei haMikdashim 4:22, Numbers 5:8 18:9-18:32, Numbers.R 8:4, Pesikta Rabbati 23/24:1, Saadia Opinions 6:5, Sifre Devarim Ki Tetze 230, y.Horayot 2:7, y.Kiddushin 2:7, z.Vayikra 24b 263 422
Leviticus 5:15-16 - mt.Hilchot Chametz uMatzah 4:2

מִקָּדְשֵׁי יְהוָה וְהֵבִיא אֶת־אֲשָׁמוֹ לַיהוָה
אַיִל תָּמִים מִן־הַצֹּאן בְּעֶרְכְּךָ כֶּסֶף־
שְׁקָלִים בְּשֶׁקֶל־הַקֹּדֶשׁ לְאָשָׁם

through error, in the holy things of the LORD, then he shall bring his penalty to the LORD, a ram without blemish out of the flock, according to your valuation in silver by shekels, after the shekel of the sanctuary, for a guilt offering.

16[1] וְאֵת אֲשֶׁר חָטָא מִן־הַקֹּדֶשׁ יְשַׁלֵּם וְאֶת־
חֲמִישִׁתוֹ יוֹסֵף עָלָיו וְנָתַן אֹתוֹ לַכֹּהֵן
וְהַכֹּהֵן יְכַפֵּר עָלָיו בְּאֵיל הָאָשָׁם וְנִסְלַח
לוֹ

And he shall make restitution for whatever he has done amiss in the holy thing, and shall add a fifth part to it, and give it to the priest; and the priest shall make atonement for him with the ram of the guilt offering, and he shall be forgiven.

17[2] וְאִם־נֶפֶשׁ כִּי תֶחֱטָא וְעָשְׂתָה אַחַת
מִכָּל־מִצְוֹת יְהוָה אֲשֶׁר לֹא תֵעָשֶׂינָה
וְלֹא־יָדַע וְאָשֵׁם וְנָשָׂא עֲוֹנוֹ

And if anyone sins, and does any of the things the LORD has commanded not to be done, though he is unaware, he is yet guilty, and *shall bear his iniquity*[3].

18[4] וְהֵבִיא אַיִל תָּמִים מִן־הַצֹּאן בְּעֶרְכְּךָ
לְאָשָׁם אֶל־הַכֹּהֵן וְכִפֶּר עָלָיו הַכֹּהֵן עַל
שִׁגְגָתוֹ אֲשֶׁר־שָׁגַג וְהוּא לֹא־יָדַע
וְנִסְלַח לוֹ

And he shall bring a ram without blemish out of the flock, *according to your valuation*[5], for a guilt offering, to the priest; and the priest shall make atonement for him *concerning the error*[6] he committed though he was unaware, and he shall be forgiven.

---

[1] Leviticus 5:16 - 1 John 2:1-2:2, Acts 2:20, b.Bava Kamma 111a, b.Bava Metzia [Rashi] 54b, b.Bava Metzia 55a, b.Horayot 10b, b.Kereitot [Rashi] 22a, b.Kereitot 26b, b.Meilah 19b, b.Temurah [Rashi] 6a, b.Zevachim [Rashi] 84ab, b.Zevachim 48a, Commandment #440, Exodus 22:1 22:3-4, Hebrews 9:13-14, Jastrow 127b 129a 436b, Leviticus 4:26 5:6 5:10 5:13 6:4-5 22:14 3:13 3:15 3:27 3:31, Luke 19:8, m.Arachin 7:2, m.Bava Metzia 4:8, m.Bava Metzia 9:6, m.Chagigah 1:8, m.Keritot 5:2, m.Pesachim 2:4, Numbers 5:7, Numbers.R 8:4, Pesikta Rabbati 23/24:1, Psalms 69:5, Sifre.z Numbers Naso 5:7, y.Avodah Zarah 3:2, y.Pesachim 2:3, z.Vayikra 428
Leviticus 5:16-19 - pap4QLXXLevb
[2] Leviticus 5:17 - Avot de R'Natan 30, b.Horayot [Rashi] 7a 8b 9a, b.Kereitot [Rashi] 24b, b.Kereitot [Tosefot] 18a, b.Kereitot 14b 19b 22b 25b, b.Kiddushin 81b, b.Menachot 4a, b.Niddah [Rashi] 14b, b.Nazir 23a 38a, b.Zevachim [Rashi] 9a, b.Zevachim [Tosefot] 10b, Ein Yaakov Kiddushin 81b, Ein Yaakov Nazir:23a, b.Zevachim 48a, Jastrow 824a, Leviticus.R 4:2, Leviticus 4:2-4 4:13 4:22 4:27 5:1-2 5:15, Luke 12:48, m.Eduyot 8:6, m.Keritot 3:1, m.Keritot 4:1, m.Temurah 7:6, m.Yevamot 4:2, m.Yoma 8:8, m.Zevachim 5:5, Psalms 19:13, Romans 14:23, t.Bikkurim 2:1, y.Horayot 2:5 2:7, y.Sheviit 2:4
Leviticus 5:17-18 - mt.Hilchot Shegagot 8:1, t.Kereitot 2:14, t.Peah 3:8
Leviticus 5:17-19 - Commandment #457 #486 Parshat Asham Tolui [variable guilt offering]
[3] LXX *have contracted guilt*
[4] Leviticus 5:18 - 1 Timothy 2:5-6, b.Horayot [Rashi] 8b 9a, b.Horayot 7a 8a, b.Kereitot [Rashi] 14b, b.Kereitot 18b 22b 24b, b.Sanhedrin [Rashi] 61b, b.Sheviit [Tosefot] 12b, b.Sheviit 19b, b.Temurah [Rashi] 34a, b.Yoma [Rashi] 85b, b.Zevachim [Rashi] 84ab, b.Zevachim 48a, Jastrow 994b, Leviticus 1:4 4:20 5:15-16 6:6-7, m.Horayot 1:1, m.Shekalim 6:6 5:5, mt.Hilchot Pesulei haMikdashim 4:22, t.Challah 2:7
[5] LXX *at a price of silver*
[6] LXX *for his trespass of ignorance*

אָשָׁם הָוּא אָשָׁם אָשַׁם לַיהוָֽה 19[1]   [2]It is a guilt offering—he is certainly guilty before the LORD.

וַיְדַבֵּר יְהוָה אֶל־מֹשֶׁה לֵּאמֹֽר 20[3]   The LORD spoke to Moses, saying:

נֶפֶשׁ כִּי תֶחֱטָא וּמָעֲלָה מַעַל בַּיהוָה וְכִחֵשׁ בַּעֲמִיתוֹ בְּפִקָּדוֹן אוֹ־בִתְשׂוּמֶת יָד אוֹ בְגָזֵל אוֹ עָשַׁק אֶת־עֲמִיתֽוֹ 21[4]   If anyone sins, and *commits a trespass against*[5] the LORD, and deals falsely with his neighbor in a matter of deposit, *or pledge, or robbery*[6], or have oppressed his neighbor;

אוֹ־מָצָא אֲבֵדָה וְכִחֶשׁ בָּהּ וְנִשְׁבַּע עַל־שָׁקֶר עַל־אַחַת מִכֹּל אֲשֶׁר־יַעֲשֶׂה הָאָדָם לַחֲטֹא בָהֵֽנָּה 22[7]   or have found what was lost, and *dealt falsely with it*[8], and swears to a lie; in any of these that a man does, sinning in that respect;

וְהָיָה כִּי־יֶחֱטָא וְאָשֵׁם וְהֵשִׁיב אֶת־הַגְּזֵלָה אֲשֶׁר גָּזָל אוֹ אֶת־הָעֹשֶׁק אֲשֶׁר עָשָׁק אוֹ אֶת־הַפִּקָּדוֹן אֲשֶׁר הָפְקַד אִתּוֹ אוֹ אֶת־הָאֲבֵדָה אֲשֶׁר מָצָֽא 23[9]   Then it shall be, if he has sinned and is guilty, he shall restore what he took by robbery, or the thing he has gotten by oppression, or the deposit that was deposited with him, or the lost thing he found,

---

[1] Leviticus 5:19 - 2 Corinthians 5:19-21, b.Menachot [Tosefot] 4ab, b.Shekalim 18a, b.Sheviit [Tosefot] 12b, b.Sheviit 12a, b.Temurah [Rashi] 34a, b.Temurah 14b 18a 23b, b.Zevachim [Rashi] 7b 12b 112a, b.Zevachim [Tosefot] 48a, b.Zevachim 103a, Ezra 10:2, m.Shekalim 6:6, m.Zevachim 5:5, Malachi 3:8, Midrash Tanchuma Ki Tissa 2, mt.Hilchot Shekalim 2:3, Psalms 51:5, t.Zevachim 1:1, y.Shekalim 6:4
[2] pap4QLXXLevb adds *For*
[3] Leviticus 5:20 - b.Bava Metzia [Rashi] 3b, Philo De Specialibus Legibus I 236
Leviticus 5:20-24 - pap4QLXXLevb
Leviticus 5:20-25 - mt.Hilchot Gezelah Vaavedah 7:2
Leviticus 5:20-26 - Jastrow 369a, Mekhilta de R'Shimon bar Yochai Nezikin 72:1 73:2, Parshat Asham Vaday [fixed guilt offering], Pseudo-Phocylides 12
[4] Leviticus 5:21 - b.Bava Batra [Rashbam] 88b 123b, b.Bava Batra 123b, b.Bava Kamma [Rashi] 105b, b.Bava Kamma 12b 13a 103b 114b, b.Bava Metzia [Rashi] 3b, b.Bava Metzia 48a 58a 111a, b.Bechorot 53b, b.Kereitot 9a, b.Ketubot 42ab, b.Kiddushin 52b, b.Sanhedrin [Rashi] 112b, b.Sheviit [Rashi] 31a 34a 36b, b.Sheviit 32a 33b 34a 35a 37b, b.Sotah 33a, b.Temurah 8a, b.Zevachim 114a, Exodus.R 20:10, Jastrow 815b 1059b 1126b 1207b, m.Bava Kamma 9:5 9:7, m.Sheviit 5:1 8:3, Mesillat Yesharim 11:Traits-of-Nekuyut, Midrash Tanchuma Tzav 14, mt.Hilchot Gezelah Vaavedah 7:1-2 7:7 8:14, mt.Hilchot Shevuot 1:8 7:4, Numbers.R 8:1 8:4-5 8:5 9:2, Pesikta Rabbati 19:2 23/24:1 29/30B:2, Philo De Specialibus Legibus II 26, y.Bava Kamma 1:1 9:7, y.Sheviit 4:2 4:6 5:1-2 6:6
Leviticus 5:21-23 - mt.Hilchot Shevuot 1:9
Leviticus 5:21-25 - mt.Hilchot Shegagot 9:7, mt.Hilchot Teshuvah 1:1 1:1
[5] LXX *willfully overlooked the commandments*
[6] LXX *or concerning fellowship, or concerning plunder*
[7] Leviticus 5:22 - b.Bava Batra [Rashbam] 123b, b.Bava Kamma 103b 105b, b.Bava Metzia [Rashi] 3b, b.Ketubot 42a, b.Pesachim 32b, b.Sheviit 37a, Genesis.R 85:11, m.Bava Kamma 9:5 9:7, m.Sheviit 8:3 5:1, mt.Hilchot Shevuot 7:4, Numbers.R 9:35, y.Bava Kamma 9:7, y.Gittin 5:3, z.Pinchas 7, z.Vayikra 273
[8] LXX *lied concerning it*
[9] Leviticus 5:23 - b.Avodah Zara 7a 71b, b.Bava Batra [Rashbam] 88ab, b.Bava Kamma 66a 67a 98b 14b 112a [Rashi] 4b 93b 94b 105b 16a [Tosefot] 11a 65b, b.Bava Metzia 48a [Rashi] 3b 41a, b.Gittin [Rashi] 53b, b.Chullin 141a [Tosefot] 81a, b.Eruvin [Rashi] 62a, b.Makkot [Rashi] 16a [Tosefot] 14b, b.Menachot [Rashi] 3a, b.Pesachim [Rashi] 32a, b.Sanhedrin [Rashi] 57a 72a, b.Sheviit [Rashi] 34a 37b, b.Temurah 6a [Rashi] 4b 6b, b.Yevamot [Rashi] 47b, b.Zevachim [Rashi] 44b, Commandment #275, Deuteronomy.R 3:15, Gates of Repentance 3.24, Genesis.R 54:3, Jastrow 945b, Midrash Tanchuma Ekev 11, Midrash Tanchuma Noach 4, Midrash Tanchuma Tzav 1, mt.Hilchot Geneivah 1:12, mt.Hilchot Gezelah Vaavedah 1:1 2:2 7:3 7:8, Numbers.R 8:1 9:36 11:7, Saadia Opinions 5:6, Siman 182:6, y.Bava Kamma 1:1, y.Kiddushin 1:4, z.Vayakhel 250, z.Vayikra 230 251 262 273

24[1] אֹ֠ו מִכֹּ֞ל אֲשֶׁר־יִשָּׁבַ֣ע עָלָ֣יו לַשֶּׁ֒קֶר֒ וְשִׁלַּ֤ם אֹתֹו֙ בְּרֹאשֹׁ֔ו וַחֲמִשִׁתָ֖יו יֹסֵ֣ף עָלָ֑יו לַאֲשֶׁ֨ר ה֥וּא לֹ֛ו יִתְּנֶ֖נּוּ בְּיֹ֥ום אַשְׁמָתֹֽו

or anything about which he has sworn falsely, he shall restore it in full, and shall add a fifth part more to it; he shall give it to whom it appertains, in the day of his guilt.

25[2] וְאֶת־אֲשָׁמֹ֣ו יָבִ֣יא לַיהוָ֑ה אַ֣יִל תָּמִ֧ים מִן־הַצֹּ֛אן בְּעֶרְכְּךָ֥ לְאָשָׁ֖ם אֶל־הַכֹּהֵֽן

And he shall bring his penalty to the LORD, a ram without blemish of the flock, *according to your valuation*[3], for a guilt offering, to the priest.

26[4] וְכִפֶּ֨ר עָלָ֧יו הַכֹּהֵ֛ן לִפְנֵ֥י יְהוָ֖ה וְנִסְלַ֣ח לֹ֑ו עַל־אַחַ֛ת מִכֹּ֥ל אֲשֶׁר־יַעֲשֶׂ֖ה לְאַשְׁמָ֥ה בָֽהּ

And the priest shall make atonement for him before the LORD, and he shall be forgiven, concerning whatever he does so as to be guilty.

[1] Leviticus 5:24 - b.Bava Kamma 65b 103b 18a 114b [Rashi] 63b 103a, b.Bava Metzia 43b 48a 54b [Rashi] 3b, b.Sanhedrin [Rashi] 3b, b.Sheviit 49a [Rashi] 31b 34a 37b, b.Temurah [Rashi] 19b, Guide for the Perplexed 3:41, Jastrow 436b 477b 1437a 1703a, m.Bava Kamma 9:5, m.Bava Metzia 9:6, Mekilta de R'Ishmael Nezikin 15:51 15:91, mt.Hilchot Gezelah Vaavedah 7:10 7:12, mt.Hilchot Shegagot 9:7, mt.Hilchot Shevuot 7:15, mt.Hilchot Terumot 10:15, Numbers.R 8:1, Saadia Opinions 5:6, Seder Olam 5:Marah, y.Sheviit 5:5 8:3
[2] Leviticus 5:25 - b.Arachin 4a, b.Bava Kamma [Rashi] 65b, b.Bava Metzia [Rashi] 3b, b.Menachot 3a 4b, b.Menachot [Rashi] 48b, b.Sanhedrin [Tosefot] 14a, b.Sheviit [Rashi] 31a, b.Temurah [Rashi] 19b, b.Zevachim [Rashi] 84ab, b.Zevachim 48a, Jastrow 1299 1200b, m.Chullin 2:10, Numbers.R 8:1 8:5
[3] LXX *of value to the amount of the thing in which he trespassed*
[4] Leviticus 5:26 - b.Bava Metzia [Rashi] 3b, b.Sheviit [Rashi] 13a, b.Sheviit 7a 13a, Leviticus.R 4:2, mt.Hilchot Shevuot 7:16, y.Kiddushin 1:1, y.Sheviit 6:1, Pesikta Rabbati 16:7

Tzav

Tzav[1] – Chapter 6

וַיְדַבֵּר יְהוָה אֶל־מֹשֶׁה לֵּאמֹר

1[2] And the LORD spoke to Moses, saying,

צַו אֶת־אַהֲרֹן וְאֶת־בָּנָיו לֵאמֹר זֹאת
תּוֹרַת הָעֹלָה הִוא הָעֹלָה עַל מֹוקְדָה[3]
עַל־הַמִּזְבֵּחַ כָּל־הַלַּיְלָה עַד־הַבֹּקֶר
וְאֵשׁ הַמִּזְבֵּחַ תּוּקַד בּוֹ

2[4] Command Aaron and his sons, saying: This is the law of the [5]burnt offering: *it is what goes up on its firewood on the altar*[6] all night until the morning; and by it, the fire of the altar shall be kept burning.

---

[1] Tzav aliyot: [1] Leviticus 6:1–11, [2] Leviticus 6:12–7:10, [3] Leviticus 7:11–38, [4] Leviticus 8:1–13, [5] Leviticus 8:14–21, [6] Leviticus 8:22–29, [7] Leviticus 8:30–36

[2] Leviticus 6:1 - Leviticus.R 7:1 7:4
Leviticus 6:1-2 - Midrash Tanchuma Tzav 1
Leviticus 6:1-3 - t.Shevuot 3:6
Leviticus 6:1-5 - pap4QLXXLevb
Leviticus 6:1-6 - Korbanot-Parshat Terumas Hadeshen [removing the ashes from the altar], Shacharit
Leviticus 6:1-7:16 - Maamodos Seder Korbanot [every day]
Leviticus 6:1-11 - Minchah [Shabbat Monday Thursday Torah reading - Parashah Tzav]
Leviticus 6:1-17 - Josephus Antiquities 4.8.29

[3] Traditional Small מ in מֹוקְדָה

[4] Leviticus 6:2 - Acts 5:4, Amos 8:5, b.Bava Batra [Rashbam] 11b, b.Chagigah 10b, b.Horayot 3a, b.Megillah 21a, b.Meilah [Rashi] 2b, b.Menachot [Rashi] 72a, b.Menachot 6b 26b 49a 82b, b.Niddah 40a, b.Pesachim [Rashi] 68b, b.Sanhedrin 34a 42b, b.Tamid [Pirush] 29a, b.Temurah 14a, b.Yoma [Tosefot] 27b, b.Yoma 20a 33a 45a, b.Zevachim [Rashi] 20a 88b, b.Zevachim 27b 51a 68b 69a 83ab 84ab 86b, Colossians 3:9, Ephesians 4:25, Exodus 22:7-10, Genesis 2:7, Genesis.R 22:5 34:9, Habakkuk 1:13, Isaiah 21:2 24:16 9:1 59:13-15, Jastrow 591a, Jeremiah 9:6, John 8:44, Leviticus 5:15 5:19 19:11, Leviticus.R 7:5 9:4 9:6 9:9, m.Berachot 1:1, m.Keritot 2:2, m.Megillah 2:6, m.Sheviit 4:8, m.Zevachim 9:1, Mekilta de R'Ishmael Kaspa 4:85, Micah 6:10-6:12, Midrash Psalms 2:15, Midrash Tanchuma Korach 12, Midrash Tanchuma Tzav 1 2 13 14, mt.Hilchot Klei haMikdash Vihaovdim Bo 10:1, mt.Hilchot Maaseh haKorbanot 4:2 6:3, mt.Hilchot Tefilah 1:6, mt.Hilchot Temidim Umusafim 1:6 2:5, Numbers 5:6-5:8, Numbers.R 13:2, Pesikta de R'Kahana 6.3, Pesikta Rabbati 5:4 16:7, Proverbs 24:28 2:19, Psalms 51:5, Revelation 22:15, Song of Songs.R 1:52 4:32, Tanna Devei Eliyahu 6, y.Megillah 1:11, y.Yoma 2:1, z.Behar 107b, z.Pekudei 238b, z.Tzav 27a, z.Behar 1 2, z.Pekudei 349 363 366 368, z.Tzav 1 15 19 21 26 35 72 73
Leviticus 6:2-3 - t.Bava Kamma 10:12

[5] LXX adds *whole*

[6] LXX *this is the whole burnt offering in its burning on the altar*

וְלָבַשׁ הַכֹּהֵן מִדּוֹ בַד וּמִכְנְסֵי־בַד יִלְבַּשׁ עַל־בְּשָׂרוֹ וְהֵרִים אֶת־הַדֶּשֶׁן אֲשֶׁר תֹּאכַל הָאֵשׁ אֶת־הָעֹלָה עַל־הַמִּזְבֵּחַ וְשָׂמוֹ אֵצֶל הַמִּזְבֵּחַ

3[7] And the priest shall put on his linen garment, and he shall put his linen breeches on his flesh; and he shall take up the ashes to where the fire has consumed the [8]burnt offering on the altar, and he shall put them beside the altar.

וּפָשַׁט אֶת־בְּגָדָיו וְלָבַשׁ בְּגָדִים אֲחֵרִים וְהוֹצִיא אֶת־הַדֶּשֶׁן אֶל־מִחוּץ לַמַּחֲנֶה אֶל־מָקוֹם טָהוֹר

4[9] And he shall remove his garments, and put on other garments, and carry the ashes outside the camp to a clean place.

וְהָאֵשׁ עַל־הַמִּזְבֵּחַ תּוּקַד־בּוֹ לֹא תִכְבֶּה וּבִעֵר עָלֶיהָ הַכֹּהֵן עֵצִים בַּבֹּקֶר בַּבֹּקֶר וְעָרַךְ עָלֶיהָ הָעֹלָה וְהִקְטִיר עָלֶיהָ חֶלְבֵי הַשְּׁלָמִים

5[10] And the fire on the altar shall be kept burning by it, it shall never go out; and the priest shall kindle wood on it every morning; and he shall lay the [11]burnt offering in order on it, and shall make smoke using the fat of the peace offerings.

אֵשׁ תָּמִיד תּוּקַד עַל־הַמִּזְבֵּחַ לֹא תִכְבֶּה

6[12] Fire shall be kept burning on the altar continually; it shall not go out.

---

[7] Leviticus 6:3 - b.Arachin 3b, b.Chullin [Tosefot] 11a, b.Chullin 114ab, b.Eruvin [Rashi] 103b, b.Kereitot 6a, b.Meilah [Tosefot] 11a, b.Meilah 9a 11b 12a, b.Menachot [Tosefot] 14b, b.Menachot 26b, b.Pesachim26a 27b 65b, b.Tamid [Pirush] 28b 29a 32b, b.Temurah 34a, b.Yoma [Rashi] 20a 59b, b.Yoma [Tosefot] 27b, b.Yoma 12b 23b 24a, b.Yoma 45b, b.Zevachim [Rashi] 18a 64a, b.Zevachim [Tosefot] 31a 86a, b.Zevachim 18b 19a 25ba 35a 46a 83b 86b, Commandment #441, Deuteronomy 22:1-22:4, Exodus 22:9-22:11 23:4, Jastrow 1696b 1699b, Jeremiah 5:2 7:9, Leviticus 19:12, m.Menachot 7:4, m.Tamid 1:2, m.Zevachim 5:6, Malachi 3:5, mt.Hilchot Biat haMikdash 9:8, mt.Hilchot Deot 6:6 7:7, mt.Hilchot Klei haMikdash Vihaovdim Bo 10:6, mt.Hilchot Temidim Umusafim 2:10 2:15, Numbers.R 4:20, Proverbs 6:9, y.Shabbat 10:3, y.Yoma 2:1, z.Pinchas 213a, Zechariah 5:4, z.Pekudei 364, z.Pinchas 674, z.Tzav 5

[8] LXX adds *whole*

[9] Leviticus 6:4 - Amos 3:10, b.Meilah [Rashi] 9a, b.Meilah [Tosefot] 10b, b.Pesachim [Rashi] 75b, b.Shabbat 114a, b.Tamid [Pirush] 28b 32b, b.Yoma [Tosefot] 28a, b.Yoma 23b, b.Zevachim [Rashi] 47b, b.Zevachim 35b 105b, Ein Yaakov Shabbat:114a, Ezekiel 18:7 18:12 18:18, Genesis 21:25, Isaiah 11:6, Job 20:19 24:2, Leviticus 4:13-15 5:3-4, Micah 2:2, mt.Hilchot Temidim Umusafim 2:14, y.Yoma 2:1-2, Zephaniah 1:9

[10] Leviticus 6:5 - 1 Samuel 12:3, 2 Samuel 12:6, b.Bava Kamma [Tosefot] 63b, b.Bava Kamma 111a, b.Bava Metzia 55a, b.Horayot [Tosefot] 4a, b.Menachot [Rashi] 89a, b.Menachot [Tosefot] 80a, b.Nedarim [Ran] 11a, b.Pesachim 58ab 59b, b.Sanhedrin [Tosefot] 14a, b.Tamid [Pirush] 29a 33a, b.Tamid 28b, b.Temurah [Rashi] 14a, b.Yoma 26b 33a 34a 45ab, b.Zevachim 103a 49a, Ein Yaakov Yoma:33a, Exodus 22:1 22:4 22:7 22:9, Isaiah 10:6 10:9, Jastrow 1585b, Korbanot-Abaye Havoh Misader, Leviticus 5:16, Luke 19:8, m.Bava Kamma 9:6, Matthew 5:23-24, Mekilta de R'Ishmael Pisha 16:39, Midrash Tanchuma Bo 11, Midrash Tanchuma Naso 10, mt.Hilchot Temidim Umusafim 2:2 2:5, Numbers 5:7-8, Numbers.R 11:6, Proverbs 6:30-31, Shacharit, t.Shevuot 2:10 3:1, y.Pesachim 6:2, y.Yoma 2:1 3:5 4:6, z.Shoftim 8, z.Tzav 23

[11] LXX adds *whole*

[12] Leviticus 6:6 - b.Yoma 45b, b.Zevachim [Rashi] 91b, Commandment #442 #443, Isaiah 53:10-11, Lamentations.R Petichata DChakimei:11, Leviticus 5:15 5:18, m.Chullin 2:10, m.Eduyot 8:6, Mekilta de R'Ishmael Shabbata 2:50, Midrash Tanchuma Terumah 11, mt.Hilchot Beit Habechirah 6:7 6:7, mt.Hilchot Sanhedrin vHainshin Hameurim Lahem 19:4, mt.Hilchot Temidim Umusafim 2:1 2:4 2:6 3:13, Numbers.R 4:17, Tanna Devei Eliyahu 1, y.Yoma 4:6, z.Tzav 25 50 50 55 76 88 151

וְזֹאת תּוֹרַת הַמִּנְחָה הַקְרֵב אֹתָהּ בְּנֵי־
אַהֲרֹן לִפְנֵי יְהוָה אֶל־פְּנֵי הַמִּזְבֵּחַ

7¹³ And this is the law of the *meal offering*[14]: the sons of Aaron shall offer it before the LORD, in front of the altar.

וְהֵרִים מִמֶּנּוּ בְּקֻמְצוֹ מִסֹּלֶת הַמִּנְחָה
וּמִשַּׁמְנָהּ וְאֵת כָּל־הַלְּבֹנָה אֲשֶׁר עַל־
הַמִּנְחָה וְהִקְטִיר הַמִּזְבֵּחַ רֵיחַ נִיחֹחַ
אַזְכָּרָתָהּ לַיהוָה

8¹⁵ And he shall take from his handful, of the fine flour of the *meal offering*[16], and of its oil, and all the frankincense on the meal offering, and shall make its memorial part smoke on the altar for a sweet savor to the LORD.

וְהַנּוֹתֶרֶת מִמֶּנָּה יֹאכְלוּ אַהֲרֹן וּבָנָיו
מַצּוֹת תֵּאָכֵל בְּמָקוֹם קָדֹשׁ בַּחֲצַר
אֹהֶל־מוֹעֵד יֹאכְלוּהָ

9¹⁷ And Aaron and his sons shall eat what is left of it; it shall be eaten without leaven in a holy place; they shall eat it in the court of the tent of meeting.

לֹא תֵאָפֶה חָמֵץ חֶלְקָם נָתַתִּי אֹתָהּ
מֵאִשָּׁי[18] קֹדֶשׁ קָדָשִׁים הִוא כַּחַטָּאת
וְכָאָשָׁם

10¹⁹ It shall not be baked with leaven. I have given it as their portion of *My offerings*[20] made by fire; it is most holy, as the sin offering, and as the guilt offering.

כָּל־זָכָר בִּבְנֵי אַהֲרֹן יֹאכְלֶנָּה חָק־
עוֹלָם לְדֹרֹתֵיכֶם מֵאִשֵּׁי יְהוָה כֹּל

11²¹ Every male among the children of Aaron may eat of it, as their due

[13] Leviticus 6:7 - 1 Corinthians 6:9-6:11, 1 John 1:7 1:9 2:1-2, b.Chullin [Rashi] 132a, b.Kereitot [Rashi] 22b, b.Kiddushin 36a, b.Menachot [Rashi] 2b 19a 52b, b.Menachot [Tosefot] 60a 84ab, b.Menachot 3b 4a 19b 53a 61a 72b 105a, b.Nedarim [Ran] 2b, b.Sotah [Rashi] 19a, b.Sotah 14b, b.Succah [Rashi] 49a, b.Yoma 45a, b.Zevachim [Rashi] 119b, b.Zevachim [Tosefot] 58a, b.Zevachim 9b 62a 63b, Ein Yaakov Menachot:110a, Exodus 10:7, Ezekiel 18:21-23 18:26-27 33:14-16 9:19, Isaiah 1:18, Leviticus 4:20 4:26 4:31 5:10 5:13 5:15-16 5:18, Leviticus.R 9:9, Matthew 12:31, Micah 7:18, Midrash Tanchuma Tzav 14, mt.Hilchot Beit Habechirah 2:17 2:17, mt.Hilchot Maaseh haKorbanot 12:6, Pesikta Rabbati 5:4, y.Sotah 3:1, z.Tzav 121
[14] LXX *sacrifice*
[15] Leviticus 6:8 - b.Menachot [Rashi] 72b 74a, b.Menachot [Tosefot] 52b 60ab 77b, b.Menachot 11ab 19b 24a 16a 61a 16b, b.Shekalim 18b, b.Sotah 14b, b.Temurah [Rashi] 34a, b.Yoma 24a 47a, b.Zevachim 63a, Jastrow 1333b, mt.Hilchot Beit HaBechirah 6:7, mt.Hilchot Maaseh haKorbanot 13:14, mt.Hilchot Pesulei haMikdashim 11:8, Tanna Devei Eliyahu 6, y.Yoma 5:1
[16] LXX *sacrifice*
[17] Leviticus 6:9 - b.Bava Batra [Tosefot] 81b, b.Chullin [Tosefot] 130b, b.Meilah 9a, b.Menachot [Rashi] 52b, b.Menachot [Tosefot] 8a, b.Menachot 9a 21b 53a 72b, b.Pesachim [Rashi] 34b 82b, b.Sheviit [Rashi] 15a, b.Temurah 23a, b.Yevamot [Rashi] 1a, b.Yevamot 39b, b.Zevachim [Rashi] 60a 11a, b.Zevachim 56a 63a, Commandment #487, Exodus 29:38-29:42, Leviticus 1:1-17 6:12-13, Mekhilta de R'Shimon bar Yochai Pisha 3:2, mt.Hilchot Maaseh haKorbanot 10:2 10:11, Numbers 4:3 4:9, Philo De Specialibus Legibus I 240 285, t.Challah 2:7, y.Yevamot 1:1
[18] , the abbreviation מאשי ' stands for מאשי יהוה *the offerings of Hashem* [confirmed by Leviticus 6:11]
[19] Leviticus 6:10 - b.Bava Kamma [Rashi] 11b, b.Bechorot [Rashi] 31a, b.Bechorot 33b, b.Menachot [Tosefot] 2a 52b 57a, b.Menachot 2b 10b 26a 53a 55a-56b 61a, b.Shabbat 111a, b.Sheviit 15b, b.Sotah 15a, b.Yevamot 40a, b.Zevachim 11a 25a [Rashi] 5b [Tosefot] 33a, Commandment #488, Exodus 28:39-43 39:27-29, Ezekiel 44:17-18, Jastrow 1556a, Leviticus 1:9 1:13 1:16-17 16:4, m.Zevachim 6:5, mt.Hilchot Maaseh haKorbanot 12:14, mt.Hilchot Sanhedrin vHainshin Hameurim Lahem 19:4, Numbers 16:21 16:35, Psalms 20:4 37:20, Revelation 7:13 19:8 19:14, t.Demai 2:8
[20] LXX *the burnt offerings of the Lord*
[21] Leviticus 6:11 - b.Kiddushin [Tosefot] 53a, b.Menachot [Rashi] 19a 82b 83a, b.Menachot [Rashi] 84b, b.Sheviit 14a, b.Sotah 23b, b.Zevachim 102a [Rashi] 98a [Tosefot] 102b, Ezekiel 20:19, Hebrews 13:11-13, Leviticus 4:12 4:21 14:40-41 16:23-24 16:27, Leviticus.R 3:6 9:6, m.Meilah 2:2

אֲשֶׁר־יִגַּע בָּהֶם יִקְדָּשׁ

forever throughout your generations, from the [22]offerings of the LORD made by fire; whatever touches them shall be holy.

וַיְדַבֵּר יְהוָה אֶל־מֹשֶׁה לֵּאמֹר

12[23] And the LORD spoke to Moses, saying:

זֶה קָרְבַּן אַהֲרֹן וּבָנָיו אֲשֶׁר־יַקְרִיבוּ לַיהוָה בְּיוֹם הִמָּשַׁח אֹתוֹ עֲשִׂירִת הָאֵפָה סֹלֶת מִנְחָה תָּמִיד מַחֲצִיתָהּ בַּבֹּקֶר וּמַחֲצִיתָהּ בָּעָרֶב

13[24] This is the offering of Aaron and of his sons, which they shall offer to the LORD in the day when he is anointed: the tenth part of an ephah of fine flour for a meal offering perpetually, half of it in the morning, and half of it in the evening.

עַל־מַחֲבַת בַּשֶּׁמֶן תֵּעָשֶׂה מֻרְבֶּכֶת תְּבִיאֶנָּה תֻּפִינֵי מִנְחַת פִּתִּים תַּקְרִיב רֵיחַ־נִיחֹחַ לַיהוָה

14[25] It shall be made with oil on a griddle; *when it is soaked, you shall bring it in; in broken pieces shall you offer the meal*[26] offering for a sweet savor to the LORD.

וְהַכֹּהֵן הַמָּשִׁיחַ תַּחְתָּיו מִבָּנָיו יַעֲשֶׂה אֹתָהּ חָק־עוֹלָם לַיהוָה כָּלִיל תָּקְטָר

15[27] And the anointed priest who shall be in his stead from among his sons shall offer it, it is a due forever; it shall be wholly made to smoke to the LORD.

---

[22] LXX adds *burnt*

[23] Leviticus 6:12 - b.Menachot [Tosefot] 51b, b.Sheviit [Rashi] 15a, b.Sheviit 14a, Exodus 29:38-42, Hebrews 10:27, Leviticus 1:7-9 3:3-5 3:9-11 3:14-16 9:24, Leviticus.R 8:4, Mark 9:48-49, Nehemiah 13:31, Numbers 4:13-14, Pesikta de R'Kahana 2.4, t.Sotah 13:7
Leviticus 6:12-16 - Leviticus.R 2:9

[24] Leviticus 6:13 - b.Chullin 132a, b.Horayot 9a, b.Menachot [Rashi] 7b, b.Menachot [Tosefot] 8b, b.Menachot 8a 50b 51ab 52a 78a, b.Moed Katan [Rashi] 16a, b.Sanhedrin [Tosefot] 14a, b.Shekalim [Taklin Chadatin] 20b, b.Sheviit [Rashi] 15ab, b.Tamid [Pirush] 30a, b.Temurah [Rashi] 14a, b.Yoma [Rashi] 25a, b.Yoma 5b, b.Zevachim [Rashi] 43a, Commandment #489, Jastrow 2049 419b, Leviticus.R 2:9 8:1 8:4, m.Megillah 1:9, m.Middot 4:5, m.Yoma 2:3, Midrash Tanchuma Ki Tissa 5, mt.Hilchot Beit Habechirah 5:17, mt.Hilchot Klei haMikdash Vihaovdim Bo 4:14 5:16, mt.Hilchot Maaseh haKorbanot 12:4 13:2, y.Horayot 2:6 3:2, y.Megillah 1:10, z.Tzav 89 98 100
Leviticus 6:13-15 - mt.Hilchot Beit HaBechirah 5:11

[25] Leviticus 6:14 - b.Menachot [Rashi] 7b 74a 78a 87b 89a, b.Menachot [Tosefot] 63a, b.Menachot 50b 51a, b.Shekalim 20b, b.Tamid [Pirush] 30a, b.Yoma [Rashi] 25a, Jastrow 530a 1441a 1655b, John 6:32, Leviticus 2:1-2:2, m.Shekalim 7:6, m.Yevamot 11:5, mt.Hilchot Beit Habechirah 5:17, mt.Hilchot Maaseh haKorbanot 12:4 13:3, mt.Hilchot Temidim Umusafim 3:18, Numbers 15:4 15:6 15:9, y.Shekalim 7:3, y.Yoma 2:2

[26] LXX *he shall offer it kneaded in rolls, an offering of fragments, an*

[27] Leviticus 6:15 - b.Horayot 11b, b.Kereitot 5b, b.Menachot [Rashi] 12b 52b, b.Menachot [Tosefot] 8b 76b, b.Menachot 8a 51b 74a 76a, b.Shekalim [Taklin Chadatin] 16a, b.Shekalim 20b, b.Sotah 23b, b.Yoma [Rashi] 34a 73a, Leviticus 2:2 2:9, m.Shekalim 7:6, m.Yevamot 11:5, mt.Hilchot Beit Habechirah 5:17, mt.Hilchot Sotah 4:15, mt.Hilchot Klei haMikdash Vihaovdim Bo 1:7, mt.Hilchot Maaseh haKorbanot 12:4, Saadia Opinions 8:9, t.Menachot 7:12, y.Horayot 3:2, y.Megillah 1:10, y.Shekalim 7:3, y.Sotah 3:7, y.Yoma 1:1

וְכָל־מִנְחַת כֹּהֵן כָּלִיל תִּהְיֶה לֹא תֵאָכֵל 16[1]

And every meal offering of the priest shall be wholly made to smoke; it shall not be eaten.

וַיְדַבֵּר יְהוָה אֶל־מֹשֶׁה לֵּאמֹר 17[2]

And the LORD spoke to Moses, saying:

דַּבֵּר אֶל־אַהֲרֹן וְאֶל־בָּנָיו לֵאמֹר זֹאת תּוֹרַת הַחַטָּאת בִּמְקוֹם אֲשֶׁר תִּשָּׁחֵט הָעֹלָה תִּשָּׁחֵט הַחַטָּאת לִפְנֵי יְהוָה קֹדֶשׁ קָדָשִׁים הִוא 18[3]

Speak to Aaron and to his sons, saying: This is the law of the sin offering: in the place where the [4]burnt offering is killed shall the sin offering be killed before the LORD; it is most holy.

הַכֹּהֵן הַמְחַטֵּא אֹתָהּ יֹאכְלֶנָּה בְּמָקוֹם קָדֹשׁ תֵּאָכֵל בַּחֲצַר אֹהֶל מוֹעֵד 19[5]

The priest who offers it for sin shall eat it; it shall be eaten in a holy place, in the court of the tent of meeting.

כֹּל אֲשֶׁר־יִגַּע בִּבְשָׂרָהּ יִקְדָּשׁ וַאֲשֶׁר יִזֶּה מִדָּמָהּ עַל־הַבֶּגֶד אֲשֶׁר יִזֶּה עָלֶיהָ תְּכַבֵּס בְּמָקוֹם קָדֹשׁ 20[6]

Whatever shall touch its flesh shall be holy; and when any garment is sprinkled by its blood, you shall wash whatever was sprinkled in a holy place.

וּכְלִי־חֶרֶשׂ אֲשֶׁר תְּבֻשַּׁל־בּוֹ יִשָּׁבֵר וְאִם־בִּכְלִי נְחֹשֶׁת בֻּשָּׁלָה וּמֹרַק וְשֻׁטַּף בַּמָּיִם 21[7]

But the earthen vessel in which it is sodden shall be broken; and if it is sodden in a brazen vessel, it shall be scoured, and rinsed in water.

---

[1] Leviticus 6:16 - 1 Corinthians 5:8 9:13-9:15, b.Arachin 4a, b.Chullin 131b, b.Makkot 18b, b.Meilah [Rashi] 10a, b.Menachot [Rashi] 12b 74a, b.Menachot [Tosefot] 57a, b.Menachot 21b 46b 51b 73b 74ab, b.Shekalim 3b, b.Sotah [Rashi] 23a, b.Yevamot [Rashi] 1a, b.Zevachim [Rashi] 102b, b.Zevachim [Tosefot] 32b, Commandment #490, Exodus 12:8, Ezekiel 20:29, Guide for the Perplexed 3:46, Leviticus 2:3 2:10-11 5:13 6:26 10:12-13, m.Shekalim 7:6, m.Yevamot 11:5, mt.Hilchot Maaseh haKorbanot 11:3 12:9, mt.Hilchot Sanhedrin vHainshin Hameurim Lahem 19:4, Numbers 18:9-10, Sifre Devarim Vezot Habracha 351, t.Menachot 1:16, y.Shekalim 1:3, y.Sotah 3:6 3:7
[2] Leviticus 6:17 - 1 Peter 2:22, Exodus 29:33-34 5:37 16:10, Leviticus 2:3 2:11 6:25 6:29 7:1 7:6, m.Yevamot 11:5, Numbers 18:9-10, t.Menachot 7:14
[3] Leviticus 6:18 - 1 Peter 1:16 2:9, b.Menachot [Rashi] 3a 82b, b.Menachot [Tosefot] 72b, b.Menachot 3b 4a 55b 11a, b.Temurah [Rashi] 32b, b.Zevachim [Rashi] 48a 49b 52b 60a 88b, b.Zevachim [Tosefot] 8a 67a, b.Zevachim 9b 48b 60a 92ab, Commandment #491, Exodus 5:37, Haggai 2:12-14, Jastrow 1234b, Leviticus 3:17 6:27 6:29 21:21-22 22:3-7, Leviticus.R 9:9 32:5, m.Zevachim 11:1 12:1, Midrash Psalms 2:15, Numbers 18:10, Philo De Specialibus Legibus I 254, y.Kiddushin 4:1, y.Pesachim 5:2, y.Sotah 8:9, y.Yevamot 8:3, Zechariah 14:20-21, z.Tzav 121
[4] LXX adds *whole*
[5] Leviticus 6:19 - b.Makkot [Rashi] 14a, b.Zevachim [Rashi] 53a 64b 112b, b.Zevachim [Tosefot] 55a, b.Zevachim 10b 52b 92ab 99a 102b, m.Zevachim 11:1, mt.Hilchot Maaseh haKorbanot 5:7 7:1 10:14, t.Challah 2:7
[6] Leviticus 6:20 - b.Avodah Zara [Rashi] 76a, b.Avodah Zara [Tosefot] 66a, b.Chullin 99a, b.Meilah 5a, b.Menachot [Rashi] 7b 83a, b.Nazir 37b, b.Pesachim 45a, b.Sheviit 14a, b.Zevachim [Rashi] 92a, b.Zevachim 38b 92b 93b-94b 97ab, Exodus 16:36 5:2 29:35-42, Hebrews 5:1 7:27 8:3-4, Leviticus 2:1-16 5:1 5:11, m.Menachot 5:3, m.Zevachim 11:1, mt.Hilchot Maaseh haKorbanot 8:1 8:15 8:19, Numbers 18:26-32 4:3 4:10, Philo Quis Rerum Divinarum Heres 174, t.Zevachim 8:29
[7] Leviticus 6:21 - 1 Chronicles 9:31, Avot de R'Natan 35, b.Avodah Zara [Rashi] 76a, b.Avodah Zara 34a, b.Menachot [Tosefot] 80a, b.Niddah [Rashi] 6a, b.Yoma [Rashi] 21a, b.Zevachim [Rashi] 96a, b.Zevachim 94b 95ab 96b 97a, Jastrow 8439 1554a, Leviticus 2:5 7:9, m.Menachot 11:3 4:5 9:1 9:7, m.Tamid 1:3, m.Temurah 2:1 2:1, m.Zevachim 11:1, Midrash Tanchuma Chukkat 2, mt.Hilchot Chametz uMatzah 5:25, mt.Hilchot Maaseh haKorbanot 8:11 8:14 8:21

כָּל־זָכָר בַּכֹּהֲנִים יֹאכַל אֹתָהּ קֹדֶשׁ קָדָשִׁים הִוא

22¹ Every male among the priests may eat of it; it is most holy².

וְכָל־חַטָּאת אֲשֶׁר יוּבָא מִדָּמָהּ אֶל־אֹהֶל מוֹעֵד לְכַפֵּר בַּקֹּדֶשׁ לֹא תֵאָכֵל בָּאֵשׁ תִּשָּׂרֵף

23³ And no sin offering, from which any of the blood is brought into the tent of meeting to make atonement in the holy place, shall be eaten; it shall be burnt with fire.

Tzav – Chapter 7

וְזֹאת תּוֹרַת הָאָשָׁם קֹדֶשׁ קָדָשִׁים הוּא

1⁴ *And this is the law of the guilt offering⁵*: it is most holy.

בִּמְקוֹם אֲשֶׁר יִשְׁחֲטוּ אֶת־הָעֹלָה יִשְׁחֲטוּ אֶת־הָאָשָׁם וְאֶת־דָּמוֹ יִזְרֹק עַל־הַמִּזְבֵּחַ סָבִיב

2⁶ In the place where they kill the ⁷burnt offering they shall kill the guilt offering: and its blood shall be dashed against the altar.

וְאֵת כָּל־חֶלְבּוֹ יַקְרִיב מִמֶּנּוּ אֵת הָאַלְיָה וְאֶת־הַחֵלֶב הַמְכַסֶּה אֶת־הַקֶּרֶב

3⁸ And he shall offer of it all its fat: *the fat tail⁹*, and the fat that covers the inwards¹⁰,

וְאֵת שְׁתֵּי הַכְּלָיֹת וְאֶת־הַחֵלֶב אֲשֶׁר

4¹¹ and the two kidneys, and the fat that is on them, which is by the *loins¹²*, and

---

¹ Leviticus 6:22 - b.Menachot [Tosefot] 82b, b.Zevachim [Rashi] 82a 92b, b.Zevachim [Tosefot] 102b, b.Zevachim 93 96b-97b 99a 102a, Deuteronomy 10:6, Esther.R 3:6, Exodus 29:22-25, Hebrews 7:23, Isaiah 5:10, Leviticus 4:3 8:21, m.Menachot 3:2, m.Zevachim 4:3, mt.Hilchot Bikkurim 1:9, mt.Hilchot Maaseh haKorbanot 8:14
² LXX adds *to the LORD*
³ Leviticus 6:23 - b.Bechorot [Tosefot] 10a, b.Chullin [Rashi] 11a, b.Horayot [Rashi] 6a, b.Meilah [Rashi] 11b, b.Menachot [Tosefot] 56b 11b, b.Pesachim [Rashi] 49a 82a-83a, b.Pesachim 23b 24a, b.Temurah [Rashi] 33a, b.Zevachim [Rashi] 27b 36a 38b 81b 92b 94b 42a [Tosefot] 26b, b.Zevachim 10b 11a 82a-83a 92a, Commandment #492, Leviticus 2:10 6:16-17, m.Menachot 3:2 6:1, m.Zevachim 10:8 4:3, mt.Hilchot Maaseh haKorbanot 11:3, mt.Hilchot Pesulei haMikdashim 2:13, y.Orlah 3:1, y.Pesachim 2:1 7:9
⁴ Leviticus 7:1 - b.Kereitot 22b, b.Menachot [Tosefot] 4a 73a, b.Menachot 11a, b.Moed Katan 14b, b.Temurah [Rashi] 32b, b.Zevachim [Rashi] 49ab 88b, b.Zevachim 48a, Commandment #493, Ein Yaakov Menachot:110a, Ezekiel 16:39 20:29 22:20, Leviticus 5:1-6 5:8 5:11 5:14-6:7 6:17 6:25 14:12-13 19:21-22 21:22, Leviticus.R 9:9, Midrash Psalms 2:15, Midrash Tanchuma Tzav 5, Numbers 6:12, Pesikta Rabbati 5:4, Song of Songs.R 1:52, Tanna Devei Eliyahu 6, z.Tzav 121
Leviticus 7:1-6 - Parshat Asham [guilt offering]
⁵ LXX *And this is the law of the ram for the trespass-offering*
⁶ Leviticus 7:2 - 1 Peter 1:2, b.Menachot [Rashi] 3a, b.Menachot [Rashi] 8b, b.Moed Katan 14b, b.Zevachim [Rashi] 53b 54b, b.Zevachim [Tosefot] 36b, b.Zevachim 49a, Ezekiel 12:25 16:39, Hebrews 9:19-9:22 11:28 12:24, Isaiah 4:15, Leviticus 1:3 1:5 1:11 3:2 3:8 4:24 4:29 4:33 5:9 6:25, m.Megillah 2:5, mt.Hilchot Maaseh haKorbanot 5:3 5:6, Numbers 6:12, Pesikta Rabbati 48:3
⁷ LXX adds *whole*
⁸ Leviticus 7:3 - b.Chullin 75a, b.Moed Katan 14b, b.Pesachim [Rashi] 96b, Exodus 5:13, Leviticus 3:3-5 3:9-11 3:15-16 4:8-10, Psalms 51:7 51:18
⁹ LXX *and the loins*
¹⁰ LXX adds *and all the fat that is upon the inwards*
¹¹ Leviticus 7:4 - b.Bechorot 39a, b.Chullin 75a, b.Moed Katan 14b, Leviticus 3:4
¹² LXX *thighs*

עֲלֵיהֶ֔ן אֲשֶׁ֖ר עַל־הַכְּסָלִ֑ים וְאֶת־
הַיֹּתֶ֙רֶת֙ עַל־הַכָּבֵ֔ד עַל־הַכְּלָיֹ֖ת יְסִירֶֽנָּה

the *lobe above*[1] the liver, which he shall remove with the kidneys.

5[2] וְהִקְטִ֤יר אֹתָם֙ הַכֹּהֵן֙ הַמִּזְבֵּ֔חָה אִשֶּׁ֖ה
לַיהוָ֑ה אָשָׁ֖ם הֽוּא

And the priest shall make them smoke on the altar for an [3]offering made by fire to the LORD; it is a guilt offering.

6[4] כָּל־זָכָ֥ר בַּכֹּהֲנִ֖ים יֹאכְלֶ֑נּוּ בְּמָק֤וֹם
קָדוֹשׁ֙ יֵֽאָכֵ֔ל קֹ֥דֶשׁ קָֽדָשִׁ֖ים הֽוּא

Every male among the priests may eat of it; it shall be eaten in a holy place; it is most holy.

7[5] כַּֽחַטָּאת֙ כָּֽאָשָׁ֔ם תּוֹרָ֥ה אַחַ֖ת לָהֶ֑ם
הַכֹּהֵ֛ן אֲשֶׁ֥ר יְכַפֶּר־בּ֖וֹ ל֥וֹ יִהְיֶֽה

As is the sin offering, so is the guilt offering; there is one law for them; the priest who makes atonement with it, shall have it.

8[6] וְהַכֹּהֵ֗ן הַמַּקְרִיב֙ אֶת־עֹ֣לַת אִ֔ישׁ ע֤וֹר
הָֽעֹלָה֙ אֲשֶׁ֣ר הִקְרִ֔יב לַכֹּהֵ֖ן ל֥וֹ יִהְיֶֽה

And the priest who offers any man's [7]burnt offering, even the priest shall have to himself the skin of the [8]burnt offering, which he has offered.

9[9] וְכָל־מִנְחָ֗ה אֲשֶׁ֤ר תֵּֽאָפֶה֙ בַּתַּנּ֔וּר וְכָל־
נַעֲשָׂ֥ה בַמַּרְחֶ֖שֶׁת וְעַל־מַֽחֲבַ֑ת לַכֹּהֵ֛ן
הַמַּקְרִ֥יב אֹתָ֖הּ ל֥וֹ תִֽהְיֶֽה

And every *meal offering*[10] that is baked in the oven, and all that is dressed in the stewing pan, and on the griddle, shall belong to the priest who offers it.

10[11] וְכָל־מִנְחָ֥ה בְלוּלָֽה־בַשֶּׁ֖מֶן וַחֲרֵבָ֑ה
לְכָל־בְּנֵ֧י אַהֲרֹ֛ן תִּהְיֶ֖ה אִ֥ישׁ כְּאָחִֽיו

And every meal offering, mingled with oil, *or dry*[12], shall all the sons of Aaron have, *one as well as another*[1].

---

[1] LXX *caul upon*

[2] Leviticus 7:5 - 1 Peter 4:1-2, b.Horayot [Rashi] 5b, b.Menachot [Rashi] 83a, b.Menachot 4a, b.Moed Katan 14b, b.Zevachim [Tosefot] 98b, b.Zevachim 12b, Galatians 2:20 5:24, Leviticus 1:9 1:13 2:2 2:9 2:16 3:16, Philo De Specialibus Legibus I 225

[3] LXX adds *burnt*

[4] Leviticus 7:6 - b.Meilah [Tosefot] 7b, b.Menachot [Tosefot] 82b, b.Moed Katan 14b, b.Sotah [Rashi] 23a, b.Zevachim [Tosefot] 102b, b.Zevachim 97b 102a, Leviticus 2:3 6:16-18 6:29, m.Zevachim 5:5, Numbers 18:9-18:10, t.Challah 2:7, y.Sotah 3:7

[5] Leviticus 7:7 - 1 Corinthians 9:13, b.Bava Metzia [Tosefot] 114a, b.Menachot [Tosefot] 83a, b.Menachot 28a, b.Moed Katan 14b, b.Nedarim 4b, b.Pesachim [Rashi] 73a, b.Sheviit [Rashi] 12a, b.Zevachim [Rashi] 98a 103a, b.Zevachim [Tosefot] 98b, b.Zevachim 10b 81b 86a 103b, Leviticus 6:25-26 14:13, m.Zevachim 5:5, mt.Hilchot Maaseh haKorbanot 9:1 10:14, t.Zevachim 8:24, y.Horayot 2:7 3:2, y.Sheviit 2:1

[6] Leviticus 7:8 - b.Chullin [Rashi] 133b, b.Meilah [Rashi] 9a, b.Menachot [Tosefot] 83a, b.Moed Katan 14b, b.Pesachim [Rashi] 57a, b.Zevachim [Rashi] 43a 85a 104a, b.Zevachim [Tosefot] 98ab, b.Zevachim 86a 103ab, Exodus 5:14, Genesis 3:21, Leviticus 1:6 4:11, m.Zevachim 12:2 4:4, mt.Hilchot Maaseh haKorbanot 10:14, Numbers 19:5, Numbers.R 8:6, Romans 13:14, t.Zevachim 11:5-7

[7] LXX adds *whole*

[8] LXX adds *whole*

[9] Leviticus 7:9 - 1 Corinthians 9:7 9:13, b.Kiddushin 53a, b.Menachot 63ab 73a, b.Moed Katan 14b, b.Yoma 56a, b.Zevachim [Rashi] 13a, b.Zevachim [Tosefot] 96a, b.Zevachim 102b, Ezekiel 20:29, Galatians 6:6, Leviticus 2:3-7 2:10 5:13 6:16-18, m.Zevachim 5:4, mt.Hilchot Maaseh haKorbanot 10:14 10:15 13:7, Numbers 18:9

[10] LXX *sacrifice*

[11] Leviticus 7:10 - 2 Corinthians 8:14, b.Bava Kamma [Rashi] 11b, b.Chullin [Tosefot] 1a, b.Kiddushin 53a, b.Menachot 3b 54a 63b 72b 73a 103b, b.Moed Katan 14b, b.Zevachim [Rashi] 99a 102b, b.Zevachim [Tosefot] 72a, Exodus 16:18, m.Chullin 10:2, m.Menachot 9:7, m.Temurah 1:1, mt.Hilchot Maaseh haKorbanot 10:15, mt.Hilchot Pesulei haMikdashim 11:14, Numbers.R 20:18, y.Sotah 3:1

[12] LXX *or not made up with oil*

וְזֹאת תּוֹרַת זֶבַח הַשְּׁלָמִים אֲשֶׁר 11[2]
יַקְרִיב לַיהוָה

אִם עַל־תּוֹדָה יַקְרִיבֶנּוּ וְהִקְרִיב עַל־ 12[3]
זֶבַח הַתּוֹדָה חַלּוֹת מַצּוֹת בְּלוּלֹת
בַּשֶּׁמֶן וּרְקִיקֵי מַצּוֹת מְשֻׁחִים בַּשָּׁמֶן
וְסֹלֶת מֻרְבֶּכֶת חַלֹּת בְּלוּלֹת בַּשָּׁמֶן

עַל־חַלֹּת לֶחֶם חָמֵץ יַקְרִיב קָרְבָּנוֹ 13[6]
עַל־זֶבַח תּוֹדַת שְׁלָמָיו

וְהִקְרִיב מִמֶּנּוּ אֶחָד מִכָּל־קָרְבָּן 14[7]
תְּרוּמָה לַיהוָה לַכֹּהֵן הַזֹּרֵק אֶת־דַּם
הַשְּׁלָמִים לוֹ יִהְיֶה

And this is the law of the sacrifice of peace offerings, which one may offer to the LORD.

If he offers it as a *thanksgiving*[4], then he shall offer it with the sacrifice of thanksgiving unleavened cakes mingled with oil, and unleavened wafers spread with oil, and cakes of fine flour mingled with oil, *soaked*[5].

With cakes of leavened bread, he shall present his offering with the sacrifice of his peace offerings for thanksgiving.

And of it he shall present one of each offering *as a gift*[8] to the LORD; it shall belong to the priest who dashes the peace offerings' blood *against the altar*[9].

---

[1] LXX *an equal portion to each*
[2] Leviticus 7:11 - b.Kiddushin [Tosefot] 53a, b.Menachot [Rashi] 19a 78a, b.Zevachim [Rashi] 50b 55a 57a 88b, b.Zevachim 50a 125ab, Commandment #494, Ezekiel 21:15, Genesis.R 22:5 34:9, Leviticus 3:1-17 22:18-21, Leviticus.R 9:9, Midrash Tanchuma Tzav 3 4 5 7, Numbers.R 13:2, Pesikta Rabbati 5:4, Sifre.z Numbers Naso 7:3, Song of Songs.R 1:52 4:32, y.Megillah 1:11, z.Tzav 121, z.Vayikra 199
Leviticus 7:11-12 - Leviticus.R 9:1
Leviticus 7:11-18 - 4QMMT B 9-13, Parshat Todah [thanks offering]
[3] Leviticus 7:12 - 1 Peter 2:5, 2 Chronicles 5:31 9:16, 2 Corinthians 9:11-15, b.Kiddushin [Rashi] 53a, b.Meilah [Rashi] 13b, b.Menachot [Rashi] 18a 19a 78ab, b.Menachot [Tosefot] 75a, b.Menachot 15a 73a 76b 77b 79b 80ab 89a, b.Pesachim [Rashi] 63b, b.Temurah 18ab, b.Zevachim [Rashi] 50b 55a 57a, b.Zevachim 50a, Ephesians 5:20, Hebrews 13:15, Hosea 14:4, Jastrow 1441a 1442b, Jeremiah 9:11, Leviticus 2:4 6:16 7:15 22:29, Luke 17:16 17:18, m.Challah 1:6, m.Menachot 3:6 7:1 7:4 9:3, m.Pesachim 2:5, m.Zevachim 5:6, Midrash Tanchuma Tzav 6, mt.Hilchot Chametz uMatzah 6:9, mt.Hilchot Maaseh haKorbanot 10:21, mt.Hilchot Temurah 3:1 4:1, Nehemiah 12:43, Numbers 6:15, Numbers.R 10:19, Psalms 50:13-14 50:23 103:1-2 11:8 107:21-22 20:17, Romans 1:21, t.Menachot 8:7, z.Vayikra 193 196
[4] LXX *praise*
[5] LXX *kneaded with oil*
[6] Leviticus 7:13 - 1 Timothy 4:4, Amos 4:5, b.Beitzah [Rashi] 19b, b.Chullin [Tosefot] 23b, b.Eruvin [Rashi] 50a, b.Horayot [Rashi] 4a [Tosefot] 7a, b.Meilah [Tosefot] 13b, b.Menachot [Rashi] 15a 19a 46ab 47ab 48b 52b, b.Menachot [Tosefot] 76b, b.Menachot 16a 47b 76a 77b-78b, b.Pesachim [Rashi] 13b, b.Pesachim 37a, b.Zevachim [Tosefot] 50a, b.Zevachim 57b, Jastrow 799a, Leviticus 23:17, m.Demai 1:3, m.Menachot 2:3 3:6, m.Pesachim 1:5, Matthew 13:33, Midrash Tanchuma Pinchas 12, z.Vayikra 194 341
[7] Leviticus 7:14 - b.Bava Kamma [Rashi] 11b, b.Chullin [Rashi] 133b, b.Horayot 4a, b.Menachot [Rashi] 46a, b.Menachot 3b 76a 77b 78b, b.Nedarim 12b, b.Niddah 6b, b.Pesachim 37ab, b.Zevachim [Rashi] 36b 55a 57b 114b, b.Zevachim [Tosefot] 50a 99a, b.Zevachim 102b, Exodus 29:27-28, Jastrow 1221a, Leviticus 6:26, m.Zevachim 5:6, mt.Hilchot Maaseh haKorbanot 9:13 9:21 10:14, Numbers 15:19-21 18:8-11 18:19 18:24-32 7:29 7:41, t.Challah 2:8, y.Yevamot 8:1
[8] LXX *a separate offering*
[9] Missing in LXX

וּבְשַׂר זֶבַח תּוֹדַת שְׁלָמָיו בְּיוֹם קָרְבָּנוֹ 15¹
יֵאָכֵל לֹא־יַנִּיחַ מִמֶּנּוּ עַד־בֹּקֶר

And the flesh of the sacrifice of his peace offerings for thanksgiving² shall be eaten on the day of his offering; he shall not leave any of it until the morning.

וְאִם־נֶדֶר אוֹ נְדָבָה זֶבַח קָרְבָּנוֹ בְּיוֹם 16³
הַקְרִיבוֹ אֶת־זִבְחוֹ יֵאָכֵל וּמִמָּחֳרָת
וְהַנּוֹתָר מִמֶּנּוּ יֵאָכֵל

But if the sacrifice of his offering is a vow or a freewill offering, it shall be eaten on the day that he offers his sacrifice; and on the following day *what remains of it may be eaten⁴*.

וְהַנּוֹתָר מִבְּשַׂר הַזָּבַח בַּיּוֹם הַשְּׁלִישִׁי 17⁵
בָּאֵשׁ יִשָּׂרֵף

But what remains of the meat of the sacrifice on the third day shall be burnt with fire.

וְאִם הֵאָכֹל יֵאָכֵל מִבְּשַׂר־זֶבַח שְׁלָמָיו 18⁶
בַּיּוֹם הַשְּׁלִישִׁי לֹא יֵרָצֶה הַמַּקְרִיב
אֹתוֹ לֹא יֵחָשֵׁב לוֹ פִּגּוּל יִהְיֶה וְהַנֶּפֶשׁ
הָאֹכֶלֶת מִמֶּנּוּ עֲוֺנָהּ תִּשָּׂא

And if any of the flesh of the sacrifice of his peace offerings is eaten on the third day, it shall not be accepted, nor shall it be imputed to he who offers it; it shall be an abhorred thing, and the soul who eats of it shall bear his iniquity.

¹ Leviticus 7:15 - b.Berachot [Rashi] 2a 9a, b.Chullin [Rashi] 83a, b.Horayot [Tosefot] 9a, b.Horayot 51 7a, b.Menachot [Rashi] 11b 46a 47b 81b, b.Menachot [Tosefot] 83b, b.Pesachim [Rashbam] 125ab, b.Pesachim [Rashi] 3a 38b, b.Pesachim [Tosefot] 71b, b.Temurah [Rashi] 14a, b.Zevachim [Rashi] 21a 53a 55a 56b, b.Zevachim [Tosefot] 57a, b.Zevachim 36a, Guide for the Perplexed 3:46, Leviticus 22:29-30, m.Korayot 3:9, m.Nazir 4:4, Mas.Soferim 9:3, mt.Hilchot Maaseh haKorbanot 4:10 10:7, mt.Hilchot Pesulei haMikdashim 15:13, Siman 14:5
Leviticus 7:15-27 - Josephus Antiquities 3.11.2
² LXX adds *shall be his and*
³ Leviticus 7:16 - b.Menachot [Rashi] 20b, b.Pesachim 71b, b.Rosh Hashanah 5b, b.Zevachim 56ab, Deuteronomy 12:6 12:11 12:17 12:26, Ezekiel 22:12, Leviticus 19:5-19:8 22:18-21 22:23 22:29 23:38, mt.Hilchot Maaseh haKorbanot 10:6, Nahum 2:1, Numbers 15:3, Psalms 66:13 20:14 20:18, Sifre Devarim Ki Tetze 264, Sifre Devarim Reeh 131
⁴ Missing in LXX
⁵ Leviticus 7:17 - 1 Corinthians 15:4, b.Beitzah [Rashi] 16a, b.Menachot [Rashi] 83a, b.Menachot [Tosefot] 83a, b.Menachot 102b, b.Nedarim 10b, b.Pesachim 3a, b.Taanit [Rashi] 30a, b.Temurah 2b, b.Yevamot [Rashi] 72b, b.Zevachim [Rashi] 29a 86a, b.Zevachim [Tosefot] 98b, b.Zevachim 56b, Commandment #495, Exodus 12:10 19:11 5:14, Genesis 22:4, Hosea 6:2, Leviticus 6:22-6:23 10:16 19:7, m.Keritot 5:8, m.Maaser Sheni 3:2, m.Makkot 3:2, m.Meilah 1:1 1:2, m.Orlah 2:16, m.Zevachim 3:4 8:11, mt.Hilchot Maaseh haKorbanot 10:6, mt.Hilchot Pesulei haMikdashim 19:1, y.Pesachim 7:10, y.Shabbat 2:1, z.Tzav 135
⁶ Leviticus 7:18 - 1 Peter 2:24, Amos 5:22, Avot de R'Natan 35, b.Bechorot [Tosefot] 27b, b.Chullin [Rashi] 38b, b.Chullin 39a 81b, b.Gittin [Rashi] 55b, b.Kereitot [Rashi] 2a, b.Kereitot 5a, b.Meilah [Rashi] 2a 15b, b.Menachot [Rashi] 2b 11b 12a 14a 79a 83a, b.Menachot [Tosefot] 50b 58b, b.Menachot 13b 14ab 25a, b.Nedarim 36a, b.Pesachim [Rashi] 61b 82b 60a, b.Pesachim 16b, b.Rosh Hashanah 6a, b.Temurah 2b 3a, b.Zevachim [Rashi] 10a 32a 36a 43a 44a 46b 125ab, b.Zevachim [Tosefot] 26b 98a, b.Zevachim 13ab 14a 23b 16ab 28ab 29ab 44a 45ab 82b, Commandment #496 [the penalty is excision], Ezekiel 18:20, Hebrews 9:28, Hosea 8:13, Isaiah 1:11-14 53:11-12 17:4 18:3, Jastrow 1159a, Jeremiah 14:10 14:12, Leviticus 5:17 10:17 10:19 11:10-11 11:41 17:16 19:7-8 20:17 20:19 22:16 22:23 22:25, Luke 16:15, m.Keritot 1:1, m.Maaser Sheni 3:2, m.Makkot 3:2, m.Meilah 4:4, m.Oholot 3:3, m.Orlah 2:16, m.Zevachim 2:2, Malachi 1:10 1:13, mt.Hilchot Maaseh haKorbanot 10:6, mt.Hilchot Pesulei haMikdashim 13:1 18:1 18:6, mt.Hilchot Sanhedrin vHainshin Hameurim Lahem 19:1, Numbers 18:27, Pesikta Rabbati 10:3, Romans 4:11, Tanya Kuntress Acharon §4-5

וְהַבָּשָׂר אֲשֶׁר־יִגַּע בְּכָל־טָמֵא לֹא 19[1]
יֵאָכֵל בָּאֵשׁ יִשָּׂרֵף וְהַבָּשָׂר כָּל־טָהוֹר
יֹאכַל בָּשָׂר

And the meat that touches any unclean thing shall not be eaten; it shall be burnt with fire. And as for the meat, everyone who is clean may eat it.

וְהַנֶּפֶשׁ אֲשֶׁר־תֹּאכַל בָּשָׂר מִזֶּבַח 20[2]
הַשְּׁלָמִים אֲשֶׁר לַיהוָה וְטֻמְאָתוֹ עָלָיו
וְנִכְרְתָה הַנֶּפֶשׁ הַהִוא מֵעַמֶּיהָ

But the soul who eats of the flesh of the sacrifice of peace offerings, that pertains to the LORD, having his uncleanness on him, that soul shall be *cut off*[3] from his people.

וְנֶפֶשׁ כִּי־תִגַּע בְּכָל־טָמֵא בְּטֻמְאַת 21[4]
אָדָם אוֹ בִּבְהֵמָה טְמֵאָה אוֹ בְּכָל־
שֶׁקֶץ טָמֵא וְאָכַל מִבְּשַׂר־זֶבַח
הַשְּׁלָמִים אֲשֶׁר לַיהוָה וְנִכְרְתָה הַנֶּפֶשׁ
הַהִוא מֵעַמֶּיהָ

And when anyone touches any unclean thing, whether it is the uncleanness of man, or an unclean beast, or any unclean detestable thing, and eat of the flesh of the sacrifice of peace offerings that *pertains to*[5] the LORD, that soul shall be cut off from his people.

וַיְדַבֵּר יְהוָה אֶל־מֹשֶׁה לֵּאמֹר 22[6]

And the LORD spoke to Moses, saying:

דַּבֵּר אֶל־בְּנֵי יִשְׂרָאֵל לֵאמֹר כָּל־חֵלֶב 23[7]
שׁוֹר וְכֶשֶׂב וָעֵז לֹא תֹאכֵלוּ

Speak to the children of Israel, saying: You shall eat no fat: of ox, or sheep, or goat.

---

[1] Leviticus 7:19 - 2 Corinthians 6:17, Acts 10:15-16 10:28, b.Bava Kamma [Tosefot] 77a, b.Chagigah 24a 74b, b.Chullin [Rashi] 33a 101a, b.Chullin [Tosefot] 86b, b.Chullin 36b, b.Makkot [Rashi] 13a 14b, b.Menachot [Rashi] 15a 21a 101a 102b, b.Menachot 25b, b.Niddah [Tosefot] 2a, b.Pesachim 16a 18b 19a 24a-25b 35a 82ab 95b, b.Sotah 29ab, b.Yevamot [Rashi] 82a, b.Zevachim [Rashi] 43b, b.Zevachim [Tosefot] 33b, b.Zevachim 34a 46b, Commandment #497 #498, Guide for the Perplexed 3:46, Leviticus 11:24-39, Luke 11:41, m.Makkot 3:2, mt.Hilchot Pesulei haMikdashim 18:12 19:1, mt.Hilchot Sanhedrin vHainshin Hameurim Lahem 19:4, mt.Hilchot Shaar Avot Hatuman 11:4, mt.Hilchot Shevitat Yom Tov 3:8, Numbers 19:11-16, Romans 14:14 14:20, Titus 1:15, y.Bikkurim 2:1, y.Chagigah 3:2, y.Pesachim 7:4-5 9:5, y.Sotah 5:2
Leviticus 7:19-20 - t.Pisha 8:9
Leviticus 7:19-26 - 4QLevg
[2] Leviticus 7:20 - 1 Corinthians 11:28, b.Chullin [Rashi] 101a, b.Kereitot 2b, b.Makkot 14b, b.Menachot [Tosefot] 55b, b.Menachot 25b, b.Pesachim 24b 95b 96a, b.Sheviit [Rashi] 6b, b.Sheviit 7a, b.Yevamot [Rashi] 82a, b.Yevamot 7a, b.Zevachim [Rashi] 33b 43b 46a 90a 106a 120b, b.Zevachim [Tosefot] 37b 43a, b.Zevachim 34a 36b 43a 46b, Commandment #499, Genesis 17:14, Jastrow 644b, Leviticus 15:2-33 22:3-7, m.Makkot 3:2, m.Meilah 1:2, m.Oholot 3:3, m.Zevachim 13:2 3:4, mt.Hilchot Pesulei haMikdashim 18:13, mt.Hilchot Sanhedrin vHainshin Hameurim Lahem 19:1, Saadia Opinions 6:5, y.Pesachim 9:4, z.Acharei Mot 259
[3] LXX *perish*
[4] Leviticus 7:21 - b.Chullin 71a, b.Kereitot 23b [Rashi] 23a, b.Sheviit 6a 7a, b.Zevachim 43b [Rashi] 43b 44a 46a, Deuteronomy 14:3 14:7-8 14:10 14:12-20, Exodus 12:15 12:19 30:33-38, Ezekiel 4:14, Genesis 17:14, Leviticus 5:2-3 7:20 7:25 7:27 11:10-13 11:20 11:24-42 12:1-59 15:1-33 17:10 17:14 18:29 22:4, m.Bechorot 8:1, mt.Hilchot Pesulei haMikdashim 18:13, Numbers 19:11-16, Saadia Opinions 6:5, y.Sheviit 1:2
[5] LXX *is*
[6] Leviticus 7:22 - y.Nazir 6:1, y.Orlah 3:1, y.Pesachim 2:1
[7] Leviticus 7:23 - 1 Samuel 2:15-17 2:29, Acts 4:27, b.Chullin 8b 114a [Rashi] 49b 98a [Tosefot] 22b 89b, b.Kereitot 4ab 21a, b.Makkot 13a, b.Menachot [Tosefot] 58b, b.Niddah [Tosefot] 28a, b.Pesachim [Rashi] 23b 24a, b.Yoma 74a, b.Zevachim 70b, Commandment #166, Leviticus 3:16-17 4:8-10 17:6, Deuteronomy 8:38, Guide for the Perplexed 3:48, m.Keritot 3:1, Mas.Soferim 9:3, Romans 8:13 13:13, t.Menachot 8:7, Midrash Psalms 119:1 119:6, mt.Hilchot Sanhedrin vHainshin Hameurim Lahem 19:1

וְחֵ֤לֶב נְבֵלָה֙ וְחֵ֣לֶב טְרֵפָ֔ה יֵעָשֶׂ֖ה לְכָל־
מְלָאכָ֑ה וְאָכֹ֖ל לֹ֥א תֹאכְלֻֽהוּ

24[1] And the fat of those that die of itself and the fat of that which is torn of beasts, may be used for any other purpose; but in no way shall you eat of it.

כִּ֚י כָּל־אֹכֵ֣ל חֵ֔לֶב מִן־הַבְּהֵמָ֔ה אֲשֶׁ֨ר
יַקְרִ֥יב מִמֶּ֛נָּה אִשֶּׁ֖ה לַיהֹוָ֑ה וְנִכְרְתָ֛ה
הַנֶּ֥פֶשׁ הָאֹכֶ֖לֶת מֵעַמֶּֽיהָ

25[2] For whoever eats the fat of the beast, of which *men*[3] present an [4]offering made by fire to the LORD, even the soul who eats it shall be cut off from his people.

וְכָל־דָּם֙ לֹ֣א תֹאכְל֔וּ בְּכֹ֖ל מוֹשְׁבֹתֵיכֶ֑ם
לָע֖וֹף וְלַבְּהֵמָֽה

26[5] And you shall eat no manner of *blood, whether it is of fowl, or of beast, in any of your dwellings*[6].

כָּל־נֶ֗פֶשׁ אֲשֶׁר־תֹּאכַ֣ל כָּל־דָּ֔ם וְנִכְרְתָ֛ה
הַנֶּ֥פֶשׁ הַהִ֖וא מֵעַמֶּֽיהָ

27[7] Whoever eats any blood, that soul shall be cut off from his people.

וַיְדַבֵּ֥ר יְהֹוָ֖ה אֶל־מֹשֶׁ֥ה לֵּאמֹֽר

28[8] And the LORD spoke to Moses, saying:

דַּבֵּ֞ר אֶל־בְּנֵ֤י יִשְׂרָאֵל֙ לֵאמֹ֔ר הַמַּקְרִ֞יב
אֶת־זֶ֤בַח שְׁלָמָיו֙ לַֽיהֹוָ֔ה יָבִ֧יא אֶת־
קָרְבָּנ֛וֹ לַיהֹוָ֖ה מִזֶּ֥בַח שְׁלָמָֽיו

29[9] [10]Speak to the children of Israel, saying: He who offers his sacrifice of peace offerings *to the LORD*[11] shall bring his offering to the LORD out of his sacrifice of peace offerings.

יָדָ֣יו תְּבִיאֶ֔ינָה אֵ֖ת אִשֵּׁ֣י יְהֹוָ֑ה אֶת־

30[12] His own hands shall bring the [1]offerings of the LORD made by fire:

---

[1] Leviticus 7:24 - 4Q251 7, b.Bechorot [Rashi] 10a, b.Chullin [Rashi] 103a 126b 129a, b.Chullin 37ab, b.Horayot 3a, b.Meilah [Tosefot] 16a, b.Menachot [Tosefot] 74b, b.Pesachim 23a, b.Zevachim 69b-70b, Deuteronomy 14:21, Exodus 22:31, Ezekiel 4:14 20:31, Leviticus 17:15 22:8, Leviticus.R 13:3, m.Bechorot 2:9, Midrash Psalms 18:25, mt.Hilchot Maachalot Assurot 8:15, mt.Hilchot Shaar Avot Hatuman 1:5, Siman 64:1, t.Uktsin 3:3, y.Orlah 3:1, y.Pesachim 2:1

[2] Leviticus 7:25 - b.Bechorot 15a, b.Chullin [Rashi] 114a, b.Chullin [Tosefot] 92b, b.Chullin 75a 120a, b.Horayot 2a 3a, b.Kereitot 4a [Rashi] 2a, b.Pesachim 43b, b.Zevachim [Rashi] 70b, m.Chullin 8:6

[3] 4QLevg *they*

[4] LXX adds *burnt*

[5] Leviticus 7:26 - 1 Samuel 14:33-34, 1 Timothy 4:4, Acts 15:20 15:29, b.Bechorot [Tosefot] 15a, b.Horayot 3a, b.Kereitot [Rashi] 4b, b.Kereitot 4b 20a 21ab, Commandment #167, Ephesians 1:7, Ezekiel 9:25, Genesis 9:4, Guide for the Perplexed 3:41, John 6:53, Jubilees 21:5, Leviticus 3:17 17:10-14, m.Bikkurim 2:7, m.Keritot 5:1, mt.Hilchot Maachalot Assurot 6:1, mt.Hilchot Sanhedrin vHainshin Hameurim Lahem 19:1, Siman 46:1, y.Nazir 6:1

[6] LXX *blood in all your habitations, either of beasts or of birds*

[7] Leviticus 7:27 - b.Chullin [Rashi] 74b, b.Horayot 2a 3a, b.Kereitot [Rashi] 4b, b.Kereitot 21a, Hebrews 10:29, Jubilees 7:28, Leviticus 7:20-21 7:25

[8] Leviticus 7:28-34 - Parshat Todah [thanks offering]

[9] Leviticus 7:29 - 1 John 1:7, b.Chullin [Rashi] 132b, b.Kiddushin 36a, b.Makkot [Rashi] 18b, b.Menachot [Rashi] 14a, b.Menachot [Rashi] 62a, b.Menachot 61b, b.Sanhedrin [Tosefot] 86a, Colossians 1:20, Leviticus 3:1-3:17, m.Chullin 9:1, m.Menachot 5:6, Sifre.z Numbers Naso 6:19

[10] LXX adds *You shall*

[11] Missing in LXX

[12] Leviticus 7:30 - 2 Corinthians 8:12, b.Bava Batra [Tosefot] 81b, b.Chullin 130a, b.Kiddushin 36ab, b.Makkot [Rashi] 18b, b.Makkot 18b, b.Menachot [Rashi] 62a, b.Menachot [Tosefot] 48a, b.Menachot 61a-b 81a 93b 94a, b.Sotah 19a, b.Succah 47b, b.Zevachim [Rashi] 120a, b.Zevachim [Tosefot] 77a, Exodus 29:24-28, John 10:18, Leviticus 3:3-4 3:9 3:14 8:27 9:21, m.Kelim 1:8, m.Megillah 2:5, m.Menachot 5:6, mt.Hilchot Beit Habechirah 7:19, Numbers 6:20, Numbers.R 9:22, Psalms 14:3

הַחֵ֫לֶב עַל־הֶחָזֶה֮ יְבִיאֶ֒נּוּ֒ אֵ֣ת הֶֽחָזֶ֗ה לְהָנִ֥יף אֹת֛וֹ תְּנוּפָ֖ה לִפְנֵ֥י יְהוָֽה

the fat with the breast[2] shall he bring, *so the breast may be waved for a wave-offering*[3] before the LORD.

31[4] וְהִקְטִ֧יר הַכֹּהֵ֛ן אֶת־הַחֵ֖לֶב הַמִּזְבֵּ֑חָה וְהָיָה֙ הֶֽחָזֶ֔ה לְאַהֲרֹ֖ן וּלְבָנָֽיו

And the priest shall make the fat smoke on the altar; but the breast shall be Aaron's and his sons'.

32[5] וְאֵת֙ שׁ֣וֹק הַיָּמִ֔ין תִּתְּנ֥וּ תְרוּמָ֖ה לַכֹּהֵ֑ן מִזִּבְחֵ֖י שַׁלְמֵיכֶֽם

And you shall give the right thigh to the priest for a heave offering out of your sacrifices of peace offerings.

33[6] הַמַּקְרִ֞יב אֶת־דַּ֤ם הַשְּׁלָמִים֙ וְאֶת־הַחֵ֔לֶב מִבְּנֵ֖י אַהֲרֹ֑ן ל֧וֹ תִהְיֶ֛ה שׁ֥וֹק הַיָּמִ֖ין לְמָנָֽה

He among the sons of Aaron, who offers the blood of the peace offerings, and the fat, shall have the right *thigh*[7] as a portion.

34[8] כִּי֩ אֶת־חֲזֵ֨ה הַתְּנוּפָ֜ה וְאֵ֣ת שׁ֣וֹק הַתְּרוּמָ֗ה לָקַ֙חְתִּי֙ מֵאֵ֣ת בְּנֵֽי־יִשְׂרָאֵ֔ל מִזִּבְחֵ֖י שַׁלְמֵיהֶ֑ם וָאֶתֵּ֣ן אֹתָ֡ם לְאַהֲרֹ֨ן הַכֹּהֵ֤ן וּלְבָנָיו֙ לְחׇק־עוֹלָ֔ם מֵאֵ֖ת בְּנֵ֥י יִשְׂרָאֵֽל

For the breast of waving and the *thigh*[9] of *heaving*[10] I have taken of the children of Israel out of their sacrifices of peace offerings, and have given them to Aaron the priest and to his sons as a due forever from the children of Israel.

35[11] זֹ֣את מִשְׁחַ֤ת אַהֲרֹן֙ וּמִשְׁחַ֣ת בָּנָ֔יו מֵאִשֵּׁ֖י יְהוָ֑ה בְּיוֹם֙ הִקְרִ֣יב אֹתָ֔ם לְכַהֵ֖ן לַֽיהוָֽה

This is the consecrated portion of Aaron, and the consecrated portion of his sons, out of the [12]offerings of the LORD made by fire, in the day when they were presented to minister to the LORD in the priest's office;

36[13] אֲשֶׁר֩ צִוָּ֨ה יְהוָ֜ה לָתֵ֤ת לָהֶם֙ בְּי֣וֹם

Which the LORD commanded to be given to them *from the children of*

---

[1] LXX adds *burnt*

[2] LXX adds *and the lobe of the liver*

[3] LXX *so as to set them for a gift*

[4] Leviticus 7:31 - b.Pesachim 59b, b.Yoma [Tosefot] 5a, Leviticus 3:5 3:11 3:16 5:13 6:16 6:26 7:34 8:29, m.Chullin 10:1, mt.Hilchot Beit Habechirah 7:19, Numbers 18:18
Leviticus 7:31-32 - Sifre Devarim Reeh 71 75
Leviticus 7:31-39 - m.Chagigah 1:4

[5] Leviticus 7:32 - 1 Corinthians 9:13-14, b.Chullin 134b, Deuteronomy 18:3, Leviticus 7:34 8:25-26 9:21 10:14, m.Zevachim 5:6, Numbers 6:20 18:18-19, z.Vaera 95

[6] Leviticus 7:33 - b.Bechorot [Rashi] 31a, b.Bechorot 30b, b.Chullin [Rashi] 134b, b.Chullin 132b 133a, b.Horayot 4a, b.Menachot 3b 18b, b.Zevachim [Tosefot] 98b, b.Zevachim 98b 102b, Leviticus 6:1-30 7:3 26:1-46, m.Zevachim 12:1, mt.Hilchot Maaseh haKorbanot 10:21, t.Demai 2:7

[7] LXX *shoulder*

[8] Leviticus 7:34 - b.Chullin 130a, b.Menachot [Rashi] 81a, b.Menachot 62b, Deuteronomy 18:3, Exodus 5:9 29:27-28, Jastrow 1541a, Leviticus 3:17 7:30-32 10:14-15, m.Chullin 10:1, mt.Hilchot Maaseh haKorbanot 9:11, Numbers 18:18-19, Numbers.R 10:23, Philo Legum Allegoriae III 133, y.Yevamot 8:6

[9] LXX *shoulder*

[10] LXX *separation*

[11] Leviticus 7:35 - 1 John 2:20 2:27, 2 Corinthians 1:21, Exodus 4:1 5:1 5:7 5:21 40:13-15, Isaiah 10:27 13:1, Jastrow 852a, John 3:34, Leviticus 8:10-12 8:30, Numbers 18:7-19, Numbers.R 14:13, z.Tzav 162, z.Vayikra 415

[12] LXX adds *burnt*

[13] Leviticus 7:36 - Exodus 40:13-15, Jubilees 2:33, Leviticus 8:12 8:30, Numbers.R 14:13

מָשְׁחוּ אֹתָם מֵאֵת בְּנֵי יִשְׂרָאֵל חֻקַּת
עוֹלָם לְדֹרֹתָם

37² זֹאת הַתּוֹרָה לָעֹלָה לַמִּנְחָה וְלַחַטָּאת
וְלָאָשָׁם וְלַמִּלּוּאִים וּלְזֶבַח הַשְּׁלָמִים

38⁶ אֲשֶׁר צִוָּה יְהוָה אֶת־מֹשֶׁה בְּהַר סִינָי
בְּיוֹם צַוֹּתוֹ אֶת־בְּנֵי יִשְׂרָאֵל לְהַקְרִיב
אֶת־קָרְבְּנֵיהֶם לַיהוָה בְּמִדְבַּר סִינָי

Israel, in the day they were anointed[1].
It is a due forever throughout their generations.

37² This is the law of the [3]burnt offering, of the *meal offering*[4], and of the sin offering, and of the guilt offering, and of the consecration offering, and of the sacrifice of peace *offerings*[5];

38⁶ That the LORD commanded Moses in mount Sinai, in the day that he commanded the children of Israel to *present their offerings*[7] to the LORD, in the wilderness of Sinai.

Tzav – Chapter 8[8]

וַיְדַבֵּר יְהוָה אֶל־מֹשֶׁה לֵּאמֹר 1⁹

קַח אֶת־אַהֲרֹן וְאֶת־בָּנָיו אִתּוֹ וְאֵת 2¹⁰
הַבְּגָדִים וְאֵת שֶׁמֶן הַמִּשְׁחָה וְאֵת פַּר
הַחַטָּאת וְאֵת שְׁנֵי הָאֵילִים וְאֵת סַל
הַמַּצּוֹת

וְאֵת כָּל־הָעֵדָה הַקְהֵל אֶל־פֶּתַח אֹהֶל 3¹¹

1⁹ And the LORD spoke to Moses, saying

2¹⁰ Take Aaron and his sons with him, and the garments, and the anointing oil, and the calf of the sin offering, and the two rams, and the basket of unleavened bread;

3¹¹ and assemble all the congregation at the door of the tent of meeting.'

---

[1] LXX *in the day in which he anointed them of the sons of Israel*
[2] Leviticus 7:37 - b.Chullin [Tosefot] 21ab, b.Horayot 7b 8a, b.Menachot [Rashi] 19a 25ab, b.Menachot [Tosefot] 2ab 10b 96a, b.Menachot 82b 83a 11a, b.Zevachim [Tosefot] 24b 28b 44a 47b 60a 61a 65a 86a 92a, b.Zevachim 97b 98a, Ein Yaakov Menachot:110a, Exodus 5:1 29:38-242, Jastrow 644b 936a, Leviticus 1:1-6 6:9-18 6:20-7:7 7:11-21, Leviticus.R 9:8 9:9, m.Menachot 7:2, Mekhilta de R'Shimon bar Yochai Kaspa 82:1, Midrash Psalms 27:4, Midrash Tanchuma Tzav 14, mt.Hilchot Maaseh haKorbanot 8:16, Tanya Kuntress Acharon §04, z.Kedoshim 10, z.Naso 15, z.Vayera 117
[3] LXX adds *whole*
[4] LXX *sacrifice*
[5] LXX singular
[6] Leviticus 7:38 - b.Bava Kamma [Rashi] 11a, b.Chullin [Tosefot] 21a 81a, b.Chullin 22a, b.Horayot [Rashi] 4a, b.Horayot 7b, b.Kereitot [Rashi] 7b, b.Kiddushin [Tosefot] 36a, b.Megillah 20b, b.Menachot [Rashi] 20b 26b 72a 1a, b.Menachot [Tosefot] 2a 92b, b.Menachot 83a, b.Pesachim [Rashi] 65b, b.Shabbat [Rashi] 138a, b.Shabbat 132a, b.Temurah [Rashi] 14a, b.Yoma [Tosefot] 48a, b.Yoma 2b, b.Zevachim [Rashi] 68a, b.Zevachim [Tosefot] 56a 65a, b.Zevachim 98a, Leviticus 1:1-2, Midrash Tanchuma Naso 28, mt.Hilchot Maaseh haKorbanot 4:1, Numbers.R 14:19, y.Megillah 2:6
[7] LXX *offer their gifts*
[8] Avot de R'Natan 1 41
[9] Leviticus 8:1 - b.Nedarim 25a, Numbers.R 9:45
Leviticus 8:1-2 - Midrash Tanchuma Tzav 8
Leviticus 8:1-4 - Leviticus.R 10:1
Leviticus 8:1-35 - Josephus Antiquities 4.11.1 8.8.4
[10] Leviticus 8:2 - b.Zevachim [Rashi] 88b, Exodus 28:2-4 28:40-44 30:23-37 39:1-31 15:41 40:12-15, Hebrews 7:27, Jastrow 354a, Leviticus.R 10:5-6, Midrash Tanchuma Chukkat 17, Midrash Tanchuma Korach 1, Midrash Tanchuma Tzav 9 10, Numbers.R 18:2 19:19, Pesikta Rabbati 33:3, z.Tzav 165
[11] Leviticus 8:3 - 1 Chronicles 13:5 15:3, 2 Chronicles 5:2 5:6 6:2 6:13 6:25, Acts 2:1, Midrash Tanchuma Chukkat 9, Midrash Tanchuma Tzav 11 12, Nehemiah 8:1, Numbers 20:8 21:16, Numbers.R 19:9, Psalms 22:26

מוֹעֵד

וַיַּעַשׂ מֹשֶׁה כַּאֲשֶׁר צִוָּה יְהוָה אֹתוֹ 4[1]
וַתִּקָּהֵל הָעֵדָה אֶל־פֶּתַח אֹהֶל מוֹעֵד

And Moses did as the LORD
commanded him; and the congregation
was assembled at the door of the tent of
meeting.

וַיֹּאמֶר מֹשֶׁה אֶל־הָעֵדָה זֶה הַדָּבָר 5[2]
אֲשֶׁר־צִוָּה יְהוָה לַעֲשׂוֹת

And Moses said to the congregation:
'This is the thing that the LORD has
commanded to be done.'

וַיַּקְרֵב מֹשֶׁה אֶת־אַהֲרֹן וְאֶת־בָּנָיו 6[3]
וַיִּרְחַץ אֹתָם בַּמָּיִם

And Moses brought Aaron and his
sons, and washed them with water.

וַיִּתֵּן עָלָיו אֶת־הַכֻּתֹּנֶת וַיַּחְגֹּר אֹתוֹ 7[4]
בָּאַבְנֵט וַיַּלְבֵּשׁ אֹתוֹ אֶת־הַמְּעִיל וַיִּתֵּן
עָלָיו אֶת־הָאֵפֹד וַיַּחְגֹּר אֹתוֹ בְּחֵשֶׁב
הָאֵפֹד וַיֶּאְפֹּד לוֹ בּוֹ

And he put the tunic on him, and girded
him with the girdle, and clothed him
with the robe, and put the ephod on
him, and he girded him with the
skillfully woven band of the ephod, and
bound it to him with it.

וַיָּשֶׂם עָלָיו אֶת־הַחֹשֶׁן וַיִּתֵּן אֶל־הַחֹשֶׁן 8[5]
אֶת־הָאוּרִים וְאֶת־הַתֻּמִּים

And he placed the breastplate on him;
and in the breastplate he put *the Urim
and the Thummim*[6].

וַיָּשֶׂם אֶת־הַמִּצְנֶפֶת עַל־רֹאשׁוֹ וַיָּשֶׂם 9[7]
עַל־הַמִּצְנֶפֶת אֶל־מוּל פָּנָיו אֵת צִיץ
הַזָּהָב נֵזֶר הַקֹּדֶשׁ כַּאֲשֶׁר צִוָּה יְהוָה
אֶת־מֹשֶׁה

And he set the turban on his head; and
on the turban, in front, he sat the
golden plate, *the holy crown*[8]; as the
LORD commanded Moses.

וַיִּקַּח מֹשֶׁה אֶת־שֶׁמֶן הַמִּשְׁחָה וַיִּמְשַׁח 10[9]
אֶת־הַמִּשְׁכָּן וְאֶת־כָּל־אֲשֶׁר־בּוֹ וַיְקַדֵּשׁ
אֹתָם

And Moses took the anointing oil, *and
anointed the tabernacle and all that
was inside, and sanctified them*[10].

וַיַּז מִמֶּנּוּ עַל־הַמִּזְבֵּחַ שֶׁבַע פְּעָמִים 11[11]

And with it, *he[1]* sprinkled on the altar

---

[1] Leviticus 8:4 - 1 Corinthians 11:23 15:3, Deuteronomy 13:1, Exodus 15:5 15:7 15:21 15:26 15:29 39:31-32 39:42-43 15:1, Leviticus 8:9 8:13 8:17 8:29 8:35, Matthew 4:20, Song of Songs.R 2:39, t.Megillah 3:21

[2] Leviticus 8:5 - b.Yoma 5b, Exodus 29:4-29:37, Jastrow 1275b

[3] Leviticus 8:6 - 1 Corinthians 6:11, Ephesians 5:26, Exodus 5:4 6:19 16:12, Ezekiel 12:25, Hebrews 9:10 10:22, Isaiah 1:16, John 13:8-13:10, Psalms 26:6 51:3 51:8, Revelation 1:5-1:6 7:14, y.Yoma 1:1, Zechariah 13:1

[4] Leviticus 8:7 - b.Yoma 5b, Exodus 4:4 5:5 39:1-39:7, Galatians 3:27, Isaiah 13:3 13:10, mt.Hilchot Klei haMikdash Vihaovdim Bo 10:3, Romans 3:22 13:14, The Massorah says this is the middle verse of the Torah, y.Yoma 1:1, z.Chukat 64, z.Vayechi 178

[5] Leviticus 8:8 - 1 Thessalonians 5:8, Ephesians 6:14, Exodus 28:15-28:30 39:8-39:21, Ezra 3:3, Genesis.R 5:7, Isaiah 11:17, mt.Hilchot Klei haMikdash Vihaovdim Bo 10:3, Song of Songs 8:6

[6] LXX *the Manifestation and the Truth*

[7] Leviticus 8:9 - Exodus 4:4 28:36-28:38 5:6 39:28-39:30, mt.Hilchot Klei haMikdash Vihaovdim Bo 10:3, Philippians 2:9-2:11, Song of Songs.R 4:8, Zechariah 3:5 6:11-6:14

[8] LXX *the most holy thing*

[9] Leviticus 8:10 - b.Horayot 11b, b.Kereitot 5b, b.Shabbat [Rashi] 19b, Exodus 30:23-30:29 40:9-40:11, Leviticus 8:2, Numbers.R 12:15

[10] Mising in LXX

[11] Leviticus 8:11 - Exodus 4:6 4:17 16:14 16:19 6:29, Ezekiel 12:25, Isaiah 4:15, Titus 3:6, y.Pesachim 5:10

וַיִּמְשַׁח אֶת־הַמִּזְבֵּחַ וְאֶת־כָּל־כֵּלָיו
וְאֶת־הַכִּיֹּר וְאֶת־כַּנּוֹ לְקַדְּשָׁם

12³ וַיִּצֹק מִשֶּׁמֶן הַמִּשְׁחָה עַל רֹאשׁ אַהֲרֹן
וַיִּמְשַׁח אֹתוֹ לְקַדְּשׁוֹ

13⁴ וַיַּקְרֵב מֹשֶׁה אֶת־בְּנֵי אַהֲרֹן וַיַּלְבִּשֵׁם
כֻּתֳּנֹת וַיַּחְגֹּר אֹתָם אַבְנֵט וַיַּחֲבֹשׁ לָהֶם
מִגְבָּעוֹת כַּאֲשֶׁר צִוָּה יְהוָה אֶת־מֹשֶׁה

14⁶ וַיַּגֵּשׁ אֵת פַּר הַחַטָּאת וַיִּסְמֹךְ אַהֲרֹן
וּבָנָיו אֶת־יְדֵיהֶם עַל־רֹאשׁ פַּר
הַחַטָּאת

15⁸ וַיִּשְׁחָט וַיִּקַּח מֹשֶׁה אֶת־הַדָּם וַיִּתֵּן עַל־
קַרְנוֹת הַמִּזְבֵּחַ סָבִיב בְּאֶצְבָּעוֹ וַיְחַטֵּא
אֶת־הַמִּזְבֵּחַ וְאֶת־הַדָּם יָצַק אֶל־יְסוֹד
הַמִּזְבֵּחַ וַיְקַדְּשֵׁהוּ לְכַפֵּר עָלָיו

16⁹ וַיִּקַּח אֶת־כָּל־הַחֵלֶב אֲשֶׁר עַל־הַקֶּרֶב
וְאֵת יֹתֶרֶת הַכָּבֵד וְאֶת־שְׁתֵּי הַכְּלָיֹת
וְאֶת־חֶלְבְּהֶן וַיַּקְטֵר מֹשֶׁה הַמִּזְבֵּחָה

17¹⁰ וְאֶת־הַפָּר וְאֶת־עֹרוֹ וְאֶת־בְּשָׂרוֹ וְאֶת־
פִּרְשׁוֹ שָׂרַף בָּאֵשׁ מִחוּץ לַמַּחֲנֶה
כַּאֲשֶׁר צִוָּה יְהוָה אֶת־מֹשֶׁה

seven times, and anointed the altar and all its vessels, and the laver and its base, to sanctify them[2].

And he poured of the anointing oil upon Aaron's head, and anointed him, to sanctify him.

And Moses brought Aaron's sons, and clothed them with tunics, and girded them with girdles, and bound *head tires*[5] on them; as the LORD commanded Moses.

And the bullock of the sin offering was brought[7]; and Aaron and his sons laid their hands on the head of the bullock of the sin offering.

And when it was slain, Moses took the blood, and put it on the horns around the altar with his finger, and purified the altar, and poured out the remaining blood at the base of the altar, and sanctified it, to make atonement for it.

And he took all the fat that was on the innards, and the lobe of the liver, and the two kidneys, and their fat, and Moses made it smoke on the altar.

But the bullock, and its skin, and its flesh, and its dung, were burnt with fire outside the camp; as the LORD commanded Moses.

---

[1] Missing in LXX

[2] LXX adds *and anointed the tabernacle and all its furniture, and hallowed it*

[3] Leviticus 8:12 - b.Horayot 12a, b.Kereitot 5b, Exodus 4:41 5:7 6:30, Leviticus 4:3 21:10-12, Mesillat Yesharim 24:Trait of Yiras Cheit, mt.Hilchot Klei haMikdash Vihaovdim Bo 1:9, Numbers.R 12:15, Psalms 13:2
Leviticus 8:12-13 - 6QpaleoLev

[4] Leviticus 8:13 - 1 Peter 2:5 2:9, b.Yoma 5b, Exodus 28:40-41 29:8-9 40:14-15, Genesis.R 100 [Excl]:7, Isaiah 13:6 13:10, mt.Hilchot Klei haMikdash Vihaovdim Bo 10:2, Numbers.R 4:8, Psalms 12:9, Revelation 1:6 5:10, y.Yoma 1:1

[5] LXX *bonnets*

[6] Leviticus 8:14 - 1 Peter 3:18, 2 Corinthians 5:21, Exodus 29:10-14, Ezekiel 19:19, Genesis.R 93:7, Hebrews 7:26-7:28, Isaiah 5:10, Leviticus 1:4 4:3-12 8:2 16:6 16:21, Psalms 66:15, Romans 8:3
Leviticus 8:14-22 - Josephus Antiquities 4.11.1 8.8.4

[7] LXX *And Moses brought near the calf for the sin offering*

[8] Leviticus 8:15 - 2 Chronicles 5:24, 2 Corinthians 5:18-21, b.Sanhedrin [Tosefot] 4a, b.Succah [Rashi] 49a, b.Yoma [Tosefot] 5a, b.Zevachim 53b 57a [Tosefot] 51b, Colossians 1:21-22, Daniel 9:24, Ephesians 2:16, Exodus 29:10-12 29:36-37, Ezekiel 43:19-27 21:20, Hebrews 2:17 9:18-23, Jastrow 863b, Leviticus 1:5 1:11 3:2 3:8 4:7 4:17-18 4:30 6:30 16:20, Leviticus.R 1:9, Mas.Soferim 9:3, Romans 5:10

[9] Leviticus 8:16 - Exodus 5:13, Leviticus 3:3-3:5 4:8-4:9

[10] Leviticus 8:17 - b.Zevachim [Rashi] 103b, Exodus 5:14, Galatians 3:13, Hebrews 13:11-13, Leviticus 4:11-12 4:21 6:30 16:27

וַיַּקְרֵב אֵת אֵיל הָעֹלָה וַיִּסְמְכוּ אַהֲרֹן וּבָנָיו אֶת־יְדֵיהֶם עַל־רֹאשׁ הָאָיִל	18[1]	And the ram of the [2]burnt offering was presented; and Aaron and his sons pressed their hands on the head of the ram.
וַיִּשְׁחָט וַיִּזְרֹק מֹשֶׁה אֶת־הַדָּם עַל־הַמִּזְבֵּחַ סָבִיב	19	And when it was killed, Moses dashed the blood against the altar on all sides.
וְאֶת־הָאַיִל נִתַּח לִנְתָחָיו וַיַּקְטֵר מֹשֶׁה אֶת־הָרֹאשׁ וְאֶת־הַנְּתָחִים וְאֶת־הַפָּדֶר	20[3]	And *when the ram was cut into its pieces*[4], Moses made the head, and the pieces, and the suet smoke.
וְאֶת־הַקֶּרֶב וְאֶת־הַכְּרָעַיִם רָחַץ בַּמָּיִם וַיַּקְטֵר מֹשֶׁה אֶת־כָּל־הָאַיִל הַמִּזְבֵּחָה עֹלָה הוּא לְרֵיחַ־נִיחֹחַ אִשֶּׁה הוּא לַיהֹוָה כַּאֲשֶׁר צִוָּה יְהֹוָה אֶת־מֹשֶׁה	21[5]	And when the innards and the legs were washed with water, Moses made the whole ram smoke on the altar; it was a [6]burnt offering for a sweet savor; it was an [7]offering made by fire to the LORD; as the LORD commanded Moses.
וַיַּקְרֵב אֶת־הָאַיִל הַשֵּׁנִי אֵיל הַמִּלֻּאִים וַיִּסְמְכוּ אַהֲרֹן וּבָנָיו אֶת־יְדֵיהֶם עַל־רֹאשׁ הָאָיִל	22[8]	And the *other*[9] ram was presented, the ram of consecration, and Aaron and his sons pressed their hands on the head of the ram.
וַיִּשְׁחָט וַיִּקַּח מֹשֶׁה מִדָּמוֹ וַיִּתֵּן עַל־תְּנוּךְ אֹזֶן־אַהֲרֹן הַיְמָנִית וְעַל־בֹּהֶן יָדוֹ הַיְמָנִית וְעַל־בֹּהֶן רַגְלוֹ הַיְמָנִית	23[10]	And when it was slain, Moses took of its blood, and put it on the tip of Aaron's right ear, and on the thumb of his right hand, and on the great toe of his right foot.
וַיַּקְרֵב אֶת־בְּנֵי אַהֲרֹן וַיִּתֵּן מֹשֶׁה מִן־הַדָּם עַל־תְּנוּךְ אָזְנָם הַיְמָנִית וְעַל־בֹּהֶן יָדָם הַיְמָנִית וְעַל־בֹּהֶן רַגְלָם הַיְמָנִית וַיִּזְרֹק מֹשֶׁה אֶת־הַדָּם עַל־הַמִּזְבֵּחַ סָבִיב	24[11]	And Aaron's sons were brought, and Moses put of the blood on the tips of their right ears, and on the thumbs of their right hands, and on the great toes of their right feet; and Moses dashed the blood against the altar all around it.

---

[1] Leviticus 8:18 - Exodus 29:15-18, Leviticus 1:4-13 8:2, y.Yoma 1:1

[2] LXX adds *whole*

[3] Leviticus 8:20 - Leviticus 1:8, Midrash Tanchuma Noach 14

[4] LXX *he divided the ram by its limbs*

[5] Leviticus 8:21 - b.Chullin [Tosefot] 113a, Ephesians 5:2, Exodus 5:18, Genesis 8:21, Jastrow 1411a, Leviticus 1:17 2:9

[6] LXX adds *whole*

[7] LXX adds *burnt*

[8] Leviticus 8:22 - 1 Corinthians 1:30, 2 Corinthians 5:21, Ephesians 5:25 5:27, Exodus 29:19-31, John 17:19, Leviticus 7:37 8:2 8:29, Revelation 1:5-6, t.Menachot 7:14

[9] LXX *second*

[10] Leviticus 8:23 - 1 Corinthians 1:2 1:30 6:20, 1 Thessalonians 5:22, b.Chullin [Tosefot] 22a, b.Ketubot [Rashi] 5b, Exodus 5:20, Hebrews 2:10 5:8, Leviticus 14:14 14:17 14:28, Mas.Soferim 9:3, mt.Hilchot Deot 5:6, Philippians 1:20 2:17, Romans 6:13 6:19 12:1, Siman 3:4, Yalchut says this is the middle verse of the Torah

[11] Leviticus 8:24 - b.Ketubot [Rashi] 5b, Hebrews 9:18-22, Seder Olam 7:Eat meat

וַיִּקַּ֣ח אֶת־הַחֵ֗לֶב וְאֶת־הָֽאַלְיָה֙ וְאֶת־ **25[1]** And he took the fat, and the *fat tail*[2],
כָּל־הַחֵלֶב֮ אֲשֶׁ֣ר עַל־הַקֶּ֒רֶב֒ וְאֵת֙ יֹתֶ֣רֶת and all the fat on the inwards, and the
הַכָּבֵ֔ד וְאֶת־שְׁתֵּ֥י הַכְּלָיֹ֖ת וְאֶת־חֶלְבְּהֶ֑ן lobe of the liver, and the two kidneys,
וְאֵ֖ת שֹׁ֥וק הַיָּמִֽין and their fat, and the right *thigh*[3].

וּמִסַּ֣ל הַמַּצֹּ֡ות אֲשֶׁר֩ לִפְנֵ֨י יְהֹוָ֜ה לָקַ֣ח **26[4]** And out of the [5]basket of unleavened
חַלַּ֣ת מַצָּ֣ה אַחַת֩ וְֽחַלַּ֨ת לֶ֤חֶם שֶׁ֙מֶן֙ אַחַ֔ת bread, that was before the LORD, he
וְרָקִ֖יק אֶחָ֑ד וַיָּ֙שֶׂם֙ עַל־הַֽחֲלָבִ֔ים וְעַ֖ל took one unleavened cake, and one
שֹׁ֥וק הַיָּמִֽין cake of oiled bread, and one wafer, and
placed them on the fat, and on the right
thigh[6].

וַיִּתֵּ֣ן אֶת־הַכֹּ֗ל עַ֚ל כַּפֵּ֣י אַהֲרֹ֔ן וְעַ֖ל כַּפֵּ֣י **27[7]** And he put the whole on the hands of
בָנָ֑יו וַיָּ֧נֶף אֹתָ֛ם תְּנוּפָ֖ה לִפְנֵ֥י יְהֹוָֽה Aaron, and on the hands of his sons,
and waved them for a wave offering
before the LORD.

וַיִּקַּ֨ח מֹשֶׁ֤ה אֹתָם֙ מֵעַ֣ל כַּפֵּיהֶ֔ם וַיַּקְטֵ֥ר **28[8]** And Moses took them from off their
הַמִּזְבֵּ֖חָה עַל־הָעֹלָ֑ה מִלֻּאִ֥ים הֵם֙ לְרֵ֣יחַ hands, and made them smoke on the
נִיחֹ֔חַ אִשֶּׁ֥ה ה֖וּא לַיהֹוָֽה altar on the [9]burnt offering; they were a
consecration offering for a sweet savor;
it was an offering made by fire to the
LORD.

וַיִּקַּ֤ח מֹשֶׁה֙ אֶת־הֶ֣חָזֶ֔ה וַיְנִיפֵ֥הוּ תְנוּפָ֖ה **29[10]** And Moses took the breast, and
לִפְנֵ֣י יְהֹוָ֑ה מֵאֵ֣יל הַמִּלֻּאִ֗ים לְמֹשֶׁ֤ה הָיָה֙ *waved*[11] it for a *wave*[12] offering before
לְמָנָ֔ה כַּאֲשֶׁ֛ר צִוָּ֥ה יְהֹוָ֖ה אֶת־מֹשֶֽׁה the LORD; it was Moses' portion of the
ram of consecration; as the LORD
commanded Moses.

וַיִּקַּ֨ח מֹשֶׁ֜ה מִשֶּׁ֣מֶן הַמִּשְׁחָ֗ה וּמִן־הַדָּם֮ **30[13]** And Moses took of the anointing oil,
אֲשֶׁ֣ר עַל־הַמִּזְבֵּחַ֒ וַיַּ֤ז עַל־אַהֲרֹן֙ עַל־ and of the blood, which was on the
בְּגָדָ֔יו וְעַל־בָּנָ֛יו וְעַל־בִּגְדֵ֥י בָנָ֖יו אִתֹּ֑ו altar, and sprinkled it on Aaron, and on
his garments, and on his sons, and on

---

[1] Leviticus 8:25 - b.Bava Batra 74b, Exodus 29:22-25, Isaiah 5:10, Leviticus 3:3-5 3:9, Proverbs 23:26
[2] LXX *rump*
[3] LXX *shoulder*
[4] Leviticus 8:26 - 1 Timothy 2:5, Acts 5:12, b.Menachot [Rashi] 62a, b.Menachot 78a, Exodus 5:23, John 1:14, m.Menachot 7:2, Sifre Devarim Ekev 41, t.Menachot 7:20, y.Challah 2:1
Leviticus 8:26-28 - 4QLevc
[5] LXX adds *consecrated*
[6] LXX *shoulder*
[7] Leviticus 8:27 - b.Menachot [Tosefot] 62a, Exodus 29:24-37, Hebrews 9:14, Jeremiah 6:21, Leviticus 7:30-31
[8] Leviticus 8:28 - Exodus 5:25, Hebrews 10:14-22, Psalms 22:14-15, Zechariah 13:7
[9] LXX adds *whole*
[10] Leviticus 8:29 - 1 Corinthians 10:31, 1 Peter 4:11, b.Zevachim 11b, Exodus 29:26-27, Isaiah 18:20, Leviticus 7:30-34, Numbers.R 14:12, Philo De Migratione Abrahami 67, Philo Legum Allegoriae III 129
Leviticus 8:29-9:14 - Philo Legum Allegoriae III 147
[11] LXX *seaprated*
[12] LXX *heave*
[13] Leviticus 8:30 - 1 John 2:27, 1 Peter 1:2, b.Yoma [Rashi] 4a, Exodus 5:21 6:30, Galatians 5:22-25, Hebrews 2:11, Isaiah 13:1 13:3, Leviticus 10:3, Numbers 3:3, Numbers.R 12:15, Revelation 7:14, Saadia Opinions 4:3, Sifre.z Numbers Naso 7:1

וַיְקַדֵּשׁ אֶת־אַהֲרֹן אֶת־בְּגָדָיו וְאֶת־
בָּנָיו וְאֶת־בִּגְדֵי בָנָיו אִתּוֹ

his sons' garments with him, and sanctified Aaron and his garments, and his sons and his sons' garments with him.

31[1] וַיֹּאמֶר מֹשֶׁה אֶל־אַהֲרֹן וְאֶל־בָּנָיו
בַּשְּׁלוּ אֶת־הַבָּשָׂר פֶּתַח אֹהֶל מוֹעֵד
וְשָׁם תֹּאכְלוּ אֹתוֹ וְאֶת־הַלֶּחֶם אֲשֶׁר
בְּסַל הַמִּלֻּאִים כַּאֲשֶׁר צִוֵּיתִי לֵאמֹר
אַהֲרֹן וּבָנָיו יֹאכְלֻהוּ

And Moses said to Aaron and to his sons, "Boil the flesh *at the door of the tent of meeting; and there eat it and the bread*[2] that is in the basket of consecration, as I commanded, saying: Aaron and his sons shall eat it.

32[3] וְהַנּוֹתָר בַּבָּשָׂר וּבַלָּחֶם בָּאֵשׁ תִּשְׂרֹפוּ

And what remains of the flesh and of the bread you shall burn with fire.

33[4] וּמִפֶּתַח אֹהֶל מוֹעֵד לֹא תֵצְאוּ שִׁבְעַת
יָמִים עַד יוֹם מְלֹאת יְמֵי מִלֻּאֵיכֶם כִּי
שִׁבְעַת יָמִים יְמַלֵּא אֶת־יֶדְכֶם

And you shall not go out from the door of the tent of meeting for seven days, until the days of your consecration be fulfilled; for He shall consecrate you seven days.

34[5] כַּאֲשֶׁר עָשָׂה בַּיּוֹם הַזֶּה צִוָּה יְהוָה
לַעֲשֹׂת לְכַפֵּר עֲלֵיכֶם

As has been done this day, so the LORD has commanded to do, to make atonement for you.

35[6] וּפֶתַח אֹהֶל מוֹעֵד תֵּשְׁבוּ יוֹמָם וָלַיְלָה
שִׁבְעַת יָמִים וּשְׁמַרְתֶּם אֶת־מִשְׁמֶרֶת
יְהוָה וְלֹא תָמוּתוּ כִּי־כֵן צֻוֵּיתִי

And at the door of the tent of meeting you shall you stay, day and night for seven days, and keep the charge of the LORD, so you will not die; for so I am commanded.

36[7] וַיַּעַשׂ אַהֲרֹן וּבָנָיו אֵת כָּל־הַדְּבָרִים
אֲשֶׁר־צִוָּה יְהוָה בְּיַד־מֹשֶׁה

And Aaron and his sons did all the things the LORD commanded by the hand of Moses.

---

[1] Leviticus 8:31 - 1 Samuel 2:13-17, b.Zevachim [Rashi] 11b, b.Zevachim 56a, Deuteronomy 12:6-7, Exodus 29:31-32, Ezekiel 46:20-24, Galatians 2:20, John 6:33 6:35 6:51 6:53-56, Leviticus 6:28 7:15 10:17, MasLevb, Numbers.R 18:3

[2] LXX *in the tent of the tabernacle of witness in the holy place; and there ye shall eat it and the loaves*

[3] Leviticus 8:32 - 2 Corinthians 6:2, Ecclesiastes 9:10, Exodus 12:10 5:34, Guide for the Perplexed 1:41, Hebrews 3:13-14, Leviticus 7:17, Proverbs 3:1

[4] Leviticus 8:33 - Avot de R'Natan 1, b.Kereitot [Rashi] 5b, b.Yoma [Rashi] 5a, b.Zevachim [Tosefot] 56a, Ecclesiastes.R 11:2, Exodus 5:30 5:35, Ezekiel 43:25-27, Genesis.R 97:1, Jastrow 483b, Leviticus 14:8, Leviticus.R 11:3-4, Midrash Tanchuma Shemini 1 3, Midrash Tanchuma Vayechi 17, Numbers 19:12, Pesikta de R'Kahana 28.4, Pesikta Rabbati 47:2 52:4, z.Pekudei 236b, z.Shemini 26 37a, z.Emor 21 23, z.Tzav 170
Leviticus 8:33-34 - MasLevb, mt.Hilchot Avodat Yom haKippurim 1:3

[5] Leviticus 8:34 - b.Yoma [Tosefot] 2b, b.Yoma 2a, Hebrews 7:16 7:27 10:11-12, y.Yoma 1:1

[6] Leviticus 8:35 - 1 Kings 2:3, 1 Timothy 1:3-4 1:18 5:21 6:13 6:17 6:20, 2 Corinthians 7:1, 2 Timothy 4:1, b.Succah [Rashi] 43a, b.Succah 43b, b.Yoma [Rashi] 2a, b.Yoma 5b, Colossians 2:9-10, Deuteronomy 11:1, Exodus 5:35, Ezekiel 19:25 24:11, Genesis.R 100 [Excl]:7, Hebrews 7:28 9:23-24, Jastrow 1069b, Leviticus 8:30 10:1 14:8, Midrash Tanchuma Shemini 1, Numbers 3:7 9:19 19:12, Seder Olam 7:Eat meat, y.Moed Katan 3:5, y.Sukkah 2:7

[7] Leviticus 8:36 - 1 Samuel 15:22, Deuteronomy 4:2 13:1, Exodus 15:43 16:16, Seder Olam 7:Eat meat

Shemini

Shemini[1] – Chapter 9

וַיְהִי֙ בַּיּ֣וֹם הַשְּׁמִינִ֔י קָרָ֣א מֹשֶׁ֔ה לְאַהֲרֹ֖ן
וּלְבָנָ֑יו וּלְזִקְנֵ֖י יִשְׂרָאֵֽל

1[2] And it came to pass on the eighth day, that Moses called Aaron and his sons, and the elders of Israel;

וַיֹּ֣אמֶר אֶֽל־אַהֲרֹ֗ן קַח־לְ֠ךָ עֵ֣גֶל בֶּן־
בָּקָ֧ר לְחַטָּ֛את וְאַ֥יִל לְעֹלָ֖ה תְּמִימִ֑ם
וְהַקְרֵ֖ב לִפְנֵ֥י יְהוָֽה

2[3] And *he*[4] said to Aaron, 'Take a young bull for a sin offering, and a ram for a [5]burnt offering, without blemish, and offer them before the LORD.

וְאֶל־בְּנֵ֥י יִשְׂרָאֵ֖ל תְּדַבֵּ֣ר לֵאמֹ֑ר קְח֤וּ
שְׂעִיר־עִזִּים֙ לְחַטָּ֔את וְעֵ֣גֶל וָכֶ֫בֶשׂ בְּנֵֽי־
שָׁנָ֥ה תְּמִימִ֖ם לְעֹלָֽה

3[6] And *to the children of Israel you shall speak*[7], saying, "Take a male goat for a sin offering, and a calf and a lamb, both of the first year, without blemish, for a [8]burnt offering;

וְשׁ֨וֹר וָאַ֜יִל לִשְׁלָמִ֗ים לִזְבֹּ֙חַ֙ לִפְנֵ֣י יְהוָ֔ה
וּמִנְחָ֖ה בְּלוּלָ֣ה בַשָּׁ֑מֶן כִּ֣י הַיּ֔וֹם יְהוָ֖ה

4[9] and an ox and a ram for peace offerings, to sacrifice before the LORD; and a meal offering mingled

---

[1] Shemini aliyot: [1] Leviticus 9:1–16, [2] Leviticus 9:17–23, [3] Leviticus 9:24–10:11, [4] Leviticus 10:12–15, [5] Leviticus 10:16–20, [6] Leviticus 11:1–32, [7] Leviticus 11:33–47

[2] Leviticus 9:1 - b.Gittin 60a, b.Megillah 10b, b.Menachot [Rashi] 59a 93b, b.Yoma [Rashi] 2a, Ecclesiastes.R 1:31 11:2, Esther.R Petichata:11, Exodus.R 5:12, Ezekiel 43:26-27, Genesis.R 42:3, Jastrow 679a, Leviticus 8:33 14:10 14:23 15:14 15:29, Leviticus.R 11:1 11:8, Mas.Sefer Torah 5:11, Mas.Soferim 5:9, Matthew 4:1, Mekhilta de R'Shimon bar Yochai Shirata 33:1, Mekilta de R'Ishmael Shirata 7:3, Midrash Psalms 18:22, Midrash Tanchuma Shemini 1-4 9-11, Midrash Tanchuma Shemot 29, Numbers 6:10, Numbers.R 12:15 13:5 14:21, Pesikta de R'Kahana 28.4, Pesikta Rabbati 5:8 52:4, Ruth.R Petichata:7, Seder Olam 7:Eat meat, Song of Songs.R 1:45, y.Megillah 3:1, z.Shemini 35b 1 26
Leviticus 9:1-10 - MasLevb
Leviticus 9:1-16 - Minchah [Shabbat Monday Thursday Torah reading - Parashah Shemini]
Leviticus 9:1-24 - Josephus Antiquities 4.11.1 8.8.4

[3] Leviticus 9:2 - 2 Corinthians 5:21, b.Beitzah [Rashi] 20a, b.Menachot [Rashi] 45a, b.Rosh Hashanah [Rashi] 10a, b.Yoma [Rashi] 3a, Ein Yaakov Yoma:3b, Exodus 5:1, Exodus.R 38:3, Guide for the Perplexed 3:46, Hebrews 5:3 7:27 10:10-14, Leviticus 4:3 8:14 8:18 9:7-8, Midrash Tanchuma Ki Tissa 26, Midrash Tanchuma Shemini 4 10, t.Parah 1:5, y.Nazir 5:1, z.Shmini 31, z.Vayakhel 480

[4] LXX *Moses*

[5] LXX adds *whole*

[6] Leviticus 9:3 - 1 Peter 2:24 3:18, 2 Corinthians 5:21, b.Menachot [Rashi] 93b, b.Pesachim [Rashi] 82b, b.Rosh Hashanah [Rashi] 10a, b.Sheviit [Rashi] 9b, b.Sotah [Rashi] 38a, b.Yoma 3b, b.Zevachim [Rashi] 101ab, Exodus 12:5, Ezra 6:17 10:19, Hebrews 9:26-28, Isaiah 5:10, Leviticus 4:23 12:6 14:10 16:5 16:15 23:12, Midrash Tanchuma Shemini 4, Revelation 5:9, Romans 8:3, t.Parah 1:5, Titus 2:14, z.Shmini 49

[7] LXX *speak to the elders of Israel*

[8] LXX adds *whole*

[9] Leviticus 9:4 - 1 Kings 8:10-12, b.Menachot [Rashi] 59a, Exodus 16:10 19:11 24:16 5:43 40:34-35, Ezekiel 19:2, Genesis.R 48:5 82:2, Leviticus 2:1-3:17 6:14-23 9:6 9:23, Leviticus.R 11:6, Numbers 14:10 15:3-9 16:19, Pesikta de R'Kahana 4.5, Pesikta Rabbati 14:1, y.Yoma 1:1, z.Shmini 32

נִרְאָה אֲלֵיכֶם

וַיִּקְחוּ אֶת אֲשֶׁר צִוָּה מֹשֶׁה אֶל־פְּנֵי
אֹהֶל מוֹעֵד וַיִּקְרְבוּ כָּל־הָעֵדָה וַיַּעַמְדוּ
לִפְנֵי יְהוָה

וַיֹּאמֶר מֹשֶׁה זֶה הַדָּבָר אֲשֶׁר־צִוָּה
יְהוָה תַּעֲשׂוּ וְיֵרָא אֲלֵיכֶם כְּבוֹד יְהוָה

וַיֹּאמֶר מֹשֶׁה אֶל־אַהֲרֹן קְרַב אֶל־
הַמִּזְבֵּחַ וַעֲשֵׂה אֶת־חַטָּאתְךָ וְאֶת־
עֹלָתֶךָ וְכַפֵּר בַּעַדְךָ וּבְעַד הָעָם וַעֲשֵׂה
אֶת־קָרְבַּן הָעָם וְכַפֵּר בַּעֲדָם כַּאֲשֶׁר
צִוָּה יְהוָה

וַיִּקְרַב אַהֲרֹן אֶל־הַמִּזְבֵּחַ וַיִּשְׁחַט אֶת־
עֵגֶל הַחַטָּאת אֲשֶׁר־לוֹ

וַיַּקְרִבוּ בְּנֵי אַהֲרֹן אֶת־הַדָּם אֵלָיו
וַיִּטְבֹּל אֶצְבָּעוֹ בַּדָּם וַיִּתֵּן עַל־קַרְנוֹת
הַמִּזְבֵּחַ וְאֶת־הַדָּם יָצַק אֶל־יְסוֹד
הַמִּזְבֵּחַ

וְאֶת־הַחֵלֶב וְאֶת־הַכְּלָיֹת וְאֶת־הַיֹּתֶרֶת
מִן־הַכָּבֵד מִן־הַחַטָּאת הִקְטִיר
הַמִּזְבֵּחָה כַּאֲשֶׁר צִוָּה יְהוָה אֶת־מֹשֶׁה

וְאֶת־הַבָּשָׂר וְאֶת־הָעוֹר שָׂרַף בָּאֵשׁ
מִחוּץ לַמַּחֲנֶה

5[1] And they brought what Moses commanded before the tent of meeting; and all the congregation drew near and stood before the LORD.

6[2] And Moses said, "This is the thing that the LORD commanded you should do, so the glory of the LORD *may*[3] appear to you."

7[4] And Moses said to Aaron, "Draw close to the altar, and offer your sin offering, and your [5]burnt offering, and make atonement for yourself, and for *the people*[6]; and present the offering of the people and make atonement for them; as the LORD commanded[7]."

8[8] And Aaron drew near to the altar, and killed the calf of the sin offering, that was for himself.

9[9] And the sons of Aaron presented the blood to him; and he dipped his finger in the blood, and put it on the horns of the altar, and poured out the blood at the base of the altar.

10[10] But the fat, and the kidneys, and the lobe of the liver of the sin offering, he made smoke on the altar; as the LORD commanded Moses.

11[11] And the flesh and the skin were burnt with fire outside the camp.

---

[1] Leviticus 9:5 - 1 Chronicles 15:3, 2 Chronicles 5:2-3, Deuteronomy 7:12, Exodus 19:17, Mekhilta de R'Shimon bar Yochai Bachodesh 50:2, Mekhilta de R'Shimon bar Yochai Pisha 3:1, Mekilta de R'Ishmael Bahodesh 3:129, Nehemiah 8:1, Seder Olam 15:Shlomo, Song of Songs.R 2:39

[2] Leviticus 9:6 - 1 Kings 8:10-12, 2 Chronicles 5:13-14, Exodus 16:10 24:16 40:34-35, Ezekiel 19:2, Leviticus 9:23, Numbers.R 12:8

[3] LXX *shall*

[4] Leviticus 9:7 - 1 Samuel 3:14, b.Yoma [Rashi] 2a 4a, b.Zevachim [Rashi] 101a 112b, Hebrews 5:1 5:3 7:27-28 9:7, Leviticus 4:3 4:16-20 8:34 9:2

[5] LXX adds *whole*

[6] LXX *your house*

[7] LXX adds *Moses*

[8] Leviticus 9:8 - b.Chullin [Tosefot] 21a, Leviticus 1:4-5 4:1-12 4:29

[9] Leviticus 9:9 - b.Moed Katan 28b, Ein Yaakov Moed Katan:28b, Hebrews 2:10 9:22-23 10:4-19, Leviticus 4:6-7 4:17-18 4:25 4:30 8:15 9:12 9:18 16:18, z.Pekudei 236b

[10] Leviticus 9:10 - b.Taanit 6b, Isaiah 5:10 9:15 18:2, Leviticus 3:3-5 3:9-11 4:8-12 4:34-35 8:16-17, Proverbs 23:26, Psalms 51:18, z.Pinchas 362

[11] Leviticus 9:11 - Hebrews 13:11-12, Leviticus 4:11-12 4:21 8:17 16:27-28

וַיִּשְׁחַט אֶת־הָעֹלָה וַיַּמְצִאוּ בְּנֵי אַהֲרֹן אֵלָיו אֶת־הַדָּם וַיִּזְרְקֵהוּ עַל־הַמִּזְבֵּחַ סָבִיב	12[1]	And he slew the [2]burnt offering; and Aaron's sons delivered to him the blood, and he dashed it against the altar, all around it.
וְאֶת־הָעֹלָה הִמְצִיאוּ אֵלָיו לִנְתָחֶיהָ וְאֶת־הָרֹאשׁ וַיַּקְטֵר עַל־הַמִּזְבֵּחַ	13[3]	And they delivered the [4]burnt offering to him, piece by piece, and the head; and he made them smoke on the altar.
וַיִּרְחַץ אֶת־הַקֶּרֶב וְאֶת־הַכְּרָעָיִם וַיַּקְטֵר עַל־הָעֹלָה הַמִּזְבֵּחָה	14[5]	And he washed the innards and the legs[6], and made them smoke on the [7]burnt offering on the altar.
וַיַּקְרֵב אֵת קָרְבַּן הָעָם וַיִּקַּח אֶת־שְׂעִיר הַחַטָּאת אֲשֶׁר לָעָם וַיִּשְׁחָטֵהוּ וַיְחַטְּאֵהוּ כָּרִאשׁוֹן	15[8]	And the people's offering was presented; and he took the goat of the sin offering that was for the people, and killed it, and offered it for sin[9], as the first.
וַיַּקְרֵב אֶת־הָעֹלָה וַיַּעֲשֶׂהָ כַּמִּשְׁפָּט	16[10]	And the [11]burnt offering was presented; and he offered it according to the ordinance[12].
וַיַּקְרֵב אֶת־הַמִּנְחָה וַיְמַלֵּא כַפּוֹ מִמֶּנָּה וַיַּקְטֵר עַל־הַמִּזְבֵּחַ מִלְּבַד עֹלַת הַבֹּקֶר	17[13]	And the meal offering[14] was presented; and he filled his hand with it, and made it smoke on the altar, besides the [15]burnt offering of the morning[16].
וַיִּשְׁחַט אֶת־הַשּׁוֹר וְאֶת־הָאַיִל זֶבַח הַשְּׁלָמִים אֲשֶׁר לָעָם וַיַּמְצִאוּ בְּנֵי אַהֲרֹן אֶת־הַדָּם אֵלָיו וַיִּזְרְקֵהוּ עַל־הַמִּזְבֵּחַ סָבִיב	18[17]	He also killed the ox and the ram, the sacrifice of peace offerings that was for the people; and Aaron's sons delivered the blood to him, and he dashed it against the altar all around it,
וְאֶת־הַחֲלָבִים מִן־הַשּׁוֹר וּמִן־הָאַיִל	19[18]	And the fat of the ox[1], and [2]of the ram,

---

[1] Leviticus 9:12 - Ephesians 5:2 5:25-27, Leviticus 1:1-17 8:18-21
Leviticus 9:12-13 - MasLevb
[2] LXX adds whole
[3] Leviticus 9:13 - Midrash Tanchuma Noach 4
[4] LXX adds whole
[5] Leviticus 9:14 - Leviticus 8:21, Philo De Migratione Abrahami 67, Philo Legum Allegoriae III 141 144
[6] LXX feet with water
[7] LXX adds whole
[8] Leviticus 9:15 - 2 Corinthians 5:21, Hebrews 2:17 5:3, Isaiah 5:10, Leviticus 4:27-31 9:3, MasLevb, Numbers 28:1-29, t.Sanhedrin 6:2, Titus 2:14
[9] LXX purified it
[10] Leviticus 9:16 - b.Chullin [Tosefot] 21a, b.Menachot 93b, b.Zevachim [Rashi] 24b, b.Zevachim [Tosefot] 50a, Hebrews 10:1-22, Leviticus 1:1-13 8:18-21 9:12-14
[11] LXX adds whole
[12] LXX in due form
[13] Leviticus 9:17 - b.Beitzah [Rashi] 20a, b.Menachot [Tosefot] 36b, b.Menachot9b 10ab 19b, b.Niddah [Tosefot] 66b, Exodus 29:38-42, Galatians 2:20, John 6:53, Leviticus 2:1-2 3:5 9:1
[14] LXX sacrifice
[15] LXX adds whole
[16] i.e., Tamid
[17] Leviticus 9:18 - Colossians 1:20, Ephesians 2:14-17, Leviticus 3:1-17 7:11-18, Romans 5:1 5:10
[18] Leviticus 9:19 - Leviticus 3:5 3:9 3:16 9:10

הָאַלְיָה וְהַמְכַסֶּה וְהַכְּלָיֹת וְיֹתֶרֶת הַכָּבֵד

ram, *the fat tail, and that covers the innards, and the kidneys, and the lobe of the liver*[3].

וַיָּשִׂימוּ אֶת־הַחֲלָבִים עַל־הֶחָזוֹת וַיַּקְטֵר הַחֲלָבִים הַמִּזְבֵּחָה

20[4] And *they*[5] put the fat on the breasts, and he made the fat smoke on the altar.

וְאֵת הֶחָזוֹת וְאֵת שׁוֹק הַיָּמִין הֵנִיף אַהֲרֹן תְּנוּפָה לִפְנֵי יְהוָה כַּאֲשֶׁר צִוָּה מֹשֶׁה

21[6] And the breasts and the right *thigh*[7] Aaron waved for a *wave*[8] offering before the LORD, as *Moses commanded*[9].

וַיִּשָּׂא אַהֲרֹן אֶת־יָדוֹ "אֶת־יָדָיו" אֶל־הָעָם וַיְבָרְכֵם וַיֵּרֶד מֵעֲשֹׂת הַחַטָּאת וְהָעֹלָה וְהַשְּׁלָמִים

22[10] And Aaron lifted up his hands toward the people, and blessed them[11]; and he came down from offering the sin offering, and the [12]burnt offering, and the peace offerings.

וַיָּבֹא מֹשֶׁה וְאַהֲרֹן אֶל־אֹהֶל מוֹעֵד וַיֵּצְאוּ וַיְבָרְכוּ אֶת־הָעָם וַיֵּרָא כְבוֹד־יְהוָה אֶל־כָּל־הָעָם

23[13] And Moses and Aaron went into the tent of meeting, and came out, and blessed the *people*[14]; and the glory of the LORD appeared to all the people.

וַתֵּצֵא אֵשׁ מִלִּפְנֵי יְהוָה וַתֹּאכַל עַל־

24[15] And fire came forth from before the

---

[1] LX *calf*

[2] LXX adds *the hind quarters*

[3] LXX *and the fat covering the belly, and the two kidneys, and the fat upon them, and the caul on the liver*

[4] Leviticus 9:20 - b.Chullin [Tosefot] 8b, b.Menachot 62a, Leviticus 3:14-17 7:29-34
Leviticus 9:20-23 - Pirkei de R'Eliezer 9

[5] LXX *he*

[6] Leviticus 9:21 - 1 Peter 4:11, Exodus 5:24 29:26-28, Isaiah 1:3, Leviticus 7:24 7:26 7:30-34, Luke 2:13

[7] LXX *shoulder*

[8] LXX *choice*

[9] LXX *the LORD commanded Moses*

[10] Leviticus 9:22 - 1 Chronicles 23:13, 1 Kings 8:55, 1 Peter 3:9, 2 Chronicles 6:3, 2 Corinthians 13:14, Acts 3:26, b.Chullin 133a, b.Megillah 18a, b.Menachot [Rashi] 18b, b.Sotah 38ab, b.Tamid 33b, Bahir 109 123, Deuteronomy 10:8 21:5, Ein Yaakov Megillah:18a, Genesis 14:18-20, Genesis.R 99 [Excl]:6, Hebrews 7:6-7, Luke 24:50, m.Sotah 7:6, Mark 10:16, Midrash Tanchuma Vayechi 9, mt.Hilchot Nesiat Kapayim 14:3, mt.Hilchot Tefilah 8:5, Numbers 6:23-27, Numbers.R 6:2 11:4 11:4 13:10, Psalms 72:17, Sefer Yetzirah 1:3, Siman 100:9, t.Demai 2:7, y.Sotah 7:6, y.Taanit 4:1, z.Yitro 1 67a, z.Beshalach 283, z.Emor 81, z.Naso 155, z.Pinchas 673 836
Leviticus 9:22-24 - MasLevb

[11] Cf. Numbers 6:23-27

[12] LXX adds *whole*

[13] Leviticus 9:23 - b.Yoma [Rashi] 53a, Ecclesiastes.R 4:8, Hebrews 9:24-28, Leviticus 9:6, Leviticus.R 11:6, Luke 1:21-22, Midrash Psalms 33:1 149:1, Midrash Tanchuma Vezot Habracha 1, mt.Hilchot Nesiat Kapayim 14:11, Numbers 14:10 16:19 17:7, Pesikta de R'Kahana S1.4 S1.11, y.Yoma 1:1, z.Shmini 36, z.Tzav 134
Leviticus 9:23-24 - 11QLevb

[14] 11QLEvb *whole congregation*

[15] Leviticus 9:24 - 1 Chronicles 21:26, 1 Kings 18:38-39, 2 Chronicles 6:2 7:1-3, 2 Kings 19:15, b.Menachot [Tosefot] 14b, b.Shabbat [Rashi] 87b, Ein Yaakov Eruvin:63a, Ein Yaakov Shabbat:87b, Exodus 3:2, Ezra 3:11, Genesis 4:3-4 15:17 17:3, Genesis.R 3:9, Judges 6:21 13:19-20 13:23, Leviticus 6:13, Leviticus.R 11:6, Matthew 2:39, Midrash Psalms 33:1 149:1, mt.Hilchot Temidim Umusafim 2:1, Numbers 14:5 16:22, Numbers.R 12:8 13:6 13:10 14:21, Pesikta Rabbati 4:2, Philo Quis Rerum Divinarum Heres 251, Pirkei de R'Eliezer 53, Psalms 20:4-5 80:2, Revelation 4:9 5:8 7:11, Song of Songs.R 2:39, Midrash Tanchuma Shemini 4, Seder Olam 15:Shlomo, z.Tzav 31b, z.Tzav 131 134

הַמִּזְבֵּ֙חָה֙ אֶת־הָעֹלָ֣ה וְאֶת־הַחֲלָבִ֑ים
וַיַּ֤רְא כָּל־הָעָם֙ וַיָּרֹ֔נּוּ וַֽיִּפְּל֖וּ עַל־פְּנֵיהֶֽם

LORD, and consumed on the altar *the burnt offering and the fat*[1]; and when all the people saw it, *they shouted*[2], and fell on their faces.

Shemini – Chapter 10[3]

וַיִּקְח֣וּ בְנֵֽי־אַ֠הֲרֹן נָדָ֨ב וַאֲבִיה֜וּא אִ֣ישׁ
מַחְתָּת֗וֹ וַיִּתְּנ֤וּ בָהֵן֙ אֵ֔שׁ וַיָּשִׂ֥ימוּ עָלֶ֖יהָ
קְטֹ֑רֶת וַיַּקְרִ֜בוּ לִפְנֵ֤י יְהוָה֙ אֵ֣שׁ זָרָ֔ה
אֲשֶׁ֧ר לֹ֦א צִוָּ֖ה אֹתָֽם

1[4] And Nadab and Abihu, the[5] sons of Aaron, each took his censer, and put fire in it, and *laid*[6] incense on it, and offered strange fire before the LORD, which *He*[7] had not commanded them.

וַתֵּ֥צֵא אֵ֛שׁ מִלִּפְנֵ֥י יְהוָ֖ה וַתֹּ֣אכַל אוֹתָ֑ם
וַיָּמֻ֖תוּ לִפְנֵ֥י יְהוָֽה

2[8] And fire came forth from before the LORD, and devoured them, and they died before the LORD.

וַיֹּ֨אמֶר מֹשֶׁ֜ה אֶֽל־אַהֲרֹ֗ן ה֩וּא אֲשֶׁר־
דִּבֶּ֨ר יְהוָ֤ה ׀ לֵאמֹר֙ בִּקְרֹבַ֣י אֶקָּדֵ֔שׁ
וְעַל־פְּנֵ֥י כָל־הָעָ֖ם אֶכָּבֵ֑ד וַיִּדֹּ֖ם אַהֲרֹֽן

3[9] Then Moses said to Aaron, "This is the thing the LORD spoke, saying: Through those who are near to Me I will be sanctified, and before all the people I will be glorified." And *Aaron*

---

[1] 11QLevb *fat of the offering of well being*

[2] LXX *and were amazed*

[3] z.Vaera 26b

[4] Leviticus 10:1 - 1 Kings 13:1-2, 2 Chronicles 26:16-20, Deuteronomy 4:2 13:1 17:3, Ecclesiastes.R 7:2, Exodus 6:23 24:1 24:9 3:3 4:1 30:1-39 30:34-36 7:11 13:29 14:3 16:27, Hebrews 9:4, Jastrow 365a, Jeremiah 7:31 19:5 8:35 20:8 20:15 44:19-21, Leviticus 9:24 16:1 16:12 22:9, Leviticus.R 20:8, Luke 1:9-11, MasLevb, Mekhilta de R'Shimon bar Yochai Shabbata 85:2, Mekilta de R'Ishmael Vayassa 7:44, Midrash Tanchuma Acharei Mot 6, Numbers 3:2-4 16:6-7 16:16-18 17:11 26:61, Numbers.R 4:20, Pesikta de R'Kahana 26.8, Philo Legum Allegoriae II 57, Psalms 21:2, Revelation 8:3-5, the sons of Aaron", z.Ki Tissa 193a, z.Noach 73b, z.Acharei Mot 70, z.Ki Tisa 93, z.Noach 309, z.Shmini 36 38, z.Tzav 156, z.Vayera 439

Leviticus 10:1-2 - 11QLevb, Midrash Tanchuma Beshallach 21, Midrash Tanchuma Tzav 9

Leviticus 10:1-3 - Ein Yaakov Eruvin:63a

Leviticus 10:1-11 - Gates of Repentance 3.116

Leviticus 10:1-20 - Josephus Antiquities 4.12.2

[5] 11QLevb LXX adds *two*

[6] LXX *threw*

[7] 11QLevb LXX *the LORD*

[8] Leviticus 10:2 - 1 Chronicles 13:10 15:13 24:2, 1 Corinthians 10:11, 1 Samuel 6:19, 2 Kings 1:10 1:12, 2 Samuel 6:7, Acts 5:5 5:10, b.Sanhedrin 52a, Bahir 34, Ein Yaakov Sanhedrin:52a, Esther.R 5:1, Isaiah 6:33, Leviticus 9:24 10:5 16:1, Leviticus.R 12:1 20:10, Midrash Psalms 75:2, Midrash Tanchuma Acharei Mot 1 4, Midrash Tanchuma Noach 15, Midrash Tanchuma Shemini 1 2 12, Midrash Tanchuma Vayakhel 1, Numbers 3:3-3:4 16:32-16:33 16:35 17:14 26:61, Numbers.R 2:23 5:4, Pesikta de R'Kahana 26.9, Philo De Fuga et Inventione 59, Ruth.R Petichata:6, z.Shmini 52, z.Tzav 135 154 156, z.Vayikra 64 66

[9] Leviticus 10:3 - 1 Chronicles 15:12-13, 1 Peter 4:17, 1 Samuel 2:30 3:18 6:20, 2 Thessalonians 1:10, Acts 5:11-13, Avot de R'Natan 14, b.Gittin [Tosefot] 7a, b.Zevachim 115b, Deuteronomy 8:51, Exodus 14:4 19:22 29:43-44, Ezekiel 20:41 4:22 18:13, Genesis 18:25, Guide for the Perplexed 1:37, Hebrews 12:28-29, Isaiah 15:8 1:3 4:11, Jastrow 365a 1263a, Job 1:20-21 2:10, John 12:28 13:31-32 14:13, Leviticus 8:35 21:6 21:8 21:15 21:17 21:21 22:9, Leviticus.R 12:2, Matthew 10:37, Mekhilta de R'Shimon bar Yochai Shirata 34:2, Mekilta de R'Ishmael Pisha 12:6, Mekilta de R'Ishmael Shirata 8:57, Midrash Tanchuma Shemini 1 12, Numbers 20:12, Numbers.R 2:23, Philo De Fuga et Inventione 59, Philo De Specialibus Legibus II 33, Psalms 39:10 46:11 89:8 119:120

held his peace[1].

4[2] And Moses called *Mishael*[3] and Elzaphan, *the sons of Uzziel, the uncle of Aaron*[4], and said to them, 'Draw near and carry your brethren from before the sanctuary out of the camp.'

5[5] And they drew near, and carried them in their tunics out of the camp, as Moses said.

6[6] And Moses said to Aaron, and to Eleazar and to Ithamar, his sons[7], "*Do not let not the hair of your heads go loose*[8], neither rend your clothes, so you will not die, and that He will not be angry with all the congregation; but let your brethren, the whole house of Israel, lament the burning that the LORD has kindled.

7[9] And you shall not go out *from*[10] the door of the tent of meeting, lest you die; for the anointing oil of the LORD is on you." And they did according to the word of Moses.

8[11] And the LORD spoke to Aaron, saying:

וַיִּקְרָא מֹשֶׁה אֶל־מִישָׁאֵל וְאֶל אֶלְצָפָן בְּנֵי עֻזִּיאֵל דֹּד אַהֲרֹן וַיֹּאמֶר אֲלֵהֶם קִרְבוּ שְׂאוּ אֶת־אֲחֵיכֶם מֵאֵת פְּנֵי־הַקֹּדֶשׁ אֶל־מִחוּץ לַמַּחֲנֶה

וַיִּקְרְבוּ וַיִּשָּׂאֻם בְּכֻתֳּנֹתָם אֶל־מִחוּץ לַמַּחֲנֶה כַּאֲשֶׁר דִּבֶּר מֹשֶׁה

וַיֹּאמֶר מֹשֶׁה אֶל־אַהֲרֹן וּלְאֶלְעָזָר וּלְאִיתָמָר בָּנָיו רָאשֵׁיכֶם אַל־תִּפְרָעוּ וּבִגְדֵיכֶם לֹא־תִפְרֹמוּ וְלֹא תָמֻתוּ וְעַל כָּל־הָעֵדָה יִקְצֹף וַאֲחֵיכֶם כָּל־בֵּית יִשְׂרָאֵל יִבְכּוּ אֶת־הַשְּׂרֵפָה אֲשֶׁר שָׂרַף יְהוָה

וּמִפֶּתַח אֹהֶל מוֹעֵד לֹא תֵצְאוּ פֶּן־תָּמֻתוּ כִּי־שֶׁמֶן מִשְׁחַת יְהוָה עֲלֵיכֶם וַיַּעֲשׂוּ כִּדְבַר מֹשֶׁה

וַיְדַבֵּר יְהוָה אֶל־אַהֲרֹן לֵאמֹר

---

[1] LXX *was pricked [in his heart]*

[2] Leviticus 10:4 - 1 Chronicles 5:28, Acts 5:6 5:9-10 8:2, Exodus 6:18 6:22, Leviticus.R 20:4, Luke 7:12, Midrash Tanchuma Acharei Mot 3, Midrash Tanchuma Shemini 12, Numbers 3:19 3:30, Pesikta de R'Kahana 26.4, Pesikta Rabbati 47:3
Leviticus 10:4-7 - 11QpaleoLeva

[3] LXX *Misadae*

[4] LXX *sons of the brother of Aaron's father*

[5] Leviticus 10:5 - b.Sanhedrin [Tosefot] 52a, Leviticus 8:13, Leviticus.R 20:9, Midrash Tanchuma Shemini 12, t.Berachot 4:17

[6] Leviticus 10:6 - 2 Samuel 24:1 24:15-17, b.Moed Katan 14b 15a 19b 24a 28b, b.Sanhedrin [Rashi] 52a, b.Taanit [Tosefot] 23b, b.Taanit 15b, b.Yevamot [Rashi] 102b, Commandment #444 #445, Deuteronomy 9:9, Ein Yaakov Moed Katan 28b, Esther.R Petichata:11, Exodus 9:5, Ezekiel 24:16-217, Genesis.R 20:3, Jeremiah 7:29, Joshua 7:1 7:11 22:18 22:20, Leviticus 13:45 21:1-15, m.Demai 1:3, Micah 1:16, mt.Hilchot Beit HaBechirah 7:20, mt.Hilchot Evel 5:2 8:1, mt.Hilchot Sanhedrin vHainshin Hameurim Lahem 15:3 19:2 19:4, Numbers 1:53 5:18 6:6-7 14:6 16:22 17:6-47 18:5, Philo De Somniis II 67, z.Acharei Mot 11, z.Shmini 53

[7] LXX adds *that were left*

[8] LXX *You shall not make bare your heads*

[9] Leviticus 10:7 - 2 Corinthians 1:21, Acts 10:38, Commandment #446, Exodus 4:41 6:30 40:13-15, Genesis.R 97:1, Leviticus 8:12 8:30 21:12, Matthew 8:21-22, mt.Hilchot Biat haMikdash 2:5, mt.Hilchot Sanhedrin vHainshin Hameurim Lahem 19:2, z.Shmini 53

[10] Missing in 11QPaleoLeva

[11] Leviticus 10:8 - Avot de R'Natan 37, b.Gittin 60b, b.Zevachim [Tosefot] 115b, Jastrow 573a, Leviticus.R 12:3, Mesillat Yesharim 26:Trait of Kedushah, Philo De Ebrietate 127, y.Moed Katan 3:5
Leviticus 10:8-9 - Midrash Tanchuma Shemini 5

יַ֥יִן וְשֵׁכָ֣ר אַל־תֵּ֣שְׁתְּ ׀ אַתָּ֣ה ׀ וּבָנֶ֣יךָ
אִתָּ֗ךְ בְּבֹאֲכֶ֛ם אֶל־אֹ֥הֶל מוֹעֵ֖ד וְלֹ֣א
תָמֻ֑תוּ חֻקַּ֥ת עוֹלָ֖ם לְדֹרֹתֵיכֶֽם

9[1] "Do not drink wine nor strong drink, you, nor your sons with you, when you go into the tent of meeting, so you will not die; it shall be a statute forever throughout your generations.

וּֽלְהַבְדִּ֔יל בֵּ֥ין הַקֹּ֖דֶשׁ וּבֵ֣ין הַחֹ֑ל וּבֵ֥ין
הַטָּמֵ֖א וּבֵ֥ין הַטָּהֽוֹר

10[2] And that you may put difference between *the holy and the common, and between the unclean and the clean*[3];

וּלְהוֹרֹ֖ת אֶת־בְּנֵ֣י יִשְׂרָאֵ֑ל אֵ֚ת כָּל־
הַ֣חֻקִּ֔ים אֲשֶׁ֨ר דִּבֶּ֧ר יְהוָ֛ה אֲלֵיהֶ֖ם בְּיַד־
מֹשֶֽׁה:

11[4] and that you may teach the children of Israel all the statutes the LORD has spoken to them by *the hand of*[5] Moses."

וַיְדַבֵּ֣ר מֹשֶׁ֗ה אֶֽל־אַהֲרֹ֜ן וְאֶ֣ל אֶלְעָזָ֣ר
וְאֶל־אִֽיתָמָ֣ר ׀ בָּנָ֣יו הַנּֽוֹתָרִים֮ קְח֣וּ אֶת־
הַמִּנְחָ֗ה הַנּוֹתֶ֙רֶת֙ מֵאִשֵּׁ֣י יְהוָ֔ה וְאִכְל֥וּהָ
מַצּ֖וֹת אֵ֣צֶל הַמִּזְבֵּ֑חַ כִּ֛י קֹ֥דֶשׁ קָֽדָשִׁ֖ים
הֽוּא

12[6] And Moses spoke to Aaron, and to Eleazar and to Ithamar, his sons *who were left*[7], "Take the *meal offering*[8] that remains of the *offerings*[9] of the LORD made by fire, and eat it without leaven beside the altar; for it is most holy.

וַאֲכַלְתֶּ֤ם אֹתָהּ֙ בְּמָק֣וֹם קָדֹ֔שׁ כִּ֣י חָקְךָ֤
וְחָק־בָּנֶ֙יךָ֙ הִ֔וא מֵאִשֵּׁ֖י יְהוָ֑ה כִּי־כֵ֖ן

13[10] And you shall eat it in a holy place, because it is your due, and your sons' due, of the offerings of the LORD

---

[1] Leviticus 10:9 - 1 Timothy 3:3 3:8 5:23, b.Bava Metzia 84ab, b.Bechorot [Rashi] 45b, b.Gittin 60b, b.Chullin [Tosefot] 24a, b.Kereitot 13b, b.Nazir [Rashi] 38a, b.Nazir 4a, b.Sanhedrin 22b 83b, b.Sheviit [Rashi] 36b, b.Sheviit [Tosefot] 23a, b.Taanit [Rashi] 26b, b.Taanit 14b, b.Yoma [Rashi] 76b, b.Zevachim [Rashi] 18a 112b, b.Zevachim 14b, Ephesians 5:18, Esther.R 5:1, Ezekiel 20:21, Gates of Repentance 3.48, Hosea 4:11, Isaiah 4:7, Jastrow 1577a, Jeremiah 35:5-6, Leviticus 3:17, Leviticus.R 12:1 12:4 20:9, Luke 1:15, Midrash Tanchuma Acharei Mot 6, Midrash Tanchuma Shemini 5 11, mt.Hilchot Biat haMikdash 1:1, mt.Hilchot Nesiat Kapayim 14:1, mt.Hilchot Deot 5:3, mt.Hilchot Pesulei haMikdashim 1:12, mt.Hilchot Sanhedrin vHainshin Hameurim Lahem 19:2 19:4, Numbers 6:3 6:20, Pesikta de R'Kahana 26.9, Philo De Ebrietate 140, Philo De Specialibus Legibus IV 191, Proverbs 20:1 31:4-5, Titus 1:7, y.Terumot 9:1, z.Mishpatim 124b, z.Naso 127a 124, z.Shmini 55
Leviticus 10:9-11 - Commandment #447
Leviticus 10:9-20 - MasLevb
[2] Leviticus 10:10 - 1 Peter 1:14-16, b.Bava Metzia 84ab, b.Chullin [Rashi] 26b, b.Gittin 60b, b.Kereitot 13b, b.Nazir [Rashi] 38a, b.Pesachim [Rashi] 14a, b.Sanhedrin [Rashi] 22b, b.Sheviit [Tosefot] 23a, b.Sheviit 18b, b.Zevachim 14b 18a, Ein Yaakov Shevuot 18b, Ezekiel 22:26 20:23, Gates of Repentance 3.48, Jastrow 329a, Jeremiah 15:19, Leviticus 11:47 20:25-26, mt.Hilchot Deot 5:3, Tanya Igeret Hakodesh §31, Titus 1:15, z.Pekudei 120
[3] LXX *sacred and profane, and between clean and unclean*
[4] Leviticus 10:11 - 1 Thessalonians 4:2, 2 Chronicles 17:9 6:22, Acts 20:27, b.Gittin 60b, b.Kereitot 13b, b.Nazir [Rashi] 38a, b.Sheviit [Tosefot] 23a, b.Sheviit 18b, b.Zevachim [Rashi] 18a, Deuteronomy 24:8 9:10, Ein Yaakov Shevuot:18b, Gates of Repentance 3.048, Jastrow 353a, Jeremiah 2:8 18:18, Malachi 2:7, Matthew 4:20, mt.Hilchot Biat haMikdash 1:3, mt.Hilchot Deot 5:3, Nehemiah 8:2 8:8 9:13-14
[5] Missing in LXX
[6] Leviticus 10:12 - b.Berachot 61a, b.Chagigah [Rashi] 11b, b.Menachot [Tosefot] 19b, b.Sanhedrin [Tosefot] 45a, b.Yoma 5b 87a, b.Zevachim [Rashi] 101a, b.Zevachim [Tosefot] 59a, b.Zevachim 60a, Exodus 5:2, Ezekiel 20:29, Leviticus 2:1-16 6:14-18 7:9 21:22, Numbers 18:9-10, Pesikta Rabbati 47:1
[7] LXX *who survived*
[8] LXX *sacrifice*
[9] LXX *burnt offerings*
[10] Leviticus 10:13 - b.Yoma 5b, b.Zevachim 55a 101a, Leviticus 2:3 6:16, Numbers 18:10

צִוֵּיתִי

וְאֵת֩ חֲזֵ֨ה הַתְּנוּפָ֜ה וְאֵ֣ת׀ שׁ֣וֹק הַתְּרוּמָ֗ה תֹּֽאכְלוּ֙ בְּמָק֣וֹם טָה֔וֹר אַתָּ֗ה וּבָנֶ֤יךָ וּבְנֹתֶ֙יךָ֙ אִתָּ֔ךְ כִּֽי־חָקְךָ֣ וְחָק־בָּנֶ֔יךָ נִתְּנ֖וּ מִזִּבְחֵ֣י שַׁלְמֵ֑י בְּנֵ֖י יִשְׂרָאֵֽל

שׁ֣וֹק הַתְּרוּמָ֗ה וַחֲזֵ֣ה הַתְּנוּפָ֔ה עַ֠ל אִשֵּׁ֨י הַחֲלָבִ֜ים יָבִ֗יאוּ לְהָנִ֛יף תְּנוּפָ֖ה לִפְנֵ֣י יְהוָ֑ה וְהָיָ֨ה לְךָ֜ וּלְבָנֶ֤יךָ אִתְּךָ֙ לְחָק־ עוֹלָ֔ם כַּאֲשֶׁ֖ר צִוָּ֥ה יְהוָֽה

וְאֵ֣ת׀ שְׂעִ֣יר הַֽחַטָּ֗את דָּרֹ֥שׁ דָּרַ֛שׁ מֹשֶׁ֖ה וְהִנֵּ֣ה שֹׂרָ֑ף וַיִּקְצֹ֨ף עַל־אֶלְעָזָ֜ר וְעַל־ אִֽיתָמָ֗ר בְּנֵ֣י אַהֲרֹ֛ן הַנּוֹתָרִ֖ם לֵאמֹֽר

מַדּ֗וּעַ לֹֽא־אֲכַלְתֶּ֤ם אֶת־הַֽחַטָּאת֙ בִּמְק֣וֹם הַקֹּ֔דֶשׁ כִּ֛י קֹ֥דֶשׁ קָֽדָשִׁ֖ים הִ֑וא וְאֹתָ֣הּ׀ נָתַ֣ן לָכֶ֗ם לָשֵׂאת֙ אֶת־עֲוֹ֣ן הָֽעֵדָ֔ה לְכַפֵּ֥ר עֲלֵיהֶ֖ם לִפְנֵ֥י יְהוָֽה

made by fire; for so I am commanded.

14¹ And you shall eat the breast of *waving and the thigh of heaving*² in a clean place; you, and your sons, and your *daughters*³ with you; for they are given as your due, and your sons' due, out of the sacrifices of the peace offerings of the children of Israel.

15⁴ They shall bring the *thigh*⁵ of heaving and the breast of *waving*⁶ with the ⁷offerings of the fat made by fire, to wave it for a wave offering before the LORD; and it shall be yours, and your sons'⁸ with you, as a due forever; as the LORD has commanded⁹."

16¹⁰ And Moses diligently inquired for the goat of the sin offering, and, behold, it was burnt; and he was angry with Eleazar and with Ithamar, the sons of Aaron that were left, saying:

17¹¹ "Why have you not eaten the sin offering in the place of the sanctuary, seeing it is most holy, and He has given it you to *bear*¹² the iniquity of the congregation, to make atonement for them before the LORD?

---

¹ Leviticus 10:14 - b.Bechorot [Rashi] 32b, b.Yevamot [Rashi] 68b 74b, b.Yevamot 87a, b.Zevachim 55a, Commandment #500, Exodus 29:24-28, John 4:34, Leviticus 7:29-34 9:21, mt.Hilchot Maaseh haKorbanot 10:5, Numbers 18:11
² LXX *separation, and the shoulder of the choice offering*
³ LXX *house*
⁴ Leviticus 10:15 - 1 Corinthians 9:13-14, b.Makkot 14b, b.Menachot [Rashi] 61a, b.Menachot 62a, b.Yoma 5b, b.Zevachim [Rashi] 114b, b.Zevachim 101a 119b, Genesis 13:15 17:8 17:13 17:17, Leviticus 7:29-30 7:34, m.Menachot 5:6
⁵ LXX *shoulder*
⁶ LXX *separation*
⁷ LXX adds *burnt*
⁸ LXX adds *and thy daughters'*
⁹ LXX adds *Moses*
¹⁰ Leviticus 10:16 - Avot de R'Natan 37, b.Chullin [Rashi] 68b, b.Kiddushin 30a, b.Kiddushin 30a [states this is the middle of the words of the Torah], b.Pesachim 23b, b.Zevachim [Tosefot] 39b, b.Zevachim 11b, Ephesians 4:26, Exodus 32:19-22, Jastrow 1407a, Leviticus 6:26 6:30 9:3 9:15, Leviticus.R 13:1, Mark 3:5 10:14, Mas.Soferim 9:2, Matthew 5:22, Numbers 12:3, Philo De Fuga et Inventione 157, Sifre.z Numbers Mattot 30:21
¹¹ Leviticus 10:17 - 1 Peter 2:24, 2 Corinthians 5:21, b.Chullin [Rashi] 68b, b.Menachot [Rashi] 25a, b.Menachot 4a, b.Rosh Hashanah [Rashi] 4b, b.Sheviit 9b 10b, b.Yoma [Rashi] 5b, b.Zevachim [Tosefot] 5b 10b 82b, b.Zevachim 101ab, Exodus 4:38 4:43, Ezekiel 4:4-6 18:19-20, Hebrews 9:28, Isaiah 53:6-11, John 1:29, Leviticus 6:24-30 7:6-7 16:22 22:16, Numbers 18:1, Sifre Numbers 157:12 157:12, y.Sheviit 1:4
¹² LCC *take away*

הֵן לֹא־הוּבָא אֶת־דָּמָהּ אֶל־הַקֹּדֶשׁ פְּנִימָה אָכוֹל תֹּאכְלוּ אֹתָהּ בַּקֹּדֶשׁ כַּאֲשֶׁר צִוֵּיתִי

18[1]   Behold, the blood of it was not brought into the sanctuary; you should certainly have eaten it in the sanctuary, as *I commanded*[2]."

וַיְדַבֵּר אַהֲרֹן אֶל־מֹשֶׁה הֵן הַיּוֹם הִקְרִיבוּ אֶת־חַטָּאתָם וְאֶת־עֹלָתָם לִפְנֵי יְהֹוָה וַתִּקְרֶאנָה אֹתִי כָּאֵלֶּה וְאָכַלְתִּי חַטָּאת הַיּוֹם הַיִּיטַב בְּעֵינֵי יְהֹוָה

19[3]   And Aaron spoke unto Moses, "Behold, this day have they offered their sin offering and their [4]burnt offering before the LORD, and there have befallen me such things as these; and if I had eaten the sin offering today, would it have been well pleasing in the sight of the LORD?"

וַיִּשְׁמַע מֹשֶׁה וַיִּיטַב בְּעֵינָיו

20[5]   And when Moses heard that, it *was well pleasing in his sight.*[6]

Shemini – Chapter 11[7]

וַיְדַבֵּר יְהֹוָה אֶל־מֹשֶׁה וְאֶל־אַהֲרֹן לֵאמֹר אֲלֵהֶם

1[8]   And the LORD spoke to Moses and to Aaron, saying *to them*[9]:

דַּבְּרוּ אֶל־בְּנֵי יִשְׂרָאֵל לֵאמֹר זֹאת

2[10]   Speak to the children of Israel, saying: These are the *living things*[1] that you

---

[1] Leviticus 10:18 - b.Chullin [Tosefot] 68b, b.Menachot [Rashi] 6b, b.Pesachim 82a 83a, b.Yoma 5b, b.Zevachim [Rashi] 26a 120a, b.Zevachim [Tosefot] 16b, b.Zevachim 82ab 101a, Leviticus 6:26 6:30, t.Zevachim 8:25, y.Pesachim 7:9

[2] LXX *the Lord commanded me*

[3] Leviticus 10:19 - 1 Samuel 1:7-1:8, Avot de R'Natan 37, b.Pesachim [Rashi] 91ab, b.Pesachim 82b, b.Taanit [Rashi] 14b, b.Zevachim 16ab 1b 101ab, Deuteronomy 12:7 2:14, Hebrews 7:27 9:8, Hosea 9:4, Isaiah 1:11 1:15, Jeremiah 6:20 14:12, Leviticus 9:8 9:12, Leviticus.R 13:1, Malachi 1:10 1:13 2:13, mt.Hilchot Biat haMikdash 2:8, mt.Hilchot Maaser Sheni vneta Revai 3:6, mt.Hilchot Sanhedrin vHainshin Hameurim Lahem 13:6 19:4, Philippians 4:4

[4] LXX adds *whole*

[5] Leviticus 10:20 - 2 Chronicles 30:18-20, Avot de R'Natan 37, b.Pesachim [Rashi] 82b, Leviticus.R 13:1, Mas.Kallah Rabbati 4:4, Matthew 12:3-7 12:20, mt.Hilchot Evel 1:1, Zechariah 7:8-9

[6] LXX *pleased him*

[7] Jastrow 589a, Midrash Proverbs 10, mt.Hilchot Korban Pesach 6:1, Sifre Devarim Reeh 98, Tanya Likutei Aramim §06

[8] Leviticus 11:1 - Jastrow 450b 556a, Leviticus.R 13:1, m.Niddah 6:9, m.Uktzin 3:2 3:9, Mekhilta de R'Shimon bar Yochai Pisha 3:2
Leviticus 11:1-8 - Leviticus.R 2:10, m.Chullin 3:6
Leviticus 11:1-21 - MasLevb
Leviticus 11:1-23 - 4 Maccabees 5:26
Leviticus 11:1-47 - Josephus Antiquities 4.12.2

[9] Missing in LXX

[10] Leviticus 11:2 - 1 Timothy 4:4-6, Acts 10:12-14, b.Chullin [Rashi] 59a 70b, b.Chullin 37ab 42a 71a, b.Menachot [Rashi] 29a, b.Sheviit [Rashi] 7a, Commandment #143, Daniel 1:8, Deuteronomy 14:3-21, Ein Yaakov Chullin:42a, Ezekiel 4:14, Hebrews 9:10 13:9, Leviticus 11:4 11:9 11:11 11:13 11:21 11:29 11:34 11:39 11:41-44, Leviticus.R 1:8 13:2 13:3, Mark 7:15-7:19, Matthew 15:11, Midrash Psalms 139:5, Midrash Tanchuma Shemini 8, Midrash Tanchuma Shemini 6 7, Midrash Tanchuma Shemini 6 7, mt.Hilchot Maachalot Assurot 2:3, Numbers.R 15:4, Romans 14:2-3 14:14-15, Saadia Opinions 10:15, Sifre Devarim Reeh 100, z.Shemini 41a, z.Shmini 102
Leviticus 11:2-7 - Midrash Tanchuma Shemini 8
Leviticus 11:2-8 - Jastrow 706b

הַחַיָּה֙ אֲשֶׁ֣ר תֹּאכְל֔וּ מִכָּל־הַבְּהֵמָ֖ה אֲשֶׁ֥ר עַל־הָאָֽרֶץ

may eat among all the beasts that are on the earth.

כֹּ֣ל ׀ מַפְרֶ֣סֶת פַּרְסָ֗ה וְשֹׁסַ֤עַת שֶׁ֙סַע֙ פְּרָסֹ֔ת מַעֲלַ֥ת גֵּרָ֖ה בַּבְּהֵמָ֑ה אֹתָ֖הּ תֹּאכֵֽלוּ

3[2] *Whatever*[3] parts the hoof, and *has a wholly cloven footed*[4], and chews the cud, among the beasts, that you may eat.

אַ֣ךְ אֶת־זֶ֞ה לֹ֤א תֹֽאכְלוּ֙ מִֽמַּעֲלֵ֣י הַגֵּרָ֔ה וּמִמַּפְרִיסֵ֖י הַפַּרְסָ֑ה אֶֽת־הַ֠גָּמָל כִּֽי־מַעֲלֵ֨ה גֵרָ֜ה ה֗וּא וּפַרְסָה֙ אֵינֶ֣נּוּ מַפְרִ֔יס טָמֵ֥א ה֖וּא לָכֶֽם

4[5] Nevertheless, these shall you not eat of them that only chew the cud, or of those that only part the hoof: the camel, because he chews the cud but does not part the hoof, he is unclean to you.

וְאֶת־הַשָּׁפָ֗ן כִּֽי־מַעֲלֵ֤ה גֵרָה֙ ה֔וּא וּפַרְסָ֖ה לֹ֣א יַפְרִ֑יס טָמֵ֥א ה֖וּא לָכֶֽם

5[6] And the *rock badger*[7], because he chews the cud but does not part the hoof, he is unclean to you.

וְאֶת־הָאַרְנֶ֗בֶת כִּֽי־מַעֲלַ֤ת גֵּרָה֙ הִ֔וא וּפַרְסָ֖ה לֹ֣א הִפְרִ֑יסָה טְמֵאָ֥ה הִ֖וא לָכֶֽם

6[8] And the hare, because she chews the cud but does not part the hoof, she is unclean to you.

וְאֶת־הַ֠חֲזִיר כִּֽי־מַפְרִ֨יס פַּרְסָ֜ה ה֗וּא וְשֹׁסַ֥ע שֶׁ֙סַע֙ פַּרְסָ֔ה וְה֖וּא גֵּרָ֣ה לֹֽא־יִגָּ֑ר טָמֵ֥א ה֖וּא לָכֶֽם

7[9] And the swine, because he parts the hoof, and *is cloven-footed*[10], but does not chew the cud, he is unclean to you.

---

[1] LXX *beasts*
[2] Leviticus 11:3 - 1 Timothy 4:15, 2 Corinthians 6:17, Acts 17:11, b.Chullin [Rashi] 70b 74a, b.Chullin 59a 71a, b.Niddah [Rashi] 23b 24a, b.Sheviit [Rashi] 7a, b.Zevachim 34a, Deuteronomy 6:6-7 16:3-8, Jastrow 1233b, Lamentations.R 4:7, mt.Hilchot Maachalot Assurot 1:1, Pesikta Rabbati 14:5, Philo De Agricultura 131, Philo De Specialibus Legibus IV 106, Proverbs 2:1-2 2:10 9:6, Psalms 1:1-2, t.Shechitat Chullin 3[4]:20, z.Acharei Mot 269, z.Shmini 105
Leviticus 11:3-19 - m.Sheviit 7:3
[3] LXX *Every beast that*
[4] LXX *making divisions of two claws*
[5] Leviticus 11:4 - b.Bava Kamma [Rashi] 78b, b.Bechorot 6ab 7a 10a 16a, b.Chullin [Rashi] 68b, b.Chullin [Tosefot] 99b, b.Chullin 59a, b.Ketubot 60a, b.Menachot [Tosefot] 11b, Commandment #144, Genesis.R 32:4 60:14, Jastrow 272b 1605b, Jastrow 400a, Leviticus.R 1:8 13:5 26:1, m.Sanhedrin 8:2, Midrash Psalms 1:3 8:2, Midrash Tanchuma Bechukkotai 4, Midrash Tanchuma Chukkat 4, Midrash Tanchuma Shemini 6, Midrash Tanchuma Vayishlach 9, mt.Hilchot Issurei Mizbeiach 5:6, mt.Hilchot Maachalot Assurot 2:1, Numbers.R 15:4 19:2, Pesikta de R'Kahana 4.2, Pesikta Rabbati 14:5 25:3
[6] Leviticus 11:5 - 2 Timothy 3:5, b.Bechorot [Tosefot] 7a, b.Bechorot 6b 10a, Genesis.R 32:4, Jastrow 1294a, Jastrow 930b, Job 12:14, Matthew 7:26, Pesikta de R'Kahana 4.2, Philippians 3:18-3:19, Proverbs 6:26, Psalms 8:18, Romans 2:18-2:24, Titus 1:16
[7] LXX *rabbit*
[8] Leviticus 11:6 - b.Bechorot 6b 10a, b.Megillah 9b, Deuteronomy 14:7, Ein Yaakov Megillah:9b, Genesis.R 32:4, Jastrow 123b 1294a, Mas.Soferim 1:8, Mekilta de R'Ishmael Pisha 14:75, Midrash Tanchuma Chukkat 4, Midrash Tanchuma Shemot 22, Numbers.R 19:2, Pesikta de R'Kahana 4.2, Testament of Asher 2:9, y.Megillah 1:9
[9] Leviticus 11:7 - 2 Peter 2:18-2:22, b.Bechorot 10a, b.Chullin 59a, Deuteronomy 14:8, Genesis.R 32:4, Guide for the Perplexed 3:48, Isaiah 17:4 18:3 18:17, Leviticus.R 13:5, Luke 8:33 15:15, m.Nedarim 2:1, Matthew 7:6, Midrash Psalms 1:3 80:6, Midrash Tanchuma Chukkat 4, Numbers.R 19:2, Pesikta de R'Kahana 4.2, Pesikta Rabbati 14:5
[10] LXX *makes claws of the hoof*

מִבְּשָׂרָם֙ לֹ֣א תֹאכֵ֔לוּ וּבְנִבְלָתָ֖ם לֹ֥א תִגָּ֑עוּ טְמֵאִ֥ים הֵ֖ם לָכֶֽם

8[1] Of their flesh you shall not eat, and their carcasses you shall not touch; they are unclean to you.

אֶת־זֶה֙ תֹּֽאכְל֔וּ מִכֹּ֖ל אֲשֶׁ֣ר בַּמָּ֑יִם כֹּ֣ל אֲשֶׁר־לוֹ֩ סְנַפִּ֨יר וְקַשְׂקֶ֜שֶׂת בַּמַּ֗יִם בַּיַּמִּ֛ים וּבַנְּחָלִ֖ים אֹתָ֥ם תֹּאכֵֽלוּ

9[2] These you may eat of all that are in the waters: whatever has fins and scales in the waters, in the seas, and in the rivers, those you may eat.

וְכֹ֣ל אֲשֶׁ֣ר אֵֽין־לוֹ֩ סְנַפִּ֨יר וְקַשְׂקֶ֜שֶׂת בַּיַּמִּ֣ים וּבַנְּחָלִ֗ים מִכֹּל֙ שֶׁ֣רֶץ הַמַּ֔יִם וּמִכֹּ֛ל נֶ֥פֶשׁ הַֽחַיָּ֖ה אֲשֶׁ֣ר בַּמָּ֑יִם שֶׁ֥קֶץ הֵ֖ם לָכֶֽם

10[3] And all that do not have fins and scales in the seas, and in the rivers, of all that swarm in the waters, and of all the living creatures that are in the waters, they are *a detestable thing unto you*[4],

וְשֶׁ֖קֶץ יִהְי֣וּ לָכֶ֑ם מִבְּשָׂרָם֙ לֹ֣א תֹאכֵ֔לוּ וְאֶת־נִבְלָתָ֖ם תְּשַׁקֵּֽצוּ

11[5] *and they shall be a detestable thing to you; you shall not eat of their flesh, and their carcasses you shall hold as detestable*[6].

כֹּ֣ל אֲשֶׁ֣ר אֵֽין־ל֗וֹ סְנַפִּ֤יר וְקַשְׂקֶ֙שֶׂת֙ בַּמָּ֔יִם שֶׁ֥קֶץ ה֖וּא לָכֶֽם

12[7] Whatever does not have fins and scales in the waters, that is a detestable thing to you.

וְאֶת־אֵ֙לֶּה֙ תְּשַׁקְּצ֣וּ מִן־הָע֔וֹף לֹ֥א יֵאָכְל֖וּ שֶׁ֣קֶץ הֵ֑ם אֶת־הַנֶּ֙שֶׁר֙ וְאֶת־הַפֶּ֔רֶס וְאֵ֖ת הָעָזְנִיָּֽה

13[8] And these you shall hold as detestable among the fowls; they shall not be eaten, they are a detestable thing: *the great vulture, and the bearded vulture,*

---

[1] Leviticus 11:8 - 1 Corinthians 8:8, 2 Corinthians 6:17, Acts 10:10-15 10:28 15:29, b.Beitzah [Rashi] 14b, b.Bechorot [Tosefot] 6b, b.Rosh Hashanah 16b, Colossians 2:16 2:21-23, Ephesians 5:7 5:11, Hebrews 9:10, Hosea 9:3, Isaiah 4:11, Jastrow 1387b, Leviticus 5:2, m.Bikkurim 2:11, Mark 7:2 7:15 7:18, Matthew 15:11 15:20, Mekhilta de R'Shimon bar Yochai Pisha 13:1, mt.Hilchot Tumat Ochalin 16:10, mt.Hilchot Maachalot Assurot 3:6, Romans 14:14-17 14:21, y.Bava Kamma 7:7, y.Terumot 8:1

[2] Leviticus 11:9 - 1 John 5:2-5, Acts 20:21, b.Avodah Zara [Rashi] 43a, b.Avodah Zara 40a, b.Bava Kamma [Rashi] 64b, b.Bechorot 51a, b.Chullin [Tosefot] 22b, b.Chullin 66b 67a, b.Pesachim 23a, b.Sheviit 5a, Commandment #145, Deuteronomy 14:9-10, Galatians 5:6, James 2:18, Leviticus.R 1:8, m.Uktzin 3:9, Midrash Psalms 8:2, Midrash Tanchuma Bechukkotai 4, Midrash Tanchuma Shemini 6, Pesikta Rabbati 25:3, Philo De Specialibus Legibus IV 110, y.Bikkurim 2:1, y.Sanhedrin 7:9, z.Toldot 57

[3] Leviticus 11:10 - b.Chullin [Tosefot] 99b, b.Chullin 66b 67a, b.Eruvin [Rashi] 28a, Deuteronomy 14:3, Leviticus 7:18, m.Bechorot 81, Philo De Specialibus Legibus IV 115, Proverbs 13:20 5:27, Psalms 139:21-22, Revelation 21:8, y.Bikkurim 2:1, y.Sanhedrin 7:9

Leviticus 11:10-11 - 11QpaleoLev

[4] LXX *an abomination; and they shall be abominations to you*

[5] Leviticus 11:11 - b.Chullin [Rashi] 67a, b.Chullin [Tosefot] 66b, b.Chullin 67b, b.Eruvin [Rashi] 28a, b.Makkot 16b, b.Pesachim 23a, Commandment #146, Jastrow 1642a, m.Nedarim 2:1, mt.Hilchot Maachalot Assurot 2:4, mt.Hilchot Sanhedrin vHainshin Hameurim Lahem 19:4

[6] LXX *You shall not eat of their flesh, and you shall abhor their carcasses*

[7] Leviticus 11:12 - b.Bava Kamma [Tosefot] 82b, b.Bechorot [Tosefot] 6b, b.Chullin 66b, Jastrow 1280b, Jastrow 589a

Leviticus 11:12-30 - m.Sheviit 7:3

[8] Leviticus 11:13 - b.Bechorot [Rashi] 7b, b.Chullin [Rashi] 61b 102a 139b, b.Chullin 60b, b.Sanhedrin [Rashi] 70b, Commandment #148, Deuteronomy 14:12-20, Habakkuk 1:8, Hosea 8:1, Jastrow 942b, Jeremiah 4:13 4:22 24:40, Job 4:7 14:41 39:27-30, Lamentations 4:19, Leviticus.R 1:8, m.Kelim 17:14, m.Parah 8:4, m.Uktzin 3:2, Matthew 24:28, mt.Hilchot Maachalot Assurot 2:4, mt.Hilchot Sanhedrin vHainshin Hameurim Lahem 19:4, Romans 1:28-32 3:13-17, Sifre Devarim Reeh 103, Titus 3:3

Leviticus 11:13-19 - mt.Hilchot Maachalot Assurot 1:14

Leviticus 11:13-23 - m.Chullin 3:6

וְאֶת־הַדָּאָה וְאֶת־הָאַיָּה לְמִינָהּ

אֵת כָּל־עֹרֵב לְמִינוֹ

וְאֵת בַּת הַיַּעֲנָה וְאֶת־הַתַּחְמָס וְאֶת־הַשָּׁחַף וְאֶת־הַנֵּץ לְמִינֵהוּ

וְאֶת־הַכּוֹס וְאֶת־הַשָּׁלָךְ וְאֶת־הַיַּנְשׁוּף

וְאֶת־הַתִּנְשֶׁמֶת וְאֶת־הַקָּאָת וְאֶת־הָרָחָם

וְאֵת הַחֲסִידָה הָאֲנָפָה לְמִינָהּ וְאֶת־הַדּוּכִיפַת וְאֶת־הָעֲטַלֵּף

כֹּל שֶׁרֶץ הָעוֹף הַהֹלֵךְ עַל־אַרְבַּע שֶׁקֶץ הוּא לָכֶם

אַךְ אֶת־זֶה תֹּאכְלוּ מִכֹּל שֶׁרֶץ הָעוֹף הַהֹלֵךְ עַל־אַרְבַּע אֲשֶׁר־לֹא אֲשֶׁר־לוֹ כְרָעַיִם מִמַּעַל לְרַגְלָיו לְנַתֵּר בָּהֵן עַל־הָאָרֶץ

14^2 and the osprey[1]; and the kite, and the falcon after its kinds[3];

15^4 every raven after its kinds[5];

16^6 and the ostrich, and the night hawk, and the sea mew, and the hawk after its kinds[7];

17^8 and the little owl, and the cormorant, and the great owl[9];

18^{10} and the horned owl, and the pelican, and the carrion vulture[11];

19^{12} and the stork, and the heron after its kinds, and the hoopoe, and the bat[13].

20^{14} All winged swarming things that *go on all fours*[15] are a detestable thing to you.

21^{16} Yet these may you eat of all winged swarming things that go on all fours: that have jointed legs above their feet, with which to leap on the earth;

---

[1] LXX *the eagle, and the ossifrage, and the sea eagle*
[2] Leviticus 11:14 - b.Chullin [Tosefot] 63b, b.Chullin 63a, Sifre Devarim Reeh 103
[3] LXX *And the vulture, and the kite, and the like to it*
[4] Leviticus 11:15 - 1 Kings 17:4 17:6, b.Bava Batra [Rashbam] 91a, b.Chullin 62a 63a, Genesis 8:7, Genesis.R 65:3, Luke 12:24, Proverbs 6:17
[5] LXX *and the sparrow, and the owl, and the sea mew, and the like to it*
[6] Leviticus 11:16 - 1 Thessalonians 5:5-7, b.Chullin [Tosefot] 64a, b.Chullin 63a, Deuteronomy 14:15-18, Ephesians 2:2-3 4:18-19 5:7-11, Isaiah 13:21-22 34:11-15, John 3:19-21, mt.Hilchot Maachalot Assurot 3:1, Philippians 3:18-19, Psalms 6:7, Revelation 18:2, y.Shabbat 1:5
[7] LXX *and every raven, and the birds like it, and the hawk, and his like*
[8] Leviticus 11:17 - b.Bechorot [Tosefot] 8a, b.Chullin [Tosefot] 61b, b.Chullin 63a 64b, b.Niddah [Tosefot] 23a, Ein Yaakov Chullin:63a, Jastrow 1582a
[9] LXX *and the night-raven and the cormorant and the stork*
[10] Leviticus 11:18 - b.Bechorot [Tosefot] 8a, b.Chullin [Tosefot] 61b, b.Chullin 63a, Jastrow 135a 1467b, y.Shabbat 2:2
[11] LXX *and the red-bill, and the pelican, and swan*
[12] Leviticus 11:19 - b.Chullin 63a, Jastrow 295b
[13] LXX *and the heron, and the lapwing, and the like to it, and the hoopoe, and the bat*
[14] Leviticus 11:20 - 1 John 2:15-17, 2 Kings 17:28-41, 2 Timothy 4:10, Deuteronomy 14:19, Ecclesiastes.R 1:28 4:8, Esther.R 4:12, Jude 1:10 1:19, Leviticus 11:23 11:27, Matthew 6:24, Philippians 3:18-19, Philo De Specialibus Legibus IV 113, Psalms 17:14
Leviticus 11:20-23 - Cairo Damascus 12:11-15
[15] LXX *creep*
[16] Leviticus 11:21 - b.Avodah Zara [Rashi] 37b, b.Bava Kamma 38a, b.Bechorot [Rashi] 7ab, b.Chullin [Rashi] 65b, b.Chullin 65a 66a, Commandment #149, Jastrow 946b, Leviticus.R 20:5, Mas.Soferim 6:5, Midrash Tanchuma Acharei Mot 4, Midrash Tanchuma Vezot Habracha 4, Pesikta de R'Kahana 26.5, Philo Quis Rerum Divinarum Heres 239

אַךְ אֶת־זֶה תֹּאכְלוּ מִכֹּל שֶׁרֶץ הָעֹוף הַהֹלֵךְ עַל־אַרְבַּע אֲשֶׁר־לֹא אֲשֶׁר־לֹו כְרָעַיִם מִמַּעַל לְרַגְלָיו לְנַתֵּר בָּהֵן עַל־הָאָרֶץ	22[1] And of these of them you may eat: *the locust after its kinds, and the bald locust after its kinds, and the cricket after its kinds, and the grasshopper after its kinds*[2].
וְכֹל שֶׁרֶץ הָעֹוף אֲשֶׁר־לֹו אַרְבַּע רַגְלָיִם שֶׁקֶץ הוּא לָכֶם	23 But all winged swarming things[3] that have four feet, are a detestable thing to you.
וּלְאֵלֶּה תִּטַּמָּאוּ כָּל־הַנֹּגֵעַ בְּנִבְלָתָם יִטְמָא עַד־הָעָרֶב	24[4] And by these you shall become unclean; whoever touches their carcasses shall be unclean until evening.
וְכָל־הַנֹּשֵׂא מִנִּבְלָתָם יְכַבֵּס בְּגָדָיו וְטָמֵא עַד־הָעָרֶב	25[5] And whoever touches their carcass shall wash his clothes, and be unclean until the evening.
לְכָל־הַבְּהֵמָה אֲשֶׁר הִוא מַפְרֶסֶת פַּרְסָה וְשֶׁסַע אֵינֶנָּה שֹׁסַעַת וְגֵרָה אֵינֶנָּה מַעֲלָה טְמֵאִים הֵם לָכֶם כָּל־הַנֹּגֵעַ בָּהֶם יִטְמָא	26[6] Every beast that parts the hoof[7], *but is not cloven footed*[8], *nor*[9] chews the cud, is unclean unto you; everyone who touches them shall be unclean[10].
וְכֹל הֹולֵךְ עַל־כַּפָּיו בְּכָל־הַחַיָּה הַהֹלֶכֶת עַל־אַרְבַּע טְמֵאִים הֵם לָכֶם כָּל־הַנֹּגֵעַ בְּנִבְלָתָם יִטְמָא עַד־הָעָרֶב	27[11] And whatever goes on its *paws*[12], among all beasts that go on all fours, they are unclean to you; Whomever touches their carcass shall be unclean until the evening.

---

[1] Leviticus 11:22 - b.Bava Kamma 38a, b.Chullin 65ab 66a, Exodus 10:4-5, Hebrews 5:11 12:12-13, Isaiah 11:3, Jastrow 879a 907a 1499a, Lives of the Prophets 2:7, m.Berachot 6:3, m.Chullin 3:7, Mark 1:6, Matthew 3:4, Philo Legum Allegoriae II 105, Romans 14:1 15:1
Leviticus 11:22-29 - 2QpaleoLev

[2] LXX *the caterpillar and his like, and the attacus and his like, and the cantharus and his like, and the locust and his like*

[3] LXX *from among the birds*

[4] Leviticus 11:24 - 1 Corinthians 15:33, 1 John 1:7, 2 Corinthians 6:17, b.Chullin [Rashi] 20b, b.Chullin [Tosefot] 114b, b.Nedarim [Ran] 76b, b.Pesachim [Rashi] 20b, b.Zevachim [Rashi] 70a, Colossians 2:16-17 2:20, Ephesians 2:1-3 5:11, Hebrews 9:26, Isaiah 22:14, Leviticus 11:8 11:27-28 11:31 11:38-40 17:15-16, mt.Hilchot Shaar Avot Hatuman 3:15
Leviticus 11:24-40 - MasLevb

[5] Leviticus 11:25 - 1 John 1:7, 1 Peter 3:21, 4QMMT B 22-23, Acts 22:16, Exodus 19:10 19:14, Hebrews 9:10 10:22, John 13:8, Leviticus 11:28 11:40 14:8 14:47 15:5 15:7-11 15:13 16:28, mt.Hilchot Shaar Avot Hatuman 3:15, Numbers 19:8 19:10 19:19 19:21-22 7:24, Psalms 51:3 51:8, Revelation 7:14, Zechariah 13:1

[6] Leviticus 11:26 - b.Chullin [Rashi] 72b, b.Chullin [Tosefot] 99b, b.Zevachim [Rashi] 70a, Jastrow 1608a, mt.Hilchot Shaar Avot Hatuman 3:15

[7] 2QpaleoLev adds *and cleaves the foot*; SP *cleaves not the foot*

[8] LXX *and makes claws*

[9] LXX *and does not*

[10] LXX adds *until evening*

[11] Leviticus 11:27 - b.Bechorot [Tosefot] 6a, b.Chullin [Rashi] 124b, b.Chullin 70b, Guide for the Perplexed 3:47, Jastrow 360b 657a, Leviticus 11:20 11:23, y.Terumot 8:1
Leviticus 11:27-32 - 11QpaleoLeva

[12] 11QpaleoLeva *belly*

וְהַנֹּשֵׂא אֶת־נִבְלָתָם יְכַבֵּס בְּגָדָיו   28[1]   And he who bears their carcass shall
וְטָמֵא עַד־הָעֶרֶב טְמֵאִים הֵמָּה לָכֶם   wash his clothes, and be unclean until
                                                          the evening; they are unclean to you.

וְזֶה לָכֶם הַטָּמֵא בַּשֶּׁרֶץ הַשֹּׁרֵץ עַל־   29[2]   And these are they that are unclean to
הָאָרֶץ הַחֹלֶד וְהָעַכְבָּר וְהַצָּב לְמִינֵהוּ   you among the swarming things[3] that
                                                          swarm on the earth: the weasel, and the
                                                          mouse, and the *great lizard after its
                                                          kinds*[4],

וְהָאֲנָקָה וְהַכֹּחַ וְהַלְּטָאָה וְהַחֹמֶט   30[5]   *And the gecko, and the land crocodile,
וְהַתִּנְשָׁמֶת   and the lizard, and the sand lizard, and
                                                          the chameleon*[6].

אֵלֶּה הַטְּמֵאִים לָכֶם בְּכָל־הַשָּׁרֶץ כָּל־   31[7]   These are they that are unclean to you
הַנֹּגֵעַ בָּהֶם בְּמֹתָם יִטְמָא עַד־הָעֶרֶב   *among all that swarm; whoever
                                                          touches them, when they are dead*[8],
                                                          shall be unclean until the evening.

וְכֹל אֲשֶׁר־יִפֹּל־עָלָיו מֵהֶם בְּמֹתָם   32[9]   And on whatever any of them fall,

---

[1] Leviticus 11:28 - b.Chullin [Rashi] 124b, Leviticus 11:24-11:25, mt.Hilchot Shaar Avot Hatuman 1:1, y.Sheviit 7:1

[2] Leviticus 11:29 - 2 Timothy 3:2-5, b.Bava Batra [Rashbam] 134a, b.Bava Kamma [Tosefot] 80b, b.Berachot [Tosefot] 12b, b.Chullin 67b 122b 126b 116a, b.Kereitot [Rashi] 21b, b.Kereitot 4b 22a, b.Makkot [Rashi] 13a, b.Menachot [Tosefot] 51b 14a, b.Menachot 29b, b.Moed Katan 13a, b.Niddah [Rashi] 43b, b.Shabbat [Rashi] 107b, b.Sheviit [Rashi] 14b, b.Sheviit 11b, Colossians 3:5, Ein Yaakov Meilah:17ab, Ein Yaakov Menachot 29a, Ephesians 4:14, Exodus.R 15:28, Genesis.R 60:8, Guide for the Perplexed 3:47, Haggai 2:6, Hebrews 13:5, Isaiah 18:17, Jastrow 1257a, Jastrow 1633b, John 6:26 7:6, Leviticus 11:20-21 11:41-42, Leviticus.R 1:8, Luke 12:15 16:14, m.Bikkurim 2:7, m.Chullin 9:2, m.Kelim 1:1 2:6 19:6, m.Machshirin 6:5, m.Meilah 4:3, m.Nedarim 2:1, m.Oholot 1:9 13:5 3:7 4:1 5:1 9:1 10:7, m.Parah 5:2 9:2, m.Shabbat 13:2, m.Tamid 5:5, Mekilta de R'Ishmael Pisha 2:5, Midrash Tanchuma Shemini 8, mt.Hilchot Beit Habechirah 7:14, mt.Hilchot Biat haMikdash 1:3, mt.Hilchot Chametz uMatzah 18:18, mt.Hilchot Sanhedrin vHainshin Hameurim Lahem 19:4, mt.Hilchot Shaar Avot Hatuman 4:1 14:3, Numbers.R 19:3, Pesikta de R'Kahana 5.15, Pesikta Rabbati 15:2, Philippians 3:19, Psalms 10:4 17:13-14, z.BereshitA 123
Leviticus 11:29-30 - Commandment #561, mt.Hilchot Maachalot Assurot 2:7
Leviticus 11:29-35 - Ein Yaakov Eruvin

[3] LXX *reptiles*

[4] LXX *lizard*

[5] Leviticus 11:30 - b.Bava Batra [Rashi] 4a, b.Chullin 63a 122b, b.Meilah 14ab, b.Moed Katan 13a, b.Shabbat [Tosefot] 54b, b.Sheviit 11b, Ein Yaakov Eruvin, Jastrow 135a, m.Kelim 1:1 19:6, m.Kelim 2:6, m.Machshirin 6:5, m.Meilah 4:3, m.Negaim 14:2, m.Oholot 3:7 4:1 5:1 9:1 10:7, m.Shabbat 13:2, m.Tamid 5:5, mt.Hilchot Beit Habechirah 7:14, mt.Hilchot Biat haMikdash 1:3, mt.Hilchot Chametz uMatzah 18:18 20:11, mt.Hilchot Shaar Avot Hatuman 4:1

[6] LXX *the ferret, and the chameleon, and the evet, and the newt, and the mole*

[7] Leviticus 11:31 - b.Avodah Zara [Tosefot] 40a, b.Bechorot 6b, b.Chagigah 11a, b.Chullin [Rashi] 116a, b.Chullin [Tosefot] 64a 99b 118b, b.Chullin 74a 11b 120a 122b 126b 128b, b.Kereitot [Rashi] 4b, b.Meilah 14a, b.Moed Katan 13a, b.Nazir 52a, b.Niddah 56a, b.Shabbat 107a, Leviticus 11:8 11:24-11:25, m.Kelim 2:6, m.Negaim 14:2, Midrash Psalms 15:7, mt.Hilchot Shaar Avot Hatuman 4:2

[8] LXX *of all the reptiles which are on the earth; everyone who touches their carcasses*

[9] Leviticus 11:32 - 4Q266 1 ii 10-13, b.Bava Batra [Rashbam] 66a, b.Bava Kamma 25b, b.Bechorot [Rashi] 38a, b.Chagigah [Rashi] 26b, b.Chullin [Rashi] 25a, b.Chullin 74a, b.Megillah [Rashi] 26b, b.Menachot [Rashi] 29a, b.Menachot [Tosefot] 31a 39b 96b, b.Moed Katan 13a, b.Nazir 52a, b.Niddah 56a, b.Sanhedrin [Tosefot] 83b, b.Shabbat 16a 63b 64a 123b, b.Sotah [Rashi] 29b, b.Yevamot 43a 75a, b.Yoma [Rashi] 21b, b.Zevachim [Tosefot] 14a, b.Zevachim 94a, Jastrow 577a 907a 1361a 1380b 1620b, Leviticus 6:28 15:12, m.Kelim 27:1, mt.Hilchot Tumat Meit 6:2, mt.Hilchot Keilim 1:1 4:4, mt.Hilchot Shaar Avot Hatuman 10:1, Titus 2:14 3:5, y.Pesachim 6:1

יִטְמָא מִכָּל־כְּלִי־עֵץ אוֹ בֶגֶד אוֹ־עוֹר
אוֹ שָׂק כָּל־כְּלִי אֲשֶׁר־יֵעָשֶׂה מְלָאכָה
בָּהֶם בַּמַּיִם יוּבָא וְטָמֵא עַד־הָעֶרֶב
וְטָהֵר

when they are dead, it shall be unclean; whether it is any vessel of wood, or raiment, or skin, or sack, whatever vessel it is, with which any work is done, it must be put in water, and it shall be unclean until the evening; then shall it be clean.

וְכָל־כְּלִי־חֶרֶשׂ אֲשֶׁר־יִפֹּל מֵהֶם אֶל־
תּוֹכוֹ כֹּל אֲשֶׁר בְּתוֹכוֹ יִטְמָא וְאֹתוֹ
תִשְׁבֹּרוּ

33[1] And every earthen vessel into which any of them fall, whatever is in it shall be unclean, and you shall break it.

מִכָּל־הָאֹכֶל אֲשֶׁר יֵאָכֵל אֲשֶׁר יָבוֹא
עָלָיו מַיִם יִטְמָא וְכָל־מַשְׁקֶה אֲשֶׁר
יִשָּׁתֶה בְּכָל־כְּלִי יִטְמָא

34[2] All edible food in it, upon which water comes [from such a vessel], shall be unclean; and all potable drink in every such vessel shall [likewise] be unclean.

וְכֹל אֲשֶׁר־יִפֹּל מִנִּבְלָתָם עָלָיו יִטְמָא
תַּנּוּר וְכִירַיִם יֻתָּץ טְמֵאִים הֵם
וּטְמֵאִים יִהְיוּ לָכֶם

35[3] And everything upon which any part of their carcass falls shall be unclean; whether oven, or *range*[4] for pots; it shall be broken in pieces; they are unclean, and shall be unclean to you.

אַךְ מַעְיָן וּבוֹר מִקְוֵה־מַיִם יִהְיֶה טָהוֹר
וְנֹגֵעַ בְּנִבְלָתָם יִטְמָא

36[5] Nevertheless, *a fountain or a cistern in which is a gathering of water*[6] shall be clean; but he who touches their carcass shall be unclean.

---

[1] Leviticus 11:33 - 2 Corinthians 5:1-5:8, Avot de R'Natan 12, b.Chullin [Rashi] 3a 118a, b.Chullin 24b 25a 33b, b.Eruvin [Rashi] 42a, b.Moed Katan 13a, b.Niddah [Rashi] 6a 14a, b.Niddah 42b, b.Pesachim [Rashi] 14a 25ba, b.Pesachim 16a 18a 25ab, b.Shabbat [Rashi] 16a 138b, b.Sotah [Rashi] 29ab, b.Sotah 27b, b.Zevachim [Rashi] 105b, b.Zevachim 3a, Jeremiah 24:38, Leviticus 6:28 11:35 14:45 15:12, m.Sotah 5:2, mt.Hilchot Keilim 1:1 1:8 6:1 13:1, mt.Hilchot Mikvaot 1:3, mt.Hilchot Shaar Avot Hatuman 11:2, Philippians 3:21, t.Sotah 5:13, y.Sotah 5:2

[2] Leviticus 11:34 - b.Avodah Zara [Rashi] 37b, b.Bava Batra [Rashbam] 80a 97a, b.Bava Kamma [Rashi] 76a, b.Bechorot 9b, b.Chullin [Rashi] 3a 16a 25a 34a 35b 36a 81b 128a, b.Chullin [Tosefot] 36b 85a, b.Chullin 13a 129ab, b.Meilah [Tosefot] 5a, b.Menachot 11b, b.Moed Katan 13a, b.Nedarim [Rashi] 19a, b.Niddah [Rashi] 19b, b.Pesachim [Rashbam] 18b, b.Pesachim [Rashi] 14a 33b, b.Pesachim 16a 18a, b.Rosh Hashanah [Rashi] 13a, b.Shabbat 14b 138b, b.Sheviit [Rashi] 11b, Commandment #562, Jastrow 677a 858a, m.Avodah Zarah 2:7, m.Bikkurim 2:7, m.Chullin 2:5 9:7, m.Oholot 2:5 9:1, m.Parah 11:6, m.Uktzin 3:1, mt.Hilchot Shaar Avot Hatuman 7:1, mt.Hilchot Tumat Ochalin 1:2 2:8 4:1, mt.Hilcnot Shofar Sukkah vLulav 8:2, Proverbs 15:8 21:4 21:27 4:8, Titus 1:15, y.Chagigah 3:2, y.Eruvin 1:7, y.Gittin 2:3, y.Terumot 11:2
Leviticus 11:34-38 - 4QMMT B 55-58

[3] Leviticus 11:35 - 2 Corinthians 5:1-5:7, Avot de R'Natan 12, b.Chullin [Rashi] 28b 72b 127b, b.Chullin [Tosefot] 24b, b.Chullin 118a, b.Pesachim [Rashi] 14a, b.Shabbat 125a, b.Sotah [Rashi] 29b, b.Zevachim [Tosefot] 96a, Gates of Repentance 1.015, Jastrow 944a, Leviticus 6:28 11:33 15:12, mt.Hilchot Keilim 1:13, y.Pesachim 3:2, y.Sheviit 7:1

[4] LXX *stand*

[5] Leviticus 11:36 - b.Bava Batra [Rashbam] 66a, b.Bava Batra [Tosefot] 66b, b.Chagigah [Rashi] 19a, b.Chagigah [Tosefot] 11a, b.Chullin 74a 84a 118a, b.Nazir 64a, b.Pesachim [Rashi] 14b, b.Pesachim 16a, b.Shabbat [Rashi] 14a, b.Zevachim 25b, John 4:14, mt.Hilchot Mikvaot 4:1, mt.Hilchot Shaar Avot Hatuman 6:16, Song of Songs.R 1:18, y.Avodah Zarah 5:4, y.Chagigah 1:7, Zechariah 13:1

[6] LXX *fountains of water, or a pool, or confluence of water*

87   Rabbinic Reference Bible

וְכִי יִפֹּל מִנִּבְלָתָם עַל־כָּל־זֶרַע זֵרוּעַ אֲשֶׁר יִזָּרֵעַ טָהוֹר הוּא	37[1]	And if one of their carcasses falls on any sowing seed to be sown, it is clean.
וְכִי יֻתַּן־מַיִם עַל־זֶרַע וְנָפַל מִנִּבְלָתָם עָלָיו טָמֵא הוּא לָכֶם	38[2]	But if water is put on the seed, and one of their carcasses falls upon it, it is unclean to you.
וְכִי יָמוּת מִן־הַבְּהֵמָה אֲשֶׁר־הִיא לָכֶם לְאָכְלָה הַנֹּגֵעַ בְּנִבְלָתָהּ יִטְמָא עַד־הָעָרֶב	39[3]	And if any *beast*[4], of which you may eat, dies, he who touches its carcass shall be unclean until the evening.
וְהָאֹכֵל מִנִּבְלָתָהּ יְכַבֵּס בְּגָדָיו וְטָמֵא עַד־הָעָרֶב וְהַנֹּשֵׂא אֶת־נִבְלָתָהּ יְכַבֵּס בְּגָדָיו וְטָמֵא עַד־הָעָרֶב	40[5]	And he who eats of the carcass shall wash his clothes, and be unclean until the evening; also, he who bears the carcass shall wash his clothes, and be unclean until the evening.
וְכָל־הַשֶּׁרֶץ הַשֹּׁרֵץ עַל־הָאָרֶץ שֶׁקֶץ הוּא לֹא יֵאָכֵל	41[6]	And every *swarming thing*[7] that swarms on the earth is a detestable thing; it shall not be eaten.
כֹּל הוֹלֵךְ עַל־גָּחוֹן[8] וְכֹל הוֹלֵךְ עַל־אַרְבַּע עַד כָּל־מַרְבֵּה רַגְלַיִם לְכָל־	42[9]	*Whatever*[1] goes on the belly, and whatever goes upon all fours, or

---

[1] Leviticus 11:37 - 1 Corinthians 15:37, 1 John 3:9 5:18, 1 Peter 1:23, b.Chullin [Rashi] 74a 118a, b.Chullin [Tosefot] 126b, b.Chullin 114b 118b 119ab 127b, b.Kereitot 21a, b.Menachot 70b, b.Nedarim [Ran] 76a, b.Niddah 51a, b.Shabbat 95b, b.Zevachim 105a, y.Kilayim 7:6 8:1, y.Maasrot 5:1, y.Peah 1:4, y.Shabbat 10:6

[2] Leviticus 11:38 - b.Arachin 18b, b.Bava Batra [Rashbam] 66b 97a, b.Bava Kamma [Tosefot] 98a, b.Bava Metzia 22ab, b.Bechorot [Rashi] 10a, b.Chullin [Rashi] 36b 114b 118b, b.Chullin 13a 16a 31b 36a 118a 121a, b.Kiddushin 59b, b.Niddah [Tosefot] 15a, b.Pesachim [Rashi] 19a, b.Pesachim [Tosefot] 16a, b.Pesachim 14a 18b, b.Succah [Rashi] 35b, b.Zevachim [Tosefot] 40a, Jastrow 677a 944b 1482b, m.Machshirin 1:3, m.Oholot 2:5 9:1, m.Parah 11:6, m.Uktzin 3:1, mt.Hilchot Tumat Ochalin 12:1 13:2, Song of Songs.R 1:18

[3] Leviticus 11:39 - 4QMMT B 22-23, Avot de R'Natan 34, b.Chullin 37a 70b 74a 77b 85b 114b 118a 121b 124b 125a 126b 28b [Rashi] 9a 13b 68a,, b.Meilah [Rashi] 16a, b.Nazir 5a, b.Niddah 56a [Rashi] 55b, b.Shabbat 136a, b.Zevachim 69b [Rashi] 50b, Commandment #563, Jastrow 870a, Leviticus 11:24 11:28 11:31 11:40 15:5 15:7, m.Chullin 4:4 9:5, m.Meilah 4:3, m.Nazir 6:6, m.Oholot 1:4, m.Zevachim 7:3 7:6, Midrash Tanchuma Emor 15, mt.Hilchot Shemitah vYovel 4:2, Numbers 19:11 19:16

[4] LXX *cattle*

[5] Leviticus 11:40 - 1 Corinthians 6:11 10:21, 1 John 1:7, b.Bava Batra [Rashi] 9b, b.Chullin [Rashi] 13b 25ab 71b, b.Chullin 71a 124b 125a, b.Eruvin [Rashi] 28a, b.Nazir 5a, b.Niddah [Rashi] 55b, b.Niddah 42b, Deuteronomy 14:21, Exodus 22:31, Ezekiel 4:14 12:25 20:31, Isaiah 1:16, Leviticus 11:25 11:28 14:8-9 15:5-10 15:27 16:26 16:28 17:15-16 22:8, m.Chullin 9:5, m.Zevachim 7:6, mt.Hilchot Tumat Meit 1:2, Numbers 19:7-8 19:19, Zechariah 13:1

[6] Leviticus 11:41 - b.Arachin 28a, b.Bava Kamma [Tosefot] 82b, b.Chullin [Rashi] 58a, b.Chullin 64a 67ab 116a, b.Makkot 16b, b.Nazir 5a, b.Pesachim 23a, Commandment #150 #151, Leviticus 11:20 11:23 11:29, m.Makkot 3:2, mt.Hilchot Maachalot Assurot 2:6, mt.Hilchot Sanhedrin vHainshin Hameurim Lahem 19:4, Siman 46:34, y.Terumot 8:1

[7] LXX *reptile*

[8] Traditional Enlarged ו in עַל־גָּחוֹן, the ו in גחון is the middle letter of the Torah per b.Kiddushin 30a

[9] Leviticus 11:42 - 2 Corinthians 11:3 11:13, b.Avodah Zara 68b, b.Beitzah 6b, b.Chullin 67b, b.Eruvin 28a, b.Kiddushin 30a, b.Meilah [Rashi] 16b, b.Nazir 5a, b.Sanhedrin [Tosefot] 14a, b.Yevamot 114a, Commandment #151, Ein Yaakov Kiddushin 30a, Genesis 3:14-15, Isaiah 17:25, Jastrow 371b 879a 1589b, John 8:44, Kuzari 3.31, Mas.Soferim 9:2, Matthew 3:7 23:23, Micah 7:17, mt.Hilchot Maachalot

הַשֶּׁרֶץ הַשֹּׁרֵץ עַל־הָאָרֶץ לֹא תֹאכְלוּם
כִּי־שֶׁקֶץ הֵם

אַל־תְּשַׁקְּצוּ אֶת־נַפְשֹׁתֵיכֶם בְּכָל־
הַשֶּׁרֶץ הַשֹּׁרֵץ וְלֹא תִטַּמְּאוּ בָּהֶם
וְנִטְמֵתֶם בָּם

כִּי אֲנִי יְהוָה אֱלֹהֵיכֶם וְהִתְקַדִּשְׁתֶּם
וִהְיִיתֶם קְדֹשִׁים כִּי קָדוֹשׁ אָנִי וְלֹא
תְטַמְּאוּ אֶת־נַפְשֹׁתֵיכֶם בְּכָל־הַשֶּׁרֶץ
הָרֹמֵשׂ עַל־הָאָרֶץ

כִּי אֲנִי יְהוָה הַמַּעֲלֶה אֶתְכֶם מֵאֶרֶץ
מִצְרַיִם לִהְיֹת לָכֶם לֵאלֹהִים וִהְיִיתֶם
קְדֹשִׁים כִּי קָדוֹשׁ אָנִי

זֹאת תּוֹרַת הַבְּהֵמָה וְהָעוֹף וְכֹל נֶפֶשׁ
הַחַיָּה הָרֹמֶשֶׂת בַּמָּיִם וּלְכָל־נֶפֶשׁ

whatever has many feet, even all *swarming things*[2] that swarm on the earth, you shall not eat them; for they are a detestable thing.

43[3] You shall not *make yourselves detestable*[4] with any *swarming thing*[5] that swarms, nor shall you make yourselves unclean with them, that you should be defiled by them.

44[6] For I am the LORD your God; therefore, sanctify yourselves *and be holy; for I am holy*[7]; nor shall you defile yourselves with any manner of swarming thing that moves on the earth.

45[8] For I am the LORD who brought you up out of the land of the Egyptians, to be your God; you shall, therefore, be holy, for I am holy.

46[9] This is the law of the beast, and of the fowl, and of every living creature that

---

Assurot 2:14, Philo De Migratione Abrahami 64, Philo Legum Allegoriae III 139, Titus 1:12, y.Orlah 3:1, y.Pesachim 2:1, z.BereshitA 250, z.Vayechi 35

[1] LXX *And every animal*

[2] LXX *reptiles*

[3] Leviticus 11:43 - b.Arachin [Rashi] 28a, b.Avodah Zara [Tosefot] 37b 38a, b.Avodah Zara 68b, b.Chullin [Rashi] 35a, b.Chullin [Tosefot] 34b 96b, b.Makkot [Rashi] 16b, b.Nazir 5a 64a, b.Pesachim [Rashi] 24a, b.Shabbat 84ab, b.Yoma 39a 80b, Commandment #153, Ein Yaakov Yoma:39a, Gates of Repentance 3.093, Jastrow 532a 869b 1642a, Leviticus 11:41-42 20:25, Mesillat Yesharim 11 Nekiyut-in-Treif, Midrash Tanchuma Shemini 6, mt.Hilchot Maachalot Assurot 2:12, mt.Hilchot Sanhedrin vHainshin Hameurim Lahem 19:4, Numbers.R 10:1, Philo De Migratione Abrahami 65, Shepherd Vision III 9:7, Siman 150:5 46:45, Song of Songs.R 6:4, z.Bereshit 54a, z.Mishpatim 125b, z.Acharei Mot 341, z.BereshitB 327, z.Kedoshim 5 9, z.Mishpatim 567, z.Shmini 112

[4] LXX *defile your souls*

[5] LXX *reptiles*

[6] Leviticus 11:44 - 1 Peter 1:15-16 2:9, 1 Samuel 6:20, 1 Thessalonians 4:7, Amos 3:3, b.Arachin [Rashi] 28a, b.Chullin [Tosefot] 2b 105a, b.Makkot 16b, b.Nazir 5a, b.Pesachim [Rashi] 24a, b.Sheviit 18b, b.Yevamot 20b, b.Yoma 39a 80a, Commandment #152, Deuteronomy 14:2, Ein Yaakov Shevuot:18b, Ein Yaakov Yoma:39a, Exodus 6:7 19:6 20:2 23:25, Exodus.R 43:5, Gates of Repentance 3.017, Guide for the Perplexed 3:47, Isaiah 6:3-5 19:3 3:15, Jastrow 1319a, Leviticus 10:3 11:43 19:2 20:7 20:26 21:8, Matthew 5:48, Midrash Tanchuma Kedoshim 1, Midrash Tanchuma Shemini 6, mt.Hilchot Berachot 6:3, mt.Hilchot Maachalot Assurot 17:32, mt.Hilchot Sanhedrin vHainshin Hameurim Lahem 19:4, mt.Hilchot Tumat Ochalin 16:12, Psalms 99:5 99:9, Revelation 22:11, Tanya Igeret Hateshuvah §12, z.Acharei Mot 78b 363, z.Balak 190b, z.Bereshit 54a, z.Mishpatim 125b 567, z.Shemot 11b 184, z.Vayikra 24b, z.Vayishlach 167b 38, z.BereshitB 328, z.Kedoshim 15, z.Pekudei 881, z.Pinchas 638, z.Shmini 110 117, z.Vayetze 182

[7] LXX *because I the LORD your God am holy*

[8] Leviticus 11:45 - 1 Peter 1:16, 1 Thessalonians 4:7, b.Bava Metzia 61b, Exodus 6:7 20:2, Ein Yaakov Bava Metzia 61b, b.Eruvin 19a, Hosea 11:1, Leviticus 11:44 1:38, Psalms 105:43-45, z.Acharei Mot 78b

[9] Leviticus 11:46 - b.Avodah Zara [Tosefot] 38a, b.Chullin [Rashi] 4a 20b 66a, b.Chullin 27b, b.Pesachim 49b, b.Zevachim [Rashi] 51a, b.Zevachim [Tosefot] 50b, b.Zevachim 69b, Commandment #153, Ein Yaakov Pesachim:49b, Ezekiel 19:12, Leviticus 7:37 14:54 15:32, Leviticus.R 14:1, Midrash Psalms 139:5, Midrash Tanchuma Chukkat 6

הַשֹּׁרֶצֶת עַל־הָאָרֶץ

לְהַבְדִּיל בֵּין הַטָּמֵא וּבֵין הַטָּהֹר וּבֵין הַחַיָּה הַנֶּאֱכֶלֶת וּבֵין הַחַיָּה אֲשֶׁר לֹא תֵאָכֵל

47[2]

moves in the waters, and of every [1]creature that swarms on the earth; to make a difference between the unclean and the clean, and between *the living thing*[3] that may be eaten and the living thing that may not be eaten.

---

[1] LXX adds *living*

[2] Leviticus 11:47 - b.Chullin [Rashi] 42b, b.Chullin 42a, b.Sheviit 18b, Ein Yaakov Shevuot:18b, Ezekiel 20:23, Leviticus 10:10, Malachi 3:18, Mesillat Yesharim 11:Nekiyut-in-Treif, Midrash Psalms 139:5, mt.Hilchot Maachalot Assurot 1:1, Romans 14:2-3 14:13-23, Saadia Opinions 10:15, z.Shmini 98

[3] LXX *those that bring forth alive*

Tazria

Tazria[1] – Chapter 12[2]

וַיְדַבֵּר יְהוָה אֶל־מֹשֶׁה לֵּאמֹר

1[3] And the LORD spoke to Moses, saying:

דַּבֵּר אֶל־בְּנֵי יִשְׂרָאֵל לֵאמֹר אִשָּׁה כִּי תַזְרִיעַ וְיָלְדָה זָכָר וְטָמְאָה שִׁבְעַת יָמִים כִּימֵי נִדַּת דְּוֹתָהּ תִּטְמָא

2[4] Speak to the children of Israel, saying: If a woman delivers, and bears a male child, she shall be unclean seven days; *as in the days of the impurity of her sickness shall she be unclean*[5].

---

[1] Tazria aliyot: [1] Leviticus 12:1–13:5, [2] Leviticus 13:6–17, [3] Leviticus 13:18–23, [4] Leviticus 13:24–28, [5] Leviticus 13:29–39, [6] Leviticus 13:40–54, [7] Leviticus 13:55–59
Tazria and Metzora are combined when there are only 52 available reading days in the year.

[2] Ein Yaakov Berachot:4a, Midrash Proverbs 10, mt.Hilchot Parah Adumah 11:3, mt.Hilchot Issurei Biah 11:15

[3] Leviticus 12:1 - b.Nazir [Rashi] 64b, Ein Yaakov Shevuot:18b, Leviticus.R 15:5, Sifre.z Numbers Naso 5:2, t.Bikkurim 2:6, t.Eduyot 2:4
Leviticus 12:1-8 - m.Eduyot 5:1 5:4, m.Pesachim 9:4, m.Sotah 1:5, mt.Hilchot Beit Habechirah 7:15
Leviticus 12:1-8 - Josephus Antiquities 4.12.5
Leviticus 12:1-13:5 - Minchah [Shabbat Monday Thursday Torah reading - Parashah Tazria]
Leviticus 12:1-13:59 - mt.Hilchot Mamrim 4:2

[4] Leviticus 12:2 - Avot de R'Natan 25, b.Bava Batra 116a, b.Bava Kamma [Rashi] 38b, b.Berachot 60a, b.Chagigah 18b, b.Chullin [Tosefot] 38a, b.Kereitot 7b, b.Niddah [Rashi] 21a 26a 30b, b.Niddah [Tosefot] 18a, b.Niddah 24b 27b 31a 35b 37b 40a, b.Pesachim [Rashi] 84ab, b.Sanhedrin [Tosefot] 86a, b.Shabbat 135a, b.Sheviit 18b, b.Yevamot 74b, b.Yoma [Rashi] 6a, Genesis 1:28 3:16, Job 14:4 15:14 1:4, Leviticus 15:19 18:19, Leviticus.R 14:1 27:10, Luke 2:22, m.Niddah 4:3 4:5, m.Chullin 4:7, m.Keritot 2:1, Midrash Psalms 8:2 139:5, Midrash Tanchuma Bechukkotai 4, Midrash Tanchuma Tazria 1-3, mt.Hilchot Issurei Biah 4:2 4:5 10:5, mt.Hilchot Metamei Mishkav Umoshav 1:1, mt.Hilchot Tumat Tzaraat 6:1, Numbers.R 4:20, Psalms 51:6, Romans 5:12-19, Sifre Devarim Reeh 78, Siman 143:1, y.Pesachim 2:1, z.Tazria 42ab 43b 1 9-11 23 26 37 60
Leviticus 12:2-3 - Midrash Tanchuma Emor 15
Leviticus 12:2-5 - 4Q265 7 ii 11-17, Commandment #564, Jubilees 3:8, mt.Hilchot Metamei Mishkav Umoshav 4:6
Leviticus 12:2-6 - mt.Hilchot Mechusrei Kapparah 1:5

[5] LXX *according to the days of separation for her monthly courses*

וּבַיּוֹם הַשְּׁמִינִ֖י יִמּ֖וֹל בְּשַׂ֥ר עָרְלָתֽוֹ

3[1] And in the eighth day *the flesh of his foreskin shall be circumcised*[2].

וּשְׁלֹשִׁ֥ים יוֹם֙ וּשְׁלֹ֣שֶׁת יָמִ֔ים תֵּשֵׁ֖ב בִּדְמֵ֣י טָהֳרָ֑ה בְּכָל־קֹ֣דֶשׁ לֹֽא־תִגָּ֗ע וְאֶל־הַמִּקְדָּשׁ֙ לֹ֣א תָבֹ֔א עַד־מְלֹ֖את יְמֵ֥י טָהֳרָֽהּ

4[3] *And she shall continue in the blood of purification thirty-three days*[4]; she shall touch no hallowed thing, nor come into the sanctuary, until the days of her purification are fulfilled.

וְאִם־נְקֵבָ֣ה תֵלֵ֔ד וְטָמְאָ֥ה שְׁבֻעַ֖יִם כְּנִדָּתָ֑הּ וְשִׁשִּׁ֥ים יוֹם֙ וְשֵׁ֣שֶׁת יָמִ֔ים תֵּשֵׁ֖ב עַל־דְּמֵ֥י טָהֳרָֽה

5[5] But if she bears a female child, she shall be unclean *two weeks*[6], *as in her impurity*[7]; and she shall continue in the blood of purification for sixty-six days.

וּבִמְלֹ֣את ׀ יְמֵ֣י טָהֳרָ֗הּ לְבֵן֮ א֣וֹ לְבַת֒ תָּבִ֞יא כֶּ֤בֶשׂ בֶּן־שְׁנָתוֹ֙ לְעֹלָ֔ה וּבֶן־יוֹנָ֥ה אֽוֹ־תֹ֖ר לְחַטָּ֑את אֶל־פֶּ֥תַח אֹֽהֶל־מוֹעֵ֖ד אֶל־הַכֹּהֵֽן

6[8] And when the days of her purification are fulfilled, for a son, or for a daughter, she shall bring a lamb of the first year for a [9]burnt offering, and a young pigeon or a turtle dove, for a sin offering, to the door of the tent of

---

[1] Leviticus 12:3 - b.Arachin 8b, b.Bava Batra 116a, b.Chullin [Rashi] 84b, b.Kereitot [Rashi] 2a, b.Kiddushin 29a, b.Megillah 20a, b.Nedarim 31b-32a [Rashi] 31b, b.Niddah 24b, b.Pesachim [Rashi] 84a, b.Sanhedrin 59b, b.Shabbat 132ab 134b 137b [Rashi] 135b, b.Yevamot 72b, b.Yoma 28b 34b, Colossians 2:11, Commandment #17, Deuteronomy 6:6, Ecclesiastes.R 3:21 11:2, Galatians 3:17 5:3, Genesis 17:11-12, Genesis.R 11:6 46:12, Guide for the Perplexed 3:49, John 7:22-23, Leviticus.R 14:7 27:1 27:10, Luke 1:59 2:21, m.Demai 1:3, m.Megillah 2:4, m.Nedarim 3:11, m.Niddah 24b, Midrash Tanchuma Chayyei Sarah 7, Midrash Tanchuma Emor 6 12, Midrash Tanchuma Lech Lecha 16, Midrash Tanchuma Massei 1, Midrash Tanchuma Tazria 5, Midrash Tanchuma Vayera 6, mt.Hilchot Issurei Biah 4:5, mt.Hilchot Melachim uMichamoteihem 9:1, mt.Hilchot Milah 1:1 1:7-8, Pesikta de R'Kahana 9.1 9.10 28.4, Pesikta Rabbati 48:4 52:4, Philippians 3:5, Romans 3:19 4:11-12, Sefer Yetzirah 1:3, y.Kiddushin 1:7, y.Megillah 2:5, y.Nedarim 3:9, y.Pesachim 2:1, y.Rosh Hashanah 1:1, y.Shabbat 2:1, y.Yevamot 8:1, z.Pinchas 830, z.Tazria 31
[2] LXX *she shall circumcise the flesh of his foreskin*
[3] Leviticus 12:4 - b.Chullin [Tosefot] 33b 81a, b.Kereitot [Rashi] 2ab, b.Kereitot 10a, b.Makkot [Tosefot] 15a, b.Makkot 14b, b.Niddah [Rashi] 29b 71b, b.Niddah [Tosefot] 37a, b.Niddah 38b, b.Pesachim [Tosefot] 92a, b.Sheviit [Tosefot] 16b, b.Sheviit 6a 7a 14b, b.Yevamot 74b 75a, b.Zevachim [Tosefot] 14a 114b, b.Zevachim 32b 33b 34a, Guide for the Perplexed 3:47, Haggai 2:13, Leviticus 15:25-28, Luke 2:22-23, m.Niddah 1:7 4:3 3:2 10:6, mt.Hilchot Tumat Tzaraat 7:3, mt.Hilchot Biat haMikdash 3:11, mt.Hilchot Issurei Biah 4:5, mt.Hilchot Pesulei haMikdashim 18:13, mt.Hilchot Tumat Ochalin 16:8, Sifre.z Numbers Naso 5:2, y.Pesachim 9:4, y.Shabbat 16:3, z.Tazria 43b 44a 26 29
[4] LXX *And for thirty-three days she shall continue in her unclean blood*
[5] Leviticus 12:5 - 1 Timothy 2:14-15, b.Avodah Zara [Rashi] 23b, b.Bava Batra [Rashbam] 116a, b.Bechorot 47b, b.Chullin [Rashi] 51b, b.Kereitot 7b 10ab, b.Niddah [Tosefot] 35b 37a, b.Niddah 30b 36b 38b 40a, b.Sanhedrin 4a, b.Zevachim 38a, Genesis 3:13, Leviticus 12:2 12:4, m.Keritot 1:6, m.Niddah 4:6, mt.Hilchot Issurei Biah 4:2 4:5, mt.Hilchot Metamei Mishkav Umoshav 1:1, mt.Hilchot Mechusrei Kapparah 1:1, z.Tazria 25 28 30
[6] LXX *twice seven days*
[7] LXX *according to the time of her monthly courses*
[8] Leviticus 12:6 - 1 Peter 1:18-1:19, 2 Corinthians 5:21, b.Arachin [Rashi] 21a, b.Arachin 18b, b.Bava Kamma [Tosefot] 65b, b.Bechorot 27b, b.Kereitot 8a 28a, b.Menachot [Rashi] 48b, b.Menachot 4b, b.Nazir [Rashi] 29a, b.Nazir 64b, b.Niddah 40a 47b, b.Temurah [Rashi] 34a, b.Zevachim [Rashi] 25b 80a, Commandment #501, Genesis.R 46:11 85:12, Hebrews 7:26, John 1:29, Leviticus 1:10-1:13 5:6-10 12:2 14:22 15:14 15:29, Leviticus.R 36:1, Luke 2:22, m.Chullin 5:1, m.Kenim 1:4 3:6, m.Keritot 1:3 5:3, m.Niddah 5:1, m.Zevachim 14:3, Mas.Kutim 1:2, Midrash Tanchuma Tazria 4, mt.Hilchot Mechusrei Kapparah 1:3 1:5 1:8 3:4, mt.Hilchot Pesulei haMikdashim 4:27, Numbers 6:10, Siman 211:11
[9] LXX adds *whole*

meeting, to the priest.

וְהִקְרִיבוֹ לִפְנֵי יְהוָה וְכִפֶּר עָלֶיהָ 7[1]

And he shall offer it before the LORD, and make atonement for her; and she shall be cleansed from the fountain of her blood. This is the law for she who bears, either a male or a female.

וְטָהֲרָה מִמְּקֹר דָּמֶיהָ זֹאת תּוֹרַת
הַיֹּלֶדֶת לַזָּכָר אוֹ לַנְּקֵבָה

וְאִם־לֹא תִמְצָא יָדָהּ דֵּי שֶׂה וְלָקְחָה 8[2]
שְׁתֵּי־תֹרִים אוֹ שְׁנֵי בְּנֵי יוֹנָה אֶחָד
לְעֹלָה וְאֶחָד לְחַטָּאת וְכִפֶּר עָלֶיהָ
הַכֹּהֵן וְטָהֵרָה

And if her means cannot afford a lamb, then she shall take two turtle doves, or two young pigeons: one for a [3]burnt offering, and the other for a sin offering; and the priest shall make atonement for her, and she shall be clean.

Tazria – Chapter 13[4]

וַיְדַבֵּר יְהוָה אֶל־מֹשֶׁה וְאֶל־אַהֲרֹן 1[5]
לֵאמֹר

And the LORD spoke to Moses and to Aaron, saying:

אָדָם כִּי־יִהְיֶה בְעוֹר־בְּשָׂרוֹ שְׂאֵת אוֹ־ 2[6]
סַפַּחַת אוֹ בַהֶרֶת וְהָיָה בְעוֹר־בְּשָׂרוֹ
לְנֶגַע צָרָעַת וְהוּבָא אֶל־אַהֲרֹן הַכֹּהֵן
אוֹ אֶל־אַחַד מִבָּנָיו הַכֹּהֲנִים

When a man shall have in the skin of his flesh *a rising, a scab, a bright spot*[7], and it becomes in the skin of his flesh the plague of leprosy, then he shall be brought to Aaron the priest, or to one of his sons the priests.

---

[1] Leviticus 12:7 - 1 Corinthians 7:14, b.Bava Batra [Rashbam] 166a, b.Kereitot [Rashi] 8a, b.Kereitot 9b, b.Nedarim [Ran] 38b, b.Nedarim 35b, b.Niddah 19a 38b 40a [Tosefot] 19b 32b, b.Pesachim [Rashi] 59a, b.Sanhedrin [Tosefot] 69a, Galatians 3:28, Hebrews 9:12-14, Job 1:5 14:4, Leviticus 1:4 4:20 4:26 4:31 4:35 15:28-30, Romans 3:23 3:26, Siman 211:11, t.Shabbat 8:27, y.Niddah 2:3, z.Beha'alotcha 77
[2] Leviticus 12:8 - 2 Corinthians 8:9, b.Bava Batra 166a, b.Eruvin [Rashi] 37b, b.Kereitot 28a, b.Menachot [Rashi] 4b 73a, b.Nazir 26b 16a, b.Nedarim [Ran] 4b, b.Sanhedrin 11a 83b, b.Shekalim 9b, b.Yevamot 74b, b.Yoma 41a, b.Zevachim [Rashi] 19b 80a, b.Zevachim [Tosefot] 14a, Genesis.R 20:7, Guide for the Perplexed 3:45, Lamentations.R 2:4, Leviticus 1:14 4:26 5:7 14:22 15:14 15:29, Leviticus.R 15:6, Luke 2:22-24, m.Shekalim 2:5, m.Temurah 7:6, m.Zevachim 10:4, Mas.Kutim 1:2, mt.Hilchot Biat haMikdash 3:7 4:5, mt.Hilchot Kiddush HaChodesh 4:7, Numbers.R 10:15 14:11, Siman 211:11, Song of Songs.R 1:9, t.Sotah 6:7, y.Shabbat 1:3, y.Shekalim 3:3
[3] LXX adds *whole*
[4] 4Q274, Jastrow 342a, Josephus Antiquities 4.11.3, Midrash Proverbs 10, mt.Hilchot Issurei Biah 7:10, mt.Hilchot Mamrim 4:2
[5] Leviticus 13:1 - Leviticus.R 18:2, m.Moed Katan 1:5, m.Oholot 3:3, z.Tazria 45b
Leviticus 13:1-15:33 - Deuteronomy.R 6:13
[6] Leviticus 13:2 - 2 Chronicles 26:19-21, 2 Kings 5:1 5:27, 2 Samuel 3:29, b.Arachin 3a, b.Chullin [Rashi] 8a, b.Horayot 10a, b.Niddah 44a 50a, b.Sanhedrin [Tosefot] 59a, b.Sanhedrin 34b, b.Shabbat 54a, b.Sheviit [Rashi] 2a, b.Yoma [Rashi] 34b 42a, b.Zevachim [Rashi] 102a, Deuteronomy 17:8-9 24:8 4:27, Exodus 4:6-4:7, Isaiah 1:6 3:17, Jastrow 143a 204a 1012b 1087b, Leviticus 14:3 14:35 14:56, Leviticus.R 2:6 15:1, Luke 5:14 17:14, m.Keritot 2:1, m.Negaim 1:1, m.Sheviit 1:1, Malachi 2:7, Mark 1:44, Mas.Kallah Rabbati 2:4 6:1, Matthew 8:4, Midrash Tanchuma Tazria 6-11, mt.Hilchot Shevitat Yom Tov 7:16, mt.Hilchot Tumat Tzaraat 1:2 6:4 9:1 9:5, Numbers 12:10 12:12, Numbers.R 7:5 19:1, Pesikta de R'Kahana 17.6, Pesikta Rabbati 31:7, Sifre Devarim Shoftim 208, y.Niddah 2:6, y.Sheviit 1:1, z.Tazria 47a 62 71 107
Leviticus 13:2-46 - Commandment #565
[7] LXX *a bright clear spot*

וְרָאָה הַכֹּהֵן אֶת־הַנֶּגַע בְּעוֹר־הַבָּשָׂר וְשֵׂעָר בַּנֶּגַע הָפַךְ לָבָן וּמַרְאֵה הַנֶּגַע עָמֹק מֵעוֹר בְּשָׂרוֹ נֶגַע צָרַעַת הוּא וְרָאָהוּ הַכֹּהֵן וְטִמֵּא אֹתוֹ

3[1]

וְאִם־בַּהֶרֶת לְבָנָה הִוא בְּעוֹר בְּשָׂרוֹ וְעָמֹק אֵין־מַרְאֶהָ מִן־הָעוֹר וּשְׂעָרָה לֹא־הָפַךְ לָבָן וְהִסְגִּיר הַכֹּהֵן אֶת־הַנֶּגַע שִׁבְעַת יָמִים

4[5]

וְרָאָהוּ הַכֹּהֵן בַּיּוֹם הַשְּׁבִיעִי וְהִנֵּה הַנֶּגַע עָמַד בְּעֵינָיו לֹא־פָשָׂה הַנֶּגַע בָּעוֹר וְהִסְגִּירוֹ הַכֹּהֵן שִׁבְעַת יָמִים שֵׁנִית

5[8]

וְרָאָה הַכֹּהֵן אֹתוֹ בַּיּוֹם הַשְּׁבִיעִי שֵׁנִית וְהִנֵּה כֵּהָה הַנֶּגַע וְלֹא־פָשָׂה הַנֶּגַע בָּעוֹר וְטִהֲרוֹ הַכֹּהֵן מִסְפַּחַת הִיא וְכִבֶּס בְּגָדָיו וְטָהֵר

6[11]

3[1] And the priest shall look on the *plague*[2] in the skin of the flesh; and if the hair in the *plague*[3] has turned white, and the appearance of the *plague*[4] is deeper than the skin of his flesh, it is the plague of leprosy; and the priest shall look on him, and pronounce him unclean.

4[5] And if the bright spot is *white*[6] in the skin of his flesh, and its appearance is not deeper than the skin, and its hair has not turned white, then the priest shall quarantine he who has the *plague*[7] for seven days.

5[8] And the priest shall look on *him*[9] on the seventh day; and, behold, if the plague stayed in its appearance, and the *plague*[10] has not spread in the skin, then the priest shall quarantine him seven days more.

6[11] And the priest shall look on him again on the seventh day; and, behold, if the plague is *dim*[12], and the plague has not spread in the skin, then the priest shall pronounce him clean: it is a *scab*[13]; and he shall wash his clothes, and be clean.

---

[1] Leviticus 13:3 - 1 Corinthians 5:4-6, 1 Timothy 1:20, 2 Thessalonians 3:14-15, 2 Timothy 2:16-17 3:13, Acts 20:28, b.Nazir 14b, Ezekiel 16:30 20:23, Genesis 13:3, Haggai 2:11, Hebrews 13:7, Hosea 7:9, Jastrow 834b 875b, John 20:23, Leviticus 10:10 13:2, Leviticus.R 15:4, m.Nazir 7:5, Malachi 2:7, Matthew 16:19 18:17-18, mt.Hilchot Tumat Tzaraat 1:6 2:1 6:1 9:10, Philo De Posteritate Caini 47, Revelation 2:23, Romans 3:19-20 7:7, t.Negaim 2:12, z.Tazria 71 135
Leviticus 13:3-9 - 11QpaleoLeva
Leviticus 13:3-12 - mt.Hilchot Tumat Tzaraat 1:9
[2] LXX *spot*
[3] LXX *spot*
[4] LXX *spot*
[5] Leviticus 13:4 - 1 Corinthians 4:5, 1 Timothy 5:24, b.Bava Btra [Rashbam] 84a, b.Nazir [Rashi] 54b, b.Sheviit 6b, Deuteronomy 13:15, Ezekiel 20:10, Genesis.R 100 [Excl]:7, Jastrow 359a 956a, Leviticus.R 18:5 18:5 18:5, m.Kelim 1:5, m.Negaim 1:3, Numbers 12:15, Ruth.R 2:10, Sifre Devarim Haazinu Hashamayim 323, Sifre Devarim Nitzavim 323
[6] LXX *clear and white*
[7] LXX *spot*
[8] Leviticus 13:5 - Guide for the Perplexed 3:32, Jastrow 834b, Leviticus.R 17:3, m.Negaim 1:4, Midrash Tanchuma Metzora 4, mt.Hilchot Tumat Tzaraat 9:6, Numbers.R 6:2 7:5 9:17, z.Balak 386
[9] LXX *the spot*
[10] LXX *spot*
[11] Leviticus 13:6 - 1 John 1:7-9, 1 Kings 8:38 8:45, 2 Corinthians 7:1, b.Chullin [Rashi] 38a, b.Chullin [Tosefot] 71b, b.Megillah 8b, b.Niddah [Rashi] 19a, Deuteronomy 8:5, Ecclesiastes 7:20, Hebrews 9:10 10:22, Isaiah 11:3-4 18:3, James 3:2, John 13:8-10, Jude 1:22-23, Leviticus 11:25 11:28 11:40 13:2 14:8, Mas.Kallah Rabbati 6:1, Pesikta Rabbati 48:3, Proverbs 20:9, Psalms 19:13, Romans 14:1, z.Tazria 165
[12] LXX *dark*
[13] LXX *mark*

וְאִם־פָּשֹׂה תִפְשֶׂה הַמִּסְפַּחַת בָּעוֹר אַחֲרֵי הֵרָאֹתוֹ אֶל־הַכֹּהֵן לְטָהֳרָתוֹ וְנִרְאָה שֵׁנִית אֶל־הַכֹּהֵן	7[1]	*But if the scab spread abroad[2] in the skin after that he has shown himself to the priest for his cleansing[3], he shall show himself to the priest again.*
וְרָאָה הַכֹּהֵן וְהִנֵּה פָּשְׂתָה הַמִּסְפַּחַת בָּעוֹר וְטִמְּאוֹ הַכֹּהֵן צָרַעַת הִוא	8[4]	And the priest shall look[5], and, behold, if the *scab*[6] has spread in the skin, then the priest shall pronounce him unclean: it is leprosy.
נֶגַע צָרַעַת כִּי תִהְיֶה בְּאָדָם וְהוּבָא אֶל־הַכֹּהֵן	9[7]	*When the plague of leprosy is in a man, then he shall be brought to the priest[8].*
וְרָאָה הַכֹּהֵן וְהִנֵּה שְׂאֵת־לְבָנָה בָּעוֹר וְהִיא הָפְכָה שֵׂעָר לָבָן וּמִחְיַת בָּשָׂר חַי בַּשְׂאֵת	10[9]	And the priest shall look, and, behold, if there is a white *rising*[10] in the skin, and it have turned the hair white, and there is quick raw flesh in the rising,
צָרַעַת נוֹשֶׁנֶת הִוא בְּעוֹר בְּשָׂרוֹ וְטִמְּאוֹ הַכֹּהֵן לֹא יַסְגִּרֶנּוּ כִּי טָמֵא הוּא	11[11]	It is an old leprosy in the skin of his flesh, and the priest shall pronounce him unclean; *he shall not quarantine him[12]*, for he is unclean.
וְאִם־פָּרוֹחַ תִּפְרַח הַצָּרַעַת בָּעוֹר וְכִסְּתָה הַצָּרַעַת אֵת כָּל־עוֹר הַנֶּגַע מֵרֹאשׁוֹ וְעַד־רַגְלָיו לְכָל־מַרְאֵה עֵינֵי הַכֹּהֵן	12[13]	And if the leprosy breaks out abroad in the skin, and the leprosy covers all the skin of he who has the plague from his head even to his feet, as far as the priest can see;

---

[1] Leviticus 13:7 - 2 Timothy 2:16-17, Isaiah 1:5-6, Jastrow 1194b, Leviticus 13:27 13:35-36, m.Negaim 1:3, Psalms 38:4, Romans 6:12-14, y.Sheviit 1:1

[2] LXX *But if the bright spot should have changed and spread*

[3] LXX *for the purpose of purifying him*

[4] Leviticus 13:8 - 2 Peter 2:19, Acts 8:21, Leviticus 13:3, m.Nazir 7:5, Matthew 15:7-8, Numbers.R 9:17, Philippians 3:18-19

[5] LXX adds *upon him*

[6] LXX *mark*

[7] Leviticus 13:9 - b.Sanhedrin [Rashi] 101a, b.Sanhedrin [Tosefot] 59a, Ein Yaakov Sanhedrin:101a, y.Sanhedrin 10:1, z.Tazria 88 135 136

[8] LXX *And if a man has a plague of leprosy, then he shall come to the priest*

[9] Leviticus 13:10 - 2 Chronicles 26:19-20, 2 Kings 5:27, Amos 5:10, Avot de R'Natan 34, b.Kiddushin [Rashi] 25a, Guide for the Perplexed 1:42, Jastrow 468b, John 3:19-20 7:7, Leviticus 13:3-4 13:14-15 13:24, m.Negaim 1:3 1:5, mt.Hilchot Tumat Tzaraat 2:6 3:4, Numbers 12:10-12, Pesikta Rabbati 6:5, Proverbs 12:1, t.Negaim 3:8

[10] LXX *spot*

[11] Leviticus 13:11 - Jastrow 1303b, m.Nazir 7:5, mt.Hilchot Tumat Tzaraat 7:1, mt.Nizirut 7:9, Philo Quod Deus Immutabilis Sit 127, z.Tazria 165

[12] LXX *and shall separate him*

[13] Leviticus 13:12 - 1 John 1:8-1:10, 1 Kings 8:38, b.Arachin 18b, b.Gittin [Rashi] 42b, b.Kiddushin [Rashi] 25a, b.Moed Katan 8a, b.Niddah [Rashi] 19a 67a, b.Niddah 50a, b.Sanhedrin [Rashi] 88a, b.Sanhedrin 34b, b.Zevachim 49b, Exodus.R 11:6, Isaiah 16:7, Jastrow 1223a 1225b, Job 16:4 18:6, John 16:8-9, Leviticus.R 15:7, m.Negaim 8:1, Mekhilta de R'Shimon bar Yochai Pisha 10:2, Midrash Tanchuma Metzora 4, mt.Hilchot Tumat Tzaraat 7:4, Numbers.R 7:5, Philo De Plantatione 111, Philo De Sobrietate 49, Romans 7:14, t.Negaim 1:7, z.Balak 195 393

וְרָאָה הַכֹּהֵן וְהִנֵּה כִסְּתָה הַצָּרַעַת אֶת־כָּל־בְּשָׂרוֹ וְטִהַר אֶת־הַנָּגַע כֻּלּוֹ הָפַךְ לָבָן טָהוֹר הוּא

13[1] Then the priest shall look; and, behold, if the leprosy has covered all his flesh, he shall pronounce he who has the plague clean; it has all turned white: he is clean.

וּבְיוֹם הֵרָאוֹת בּוֹ בָּשָׂר חַי יִטְמָא

14[2] But whenever raw flesh appears in him, he shall be unclean.

וְרָאָה הַכֹּהֵן אֶת־הַבָּשָׂר הַחַי וְטִמְּאוֹ הַבָּשָׂר הַחַי טָמֵא הוּא צָרַעַת הוּא

15[3] And the priest shall look on the *raw*[4] flesh, and pronounce him unclean; the *raw*[5] flesh is unclean: it is leprosy.

אוֹ כִי יָשׁוּב הַבָּשָׂר הַחַי וְנֶהְפַּךְ לְלָבָן וּבָא אֶל־הַכֹּהֵן

16[6] But if the *raw*[7] flesh[8] again has turned to white, then he shall come to the priest;

וְרָאָהוּ הַכֹּהֵן וְהִנֵּה נֶהְפַּךְ הַנֶּגַע לְלָבָן וְטִהַר הַכֹּהֵן אֶת־הַנֶּגַע טָהוֹר הוּא

17 and the priest shall look on him; and, behold, if the plague be turned to white, then the priest shall pronounce him clean *who has the plague*[9]: he is clean.

וּבָשָׂר כִּי־יִהְיֶה בוֹ־בְעֹרוֹ שְׁחִין וְנִרְפָּא

18[10] And when the flesh *has in its skin a boil*[11], and it is healed,

וְהָיָה בִּמְקוֹם הַשְּׁחִין שְׂאֵת לְבָנָה אוֹ בַהֶרֶת לְבָנָה אֲדַמְדָּמֶת וְנִרְאָה אֶל־הַכֹּהֵן

19[12] and in the place of the *boil*[13] there is a white *rising, or a bright spot, reddish white*[14], then it shall be shown to the priest.

וְרָאָה הַכֹּהֵן וְהִנֵּה מַרְאֶהָ שָׁפָל מִן־הָעוֹר וּשְׂעָרָהּ הָפַךְ לָבָן וְטִמְּאוֹ הַכֹּהֵן נֶגַע־צָרַעַת הִוא בַּשְּׁחִין פָּרָחָה

20[15] And the priest shall look; and, behold, if the appearance is lower than the skin, and its hair has turned white, then the priest shall pronounce him unclean: it is the plague of leprosy, it has broken out

---

[1] Leviticus 13:13 - b.Bechorot [Rashi] 34b, b.Chullin [Tosefot] 76b, b.Niddah 19a, b.Sanhedrin 97a, Ein Yaakov Sanhedrin:97a, Isaiah 16:7, John 9:41, m.Negaim 4:3

[2] Leviticus 13:14 - b.Bechorot [Tosefot] 14b, b.Moed Katan 7b, b.Niddah 50a, b.Sanhedrin 34b, b.Yevamot [Rashi] 14a, m.Negaim 1:5, mt.Hilchot Sanhedrin vHainshin Hameurim Lahem 3:3, Philo Quod Deus Immutabilis Sit 123, t.Negaim 3:8 3:9

[3] Leviticus 13:15 - b.Moed Katan 7b, z.Tazria 135

[4] LXX *sound*

[5] LXX *sound*

[6] Leviticus 13:16 - 1 Timothy 1:13-15, Galatians 1:14-16, Jastrow 1014a, Philippians 3:6-8, Romans 7:14-24

[7] LXX *sound*

[8] LXX adds *is restored and*

[9] Missing in LXX

[10] Leviticus 13:18 - 2 Kings 20:7, b.Chullin 8a, b.Sotah 5a, Ein Yaakov Sotah:4b, Exodus 9:9 15:26, Isaiah 14:21, Job 2:7, m.Negaim 1:5 9:3, Midrash Tanchuma Metzora 4, mt.Hilchot Tumat Tzaraat 5:3, Psalms 38:4-8
Leviticus 13:18-28 - mt.Hilchot Tumat Tzaraat 5:1

[11] LXX *should have become an ulcer in his skin*

[12] Leviticus 13:19 - Leviticus 13:24, mt.Hilchot Tumat Tzaraat 1:4

[13] LXX *ulcer*

[14] LXX *sore, or one looking white and bright, or fiery*

[15] Leviticus 13:20 - 2 Peter 2:20, b.Arachin 8b, John 5:14, Leviticus 13:3, Matthew 12:45

in the *boil*[1].

21[2] But if the priest looks on it, and, behold, there are no white hairs in it, and it is not lower than the skin, but is *dim*[3], then the priest shall quarantine him for seven days.

וְאִם ׀ יִרְאֶנָּה הַכֹּהֵן וְהִנֵּה אֵין־בָּהּ שֵׂעָר לָבָן וּשְׁפָלָה אֵינֶנָּה מִן־הָעוֹר וְהִיא כֵהָה וְהִסְגִּירוֹ הַכֹּהֵן שִׁבְעַת יָמִים

22[4] And if it spreads abroad in the skin, then the priest shall pronounce him unclean: it is a plague[5].

וְאִם־פָּשֹׂה תִפְשֶׂה בָּעוֹר וְטִמֵּא הַכֹּהֵן אֹתוֹ נֶגַע הִוא

23[6] But if the bright spot stays in its place, and has not spread, it is the scar of the boil; and the priest shall pronounce him clean.

וְאִם־תַּחְתֶּיהָ תַּעֲמֹד הַבַּהֶרֶת לֹא פָשָׂתָה צָרֶבֶת הַשְּׁחִין הִוא וְטִהֲרוֹ הַכֹּהֵן

24[7] Or when the flesh has in the skin a *burning by fire*[8], and *the quick flesh of the burning becomes a bright spot, reddish white, or white*[9];

אוֹ בָשָׂר כִּי־יִהְיֶה בְעֹרוֹ מִכְוַת־אֵשׁ וְהָיְתָה מִחְיַת הַמִּכְוָה בַּהֶרֶת לְבָנָה אֲדַמְדֶּמֶת אוֹ לְבָנָה

25[10] then the priest shall look on it; and, behold, if the hair in the bright spot has turned white, and its appearance is deeper than the skin, it is leprosy, it has broken out in the *burning*[11]; and the priest shall pronounce him unclean: it is the plague of leprosy.

וְרָאָה אֹתָהּ הַכֹּהֵן וְהִנֵּה נֶהְפַּךְ שֵׂעָר לָבָן בַּבַּהֶרֶת וּמַרְאֶהָ עָמֹק מִן־הָעוֹר צָרַעַת הִוא בַּמִּכְוָה פָּרָחָה וְטִמֵּא אֹתוֹ הַכֹּהֵן נֶגַע צָרַעַת הִוא

26[12] But if the priest looks on it, and, behold, there is no white hair in the bright spot, and it is no lower than the skin, but is *dim*[13]; then the priest shall quarantine him for seven days.

וְאִם ׀ יִרְאֶנָּה הַכֹּהֵן וְהִנֵּה אֵין־בַּבַּהֶרֶת שֵׂעָר לָבָן וּשְׁפָלָה אֵינֶנָּה מִן־הָעוֹר וְהִוא כֵהָה וְהִסְגִּירוֹ הַכֹּהֵן שִׁבְעַת יָמִים

27 And the priest shall look on him on the seventh day; if it spread abroad in the

וְרָאָהוּ הַכֹּהֵן בַּיּוֹם הַשְּׁבִיעִי אִם־פָּשֹׂה תִפְשֶׂה בָּעוֹר וְטִמֵּא הַכֹּהֵן אֹתוֹ נֶגַע

---

[1] LXX *ulcer*

[2] Leviticus 13:21 - 1 Corinthians 5:5, Avot de R'Natan 34, m.Megillah 1:7, z.Pinchas 246 689, z.Tazria 134

[3] LXX *dark colored*

[4] Leviticus 13:22 - y.Nazir 9:4

[5] LXX adds *leprosy, it has broken out in the ulcer*

[6] Leviticus 13:23 - 1 Peter 4:2-3, 2 Chronicles 19:2-3, 2 Corinthians 2:7, 2 Samuel 12:13, b.Beitzah [Rashi] 7a, b.Temurah 16a, Galatians 6:1, Genesis 14:26, Jastrow 1688b, Job 34:31-32 40:4-5, m.Negaim 9:2, Matthew 26:75, mt.Hilchot Tumat Tzaraat 5:4, Proverbs 4:13, y.Nazir 9:4

[7] Leviticus 13:24 - b.Chullin 8a, b.Pesachim 75ab, Isaiah 3:24, Jastrow 760b, m.Negaim 1:3 1:5, Pesikta Rabbati 6:5, y.Pesachim 7:2, z.Tazria 135

[8] LXX *fiery inflammation*

[9] LXX *there should be in his skin the part which is healed of the inflammation, bright, clear, and white, suffused with red or very white*

[10] Leviticus 13:25 - b.Bava Metzia [Rashi] 86a, b.Bechorot [Rashi] 41a, b.Bechorot 41a, b.Chullin 63a, b.Ketubot [Rashi] 75b, b.Niddah [Rashi] 19a, b.Sheviit 6b, Leviticus 13:4 13:18-20

[11] LXX *inflammation*

[12] Leviticus 13:26 - Leviticus 13:4-5 13:23, Leviticus.R 21:2

[13] LXX *dark*

צָרַעַת הִוא

וְאִם־תַּחְתֶּיהָ תַעֲמֹד הַבַּהֶרֶת לֹא־
פָשְׂתָה בָעוֹר וְהִוא כֵהָה שְׂאֵת הַמִּכְוָה
הִוא וְטִהֲרוֹ הַכֹּהֵן כִּי־צָרֶבֶת הַמִּכְוָה
הִוא

וְאִישׁ אוֹ אִשָּׁה כִּי־יִהְיֶה בוֹ נָגַע
בְּרֹאשׁ אוֹ בְזָקָן

וְרָאָה הַכֹּהֵן אֶת־הַנֶּגַע וְהִנֵּה מַרְאֵהוּ
עָמֹק מִן־הָעוֹר וּבוֹ שֵׂעָר צָהֹב דָּק
וְטִמֵּא אֹתוֹ הַכֹּהֵן נֶתֶק הוּא צָרַעַת
הָרֹאשׁ אוֹ הַזָקָן הוּא

וְכִי־יִרְאֶה הַכֹּהֵן אֶת־נֶגַע הַנֶּתֶק וְהִנֵּה
אֵין־מַרְאֵהוּ עָמֹק מִן־הָעוֹר וְשֵׂעָר
שָׁחֹר אֵין בּוֹ וְהִסְגִּיר הַכֹּהֵן אֶת־נֶגַע
הַנֶּתֶק שִׁבְעַת יָמִים

וְרָאָה הַכֹּהֵן אֶת־הַנֶּגַע בַּיּוֹם הַשְּׁבִיעִי
וְהִנֵּה לֹא־פָשָׂה הַנֶּתֶק וְלֹא־הָיָה בוֹ
שֵׂעָר צָהֹב וּמַרְאֵה הַנֶּתֶק אֵין עָמֹק
מִן־הָעוֹר

skin, then the priest shall pronounce him unclean: it is the plague of leprosy[1].

28[2] And if the bright spot *stays in its place*[3], and has not spread in the skin, but is *dim*[4], it is *the rising of the burning*[5], and the priest shall pronounce him clean; for it is the *scar of the burning*[6].

29[7] And when a man or woman has a plague[8] on the head or on the beard,

30[9] Then the priest shall look on the plague; and, behold, if its appearance is deeper than the skin, and there is thin yellow hair in it, then the priest shall pronounce him unclean: it is a *scall*[10], it is leprosy of the head or [11]of the beard.

31[12] And if the priest looks on the plague of the *scall*[13] and, behold, its appearance is not deeper than the skin, and there be no *black*[14] hair in it, then the priest shall quarantine he who has the plague of the *scall*[15] for seven days.

32[16] And in the seventh day the priest shall look on the plague; and, behold, if the *scall*[17] has not spread, and there is no yellow hair in it, and the appearance of the *scall*[18] is not *deeper than*[19] the skin,

---

[1] LXX adds *it has broken out in the ulcer*

[2] Leviticus 13:28 - Jastrow 1086a, y.Pesachim 7:2

[3] LX *remains stationary*

[4] LXX *dark*

[5] LXX *a scar of inflammation*

[6] LXX *mark of the inflammation*

[7] Leviticus 13:29 - 1 Kings 8:38 12:28, 2 Chronicles 6:29, 2 Corinthians 4:3-4, 2 Thessalonians 2:11-12, Acts 22:3-4 26:9-10, b.Arachin [Tosefot] 3a, b.Kiddushin 35b, b.Menachot 37b, Isaiah 1:5 5:20 9:16, John 16:2-3, Matthew 6:23 13:14-15, Micah 3:11, Psalms 53:5, z.Tazria 108
Leviticus 13:29-37 - mt.Hilchot Tumat Tzaraat 8:1

[8] LXX adds *of leprosy*

[9] Leviticus 13:30 - b.Bava Batra 84a, b.Menachot 37b, Jastrow 718b 1264b, Leviticus 13:34-37 14:54, mt.Hilchot Tumat Tzaraat 8:4 8:14

[10] LXX *scurf*

[11] LXX adds *leprosy*

[12] Leviticus 13:31 - m.Negaim 10:2 10:6, mt.Hilchot Tumat Tzaraat 8:1

[13] LXX *scurf*

[14] LXX *yellowish*

[15] LXX *scurf*

[16] Leviticus 13:32 - Leviticus 13:30, Luke 18:9-18:12, m.Negaim 10:2, Matthew 23:5, Romans 2:23
Leviticus 13:32-33 - 4QLev-Numa

[17] LXX *scurf*

[18] LXX *scurf*

[19] LXX *hollow under*

וְהִתְגַּלָּח[1] וְאֶת־הַנֶּתֶק לֹא יְגַלֵּחַ
וְהִסְגִּיר הַכֹּהֵן אֶת־הַנֶּתֶק שִׁבְעַת יָמִים
שֵׁנִית

33[2] then he shall be shaven, but the *scall*[3] shall not be shaven; and the priest shall quarantine he who has the *scall*[4] seven days more.

וְרָאָה הַכֹּהֵן אֶת־הַנֶּתֶק בַּיּוֹם הַשְּׁבִיעִי
וְהִנֵּה לֹא־פָשָׂה הַנֶּתֶק בָּעוֹר וּמַרְאֵהוּ
אֵינֶנּוּ עָמֹק מִן־הָעוֹר וְטִהַר אֹתוֹ הַכֹּהֵן
וְכִבֶּס בְּגָדָיו וְטָהֵר

34[5] And in the seventh day the priest shall look on the *scall*[6]; and, behold, if the *scall*[7] has not spread in the skin[8], and the appearance[9] is not *deeper than*[10] the skin, then the priest shall pronounce him clean; and he shall wash his clothes, and be clean.

וְאִם־פָּשֹׂה יִפְשֶׂה הַנֶּתֶק בָּעוֹר אַחֲרֵי
טָהֳרָתוֹ

35[11] But if the *scall*[12] spread abroad in the skin after his cleansing,

וְרָאָהוּ הַכֹּהֵן וְהִנֵּה פָּשָׂה הַנֶּתֶק בָּעוֹר
לֹא־יְבַקֵּר הַכֹּהֵן לַשֵּׂעָר הַצָּהֹב טָמֵא
הוּא

36[13] Then the priest shall look on him; and, behold, if the *scall*[14] has spread in the skin, the priest shall not search for the yellow hair: he is unclean.

וְאִם־בְּעֵינָיו עָמַד הַנֶּתֶק וְשֵׂעָר שָׁחֹר
צָמַח־בּוֹ נִרְפָּא הַנֶּתֶק טָהוֹר הוּא
וְטִהֲרוֹ הַכֹּהֵן

37[15] But if the *scall*[16] stays in its appearance, and *black*[17] hair has grown up in it; the *scall*[18] is healed, he is clean; and the priest shall pronounce him clean.

וְאִישׁ אוֹ־אִשָּׁה כִּי־יִהְיֶה בְעוֹר־בְּשָׂרָם
בֶּהָרֹת בֶּהָרֹת לְבָנֹת

38[19] And if a man or a woman has in the skin of his flesh *bright spots, even white bright spots*[20];

---

[1] Traditional Enlarged ג in וְהִתְגַּלָּח
[2] Leviticus 13:33 - 4Q266 9 9, 4Q266 frag 6 1.9, 4Q272 frag 1 1.17-18, b.Kiddushin 30a, b.Kiddushin 30a [states this is the middle of the verses of the Torah], Commandment #577, Ein Yaakov Kiddushin:30a, Jastrow 1193b, m.Negaim 10:5, Mas.Soferim 9:3, mt.Hilchot Tumat Tzaraat 8:2 8:3 10:1, mt.Hilchot Sanhedrin vHainshin Hameurim Lahem 19:4, t.Negaim 1:9
[3] LXX *scurf*
[4] LXX *scurf*
[5] Leviticus 13:34 - 1 John 4:1, Jastrow 1227a, Jude 1:22, Revelation 2:2
[6] LXX *scurf*
[7] LXX *scurf*
[8] LXX adds *after the man was shaved*
[9] LXX adds *of the scurf*
[10] LXX *hollow under*
[11] Leviticus 13:35 - 2 Timothy 2:16-17 3:13, Leviticus 13:7 13:27
[12] LXX *scurf*
[13] Leviticus 13:36 - Ein Yaakov Berachot:5a, Lamentations.R 2:3
[14] LXX *scurf*
[15] Leviticus 13:37 - Jastrow 1277a 1287a, Leviticus.R 15:3, m.Negaim 10:2, mt.Hilchot Tumat Tzaraat 8:2 8:8 8:13 9:3, t.Negaim 1:16, y.Pesachim 6:1
[16] LXX *scurf*
[17] LXX *dark*
[18] LXX *scurf*
[19] Leviticus 13:38 - b.Niddah 43b, z.Tazria 50b, z.Tazria 108 162
[20] LXX *spots of a bright whiteness*

וְרָאָה הַכֹּהֵן וְהִנֵּה בְעוֹר־בְּשָׂרָם בֶּהָרֹת כֵּהוֹת לְבָנֹת בֹּהַק הוּא פָּרַח בָּעוֹר טָהוֹר הוּא	39[1]	Then the priest shall look; and, behold, *if the bright spots in the skin of their flesh is of a dull white*[2], it is a tetter, it has broken out in the skin: he is clean.
וְאִישׁ כִּי יִמָּרֵט רֹאשׁוֹ קֵרֵחַ הוּא טָהוֹר הוּא	40[3]	And if a man's hair has fallen off his head, he is bald; yet is he clean.
וְאִם מִפְּאַת פָּנָיו יִמָּרֵט רֹאשׁוֹ גִּבֵּחַ הוּא טָהוֹר הוּא	41[4]	And if his hair has fallen off from the front part of his head, he is forehead bald; yet is he clean.
וְכִי־יִהְיֶה בַקָּרַחַת אוֹ בַגַּבַּחַת נֶגַע לָבָן אֲדַמְדָּם צָרַעַת פֹּרַחַת הִוא בְּקָרַחְתּוֹ אוֹ בְגַבַּחְתּוֹ	42[5]	But if there is in *the*[6] baldhead, or the bald forehead, a *reddish white*[7] plague, it is leprosy breaking out in his baldhead, or his bald forehead.
וְרָאָה אֹתוֹ הַכֹּהֵן וְהִנֵּה שְׂאֵת־הַנֶּגַע לְבָנָה אֲדַמְדֶּמֶת בְּקָרַחְתּוֹ אוֹ בְגַבַּחְתּוֹ כְּמַרְאֵה צָרַעַת עוֹר בָּשָׂר	43	Then the priest shall look on him; and, behold, if the rising of the plague is *reddish white*[8] in his bald head, or in his bald forehead, as the appearance of leprosy in the skin of the flesh,
אִישׁ־צָרוּעַ הוּא טָמֵא הוּא טַמֵּא יְטַמְּאֶנּוּ הַכֹּהֵן בְּרֹאשׁוֹ נִגְעוֹ	44[9]	He is a leprous man, *he is unclean, unclean*[10]; the priest shall pronounce him unclean: his plague is in his head.
וְהַצָּרוּעַ אֲשֶׁר־בּוֹ הַנֶּגַע בְּגָדָיו יִהְיוּ פְרֻמִים וְרֹאשׁוֹ יִהְיֶה פָרוּעַ וְעַל־שָׂפָם	45[11]	And the leper in whom the plague is, his clothes shall be *torn*[12], and the hair of

---

[1] Leviticus 13:39 - Ecclesiastes 7:20, James 3:2, Jastrow 143a, m.Negaim 1:5, mt.Hilchot Tumat Tzaraat 1:1, Romans 7:22-7:25
Leviticus 13:39-43 - 11QpaleoLeva

[2] LXX *there [being] bright spots of a bright whiteness in the skin of their flesh*

[3] Leviticus 13:40 - 2 Kings 2:23, Amos 8:10, Galatians 4:13, Isaiah 15:2, Leviticus 13:41, Midrash Tanchuma Metzora 4, mt.Hilchot Tumat Tzaraat 8:12, Romans 6:12 6:19 8:10, Song of Songs 5:11, z.Tazria 47a, z.Tazria 96 119 126

[4] Leviticus 13:41 - m.Negaim 10:9, z.Tazria 49a, z.Tazria 129
Leviticus 13:41-44 - t.Negaim 1:4

[5] Leviticus 13:42 - b.Niddah 19a, b.Succah 28b, b.Zevachim 49b, Jastrow 17a, z.Tazria 49a 131 163

[6] 11QpaleoLeva *his*

[7] LXX *white or fiery*

[8] LXX *white or fiery*

[9] Leviticus 13:44 - 2 John 1:8-1:10, 2 Peter 2:1-2:2, b.Arachin 3a, b.Kereitot 8b, Isaiah 1:5, Job 12:14, Matthew 6:23, mt.Hilchot Tumat Tzaraat 9:3 10:8, y.Nazir 4:6, y.Sotah 3:8

[10] Missing in LXX

[11] Leviticus 13:45 - 2 Samuel 13:19, 4Q274 1 i 3, 4Q274 frag 1 1.3, b.Arachin 3a, b.Bava Kamma 92b, b.Chullin 78a, b.Kereitot 8b, b.Megillah 8b, b.Moed Katan 5a 14b 15a, b.Niddah 66a, b.Sanhedrin 26a, b.Shabbat [Rashi] 129b, b.Shabbat 67a, b.Shekalim 3a, b.Sotah 23b 32b, Commandment #566, Ein Yaakov Bava Kamma 92b, Ein Yaakov Sotah 32b, Ezekiel 24:17 24:22, Genesis 13:29, Isaiah 6:5 4:11 16:7, Jastrow 1227a 1235a 1236a 1242a 1613b, Jeremiah 3:25 12:24, Job 1:20 18:6, Lamentations 4:15, Lamentations.R 5:21, Joel 2:13, Leviticus 10:6 21:10, Leviticus.R 5:5 16:1 16:4 17:3-4 18:4, Luke 5:8 7:6-7 17:12, m.Kelim 1:5, m.Negaim 8:8, m.Sotah 3:8, Micah 3:7, Midrash Tanchuma Metzora 4, mt.Hilchot Evel 5:19, mt.Hilchot Tumat Tzaraat 10:6 10:8, Numbers.R 7:1 9:46 13:8, Pesikta Rabbati 7:7 47:2, Psalms 51:4 51:6, Ralbag SOS 1, Song of Songs.R 1:43, y.Chagigah 3:8, y.Maaser Sheni 5:1, y.Shekalim 1:1, y.Sotah 9:1, z.Chayyei Sarah 125b, z.Vayishlach 167b 39, z.Balak 386

[12] LXX *ungirt*

יַעְטֶה וְטָמֵא| טָמֵא יִקְרָא

כָּל־יְמֵי אֲשֶׁר הַנֶּגַע בּוֹ יִטְמָא טָמֵא הוּא בָּדָד יֵשֵׁב מִחוּץ לַמַּחֲנֶה מוֹשָׁבוֹ

וְהַבֶּגֶד כִּי־יִהְיֶה בוֹ נֶגַע צָרָעַת בְּבֶגֶד צֶמֶר אוֹ בְּבֶגֶד פִּשְׁתִּים

אוֹ בִשְׁתִי אוֹ בְעֵרֶב לַפִּשְׁתִּים וְלַצָּמֶר אוֹ בְעוֹר אוֹ בְּכָל־מְלֶאכֶת עוֹר

וְהָיָה הַנֶּגַע יְרַקְרַק אוֹ אֲדַמְדָּם בַּבֶּגֶד אוֹ בָעוֹר אוֹ־בַשְּׁתִי אוֹ־בָעֵרֶב אוֹ בְכָל־כְּלִי־עוֹר נֶגַע צָרַעַת הוּא וְהָרְאָה אֶת־הַכֹּהֵן

וְרָאָה הַכֹּהֵן אֶת־הַנָּגַע וְהִסְגִּיר אֶת־הַנֶּגַע שִׁבְעַת יָמִים

וְרָאָה אֶת־הַנֶּגַע בַּיּוֹם הַשְּׁבִיעִי כִּי־פָשָׂה הַנֶּגַע בַּבֶּגֶד אוֹ־בַשְּׁתִי אוֹ־בָעֵרֶב אוֹ בָעוֹר לְכֹל אֲשֶׁר־יֵעָשֶׂה הָעוֹר לִמְלָאכָה צָרַעַת מַמְאֶרֶת הַנֶּגַע טָמֵא

his head shall go loose, and he shall cover his upper lip, and shall *cry: 'Unclean, unclean.*[1]'

46[2] All the days that the plague is in him he shall be unclean; he is unclean; he shall dwell alone; his dwelling shall be outside the camp.

47[3] And when the plague of leprosy is in a garment, whether it is a garment of wool, or a *linen*[4] garment;

48[5] or in the warp, or in the woof, whether of linen, or of wool; or in a skin, or in anything made of skin.

49[6] If the plague is greenish or reddish in the garment, or in the skin, or in the warp, or in the woof, or in any *thing*[7] of skin, it is the plague of leprosy, and shall be shown to the priest.

50[8] And the priest shall look on the plague, and quarantine whatever has the plague for seven days.

51[9] And he shall look on the plague on the seventh day; if the plague has spread in the garment, or in the warp, or in the woof, or in the skin, whatever service skin is used for, the plague is a *malignant*[10] leprosy: it is unclean.

[1] LXX *be called unclean*
[2] Leviticus 13:46 - 1 Corinthians 5:5 5:9-13, 1 Timothy 6:5, 2 Chronicles 2:21, 2 Kings 7:3 15:5, 2 Thessalonians 3:6 3:14, b.Arachin [Tosefot] 32b, b.Arachin 16b, b.Berachot 25a, b.Megillah 8b, b.Pesachim 67a, b.Zevachim [Tosefot] 114b, b.Zevachim 114a, Ein Yaakov Arachin:16b, Hebrews 12:15-16, Lamentations 1:1 1:8, Lamentations.R 5:21, Leviticus.R 16:3 17:4 18:5, Luke 17:12, Midrash Tanchuma Metzora 3, mt.Hilchot Tumat Tzaraat 10:7 10:12, mt.Hilchot Beit Habechirah 7:13 7:13 7:15, mt.Hilchot Biat haMikdash 3:2, Numbers 5:1-4 12:14-15, Numbers.R 7:8, Pesikta de R'Kahana 7.1, Pesikta Rabbati 17:6 47:2, Proverbs 6:12, Revelation 21:27 22:15, Ruth.R 2:10, Sifre Numbers 1:4, t.Negaim 6:7, y.Megillah 1:8, z.Noach 64b, z.Vayishlach 167b, z.Naso Idra Raba 337, z.Noach 114, z.Pekudei 125, z.Vayishlach 39
[3] Leviticus 13:47 - b.Bechorot 14a, b.Chullin [Tosefot] 36b, b.Menachot 39b, b.Shabbat 26b, b.Yevamot [Rashi] 42a, b.Zevachim [Tosefot] 95a, Colossians 3:3, Ephesians 4:22, Ezekiel 16:16, Isaiah 3:16-3:24 11:6 16:7, Jastrow 1249b, Jude 1:23, m.Negaim 11:1, Midrash Tanchuma Metzora 4, Midrash Tanchuma Tazria 10, mt.Hilchot Tumat Tzaraat 13:1, Romans 13:12, y.Kilayim 9:1
Leviticus 13:47-49 - Commandment #567
[4] LXX *flaxen*
[5] Leviticus 13:48 - b.Chullin [Tosefot] 36b, b.Shabbat 28a, Deuteronomy 8:11, Jude 1:23, Leviticus 13:51, mt.Hilchot Tumat Tzaraat 13:1, Revelation 3:4, Siman 122:1, y.Kilayim 9:1
[6] Leviticus 13:49 - Jastrow 598b, mt.Hilchot Tumat Tzaraat 12:1
[7] LXX *utensil*
[8] Leviticus 13:50 - Ezekiel 20:23, mt.Hilchot Tumat Tzaraat 12:1
[9] Leviticus 13:51 - b.Arachin [Tosefot] 20b, Exodus.R 3:13, Jastrow 724a, Leviticus 14:44, mt.Hilchot Tumat Tzaraat 12:1 12:5
[10] LXX *confirmed*

הוּא

וְשָׂרַף אֶת־הַבֶּגֶד אוֹ אֶת־הַשְּׁתִי אוֹ אֶת־הָעֵרֶב בַּצֶּמֶר אוֹ בַפִּשְׁתִּים אוֹ אֶת־כָּל־כְּלִי הָעוֹר אֲשֶׁר־יִהְיֶה בוֹ הַנָּגַע כִּי־צָרַעַת מַמְאֶרֶת הִוא בָּאֵשׁ תִּשָּׂרֵף

52[1] And he shall burn the garment, or the warp, or the woof, whether it is of wool or of *linen*[2], or anything of skin, where the plague is; for it is a *malignant*[3] leprosy; it shall be burnt in the fire.

וְאִם יִרְאֶה הַכֹּהֵן וְהִנֵּה לֹא־פָשָׂה הַנֶּגַע בַּבֶּגֶד אוֹ בַשְּׁתִי אוֹ בָעֵרֶב אוֹ בְּכָל־כְּלִי־עוֹר

53[4] And if the priest shall look, and, behold, the plague has not spread in the garment, or in the warp, or in the woof, or in any *thing*[5] of skin,

וְצִוָּה הַכֹּהֵן וְכִבְּסוּ אֵת אֲשֶׁר־בּוֹ הַנָּגַע וְהִסְגִּירוֹ שִׁבְעַת־יָמִים שֵׁנִית

54[6] Then the priest shall command they wash the thing where the plague is, and he shall quarantine it for seven days more.

וְרָאָה הַכֹּהֵן אַחֲרֵי הֻכַּבֵּס אֶת־הַנֶּגַע וְהִנֵּה לֹא־הָפַךְ הַנֶּגַע אֶת־עֵינוֹ וְהַנֶּגַע לֹא־פָשָׂה טָמֵא הוּא בָּאֵשׁ תִּשְׂרְפֶנּוּ פְּחֶתֶת הִוא בְּקָרַחְתּוֹ אוֹ בְגַבַּחְתּוֹ

55[7] And the priest shall look, after that the plague is washed; and, behold, if the plague has not changed its color, and the plague has not spread, it is unclean; you shall burn it in the fire; *it is a fret, whether the bareness is within or without*[8].

וְאִם רָאָה הַכֹּהֵן וְהִנֵּה כֵּהָה הַנֶּגַע אַחֲרֵי הֻכַּבֵּס אֹתוֹ וְקָרַע אֹתוֹ מִן־הַבֶּגֶד אוֹ מִן־הָעוֹר אוֹ מִן־הַשְּׁתִי אוֹ מִן־הָעֵרֶב

56[9] And if the priest looks, and, behold, the plague is *dim*[10] after the washing, then he shall tear it out of the garment, or out of the skin, or out of the warp, or out of the woof.

וְאִם־תֵּרָאֶה עוֹד בַּבֶּגֶד אוֹ־בַשְּׁתִי אוֹ־בָעֵרֶב אוֹ בְכָל־כְּלִי־עוֹר פֹּרַחַת הִוא בָּאֵשׁ תִּשְׂרְפֶנּוּ אֵת אֲשֶׁר־בּוֹ הַנָּגַע

57[11] And if it still appears in the garment, or in the warp, or in the woof, or in any *thing*[12] of skin, it is breaking out, you shall burn whatever has the plague with

---

[1] Leviticus 13:52 - Acts 19:19-20, b.Yevamot 103b, Deuteronomy 7:25-26, Isaiah 6:22, Leviticus 11:33 11:35 14:44-45, Midrash Tanchuma Metzora 2, mt.Hilchot Tumat Tzaraat 13:4 13:10 16:1, Pesikta de R'Kahana 7.1, Pesikta Rabbati 17:6, Ruth.R 2:10

[2] LXX *flaxen*

[3] LXX *confirmed*

[4] Leviticus 13:53 - b.Chullin [Rashi] 31b

[5] LXX *utensil*

[6] Leviticus 13:54 - b.Chullin [Rashi] 31b, b.Zevachim [Rashi] 95a, Jastrow 1667b, mt.Hilchot Tumat Tzaraat 12:1 12:5, Ruth.R 2:10, y.Megillah 2:5, y.Shabbat 2:1

[7] Leviticus 13:55 - 2 Peter 1:9 2:20-22, b.Niddah 19a, b.Zevachim 49b, Ezekiel 24:13, Hebrews 6:4-8, Jastrow 205b 1416a 1551a 1624a, mt.Hilchot Tumat Tzaraat 12:1 12:9

[8] LXX *it is fixed in the garment, in the warp, or in the woof*

[9] Leviticus 13:56 - Jastrow 1619b, Pesikta de R'Kahana 7.1, Pesikta Rabbati 17:6, Ruth.R 2:10

[10] LXX *dark*

[11] Leviticus 13:57 - Isaiah 9:14, Jastrow 1424b, Matthew 3:12 22:7 1:41, mt.Hilchot Tumat Tzaraat 12:1 12:6, Revelation 21:8 21:27

[12] LXX *article*

וְהַבֶּ֫גֶד אֽוֹ־הַשְּׁתִ֤י אֽוֹ־הָעֵ֫רֶב אֽוֹ־כָל־ 58¹
כְּלִ֣י הָעוֹר֙ אֲשֶׁ֣ר תְּכַבֵּ֔ס וְסָ֥ר מֵהֶ֖ם
הַנָּ֑גַע וְכֻבַּ֥ס שֵׁנִ֖ית וְטָהֵֽר׃

זֹ֠את תּוֹרַ֨ת נֶֽגַע־צָרַ֜עַת בֶּ֤גֶד הַצֶּ֨מֶר֙ א֣וֹ 59³
הַפִּשְׁתִּ֔ים א֤וֹ הַשְּׁתִי֙ א֣וֹ הָעֵ֔רֶב א֖וֹ כָּל־
כְּלִי־ע֑וֹר לְטַהֲר֖וֹ א֥וֹ לְטַמְּאֽוֹ׃

fire.

58¹ And the garment, or the warp, or the woof, or whatever *thing*² of skin it is, which you shall wash, if the plague has departed from them, then it shall be washed the second time, and shall be clean.

59³ This is the law of the plague of leprosy in a garment of wool or linen, or in the warp, or in the woof, or in any thing of leather, *to pronounce it clean*⁴, or *to pronounce it*⁵ unclean.

¹ Leviticus 13:58 - 2 Corinthians 7:1 12:8, 2 Kings 5:10 5:14, b.Chullin [Rashi] 31b, b.Chullin 31b, b.Zevachim 94a, Hebrews 9:10, mt.Hilchot Tumat Tzaraat 12:1, Psalms 51:3, Revelation 1:5, y.Megillah 2:5, y.Shabbat 2:1
Leviticus 13:58-59 - 11QLevb
² LXX *article*
³ Leviticus 13:59 - b.Chullin [Tosefot] 22b, b.Moed Katan 7b, b.Nazir 65b, Leviticus.R 16:6, mt.Hilchot Tumat Tzaraat 11:6, t.Negaim 8:1, z.Tazria 168
⁴ 11QLeva *for its cleansing*
⁵ Missing in LXX

Metzora

Metzora[1] – Chapter 14[2]

וַיְדַבֵּר יְהוָה אֶל־מֹשֶׁה לֵּאמֹר

1[3] And the LORD spoke to Moses, saying:

זֹאת תִּהְיֶה תּוֹרַת הַמְּצֹרָע בְּיוֹם טָהֳרָתוֹ וְהוּבָא אֶל־הַכֹּהֵן

2[4] This shall be the law of the leper in the day of his cleansing: he shall be brought to the priest.

וְיָצָא הַכֹּהֵן אֶל־מִחוּץ לַמַּחֲנֶה וְרָאָה הַכֹּהֵן וְהִנֵּה נִרְפָּא נֶגַע־הַצָּרַעַת מִן־הַצָּרוּעַ

3[5] And the priest shall go forth out of the camp; and the priest shall look, and, behold, if the plague of leprosy is healed in the leper;

וְצִוָּה הַכֹּהֵן וְלָקַח לַמִּטַּהֵר שְׁתֵּי־צִפֳּרִים חַיּוֹת טְהֹרוֹת וְעֵץ אֶרֶז וּשְׁנִי תוֹלַעַת וְאֵזֹב

4[6] Then shall the priest command to take for he who is to be cleansed two living clean birds, and cedar wood, and [7]scarlet, and hyssop.

---

[1] Metzora aliyot: [1] Leviticus 14:1–12, [2] Leviticus 14:13–20, [3] Leviticus 14:21–32, [4] Leviticus 14:33–53, [5] Leviticus 14:54–15:15, [6] Leviticus 15:16–28, [7] Leviticus 15:29–33
Tazria and Metzora are combined when there are only 52 available reading days in the year.

[2] 4Q274, HaMadrikh 35:4, Josephus Antiquities 4.11.3, Midrash Proverbs 10, mt.Hilchot Mamrim 4:2, mt.Hilchot Mechusrei Kapparah 4:1, mt.Hilchot Pesulei haMikdashim 19:11

[3] Leviticus 14:1 - Sifre Devarim Shoftim 152, t.Demai 2:7, z.Metzorah 1 52b 53a
Leviticus 14:1-7 - Commandment #578
Leviticus 14:1-12 - Minchah [Shabbat Monday Thursday Torah reading - Parashah Metzorah]
Leviticus 14:1-32 - m.Megillah 2:5

[4] Leviticus 14:2 - b.Arachin 15b, b.Avodah Zara 74a, b.Kereitot 9b 28a, b.Ketubot [Rashi] 5b, b.Kinnim [Pirush] 23b, b.Megillah 21a, b.Menachot [Tosefot] 4b, b.Menachot 5a 19a 16a, b.Nedarim [Ran] 38b, b.Nedarim 36a, b.Shabbat 132a, b.Yoma 41b 62b, b.Zevachim [Rashi] 40a, b.Zevachim [Tosefot] 5a, Ein Yaakov Arachin:15b, Leviticus 13:59 14:54-57, Leviticus.R 16:6, Luke 5:12-14 17:14, m.Negaim 14:1, Mark 1:40-44, Matthew 8:2-4, Midrash Psalms 8:2 52:1, Midrash Tanchuma Metzora 1-4, mt.Hilchot Mechusrei Kapparah 5:6, Numbers 6:9, y.Megillah 1:8, y.Nazir 6:9, y.Sotah 2:1, z.Metzora 1 12 14 16, z.Tazria 108
Leviticus 14:2-6 - Liber Antiquitatum Biblicarum 13:3
Leviticus 14:2-8 - Jastrow 1646b, m.Kelim 1:4
Leviticus 14:2-9 - 4QMMT B 64-72

[5] Leviticus 14:3 - 1 Corinthians 6:9-11, 2 Kings 5:3 5:7-8 5:14, b.Megillah 8b, Exodus 15:26, Job 5:18, Leviticus 13:46, Luke 4:27 7:22 17:15-19, Matthew 10:8 11:5, y.Megillah 1:8, z.Metzora 16

[6] Leviticus 14:4 - b.Arachin 8b 16b, b.Chullin [Rashi] 62a, b.Chullin [Rashi] 82a, b.Kiddushin [Rashi] 57a, b.Chullin 140a, b.Menachot 42b, b.Yoma 62b, b.Zevachim [Tosefot] 116a, Ein Yaakov Arachin 16b, Exodus 12:22, Genesis.R 31:9, Hebrews 9:19, Jastrow 322b 1169b 1329a, Leviticus 1:14 5:7 12:8 14:6 14:49-52, Leviticus.R 16:7, m.Chullin 12:5, m.Keritot 2:3, m.Kiddushin 2:9, m.Megillah 1:7, m.Parah 11:8, Midrash Tanchuma Metzora 3, mt.Hilchot Tumat Tzaraat 11:1 11:8, Numbers 19:6 19:18, Numbers.R 19:3, Pesikta Rabbati 14:9, Psalms 51:8, Sifre Devarim Ki Tetze 227, Sifre Devarim Reeh 103, t.Bechorot 1:8, t.Shechitat Chullin 10:14, y.Sanhedrin 3:9, y.Sheviit 4:1, z.Metzora 17 18 25

[7] LXX adds *spun*

וְצִוָּה֙ הַכֹּהֵ֔ן וְשָׁחַ֖ט אֶת־הַצִּפּ֣וֹר הָאֶחָ֑ת ⁵⁸   And the priest shall command to kill one
אֶל־כְּלִי־חֶ֖רֶשׂ עַל־מַ֥יִם חַיִּֽים   of the birds in an earthen vessel over
                                                              running water.

אֶת־הַצִּפֹּ֣ר הַֽחַיָּ֗ה יִקַּ֤ח אֹתָהּ֙ וְאֶת־עֵ֣ץ ⁶⁹   As for the living bird, he shall take it,
הָאֶ֔רֶז וְאֶת־שְׁנִ֥י הַתּוֹלַ֖עַת וְאֶת־הָאֵזֹ֑ב   and the cedar wood, and the ¹⁰scarlet,
וְטָבַ֣ל אוֹתָ֗ם וְאֵ֣ת ׀ הַצִּפֹּ֣ר הַֽחַיָּ֔ה בְּדַם֙   and the hyssop, and shall dip them and
הַצִּפֹּ֣ר הַשְּׁחֻטָ֔ה עַ֖ל הַמַּ֥יִם הַֽחַיִּֽים   the living bird in the blood of the bird
                                                              that was killed over the running water.

וְהִזָּ֗ה עַ֧ל הַמִּטַּהֵ֛ר מִן־הַצָּרַ֖עַת שֶׁ֣בַע ⁷¹¹ And he shall sprinkle upon he who is to
פְּעָמִ֑ים וְטִ֣הֲר֔וֹ וְשִׁלַּ֛ח אֶת־הַצִּפֹּ֥ר   be cleansed from the leprosy seven
הַֽחַיָּ֖ה עַל־פְּנֵ֥י הַשָּׂדֶֽה   times, and shall pronounce him clean,
                                                              and shall let go the living bird into the
                                                              open field.

וְכִבֶּס֩ הַמִּטַּהֵ֨ר אֶת־בְּגָדָ֜יו וְגִלַּ֣ח אֶת־ ⁸¹² And he who is to be cleansed shall wash
כָּל־שְׂעָר֗וֹ וְרָחַ֤ץ בַּמַּ֙יִם֙ וְטָהֵ֔ר וְאַחַ֖ר   his clothes, and shave off all his hair,
יָב֣וֹא אֶל־הַֽמַּחֲנֶ֑ה וְיָשַׁ֛ב מִח֥וּץ לְאׇהֳל֖וֹ   and bathe himself in water, and he shall
שִׁבְעַ֥ת יָמִֽים   be clean; and after that he may come
                                                              into the camp, but shall dwell outside
                                                              his tent seven days.

וְהָיָה֩ בַיּ֨וֹם הַשְּׁבִיעִ֜י יְגַלַּ֣ח אֶת־כׇּל־ ⁹¹³ And it shall be on the seventh day, that
שְׂעָר֗וֹ אֶת־רֹאשׁ֤וֹ וְאֶת־זְקָנוֹ֙ וְאֵת֙ גַּבֹּ֣ת   he shall shave off all his hair from his
עֵינָ֔יו וְאֶת־כׇּל־שְׂעָר֖וֹ יְגַלֵּ֑חַ וְכִבֶּ֣ס אֶת־   head and his beard and his eyebrows,
בְּגָדָ֗יו וְרָחַ֧ץ אֶת־בְּשָׂר֛וֹ בַּמַּ֖יִם וְטָהֵֽר   even all his hair he shall shave off; and
                                                              he shall wash his clothes, and he shall
                                                              bathe his flesh in water, and he shall be

---

⁸ Leviticus 14:5 - 2 Corinthians 4:7 5:1 13:4, b.Chullin [Rashi] 62a 140a, b.Menachot [Rashi] 88a, b.Moed
Katan 14b, b.Nazir [Rashi] 38a, b.Shabbat [Rashi] 109a, b.Sotah 15b 16b, Hebrews 2:14, Jastrow 830b,
Leviticus 14:50, Leviticus.R 16:9, m.Mikvaot 1:8, m.Parah 6:5, Midrash Tanchuma Metzora 3, mt.Nizirut
7:9, Numbers 5:17, y.Sotah 2:2, z.Metzorah 53a
⁹ Leviticus 14:6 - b.Menachot [Tosefot] 16a, b.Moed Katan 14b, b.Sotah 16b, Hebrews 1:3, John 14:19,
Leviticus 14:4 14:51-14:53, m.Menachot 3:6, Mekhilta de R'Shimon bar Yochai Pisha 13:1, mt.Hilchot
Chametz uMatzah 18:7, mt.Nizirut 7:9, Numbers.R 9:16, Philippians 2:9-2:11, Revelation 1:5 1:18,
Romans 4:25 5:10, t.Sotah 1:8, y.Sotah 2:2, Zechariah 13:1
¹⁰ LXX adds *spun*
¹¹ Leviticus 14:7 - 1 John 5:6, 1 Peter 1:2, 2 Kings 5:10 5:14, b.Chullin [Rashi] 82a, b.Moed Katan 14b,
Daniel 9:24, Ephesians 5:26-27, Ezekiel 12:25, Hebrews 9:13 9:19 9:21 9:26 10:22 12:24, Isaiah 4:15,
Jastrow 1563a 1691b, John 19:34, Leviticus 4:6 4:17 8:11 13:13 13:17 14:51 16:14 16:19 16:22, Micah
7:19, mt.Nizirut 7:9, Numbers 19:18-19, Psalms 51:3 51:8
¹² Leviticus 14:8 - 1 Peter 3:21, 2 Chronicles 2:21, b.Bava Batra [Rashi] 9b, b.Chullin 141a, b.Kereitot 8b,
b.Kiddushin [Tosefot] 62a, b.Megillah [Rashi] 8a, b.Moed Katan 7b 15b 14b, b.Nazir [Rashi] 40a 44b 56a,
b.Niddah [Rashi] 34b, b.Pesachim [Rashi] 67b, b.Yevamot [Rashi] 73a, b.Zevachim [Rashi] 14b, Exodus
19:10 19:14, Jastrow 1017b, Leviticus 8:6 8:33-35 11:25 13:5-6 14:9 14:20 15:5-8, m.Kelim 1:1,
m.Negaim 4:2 4:4, m.Oholot 3:3, mt.Hilchot Melachim uMichamoteihem 8:5, mt.Hilchot Shevitat Yom
Tov 7:19, mt.Nizirut 7:9 7:15, mt.Hilchot Tumat Tzaraat 11:1, Numbers 5:2-3 8:7 12:14-15, Pesikta
Rabbati 48:2, Revelation 1:5-1:6 7:14, y.Shabbat 1:3
Leviticus 14:8-10 - mt.Hilchot Mechusrei Kapparah 1:3
¹³ Leviticus 14:9 - b.Bava Batra [Rashi] 9b, b.Bava Kamma 82a, b.Megillah [Rashi] 8a, b.Moed Katan 14b,
b.Menachot [Tosefot] 40a, b.Nazir [Rashi] 44b [Tosefot] 39b, b.Nazir 40b 41a 44a 57b, b.Sheviit [Tosefot]
2b, b.Sotah 16ab, b.Succah 6a, b.Yevamot 5a, b.Yoma [Rashi] 30b, Commandment #579, Leviticus 14:8,
m.Nazir 6:5, m.Negaim 2:4, mt.Hilchot Tumat Tzaraat 11:2, mt.Hilchot Mikvaot 1:2, mt.Hilchot Shevitat
Yom Tov 7:19, Numbers 6:9 8:7, Numbers.R 10:11, t.Negaim 1:9, y.Kiddushin 1:2

clean.

10^{14} And on the eighth day he shall take two male lambs[15] without blemish, and one ewe lamb of the first year without blemish, and three-tenth parts of an ephah of fine flour for a *meal offering, mingled*[16] with oil, and one *log*[17] of oil.

וּבַיּוֹם הַשְּׁמִינִי יִקַּח שְׁנֵי־כְבָשִׂים תְּמִימִים וְכַבְשָׂה אַחַת בַּת־שְׁנָתָהּ תְּמִימָה וּשְׁלֹשָׁה עֶשְׂרֹנִים סֹלֶת מִנְחָה בְּלוּלָה בַשֶּׁמֶן וְלֹג אֶחָד שָׁמֶן

11^{18} And the priest who cleanses him shall set the man who is to be cleansed, and those things, before the LORD, at the door of the tent of meeting.

וְהֶעֱמִיד הַכֹּהֵן הַמְטַהֵר אֵת הָאִישׁ הַמִּטַּהֵר וְאֹתָם לִפְנֵי יְהוָה פֶּתַח אֹהֶל מוֹעֵד

12^{19} And the priest shall take one of the male lambs, and offer him for a *guilt*[20] offering, and the *log*[21] of oil, and wave them for a wave[22] offering before the LORD.

וְלָקַח הַכֹּהֵן אֶת־הַכֶּבֶשׂ הָאֶחָד וְהִקְרִיב אֹתוֹ לְאָשָׁם וְאֶת־לֹג הַשָּׁמֶן וְהֵנִיף אֹתָם תְּנוּפָה לִפְנֵי יְהוָה

13^{23} And he shall kill the male lamb in the place where they kill the sin offering and the [24]burnt offering, in the place of the sanctuary; for as the sin offering is the priest's, so is the guilt offering; it is most holy.

וְשָׁחַט אֶת־הַכֶּבֶשׂ בִּמְקוֹם אֲשֶׁר יִשְׁחַט אֶת־הַחַטָּאת וְאֶת־הָעֹלָה בִּמְקוֹם הַקֹּדֶשׁ כִּי כַּחַטָּאת הָאָשָׁם הוּא לַכֹּהֵן קֹדֶשׁ קָדָשִׁים הוּא

---

[14] Leviticus 14:10 - 1 Peter 1:19, b.Kereitot [Tosefot] 9b, b.Menachot [Rashi] 3a 48b, b.Menachot 15b 91a 18a, b.Nazir [Rashi] 14b, b.Yoma [Rashi] 61a, b.Yoma 62b, b.Zevachim [Rashi] 76b, Commandment #502, Exodus 5:40, John 1:29 6:33 6:51, Leviticus 1:10 2:1 2:11 2:13 4:32 9:1 14:12 14:15 14:21 14:23-24 15:13-14 23:13, Luke 5:14, m.Menachot 5:6 9:6, m.Nazir 6:6, m.Shekalim 5:3, m.Zevachim 4:3 14:3, Mark 1:44, Matthew 8:4, Midrash Psalms 119:3, mt.Hilchot Maaseh haKorbanot 2:2, mt.Hilchot Mechusrei Kapparah 1:3, mt.Hilchot Pesulei haMikdashim 4:22 4:27, Numbers 6:14 15:4-15 4:20, Numbers.R 10:19, One of 32 readings called Severin, t.Challah 2:7, y.Sanhedrin 3:9, y.Sheviit 4:1
[15] LXX adds *of a year old*
[16] LCC *sacrifice kneaded*
[17] LXX *small cup*
[18] Leviticus 14:11 - b.Pesachim [Rashi] 85b 92a, b.Sotah 8a, b.Zevachim [Tosefot] 32a, Ephesians 5:26-5:27, Exodus 29:1-29:4, Jude 1:24, Leviticus 8:3, m.Sotah 1:5, mt.Hilchot Mechusrei Kapparah 4:2, mt.Hilchot Pesulei haMikdashim 4:22, Numbers 8:6-8:11 8:21
[19] Leviticus 14:12 - b.Bava Kamma [Rashi] 11b, b.Chullin [Rashi] 133b, b.Menachot [Rashi] 48b 58a, b.Menachot 3a 4b 61a, b.Temurah [Rashi] 14a 19b, b.Yoma [Tosefot] 48a, b.Yoma 61b, b.Zevachim [Rashi] 19a 44b 75b, b.Zevachim [Tosefot] 58a, Exodus 5:24, Isaiah 5:10, Leviticus 5:2-3 5:6-7 5:18-19 6:6-7 8:27-29, m.Chullin 2:10, m.Edoyot 8:6, m.Menachot 5:6, m.Parah 1:4, mt.Hilchot Maaseh haKorbanot 9:6, mt.Hilchot Mechusrei Kapparah 4:2, mt.Hilchot Pesulei haMikdashim 4:22, z.Mishpatim 121a, zevachim 5:5 10:5 10:8 14:10
[20] LXX *trespass*
[21] LXX *small cup*
[22] LX *special*
[23] Leviticus 14:13 - b.Menachot 73a, b.Yevamot 7ab, b.Yoma 61b, b.Zevachim [Rashi] 44b, b.Zevachim 10b 47b 49ab, Exodus 5:11, Jastrow 349b, Leviticus 1:5 1:11 2:3 4:4 4:24 6:24-6:30 7:6-7:7 10:17 21:22, Mekilta de R'Ishmael Bahodesh 11:31, mt.Hilchot Maaseh haKorbanot 9:2
[24] LXX adds *whole*

וְלָקַח הַכֹּהֵן מִדַּם הָאָשָׁם וְנָתַן הַכֹּהֵן
עַל־תְּנוּךְ אֹזֶן הַמִּטַּהֵר הַיְמָנִית וְעַל־
בֹּהֶן יָדוֹ הַיְמָנִית וְעַל־בֹּהֶן רַגְלוֹ
הַיְמָנִית

14²⁵ And the priest shall take of the blood of the *guilt*²⁶ offering, and the priest shall put it on the tip of the right ear of he who is to be cleansed, and on the thumb of his right hand, and on the great toe of his right foot.

וְלָקַח הַכֹּהֵן מִלֹּג הַשָּׁמֶן וְיָצַק עַל־כַּף
הַכֹּהֵן הַשְּׂמָאלִית

15²⁷ And the priest shall take of the *log*²⁸ of oil, and pour it into the palm of his own left hand.

וְטָבַל הַכֹּהֵן אֶת־אֶצְבָּעוֹ הַיְמָנִית מִן־
הַשֶּׁמֶן אֲשֶׁר עַל־כַּפּוֹ הַשְּׂמָאלִית וְהִזָּה
מִן־הַשֶּׁמֶן בְּאֶצְבָּעוֹ שֶׁבַע פְּעָמִים לִפְנֵי
יְהוָה

16²⁹ And the priest shall dip his right finger in the oil that is in his left hand, and shall sprinkle of the oil with his finger seven times before the LORD.

וּמִיֶּתֶר הַשֶּׁמֶן אֲשֶׁר עַל־כַּפּוֹ יִתֵּן הַכֹּהֵן
עַל־תְּנוּךְ אֹזֶן הַמִּטַּהֵר הַיְמָנִית וְעַל־
בֹּהֶן יָדוֹ הַיְמָנִית וְעַל־בֹּהֶן רַגְלוֹ
הַיְמָנִית עַל דַּם הָאָשָׁם

17³⁰ And of the rest of the oil that is in his hand the priest shall put on the tip³¹ of the right ear of he who is to be cleansed, and on the thumb of his right hand, and on the great toe of his right foot, on the blood of the *guilt*³² offering.

וְהַנּוֹתָר בַּשֶּׁמֶן אֲשֶׁר עַל־כַּף הַכֹּהֵן
יִתֵּן עַל־רֹאשׁ הַמִּטַּהֵר וְכִפֶּר עָלָיו
הַכֹּהֵן לִפְנֵי יְהוָה

18³³ And the rest of the oil that is in the priest's hand he shall put on the head of he who is to be cleansed; and the priest shall make atonement for him before the LORD.

וְעָשָׂה הַכֹּהֵן אֶת־הַחַטָּאת וְכִפֶּר עַל־
הַמִּטַּהֵר מִטֻּמְאָתוֹ וְאַחַר יִשְׁחַט אֶת־

19³⁴ And the priest shall offer the sin offering, and make atonement for he who is to be cleansed because of his

---

²⁵ Leviticus 14:14 - 1 Corinthians 6:20, 1 Peter 1:14-15 2:5 2:9-10, 2 Corinthians 7:1, b.Kiddushin 15a, b.Menachot 9b 10a 90a, b.Nazir [Rashi] 46b, b.Yevamot 14a, b.Yoma 61b, b.Zevachim [Rashi] 24ab, b.Zevachim [Tosefot] 25a, b.Zevachim 47b, Exodus 5:20, Isaiah 1:5, Jastrow 887a, Leviticus 8:23-24, Mekhilta de R'Shimon bar Yochai Nezikin 59:3, mt.Hilchot Mechusrei Kapparah 5:1, Philippians 1:20, Revelation 1:5-6, Romans 6:13 6:19 12:1, Sifre Devarim Ki Tetze 291, Sifre Devarim Reeh 122, y.Yevamot 12:2

²⁶ LXX *trespass*

²⁷ Leviticus 14:15 - 1 John 2:20, b.Menachot [Rashi] 10a, b.Menachot 9b, John 3:34, Psalms 45:8

²⁸ LXX *cup*

²⁹ Leviticus 14:16 - 1 Corinthians 10:31, b.Chullin [Rashi] 22a, b.Menachot [Rashi] 5a 75a, b.Menachot 9b 10a, b.Yoma [Rashi] 24a 61a, b.Zevachim [Rashi] 24a 30a 47b 76b, b.Zevachim [Tosefot] 11a, b.Zevachim 24b, Jastrow 580b, Leviticus 4:6 4:17, Luke 17:18, m.Zevachim 2:3
Leviticus 14:16-21 - 11QpaleoLev

³⁰ Leviticus 14:17 - 1 Peter 1:2, b.Menachot [Rashi] 9b 16a, b.Menachot [Tosefot] 19b 36b, b.Menachot 10ab, b.Yoma 61a, Exodus 29:20-29:21, Ezekiel 12:27, John 1:16, Leviticus 8:30 14:14, Mekilta de R'Ishmael Nezikill 2:71, mt.Hilchot Mechusrei Kapparah 5:5, Titus 3:3-3:6

³¹ 11QpaleoLeva has an indecipherable scribal error here

³² LXX *trespass*

³³ Leviticus 14:18 - 2 Corinthians 1:21-1:22, b.Arachin [Rashi] 14b, b.Menachot [Tosefot] 93b, b.Yoma 61a, b.Zevachim 6b, Ephesians 1:17-1:18, Exodus 5:7, Leviticus 4:26 4:31 5:16 8:12, mt.Hilchot Mechusrei Kapparah 5:5

³⁴ Leviticus 14:19 - 2 Corinthians 5:21, b.Zevachim 8a, Leviticus 5:1 5:6 12:6-12:8 14:12, m.Keritot 2:3, m.Negaim 14:11, Romans 8:3, y.Pesachim 5:2

הָעֹלָה

uncleanness; and afterward he shall kill the [1]burnt offering.

וְהֶעֱלָה הַכֹּהֵן אֶת־הָעֹלָה וְאֶת־הַמִּנְחָה הַמִּזְבֵּחָה וְכִפֶּר עָלָיו הַכֹּהֵן וְטָהֵר

20[2] And the priest shall offer the [3]burnt offering and the meal offering upon the altar; and the priest shall make atonement for him, and he shall be clean.

וְאִם־דַּל הוּא וְאֵין יָדוֹ מַשֶּׂגֶת וְלָקַח כֶּבֶשׂ אֶחָד אָשָׁם לִתְנוּפָה לְכַפֵּר עָלָיו וְעִשָּׂרוֹן סֹלֶת אֶחָד בָּלוּל בַּשֶּׁמֶן לְמִנְחָה וְלֹג שָׁמֶן

21[4] And if he is poor, and his means do not suffice, then he shall take one male lamb for *a guilt offering to be waved*[5] to make make atonement for him, and one-tenth part of an ephah of fine flour mingled with oil for a meal offering, and a *log*[6] of oil;

וּשְׁתֵּי תֹרִים אוֹ שְׁנֵי בְּנֵי יוֹנָה אֲשֶׁר תַּשִּׂיג יָדוֹ וְהָיָה אֶחָד חַטָּאת וְהָאֶחָד עֹלָה

22[7] And two turtledoves, or two young pigeons, such as his means suffice; and the one shall be a sin offering, and the other a [8]burnt offering.

וְהֵבִיא אֹתָם בַּיּוֹם הַשְּׁמִינִי לְטָהֳרָתוֹ אֶל־הַכֹּהֵן אֶל־פֶּתַח אֹהֶל־מוֹעֵד לִפְנֵי יְהוָה

23[9] And on the eighth day he shall bring them for his cleansing to the priest, to the door of the tent of meeting, before the LORD.

וְלָקַח הַכֹּהֵן אֶת־כֶּבֶשׂ הָאָשָׁם וְאֶת־לֹג הַשָּׁמֶן וְהֵנִיף אֹתָם הַכֹּהֵן תְּנוּפָה לִפְנֵי יְהוָה

24[10] And the priest shall take the lamb of the guilt offering, and the *log*[11] of oil, and the priest shall wave them for a wave offering before the LORD.

וְשָׁחַט אֶת־כֶּבֶשׂ הָאָשָׁם וְלָקַח הַכֹּהֵן

25[12] And he shall kill the lamb of the guilt

---

[1] LXX adds *whole*

[2] Leviticus 14:20 - b.Kinnim [Pirush] 23b, b.Menachot [Tosefot] 4b, b.Menachot 91a, b.Pesachim 59b, b.Zevachim [Tosefot] 5a, Ephesians 5:2, Leviticus 14:8 14:10, Mekhilta de R'Shimon bar Yochai Bachodesh 57:3, mt.Hilchot Pesulei haMikdashim 4:27
Leviticus 14:20-21 - mt.Hilchot Mechusrei Kapparah 1:3

[3] LXX adds *whole*

[4] Leviticus 14:21 - 1 Samuel 2:8, 2 Corinthians 8:9 8:12, b.Arachin 17a 17b, b.Menachot [Rashi] 9b 11a 28a 57b, b.Menachot [Tosefot] 22a, b.Menachot 88a 89a 93b 16b, b.Nazir 26a, b.Yoma [Rashi] 61b, b.Yoma 5a 41b, b.Zevachim [Rashi] 91b, James 2:5-2:6, Jastrow 309b 1680b, Job 10:19, Leviticus 1:14 5:7 5:11 12:8 14:22, Leviticus.R 34:6, Luke 6:20 21:2-4, m.Arachin 4:2, m.Menachot 9:3, m.Negaim 14:7 14:10-11, Midrash Psalms 106:8, Midrash Tanchuma Behar 3, mt.Hilchot Mechusrei Kapparah 5:11, Numbers.R 10:24, Proverbs 17:5 22:2, t.Menachot 7:16 10:1, y.Horayot 2:6, z.Noach 64b, z.Vayikra 117 123, b.Kereitot 28a

[5] LXX *his transgression for a separate offering*

[6] LXX *cup*

[7] Leviticus 14:22 - b.Chullin [Rashi] 22b, Ezekiel 7:16, Isaiah 14:14 11:11, Jeremiah 24:28, Leviticus 5:7, Psalms 68:14, Song of Songs 2:14
Leviticus 14:22-34 - 4QLev-Numa

[8] LXX adds *whole*

[9] Leviticus 14:23 - Leviticus 14:10-14:11

[10] Leviticus 14:24 - Genesis.R 44:14, Leviticus 14:10 14:12

[11] LXX *cup*

[12] Leviticus 14:25 - b.Menachot [Rashi] 9b, b.Menachot 10a, Ecclesiastes 5:2, Leviticus 14:14-20, Psalms 40:7

מִדַּם הָאָשָׁם וְנָתַן עַל־תְּנוּךְ אֹזֶן
הַמִּטַּהֵר הַיְמָנִית וְעַל־בֹּהֶן יָדוֹ הַיְמָנִית
וְעַל־בֹּהֶן רַגְלוֹ הַיְמָנִית

offering, and the priest shall take of the blood of the guilt offering, and put it on the tip of the right ear of he who is to be cleansed, and on the thumb of his right hand, and on the great toe of his right foot.

וּמִן־הַשֶּׁמֶן יִצֹק הַכֹּהֵן עַל־כַּף הַכֹּהֵן
הַשְּׂמָאלִית

26[1] And the priest shall pour of the oil into the palm of his own left hand.

וְהִזָּה הַכֹּהֵן בְּאֶצְבָּעוֹ הַיְמָנִית מִן־
הַשֶּׁמֶן אֲשֶׁר עַל־כַּפּוֹ הַשְּׂמָאלִית שֶׁבַע
פְּעָמִים לִפְנֵי יְהוָה

27[2] And the priest shall sprinkle with his right finger some of the oil that is in his left hand seven times before the LORD.

וְנָתַן הַכֹּהֵן מִן־הַשֶּׁמֶן אֲשֶׁר עַל־כַּפּוֹ
עַל־תְּנוּךְ אֹזֶן הַמִּטַּהֵר הַיְמָנִית וְעַל־
בֹּהֶן יָדוֹ הַיְמָנִית וְעַל־בֹּהֶן רַגְלוֹ
הַיְמָנִית עַל־מְקוֹם דַּם הָאָשָׁם

28[3] And the priest shall put of the oil that is in his hand on the tip of the right ear of he who is to be cleansed, and on the thumb of his right hand, and on the great toe of his right foot, on the place of the blood of the guilt offering.

וְהַנּוֹתָר מִן־הַשֶּׁמֶן אֲשֶׁר עַל־כַּף הַכֹּהֵן
יִתֵּן עַל־רֹאשׁ הַמִּטַּהֵר לְכַפֵּר עָלָיו
לִפְנֵי יְהוָה

29[4] And the rest of the oil that is in the priest's hand he shall put on the head of he who is to be cleansed, to make atonement for him before the LORD.

וְעָשָׂה אֶת־הָאֶחָד מִן־הַתֹּרִים אוֹ מִן־
בְּנֵי הַיּוֹנָה מֵאֲשֶׁר תַּשִּׂיג יָדוֹ

30[5] And he shall offer one of the turtledoves, or of the young pigeons, such as his means can suffice;

אֵת אֲשֶׁר־תַּשִּׂיג יָדוֹ אֶת־הָאֶחָד חַטָּאת
וְאֶת־הָאֶחָד עֹלָה עַל־הַמִּנְחָה וְכִפֶּר
הַכֹּהֵן עַל הַמִּטַּהֵר לִפְנֵי יְהוָה

31[6] *For as his means suffice*[7], the one for a sin offering, and the other for a [8]burnt offering, with the meal offering; and the priest shall make atonement for he who is to be cleansed before the LORD.

זֹאת תּוֹרַת אֲשֶׁר־בּוֹ נֶגַע צָרָעַת אֲשֶׁר
לֹא־תַשִּׂיג יָדוֹ בְּטָהֳרָתוֹ

32[9] This is the law of he in whom is the plague of leprosy, and whose means do not suffice for that which pertains to his cleansing.

---

[1] Leviticus 14:26 - b.Menachot 9b 10a, b.Zevachim [Rashi] 76b

[2] Leviticus 14:27 - b.Menachot 9b 10a, b.Zevachim [Rashi] 11a 76b
Leviticus 14:27-29 - 4QLevd

[3] Leviticus 14:28 - b.Menachot [Rashi] 5a, b.Menachot 9b 10a, b.Zevachim [Rashi] 43a, m.Negaim 4:7, mt.Hilchot Mechusrei Kapparah 5:1, t.Negaim 9:3

[4] Leviticus 14:29 - 1 John 2:1-2 5:6, b.Yoma 61a, Exodus 30:15-16, John 17:19, Leviticus 14:18 14:20, m.Negaim 4:7

[5] Leviticus 14:30 - Jastrow 1387b, Lamentations.R 2:4, Leviticus 12:8 14:22 15:14-15, Luke 2:24, Romans 8:3

[6] Leviticus 14:31 - Leviticus 5:7 14:18

[7] Missing in LXX

[8] LXX adds *whole*

[9] Leviticus 14:32 - 1 Corinthians 1:27-28, b.Arachin 17b, b.Kereitot 9b, b.Nedarim [Ran] 38b, b.Niddah [Rashi] 70a, Leviticus 13:59 14:2 14:10 14:21 14:54-57, Leviticus.R 16:6, Matthew 11:5, Psalms 72:12-14 16:23

וַיְדַבֵּר יְהוָה אֶל־מֹשֶׁה וְאֶל־אַהֲרֹן לֵאמֹר׃ 33[1]

And the LORD spoke to Moses and to Aaron, saying:

כִּי תָבֹאוּ אֶל־אֶרֶץ כְּנַעַן אֲשֶׁר אֲנִי נֹתֵן לָכֶם לַאֲחֻזָּה וְנָתַתִּי נֶגַע צָרַעַת בְּבֵית אֶרֶץ אֲחֻזַּתְכֶם׃ 34[2]

When you enter the land of *Canaan*[3], which I give to you for a possession, and I put the plague of leprosy in a house of the land of your possession;

וּבָא אֲשֶׁר־לוֹ הַבַּיִת וְהִגִּיד לַכֹּהֵן לֵאמֹר כְּנֶגַע נִרְאָה לִי בַּבָּיִת׃ 35[4]

Then he who owns the house shall come and tell the priest, saying: 'There seems to me to be, as it were, a plague in the house.'

וְצִוָּה הַכֹּהֵן וּפִנּוּ אֶת־הַבַּיִת בְּטֶרֶם יָבֹא הַכֹּהֵן לִרְאוֹת אֶת־הַנֶּגַע וְלֹא יִטְמָא כָּל־אֲשֶׁר בַּבָּיִת וְאַחַר כֵּן יָבֹא הַכֹּהֵן לִרְאוֹת אֶת־הַבָּיִת׃ 36[5]

And the priest shall command that they *empty*[6] the house before the priest goes in to see the plague[7], that all that is in the house shall not be made unclean; and afterward the priest shall go in to see the house.

וְרָאָה אֶת־הַנֶּגַע וְהִנֵּה הַנֶּגַע בְּקִירֹת הַבַּיִת שְׁקַעֲרוּרֹת יְרַקְרַקֹּת אוֹ אֲדַמְדַּמֹּת וּמַרְאֵיהֶן שָׁפָל מִן־הַקִּיר׃ 37[8]

And he shall look on the plague, and, behold, if the plague is in the walls of the house *with hollow streaks, greenish or reddish, and its appearance is lower than the wall*[9];

וְיָצָא הַכֹּהֵן מִן־הַבַּיִת אֶל־פֶּתַח הַבָּיִת 38[10]

Then the priest shall leave the house to

---

[1] Leviticus 14:33 - Guide for the Perplexed 3:47
Leviticus 14:33-36 - 4QLevd
Leviticus 14:33-54 - mt.Hilchot Beit Habechirah 7:14 7:14

[2] Leviticus 14:34 - 1 Samuel 2:6, Amos 3:6 6:11, Avot de R'Natan 9 35, b.Bava Kamma 82b, b.Gittin 82a, b.Horayot 10a, b.Kiddushin [Rashi] 37a, b.Megillah 26a, b.Nedarim 56a, b.Yoma [Rashi] 12a, b.Yoma 11b, Deuteronomy 7:1-2 7:15 12:1 12:8-10 19:1 2:1 3:3 8:49, Exodus 15:26, Genesis 12:7 13:17 17:8, Genesis.R 95 [Excl]:1, Isaiah 21:7, Joshua 13:1, Leviticus 23:10 1:2, Leviticus.R 17:1, m.Negaim 1:3 12:1, Micah 6:9, Midrash Tanchuma Metzora 4, Midrash Tanchuma Tazria 10, mt.Hilchot Tumat Tzaraat 14:6 14:11, Numbers 8:22 8:32 11:10, Proverbs 3:33, z.Tazria 50a, z.Tazria 93 144 157
Leviticus 14:34-46 - Commandment #568

[3] LXX *the Canaanites*

[4] Leviticus 14:35 - 1 Kings 13:34, 1 Samuel 3:12-14, b.Arachin 16a, b.Bechorot [Tosefot] 14b, b.Chullin [Rashi] 10b, b.Megillah [Rashi] 26a, b.Menachot [Tosefot] 33a, b.Moed Katan 8a, b.Succah [Rashi] 3b, b.Yoma 11b 12a, Deuteronomy 7:26, Ein Yaakov Arachin:16a, Jastrow 573a, Joshua 7:21, Leviticus.R 17:7, m.Negaim 12:5, Midrash Tanchuma Metzora 4, mt.Hilchot Tumat Tzaraat 14:4, Pesikta Rabbati 17:6, Philo Quod Deus Immutabilis Sit 131 135, Proverbs 3:33, Psalms 91:10, y.Orlah 1:2, z.Tazria 50b, Zechariah 5:4, z.Pinchas 246, z.Tazria 157 158

[5] Leviticus 14:36 - 1 Corinthians 15:33, 2 Timothy 2:17-2:18, b.Arachin 16a, b.Chullin [Rashi] 49b, b.Menachot [Rashi] 86b, b.Moed Katan 7b, b.Rosh Hashanah [Rashi] 16a, b.Shabbat [Tosefot] 41b, b.Sheviit 14b, b.Yoma [Rashi] 39a, Deuteronomy.R 6:8, Ein Yaakov Arachin 16a, Hebrews 12:15, Jastrow 1165a, Leviticus.R 17:2 17:7, m.Negaim 12:5, Midrash Tanchuma Metzora 4, mt.Hilchot Tumat Tzaraat 9:8, Philo Quod Deterius Potiori Insidiari Soleat 16, Revelation 18:4

[6] LXXX *remove the furniture of*

[7] 4QLevd adds *of leprosy*

[8] Leviticus 14:37 - b.Bava Batra 164b, b.Nazir 8b, b.Niddah 19a, b.Sanhedrin [Rashi] 87b, b.Sanhedrin 71a, Deuteronomy.R 6:8, Jastrow 598a 696b 1625a, Leviticus 13:3 13:19-20 13:42 13:49, Leviticus.R 17:2, m.Negaim 3:7, mt.Hilchot Tumat Tzaraat 14:1-3, Numbers.R 14:10

[9] LXX *greenish or reddish cavities, and the appearance of them [will be] beneath the surface of the walls*

[10] Leviticus 14:38 - b.Chullin 10b, b.Nedarim 56b, b.Niddah [Tosefot] 2b, Leviticus 13:50, m.Negaim 12:6

וְהִסְגִּיר אֶת־הַבַּיִת שִׁבְעַת יָמִים

וְשָׁב הַכֹּהֵן בַּיּוֹם הַשְּׁבִיעִי וְרָאָה וְהִנֵּה פָּשָׂה הַנֶּגַע בְּקִירֹת הַבָּיִת

וְצִוָּה הַכֹּהֵן וְחִלְּצוּ אֶת־הָאֲבָנִים אֲשֶׁר בָּהֵן הַנָּגַע וְהִשְׁלִיכוּ אֶתְהֶן אֶל־מִחוּץ לָעִיר אֶל־מָקוֹם טָמֵא

וְאֶת־הַבַּיִת יַקְצִעַ מִבַּיִת סָבִיב וְשָׁפְכוּ אֶת־הֶעָפָר אֲשֶׁר הִקְצוּ אֶל־מִחוּץ לָעִיר אֶל־מָקוֹם טָמֵא

וְלָקְחוּ אֲבָנִים אֲחֵרוֹת וְהֵבִיאוּ אֶל־תַּחַת הָאֲבָנִים וְעָפָר אַחֵר יִקַּח וְטָח אֶת־הַבָּיִת

וְאִם־יָשׁוּב הַנֶּגַע וּפָרַח בַּבַּיִת אַחַר חִלֵּץ אֶת־הָאֲבָנִים וְאַחֲרֵי הִקְצוֹת אֶת־הַבַּיִת וְאַחֲרֵי הִטּוֹחַ

וּבָא הַכֹּהֵן וְרָאָה וְהִנֵּה פָּשָׂה הַנֶּגַע

---

the door of the house, and quarantine the house for seven days.

39[1] And the priest shall come again on the seventh day, and shall look; and, behold, if the plague has spread in the walls of the house;

40[2] Then the priest shall command that they take out the stones that contain the plague, and cast them into an unclean place outside the city.

41[3] And he shall cause the house to be scraped all around within it, and they shall pour out the mortar that they scrape off outside the city in an unclean place.

42[4] And they shall take other [5]stones, and put them in the place of those stones; and he shall take other mortar, and[6] shall take plaster and plaster the house.

43[7] And if the plague comes again, and breaks out in the house, after the stones were taken out, and after the house was scraped, and after *it was plastered*[8];

44[9] Then the priest shall come in and look; and, behold, if the plague has spread in

---

[1] Leviticus 14:39 - b.Arachin [Rashi] 8b, b.Bava Batra 164ab, b.Bava Kamma [Rashi] 83b, b.Bechorot 14b, b.Chullin 85a, b.Eruvin 51a, b.Horayot 8b, b.Makkot 13b, b.Menachot 4a 45b, b.Nazir 5a 8b, b.Niddah 22b, b.Yevamot 14b, b.Yoma 2b, Jastrow 159a 1556b, Leviticus 13:7-8 13:22 13:27 13:36 13:51, mt.Hilchot Tumat Tzaraat 14:2

[2] Leviticus 14:40 - 1 Corinthians 5:5-6 5:13, 2 John 1:10-11, b.Chullin [Rashi] 128b, b.Eruvin [Rashi] 51a, b.Niddah [Rashi] 19a, b.Sanhedrin [Rashi] 71a 87b, b.Yevamot 102b, Isaiah 1:25-26, Jastrow 469a, John 15:2, Leviticus.R 17:4, m.Negaim 12:6, Matthew 18:17, mt.Hilchot Tumat Tzaraat 14:7 15:3, Pesikta de R'Kahana 7.1, Pesikta Rabbati 17:6, Proverbs 22:10 25:4-5, Psalms 5:5 101:7-8, Revelation 2:2 2:6 2:14-16 2:20 22:15, Ruth.R 2:10, Titus 3:10, z.Tazria 149
Leviticus 14:40-42 - mt.Hilchot Tumat Tzaraat 15:4
Leviticus 14:40-54 - 4QLev-Numa

[3] Leviticus 14:41 - 1 Timothy 1:20, b.Eruvin [Rashi] 51a, Isaiah 17:4, Job 36:13-14, Leviticus.R 17:7, Matthew 8:28 24:51, Revelation 22:15, t.Negaim 6:8

[4] Leviticus 14:42 - 1 Timothy 5:9-10 5:21-22, 2 Chronicles 17:7-9 19:5-7 29:4-5, 2 Timothy 2:2, Acts 1:20-26, b.Bava Batra [Tosefot] 11a, b.Eruvin [Rashi] 51a, Genesis 18:19, Joshua 24:15, Leviticus.R 17:7, m.Negaim 12:6, mt.Hilchot Tumat Tzaraat 15:2-4, Psalms 5:6, Titus 1:5-9, z.Pinchas 53 89, z.Tazria 149

[5] LXX adds *scraped*

[6] 4QLev-Numa adds *they*

[7] Leviticus 14:43 - 2 Peter 2:20 2:22, b.Eruvin [Rashi] 51a, Ezekiel 24:13, Hebrews 6:4-8, Jastrow 1556b, Jeremiah 6:28-30, Jude 1:12

[8] 4QLev-Numa *he has plastered the house*

[9] Leviticus 14:44 - b.Arachin 8b, b.Bava Kamma [Rashi] 83b, b.Bechorot 14b, b.Chullin 85a, b.Eruvin 51a, b.Horayot 8b, b.Makkot 13b, b.Menachot 4a 45b, b.Nazir 5a, b.Niddah 22b, b.Yevamot 14b, b.Yoma 2b, Jastrow 159a, Leviticus 13:51-52, mt.Hilchot Tumat Tzaraat 16:1-2, y.Orlah 3:3, Zechariah 5:4

בְּבֵית צָרַעַת מַמְאֶרֶת הִוא בַּבַּיִת טָמֵא
הוּא

וְנָתַץ אֶת־הַבַּיִת אֶת־אֲבָנָיו וְאֶת־עֵצָיו
וְאֵת כָּל־עֲפַר הַבָּיִת וְהוֹצִיא אֶל־
מִחוּץ לָעִיר אֶל־מָקוֹם טָמֵא

וְהַבָּא אֶל־הַבַּיִת כָּל־יְמֵי הִסְגִּיר אֹתוֹ
יִטְמָא עַד־הָעָרֶב

וְהַשֹּׁכֵב בַּבַּיִת יְכַבֵּס אֶת־בְּגָדָיו וְהָאֹכֵל
בַּבַּיִת יְכַבֵּס אֶת־בְּגָדָיו

וְאִם־בֹּא יָבֹא הַכֹּהֵן וְרָאָה וְהִנֵּה לֹא־
פָשָׂה הַנֶּגַע בַּבַּיִת אַחֲרֵי הִטֹּחַ אֶת־
הַבָּיִת וְטִהַר הַכֹּהֵן אֶת־הַבַּיִת כִּי נִרְפָּא
הַנָּגַע

וְלָקַח לְחַטֵּא אֶת־הַבַּיִת שְׁתֵּי צִפֳּרִים
וְעֵץ אֶרֶז וּשְׁנִי תוֹלַעַת וְאֵזֹב

וְשָׁחַט אֶת־הַצִּפֹּר הָאֶחָת אֶל־כְּלִי־
חֶרֶשׂ עַל־מַיִם חַיִּים

the house, it is a *malignant*[1] leprosy in the house: it is unclean.

45[2] And *he*[3] shall break down the house: its stones, and its timbers, and all the mortar of the house; and he shall carry them forth out of the city into an unclean place.

46[4] Moreover, he who goes into the house all the while it is quarantined shall be unclean until the evening.

47[5] And he who *lies*[6] in the house shall wash his clothes[7]; and he who eats in the house shall wash his clothes[8].

48[9] And if the priest shall come in, and look, and, behold, the plague has not spread in the house, after the house was plastered; then the priest shall pronounce the house clean, because the plague is healed.

49[10] And[11] he shall take two birds, and cedar wood, and [12]scarlet, and hyssop to cleanse the house.

50 And *he*[13] shall kill one of the birds in an earthen vessel over running water.

---

[1] LXX *confirmed*

[2] Leviticus 14:45 - 1 Kings 9:6-9, 2 Kings 10:27 17:20-23 18:4 25:4-12 25:25-26, b.Chullin [Rashi] 128b, b.Eruvin [Rashi] 51a, b.Yevamot 103b, Ezekiel 5:4, Jastrow 683b 944a 945a, Jeremiah 4:13, Leviticus.R 17:7, m.Negaim 12:2 12:7, Matthew 22:7 24:2, Midrash Psalms 52:1, Midrash Tanchuma Metzora 4, mt.Hilchot Tumat Tzaraat 14:6 15:5, Numbers.R 7:5, Pesikta de R'Kahana 7.1, Pesikta Rabbati 17:6, Revelation 11:2, Romans 11:7-11, Ruth.R 2:10, z.Balak 391, z.Pinchas 89, z.Tazria 153

[3] 4QLev-Numa LXX *they*

[4] Leviticus 14:46 - b.Arachin [Rashi] 4a 82b, b.Berachot [Rashi] 41a, b.Chullin [Rashi] 33b 71b 128b, b.Niddah [Rashi] 54b, b.Sheviit 14b, b.Succah [Rashi] 5b, b.Yevamot 103b, b.Yoma [Tosefot] 52b, Leviticus 11:24-25 11:28 15:5-8 15:10 17:15 22:6, m.Arachin 2:1, mt.Hilchot Tumat Tzaraat 16:2 16:4-5, Numbers 19:7-10 19:21-22

[5] Leviticus 14:47 - b.Avodah Zara [Rashi] 67a, b.Berachot [Rashi] 41a, b.Eruvin [Rashi] 4a 82b, b.Pesachim 44a, Leviticus 11:25 14:8-9, mt.Hilchot Tumat Tzaraat 16:6

[6] LXX *sleeps*

[7] LXX adds *and shall be unclean until the evening*

[8] LXX adds *and shall be unclean until the evening*

[9] Leviticus 14:48 - 1 Corinthians 6:11, Hosea 6:1, Job 5:18, Leviticus 14:3, Luke 7:21, Mark 5:29 5:34

[10] Leviticus 14:49 - b.Niddah 39b, Ecclesiastes.R 7:35, Leviticus 14:4, m.Negaim 13:1

[11] Missing in 4QLev-Numa

[12] LXX adds *spun*

[13] 4QLev-Numa *they*

וְלָקַח אֶת־עֵץ־הָאֶ֫רֶז וְאֶת־הָאֵזֹב וְאֵת֮ שְׁנִי הַתּוֹלַ֫עַת וְאֵת֮ הַצִּפֹּר הַֽחַיָּ֑ה וְטָבַל אֹתָם בְּדַם הַצִּפֹּר הַשְּׁחוּטָ֔ה וּבַמַּ֖יִם הַֽחַיִּ֑ים וְהִזָּ֥ה אֶל־הַבַּ֖יִת שֶׁ֥בַע פְּעָמִֽים

וְחִטֵּ֣א אֶת־הַבַּ֗יִת בְּדַם הַצִּפּ֔וֹר וּבַמַּ֖יִם הַֽחַיִּ֑ים וּבַצִּפֹּ֣ר הַֽחַיָּ֔ה וּבְעֵ֥ץ הָאֶ֖רֶז וּבָאֵזֹ֥ב וּבִשְׁנִ֥י הַתּוֹלָֽעַת

וְשִׁלַּ֞ח אֶת־הַצִּפֹּ֧ר הַֽחַיָּ֛ה אֶל־מִח֥וּץ לָעִ֖יר אֶל־פְּנֵ֣י הַשָּׂדֶ֑ה וְכִפֶּ֥ר עַל־הַבַּ֖יִת וְטָהֵֽר

זֹ֥את הַתּוֹרָ֖ה לְכָל־נֶ֣גַע הַצָּרַ֑עַת וְלַנָּֽתֶק

וּלְצָרַ֥עַת הַבֶּ֖גֶד וְלַבָּֽיִת

וְלַשְׂאֵ֥ת וְלַסַּפַּ֖חַת וְלַבֶּהָֽרֶת

לְהוֹרֹ֕ת בְּי֥וֹם הַטָּמֵ֖א וּבְי֣וֹם הַטָּהֹ֑ר זֹ֥את תּוֹרַ֥ת הַצָּרָֽעַת

51[1] And he shall take the cedar wood, and the hyssop, and the scarlet, and the living bird, and dip them in the blood of the slain bird, and in the running water, and sprinkle [2]the house seven times.

52[3] And he shall cleanse the house with the blood of the bird, and with the running water, and with the living bird, and with the cedar wood, and with the hyssop, and with the [4]scarlet.

53[5] But he shall let go the living bird out of the city into the open field; so, shall he make atonement for the house; and it shall be clean.

54[6] This is the law for all manner of plague of leprosy, and for a *scall*[7];

55[8] and for the leprosy of a garment, and for a house;

56[9] *and for a rising, and for a scab, and for a bright spot*[10];

57[11] *to teach when it is unclean, and when it is clean*[12]; this is the law of leprosy.

---

[1] Leviticus 14:51 - 4b.Menachot [Tosefot] 88a, m.Menachot 9:3, Psalms 51:8

[2] 4QLev-Numa adds *on*

[3] Leviticus 14:52 - b.Chullin 16a
Leviticus 14:52-57 - 11QpaleoLev

[4] LXX adds *spun*

[5] Leviticus 14:53 - b.Kiddushin 57b, Leviticus 14:7 14:20, m.Negaim 14:2, mt.Hilchot Tumat Tzaraat 11:1

[6] Leviticus 14:54 - b.Berachot [Rashi] 25a, Deuteronomy 24:8, Leviticus 6:9 6:14 6:25 7:1 7:37 11:46 13:30-31 14:2 14:32 15:32, Leviticus.R 16:6, mt.Hilchot Tumat Tzaraat 14:1, Numbers 5:29 6:13 19:14, Numbers.R 13:4, t.Negaim 1:2
Leviticus 14:54-55 - mt.Hilchot Tumat Tzaraat 9:6

[7] LXX *scurf*

[8] Leviticus 14:55 - b.Berachot [Rashi] 25a, Leviticus 13:47-59, mt.Hilchot Tumat Tzaraat 14:1

[9] Leviticus 14:56 - b.Kiddushin 70b, b.Shabbat 62b, b.Sheviit 6a, b.Sotah 5b, Ein Yaakov Kiddushin 70b, Ein Yaakov Sotah:5b, Lamentations.R 4:18, Leviticus 13:2, Leviticus.R 15:1 16:1, Midrash Tanchuma Metzora 4, Midrash Tanchuma Tazria 11, mt.Pirkei Avot 4:4, z.Balak 391

[10] LXX *and of a sore, and of a clear spot, and of a shining one*

[11] Leviticus 14:57 - b.Nedarim [Ran] 38b, Deuteronomy 24:8, Ezekiel 20:23, Jeremiah 15:19, Leviticus 10:10, Leviticus.R 16:6, Saadia Opinions 10:15

[12] LXX *and of declaring in what day it is unclean, and in what day it shall be purged*

Metzora – Chapter 15[1]

וַיְדַבֵּר יְהֹוָה אֶל־מֹשֶׁה וְאֶל־אַהֲרֹן לֵאמֹר

1[2] And the LORD spoke to Moses and to Aaron, saying:

דַּבְּרוּ אֶל־בְּנֵי יִשְׂרָאֵל וַאֲמַרְתֶּם אֲלֵהֶם אִישׁ אִישׁ כִּי יִהְיֶה זָב מִבְּשָׂרוֹ זוֹבוֹ טָמֵא הוּא

2[3] Speak to the children of Israel, and say to them: When any man has an issue out of his flesh, his issue is unclean.

וְזֹאת תִּהְיֶה טֻמְאָתוֹ בְּזוֹבוֹ רָר בְּשָׂרוֹ אֶת־זוֹבוֹ אוֹ־הֶחְתִּים בְּשָׂרוֹ מִזּוֹבוֹ טֻמְאָתוֹ הִוא

3[4] And this shall be his uncleanness in his issue: whether his flesh runs with his issue, or his flesh is stopped from his issue, it is his uncleanness[5].[6]

כָּל־הַמִּשְׁכָּב אֲשֶׁר יִשְׁכַּב עָלָיו הַזָּב יִטְמָא וְכָל־הַכְּלִי אֲשֶׁר־יֵשֵׁב עָלָיו יִטְמָא

4[7] Every bed upon which he who has the issue lies shall be unclean; and everything on whatever he sits shall be unclean.

---

[1] 4Q274, Josephus Antiquities 4.11.3, Josephus Antiquities 4.11.3, Midrash Proverbs 10, mt.Hilchot Korban Pesach 6:1, mt.Nizirut 7:9

[2] Leviticus 15:1 - Amos 3:7, Guide for the Perplexed 3:47, Hebrews 1:1, Leviticus 11:1 13:1, Leviticus.R 18:1, Mas.Kallah Rabbati 2:5, Psalms 25:14
Leviticus 15:1-5 - 11QpaleoLeva
Leviticus 15:1-15 - Commandment #569, Jastrow 377b, m.Berachot 3:6, m.Megillah 1:7, m.Pesachim 8:5, m.Rosh Hashanah 3:2, m.Zavim 1:1, mt.Hilchot Beit Habechirah 7:15 7:15
Leviticus 15:1-18 - 4Q266 9 14-16, 4Q272 1 ii 7

[3] Leviticus 15:2 - 2 Samuel 3:29, b.Arachin 3a, b.Chullin 51b, b.Horayot [Rashi] 10a, b.Kereitot 8b, b.Kiddushin [Rashi] 2b, b.Megillah [Rashi] 8a, b.Menachot [Tosefot] 14b, b.Niddah [Rashi] 35a 71a, b.Niddah 32b 34ab 43ab 44a 55ab 56a, b.Shabbat 83a, b.Yevamot 105a, Deuteronomy 4:7-4:8, Ecclesiastes.R 12:7, Leviticus 22:4, Leviticus.R 19:3, Luke 8:43, m.Keritot 2:1, m.Oholot 3:3, Mark 5:25 7:20-7:23, Matthew 9:20, Midrash Tanchuma Ki Tissa 17, Midrash Tanchuma Metzora 4 9, mt.Hilchot Mechusrei Kapparah 2:1 2:2, mt.Hilchot Metamei Mishkav Umoshav 1:1 1:12 2:10, mt.Hilchot Mikvaot 1:5 1:6, mt.Hilchot Shevitat Yom Tov 7:21, Nehemiah 9:13-9:14, Numbers 5:2, Psalms 78:5 147:19-147:20, Romans 3:2, Song of Songs.R 5:14

[4] Leviticus 15:3 - 11QpaleoLeva, b.Bava Kamma 24a, b.Chullin [Tosefot] 24a, b.Megillah [Rashi] 8a, b.Nazir [Rashi] 15b, b.Niddah [Tosefot] 22a, b.Niddah 43b 55b 56a, Ezekiel 16:26 23:20, Jastrow 513a 1477b, Leviticus 12:3, Midrash Tanchuma Metzora 9, mt.Hilchot Shaar Avot Hatuman 5:1, mt.Hilchot Shevitat Yom Tov 7:21

[5] LXX *And this is the law of his uncleanness; whoever has a gonorrhoea out of his body, this is his uncleanness in him by reason of the issue, by which, his body is affected through the issue: all the days of the issue of his body, by which his body is affected through the issue, there is his uncleanness*

[6] 11QpaleoLeva adds *in him all the days of the discharge of his flesh, even if his flesh obstructs his discharge, it is his uncleanness.*

[7] Leviticus 15:4 - 1 Corinthians 15:33, b.Bava Kamma [Rashi] 25b, b.Menachot 24b, b.Nazir [Rashi] 15b, b.Niddah [Tosefot] 55a, b.Niddah 54b, b.Yoma [Rashi] 6b, Ephesians 5:11, Jastrow 751b 1472b, m.Zavim 5:11, mt.Hilchot Keilim 1:10 23:1, mt.Hilchot Mikvaot 1:4, mt.Hilchot Metamei Mishkav Umoshav 7:8, Titus 1:15

וְאִ֗ישׁ אֲשֶׁ֤ר יִגַּע֙ בְּמִשְׁכָּב֔וֹ יְכַבֵּ֣ס בְּגָדָ֔יו וְרָחַ֥ץ בַּמַּ֖יִם וְטָמֵ֥א עַד־הָעָֽרֶב	5[1]	And whoever touches his bed shall wash his clothes, and bathe himself in water, and be unclean until the evening.
וְהַיֹּשֵׁב֙ עַֽל־הַכְּלִ֔י אֲשֶׁר־יֵשֵׁ֥ב עָלָ֖יו הַזָּ֑ב יְכַבֵּ֧ס בְּגָדָ֛יו וְרָחַ֥ץ בַּמַּ֖יִם וְטָמֵ֥א עַד־הָעָֽרֶב	6[2]	And he who sits on anything upon which he who has the issue sat shall wash his clothes, and bathe himself in water, and be unclean until the evening.
וְהַנֹּגֵ֖עַ בִּבְשַׂ֣ר הַזָּ֑ב יְכַבֵּ֧ס בְּגָדָ֛יו וְרָחַ֥ץ בַּמַּ֖יִם וְטָמֵ֥א עַד־הָעָֽרֶב	7[3]	And he who touches the flesh of he who has the issue shall wash his clothes, and bathe himself in water, and be unclean until the evening.
וְכִֽי־יָרֹ֥ק הַזָּ֖ב בַּטָּה֑וֹר וְכִבֶּ֣ס בְּגָדָ֗יו וְרָחַ֥ץ בַּמַּ֖יִם וְטָמֵ֥א עַד־הָעָֽרֶב	8[4]	And if he who has the issue spat on he who is clean, then he shall wash his clothes, and bathe himself in water, and be unclean until the evening[5].
וְכָל־הַמֶּרְכָּ֗ב אֲשֶׁ֨ר יִרְכַּ֥ב עָלָ֛יו הַזָּ֖ב יִטְמָֽא	9[6]	And *any*[7] saddle upon which he who has the issue rides shall be unclean.
וְכָל־הַנֹּגֵ֗עַ בְּכֹל֙ אֲשֶׁ֣ר יִהְיֶ֣ה תַחְתָּ֔יו יִטְמָ֖א עַד־הָעָ֑רֶב וְהַנּוֹשֵׂ֣א אוֹתָ֗ם יְכַבֵּ֧ס בְּגָדָ֛יו וְרָחַ֥ץ בַּמַּ֖יִם וְטָמֵ֥א עַד־הָעָֽרֶב	10[8]	And whoever touches anything that was under him shall be unclean until the even; and he who bears those things shall wash his clothes, and bathe himself in water, and be unclean until the evening.
וְכֹ֨ל אֲשֶׁ֤ר יִגַּע־בּוֹ֙ הַזָּ֔ב וְיָדָ֖יו לֹא־שָׁטַ֣ף	11[9]	And whomever he who has the issue touches, *without having*[1] rinsed his

---

[1] Leviticus 15:5 - b.Bava Kamma [Tosefot] 67b, b.Bava Kamma 66b, b.Chagigah [Tosefot] 20b, b.Chullin [Rashi] 72b, b.Menachot 24b, b.Niddah [Rashi] 32b, b.Niddah 33a, b.Shabbat 84ab, b.Yevamot [Rashi] 46b, Ezekiel 12:25 12:29, Guide for the Perplexed 3:47, Hebrews 9:14 9:26 10:22, Isaiah 1:16 22:14, James 4:8, Leviticus 11:25 11:28 11:32 13:6 13:34 14:8-14:9 14:27 14:46-14:47 16:26 16:28 17:15, mt.Hilchot Keilim 24:7, mt.Hilchot Metamei Mishkav Umoshav 6:2, mt.Hilchot Mikvaot 1:6 4:1, Numbers 19:10 19:22, Psalms 26:6 51:3 51:8, Revelation 7:14

[2] Leviticus 15:6 - b.Chagigah 23b, b.Chullin [Tosefot] 55a, b.Eruvin [Rashi] 16a 14b, b.Menachot 24b, b.Niddah 49b, b.Shabbat 59a, Isaiah 1:16, James 4:8, m.Zavim 2:4

[3] Leviticus 15:7 - b.Chullin [Rashi] 126b, b.Niddah [Rashi] 43a 55b, b.Shabbat [Rashi] 84b, b.Zevachim [Tosefot] 14a, Jastrow 1361b, m.Oholot 1:5, The Massorah says this is the middle verse of the Leviticus

[4] Leviticus 15:8 - 1 Timothy 4:1-4:3, 2 Peter 2:1-2:3, b.Bava Kamma [Rashi] 25a, b.Bava Kamma [Tosefot] 25b, b.Bechorot [Rashi] 38a, b.Chullin [Rashi] 88a, b.Kereitot [Rashi] 13b, b.Niddah [Rashi] 7b 28b 34b, b.Niddah 55b 56b, b.Pesachim [Rashi] 19b, b.Shabbat 14b, b.Zevachim [Rashi] 79b, Galatians 1:8-1:9, Isaiah 1:16, James 4:8, Jude 1:4, mt.Hilchot Issurei Biah 4:3, mt.Hilchot Shaar Avot Hatuman 7:2, One of 32 readings called Severin, Titus 1:9-1:10

[5] LXX adds *until evening*

[6] Leviticus 15:9 - b.Nazir 58a, b.Niddah [Tosefot] 32b, b.Pesachim [Rashi] 3a, b.Sanhedrin 48b, Ein Yaakov Pesachim:3a, Ein Yaakov Sanhedrin:48b, Genesis 7:34, Jastrow 844a, m.Kelim 1:3 23:3, Midrash Tanchuma Massei 12, mt.Hilchot Metamei Mishkav Umoshav 6:2, Numbers.R 23:13

[7] LXX *every ass's*

[8] Leviticus 15:10 - b.Chullin [Rashi] 126b, b.Eruvin [Rashi] 16a, b.Niddah [Rashi] 7a 33a 43a 55b, b.Niddah 32b 35a 55a, b.Shabbat [Rashi] 82b, James 4:8, Leviticus 15:5 15:8, m.Oholot 1:5, mt.Hilchot Metamei Mishkav Umoshav 6:2 6:3, mt.Hilchot Kriat Shema 4:8, Psalms 26:6
Leviticus 15:10-11 - 4QLev-Numa

[9] Leviticus 15:11 - b.Beitzah [Rashi] 32a, b.Chullin [Rashi] 71b 126b, b.Chullin 16a, b.Kiddushin 25a, b.Niddah [Rashi] 41b, b.Niddah 43a, b.Sanhedrin [Rashi] 55b, mt.Hilchot Mikvaot 1:2

בַּמַּיִם וְכִבֶּס בְּגָדָיו וְרָחַץ בַּמַּיִם וְטָמֵא
עַד־הָעָרֶב

וּכְלִי־חֶרֶשׂ אֲשֶׁר־יִגַּע־בּוֹ הַזָּב יִשָּׁבֵר
וְכָל־כְּלִי־עֵץ יִשָּׁטֵף בַּמָּיִם

וְכִי־יִטְהַר הַזָּב מִזּוֹבוֹ וְסָפַר לוֹ שִׁבְעַת
יָמִים לְטָהֳרָתוֹ וְכִבֶּס בְּגָדָיו וְרָחַץ
בְּשָׂרוֹ בְּמַיִם חַיִּים וְטָהֵר

וּבַיּוֹם הַשְּׁמִינִי יִקַּח־לוֹ שְׁתֵּי תֹרִים אוֹ
שְׁנֵי בְּנֵי יוֹנָה וּבָא לִפְנֵי יְהוָה אֶל־
פֶּתַח אֹהֶל מוֹעֵד וּנְתָנָם אֶל־הַכֹּהֵן

וְעָשָׂה אֹתָם הַכֹּהֵן אֶחָד חַטָּאת וְהָאֶחָד
עֹלָה וְכִפֶּר עָלָיו הַכֹּהֵן לִפְנֵי יְהוָה
מִזּוֹבוֹ

hands in water, he shall wash his clothes, and bathe himself in water, and be unclean until the evening.

12[2] And the earthen vessel, that he who has the issue touches, shall be broken; and every vessel of wood shall be rinsed in water.

13[3] And when he who has an issue is cleansed of his issue, then he shall number to himself seven days for his cleansing, and wash his clothes; and he shall bathe his flesh in running water, and shall be clean.

14[4] And on the eighth day he shall take two turtledoves, or two young pigeons, and come before the LORD to the door of the tent of meeting, and give them to the priest.

15[5] And the priest shall offer them, the one for a sin offering, and the other for a [6]burnt offering; and the priest shall make atonement for him before the LORD for his issue.

---

[1] LXX *if he has not*

[2] Leviticus 15:12 - 2 Corinthians 5:1, b.Bava Kamma [Rashi] 25b, b.Bechorot [Rashi] 38a, b.Niddah [Rashi] 6a 33a, b.Pesachim [Rashi] 67b, Leviticus 6:28 11:32-33, m.Eduyot 2:5, Philippians 3:21, Proverbs 1:21 1:23 3:21, Psalms 2:9
Leviticus 15:12-16 - m.Bikkurim 42

[3] Leviticus 15:13 - 2 Corinthians 7:1, 4Q514 1 i 1-11, b.Gittin [Tosefot] 28b, b.Kiddushin 25a, b.Megillah 8a, b.Menachot [Tosefot] 62b, b.Nazir [Rashi] 44b, b.Niddah [Rashi] 7b, b.Niddah 33b 37a, b.Pesachim [Rashi] 81a, b.Shabbat [Rashi] 11b 109a, b.Yoma 31a, b.Zevachim [Tosefot] 75a, Exodus 5:35 5:37, Ezekiel 36:25-29, James 4:8, Jeremiah 9:8, Leviticus 8:33 9:1 14:8 14:10 15:5 15:10-11 15:28, m.Kelim 1:4 1:5, m.Mikvaot 1:7 1:8, m.Parah 6:5, m.Pesachim 8:5, m.Zavim 1:1, mt.Hilchot Mikvaot 1:2 1:5, mt.Hilchot Sanhedrin vHainshin Hameurim Lahem 19:2, Numbers 12:14 19:11-12, Pirkei de R'Eliezer 53, Revelation 1:5
Leviticus 15:13-14 - mt.Hilchot Mechusrei Kapparah 1:3
Leviticus 15:13-15 - Commandment #503

[4] Leviticus 15:14 - 2 Corinthians 5:21, b.Megillah 8a, b.Nazir 44b, Hebrews 7:26 10:10 10:12 10:14, Leviticus 1:14 12:6 12:8 14:22-31 15:29-15:30, m.Shekalim 1:5, m.Sheviit 88, m.Zevachim 14:3, Mas.Kutim 1:2, mt.Hilchot Kiddush HaChodesh 4:7, mt.Hilchot Sanhedrin vHainshin Hameurim Lahem 19:2, Numbers 6:10
Leviticus 15:14-15 - mt.Hilchot Mechusrei Kapparah 1:3

[5] Leviticus 15:15 - b.Megillah 8a 20a, b.Nazir 16a, b.Niddah 66b, Ephesians 1:6, Hebrews 1:3, Guide for the Perplexed 3:47, Leviticus 4:20 4:26 4:31 4:35 5:7-10 12:7 14:18-20 14:30-31, m.Shekalim 1:5, Matthew 3:17, mt.Hilchot Sanhedrin vHainshin Hameurim Lahem 19:2, Numbers 15:25 1:13

[6] LXX adds *whole*

וְאִ֗ישׁ כִּי־תֵצֵ֤א מִמֶּ֙נּוּ֙ שִׁכְבַת־זָ֔רַע
וְרָחַ֥ץ בַּמַּ֛יִם אֶת־כָּל־בְּשָׂר֖וֹ וְטָמֵ֥א עַד־
הָעָֽרֶב

16[1]   *And if the flow of seed goes out from a man[2]*, then he shall bathe all his flesh in water, and be unclean until the evening.

וְכָל־בֶּ֞גֶד וְכָל־ע֗וֹר אֲשֶׁר־יִהְיֶ֥ה עָלָ֖יו
שִׁכְבַת־זָ֑רַע וְכֻבַּ֥ס בַּמַּ֖יִם וְטָמֵ֥א עַד־
הָעָֽרֶב

17[3]   And every garment, and every skin, upon which is the *flow of seed[4]*, shall be washed with water, and be unclean until the evening.

וְאִשָּׁ֕ה אֲשֶׁ֨ר יִשְׁכַּ֥ב אִ֛ישׁ אֹתָ֖הּ שִׁכְבַת־
זָ֑רַע וְרָחֲצ֣וּ בַמַּ֔יִם וְטָמְא֖וּ עַד־הָעָֽרֶב

18[5]   The woman also with whom a man *shall lie carnally[6]*, they shall both bathe themselves in water, and be unclean until the evening.

וְאִשָּׁה֙ כִּֽי־תִהְיֶ֣ה זָבָ֔ה דָּ֛ם יִהְיֶ֥ה זֹבָ֖הּ
בִּבְשָׂרָ֑הּ שִׁבְעַ֤ת יָמִים֙ תִּהְיֶ֣ה בְנִדָּתָ֔הּ
וְכָל־הַנֹּגֵ֥עַ בָּ֖הּ יִטְמָ֥א עַד־הָעָֽרֶב

19[7]   And if a woman has an issue, and her issue in her flesh is blood, she shall be in her impurity seven days; and whoever touches her shall be unclean until the evening.

וְכֹל֩ אֲשֶׁ֨ר תִּשְׁכַּ֥ב עָלָ֛יו בְּנִדָּתָ֖הּ יִטְמָ֑א
וְכֹ֛ל אֲשֶׁר־תֵּשֵׁ֥ב עָלָ֖יו יִטְמָֽא

20[8]   And everything that she lies upon in her impurity shall be unclean; everything also that she sits on shall be unclean.

---

[1] Leviticus 15:16 - 1 John 1:7, 1 Peter 2:11, 2 Corinthians 7:1, Avot de R'Natan 2 8, b.Bava Kamma 82b, b.Chagigah 11a, b.Chullin [Tosefot] 83b, b.Eruvin 4b 14a, b.Menachot [Tosefot] 18b, b.Nazir 47b, b.Niddah [Rashi] 41b, b.Niddah 32b 43a, b.Pesachim [Rashi] 67b, b.Pesachim 109a, Commandment #570 #571, Deuteronomy 23:12-12, Ein Yaakov Eruvin:14a, Leviticus 15:5 22:4, m.Berachot 3:4, m.Kelim 1:5, m.Oholot 3:3, mt.Hilchot Beit Habechirah 5:11 8:7, mt.Hilchot Kriat Shema 4:8
[2] LXX *And the man whose seed of copulation shall happen to go forth from him*
[3] Leviticus 15:17 - b.Bava Batra [Rashi] 9b, b.Bava Kamma [Rashi] 25a, b.Bava Kamma 25b, b.Niddah [Tosefot] 22a 43b, b.Shabbat 86b, m.Berachot 3:4
[4] LXX *seed of copulation*
[5] Leviticus 15:18 - 1 Corinthians 6:12 6:18, 1 Peter 2:11, 1 Samuel 21:4-5, 1 Thessalonians 4:3-5, 2 Timothy 2:22, 4Q284 1, 4Q284 2 i, b.Niddah 32a 41b 42a, b.Sanhedrin [Rashi] 55b, b.Yevamot [Rashi] 69a, b.Yevamot 34b, b.Zevachim 81ab, Ephesians 4:17-19 5:3-11, Exodus 19:15, Hebrews 13:4, Leviticus 15:5, m.Berachot 3:4, mt.Hilchot Shaar Avot Hatuman 5:9 5:19, mt.Hilchot Terumot 7:7 8:3, Psalms 51:6
[6] LXX *shall lie with her with seed of copulation*
[7] Leviticus 15:19 - 4Q284 2 ii, 4Q284 3, Avot de R'Natan 2, b.Bava Kamma [Rashi] 38b, b.Chullin [Rashi] 55a, b.Niddah [Rashi] 6a 31b 32b 42a 44a 67b 73a, b.Niddah 21b 32a 36b 40a 41b 54b 57b 58b 72b, b.Pesachim 90b, b.Rosh Hashanah [Rashi] 10a, b.Shabbat [Rashi] 16b, b.Sheviit 18a, b.Yoma [Rashi] 6a, Ein Yaakov Berachot:4a, Ezekiel 12:17, Guide for the Perplexed 3:47, Lamentations 1:8-9 1:17, Leviticus 12:2 12:4 20:18, Leviticus.R 19:3, m.Horayot 1:3, m.Megillah 2:4, m.Niddah 1:2 1:7 4:3 5:1 6:4 8:3, Mark 5:25, Mas.Kallah 1:1, Matthew 15:19, Midrash Tanchuma Ki Tissa 17, mt.Hilchot Issurei Biah 4:2 4:6 5:2 5:16 7:1, mt.Hilchot Kriat Shema 4:8, mt.Hilchot Shevitat Yom Tov 7:21, Pirkei de R'Eliezer 53, Song of Songs.R 5:14, y.Niddah 2:3 3:1, z.Pinchas 246
Leviticus 15:19-24 - 4Q278, 4QLev-Numa, Commandment #572, Jastrow 377b, m.Avot 3:18, m.Berachot 3:6, m.Zavim 1:1, mt.Hilchot Beit Habechirah 7:15-16
Leviticus 15:19-30 - 4Q266 9 ii 1-4
Leviticus 15:19-33 - m.Pesachim 9:4
[8] Leviticus 15:20 - 1 Corinthians 15:33, Ecclesiastes 7:26, Ein Yaakov Pesachim 3a, Leviticus 15:4-9, m.Megillah 2:4, Proverbs 2:16-19 5:3-13 6:24 6:35 7:10-27 9:13-18 22:27
Leviticus 15:20-24 - 4QLevd

וְכָל־הַנֹּגֵעַ בְּמִשְׁכָּבָהּ יְכַבֵּס בְּגָדָיו וְרָחַץ בַּמַּיִם וְטָמֵא עַד־הָעָרֶב	21[1]	And whoever touches her bed shall wash his clothes, and bathe himself in water, and be unclean until the evening.
וְכָל־הַנֹּגֵעַ בְּכָל־כְּלִי אֲשֶׁר־תֵּשֵׁב עָלָיו יְכַבֵּס בְּגָדָיו וְרָחַץ בַּמַּיִם וְטָמֵא עַד־הָעָרֶב	22[2]	And whoever touches anything[3] upon which she sits shall wash his clothes, and bathe himself in water, and be unclean until the evening.
וְאִם עַל־הַמִּשְׁכָּב הוּא אוֹ עַל־הַכְּלִי אֲשֶׁר־הִוא יֹשֶׁבֶת־עָלָיו בְּנָגְעוֹ־בוֹ יִטְמָא עַד־הָעָרֶב	23[4]	And if he is on the bed, or on anything upon which she sits, when he touches it, he shall be unclean until the evening.
וְאִם שָׁכֹב יִשְׁכַּב אִישׁ אֹתָהּ וּתְהִי נִדָּתָהּ עָלָיו וְטָמֵא שִׁבְעַת יָמִים וְכָל־הַמִּשְׁכָּב אֲשֶׁר־יִשְׁכַּב עָלָיו יִטְמָא	24[5]	And if any man lies with her, and her impurity comes upon him, he shall be unclean seven days; and every bed upon which he lies shall be unclean.
וְאִשָּׁה כִּי־יָזוּב זוֹב דָּמָהּ יָמִים רַבִּים בְּלֹא עֶת־נִדָּתָהּ אוֹ כִי־תָזוּב עַל־נִדָּתָהּ כָּל־יְמֵי זוֹב טֻמְאָתָהּ כִּימֵי נִדָּתָהּ תִּהְיֶה טְמֵאָה הִוא	25[6]	And if a woman has an issue of her blood many days not in the time of her impurity, or if she has an issue beyond the time of her impurity; all the days of the issue of her uncleanness she shall be as in the days of her impurity: she is unclean.
כָּל־הַמִּשְׁכָּב אֲשֶׁר־תִּשְׁכַּב עָלָיו כָּל־יְמֵי זוֹבָהּ כְּמִשְׁכַּב נִדָּתָהּ יִהְיֶה־לָּהּ וְכָל־הַכְּלִי אֲשֶׁר תֵּשֵׁב עָלָיו טָמֵא	26[7]	Every bed upon which she lies all the days of her *issue*[8] shall be to her as the bed of her impurity; and everything upon which she sits shall be unclean, as

---

[1] Leviticus 15:21 - 2 Corinthians 7:1, b.Niddah [Rashi] 5b 32b 33a, b.Yoma [Rashi] 6b, Hebrews 9:26, Isaiah 22:14, Leviticus 15:5-6, Revelation 7:14

[2] Leviticus 15:22 - b.Avodah Zara [Rashi] 47b

[3] LXX *vessel*

[4] Leviticus 15:23 - b.Niddah 54b, b.Pesachim 26a [Rashi] 3ab, b.Yoma 31b, Ein Yaakov Shabbat 82a

[5] Leviticus 15:24 - 1 Peter 2:11, 1 Thessalonians 5:22, b.Chagigah [Tosefot] 11a, b.Kiddushin 68a [Rashi] 10a, b.Niddah 33a [Rashi] 14a, b.Pesachim 68a, b.Sanhedrin [Rashi] 55b, b.Sheviit 18ab, b.Yevamot 49b [Rashi] 54a, b.Yoma 31b [Rashi] 6ab, Ezekiel 18:6 22:10, Hebrews 13:4, Leviticus 15:33 18:19 20:18, m.Niddah 2:3, m.Shabbat 1:3, m.Zavim 2:4, mt.Hilchot Beit HaBechirah 7:16, mt.Hilchot Metamei Mishkav Umoshav 3:1 3:2, mt.Hilchot Shegagot 5:6, y.Horayot 2:5, z.Shemot 25

[6] Leviticus 15:25 - b.Bava Batra 24a 166a, b.Bava Kamma [Rashi] 24a, b.Chullin [Rashi] 138a, b.Horayot [Tosefot] 4a, b.Kereitot [Rashi] 8b, b.Ketubot 75a, b.Megillah 20a [Rashi] 28b, b.Nazir [Rashi] 15b, b.Niddah [Rashi] 7b 21b 34b 44a 72b, b.Niddah 22a 32b 36b 37b 38a 73a [Tosefot] 9b 22b 32a, b.Sanhedrin [Rashi] 87a, b.Succah [Tosefot] 5b, b.Yevamot [Rashi] 83a, Ecclesiastes.R 10:18, Esther.R 2:2, Exodus.R 3:13, Guide for the Perplexed 3:47, Lamentations.R 5:17, Leviticus 15:19-24, Leviticus.R 19:1 19:4 19:6, Luke 8:43, m.Keritot 1:7, m.Moed Katan 3:2, m.Niddah 4:3 4:5 6:14, m.Oholot 3:3, m.Pesachim 8:6, m.Taanit 4:8, Mark 5:25 7:20-23, Matthew 9:20, Midrash Psalms 8:2 78:2, Midrash Tanchuma Metzora 5-7 9, Midrash Tanchuma Noach 1, mt.Hilchot Issurei Biah 4:2 6:2 6:7 6:17, mt.Hilchot Kriat Shema 4:8, mt.Hilchot Metamei Mishkav Umoshav 1:1, mt.Hilchot Mechusrei Kapparah 1:6, mt.Hilchot Mikvaot 1:5, mt.Hilchot Shevitat Yom Tov 7:21, Pesikta de R'Kahana 12.15, Song of Songs.R 8:15, y.Niddah 2:3, y.Yoma 2:4, z.Metzorah 28 30 3254a, z.Balak 315

Leviticus 15:25-27 - Commandment #573

Leviticus 15:25-30 - mt.Hilchot Beit Habechirah 7:15

[7] Leviticus 15:26 - b.Horayot 4a, b.Niddah 73a [Rashi] 54a, b.Shabbat 84a, mt.Hilchot Shegagot 14:2

[8] LXX *flux*

יִהְיֶה כְּטֻמְאַת נִדָּתָהּ

וְכָל־הַנּוֹגֵעַ בָּם יִטְמָא וְכִבֶּס בְּגָדָיו
וְרָחַץ בַּמַּיִם וְטָמֵא עַד־הָעָרֶב

וְאִם־טָהֲרָה מִזּוֹבָהּ וְסָפְרָה לָּהּ שִׁבְעַת
יָמִים וְאַחַר תִּטְהָר

וּבַיּוֹם הַשְּׁמִינִי תִּקַּח־לָהּ שְׁתֵּי תֹרִים
אוֹ שְׁנֵי בְּנֵי יוֹנָה וְהֵבִיאָה אוֹתָם אֶל־
הַכֹּהֵן אֶל־פֶּתַח אֹהֶל מוֹעֵד

וְעָשָׂה הַכֹּהֵן אֶת־הָאֶחָד חַטָּאת וְאֶת־
הָאֶחָד עֹלָה וְכִפֶּר עָלֶיהָ הַכֹּהֵן לִפְנֵי
יְהֹוָה מִזּוֹב טֻמְאָתָהּ

וְהִזַּרְתֶּם אֶת־בְּנֵי־יִשְׂרָאֵל מִטֻּמְאָתָם
וְלֹא יָמֻתוּ בְּטֻמְאָתָם בְּטַמְּאָם אֶת־
מִשְׁכָּנִי אֲשֶׁר בְּתוֹכָם

זֹאת תּוֹרַת הַזָּב וַאֲשֶׁר תֵּצֵא מִמֶּנּוּ
שִׁכְבַת־זֶרַע לְטָמְאָה־בָהּ

the uncleanness of her *impurity*[1].

27[2] And whoever touches those things shall be unclean, and shall wash his clothes, and bathe himself in water, and be unclean until the evening.

28[3] But if she is cleansed of her *issue*[4], then she shall number to herself seven days, and after that she shall be clean.

29[5] And on the eighth day she shall take two turtledoves, or two young pigeons, and bring them to the priest, to the door of the tent of meeting.

30[6] And the priest shall offer the one for a sin offering, and the other for a [7]burnt offering; and the priest shall make atonement for her before the LORD for the issue of her *uncleanness*[8].

31[9] Thus, shall you separate the children of Israel from their uncleanness; so, they will not die in their uncleanness, when they defile My tabernacle that is in their midst.

32[10] This is the law of he who has an issue, *and of him from whom the flow of seed*

---

[1] LXX *separation*

[2] Leviticus 15:27 - 1 John 1:7, 1 Peter 1:18-19, Ezekiel 12:25 12:29, Hebrews 9:14 10:22, Leviticus 15:5-8 15:13 15:21 17:15-16, Zechariah 13:1

[3] Leviticus 15:28 - 1 Corinthians 1:30 6:11, b.Arachin [Rashi] 8a, b.Horayot 4a, b.Ketubot 72a, b.Megillah [Rashi] 20b, b.Menachot [Tosefot] 65b, b.Niddah [Rashi] 7b 22a 35b 42a, b.Niddah 33b 37a 67b 68b, b.Pesachim [Rashi] 90b, b.Rosh Hashanah [Tosefot] 10a, b.Tamid [Pirush] 26a, b.Zevachim [Rashi] 29a, Chibbur Yafeh 7 {26b}, Ephesians 1:6-7, Galatians 3:13 4:4, Guide for the Perplexed 3:47, Jastrow 1012b, Leviticus 15:13-15, m.Kelim 1:4, Matthew 1:21, mt.Hilchot Issurei Biah 6:11 7:10, Numbers.R 4:20, Pirkei de R'Eliezer 53, Siman 159:6, z.Emor 162 175

Leviticus 15:28-29 - mt.Hilchot Mechusrei Kapparah 1:3

Leviticus 15:28-30 - Commandment #504

[4] LXX *flux*

[5] Leviticus 15:29 - b.Bava Batra 166a, m.Kinnim 1:4 2:1, m.Shekalim 1:5, m.Sheviit 8:8, m.Zevachim 4:3, Mas.Kutim 1:2, mt.Hilchot Kiddush HaChodesh 4:7

Leviticus 15:29-30 - mt.Hilchot Mechusrei Kapparah 1:3

[6] Leviticus 15:30 - b.Arachin [Rashi] 37b, b.Kereitot 28a, m.Shekalim 1:5

[7] LXX adds *whole*

[8] LXX *unclean flux*

[9] Leviticus 15:31 - 1 Corinthians 3:17, 4Q512 69, b.Horayot [Rashi] 8b, b.Moed Katan 5a, b.Niddah 63b, b.Pesachim [Rashi] 72b, b.Sheviit [Rashi] 18a, b.Sheviit 18b, Daniel 9:27, Deuteronomy 24:8, Ein Yaakov Shevuot:18b, Ezekiel 5:11 23:38 44:5-7 20:23, Hebrews 10:29 12:14-15, Jude 1:4, Leviticus 11:47 13:59 19:30 20:3 21:23, m.Keritot 1:1, mt.Hilchot Issurei Biah 4:12, mt.Hilchot Keilim 23:1, Numbers 5:3 19:13 19:20, Philo Legum Allegoriae III 15, Psalms 66:18, Sifre Numbers 1:10 161:2, Siman 155:1, y.Horayot 2:5, z.Metzorah 55a 47

[10] Leviticus 15:32 - b.Kereitot [Rashi] 8a, b.Megillah 20a, b.Nedarim [Ran] 38b, b.Nedarim 35b, b.Niddah [Rashi] 35b 41b, b.Niddah 22a 34b 35a 68b, b.Pesachim [Rashi] 67b, Ezekiel 19:12, Leviticus 11:46 13:59 14:2 14:32 14:54-15:18, mt.Hilchot Keilim 23:1, Numbers 5:29 6:13 19:14, y.Shabbat 9:3

וְהַדָּוָה֙ בְּנִדָּתָ֔הּ וְהַזָּב֙ אֶת־זוֹב֔וֹ לַזָּכָ֖ר
וְלַנְּקֵבָ֑ה וּלְאִ֕ישׁ אֲשֶׁ֥ר יִשְׁכַּ֖ב עִם־
טְמֵאָֽה

33[2]

goes out[1], by which he is unclean;
and of she *who endures her impurity*[3],
and of those who have an issue,[4]
whether he is a male or she is a female,
and of he who lies with her who is
unclean[5].

---

[1] LXX *and if one discharge seed of copulation*

[2] Leviticus 15:33 - Avot de R'Natan 2, b.Arachin 3a, b.Bava Kamma 24a, b.Nazir 29a 65b, b.Niddah
[Rashi] 34a, b.Niddah [Tosefot] 32a, b.Niddah 28b 32b 34b 35a 44a 54b 55b, b.Pesachim [Rashi] 72b,
b.Shabbat [Rashi] 82b, b.Shabbat 64b, b.Sheviit [Rashi] 18b, Ecclesiastes.R 10:18, Jastrow 878a,
Lamentations.R 5:17, Leviticus 15:19 15:24-25 20:18, mt.Hilchot Metamei Mishkav Umoshav 1:8,
Numbers.R 10:8, y.Gittin 9:11, y.Nazir 9:4, z.Vayeshev 232

[3] LXX *that has the issue of blood in her separation*

[4] LXX adds *of seed*

[5] LXX *set apart*

Acharei Mot

Acharei Mot[1] – Chapter 16[2]

וַיְדַבֵּר יְהֹוָה אֶל־מֹשֶׁה אַחֲרֵי מוֹת שְׁנֵי בְּנֵי אַהֲרֹן בְּקָרְבָתָם לִפְנֵי־יְהֹוָה וַיָּמֻתוּ

1[3] And the LORD spoke to Moses, after the death of the two sons of Aaron, *when they drew near before the LORD, and died*[4];

וַיֹּאמֶר יְהֹוָה אֶל־מֹשֶׁה דַּבֵּר אֶל־אַהֲרֹן אָחִיךָ וְאַל־יָבֹא בְכָל־עֵת אֶל־הַקֹּדֶשׁ מִבֵּית לַפָּרֹכֶת אֶל־פְּנֵי הַכַּפֹּרֶת אֲשֶׁר עַל־הָאָרֹן וְלֹא יָמוּת כִּי בֶּעָנָן אֵרָאֶה עַל־הַכַּפֹּרֶת

2[5] and the LORD said to Moses, "Speak to Aaron your brother, he shall not come at all times into the holy place within the veil, before the *ark cover*[6] which is on the ark; so, he will not die; for I appear in the cloud on the ark cover.

---

[1] Acharei Mot aliyot: [1] Leviticus 16:1–17, [2] Leviticus 16:18–24, [3] Leviticus 16:25–34, [4] Leviticus 17:1–7, [5] Leviticus 17:8–18:5, [6] Leviticus 18:6–21, [7] Leviticus 18:22–30
Acharei Mot and Kedoshim are combined when there are only 51 available reading days in the year.
[2] Ein Yaakov Yoma:18a, Mas.Soferim 11:2 17:6, mt.Hilchot Avodat Yom haKippurim 3:10, z.Toldot 80
[3] Leviticus 16:1 - b.Megillah 24a 30b 31a, b.Sheviit 18b, b.Sotah 40b, b.Yoma 53a, Ecclesiastes.R 2:3 9:1, Ein Yaakov Shevuot:18b, Jastrow 865a, Leviticus 10:1-10:2, Leviticus.R 17:3 20:1 20:12, m.Megillah 3:5, m.Sotah 10:7, m.Yoma 7:1, Midrash Psalms 75:2, Midrash Tanchuma Acharei Mot 1 3-6 8, Numbers.R 2:23, Pesikta de R'Kahana 26.1-5 26.6/7, Pesikta Rabbati 47:1-4, Philo Legum Allegoriae II 56, t.Megillah 3:7, y.Megillah 3:5, y.Sotah 7:6, y.Yoma 1:5 7:1, z.Acharei Mot 56a 60a 1 6 12 68 70
Leviticus 16:1-6 - 11Qpaleol.eva
Leviticus 16:1-15 - 4QtgLev
Leviticus 16:1-17 - Minchah [Shabbat Monday Thursday Torah reading - Parashah Acharei Mot]
Leviticus 16:1-34 - mt.Hilchot Tefilah 13:11, Philo De Specialibus Legibus II 193-203, Shabbat Parshat Parah, Testament of Levi 8:4, Torah reading for Yom Kippur morning, Torah Reading Yom Kippur Morning, Yom Kippur [Pesikta Rabbati 47], Josephus Antiquities 4.10.3
[4] LXX *in bringing strange fire before the Lord, so they died*
[5] Leviticus 16:2 - 1 Kings 8:6 8:10-12, 2 Chronicles 5:14, Avot de R'Natan 2, b.Eruvin [Rashi] 105a, b.Kereitot [Rashi] 6a, b.Menachot 27b, b.Yoma 19b 53a, b.Zevachim [Tosefot] 82b, Commandment #374, Exodus 25:17-22 26:33-34 6:10 40:20-21 40:34-35, Hebrews 4:14-16 9:3 9:7-8 9:25 10:19-20, Jastrow 817a 1294b, Leviticus 8:35 16:13 23:27, Leviticus.R 21:7, Matthew 3:51, Mekilta de R'Ishmael Pisha 12:55, Midrash Psalms 10:7, mt.Hilchot Avodat Yom haKippurim 1:7 5:25, mt.Hilchot Beit HaBechirah 7:20-22, mt.Hilchot Biat haMikdash 2:1, mt.Hilchot Sanhedrin vHainshin Hameurim Lahem 19:2 19:4, mt.Hilchot Yesodei haTorah 7:6, mt.Perek Chelek Intro:11, Numbers 4:19 17:25, Pesikta Rabbati 1:2 47:24, y.Yoma 1:5, z.Acharei Mot 59a 5 30 39 51, z.Lech Lecha 78, z.Miketz 26, z.Trumah 541, z.Vayera 439
[6] LXX and hereafter *mercy seat*

בְּזֹאת יָבֹא אַהֲרֹן אֶל־הַקֹּדֶשׁ בְּפַר בֶּן־ 3[7]
בָּקָר לְחַטָּאת וְאַיִל לְעֹלָה

With this shall Aaron come into the holy place: with a young bullock for a sin offering, and a ram for a [8]burnt offering.

כְּתֹנֶת־בַּד קֹדֶשׁ יִלְבָּשׁ וּמִכְנְסֵי־בַד 4[9]
יִהְיוּ עַל־בְּשָׂרוֹ וּבְאַבְנֵט בַּד יַחְגֹּר
וּבְמִצְנֶפֶת בַּד יִצְנֹף בִּגְדֵי־קֹדֶשׁ הֵם
וְרָחַץ בַּמַּיִם אֶת־בְּשָׂרוֹ וּלְבֵשָׁם

He shall put on the holy linen tunic, and he shall have the linen breeches on his flesh, and shall be girded with the linen girdle, and with the linen turban shall he be attired; they are the holy garments; and he shall bathe [10]his flesh in water and put them on.

וּמֵאֵת עֲדַת בְּנֵי יִשְׂרָאֵל יִקַּח שְׁנֵי־ 5[11]
שְׂעִירֵי עִזִּים לְחַטָּאת וְאַיִל אֶחָד
לְעֹלָה

And he shall take of the congregation of the children of Israel two *male goats*[12] for a sin offering, and one *ram*[13] for a burnt offering.

וְהִקְרִיב אַהֲרֹן אֶת־פַּר הַחַטָּאת אֲשֶׁר־ 6[14]
לוֹ וְכִפֶּר בַּעֲדוֹ וּבְעַד בֵּיתוֹ

And Aaron shall present the bullock of the sin offering, which is for himself, and make atonement for himself, and for his house.

---

[7] Leviticus 16:3 - b.Kereitot [Rashi] 6a, b.Menachot [Rashi] 16a, b.Yoma [Rashi] 49a 50a, b.Yoma 3b 4a, Exodus.R 38:8, Guide for the Perplexed 3:46, Hebrews 9:7 9:12 9:24-25, Leviticus 1:3 1:10 4:3 8:14 8:18 9:3, Leviticus.R 5:6 21:1 21:4 21:6 21:9 21:11, m.Yoma 3:8 7:8, Mesillat Yesharim 26:Trait of Kedushah, Midrash Psalms 27:4 39:3, Midrash Tanchuma Acharei Mot 6, Midrash Tanchuma Bamidbar 23, mt.Hilchot Temurah 1:10, Numbers 29:7-11, Numbers.R 5:4 5:7 18:21, Pesikta Rabbati 47:4, y.Yoma 1:1, z.Beshallach 153 280 57a, z.Metzorah 23 53b, z.Noach 281 72a, z.Shemini 37b, z.Tzav 31a, z.Acharei Mot 5 41 42 84, z.Behar 10, z.Pinchas 838, z.Shmini 37, z.Tzav 99, z.Vayikra 114
Leviticus 16:3-34 - Commandment #505
[8] LXX adds *whole*
[9] Leviticus 16:4 - b.Chullin [Rashi] 138a, b.Sanhedrin 49b, b.Succah 5a, b.Yoma [Rashi] 12a 30b, b.Yoma 25a 32a 35a, b.Zevachim 18b 19b, Exodus 4:2 28:39-28:43 5:4 6:20 39:27-39:29 16:12 40:31-40:32, Exodus.R 33:4, Ezekiel 44:17-44:18, Hebrews 2:14 7:26 10:22, Isaiah 5:2, Jastrow 137b, Lamentations.R 2:3, Leviticus 6:10 8:6-8:7 16:24, Leviticus.R 21:11, Luke 1:35, mt.Hilchot Klei haMikdash Vihaovdim Bo 10:6, Pesikta Rabbati 47:4, Philippians 2:7, Revelation 1:5-1:6, y.Kilayim 9:1, y.Yoma 3:6 7:3, z.Pekudei 229b, z.Kedoshim 121, z.Pekudei 165 364, z.Tzav 5, z.Vayechi 131
[10] LXX adds *all*
[11] Leviticus 16:5 - 2 Chronicles 5:21, b.Sheviit 14a, b.Yoma 3b 62b, Ezekiel 45:22-23, Ezra 6:17, Genesis.R 65:14, Hebrews 7:27-28 10:5-14, Leviticus 4:13-21 8:2 8:14 9:8-16, Leviticus.R 21:11, m.Eduyot 8:6, m.Meilah 2:1 2:3, m.Menachot 3:6, m.Yoma 3:9, m.Zevachim 4:4, mt.Hilchot Avodat Yom haKippurim 1:1, mt.Hilchot Klei haMikdash Vihaovdim Bo 5:10, mt.Hilchot Temidim Umusafim 10:1, Numbers 5:11, Pesikta Rabbati 47:4, Romans 8:3, y.Sanhedrin 3:9, y.Sheviit 4:1, z.Acharei Mot 130
Leviticus 16:5-9 - mt.Hilchot Temidim Umusafim 10:2
[12] LXX *kids of the goats*
[13] LXX *lamb*
[14] Leviticus 16:6 - b.Chullin [Rashi] 22a, b.Megillah 20b, b.Menachot [Tosefot] 2a, b.Menachot 83a, b.Sheviit 2b 13b 14a, b.Succah [Rashi] 24a, b.Yevamot [Rashi] 33b, b.Yoma 36b 51b, b.Zevachim 98a, Ecclesiastes.R 9:8, Ezekiel 19:19 19:27, Ezra 10:18-19, Hebrews 5:2-3 7:27 9:7, Jastrow 373a, Job 1:5, Leviticus 8:14-17 9:7, Leviticus.R 5:6 5:6 20:9, m.Eduyot 8:6, m.Megillah 1:9, m.Meilah 2:1 2:3, m.Pesachim 5:3, m.Yoma 1:1 3:8 7:8, m.Zevachim 4:4, Midrash Tanchuma Acharei Mot 6, mt.Hilchot Avodat Yom haKippurim 5:13, mt.Hilchot Shegagot 11:9, Pesikta de R'Kahana 26.9, z.Naso 145b, z.Tetzaveh 182b, z.Vayechi 233a, z.Vayikra 18a, z.Naso 142, z.Tetzaveh 64, z.Vayechi 494

וְלָקַח אֶת־שְׁנֵי הַשְּׂעִירִם וְהֶעֱמִיד
אֹתָם לִפְנֵי יְהוָה פֶּתַח אֹהֶל מוֹעֵד

7[15] And he shall take the two goats and set them before the LORD at the door of the tent of meeting.

וְנָתַן אַהֲרֹן עַל־שְׁנֵי הַשְּׂעִירִם גּוֹרָלוֹת
גּוֹרָל אֶחָד לַיהוָה וְגוֹרָל אֶחָד לַעֲזָאזֵל

8[16] And Aaron shall cast lots on the two goats: one lot for the LORD, and the other lot for *Azazel*[17].

וְהִקְרִיב אַהֲרֹן אֶת־הַשָּׂעִיר אֲשֶׁר עָלָה
עָלָיו הַגּוֹרָל לַיהוָה וְעָשָׂהוּ חַטָּאת

9[18] And Aaron shall present the goat on which the lot fell for the LORD and offer him for a sin offering.

וְהַשָּׂעִיר אֲשֶׁר עָלָה עָלָיו הַגּוֹרָל
לַעֲזָאזֵל יָעֳמַד־חַי לִפְנֵי יְהוָה לְכַפֵּר
עָלָיו לְשַׁלַּח אֹתוֹ לַעֲזָאזֵל הַמִּדְבָּרָה

10[19] But the goat, on which the lot fell for Azazel, shall be set alive before the LORD, to make atonement over him, to send him away for Azazel into the wilderness.

וְהִקְרִיב אַהֲרֹן אֶת־פַּר הַחַטָּאת אֲשֶׁר־
לוֹ וְכִפֶּר בַּעֲדוֹ וּבְעַד בֵּיתוֹ וְשָׁחַט אֶת־
פַּר הַחַטָּאת אֲשֶׁר־לוֹ

11[20] And Aaron shall present the *bullock of the sin offering, which is for himself*[21], and shall make atonement for himself and for his house and shall kill the bullock of *the sin offering which is for himself*[22].

---

[15] Leviticus 16:7 - b.Chullin 11a, b.Sheviit 13b, b.Yoma [Rashi] 37a, b.Zevachim 34b, Leviticus 1:3 4:4 12:6-12:7, m.Yoma 3:9, Matthew 16:21, mt.Hilchot Avodat Yom haKippurim 1:2, Philo Legum Allegoriae II 52, Romans 12:1, y.Yoma 1:1, z.Acharei Mot 120, z.Pinchas 679
Leviticus 16:7-11 - mt.Hilchot Teshuvah 1:2
[16] Leviticus 16:8 - 1 Samuel 14:41-42, 3 Enoch 1:1, Acts 1:23-1:26, b.Chullin [Rashi] 24a, b.Kiddushin 14a, b.Yoma [Rashi] 3b 5a, b.Yoma 37a, b.Zevachim 34b, Ezekiel 24:29, Genesis.R 98 [Excl]:2, Jastrow 332a 360a, Jonah 1:7, Joshua 18:10-11, Numbers 2:55 9:54, Pirkei de R'Eliezer 46, Proverbs 16:33, Saadia Opinions 3:10, y.Yoma 4:1, z.Acharei Mot 62b, z.Terumah 157a, z.Acharei Mot 111 116, z.Emor 39 236, z.Pinchas 679, z.Tetzaveh 104, z.Toldot 129, z.Trumah 565 566, z.Tzav 42
Leviticus 16:8-10 - z.Emor 101b
[17] LXX and hereafter: *scape goat*
[18] Leviticus 16:9 - Acts 2:23 4:27-4:28, b.Chullin [Rashi] 24a, b.Chullin 24a, b.Kereitot 28a, b.Kiddushin 14a, b.Yoma [Rashi] 5a, b.Yoma 40b, b.Zevachim 34b, Jastrow 1671b, Leviticus.R 27:9, t.Kippurim 2:10, y.Sheviit 1:4, y.Yoma 6:1, z.Toldot 129
[19] Leviticus 16:10 - 1 John 2:2 3:16, 2 Corinthians 5:21, b.Avodah Zara 74a, b.Chullin [Tosefot] 24a, b.Megillah [Rashi] 20b, b.Sheviit [Rashi] 2a, b.Sheviit [Tosefot] 14b, b.Yoma [Rashi] 36b 62a, b.Yoma 40b 65a 67b 71a, b.Zevachim 34b, Hebrews 7:26-27 9:23-24, Isaiah 53:4-11, Jastrow 1580a, Leviticus 14:7 16:21-16:22, m.Yoma 4:1, m.Zevachim 14:1, mt.Hilchot Avodat Yom haKippurim 5:18, Philo De Posteritate Caini 70, Romans 3:25 4:25, y.Sheviit 1:7, y.Yoma 5:4 6:1 6:2, z.Terumah 157a 565 566, z.Emor 237, z.Toldot 129
[20] Leviticus 16:11 - b.Chullin [Rashi] 22a, b.Kiddushin [Tosefot] 41b, b.Meilah [Tosefot] 12b, b.Meilah 11a, b.Menachot [Tosefot] 5a 19a 92a 93, b.Sheviit 2b 14a, b.Yoma [Rashi] 42a 50a, b.Yoma 51b, b.Zevachim [Rashi] 20a, Ein Yaakov Yoma:2a, Genesis.R 17:2, HaMadrikh 35:5, Hebrews 7:27 9:7, Jastrow 373a, Leviticus 16:3 16:6, mt.Hilchot Pesulei haMikdashim 1:2, y.Yoma 1:1
[21] LXX *calf for his sin*
[22] LXX *his sin offering*

וְלָקַח מְלֹא־הַמַּחְתָּה גַּחֲלֵי־אֵשׁ מֵעַל הַמִּזְבֵּחַ מִלִּפְנֵי יְהוָה וּמְלֹא חָפְנָיו קְטֹרֶת סַמִּים דַּקָּה וְהֵבִיא מִבֵּית לַפָּרֹכֶת 12²³

וְנָתַן אֶת־הַקְּטֹרֶת עַל־הָאֵשׁ לִפְנֵי יְהוָה וְכִסָּה עֲנַן הַקְּטֹרֶת אֶת־הַכַּפֹּרֶת אֲשֶׁר עַל־הָעֵדוּת וְלֹא יָמוּת 13²⁴

וְלָקַח מִדַּם הַפָּר וְהִזָּה בְאֶצְבָּעוֹ עַל־פְּנֵי הַכַּפֹּרֶת קֵדְמָה וְלִפְנֵי הַכַּפֹּרֶת יַזֶּה שֶׁבַע־פְּעָמִים מִן־הַדָּם בְּאֶצְבָּעוֹ 14²⁵

וְשָׁחַט אֶת־שְׂעִיר הַחַטָּאת אֲשֶׁר לָעָם וְהֵבִיא אֶת־דָּמוֹ אֶל־מִבֵּית לַפָּרֹכֶת וְעָשָׂה אֶת־דָּמוֹ כַּאֲשֶׁר עָשָׂה לְדַם הַפָּר וְהִזָּה אֹתוֹ עַל־הַכַּפֹּרֶת וְלִפְנֵי הַכַּפֹּרֶת 15²⁶

וְכִפֶּר עַל־הַקֹּדֶשׁ מִטֻּמְאֹת בְּנֵי יִשְׂרָאֵל 16²⁷

12²³ And he shall take a censer full of coals of fire from off the altar before the LORD, and his hands full of sweet incense beaten small, and bring it within the veil.

13²⁴ And he shall put the incense on the fire before the LORD, that the cloud of the incense may cover the ark cover that is on the testimony so he will not die.

14²⁵ And he shall take of the blood of the bullock and sprinkle it with his finger on the ark cover on the east; and before the ark cover he shall sprinkle of the blood with his finger seven times.

15²⁶ Then he shall kill the goat of the sin offering that is for the people, and bring his blood within the veil, and do with his blood as he did with the blood of the bullock, and sprinkle it on the ark cover, and before the ark cover.

16²⁷ And he shall make atonement for the holy place, because of the

---

[23] Leviticus 16:12 - 1 John 1:7, b.Chullin [Tosefot] 29b, b.Kereitot 6b, b.Menachot 11a, b.Pesachim 75b, b.Tamid [Pirush] 29a, b.Yoma [Rashi] 18b 19b, b.Yoma 45b 47a, b.Zevachim 58b 19b, b.Zevachim [Tosefot] 58a, Ein Yaakov Berachot:7a, Exodus 30:34-38 7:11 13:29, Hebrews 9:14, Isaiah 6:6-7, Jastrow 328b 491b 492a 704a, Lamentations.R 4:1, Leviticus 10:1, m.Eduyot 8:1, m.Kelim 17:11, m.Yoma 4:4, Midrash Tanchuma Tetzaveh 15, mt.Hilchot Avodat Yom haKippurim 4:1, mt.Hilchot Biat haMikdash 9:4, Numbers 16:18 17:11, Revelation 8:3-4, y.Yoma 1:5 4:3 4:6, z.Yitro 79a, z.Yitro 249
[24] Leviticus 16:13 - 1 John 2:1-2, b.Sheviit [Tosefot] 14b, b.Yoma 53a, Ecclesiastes.R 4:5, Ein Yaakov Berachot 7a, Exodus 1:21 4:43 6:1 30:7-8, Hebrews 4:14-16 7:25 9:24, Leviticus 22:9, Leviticus.R 5:6, Midrash Tanchuma Tetzaveh 15, mt.Hilchot Avodat Yom haKippurim 1:7, Numbers 16:7 16:18 17:11, Revelation 8:3-4, Sifre Devarim Vezot Habracha 351, Song of Songs.R 1:62, t.Kippurim 1:8, y.Yoma 1:5, z.Emor 260
[25] Leviticus 16:14 - b.Bechorot 39b, b.Chullin [Rashi] 22a, b.Menachot [Rashi] 10a, b.Menachot 27b, b.Sanhedrin [Tosefot] 4b, b.Succah 5a, b.Yoma 55a, b.Zevachim [Rashi] 38a 40a 14a 57a, Hebrews 9:7 9:13 9:25 10:4 10:10-12 10:19 12:24, Leviticus 4:5-4:6 4:17 8:11, Mekhilta de R'Shimon bar Yochai Bachodesh 48:2, mt.Hilchot Avodat Yom haKippurim 3:5, mt.Hilchot Pesulei haMikdashim 1:29 2:3, Romans 3:24-3:26, y.Shabbat 1:1, y.Sukkah 1:1, y.Yoma 5:4
[26] Leviticus 16:15 - b.Menachot [Tosefot] 92a, b.Niddah [Rashi] 42a, b.Sheviit [Rashi] 2a, b.Sheviit [Tosefot] 14b, b.Sheviit 13b, b.Yoma 55a, b.Zevachim [Rashi] 51a 57a, Hebrews 2:17 5:3 6:19 9:3 9:7 9:12 9:25-26, Jastrow 1125b, Leviticus 16:2 16:5-9, m.Shevuot 1:2, Mekhilta de R'Shimon bar Yochai Pisha 9:5, mt.Hilchot Avodat Yom haKippurim 3:5, y.Yoma 3:7 5:4, z.Acharei Mot 63b, z.Emor 249
Leviticus 16:15-29 - 4QLev-Numa
[27] Leviticus 16:16 - 4Q159 1 ii 1-2, b.Kereitot 25b, b.Menachot [Tosefot] 92a, b.Sheviit 7b 8ab 12b 13b, b.Yoma [Rashi] 53b, b.Yoma 53a 57a, b.Zevachim [Rashi] 47a 57a, b.Zevachim [Tosefot] 57b, b.Zevachim 52b, Exodus 29:36-37, Exodus.R 15:5, Ezekiel 45:18-19, Guide for the Perplexed 3:47, Hebrews 9:22-23, John 14:3, Leviticus 8:15 16:18, Midrash Tanchuma Metzora 9, mt.Hilchot Avodat Yom haKippurim 3:5, mt.Hilchot Shegagot 11:9, Numbers.R 7:8, Pirkei de R'Eliezer 46, Sifre Numbers 1:10 161:2, Tanya Igeret Hakodesh §24, Tanya Igeret Hateshuvah §01, Tanya Likutei Aramim §45, y.Sheviit 1:2, y.Yoma 5:4, z.Acharei Mot 180 66a, z.Vayakhel 219b 483, z.Pinchas 812, z.Tetzaveh 114
Leviticus 16:16-17 - Midrash Proverbs 9

וּמִפִּשְׁעֵיהֶם לְכָל־חַטֹּאתָם וְכֵן יַעֲשֶׂה
לְאֹהֶל מוֹעֵד הַשֹּׁכֵן אִתָּם בְּתוֹךְ
טֻמְאֹתָם

uncleannesses of the children of Israel, and because of their transgressions, for all their sins; and so shall he do for the tent of meeting that dwells with them in the midst of their uncleannesses.

וְכָל־אָדָם לֹא־יִהְיֶה। בְּאֹהֶל מוֹעֵד
בְּבֹאוֹ לְכַפֵּר בַּקֹּדֶשׁ עַד־צֵאתוֹ וְכִפֶּר
בַּעֲדוֹ וּבְעַד בֵּיתוֹ וּבְעַד כָּל־קְהַל
יִשְׂרָאֵל

17²⁸ And no man shall be in the tent of meeting when he goes in to make atonement in the holy place, until he come out, and have made atonement for himself, and for his household, and for all the assembly of Israel.

וְיָצָא אֶל־הַמִּזְבֵּחַ אֲשֶׁר לִפְנֵי־יְהוָה
וְכִפֶּר עָלָיו וְלָקַח מִדַּם הַפָּר וּמִדַּם
הַשָּׂעִיר וְנָתַן עַל־קַרְנוֹת הַמִּזְבֵּחַ סָבִיב

18²⁹ And he shall go out to the altar that is before the LORD, and make atonement for it; and shall take of the blood of the bullock, and of the blood of the goat, and put it on the horns of the altar around it.

וְהִזָּה עָלָיו מִן־הַדָּם בְּאֶצְבָּעוֹ שֶׁבַע
פְּעָמִים וְטִהֲרוֹ וְקִדְּשׁוֹ מִטֻּמְאֹת בְּנֵי
יִשְׂרָאֵל

19³⁰ And he shall sprinkle of the blood on it with his finger seven times, and cleanse it, and hallow it from the uncleannesses of the children of Israel.

וְכִלָּה מִכַּפֵּר אֶת־הַקֹּדֶשׁ וְאֶת־אֹהֶל
מוֹעֵד וְאֶת־הַמִּזְבֵּחַ וְהִקְרִיב אֶת־
הַשָּׂעִיר הֶחָי

20³¹ And when he has made an end of atoning for the holy place, and the tent of meeting, and the altar, he shall present the live goat.

[28] Leviticus 16:17 - 1 Peter 2:24 3:18, 1 Timothy 2:5, Acts 4:12, b.Chullin [Tosefot] 24a, b.Gittin 54b, b.Horayot 13a, b.Menachot [Tosefot] 19b, b.Sheviit [Tosefot] 14b, b.Tamid [Pirush] 33a, b.Yoma [Tosefot] 13b, b.Yoma 13a 43b 44a, b.Zevachim [Rashi] 88b, b.Zevachim 83a, Daniel 9:24, Exodus 10:3, Hebrews 1:3 9:7, Isaiah 5:6, Leviticus 16:10-11, Leviticus.R 5:6 21:12, Luke 1:10, m.Horayot 3:6, mt.Hilchot Avodat Yom haKippurim 2:6 4:2, mt.Hilchot Temidim Umusafim 3:3, Pesikta Rabbati 47:3, Philo De Somniis II 189 231, Philo Quis Rerum Divinarum Heres 84, t.Horayot 2:4, t.Zevachim 10:2, y.Horayot 3:4, y.Sukkah 4:6, y.Yoma 1:1 1:5 5:2, z.Acharei Mot 181 188, z.Lech Lecha 427, z.Naso 143, z.Vayikra 300
[29] Leviticus 16:18 - b.Bava Metzia [Tosefot] 61a, b.Chullin [Tosefot] 87a, b.Chullin 98b, b.Menachot [Tosefot] 22b, b.Menachot 22a, b.Nedarim [Ran] 52a, b.Sheviit [Rashi] 8b, b.Temurah 5b, b.Yoma [Rashi] 40a 59a, b.Yoma [Tosefot] 52b, b.Yoma 57b 58b, b.Zevachim [Rashi] 42ab 47a 83a 11a, b.Zevachim [Tosefot] 77b, Exodus 6:10, Hebrews 2:11 5:7-8 9:22-23, John 17:19, Leviticus 4:7 4:18 4:25 16:16, m.Yoma 5:5, mt.Hilchot Avodat Yom haKippurim 4:2, y.Yoma 5:4-5, z.Acharei Mot 64b 66a 145 176 Leviticus 16:18-21 - 4QtgLev
[30] Leviticus 16:19 - b.Shekalim 9b, b.Yoma [Rashi] 58b, b.Yoma 59a, b.Zevachim [Rashi] 38a, Ezekiel 43:18-22, Song of Songs.R 1:9, y.Shabbat 1:3, y.Shekalim 3:3, y.Yoma 2:2 5:6, Zechariah 13:1, z.Ekev 60, z.Pinchas 625
[31] Leviticus 16:20 - 2 Corinthians 5:19, b.Shekalim 9b, b.Sheviit [Tosefot] 13b, b.Yoma [Tosefot] 5a, b.Yoma 40b 57a 60b 61a, b.Zevachim [Rashi] 41b, b.Zevachim [Tosefot] 39b, b.Zevachim 40a 52ab, Colossians 1:20, Ezekiel 21:20, Guide for the Perplexed 3:46, Hebrews 7:25, Jastrow 641a 662b, Leviticus 6:30 8:15 16:16, mt.Hilchot Avodat Yom haKippurim 5:7, Philo De Fuga et Inventione 159, Revelation 1:18, Romans 4:25 8:34, Song of Songs.R 1:9, t.Kippurim 3:8 3:12, y.Shabbat 1:3, y.Shekalim 3:3, y.Sheviit 1:7, y.Yoma 5:6-7 6:2

21[32] וְסָמַךְ אַהֲרֹן אֶת־שְׁתֵּי "יָדוֹ" "יָדָיו" עַל־רֹאשׁ הַשָּׂעִיר הַחַי וְהִתְוַדָּה עָלָיו אֶת־כָּל־עֲוֺנֹת בְּנֵי יִשְׂרָאֵל וְאֶת־כָּל־פִּשְׁעֵיהֶם לְכָל־חַטֹּאתָם וְנָתַן אֹתָם עַל־רֹאשׁ הַשָּׂעִיר וְשִׁלַּח בְּיַד־אִישׁ עִתִּי הַמִּדְבָּרָה

And Aaron shall press both his hands on the head of the live goat, and confess over him all the iniquities of the children of Israel, and all their transgressions, even all their sins; and he shall put them on the head of the goat, and shall send him away by the hand of an *appointed*[33] man into the wilderness.

22[34] וְנָשָׂא הַשָּׂעִיר עָלָיו אֶת־כָּל־עֲוֺנֹתָם אֶל־אֶרֶץ גְּזֵרָה וְשִׁלַּח אֶת־הַשָּׂעִיר בַּמִּדְבָּר

And the goat shall bear on him all their iniquities *to a land that is cut off*[35]; and *he*[36] shall let go the goat in the wilderness.

23[37] וּבָא אַהֲרֹן אֶל־אֹהֶל מוֹעֵד וּפָשַׁט אֶת־בִּגְדֵי הַבַּד אֲשֶׁר לָבַשׁ בְּבֹאוֹ אֶל־הַקֹּדֶשׁ וְהִנִּיחָם שָׁם

And Aaron shall come into the tent of meeting, and shall take off the linen garments, which he put on *when he went*[38] into the holy place, and shall leave them there.

24[39] וְרָחַץ אֶת־בְּשָׂרוֹ בַמַּיִם בְּמָקוֹם קָדוֹשׁ וְלָבַשׁ אֶת־בְּגָדָיו וְיָצָא וְעָשָׂה אֶת־עֹלָתוֹ וְאֶת־עֹלַת הָעָם וְכִפֶּר בַּעֲדוֹ וּבְעַד הָעָם

And he shall bathe his flesh in water in a holy place and put on his *other*[40] vestments, and come forth, and offer his burnt offering and the burnt offering of the people, and make atonement for himself[41] and for the people[42].

---

[32] Leviticus 16:21 - 2 Corinthians 5:21, 4Q159 1 ii 1-2, b.Kereitot 14a 25b 26a, b.Menachot [Rashi] 62b, b.Menachot [Tosefot] 56a, b.Menachot 92ab 93b, b.Sheviit [Tosefot] 14b, b.Sheviit [Tosefot] 8b, b.Yoma [Rashi] 40b, b.Yoma 36b 66a 67b, b.Zevachim [Rashi] 48b, Daniel 9:3-20, Ein Yaakov Yoma 36b, Exodus 5:10, Ezra 10:1, Isaiah 5:6, Jastrow 333a 373a 1000a 1521a, Leviticus 1:4 5:5 2:40, m.Megillah 2:5, m.Sheviit 1:7, m.Yoma 6:8, Midrash Proverbs 10, mt.Hilchot Avodat Yom haKippurim 3:7 5:21, mt.Hilchot Maaseh haKorbanot 3:10 3:13, mt.Hilchot Teshuvah 1:2 1:2, Nehemiah 1:6-7 9:3-5, Numbers.R 14:12, Proverbs 4:13, Psalms 32:5 51:4, Romans 10:10, t.Kippurim 2:1, y.Horayot 1:8, y.Sheviit 1:3 1:5, y.Yoma 3:7 6:3, z.Acharei Mot 63ab, z.Acharei Mot 121 122 124 138, z.Noach 120, z.Pekudei 830 944, z.Pinchas 679
[33] LXX *ready*; i.e. *fit*
[34] Leviticus 16:22 - 1 Peter 2:24, b.Avodah Zara 74a, b.Meilah [Rashi] 11b, b.Menachot [Rashi] 109a, b.Sheviit [Tosefot] 14b, b.Yoma [Rashi] 67b, Ezekiel 18:22, Galatians 3:13, Genesis.R 65:15, Hebrews 9:28, Isaiah 53:11-12, Jastrow 231b 232b, John 1:29, m.Sheviit 1:6, Micah 7:19, Pirkei de R'Eliezer 46, Psalms 7:10 7:12, y.Sheviit 1:3, z.Toledot 138b, z.Acharei Mot 123 132 138, z.Balak 144, z.Emor 248, z.Pekudei 320 830, z.Pinchas 374 378 681, z.Toldot 31, z.Tzav 42
[35] LXX *into a desert land*
[36] LXX *Aaron*
[37] Leviticus 16:23 - b.Chullin [Rashi] 114a, b.Kereitot 6a, b.Meilah 11b, b.Yoma [Rashi] 5a 12b, b.Yoma 24a 32a 67b, b.Yoma 70b 71a, b.Zevachim 46a, Ezekiel 18:14 20:19, Hebrews 9:28, Leviticus 16:4, Leviticus.R 21:12, mt.Hilchot Avodat Yom haKippurim 2:2, mt.Hilchot Klei haMikdash Vihaovdim Bo 8:5, Philippians 2:6-2:11, Romans 8:3, y.Yoma 3:6 7:2
[38] 4QLEv-Numa *and he shall go*
[39] Leviticus 16:24 - b.Chullin 10b, b.Yoma [Rashi] 19a 36b, b.Yoma 70b 71a, Exodus 28:4-14 29:4-5, Hebrews 9:10 10:19-22, Leviticus 8:6-9 14:9 16:3-5 22:6, mt.Hilchot Avodat Yom haKippurim 2:2 4:2, Revelation 1:5-6, y.Yoma 3:6 7:2, z.Acharei Mot 66a, z.Acharei Mot 179
[40] Missing in LXX
[41] LXX adds *and for his house*

וְאֵת חֵלֶב הַחַטָּאת יַקְטִיר הַמִּזְבֵּחָה 25[43]

וְהַמְשַׁלֵּחַ אֶת־הַשָּׂעִיר לַעֲזָאזֵל יְכַבֵּס 26[44]
בְּגָדָיו וְרָחַץ אֶת־בְּשָׂרוֹ בַּמָּיִם וְאַחֲרֵי־
כֵן יָבוֹא אֶל־הַמַּחֲנֶה

וְאֵת פַּר הַחַטָּאת וְאֵת שְׂעִיר הַחַטָּאת 27[47]
אֲשֶׁר הוּבָא אֶת־דָּמָם לְכַפֵּר בַּקֹּדֶשׁ
יוֹצִיא אֶל־מִחוּץ לַמַּחֲנֶה וְשָׂרְפוּ בָאֵשׁ
אֶת־עֹרֹתָם וְאֶת־בְּשָׂרָם וְאֶת־פִּרְשָׁם

וְהַשֹּׂרֵף אֹתָם יְכַבֵּס בְּגָדָיו וְרָחַץ אֶת־ 28[48]
בְּשָׂרוֹ בַּמָּיִם וְאַחֲרֵי־כֵן יָבוֹא אֶל־
הַמַּחֲנֶה

וְהָיְתָה לָכֶם לְחֻקַּת עוֹלָם בַּחֹדֶשׁ 29[49]
הַשְּׁבִיעִי בֶּעָשׂוֹר לַחֹדֶשׁ תְּעַנּוּ אֶת־
נַפְשֹׁתֵיכֶם וְכָל־מְלָאכָה לֹא תַעֲשׂוּ
הָאֶזְרָח וְהַגֵּר הַגָּר בְּתוֹכְכֶם

25[43] And he shall make the fat of the sin offering smoke on the altar.

26[44] And he who *releases*[45] the goat for *Azazel*[46] shall wash his clothes, and bathe his flesh in water, and afterward he may come in the camp.

27[47] And the bullock of the sin offering, and the goat of the sin offering, whose blood was brought in to make atonement in the holy place, shall be carried forth outside the camp; and they shall burn in the fire their skins, and their flesh, and their dung.

28[48] And he who burns them shall wash his clothes, and bathe his flesh in water, and afterward he may come in the camp.

29[49] And it shall be a statute forever to you: in the seventh month, on the tenth day of the month, you shall *afflict*[50] your souls, and shall do no *manner of*[51] work, the homeborn, or the stranger who sojourns among you.

---

[42] LXX adds *as for the priests*

[43] Leviticus 16:25 - b.Yoma [Rashi] 67b, b.Yoma 71a, Exodus 5:13, Jastrow 1625b, Leviticus 4:8-4:10 4:19 16:6, mt.Hilchot Parah Adumah 5:4

[44] Leviticus 16:26 - b.Niddah [Rashi] 35a 55a, b.Temurah [Rashi] 7a, b.Yoma [Rashi] 67ab, Hebrews 7:19, Leviticus 11:25 14:8 15:5-11 15:27 16:10 16:21-22 16:28, m.Parah 8:3, m.Yoma 6:6, Midrash Tanchuma Chukkat 7, mt.Hilchot Parah Adumah 5:4, Numbers 19:7-8 19:21, Numbers.R 19:5, Pesikta de R'Kahana 4.6, Pesikta Rabbati 14:1, y.Yoma 6:3 6:6, z.Terumah 157a, z.Trumah 565 566

[45] LXX *sends forth*

[46] LXX *that has been set apart to be let go*

[47] Leviticus 16:27 - b.Pesachim [Rashi] 85b, b.Yoma [Rashi] 61b, b.Yoma 68a 71a, b.Zevachim [Rashi] 50b 105a, b.Zevachim [Tosefot] 47b, b.Zevachim 50a 83a 105b, Exodus.R 49:2, Hebrews 13:11-14, Leviticus 4:11-12 4:21 6:30 8:17, m.Parah 8:3, m.Yoma 6:7, Matthew 27:31-33, mt.Hilchot Maaseh haKorbanot 5:18, mt.Hilchot Temidim Umusafim 10:2, y.Yoma 6:6

[48] Leviticus 16:28 - b.Yoma [Rashi] 67b, b.Yoma 68b, b.Zevachim [Rashi] 41a 105b, b.Zevachim 83a 105a 16a, m.Parah 8:3, m.Yoma 6:7, m.Zevachim 12:5, mt.Hilchot Parah Adumah 5:7, mt.Hilchot Avodat Yom haKippurim 5:9, y.Yoma 6:6

[49] Leviticus 16:29 - 1 Corinthians 11:31, 1 Kings 8:2, 2 Corinthians 7:10-11, b.Chullin 24a, b.Menachot [Rashi] 19a, b.Nedarim 80b, b.Succah [Rashi] 28a, b.Yoma 74b 76a, b.Zevachim [Rashi] 41b 52b, b.Zevachim [Tosefot] 39b, Daniel 10:3 10:12, Exodus 12:16 20:10 6:10, Ezra 3:1, Hebrews 4:10, Isaiah 10:3 10:5 10:13, Jastrow 1294b, Jubilees 34:18, Leviticus 23:3 23:7-8 23:21 23:27-32 23:36, mt.Hilchot Shevitat Esor 1:4, Numbers 5:7, Pesikta de R'Kahana 4.6, Pirkei de R'Eliezer 46, Psalms 35:13 69:11, y.Sheviit 3:3, y.Yoma 8:1 8:3, z.Acharei Mot 69a 69b, z.Acharei Mot 131 202 223-225 236 239, z.Pinchas 812

Leviticus 16:29-30 - mt.Hilchot Teshuvah 2:7 2:7

Leviticus 16:29-31 - Apocalypse of Elijah 1:13

[50] LXX *humble*

[51] Missing inLXX

כִּי־בַיּוֹם הַזֶּה יְכַפֵּר עֲלֵיכֶם לְטַהֵר
אֶתְכֶם מִכֹּל חַטֹּאתֵיכֶם לִפְנֵי יְהוָה
תִּטְהָרוּ

30[1]   For on this day *atonement shall be made for you, to cleanse you; from all your sins you shall be clean before the LORD*[2].

שַׁבַּת שַׁבָּתוֹן הִיא לָכֶם וְעִנִּיתֶם אֶת־
נַפְשֹׁתֵיכֶם חֻקַּת עוֹלָם

31[3]   It is a [4]sabbath of solemn rest to you, and you shall *afflict*[5] your souls; it is a statute forever.

וְכִפֶּר הַכֹּהֵן אֲשֶׁר־יִמְשַׁח אֹתוֹ וַאֲשֶׁר
יְמַלֵּא אֶת־יָדוֹ לְכַהֵן תַּחַת אָבִיו וְלָבַשׁ
אֶת־בִּגְדֵי הַבָּד בִּגְדֵי הַקֹּדֶשׁ

32[6]   And the priest, who shall be anointed and who shall be consecrated to be priest in his father's stead, shall make the atonement, and shall put on the linen garments, even the holy garments.

וְכִפֶּר אֶת־מִקְדַּשׁ הַקֹּדֶשׁ וְאֶת־אֹהֶל
מוֹעֵד וְאֶת־הַמִּזְבֵּחַ יְכַפֵּר וְעַל הַכֹּהֲנִים
וְעַל־כָּל־עַם הַקָּהָל יְכַפֵּר

33[7]   And he shall make atonement for the most holy place, and *he shall make atone for*[8] the tent of meeting
and for the altar; and *he shall make atonement*[9] for the priests and [10]for all the people of the assembly.

---

[1] Leviticus 16:30 - 1 John 1:7-9, Avot de R'Natan 29, b.Chullin [Rashi] 22a, b.Kereitot [Rashi] 7a, b.Kereitot 25b, b.Megillah 20b, b.Menachot [Rashi] 83a, b.Sheviit [Rashi] 13a, b.Yoma 35a 41ab 66a 85b 86a, b.Zevachim [Rashi] 98a, Ein Yaakov Yoma 85b 86a 87a, Ephesians 5:26, Ezekiel 36:25-27, Gates of Repentance 2.14 4.3 4.6 4.17, Genesis.R 65:14, Guide for the Perplexed 3:41 3:47, Hebrews 9:13-14 10:1-2, Jeremiah 9:8, Lamentations.R Petichata DChakimei:11, Leviticus.R 20:12 21:11 27:9, m.Keritot 6:4, m.Yoma 3:8 4:2 6:2 8:9, Mekhilta de R'Shimon bar Yochai Bachodesh 54:1, Mekilta de R'Ishmael Bahodesh 7:22, Midrash Psalms 15:5 86:8 118:2, Midrash Tanchuma Acharei Mot 7, Midrash Tanchuma Emor 12 22, Midrash Tanchuma Ki Tissa 6, Midrash Tanchuma Pekudei 11, Midrash Tanchuma Shelach 13, mt.Hilchot Avodat Yom haKippurim 4:1 4:2, mt.Hilchot Shegagot 3:9, mt.Hilchot Teshuvah 1:3 2:9, Numbers.R 16:23, Pesikta de R'Kahana 2.7 9.9 26.11 S2.8, Pesikta Rabbati 11:2 45:1 45:3 51:8, Pirkei de R'Eliezer 29, Pirkei de R'Eliezer 46, Psalms 51:3 51:8 51:11, Siman 130:1 131:4, Song of Songs.R 1:37 6:26 8:9, t.Kippurim 2:1 4:7, Tefillat Yom Kippur [Viduy], Titus 2:14, y.Sanhedrin 10:1, y.Sheviit 1:6, y.Yoma 3:7 8:7, z.Acharei Mot 66b 68b, z.Emor 102b, z.Tetzaveh 185a, z.Acharei Mot 115 181 194 195 241, z.Balak 332, z.Ha'azinu 86, z.Tetzaveh 103 112, z.Trumah 157, z.Vayikra 250 256
[2] LXX *he shall make an atonement for you, to cleanse you from all your sins before the Lord, and ye shall be purged*
[3] Leviticus 16:31 - b.Chullin [Rashi] 21b, b.Yoma 74ab 76a, Exodus 7:15 11:2, Isaiah 10:3 10:5, Jastrow 1072b, Leviticus 23:32 1:4, mt.Hilchot Shevitat Esor 1:1, Pirkei de R'Eliezer 46, z.Acharei Mot 68b, z.Safra Det'zniuta 19
[4] LXX adds *most holy*
[5] LXX *humble*
[6] Leviticus 16:32 - b.Chullin 29a, b.Menachot [Tosefot] 92a 19b, b.Sheviit [Tosefot] 13b, b.Yoma 5a, Exodus 5:9 29:29-30, Leviticus 4:3 4:5 4:16 16:4, mt.Hilchot Klei haMikdash Vihaovdim Bo 4:20, mt.Hilchot Melachim uMichamoteihem 1:7, Numbers 20:26-28, y.Horayot 3:2, y.Megillah 1:10, y.Yoma 1:1
[7] Leviticus 16:33 - b.Chullin 131b, b.Horayot 6a, b.Menachot [Rashi] 92a, b.Menachot [Tosefot] 16a 92a, b.Menachot 27b 92a, b.Yoma 61a, b.Zevachim [Tosefot] 42a, Exodus 20:22-26, Exodus.R 15:5, Leviticus 16:6 16:11 16:16 16:18-19 16:24, Mekilta de R'Ishmael Bahodesh 4:68, y.Yoma 5:6
[8] Missing in LXX
[9] Missing in LXX
[10] LXX adds *he shall make atonement*

וְהָיְתָה־זֹּאת לָכֶם לְחֻקַּת עוֹלָם לְכַפֵּר
עַל־בְּנֵי יִשְׂרָאֵל מִכָּל־חַטֹּאתָם אַחַת
בַּשָּׁנָה וַיַּעַשׂ כַּאֲשֶׁר צִוָּה יְהוָה אֶת־
מֹשֶׁה

34[1] And this shall be an everlasting statute to you, to make atonement for the children of Israel because of all their sins once in the year.' *And he did[2]* as the LORD commanded Moses.

Acharei Mot – Chapter 17[3]

וַיְדַבֵּר יְהוָה אֶל־מֹשֶׁה לֵּאמֹר

1[4] And the LORD spoke to Moses, saying:

דַּבֵּר אֶל־אַהֲרֹן וְאֶל־בָּנָיו וְאֶל כָּל־בְּנֵי
יִשְׂרָאֵל וְאָמַרְתָּ אֲלֵיהֶם זֶה הַדָּבָר
אֲשֶׁר־צִוָּה יְהוָה לֵאמֹר

2[5] Speak to Aaron, *and to his sons[6]*, and to all the children of Israel, and say to them, this is the thing the LORD has commanded:

אִישׁ אִישׁ מִבֵּית יִשְׂרָאֵל אֲשֶׁר יִשְׁחַט
שׁוֹר אוֹ־כֶשֶׂב אוֹ־עֵז בַּמַּחֲנֶה אוֹ אֲשֶׁר
יִשְׁחַט מִחוּץ לַמַּחֲנֶה

3[7] Whatever man of the *house[8]* of Israel[9], who kills an ox, or lamb, or goat, in the camp, or who kills it outside the camp,

---

[1] Leviticus 16:34 - 11Qpaleol.eva, 3 Maccabees 1:12, b.Chullin [Tosefot] 24a 29b, b.Menachot [Rashi] 27b, b.Menachot 16a, b.Sanhedrin [Rashi] 49b, b.Sheviit 10a, b.Yoma [Rashi] 2b 42a, b.Yoma 60a, b.Zevachim [Tosefot] 39a 58a, b.Zevachim 19b 40a 19b, Exodus 6:10, Hebrews 9:7 9:25 10:3 10:14, Jubilees 34:18, Leviticus 23:31, Midrash Proverbs 9, Midrash Tanchuma Chukkat 7, Numbers 5:7, Numbers.R 19:5, Pesikta Rabbati 14:12 45:3, Pirkei de R'Eliezer 46, Seder Olam 6:Descended, y.Yoma 7:1, z.Acharei Mot 235

[2] Missing in LXX

[3] mt.Hilchot Melachim uMichamoteihem 9:5

[4] Leviticus 17:1 - Midrash Tanchuma Acharei Mot 1
Leviticus 17:1-3 - Midrash Tanchuma Acharei Mot 9
Leviticus 17:1-5 - 11QpaleoLeva
Leviticus 17:1-16 - Josephus Antiquities 4.11.2

[5] Leviticus 17:2 - b.Bava Batra 120ab, b.Nedarim 78a, b.Zevachim 107a 116b, Mekilta de R'Ishmael Nezikin 12:63, Midrash Tanchuma Acharei Mot 10, z.Pekudei 239b
Leviticus 17:2-11 - 4QLevd

[6] Missing in 11QpaleoLeva

[7] Leviticus 17:3 - b.Bava Batra [Rashbam] 120b, b.Bava Kamma [Tosefot] 71b, b.Chullin [Rashi] 29b 40b, b.Chullin [Tosefot] 16b 22b, b.Menachot [Tosefot] 91b, b.Nedarim [Ran] 78a, b.Pesachim [Rashi] 91a, b.Sanhedrin [Rashi] 42b 82b, b.Temurah 13a, b.Yoma 63a, b.Zevachim [Rashi] 4b 69a 85a 16a 111b, b.Zevachim [Tosefot] 115b, b.Zevachim 107ab 18ab 115a, Deuteronomy 12:5-7 12:11-15 12:20-22 12:26-27, Ecclesiastes.R 5:10, Jastrow 1547b, Leviticus 17:8 17:12-13 17:15, Leviticus.R 22:1, m.Zevachim 13:1, Midrash Tanchuma Acharei Mot 10 11, mt.Hilchot Maaseh haKorbanot 18:2 18:15 18:18, mt.Hilchot Sanhedrin vHainshin Hameurim Lahem 19:1, Numbers.R 14:1
Leviticus 17:3-4 - Commandment #506, Midrash Tanchuma Acharei Mot 9 11 12, Midrash Tanchuma Naso 28
Leviticus 17:3-9 - 4QMMT b 27-35

[8] LXX *children*

[9] 4QLevd LXX adds *and the stranger who resides in Israel*

וְאֶל־פֶּתַח אֹהֶל מוֹעֵד֙ לֹא הֱבִיאוֹ֙
לְהַקְרִיב קׇרְבָּן֙ לַיהֹוָה לִפְנֵי מִשְׁכַּן
יְהֹוָה דָּם יֵחָשֵׁב֙ לָאִישׁ הַהוּא דָּם שָׁפָ֔ךְ
וְנִכְרַת הָאִישׁ הַהוּא מִקֶּרֶב עַמּוֹ

4[1]   and has not brought it to the door of the tent of meeting, *to present it*[2] as an *offering*[3] unto the LORD[4] before the tabernacle of the LORD, blood shall be imputed to that man; he has shed blood; and that man shall be cut off from among his people.

לְמַ֩עַן֩ אֲשֶׁר֙ יָבִ֜יאוּ בְּנֵ֣י יִשְׂרָאֵל֮ אֶת־
זִבְחֵיהֶם֒ אֲשֶׁר֙ הֵם זֹבְחִים֙ עַל־פְּנֵי
הַשָּׂדֶ֔ה וֶהֱבִיאֻם לַיהֹוָה אֶל־פֶּתַח אֹהֶל
מוֹעֵד אֶל־הַכֹּהֵן וְזָבְחוּ זִבְחֵי שְׁלָמִים
לַיהֹוָה אוֹתָם

5[5]   To the end that the children of Israel may bring their sacrifices, which they sacrifice in the open field, even that they may bring to the LORD, to the door of the tent of meeting, to the priest, and sacrifice them for sacrifices of peace offerings to the LORD.

וְזָרַק הַכֹּהֵן אֶת־הַדָּם֙ עַל־מִזְבַּח יְהֹוָה
פֶּתַח אֹהֶל מוֹעֵד וְהִקְטִיר הַחֵלֶב לְרֵיחַ
נִיחֹחַ לַיהֹוָה

6[6]   And the priest shall dash the blood against the altar of the LORD at the door of the tent of meeting, and make the fat smoke for a sweet savor to the LORD.

וְלֹא־יִזְבְּחוּ עוֹד֙ אֶת־זִבְחֵיהֶם לַשְּׂעִירִ֔ם
אֲשֶׁר הֵם זֹנִים אַחֲרֵיהֶם חֻקַּת עוֹלָם

7[7]   And they shall no longer sacrifice their sacrifices to the *satyrs*[8], after whom they go *astray*[9]. This shall be a statute

---

[1] Leviticus 17:4 - b.Avodah Zara 51b, b.Bava Kamma [Tosefot] 76a, b.Bechorot [Rashi] 4b 16a, b.Chullin [Rashi] 16b 14a 78a 85a, b.Kereitot [Rashi] 2a, b.Kereitot 3b, b.Kiddushin 43a 157b, b.Pesachim [Rashi] 91a, b.Sanhedrin [Rashi] 42b, b.Sanhedrin 34b, b.Temurah [Tosefot] 24b, b.Temurah 6b 13a, b.Yoma [Rashi] 62b, b.Yoma 63ab, b.Zevachim [Rashi] 13a 111b 112b 114a, b.Zevachim [Tosefot] 10b, b.Zevachim 16ab 107ab 18a 112a 113b 115a, Deuteronomy 12:5-21, Deuteronomy.R 4:6, Exodus 12:15 12:19, Ezekiel 20:40, Genesis 17:14, Isaiah 18:3, John 10:7 10:9 14:6, Leviticus 1:3 7:18 17:10 17:14 18:29 20:3 20:16 20:18, m.Keritot 1:1, m.Makkot 3:2, m.Zevachim 13:1 14:1-2, Midrash Tanchuma Acharei Mot 12, mt.Hilchot Sanhedrin vHainshin Hameurim Lahem 19:1, Numbers 15:30-31, Philemon 1:18-19, Psalms 32:2, Romans 4:6 5:13 5:20, y.Ketubot 3:2, y.Rosh Hashanah 1:1, y.Terumot 7:1

[2] 4QLevd *so as to sacrifice it as a burnt offering or an offering of well-being to the LORD to be acceptable as a pleasing odor and has slaughtered it without and does not bring it to the door of the tent of meeting to offer it*

[3] LXX *whole burnt offering or peace offering*

[4] LXX adds *to be acceptable for a sweet-smelling savor*

[5] Leviticus 17:5 - 1 Kings 14:23, 2 Chronicles 4:4, 2 Kings 16:4 17:10, b.Avodah Zara 51b, b.Bechorot 12a, b.Zevachim [Rashi] 112b 114b 118a, b.Zevachim 26ab 16b 119b, Deuteronomy 12:2, Exodus 24:5, Ezekiel 20:28 22:9, Genesis 21:33 22:2 22:13 7:54, Guide for the Perplexed 3:46, Leviticus 3:1-17 7:11-21, mt.Hilchot Pesulei haMikdashim 1:14, Pesikta Rabbati 7:4

[6] Leviticus 17:6 - b.Chullin [Rashi] 114b, b.Eruvin [Rashi] 103b, b.Menachot [Rashi] 9a, b.Menachot 26a, b.Pesachim 79a, b.Yoma [Rashi] 60a, b.Zevachim [Rashi] 19b, b.Zevachim 18b 118a 119b, Exodus 5:13 5:18, Leviticus 3:2 3:5 3:8 3:11 3:13 3:16 4:31, m.Zevachim 14:10, Numbers 18:17, y.Pesachim 7:5

[7] Leviticus 17:7 - 1 Corinthians 10:20, 2 Chronicles 11:15, 2 Corinthians 4:4, b.Avodah Zara 51ab, b.Bava Batra [Rashbam] 120b, b.Bava Batra 120a, b.Kereitot [Rashi] 3b, b.Makkot [Rashi] 13a, b.Sanhedrin [Rashi] 63a, b.Sanhedrin 61a, b.Zevachim [Rashi] 112b 119b, b.Zevachim 16ab, Deuteronomy 7:16 8:17, Ephesians 2:2, Exodus 22:20 8:8 10:15, Ezekiel 23:8, Guide for the Perplexed 3:46, Jastrow 1523b, Jeremiah 3:1, John 12:31 14:30, Jubilees 7:21, Leviticus 20:5, Leviticus.R 22:8, Midrash Tanchuma Acharei Mot 11, Psalms 10:37, Revelation 9:20 17:1-5, Sifre Numbers 116:6, y.Sanhedrin 7:9-10, z.Acharei Mot 63a 123 250, z.Pinchas 681, z.Vayishlach 34, z.Yitro 357

[8] LXX *vain*

[9] LXX *whoring*

תְּהְיֶה־זֹּאת לָהֶם לְדֹרֹתָם

forever for them throughout their generations.

וַאֲלֵהֶם תֹּאמַר אִישׁ אִישׁ מִבֵּית
יִשְׂרָאֵל וּמִן־הַגֵּר אֲשֶׁר־יָגוּר בְּתוֹכָם
אֲשֶׁר־יַעֲלֶה עֹלָה אוֹ־זָבַח

8[1] And you shall say to them: Whatever man there be of the *house*[2] of Israel, or of the *strangers*[3] who sojourn among *them*[4], who offers a burnt offering or sacrifice,

וְאֶל־פֶּתַח אֹהֶל מוֹעֵד לֹא יְבִיאֶנּוּ
לַעֲשׂוֹת אֹתוֹ לַיהוָה וְנִכְרַת הָאִישׁ
הַהוּא מֵעַמָּיו

9[5] And brings it not unto the door of the tent of meeting, to sacrifice it to the LORD, even that man shall be *cut*[6] off from his people.

וְאִישׁ אִישׁ מִבֵּית יִשְׂרָאֵל וּמִן־הַגֵּר
הַגָּר בְּתוֹכָם אֲשֶׁר יֹאכַל כָּל־דָּם
וְנָתַתִּי פָנַי בַּנֶּפֶשׁ הָאֹכֶלֶת אֶת־הַדָּם
וְהִכְרַתִּי אֹתָהּ מִקֶּרֶב עַמָּהּ

10[7] And whatsoever man of the house of Israel, or of the strangers who sojourn among them, who eats *any manner of*[8] blood, I will set My face against that soul who eats blood, and will *cut him off from among his*[9] people.

כִּי נֶפֶשׁ הַבָּשָׂר בַּדָּם הִוא וַאֲנִי נְתַתִּיו
לָכֶם עַל־הַמִּזְבֵּחַ לְכַפֵּר עַל־נַפְשֹׁתֵיכֶם
כִּי־הַדָּם הוּא בַּנֶּפֶשׁ יְכַפֵּר

11[10] For the life of *the*[11] flesh is in the blood; and I have given it to you on the altar to make atonement for your souls; *for it is the blood that makes atonement by reason of the life*[12].

---

[1] Leviticus 17:8 - 1 Kings 18:30-38, 1 Samuel 7:9 10:8 16:2, 2 Samuel 24:25, b.Kereitot [Rashi] 2a, b.Menachot [Tosefot] 14b, b.Sanhedrin [Tosefot] 82b, b.Sanhedrin 34b, b.Zevachim [Rashi] 85a 16a 107b 111b, b.Zevachim 107a 18ab 109a 115b 119b, Jastrow 976b, Judges 6:26, Leviticus 1:2-3 17:4 17:10, m.Zevachim 14:4, Malachi 1:11, mt.Hilchot Maaseh haKorbanot 18:2 19:2, z.Yitro 378 Leviticus 17:8-16 - m.Megillah 3:6

[2] LXX *children*

[3] LXX *sons of the proselytes*

[4] LXX *you*

[5] Leviticus 17:9 - b.Kereitot [Rashi] 2a, b.Kereitot 3b, b.Yoma [Rashi] 60b, b.Zevachim [Rashi] 13a 16ab 111b, b.Zevachim [Tosefot] 85a 115b, b.Zevachim 107a 18ab 109ab, Deuteronomy.R 4:6, Leviticus 17:4, m.Keritot 1:1, m.Makkot 3:2, m.Zevachim 14:9, mt.Hilchot Maaseh haKorbanot 18:2 19:1 19:3

[6] LXX *destroyed*

[7] Leviticus 17:10 - 1 Samuel 14:33, Acts 15:20 15:29, b.Kereitot 22a [Rashi] 4b, Deuteronomy 12:16 12:23 15:23, Ezekiel 14:8 15:7 9:25 20:7, Genesis 9:4, Guide for the Perplexed 3:46, Hebrews 10:29, Jeremiah 21:10 20:11, Jubilees 6:11 7:32, Leviticus 3:17 7:26-27 17:11 19:26 20:3-6 2:17, mt.Hilchot Temurah 1:2, m.Keritot 5:1, Psalms 34:17, Sibylline Oracles 8.403, z.Terumah 142b, b.Sotah Rashi 9a

[8] Missing in LXX

[9] LXX *destroy it from among its*

[10] Leviticus 17:11 - 1 John 1:7 2:2, 1 Peter 1:2, b.Berachot [Rashi] 31a, b.Chullin 114a [Rashi] 16a 114b, b.Kereitot 22a [Rashi] 4b 24b, b.Menachot 93b [Rashi] 8b 25b [Tosefot] 57b, b.Nazir [Rashi] 46a, b.Pesachim [Rashi] 16b, b.Pesachim 65a, b.Yoma 5a 59b, b.Zevachim 6a 35a 46a [Rashi] 13a 16a [Tosefot] 38a, Colossians 1:14 1:20, Ephesians 1:7, Genesis 9:4, Hebrews 9:22 13:12, Jubilees 6:14 7:32, Leviticus 8:15 16:11 16:14-19 17:14, m.Meilah 3:3, m.Zevachim 3:1, Mark 14:24, Matthew 20:28 2:28, Midrash Tanchuma Tzav 14, mt.Hilchot Korban Pesach 2:6, mt.Hilchot Maachalot Assurot 6:4, mt.Hilchot Pesulei haMikdashim 13:3, Philo De Specialibus Legibus IV 122, Philo Quod Deterius Potiori Insidiari Soleat 80, Revelation 1:5, Romans 3:25 5:9, Saadia Opinions 3:10 6:1, t.Zevachim 8:17, Tanya Igeret Hakodesh §31, Tanya Likutei Aramim §1, y.Yoma 5:6, z.Lech Lecha 302

[11] Missing in LXX

[12] LXX *for its blood shall make atonement for the soul*

עַל־כֵּן אָמַרְתִּי לִבְנֵי יִשְׂרָאֵל כָּל־נֶפֶשׁ
מִכֶּם לֹא־תֹאכַל דָּם וְהַגֵּר הַגָּר
בְּתוֹכְכֶם לֹא־יֹאכַל דָּם

וְאִישׁ אִישׁ מִבְּנֵי יִשְׂרָאֵל וּמִן־הַגֵּר
הַגָּר בְּתוֹכָם אֲשֶׁר יָצוּד צֵיד חַיָּה אוֹ־
עוֹף אֲשֶׁר יֵאָכֵל וְשָׁפַךְ אֶת־דָּמוֹ
וְכִסָּהוּ בֶּעָפָר

כִּי־נֶפֶשׁ כָּל־בָּשָׂר דָּמוֹ בְנַפְשׁוֹ הוּא
וָאֹמַר לִבְנֵי יִשְׂרָאֵל דַּם כָּל־בָּשָׂר לֹא
תֹאכֵלוּ כִּי נֶפֶשׁ כָּל־בָּשָׂר דָּמוֹ הִוא
כָּל־אֹכְלָיו יִכָּרֵת

וְכָל־נֶפֶשׁ אֲשֶׁר תֹּאכַל נְבֵלָה וּטְרֵפָה
בָּאֶזְרָח וּבַגֵּר וְכִבֶּס בְּגָדָיו וְרָחַץ
בַּמַּיִם וְטָמֵא עַד־הָעֶרֶב וְטָהֵר

וְאִם לֹא יְכַבֵּס וּבְשָׂרוֹ לֹא יִרְחָץ וְנָשָׂא
עֲוֹנוֹ

12[1] Therefore, I said to the children of Israel: No soul among you shall eat blood, nor shall any stranger who sojourns among you eat blood.

13[2] And whatever man of the children of Israel, or of the strangers who sojourn among them, who takes in hunting any beast or fowl that may be eaten, he shall pour out its blood, and cover it with dust.

14[3] For as to the life of all flesh, its blood is all one with its life; therefore, I said to the children of Israel: You shall eat the blood of no manner of flesh; for the life of all flesh is its blood; whoever eats it shall be cut off.

15[4] And every soul who eats what dies of itself, or what is torn of beasts, whether he is homeborn or a stranger, he shall wash his clothes, and bathe himself in water, and will be unclean until the evening; then he shall be clean.

16[5] But if he will not wash them, nor bathe his flesh, then he shall bear his iniquity.

---

[1] Leviticus 17:12 - b.Bechorot [Tosefot] 15a, b.Chullin [Tosefot] 33a, b.Kereitot [Rashi] 4b, Exodus 12:49, b.Pesachim 22a, b.Yevamot 114a, Guide for the Perplexed 3:48, Jubilees 6:11, y.Maaser Sheni 2:1, y.Sheviit 3:2, y.Yoma 8:3

[2] Leviticus 17:13 - 1 Samuel 14:32-34, b.Bava Kamma 91b, b.Bechorot [Rashi] 19a [Tosefot] 3a 9b, b.Beitzah 7b [Tosefot] 8a, b.Chullin 27b 31a 83b 84a 85a 86b 87a 88a [Rashi] 14a 28a 88b 120a, b.Menachot [Tosefot] 11b, b.Shabbat 22a, b.Sotah 16a, Commandment #168, Deuteronomy.R 4:5, Deuteronomy 12:16 12:24 15:23, Ecclesiastes.R 3:19 10:5, Ein Yaakov Shabbat:22a, Ezekiel 24:7, Guide for the Perplexed 3:46, Jastrow 634a 1000a, Job 16:18, Lamentations.R 1:37 2:4 4:16 4:16, Jubilees 21:18 7:30, Petichata DChakimei 4-5 23, Leviticus 7:26, m.Chullin 6:1, m.Beitzah 1:2, Sifre Devarim Reeh 122, m.Bikkurim 2:9, Mekhilta de R'Shimon bar Yochai Nezikin 69:3, Midrash Psalms 22:17 119:32, Midrash Tanchuma Shelach 15, mt.Hilchot Chametz uMatzah 18:11, mt.Hilchot Shechitah 1:1 14:1, Numbers.R 9:15 17:5, Pesikta de R'Kahana 15.7, y.Kiddushin 1:2, y.Taanit 4:5

[3] Leviticus 17:14 - b.Bechorot [Tosefot] 15a, b.Chullin [Rashi] 16a 74b, b.Chullin 86b 87a, b.Kereitot [Rashi] 2a 4b 20b, b.Pesachim [Rashi] 65a, b.Sheviit [Tosefot] 23a, Derech Hashem Part III 1§02, Deuteronomy 12:23, Genesis 9:4, Jubilees 7:32, Leviticus 17:11-12, m.Keritot 5:1, m.Zevachim 3:3, Midrash Tanchuma Tzav 14, Saadia Opinions 8:9, y.Yoma 5:6

[4] Leviticus 17:15 - b.Chullin [Rashi] 20b, b.Chullin 120a, b.Sheviit [Rashi] 7b, b.Zevachim 69a 70a, Deuteronomy 14:21, Exodus 22:31, Ezekiel 4:14 20:31, Leviticus 11:25 15:5 15:10 15:21 22:8, Mekilta de R'Ishmael Kaspa 2:9, mt.Hilchot Shaar Avot Hatuman 3:1, Numbers 19:8 19:19 19:21, Revelation 7:14, Song of Songs.R 1:19, y.Nazir 6:1
Leviticus 17:15-16 - Sifre Numbers 1:7

[5] Leviticus 17:16 - 1 Peter 2:24, Hebrews 9:28, Isaiah 5:11, John 13:8, Leviticus 5:1 7:18 19:8 20:17 20:19-20, mt.Hilchot Biat haMikdash 3:12, mt.Hilchot Tumat Meit 3:3, mt.Hilchot Sanhedrin vHainshin Hameurim Lahem 19:4, Numbers 19:19-20

Acharei Mot – Chapter 18[1]

וַיְדַבֵּר יְהוָה אֶל־מֹשֶׁה לֵּאמֹר

1[2] And the LORD spoke to Moses, saying:

דַּבֵּר אֶל־בְּנֵי יִשְׂרָאֵל וְאָמַרְתָּ אֲלֵהֶם אֲנִי יְהוָה אֱלֹהֵיכֶם

2[3] Speak to the children of Israel, and say to them: I am the LORD your God.

כְּמַעֲשֵׂה אֶרֶץ־מִצְרַיִם אֲשֶׁר יְשַׁבְתֶּם־בָּהּ לֹא תַעֲשׂוּ וּכְמַעֲשֵׂה אֶרֶץ־כְּנַעַן אֲשֶׁר אֲנִי מֵבִיא אֶתְכֶם שָׁמָּה לֹא תַעֲשׂוּ וּבְחֻקֹּתֵיהֶם לֹא תֵלֵכוּ

3[4] You shall not imitate the *behaviors*[5] of the land of the Egyptians, where you lived; and you shall not copy the *behaviors*[6] of the land of Canaan, into which I bring you; nor shall you walk in their statutes.

אֶת־מִשְׁפָּטַי תַּעֲשׂוּ וְאֶת־חֻקֹּתַי תִּשְׁמְרוּ לָלֶכֶת בָּהֶם אֲנִי יְהוָה אֱלֹהֵיכֶם

4[7] You shall perform My ordinances, and you shall keep My statutes, to walk in them: I am the LORD your God.

וּשְׁמַרְתֶּם אֶת־חֻקֹּתַי וְאֶת־מִשְׁפָּטַי

5[8] And you shall keep My statutes, and my ordinances, which, if a man does,

---

[1] Ein Yaakov Sotah 4b, Ein Yaakov Yevamot 21a, Jastrow 1355a, Mesillat Yesharim 5 Factors Detracting from Zehirus, mt.Hilchot Tumat Meit 1:2, mt.Hilchot Sanhedrin vHainshin Hameurim Lahem 19:1, Torah reading for Minchah [Yom Kippur], Josephus Antiquities 4.12.1

[2] Leviticus 18:1 - m.Moed Katan 1:7, Philo De Congressu Quaerendae Eruditionis Gratia 86

[3] Leviticus 18:2 - Exodus 6:7 20:2, Ezekiel 20:5 20:7 20:19-20, Genesis 17:7, Jubilees 31:16, Leviticus 11:44 18:4 19:3-4 19:10 19:34 20:7, Mekilta de R'Ishmael Bahodesh 6:11, Psalms 33:12, z.Acharei Mot 78b

[4] Leviticus 18:3 - 1 Peter 4:2-4, b.Avodah Zara 11a, b.Chullin 41b, b.Sanhedrin [Rashi] 52b, b.Shabbat [Rashi] 67a, Commandment #332, Deuteronomy 12:4 12:30-31, Ephesians 5:7-11, Exodus 23:24, Ezekiel 20:7-8 23:8, Gates of Repentance 3.104, Guide for the Perplexed 3:37, Jastrow 896b 1280a 1333a, Jeremiah 10:2-3, Leviticus 18:24-30 20:23, Leviticus.R 23:1 23:7 23:9 23:12, Mekilta de R'Ishmael Bahodesh 6:14, mt.Hilchot Avodat Kochavim vChukkoteihem 11:1, mt.Hilchot Issurei Biah 21:8, mt.Hilchot Melachim uMichamoteihem 5:8, mt.Hilchot Sotah 3:11, mt.Hilchot Teshuvah 6:3 6:3, mt.Shemonah Perakim 5:6, Psalms 10:35, Romans 12:2, Shemonah Perachim V, Sifre Devarim Ekev 38, Siman 3:2, Song of Songs.R 2:9, t.Sanhedrin 9:11, z.Acharei Mot 70a, z.Acharei Mot 250 277 289
Leviticus 18:3-18 - HaMadrikh 2

[5] LXX *devices*

[6] LXX *devices*

[7] Leviticus 18:4 - b.Sanhedrin [Rashi] 60a, b.Yoma 67b, Deuteronomy 4:1-2 6:1, Ein Yaakov Yoma 67b, Ezekiel 20:19 12:27 13:24, HaMadrikh 35:4, Jastrow 873a, John 15:14, Leviticus 18:2 18:26 19:37 20:22, Leviticus.R 23:9, Luke 1:6, Mesillat Yesharim 16 Trait of Taharah, Midrash Tanchuma Mishpatim 7, Psalms 9:45 23:4, Sifre Devarim Vaetchanan 34, z.Acharei Mot 72b 78b 295 308, z.Bechukotai 16

[8] Leviticus 18:5 - 4Q504 frag 6 1.17, b.Avodah Zara 3a 27b 54a, b.Bava Kamma 38a, b.Chagigah [Tosefot] 13a, b.Makkot [Riven] 23a, b.Makkot 23b, b.Pesachim 25a, b.Sanhedrin [Tosefot] 61b, b.Sanhedrin 59a 60a 74a, b.Sheviit [Rashi] 26b, b.Yoma [Tosefot] 85a, b.Yoma 85b, Cairo Damascus 3.16, Ecclesiastes.R 1:24, Ein Yaakov Avodah Zarah 3a 27b, Ein Yaakov Makkot 23b, Ein Yaakov Pesachim 53a, Ein Yaakov Sanhedrin 59a, Exodus 6:2 6:6 6:29, Exodus.R 30:22, Ezekiel 20:11 20:13 20:21, Galatians 3:12, Gates of Repentance 3.136, Leviticus.R 23:9, Luke 10:28, m.Makkot 3:15, Malachi 3:6, Midrash Psalms 1:18, Midrash Tanchuma Chukkat 7, Midrash Tanchuma Massei 1, Midrash Tanchuma Mishpatim 3, Midrash Tanchuma Vayakhel 8, mt.Hichot Meilah 8:8, mt.Hilchot Milah 1:18, mt.Hilchot Yesodei haTorah 5:1, Numbers.R 13:15-16, Pesikta de R'Kahana 4.6, Psalms of Solomon 14:3, Romans 10:5, Sifra Acharei Mot 13, Sifre Devarim Ki Tetze 286, t.Shabbat 15:17, y.Avodah Zarah 2:2, y.Makkot 3:12, y.Shabbat 14:4, y.Taanit 4:5, z.Acharei Mot 78b

אֲשֶׁ֤ר יַעֲשֶׂ֥ה אֹתָ֛ם הָאָדָ֖ם וָחַ֣י בָּהֶ֑ם אֲנִ֖י יְהֹוָֽה׃

he shall live by them: I am the LORD[1].

אִ֥ישׁ אִישׁ֙ אֶל־כׇּל־שְׁאֵ֣ר בְּשָׂר֔וֹ לֹ֥א תִקְרְב֖וּ לְגַלּ֣וֹת עֶרְוָ֑ה אֲנִ֖י יְהֹוָֽה׃

6[2] A man, any man shall not approach anyone near of kin to him, to uncover their nakedness. I am the LORD.

עֶרְוַ֥ת אָבִ֛יךָ וְעֶרְוַ֥ת אִמְּךָ֖ לֹ֣א תְגַלֵּ֑ה אִמְּךָ֣ הִ֔וא לֹ֥א תְגַלֶּ֖ה עֶרְוָתָֽהּ׃

7[3] The nakedness of your father, and the nakedness of your mother, *shall you not uncover: she is your mother*[4]; you shall not uncover her nakedness.

עֶרְוַ֥ת אֵֽשֶׁת־אָבִ֖יךָ לֹ֣א תְגַלֵּ֑ה עֶרְוַ֥ת אָבִ֖יךָ הִֽוא׃

8[5] The nakedness of your father's wife shall you not uncover: it is your father's nakedness.

עֶרְוַ֨ת אֲחֽוֹתְךָ֤ בַת־אָבִ֙יךָ֙ א֣וֹ בַת־אִמֶּ֔ךָ מוֹלֶ֣דֶת בַּ֔יִת א֖וֹ מוֹלֶ֣דֶת ח֑וּץ לֹ֥א תְגַלֶּ֖ה עֶרְוָתָֽן׃

9[6] The nakedness of your sister, the daughter of your father, or the daughter of your mother, whether born at home or born abroad, their nakedness you shall not uncover.

עֶרְוַ֤ת בַּת־בִּנְךָ֙ א֣וֹ בַת־בִּתְּךָ֔ לֹ֥א תְגַלֶּ֖ה עֶרְוָתָ֑ן כִּ֥י עֶרְוָתְךָ֖ הֵֽנָּה׃

10[7] The nakedness of your son's daughter, or of your daughter's daughter, their nakedness you shall not uncover; for theirs is your own nakedness.

---

[1] LXX adds *your God*

[2] Leviticus 18:6 - 4Q387 5, 4Q477 2 ii 8, Avot de R'Natan 2, b.Avodah Zara 14a, b.Bava Batra 88b, b.Chagigah 11b, b.Ketubot 3047b, b.Makkot [Riven] 23b, b.Sanhedrin 57b, b.Shabbat 13a, b.Yevamot [Rashi] 2b, b.Yevamot 97a, Commandment #82, Gates of Repentance 3.80, Genesis.R 31:5, Jastrow 1509a, Leviticus 18:7-19 20:11-12 20:17-21, m.Yevamot 10:2, Mekhilta de R'Shimon bar Yochai Nezikin 60:4, Mekilta de R'Ishmael Nezikin 3:132, Mesillat Yesharim 11 Traits-of-Nekuyut, Midrash Tanchuma Behaalotcha 16, mt.Hilchot Sanhedrin vHainshin Hameurim Lahem 19:4, Numbers.R 10:8 15:24, Philo De Gigantibus 32, y.Ketubot 5:7, y.Kiddushin 1:1, y.Shabbat 7:2, z.Acharei Mot 78b
Leviticus 18:6-18 - m.Bikkurim 4:3, m.Chagigah 1:7 1:8 2:1, m.Megillah 4:9, m.Niddah 5:4
Leviticus 18:6-19 - 4Q251 12
Leviticus 18:6-20 - Mas.Soferim 9:8
Leviticus 18:6-23 - Midrash Proverbs 6

[3] Leviticus 18:7 - b.Kereitot [Rashi] 2a, b.Sanhedrin [Rashi] 58b, b.Sanhedrin [Tosefot] 9b, b.Sanhedrin 53b 54a, Commandment #83, Commandment #84, Ezekiel 22:10, Jastrow 648b 1076b, Leviticus 18:8-18:16 20:11 20:14, m.Sanhedrin 7:4, Mas.Soferim 9:8, mt.Hilchot Shegagot 4:1, Philo De Fuga et Inventione 194, y.Sanhedrin 7:6, z.Acharei Mot 74a, z.Bereshit 27b, z.Terumah 176a, z.Acharei Mot 317 327, z.BereshitA 268 268, z.Safra Det'zniuta 32, z.Trumah 923, z.Vayikra 254

[4] LXX *for she is thy mother; thou shalt not uncover her nakedness*

[5] Leviticus 18:8 - 1 Corinthians 5:1, 2 Samuel 16:21-16:22, Amos 2:7, b.Sanhedrin 53b 54a, Commandment #85, Deuteronomy 23:1 3:20, Ezekiel 22:10, Genesis 11:22 1:4, Leviticus 20:11, m.Sanhedrin 7:4, Pseudo-Phocylides 179 181, t.Yevamot 12:1, y.Sanhedrin 7:6, z.Acharei Mot 75a, z.Acharei Mot 336 341, z.BereshitA 270
Leviticus 18:8-9 - 2QNumd

[6] Leviticus 18:9 - 2 Samuel 13:11-13:14, b.Kereitot [Rashi] 3a, b.Ketubot 32b, b.Makkot 5b, b.Sanhedrin [Rashi] 76a, b.Sanhedrin [Tosefot] 53b, b.Yevamot [Tosefot] 2b, b.Yevamot 22b 23a, b.Zevachim [Rashi] 16b, Commandment #86, Deuteronomy 3:22, Ezekiel 22:11, Leviticus 18:11 20:17, m.Nedarin 11:3, mt.Hilchot Issurei Biah 2:2, z.Acharei Mot 75b, z.Acharei Mot 379, z.Vayechi 79, z.BereshitA 270

[7] Leviticus 18:10 - b.Kereitot [Rashi] 3b, b.Kereitot 5a, b.Sanhedrin [Rashi] 51a 75b 76a, b.Yevamot 3a 22b 97a, Commandment #88 [Note: Chafetz Chayim treats this and #89 as one commandment; Rambam treats them separately], Commandment #89 [Note: Chafetz Chayim treats this and #88 as one commandment; Rambam treats them as two], m.Yevamot 1:1, y.Sanhedrin 9:1, y.Yevamot 11:1

עֶרְוַת בַּת־אֵשֶׁת אָבִיךָ מוֹלֶדֶת אָבִיךָ
אֲחוֹתְךָ הִוא לֹא תְגַלֶּה עֶרְוָתָהּ

עֶרְוַת אֲחוֹת־אָבִיךָ לֹא תְגַלֵּה שְׁאֵר
אָבִיךָ הִוא

עֶרְוַת אֲחוֹת־אִמְּךָ לֹא תְגַלֵּה כִּי־שְׁאֵר
אִמְּךָ הִוא

עֶרְוַת אֲחִי־אָבִיךָ לֹא תְגַלֵּה אֶל־אִשְׁתּוֹ
לֹא תִקְרָב דֹּדָתְךָ הִוא

עֶרְוַת כַּלָּתְךָ לֹא תְגַלֵּה אֵשֶׁת בִּנְךָ הִוא
לֹא תְגַלֵּה עֶרְוָתָהּ

עֶרְוַת אֵשֶׁת־אָחִיךָ לֹא תְגַלֵּה עֶרְוַת
אָחִיךָ הִוא

עֶרְוַת אִשָּׁה וּבִתָּהּ לֹא תְגַלֵּה אֶת־בַּת־
בְּנָהּ וְאֶת־בַּת־בִּתָּהּ לֹא תִקַּח לְגַלּוֹת
עֶרְוָתָהּ שַׁאֲרָה הֵנָּה זִמָּה הִוא

11[1] The nakedness of your father's wife's daughter, born of your father, she is your sister, you shall not uncover her nakedness.

12[2] You shall not uncover the nakedness of your father's sister: she is your father's near relatives.

13[3] You shall not uncover the nakedness of your mother's sister; for she is your mother's near relatives.

14[4] You shall not uncover the nakedness of your father's brother, you shall not approach his wife: she is your aunt.

15[5] You shall not uncover the nakedness of your daughter-in-law: she is your son's wife; you shall not uncover her nakedness.

16[6] You shall not uncover the nakedness of your brother's wife: it is your brother's nakedness.

17[7] You shall not uncover the nakedness of a woman and her daughter; you shall not take her son's daughter, or her daughter's daughter, to uncover her nakedness: they are near relatives; this is lewdness.

---

[1] Leviticus 18:11 - b.Kereitot [Rashi] 3a, b.Makkot [Rashi] 14a, b.Makkot 5b, b.Yevamot 22b 23a, b.Zevachim [Rashi] 16b, Commandment #87, mt.Hilchot Issurei Biah 2:3

[2] Leviticus 18:12 - b.Bava Batra [Rashbam] 18b, b.Bava Batra 19b, b.Sanhedrin [Rashi] 58b, b.Yevamot 54b, Commandment #91, Ein Yaakov Shabbat:33a, Exodus 6:20, Jastrow 1509a, Leviticus 20:19, y.Sanhedrin 7:5, z.Acharei Mot 76b, z.Acharei Mot 357
Leviticus 18:12-13 - 4Q545 4-7, Mekilta de R'Ishmael Nezikin 3:132-133

[3] Leviticus 18:13 - b.Bava Batra 19b, Cairo Damascus 5.07-9, Commandment #92, Jastrow 1509a, y.Sanhedrin 7:5, z.Acharei Mot 377 381

[4] Leviticus 18:14 - b.Sanhedrin 28b, Commandment #93 #94, Leviticus 20:20, mt.Hilchot Shegagot 4:1, Mas.Derek Eretz Rabbah 1:6, mt.Hilchot Malveh VLoveh 2:7, z.Acharei Mot 77b, z.BereshitA 270

[5] Leviticus 18:15 - b.Sanhedrin [Rashi] 54a, b.Sanhedrin 53b 76a, b.Yevamot 21b, Commandment #95, Ezekiel 22:11, Genesis 38:18-38:19 14:26, Jubilees 41:26, Leviticus 20:12, m.Sanhedrin 7:4, m.Shekalim 8:8, Midrash Psalms 116:9, y.Sanhedrin 7:6, z.Acharei Mot 383, z.BereshitA 270

[6] Leviticus 18:16 - b.Bava Kamma [Tosefot] 71b, b.Bechorot [Rashi] 19b, b.Yevamot [Rashi] 2a 4a 14b, b.Yevamot 55a, Commandment #96, Deuteronomy 1:5, Exodus.R 28:4, Leviticus 20:21, Luke 3:19, m.Shekalim 8:8, m.Yevamot 1:1 3:10, Mark 6:17 12:19, Matthew 14:3-4 22:24, Mekilta de R'Ishmael Bahodesh 7:58, Midrash Tanchuma Chukkat 7, Numbers.R 19:5, Pesikta de R'Kahana 4.6, Pesikta Rabbati 14:1, Sifre Devarim Ki Tetze 233, y.Nedarim 3:2, y.Sheviit 3:8, y.Yevamot 1:1
Leviticus 18:16-21 - 4QLev-Numa

[7] Leviticus 18:17 - Amos 2:7, b.Avodah Zara 14b, b.Bava Batra [Tosefot] 115a, b.Chagigah 11b, b.Kereitot 3b 5a 15a, b.Nedarim 51a, b.Sanhedrin [Rashi] 51a 75b 76a, b.Sanhedrin 75a, b.Yevamot [Rashi] 2a, b.Yevamot 21a 22b, b.Yevamot 3a, Commandment #97 #98 #99, Deuteronomy 3:23, Ein Yaakov Nedarim:51a, Jastrow 894b, Leviticus 20:14, m.Keritot 3:6, m.Kiddushin 2:7, m.Shekalim 8:8, m.Yevamot 1:1, Mas.Derek Eretz Rabbah 1:6, mt.Hilchot Shegagot 4:4, y.Sanhedrin 9:1, y.Yevamot 2:4 11:1, z.Acharei Mot 78b, z.Acharei Mot 393, z.BereshitA 269 270

וְאִשָּׁה אֶל־אֲחֹתָהּ לֹא תִקָּח לִצְרֹר לְגַלּוֹת עֶרְוָתָהּ עָלֶיהָ בְּחַיֶּיהָ

18[1] And you shall not take a woman and her sister, to be a rival to her, to uncover her nakedness, with the other during her lifetime.

וְאֶל־אִשָּׁה בְּנִדַּת טֻמְאָתָהּ לֹא תִקְרַב לְגַלּוֹת עֶרְוָתָהּ

19[2] And you shall not approach a woman to uncover her nakedness, as long as she is impure by her uncleanness.

וְאֶל־אֵשֶׁת עֲמִיתְךָ לֹא־תִתֵּן שְׁכָבְתְּךָ לְזָרַע לְטָמְאָה־בָהּ

20[3] And you shall never lie carnally with your neighbor's wife, to defile yourself with her.

וּמִזַּרְעֲךָ לֹא־תִתֵּן לְהַעֲבִיר לַמֹּלֶךְ וְלֹא תְחַלֵּל אֶת־שֵׁם אֱלֹהֶיךָ אֲנִי יְהוָה

21[4] And you shall not give any of your seed to *set them apart to Molech*[5], nor shall you profane the name of your God: I am the LORD.

וְאֶת־זָכָר לֹא תִשְׁכַּב מִשְׁכְּבֵי אִשָּׁה תּוֹעֵבָה הִוא

22[6] You shall not lie with *a male, as with a woman*[7]; it is an abomination.

---

[1] Leviticus 18:18 - 1 Samuel 1:6-1:8, b.Horayot 8a, b.Kiddushin 10b, b.Sanhedrin [Tosefot] 54b, b.Yevamot [Rashi] 41a, b.Yevamot 3b 8ab 9a 13a 19a 28b 50a 97a, b.Yoma [Rashi] 9b, Commandment #100, Exodus 2:3, Genesis 4:19 5:28 6:15, Jastrow 1115a, Jubilees 28:6, m.Shekalim 8:8, m.Yevamot 1:1 2:6 2:7 3:10 13:6 14:4 14:5 14:6, Malachi 2:15, Mas.Derek Eretz Rabbah 1:1, Mekilta de R'Ishmael Beshallah 4:74, mt.Hilchot Issurei Biah 2:9 2:11, t.Yevamot 5:3, y.Horayot 2:4, y.Sanhedrin 9:1, y.Yevamot 1:1 11:1, z.Terumah 126b, z.Trumah 4

[2] Leviticus 18:19 - Avot de R'Natan 2, b.Horayot [Rashi] 8b, b.Kereitot [Rashi] 2a 9a 15a, b.Kereitot 2b, b.Ketubot 56b, b.Makkot 14a, b.Shabbat 13b, b.Sheviit [Tosefot] 18a, b.Sheviit 18b, b.Yevamot 55a, Commandment #101, Ezekiel 18:6 22:10, Guide for the Perplexed 3:49, Leviticus 12:2 15:19 15:24 20:18, m.Horayot 1:3, m.Keritot 7:6, m.Nidah 2:2, m.Yevamot 3:10, Mas.Derek Eretz Rabbah 1:7, Mas.Kallah Rabbati 6:1, Midrash Psalms 2:15 146:4, Midrash Tanchuma Ki Tissa 2, Midrash Tanchuma Metzora 5, Numbers.R 10:8, Pesikta Rabbati 10:3, Pseudo-Phocylides 189, Siman 153:4, Song of Songs.R 7:7, y.Horayot 2:5, y.Sanhedrin 7:7, z.Acharei Mot 79a, z.Beshalach 357, z.Chayyei Sarah 126b, z.Acharei Mot 397 400 405 406, z.Behar 48, z.Chayei Sarah 86, z.Ha'azinu 84, z.Tzav 156

[3] Leviticus 18:20 - 1 Corinthians 6:9, 2 Samuel 11:3-11:4 11:27, b.Sanhedrin [Rashi] 53b, b.Sheviit [Tosefot] 18a, b.Yevamot 55b, Commandment #102, Deuteronomy 5:18 22:22 22:25, Exodus 20:13, Galatians 5:19, Hebrews 13:4, Leviticus 20:10, m.Niddah 5:4, m.Sanhedrin 7:4 11:6, m.Yevamot 3:10 4:13 14:3 15:3, Malachi 3:5, Matthew 5:27-5:28, mt.Hilchot Avodat Kochavim vChukkoteihem 6:3, Proverbs 6:25 6:29-6:33, Romans 2:22, y.Sotah 5:1, z.Bereshit 8b, z.Chayei Sarah 86, z.Prologue 132

[4] Leviticus 18:21 - 1 Kings 11:7 11:33, 2 Kings 16:3 21:6 23:10, Acts 7:43, Amos 5:26, b.Bava Batra [Tosefot] 115a, b.Kereitot [Rashi] 2a, b.Megillah 25a, b.Sanhedrin [Rashi] 74a, b.Sanhedrin 64b, Commandment #333, Deuteronomy 12:31 18:10, Deuteronomy.R 2:33, Ezekiel 20:31 23:37 36:20-36:23, Jastrow 123a 359b, Jeremiah 7:31 19:5, Leviticus 19:12 20:2-20:5 21:6 22:2 22:32, m.Megillah 4:9, m.Sanhedrin 7:7, Malachi 1:12, Mas.Derek Eretz Rabbah 1:11, Mas.Soferim 9:8, Mekilta de R'Ishmael Bahodesh 6:48, mt.Hilchot Avodat Kochavim vChukkoteihem 6:3 6:4, Psalms 106:37-106:38, Romans 1:23 2:24, Sifre Devarim Shoftim 171, Testament of Solomon 26:1, y.Megillah 4:10, y.Sanhedrin 7:10, z.Chayei Sarah 86

[5] LXX *serve a ruler*

[6] Leviticus 18:22 - 1 Corinthians 6:9, 1 Kings 14:24, 1 Timothy 1:10, b.Kereitot [Rashi] 11a, b.Kereitot 3a, b.Nedarim [Ran] 51a, b.Sanhedrin [Rashi] 66b, b.Sanhedrin [Tosefot] 73a, b.Sanhedrin 54ab 55a 82a, b.Yevamot 55b 83b, Commandment #103, Deuteronomy 23:20, Genesis 19:5, Guide for the Perplexed 3:49, Jastrow 1570b, Jude 1:7, Judges 19:22, Leviticus 20:13, mt.Hilchot Issurei Biah 1:14 3:15, mt.Hilchot Shegagot 4:1, Pseudo-Phocylides 4, Romans 1:26-1:27, Sifre Devarim Haazinu Hashamayim 318, Sifre Devarim Nitzavim 318, y.Sanhedrin 7:7, y.Yevamot 8:6

[7] LXX *a man as with a woman*

וּבְכָל־בְּהֵמָה לֹא־תִתֵּן שְׁכָבְתְּךָ לְטָמְאָה־בָהּ וְאִשָּׁה לֹא־תַעֲמֹד לִפְנֵי בְהֵמָה לְרִבְעָהּ תֶּבֶל הוּא 23[1]

אַל־תִּטַּמְּאוּ בְּכָל־אֵלֶּה כִּי בְכָל־אֵלֶּה נִטְמְאוּ הַגּוֹיִם אֲשֶׁר־אֲנִי מְשַׁלֵּחַ מִפְּנֵיכֶם 24[2]

וַתִּטְמָא הָאָרֶץ וָאֶפְקֹד עֲוֹנָהּ עָלֶיהָ וַתָּקִא הָאָרֶץ אֶת־יֹשְׁבֶיהָ 25[3]

וּשְׁמַרְתֶּם אַתֶּם אֶת־חֻקֹּתַי וְאֶת־מִשְׁפָּטַי וְלֹא תַעֲשׂוּ מִכֹּל הַתּוֹעֵבֹת הָאֵלֶּה הָאֶזְרָח וְהַגֵּר הַגָּר בְּתוֹכְכֶם 26[5]

כִּי אֶת־כָּל־הַתּוֹעֵבֹת הָאֵל עָשׂוּ אַנְשֵׁי־הָאָרֶץ אֲשֶׁר לִפְנֵיכֶם וַתִּטְמָא הָאָרֶץ 27[6]

וְלֹא־תָקִיא הָאָרֶץ אֶתְכֶם בְּטַמַּאֲכֶם אֹתָהּ כַּאֲשֶׁר קָאָה אֶת־הַגּוֹי אֲשֶׁר לִפְנֵיכֶם 28[7]

23[1] And you shall not lie with any beast to defile yourself with it; nor shall any woman stand before a beast, to lie down with it; it is perversion.

24[2] Do not defile yourselves in any of these things; for in all these the nations are defiled, which I cast out from before you.

25[3] And the land was defiled, therefore I visited its iniquity upon it, *and the land vomited out her inhabitants*[4].

26[5] And you shall keep My statutes and My ordinances, and shall not do any of these abominations, neither the homeborn, nor the stranger who sojourns among you,

27[6] for the men of the land who were before you have done all these abominations, and the land is defiled,

28[7] *so the land does not vomit you out also, when you defile it, as it vomited out the nation that was before you*[8].

---

[1] Leviticus 18:23 - b.Nedarim 51a, b.Sanhedrin 54b, Commandment #104 #105, Deuteronomy 3:21, Ein Yaakov Nedarim:51a, Exodus 22:19, Jastrow 1573a 1644b, Leviticus 20:12 20:15-16, Mas.Derek Eretz Rabbah 1:11, Mekhilta de R'Shimon bar Yochai Nezikin 74:4, Mekilta de R'Ishmael Nezikin 17:77, mt.Hilchot Issurei Biah 1:16, Pseudo-Phocylides 188, y.Sanhedrin 7:7
[2] Leviticus 18:24 - 1 Corinthians 3:17, b.Makkot 24a, b.Sanhedrin 81a, b.Yevamot [Rashi] 11a, Deuteronomy 12:31 18:12, Ein Yaakov Makkot:24a, Ein Yaakov Sanhedrin:81a, Guide for the Perplexed 3:47, Jeremiah 20:4, Leviticus 18:3 18:6-23 18:30 20:22-23, Leviticus.R 23:8, Mark 7:10-23, Matthew 15:18-20, Midrash Psalms 15:7, mt.Hilchot Yibbum Va'Chalitzah 6:19, z.Balak 426
[3] Leviticus 18:25 - b.Arachin [Rashi] 16a, b.Shabbat 33a, Deuteronomy 9:5 18:12, Ein Yaakov Shabbat:33a, Ezekiel 36:17-18, Hosea 2:13 8:13 9:9, Isaiah 24:5 2:21, Jastrow 1323a, Jeremiah 2:7 5:9 5:29 9:10 14:10 16:18 23:2, Leviticus 18:28 20:22-23, Numbers 35:33-34, Psalms 89:33 10:38, Romans 8:22, y.Orlah 1:1, z.Noach 62a 56
[4] LXX *and the land is aggrieved with them who dwell upon it*
[5] Leviticus 18:26 - b.Bechorot 56b, Deuteronomy 4:1-2 4:40 13:1, John 14:15 14:21-23 15:14, Leviticus 17:8 17:10 18:5 18:30, Luke 8:15 11:28, Pesikta Rabbati 14:1, Psalms 105:44-45
Leviticus 18:26-28 - Jubilees 6:2
[6] Leviticus 18:27 - 1 Kings 14:24, 2 Chronicles 12:14, 2 Kings 16:3 21:2, b.Sanhedrin [Rashi] 54b 59a, b.Bava Batra 88b, b.Shabbat 33a, b.Sotah 4b, b.Temurah [Rashi] 29b, b.Yevamot 21a, Deuteronomy 20:18 23:20 1:16 3:15, Ein Yaakov Shabbat 33a, Ein Yaakov Sotah 4b, Ein Yaakov Yevamot 21a, Ezekiel 16:50 22:11, Hosea 9:10, Jastrow 1606b, Leviticus 18:24, mt.Pirkei Avot 4:4, y.Yevamot 2:4, z.Acharei Mot 289
Leviticus 18:27-30 - 11QpaleoLeva
[7] Leviticus 18:28 - b.Shabbat 33a, Ecclesiastes.R 1:9, Ein Yaakov Shabbat:33a, Ezekiel 12:13 12:17, Jeremiah 9:20, Leviticus 18:25 20:22, Revelation 3:16, Romans 8:22, Sifre Devarim Ekev 38
[8] LXX *and lest the land be aggrieved with you in your polluting it, as it was aggrieved with the nations before you*

כִּי כָּל־אֲשֶׁר יַעֲשֶׂה מִכֹּל הַתּוֹעֵבוֹת
הָאֵלֶּה וְנִכְרְתוּ הַנְּפָשׁוֹת הָעֹשֹׂת מִקֶּרֶב
עַמָּם

29[1]　For whoever shall do any of these abominations, even the souls who do them shall be cut off from among their people.

וּשְׁמַרְתֶּם אֶת־מִשְׁמַרְתִּי לְבִלְתִּי עֲשׂוֹת
מֵחֻקּוֹת הַתּוֹעֵבֹת אֲשֶׁר נַעֲשׂוּ לִפְנֵיכֶם
וְלֹא תִטַּמְּאוּ בָּהֶם אֲנִי יְהוָה אֱלֹהֵיכֶם

30[2]　And shall you keep My charge; do not do any of these abominable customs, which were done before you, and that you not defile yourselves with them: [3]I am the LORD your God.

---

[1] Leviticus 18:29 - b.Bava Batra 88b, b.Bava Kamma 32a, b.Kereitot [Rashi] 2a 3a 10b, b.Kereitot 2b, b.Kiddushin 10b 67b, b.Makkot [Rashi] 13b, b.Makkot 14a 23a, b.Megillah [Rashi] 7b, b.Sanhedrin [Rashi] 55a, b.Sanhedrin [Tosefot] 64b 74b, b.Sheviit 13a, b.Temurah 29b, b.Yevamot [Rashi] 33b, b.Yevamot 3b 8a 54b, Ein Yaakov Makkot:23a, Exodus 12:15, Jastrow 674b 956a, Leviticus 17:10 20:6, m.Makkot 3:15, m.Yevamot 4:13 11:11, mt.Hilchot Issurei Biah 1:1, Numbers.R 9:10, Sifre Devarim Ki Tetze 286, y.Avodah Zarah 3:6, y.Makkot 3:12, y.Sanhedrin 7:5 7:6 7:7 7:11, y.Shabbat 7:2 9:1, y.Yevamot 1:1
[2] Leviticus 18:30 - b.Chagigah 11b, b.Moed Katan 5a, b.Nedarim [Rashi] 10a, b.Sheviit 7b, b.Yevamot 21a, Deuteronomy 11:1 18:9-18:12, Ein Yaakov Midrash Shmuel 1:1, Ein Yaakov Yevamot:21a, Gates of Repentance 1.50 3.7, Jastrow 856b, Leviticus 18:2-18:4 18:26-18:27 20:23 22:9, Mas.Kallah Rabbati 3:21, Mekhilta de R'Shimon bar Yochai Amalek 47:1, Mekhilta de R'Shimon bar Yochai Vayassa 37:2, Mekhilta de R'Ishmael Amalek 4:26, Mekhilta de R'Ishmael Amalek 4:50, Mekhilta de R'Ishmael Vayassa 1:140, Mesillat Yesharim 11:Traits-of-Nekuyut, Midrash Psalms 4:9, mt.Hilchot Issurei Biah 21:1, mt.Introduction, mt.Pirkei Avot 1:1, y.Sheviit 1:2, z.Acharei Mot 78b
[3] 11QpaleoLeva adds *For*

Kedoshim

Kedoshim[1] – Chapter 19[2]

וַיְדַבֵּר יְהוָה אֶל־מֹשֶׁה לֵּאמֹר

1[3] And the LORD spoke to Moses, saying:

דַּבֵּר אֶל־כָּל־עֲדַת בְּנֵי־יִשְׂרָאֵל וְאָמַרְתָּ אֲלֵהֶם קְדֹשִׁים תִּהְיוּ כִּי קָדוֹשׁ אֲנִי יְהוָה אֱלֹהֵיכֶם

2[4] Speak to all the congregation of the children of Israel and say to them: You shall be holy; for I the LORD your God am holy.

אִישׁ אִמּוֹ וְאָבִיו תִּירָאוּ וְאֶת־שַׁבְּתֹתַי תִּשְׁמֹרוּ אֲנִי יְהוָה אֱלֹהֵיכֶם

3[5] Every man shall *fear*[6] his *mother, and his father*[7], and you shall keep My Sabbaths; I am the LORD your God.

---

[1] Kedoshim aliyot: [1] Leviticus 19:1–14, [2] Leviticus 19:15–22, [3] Leviticus 19:23–32, [4] Leviticus 19:33–37, [5] Leviticus 20:1–7, [6] Leviticus 20:8–22, [7] Leviticus 20:23–27
Acharei Mot and Kedoshim are combined when there are only 51 available reading days in the year.
[2] Jastrow 1314a 1322b 1355a
[3] Leviticus 19:1 - Lamentations.R 1:28, Midrash Tanchuma Kedoshim 3, mt.Hilchot Avadim 6:6, Philo De Specialibus Legibus I 224, t.Maaserot 3:12, z.Kedoshim 1
Leviticus 19:1-2 - Midrash Tanchuma Kedoshim 1
Leviticus 19:1-4 - 11QpaleoLeva
Leviticus 19:1-14 - Minchah [Shabbat Monday Thursday Torah reading - Parashah Kedoshim]
Leviticus 19:1-20:23 - Pesikta Rabbati 15:16
[4] Leviticus 19:2 - 1 Peter 1:15-1:16, 2 Corinthians 6:14-16 7:1, Amos 3:3, b.Megillah [Rashi] 7b, b.Shekalim [Taklin Chadatin] 9b, Exodus 19:6, Exodus.R 38:2 38:7, Genesis.R 90:2, Guide for the Perplexed 3:47, Isaiah 6:3-4, Jastrow 496a 1222a, Kuzari 4.3, Leviticus 11:44-45 20:7 20:26 21:8, Leviticus.R 24:1 24:6, m.Bava Metzia 7:7, Matthew 5:48, Mesillat Yesharim 13 Trait of Perishus, Midrash Psalms 10:1, Midrash Tanchuma Bereshit 1, Midrash Tanchuma Kedoshim 2-6 9, mt.Hilchot Avadim 6:6, mt.Hilchot Deot 1:5, mt.Hilchot Teshuvah 1:1, Numbers.R 9:45, Pirkei de R'Eliezer 51, Tanya Igeret Hakodesh §7, Tanya Likutei Aramim §30, y.Megillah 4:4, z.Kedoshim 80ab 1 7 13 28, z.Mikketz 204b, z.Pekudei 225b 90, z.Yitro 89a 467, z.Miketz 250, z.Tazria 38, z.Vayechi 443
[5] Leviticus 19:3 - b.Bava Kamma [Tosefot] 41b, b.Bava Metzia 32a, b.Kereitot 28a, b.Kiddushin 29a 30b, b.Shabbat 69b, b.Yevamot 5b 6a, Commandment #62, Deuteronomy 21:18-21 3:16, Ein Yaakov Keritot 6b, Ein Yaakov Kiddushin 30b-31b, Ein Yaakov Yevamot 6a, Ein Yaakov Yoma 67b, Ephesians 6:1-3, Exodus 16:29 20:8 20:12 21:15 21:17 31:13-17, Ezekiel 20:12 22:7-8, Gates of Repentance 3.21, Genesis.R 1:15, HaMadrikh 35:4, Hebrews 12:9, Isaiah 56:4-6 10:13, Jastrow 630b 748b, Leviticus 11:44 2:2, Leviticus.R 24:5 36:1, m.Keritot 6:9, Malachi 1:6, Matthew 15:4-15:6, Mekhilta de R'Shimon bar Yochai Bachodesh 55:1, Mekilta de R'Ishmael Bahodesh 8:9 8:17, Mekilta de R'Ishmael Pisha 1:30, Midrash Tanchuma Kedoshim 3, mt.Hilchot Gezelah Vaavedah 11:19, mt.Hilchot Kriat Shema 2:16, mt.Hilchot Mamrim 6:1, mt.Hilchot Talmud Torah 5:1, Numbers.R 14:6, Pesikta Rabbati 23/24:2, Philo De Specialibus Legibus II 239 56-139, Proverbs 1:8 6:20-21 23:22 6:11 6:17, Pseudo-Phocylides 19-21 6, Siman 143:1 143:11, y.Kiddushin 1:7, y.Peah 1:1, y.Sanhedrin 7:11, z.Acharei Mot 78b, z.Kedoshim 81b 82a, z.Emor 314 26 30
Leviticus 19:3-8 - 4QLev-Numa
[6] LXX *reverence*
[7] LXX *father and his mother*

אַל־תִּפְנוּ אֶל־הָאֱלִילִים וֵאלֹהֵי מַסֵּכָה
לֹא תַעֲשׂוּ לָכֶם אֲנִי יְהוָה אֱלֹהֵיכֶם

4^1 *Do not turn to the idols*[2], nor make molten gods for yourselves: I am the LORD your God.

וְכִי תִזְבְּחוּ זֶבַח שְׁלָמִים לַיהוָה
לִרְצֹנְכֶם תִּזְבָּחֻהוּ

5^3 And when you offer a sacrifice of peace offerings to the LORD, you shall offer it so you may be accepted.

בְּיוֹם זִבְחֲכֶם יֵאָכֵל וּמִמָּחֳרָת וְהַנּוֹתָר
עַד־יוֹם הַשְּׁלִישִׁי בָּאֵשׁ יִשָּׂרֵף

6^4 It shall be eaten the same day you offer it, and on the next day; and if any remains the third day, it shall be burnt with fire.

וְאִם הֵאָכֹל יֵאָכֵל בַּיּוֹם הַשְּׁלִישִׁי פִּגּוּל
הוּא לֹא יֵרָצֶה

7^5 And if any of it is eaten on the third day, *it is a vile thing; it shall not be accepted*[6].

וְאֹכְלָיו עֲוֹנוֹ יִשָּׂא כִּי־אֶת־קֹדֶשׁ יְהוָה
חִלֵּל וְנִכְרְתָה הַנֶּפֶשׁ הַהִוא מֵעַמֶּיהָ

8^7 *But everyone*[8] who eats it shall bear his iniquity, because he has profaned the holy thing of the LORD; and that soul shall be *cut off from*[9] his people.

---

[1] Leviticus 19:4 - 1 Corinthians 10:14, 1 John 5:21, Avot de R'Natan 34, b.Avodah Zara [Tosefot] 50a, b.Sanhedrin [Rashi] 63a, b.Shabbat 149a, Commandment #314, Commandment #331, Deuteronomy 3:15, Ecclesiastes.R 9:10, Ein Yaakov Shabbat:149a, Exodus 20:3-20:5 20:20 8:4 10:17, Haggai 2:18, Jastrow 1187b 1188a, Leviticus 2:1, Leviticus.R 24:5, Mekilta de R'Ishmael Bahodesh 6:67, Midrash Tanchuma Kedoshim 3, mt.Hilchot Avodat Kochavim vChukkoteihem 2:2 3:9, mt.Hilchot Sanhedrin vHainshin Hameurim Lahem 19:4, Pesikta Rabbati 21:14, Philo De Specialibus Legibus I 25, Philo Legum Allegoriae III 22, Psalms 96:5 115:4-115:7, Siman 167:5 168:4, t.Shabbat 17:1, y.Avodah Zarah 3:1, z.Acharei Mot 78b, z.Kedoshim 83b, z.Tetzaveh 182b, z.Kedoshim 65 78 93, z.Tetzaveh 56
[2] LXX *You shall not follow idols*
[3] Leviticus 19:5 - 2 Chronicles 7:2, b.Chullin [Rashi] 31b, b.Chullin 13a 29ab, b.Menachot 11a, b.Zevachim 28b 47a, Ein Yaakov Menachot:110a, Ephesians 2:13-2:14, Exodus 24:5, Ezekiel 45:15-45:17 22:2 22:12, Gates of Repentance 3.087, Leviticus 1:3 3:1-3:17 7:16 22:19 22:21 22:23 22:29
[4] Leviticus 19:6 - b.Berachot [Rashi] 9b, b.Chullin [Rashi] 90b, b.Megillah 20b, b.Menachot [Rashi] 1a, b.Menachot [Tosefot] 2a 93b, b.Pesachim [Rashbam] 120b, b.Pesachim [Rashi] 16b, b.Pesachim 3a, b.Yoma [Rashi] 27b 28a, b.Zevachim [Rashi] 36a 56b 90a 111b, b.Zevachim 28b 56b, Leviticus 7:11-7:17, m.Keritot 3:9, m.Tamid 3:2, Midrash Tanchuma Naso 28, y.Avodah Zarah 1:1
[5] Leviticus 19:7 - Avot de R'Natan 35, b.Kereitot [Rashi] 5a, b.Meilah [Rashi] 2b 10a, b.Menachot [Rashi] 11b 12a, b.Menachot 16b 25a, b.Pesachim 16b, b.Zevachim 23b 27b 28ab 29a, Isaiah 1:13 17:4 18:3, Jastrow 368b 1133b 1159a, Jeremiah 16:18, Leviticus 7:18-7:21 22:23 22:25, m.Gittin 5:4, m.Meilah 2:9, m.Menachot 2:3, m.Oholot 3:3, m.Zevachim 2:2, mt.Hilchot Pesulei haMikdashim 13:1, Pesikta Rabbati 10:3, t.Shevuot 3:1
[6] LXX *it is unfit for sacrifice: it shall not be accepted*
[7] Leviticus 19:8 - 4Q513 2 ii 1-6, b.Chullin [Tosefot] 114b 120b, b.Kereitot [Rashi] 2a, b.Kereitot 5a, b.Meilah [Rashi] 10a, b.Menachot [Rashi] 11b 12a 79a, b.Menachot [Tosefot] 50b, b.Pesachim [Rashi] 72b 82b, b.Sanhedrin [Rashi] 83a, b.Sanhedrin [Tosefot] 83a, b.Sanhedrin 83b, b.Temurah 3a, b.Zevachim [Rashi] 46a 109a 120b, b.Zevachim [Tosefot] 15b 43a, b.Zevachim 28b 44a 45ab 82a, Commandment #507, Leviticus 5:1 22:15, m.Oholot 3:3, mt.Hilchot Sanhedrin vHainshin Hameurim Lahem 19:1, Psalms of Solomon 1:8, t.Shevuot 3:1
[8] LXX *and he*
[9] LXX *destroyed from among*

וּבְקֻצְרְכֶם אֶת־קְצִיר אַרְצְכֶם לֹא 9[1] And when you reap the harvest of your
תְכַלֶּה פְּאַת שָׂדְךָ לִקְצֹר וְלֶקֶט קְצִירְךָ   land, *you shall not wholly reap the*
לֹא תְלַקֵּט   *corner of your field, nor shall you*
                                                        gather the gleaning of your harvest[2].

וְכַרְמְךָ לֹא תְעוֹלֵל וּפֶרֶט כַּרְמְךָ לֹא 10[3] And you shall not glean your vineyard,
תְלַקֵּט לֶעָנִי וְלַגֵּר תַּעֲזֹב אֹתָם אֲנִי   nor shall you gather the fallen fruit of
יְהֹוָה אֱלֹהֵיכֶם   your vineyard; you shall leave them for
                                                        the poor and for the stranger: I am the
                                                        LORD your God.

לֹא תִּגְנֹבוּ וְלֹא־תְכַחֲשׁוּ וְלֹא־תְשַׁקְּרוּ 11[4] You shall not steal; *nor shall you deal*
אִישׁ בַּעֲמִיתוֹ   *falsely, nor lie one to another*[5].

וְלֹא־תִשָּׁבְעוּ בִשְׁמִי לַשָּׁקֶר וְחִלַּלְתָּ 12[6] And you shall not swear by My name
אֶת־שֵׁם אֱלֹהֶיךָ אֲנִי יְהֹוָה   falsely, *so that you*[1] profane the [2]name
                                                        of your God: I am the LORD[3].

---

[1] Leviticus 19:9 - Avot de R'Natan 38, b.Bava Batra [Rashbam] 150a, b.Bava Batra 16a, b.Bava Kamma [Rashi] 94a, b.Bechorot [Tosefot] 2a, b.Chagigah [Tosefot] 6b, b.Chullin [Rashi] 141a, b.Chullin 131b 135b 137a 138a 141b, b.Makkot 16b, b.Nedarim 6b, b.Niddah [Rashi] 50a, b.Rosh Hashanah [Tosefot] 4b, b.Shabbat [Rashi] 68a, b.Shabbat 23ab, b.Yoma [Rashi] 36b, Commandment #41 #42 #43 #44, Deuteronomy 24:19-24:22, Ein Yaakov Shabbat:113b, Ein Yaakov Shabbat:23a, Jastrow 632a 718a 1357b 1331a, Leviticus 23:10 23:22 23:29, m.Peah 1:1 4:6, m.Pesachim 4:8, Mas.Gerim 1:3, Midrash Proverbs 30, mt.Hilchot Mamrim 4:2 4:2, mt.Hilchot Sanhedrin vHainshin Hameurim Lahem 18:2 19:4, mt.Pirkei Avot 5:8, mt.Shemonah Perakim 4:6, Numbers.R 10:1, Pesikta de R'Kahana 5.5, Pesikta Rabbati 11:1 15:5 30:3 31:7, Philo De Somniis II 23, Ruth 2:2 2:15, Sifre Devarim Ekev 41, Sifre Devarim Shoftim 152, Song of Songs.R 4:1 6:5, t.Peah 1:1 1:6 2:14, y.Peah 1:2 1:4 2:1 2:5 3:3 3:6 4:3 4:7 5:5, z.Ki Tetze 46 Leviticus 19:9-10 - 4Q284a, Midrash Tanchuma Vayetze 2, Pesikta Rabbati 23/24:2, z.Ki Tetze 46, z.Mishpatim 388

[2] LXX *you shall not complete the reaping of your field with exactness, and you shalt not gather that which falls from your reaping*

[3] Leviticus 19:10 - b.Bava Kamma [Rashi] 28a, b.Bava Kamma 94a, b.Bava Metzia [Tosefot] 12a, b.Berachot [Rashi] 35a, b.Chullin [Rashi] 141a, b.Chullin 131ab 134b, b.Kiddushin [Rashi] 54b, b.Makkot 16b, b.Nedarim [Ran] 44b 83b, b.Niddah [Rashi] 51b, b.Rosh Hashanah [Tosefot] 4b, b.Temurah 6a, b.Zevachim 28b 44a, Commandment #45 #46 #47 #48, Esther.R 3:3, Isaiah 17:6 24:13, Jastrow 604a 682a 942a 1052a 1061b 1224b, Jeremiah 1:9, Judges 8:2, Leviticus 1:6, m.Peah 1:1 4:6 6:5 7:3 7:7, m.Pesachim 4:8, Micah 7:1, mt.Hilchot Matnot Aniyim 1:4 4:21 5:16, mt.Hilchot Nedarim 7:10, mt.Pirkei Avot 5:8, mt.Shemonah Perakim 4:6, Obadiah 1:5, Pesikta de R'Kahana 17.6, Pesikta Rabbati 31:7, Sifre Devarim Reeh 110, y.Peah 4:1 4:7 6:1 6:4 7:6-7 8:1, z.Acharei Mot 78b

[4] Leviticus 19:11 - 1 Corinthians 6:8-6:10, 1 Kings 13:18, 1 Timothy 1:10, 2 Enoch 42:12, Acts 5:3-4, b.Bava Kamma 105b, b.Bava Metzia 61b, b.Sanhedrin 86a, b.Sheviit 26a, Colossians 3:9, Commandment #271 #272 #274, Deuteronomy 5:19, Ein Yaakov Bava Metzia:61b, Ephesians 4:25 4:28, Exodus 20:13 20:14 22:1 22:7 22:10-12, Gates of Repentance 3.85 3.178, Jeremiah 6:13 7:9-11 9:4-6, Lamentations.R 1:34, Leviticus 6:2-3, Leviticus.R 24:5, Mekilta de R'Ishmael Bahodesh 8:55, Mekilta de R'Ishmael Nezikin 5:76, Mesillat Yesharim 11 Traits-of-Nekuyut, Midrash Tanchuma Kedoshim 3, mt.Hilchot Geneivah 1:1, mt.Hilchot Shevuot 1:8, Pesikta Rabbati 21:18, Philo De Specialibus Legibus IV 39, Psalms 5:7 20:11, Revelation 21:8, Romans 3:4, Saadia Opinions 3:1, y.Sanhedrin 8:3 11:2, Zechariah 5:3-4 8:16-17

[5] LXX *you shall not lie, neither shall one bear false witness as an informer against his neighbor*

[6] Leviticus 19:12 - b.Bava Kamma [Rashi] 105b, b.Shabbat 33a, b.Sheviit [Rashi] 3b 35b, b.Sheviit 20b 21a 28b 39a, Commandment #205, Deuteronomy 5:11, Exodus 20:7, Ezekiel 36:20-36:23, Gates of Repentance 3.045, James 5:12, Jeremiah 4:2 7:9, Leviticus 6:3 18:21 24:11 24:15-24:16, Leviticus.R 24:5, Malachi 3:5, Matthew 5:33-5:34, Mekilta de R'Ishmael Bahodesh 7:8, Midrash Tanchuma Kedoshim 3, mt.Hilchot Sanhedrin vHainshin Hameurim Lahem 19:4, mt.Hilchot Shevuot 1:3 12:1, Pesikta Rabbati 21:18 22:4 22:5 22:6, Psalms 15:4, Pseudo-Phocylides 16-17, y.Nedarim 3:4, y.Sheviit 3:8, z.Acharei Mot 78b, Zechariah 5:4

לֹא־תַעֲשֹׁק אֶת־רֵעֲךָ וְלֹא תִגְזֹל לֹא־   13[4]   You shall not *oppress*[5] your neighbor,
תָלִין פְּעֻלַּת שָׂכִיר אִתְּךָ עַד־בֹּקֶר   nor rob him; the wages of a hired
                                                servant shall not be with you *all night*[6]
                                                until the morning.

לֹא־תְקַלֵּל חֵרֵשׁ וְלִפְנֵי עִוֵּר לֹא תִתֵּן   14[7]   You shall not *curse*[8] the deaf, nor put a
מִכְשֹׁל וְיָרֵאתָ מֵּאֱלֹהֶיךָ אֲנִי יְהוָה   stumbling block *before*[9] the blind, but
                                                you shall fear[10] your God: I am the
                                                LORD[11].

---

[1] LXX *and you shall not*

[2] LXX adds *holy*

[3] LXX adds *your God*

[4] Leviticus 19:13 - 1 Thessalonians 4:6, b.Bava Kamma 99a, b.Bava Metzia [Rashi] 5b 61b 118a, b.Bava Metzia 26b 61b 11b 111ab 112a 113a, b.Chullin 81a 141a, b.Makkot 16a, b.Sanhedrin [Rashi] 57a 86a, b.Sheviit [Rashi] 47a, b.Sheviit 45b, b.Temurah 6a, b.Zevachim [Tosefot] 114b, Commandment #184 #280 #281, Deuteronomy 24:14-15, Exodus 22:8-9 22:13 22:15 22:21 22:24-27, Ezekiel 22:29, Gates of Repentance 3.24 3.68, James 5:4, Jastrow 699b 945b 1059b 1202a 1310b, Jeremiah 22:3 22:13, Job 7:39, Josephus Antiquities 4.8.19-20 4.8.31 4.8.38, Leviticus 6:3, Luke 3:13, m.Bava Metzia 9:11, Malachi 3:5, Mark 10:19, Mas.Gerim 3:2, Mesillat Yesharim 11:Traits-of-Nekuyut, Midrash Tanchuma Kedoshim 3, mt.Hilchot Gezelah Vaavedah 1:1 1:4, mt.Hilchot Issurei Biah 1:10, mt.Hilchot Sechirot 11:1-2, mt.Hilchot Shevuot 6:2, Numbers.R 2:8, Philo De Virtutibus 88, Proverbs 20:10 22:22, Sifre Devarim Ki Tetze 278 279, Sifre Devarim Shoftim 188, Siman 182:2 182:4 185:2, t.Bava Metzia 10:3, Testament of Job 12:4, y.Bava Metzia 9:11, z.Kedoshim 84b 84, z.Mishpatim 349

[5] LXX *injure*

[6] Missing in LXX

[7] Leviticus 19:14 - 1 Corinthians 8:8-13 10:32, 1 Peter 1:17 2:17, b.Avodah Zara [Rashi] 15a 39b, b.Avodah Zara [Tosefot] 2a 26b, b.Avodah Zara 6ab 14a 21a 22a, b.Bava Metzia [Tosefot] 10b, b.Bava Metzia 5b 75b 90b, b.Bechorot [Tosefot] 2b 21b, b.Chagigah [Rashi] 25b, b.Chullin [Rashi] 3a 5b, b.Chullin [Tosefot] 4a, b.Chullin 7b, b.Kiddushin 32ab 33b, b.Moed Katan 5a 14a, b.Nedarim 62b, b.Niddah 57a, b.Pesachim 22b, b.Sanhedrin 66a, b.Sheviit [Rashi] 35b, b.Sheviit 36a, b.Succah [Rashi] 39a, b.Temurah 4a, Commandment #34 #35, Deuteronomy 3:18, Ein Yaakov Bava Metzia:75b, Ein Yaakov Chullin 7b, Ein Yaakov Moed Katan 17a, Gates of Repentance 3.46 3.52 3.81, Genesis 18:18, Guide for the Perplexed 3:41, Jastrow 27a 1058a 1189b 1627a, Josephus Antiquities 4.8.19-20 4.8.31 4.8.38, Leviticus 19:32 1:17, m.Bava Metzia 5:11, m.Sheviit 4:13, Mas.Kallah Rabbati 10:8, Mekhilta de R'Shimon bar Yochai Kaspa 76:3, Mekilta de R'Ishmael Nezikin 5:120, Mesillat Yesharim 2 Traits of Zehirus 11:Nekiyut-in-Giving-Advice, mt.Hilchot Chovel Umazik 5:13, mt.Hilchot Gezelah Vaavedah 5:1, mt.Hilchot Issurei Biah 22:6, mt.Hilchot Malveh VLoveh 4:2, mt.Hilchot Shabbat 13:7, mt.Hilchot Mamrim 5:4 6:9, mt.Hilchot Rotzeach Ushmirat Nefesh 12:14, mt.Hilchot Sanhedrin vHainshin Hameurim Lahem 19:4 23:2 26:1, mt.Hilchot Shemitah vYovel 8:1, mt.Hilchot Talmud Torah 5:4 6:14, Nehemiah 5:15, Philo De Specialibus Legibus IV 197, Revelation 2:14, Romans 12:14 14:13, Siman 143:18 181:6 191:6 65:1, y.Bava Metzia 5:8, z.Acharei Mot 78b, z.Beshalach 119 49b, z.Kedoshim 89 85a, z.Vayakhel 216a 412

Leviticus 19:14-16 - mt.Hilchot Teshuvah 1:1 1:1

[8] LXX *revile*

[9] LXX *in the way of*

[10] LXX adds *the LORD*

[11] LXX adds *your God*

לֹא־תַעֲשׂוּ עָוֶל בַּמִּשְׁפָּט לֹא־תִשָּׂא פְנֵי־דָל וְלֹא תֶהְדַּר פְּנֵי גָדוֹל בְּצֶדֶק תִּשְׁפֹּט עֲמִיתֶךָ

15[1] You shall *do no unrighteousness*[2] in judgment; you shall not *respect*[3] the face of the poor, nor *favor*[4] the face of the mighty; but you shall judge your neighbor *in righteousness*[5].

לֹא־תֵלֵךְ רָכִיל בְּעַמֶּיךָ לֹא תַעֲמֹד עַל־דַּם רֵעֶךָ אֲנִי יְהוָה

16[6] You shall not *go up and down as a talebearer*[7] among your people; nor shall you *stand idly by the blood*[8] of your neighbor: I am the LORD[9].

לֹא־תִשְׂנָא אֶת־אָחִיךָ בִּלְבָבֶךָ הוֹכֵחַ תּוֹכִיחַ אֶת־עֲמִיתֶךָ וְלֹא־תִשָּׂא עָלָיו חֵטְא

17[10] You shall not hate your brother in your heart; you shall rebuke, yes, rebuke your neighbor, and not bear sin because of him.

---

[1] Leviticus 19:15 - 2 Chronicles 19:6-7, b.Bava Batra [Rashbam] 94a, b.Sanhedrin 3a 32b [Rashi] 5a 27b 59a, b.Sheviit 30a, b.Kiddushin [Rashi] 33a, Deuteronomy 1:17 16:19 25:13-16 3:19, Ein Yaakov Aggadot, Ein Yaakov Shevuot 30a, Commandment #251 #252 #253 #256, Exodus 18:21 23:2-3 23:6-8, Gates of Repentance 3.218, Guide for the Perplexed 1:40, James 2:6-9, Jastrow 1088b, Leviticus 19:35, Mekhilta de R'Shimon bar Yochai Kaspa 77:3, Mekilta de R'Ishmael Kaspa 2:76, Midrash Proverbs 22, Midrash Psalms 55:1, Midrash Tanchuma Mishpatim 6, mt.Hilchot Rotzeach Ushmirat Nefesh 13:12, mt.Hilchot Sanhedrin vHainshin Hameurim Lahem 20:4 20:6 20:12 21:1, Proverbs 18:5 24:23, Psalms 82:2, Pseudo-Phocylides 9, Ruth.R 1:2, z.Kedoshim 85b 97 98, z.Balak 263

[2] LXX *not act unjustly*

[3] LXX *accept*

[4] LXX *admire*

[5] LXX *with justice*

[6] Leviticus 19:16 - 1 Kings 21:10-13, 1 Peter 2:1, 1 Timothy 3:11, 2 Timothy 3:3, Acts 6:11-13 24:4-9, b.Ketubot [Rashi] 45b, b.Ketubot 46a, b.Pesachim [Rashbam] 113b, b.Sanhedrin 29a 30a 31a 73a, Commandment #27 #29, Exodus 20:13 23:1 23:7, Ezekiel 22:9, Gates of Repentance 3.55 3.70 3.222, Jastrow 544b 1344a 1478b 1479b, Jeremiah 6:28 9:5, Leviticus.R 24:5, m.Sanhedrin 3:7, Mas.Derek Eretz Rabbah 11:13, Matthew 26:60-61 3:4, Midrash Psalms 56:1, Midrash Tanchuma Kedoshim 3, mt.Hilchot Naarah Betulah 3:1, mt.Hilchot Shabbat 2:23, mt.Hilchot Deot 7:1, mt.Hilchot Avodat Kochavim vChukkoteihem 5:4 10:1mt.Hilchot Matnot Aniyim 8:10, mt.Hilchot Rotzeach Ushmirat Nefesh 1:14 4:11, mt.Hilchot Melachim uMichamoteihem 5:1, Numbers.R 19:2, Philo De Specialibus Legibus IV 183, Proverbs 11:13 20:19, Psalms 15:3, Ruth.R 1:2, Sifre Devarim Reeh 89, Siman 30:1, Titus 2:3, y.Peah 1:1, z.Kedoshim 86a, z.Ha'azinu 160, z.Kedoshim 105

[7] LXX *walk deceitfully*

[8] LXX *rise up against the blood*

[9] LXX adds *your God*

[10] Leviticus 19:17 - 1 Corinthians 5:2, 1 John 2:9 2:11 3:12-15, 1 Timothy 5:20 5:22, 2 John 1:10-11, 2 Timothy 4:2, 4Q267 frag 91.3, 4Q270 frag 64.1, 4Q477, 5Q12 frag 1 1.2, b.Arachin 16b, b.Avodah Zara [Tosefot] 16a, Avot de R'Natan 26, b.Bava Metzia 31a, b.Berachot [Tosefot] 31b, b.Nedarim 65b, b.Pesachim 113b, b.Sanhedrin [Rashi] 75a, b.Sotah 3a, b.Yevamot [Rashi] 65b, Cairo Damascus 9.7-8, Commandment #30 #33 #36, Ecclesiastes.R 1:36, Ein Yaakov Arachin:16b, Ein Yaakov Metzia:31a, Ephesians 5:11, Galatians 2:11-14 6:1, Gates of Repentance 1.50 3.39 3.59 3.72 3.187 3.196 3.220 3.222, Genesis 3:41, Jastrow 1652a, Leviticus.R 20:11, Luke 17:3, m.Nedarim 9:4, Matthew 18:15-17, Mekilta de R'Ishmael Beshallah 1:146, Mesillat Yesharim 11 Nekiyut-from-Hatred-and-Revenge 11:Nekiyut-in-Hurtful-Speech 20 Weighing Implementation of Chassidus, Midrash Tanchuma Mishpatim 7, mt.Hilchot Deot 6:5-8, mt.Hilchot Rotzeach Ushmirat Nefesh 13:14, mt.Hilchot Teshuvah 4:2 7:8, mt.Shemonah Perakim 4:6, Numbers.R 9:12, Proverbs 9:8 26:24-26 27:5-6, Psalms 21:5, Romans 1:32, Sifre Devarim Ki Tetze 235, Sifre Devarim Shoftim 186-187, Siman 143:11 189:5 29:13 29:15 29:17, t.Sotah 5:11, Tanya Kuntress Acharon §9, Tanya Igeret Hakodesh §25, Tanya Likutei Aramim §32, Titus 1:13 2:15, y.Nedarim 9:4, z.Kedoshim 100 105

לֹא־תִקֹּם וְלֹא־תִטֹּר אֶת־בְּנֵי עַמֶּךָ
וְאָהַבְתָּ לְרֵעֲךָ כָּמוֹךָ אֲנִי יְהוָה

18[1] *You shall not take vengeance*[2], nor *bear a grudge against*[3] the children of your people, but you shall love your neighbor as yourself: I am the LORD.

אֶת־חֻקֹּתַי תִּשְׁמֹרוּ בְּהֶמְתְּךָ לֹא־
תַרְבִּיעַ כִּלְאַיִם שָׂדְךָ לֹא־תִזְרַע
כִּלְאָיִם וּבֶגֶד כִּלְאַיִם שַׁעַטְנֵז לֹא יַעֲלֶה
עָלֶיךָ

19[4] You shall keep My statutes. you shall not let your cattle mate with *a diverse*[5] kind; *you shall not sow your field with two kinds of seed*[6]; nor shall there come on you a *garment of two kinds of stuff mingled together*[7].

---

[1] Leviticus 19:18 - 1 Peter 2:1, 2 Samuel 13:22 13:28, 4Q266 frag 8 2.10, 4Q270 frag 6 3.17, Avot de R'Natan 16 39, b.Bava Kamma 51a, b.Ketubot 37b, b.Kiddushin 41a, b.Nedarim 65b, b.Niddah 14a, b.Pesachim 75a 112b, b.Sanhedrin 45a 52ab 84b, b.Sotah 8b, b.Yoma 23a, Cairo Damascus 9.2, Colossians 3:8, Commandment #26 #31 #32, Deuteronomy 8:25, Ecclesiastes.R 8:8, Ein Yaakov Yoma 23a, Ephesians 4:31, Exodus 23:4-5, Galatians 5:14 5:20, Gates of Repentance 3.38, Genesis.R 24:7 55:3, Hebrews 10:30, James 2:8, Jastrow 644a 901b 1351b, Leviticus.R 24:5, Luke 10:27-37, Mark 12:31-34, m.Keritot 1:1, m.Nedarim 9:4, Mas.Kallah Rabbati 4:9 6:1, Matthew 5:43-44 19:16 19:19 22:39-40, Mekhilta de R'Shimon bar Yochai Nezikin 61:2 62:1, Mekhilta de R'Ishmael Beshallah 1:148, Mesillat Yesharim 11 Nekiyut-from-Hatred-and-Revenge 19 Gemillut-Chassidim, mt.Hilchot Deot 1:1 6:3 6:7 7:7-8, mt.Hilchot Evel 14:1, mt.Hilchot Kriat Shema 4:6, mt.Hilchot Matnot Aniyim 8:10, mt.Hilchot Teshuvah 2:10 2:10, mt.Perek Chelek Intro:11, mt.Shemonah Perakim 4:6, Proverbs 20:22, Psalms 7:9, Romans 12:17 12:19 13:4 13:9, Shemonah Perachim 4, Sifra Qedoshim 4, Sifre Devarim Ki Tetze 235, Sifre Devarim Reeh 89, Sifre Devarim Shoftim 186-187, Siman 12:2 207:1 29:12-13 30:7 30:9, t.Sanhedrin 9:11, t.Sotah 5:11, Tanya Likutei Aramim §32, Two Letters Part II, y.Nedarim 9:4, y.Sanhedrin 6:4, y.Sotah 1:5, z.Acharei Mot 78b, z.Kedoshim 105, z.Miketz 133 190

[2] LXX *And your hand shall not avenge you*

[3] LXX *shall you be angry with*

[4] Leviticus 19:19 - 1 Kings 1:33, 2 Corinthians 6:14-17, 2 Samuel 13:29 18:9, 4Q418 frag 103 2.7, 4QMMT B 76-82, Avot de R'Natan 26, b.Avodah Zara 63b 64a 65b, b.Bava Batra [Rashbam] 156b, b.Bava Batra 36a, b.Bava Kamma [Rashi] 55a, b.Bava Kamma 54b, b.Bava Metzia 91ab, b.Beitzah 14b, b.Chullin [Rashi] 79a, b.Chullin [Tosefot] 60a 82b, b.Chullin 115a, b.Horayot [Rashi] 11a, b.Kiddushin 39a, b.Makkot 21ab 22a, b.Moed Katan 2b, b.Sanhedrin 60a, b.Tamid 27b, b.Yevamot 4b, b.Yoma 69a, Commandment #358 [Talmud applies this to birds] #359, Deuteronomy 22:9-11, Ezra 3:6, Galatians 3:9-11, Gates of Repentance 3.091, Genesis 12:24, Genesis.R 7:4, Guide for the Perplexed 3:49, Jastrow 131b 360a 438b 638b 1247a, Josephus Antiquities 4.8.11 4.8.19-20 4.8.31 4.8.38, m.Bava Kamma 5:7, m.Beitzah 1:10, m.Makkot 3:9, Mas.Derek Eretz Rabbah 1:11, Matthew 9:16-17, Midrash Psalms 1:15, Midrash Tanchuma Chukkat 7, Midrash Tanchuma Vayakhel 1, mt.Hilchot Deot 1:5, mt.Hilchot Kilayim 1:1 3:16 5:1 9:1 10:12, mt.Hilchot Melachim uMichamoteihem 10:6, mt.Hilchot Sanhedrin vHainshin Hameurim Lahem 15:1 19:4, mt.Hilchot Shegagot 9:1, mt.Hilchot Shevitat Yom Tov 7:11, mt.Hilchot Toen vNitan 12:12, Numbers.R 10:1 19:5, Pesikta de R'Kahana 4.6, Pesikta Rabbati 14:1 25:2, Pirkei de R'Eliezer 21, Romans 11:6, Sifre Devarim Ki Tetze 230 232, Sifre Devarim Reeh 59, Siman 174:1 175:1-6 176:1-8, Song of Songs.R 7:13, y.Bava Kamma 5:8, y.Kilayim 1:1 1:7 8:1-2 9:1, y.Orlah 3:7, y.Peah 3:6, z.Kedoshim 86a, z.Shemot 15b, z.Vaera 30b 168, z.Balak 470, z.Kedoshim 105 110 111, z.Shemot 266

[5] LXX *with one of a different*

[6] LXX *and you shalt not sow your vineyard with diverse seed*

[7] LXX *mingled garment woven of two [materials]*

וְאִישׁ כִּי־יִשְׁכַּב אֶת־אִשָּׁה שִׁכְבַת־זֶרַע
וְהִוא שִׁפְחָה נֶחֱרֶפֶת לְאִישׁ וְהָפְדֵּה לֹא
נִפְדָּתָה אוֹ חֻפְשָׁה לֹא נִתַּן־לָהּ בִּקֹּרֶת
תִּהְיֶה לֹא יוּמְתוּ כִּי־לֹא חֻפָּשָׁה

20[1] And whoever lies carnally with a woman, who is a bondmaid, destined for a man, and not at all redeemed, *nor was freedom given her; there shall be inquisition; they shall not be put to death, because she was not free*[2].

וְהֵבִיא אֶת־אֲשָׁמוֹ לַיהוָה אֶל־פֶּתַח
אֹהֶל מוֹעֵד אֵיל אָשָׁם

21[3] And he shall bring his forfeit to the LORD, to the door of the tent of meeting, even a ram for a guilt offering.

וְכִפֶּר עָלָיו הַכֹּהֵן בְּאֵיל הָאָשָׁם לִפְנֵי
יְהוָה עַל־חַטָּאתוֹ אֲשֶׁר חָטָא וְנִסְלַח
לוֹ מֵחַטָּאתוֹ אֲשֶׁר חָטָא

22[4] And the priest shall make atonement for him with the ram of the guilt offering before the LORD for his sin which he has sinned; and he shall be forgiven for his sin which he has sinned.

וְכִי־תָבֹאוּ אֶל־הָאָרֶץ וּנְטַעְתֶּם כָּל־עֵץ

23[5] And when you shall come into the land[6], and have planted *all manner of*

---

[1] Leviticus 19:20 - b.Avodah Zara [Tosefot] 13b, b.Bava Kamma [Rashi] 15a 88a, b.Chagigah 4a, b.Gittin [Rashi] 9a 39a, b.Gittin 39b 41b 43b, b.Kereitot [Rashi] 7b, b.Kereitot 9a 11ab, b.Kiddushin 6a, b.Makkot [Riven] 22b, b.Menachot [Tosefot] 14b, b.Sanhedrin [Rashi] 73b, b.Sanhedrin [Tosefot] 66b, b.Sanhedrin 69a, b.Shabbat [Rashi] 72a, b.Sheviit [Rashi] 13a, b.Sheviit [Tosefot] 37a, b.Yevamot 55ab, b.Zevachim [Tosefot] 48a 103a, Deuteronomy 22:23-24, Exodus 21:20-21, Genesis.R 81:1, Guide for the Perplexed 1:39, Jastrow 165a 493a 500a 505a 1116b, m.Chullin 2:10, m.Eduyot 8:6, m.Horayot 2:7, m.Keritot 2:2, m.Nazir 7:4, m.Zevachim 5:5, Mekhilta de R'Shimon bar Yochai Nezikin 66:1, mt.Hilchot Avadim 7:3 7:6, mt.Hilchot Ishut 3:6, mt.Hilchot Issurei Biah 3:13 3:15, mt.Hilchot Sanhedrin vHainshin Hameurim Lahem 16:11, mt.Hilchot Shegagot 9:1, mt.Hilchot Teshuvah 1:1, Numbers.R 10:1, Song of Songs.R 5:22, t.Gittin 2:7, y.Kiddushin 1:1, y.Sotah 1:2 2:2, y.Yevamot 6:1

[2] LXX *and her freedom has not been given to her, they shall be visited with punishment; but they shall not die, because she was not set at liberty*

[3] Leviticus 19:21 - b.Kereitot [Rashi] 9a, b.Kereitot 11a 22b, b.Sheviit [Rashi] 13a, b.Temurah [Rashi] 19b, Jastrow 129a, Leviticus 5:1-5:6 5:15 6:6-6:7, m.Chullin 2:10, m.Horayot 2:7, m.Keritot 2:2, mt.Hilchot Issurei Biah 3:14, mt.Hilchot Shegagot 9:1, mt.Hilchot Teshuvah 1:1

[4] Leviticus 19:22 - b.Kereitot 9a 22b, b.Sheviit [Rashi] 13a, b.Zevachim [Rashi] 90a, b.Zevachim 48a, Leviticus 4:20 4:26, m.Chullin 2:10, m.Horayot 2:7, m.Keritot 2:2, mt.Pirkei Avot 4:5, t.Peah 3:15

[5] Leviticus 19:23 - Acts 7:51, b.Bava Batra 36a, b.Bava Kamma 101a, b.Beitzah 25b, b.Berachot 36b, b.Gittin [Rashi] 53b, b.Kiddushin 56b, b.Pesachim 22b, b.Rosh Hashanah 9b 81b, b.Shabbat [Rashi] 18a, b.Succah 34b 35a, Commandment #360, Exodus 6:12 6:30 22:29-30, Gates of Repentance 3.83, Genesis.R 21:7 46:4, Guide for the Perplexed 3:26, Jastrow 1098b 1119b 1120a, Jeremiah 6:10 9:26-27, Jubilees 7:36, Leviticus 12:3 14:34 22:27, Leviticus.R 25:1 25:6 25:8, m.Bava Metzia 4:8, m.Orlah 1:1 1:7, m.Peah 7:6, m.Sanhedrin 1:3, m.Temurah 7:5, Mas.Kutim 1:13, Mas.Semachot 7:25, Midrash Psalms 119:1, Midrash Tanchuma Balak 12, Midrash Tanchuma Kedoshim 7 8 10-14, Midrash Tanchuma Shelach 15, mt.Hilchot Maachalot Assurot 10:9, mt.Hilchot Maaser Sheni vneta Revai 10:1-2 10:9, mt.Hilchot Sanhedrin vHainshin Hameurim Lahem 19:4, mt.Hilchot Teshuvah 1:1, mt.Hilchot Tumat Ochalin 1:25, mt.Hilchot Yesodei haTorah 5:8, mt.Hilcnot Shofar Sukkah vLulav 8:2, Numbers.R 10:1 17:5 20:19, Philo De Plantatione 95 109 113, Pirkei de R'Eliezer 29, Sifre Devarim Ekev 44, Song of Songs.R 5:22 6:5 7:13, t.Demai 5:2, t.Orlah 1:1, t.Shabbat 15:8, y.Kiddushin 1:7, y.Maasrot 4:4, y.Orlah 1:1-2 3:1, y.Rosh Hashanah 1:2, y.Sheviit 2:4, z.Kedoshim 124 87a, z.Balak 39, z.Pekudei 470, z.Vayera 395
Leviticus 19:23-24 - 4QMMT B 62-64, Siman 1731:4, Song of Songs.R 1:63
Leviticus 19:23-25 - 4Q251 6 7-9, Sifre Devarim Reeh 59
Leviticus 19:23-25 - Josephus Antiquities 4.8.19-20 4.8.31 4.8.38

[6] LLX adds *that the LORD your God gives you*

מֵאֲכָל וַעֲרַלְתֶּם עָרְלָתוֹ אֶת־פִּרְיוֹ שָׁלֹשׁ שָׁנִים יִהְיֶה לָכֶם עֲרֵלִים לֹא יֵאָכֵל

trees for food[1], then you shall count its fruit forbidden; it shall be forbidden for three years[2]; it shall not be eaten.

וּבַשָּׁנָה הָרְבִיעִת יִהְיֶה כָּל־פִּרְיוֹ קֹדֶשׁ הִלּוּלִים לַיהוָה

24[3] And in the fourth year all its fruit shall be holy, for giving praise to the LORD.

וּבַשָּׁנָה הַחֲמִישִׁת תֹּאכְלוּ אֶת־פִּרְיוֹ לְהוֹסִיף לָכֶם תְּבוּאָתוֹ אֲנִי יְהוָה אֱלֹהֵיכֶם

25[4] But in the fifth year you may eat of its fruit, *that it may yield to you more richly its increase[5]*: I am the LORD your God.

לֹא תֹאכְלוּ עַל־הַדָּם לֹא תְנַחֲשׁוּ וְלֹא תְעוֹנֵנוּ

26[6] *You shall not eat with the blood; nor shall you practice divination nor soothsaying[7].*

לֹא תַקִּפוּ פְּאַת רֹאשְׁכֶם וְלֹא תַשְׁחִית אֵת פְּאַת זְקָנֶךָ

27[8] You shall not *round the corners of your heads[9]*, nor *shall you mar the corners of[10]* your beard.

---

[1] LXX *any fruit tree*

[2] LXX *then shall you purge away its uncleanness; its fruit shall be three years uncleansed to you*

[3] Leviticus 19:24 - b.Bava Batra 36a, b.Bava Kamma 69b, b.Bava Metzia [Rashi] 55b, b.Beitzah [Rashi] 5a, b.Berachot 35a, b.Gittin [Rashi] 53b, b.Kiddushin 54b, b.Rosh Hashanah 9b 10a, b.Sotah [Rashi] 43a, Commandment #361, Deuteronomy 12:17-18 14:28-29 18:4, Ein Yaakov Berachot:35a, Jastrow 346a 456a 901a 1137a, m.Bava Metzia 4:8, m.Peah 7:6, m.Sanhedrin 1:3, Midrash Tanchuma Kedoshim 14, mt.Hilchot Maaser Sheni vneta Revai 9:1 10:1, Numbers 18:12-13, Numbers.R 8:7 10:1, Philo De Abrahamo 13, Philo De Plantatione 135, Proverbs 3:9, t.Demai 5:2, y.Berachot 6:1, y.Maaser Sheni 5:2, y.Peah 7:5, y.Rosh Hashanah 1:2, y.Sheviit 2:4, y.Sotah 8:5, z.Kedoshim 124

[4] Leviticus 19:25 - b.Berachot 35a, b.Rosh Hashanah 10a, Ecclesiastes 11:1-2, Guide for the Perplexed 3:37, Haggai 1:4-6 1:9-11 2:18-19, Leviticus 26:3-4, m.Bava Metzia 4:8, m.Peah 7:6, m.Sanhedrin 1:3, Malachi 3:8-10, mt.Hilchot Maachalot Assurot 10:18, mt.Hilchot Maaser Sheni vneta Revai 9:2, mt.Hilchot Sanhedrin vHainshin Hameurim Lahem 19:4, Philo De Plantatione 117, Proverbs 3:9-10, y.Maaser Sheni 5:3, y.Peah 7:5

[5] LXX *its produce is an increase to you*

[6] Leviticus 19:26 - 1 Samuel 15:23, 2 Chronicles 9:6, 2 Kings 17:17 21:6, b.Bava Metzia [Tosefot] 27b, b.Berachot 10b, b.Chullin [Rashi] 33a, b.Chullin 121b, b.Moed Katan 14b, b.Sanhedrin 63a 66a, Commandment #169 #335 #336, Daniel 2:10, Deuteronomy 12:23 18:10-14, Ein Yaakov Berachot 10b, Ein Yaakov Sanhedrin:66a, Exodus 7:11 8:3, Gates of Repentance 3.86, Guide for the Perplexed 3:46, Jastrow 865b 896b, Jeremiah 10:2, Jubilees 7:31, Leviticus 3:17 7:26 17:10-14, Leviticus.R 25:8, Malachi 3:5, Mas.Semachot 2:9, mt.Hilchot Avodat Kochavim vChukkoteihem 11:4 11:9, mt.Hilchot Mamrim 7:1, mt.Hilchot Sanhedrin vHainshin Hameurim Lahem 18:3 19:4, mt.Hilchot Shechitah 1:2, mt.Hilchot Tefilah 6:4, Numbers.R 10:1, Siman 166:1 200:7 8:2, Song of Songs.R 5:22, y.Sanhedrin 7:5, y.Shabbat 6:9 7:2, z.Mishpatim 122a 518, z.Vayakhel 215b 403, z.Vayigash 207b 53, z.Kedoshim 131

[7] LXX *Do not eat on the mountains, nor shall you employ auguries, nor divine by inspection of birds*

[8] Leviticus 19:27 - b.Bava Metzia [Rashi] 10b, b.Kiddushin 35b, b.Makkot [Riven] 20a, b.Makkot 21a, b.Moed Katan [Rashi] 18a, b.Nazir [Rashi] 29a, b.Nazir 40b 41a 57b, b.Sheviit [Rashi] 2b, b.Sheviit [Tosefot] 20b, b.Sheviit 3a, b.Sotah [Rashi] 16a, b.Yevamot 5a, Commandment #345, Commandment #346, Deuteronomy 14:1, Deuteronomy.R 2:18 6:3, Ezekiel 7:18 20:20, Gates of Repentance 3.078, Isaiah 15:2, Jastrow 364b 369b 934b 1131a 1262b l646b, Jeremiah 16:6 24:37, Lamentations.R 2:17 5:5, Leviticus 21:5, m.Bikkurim 4:2, m.Kiddushin 1:7, m.Makkot 3:5, Midrash Psalms 35:2, Midrash Tanchuma Shelach 15, Midrash Tanchuma Shemini 8, mt.Hilchot Avodat Kochavim vChukkoteihem 12:1 12:7 12:1-2, mt.Hilchot Avodat Kochavim vChukkoteihem 12:2, mt.Hilchot Sanhedrin vHainshin Hameurim Lahem 19:4, Numbers.R 10:5 17:5, Song of Songs.R 6:5, t.Bikkurim 2:4, y.Peah 1:4, z.Naso Idra Raba 291

[9] LXX *make a round cutting of the hair of your head*

[10] LXX *disfigure*

וְשֶׂ֣רֶט לָנֶ֗פֶשׁ לֹ֤א תִתְּנוּ֙ בִּבְשַׂרְכֶ֔ם
וּכְתֹ֣בֶת קַֽעֲקַ֔ע לֹ֥א תִתְּנ֖וּ בָּכֶ֑ם אֲנִ֖י
יְהוָֽה׃

28[1] You shall not make any cuttings in your flesh for the dead, nor imprint any marks on you: I am the LORD[2].

אַל־תְּחַלֵּ֥ל אֶת־בִּתְּךָ֖ לְהַזְנוֹתָ֑הּ וְלֹא־
תִזְנֶ֣ה הָאָ֔רֶץ וּמָלְאָ֥ה הָאָ֖רֶץ זִמָּֽה׃

29[3] Do not profane your daughter to make her a harlot, lest the land fall into harlotry, and the land become full of lewdness.

אֶת־שַׁבְּתֹתַ֣י תִּשְׁמֹ֔רוּ וּמִקְדָּשִׁ֖י תִּירָ֑אוּ
אֲנִ֖י יְהוָֽה׃

30[4] You shall keep My sabbaths, and reverence My sanctuary: I am the LORD.

אַל־תִּפְנ֤וּ אֶל־הָֽאֹבֹת֙ וְאֶל־הַיִּדְּעֹנִ֔ים
אַל־תְּבַקְשׁ֖וּ לְטָמְאָ֣ה בָהֶ֑ם אֲנִ֖י יְהוָ֥ה
אֱלֹהֵיכֶֽם׃

31[5] *Do not turn to the ghosts, nor to familiar spirits; do not seek them out, to be defiled by them[6]: I am the LORD your God.*

מִפְּנֵ֤י שֵׂיבָה֙ תָּק֔וּם וְהָדַרְתָּ֖ פְּנֵ֣י זָקֵ֑ן

32[7] You shall rise up before the grayed

---

[1] Leviticus 19:28 - 1 Kings 18:28, b.Makkot 20b 21a, b.Sanhedrin [Tosefot] 68a, Commandment #347 #348, Deuteronomy 14:1, Jastrow 678b 680b 869b 1397b, Jeremiah 16:6 24:37, Leviticus 21:1 21:5, m.Keritot 5:1, m.Makkot 3:5 3:6, Mark 5:5, Midrash Tanchuma Shemini 8, mt.Hilchot Avodat Kochavim vChukkoteihem 12:11-12, mt.Hilchot Sanhedrin vHainshin Hameurim Lahem 19:4, Revelation 13:16-17 14:9 14:11 15:2 16:2 19:20 20:4, Siman 169:1-2, Song of Songs.R 6:4, y.Makkot 3:7, z.Acharei Mot 78b
[2] LXX adds *your God*
[3] Leviticus 19:29 - 1 Corinthians 6:15, b.Sanhedrin 76a, b.Yevamot [Tosefot] 97a, b.Yevamot 37b, b.Yoma 18b, Deuteronomy 23:19-19, Ein Yaakov Sanhedrin:76a, Gates of Repentance 3.94-95, Genesis.R 11:6, Hosea 4:12-14, Jastrow 394b 406b, Leviticus 21:7, mt.Hilchot Naarah Betulah 2:17, mt.Hilchot Issurei Biah 15:29, Pseudo-Phocylides 1, t.Kiddushin 1:4 1:4, y.Kilayim 1:1, y.Sanhedrin 9:1, y.Yevamot 11:1
[4] Leviticus 19:30 - 1 Peter 4:17, 2 Chronicles 9:7 12:14, 2 Corinthians 6:16, b.Megillah 28a, b.Sheviit [Rashi] 15b, b.Yevamot 6ab, Bahir 180, Commandment #448 [now applicable to synagogues], Ecclesiastes 5:2, Ein Yaakov Yevamot:6a, Exodus 20:8, Ezekiel 9:6, Genesis 28:16-17, Guide for the Perplexed 3:47, John 2:15-2:16, Leviticus 10:3 15:31 16:2 19:3 2:2, Mas.Sefer Torah 3:10, Mas.Soferim 3:13, Matthew 21:13, Midrash Tanchuma Vayikra 6, mt.Hilchot Beit Habechirah 1:12 7:1 7:5 7:7, Psalms 89:8, Siman 13:1, z.Acharei Mot 78b, z.Bereshit 5b 6a, z.Prologue 75 80 81 82 85, z.Vaetchanan 67
Leviticus 19:30-34 - 1QpaleoLev
[5] Leviticus 19:31 - 1 Chronicles 10:13, 1 Samuel 4:3 28:7-28:9, 2 Chronicles 9:6, 2 Kings 17:17 21:6, Acts 8:11 13:6-13:8 16:16-16:18 19:19-19:20, b.Eruvin 14b, b.Kereitot [Rashi] 2a, b.Pesachim [Rashbam] 113b, b.Sanhedrin [Rashi] 65a, Commandment #337, Commandment #338, Deuteronomy 18:10-18:14, Exodus 22:18, Galatians 5:20, Isaiah 8:19 5:4 23:13, Leviticus 19:26 20:6-20:7 20:27, m.Sanhedrin 7:7, mt.Hilchot Avodat Kochavim vChukkoteihem 6:2 6:2, Revelation 21:8, Sibylline Oracles 3.218, y.Sanhedrin 7:10, z.Acharei Mot 78b
[6] LXX *You shall not attend to those who have in them divining spirits, nor attach yourselves to enchanters, to pollute yourselves with them*
[7] Leviticus 19:32 - 1 Kings 2:19, 1 Peter 2:17, 1 Timothy 5:1, b.Avodah Zara [Tosefot] 20a, b.Bava Kamma [Tosefot] 41b, b.Bava Metzia [Tosefot] 61a, b.Chagigah [Rashi] 5a, b.Chullin [Tosefot] 114b, b.Kiddushin [Rashi] 33b, b.Kiddushin 32b, b.Megillah 14b, b.Menachot [Tosefot] 19a, b.Sheviit 30b, Commandment #11, Ecclesiastes.R 7:33, Ein Yaakov Kiddushin:32b 33b, Ein Yaakov Megillah:17b, Gates of Repentance 3.012, Guide for the Perplexed 3:36, Isaiah 3:5, Jastrow 343b 409b 748b 1088a 1362a, Job 8:4 8:6, Lamentations 5:12, Lamentations.R 1:33, Leviticus 19:14, Leviticus.R 30:10-11 35:3, Mas.Kallah Rabbati 8:6, Mesillat Yesharim 19:Honoring-Torah, Midrash Psalms 119:43, Midrash Tanchuma Behaalotcha 11, Midrash Tanchuma Mishpatim 12, mt.Hilchot Talmud Torah 6:1 6:9, mt.Shemonah Perakim 4:6, Numbers.R 8:2 15:17, Pesikta de R'Kahana 27.9, Pesikta Rabbati 51:2, Philo De Sacrificiis Abelis et Cain 77, Philo De Specialibus Legibus II 238, Proverbs 16:31 20:29, Pseudo-Phocylides 220, Romans 13:7, Shemonah Perachim IV, Siman 144:2, Syriac Menander 13, t.Megillah 3:24, y.Bikkurim 3:3, y.Rosh Hashanah 1:3, z.Acharei Mot 78b, z.Kedoshim 87b, z.Kedoshim 131, z.Pinchas 266

וְיָרֵאתָ מֵּאֱלֹהֶיךָ אֲנִי יְהוָה

head, and honor the face of the old man, and you shall fear your God: I am the LORD[1].

וְכִי־יָגוּר אִתְּךָ גֵּר בְּאַרְצְכֶם לֹא תוֹנוּ אֹתוֹ

33[2] And if a stranger sojourn with you in your land, you shall not do him wrong.

כְּאֶזְרָח מִכֶּם יִהְיֶה לָכֶם הַגֵּר הַגָּר אִתְּכֶם וְאָהַבְתָּ לוֹ כָּמוֹךָ כִּי־גֵרִים הֱיִיתֶם בְּאֶרֶץ מִצְרָיִם אֲנִי יְהוָה אֱלֹהֵיכֶם

34[3] The stranger who sojourns with you shall be to you as the homeborn among you, and you shall love him as yourself; for you were strangers in the land of Egypt: I am the LORD your God.

לֹא־תַעֲשׂוּ עָוֶל בַּמִּשְׁפָּט בַּמִּדָּה בַּמִּשְׁקָל וּבַמְּשׂוּרָה

35[4] You shall do no unrighteousness in judgment, in *measure, in weight, or in capacity*[5].

מֹאזְנֵי צֶדֶק אַבְנֵי־צֶדֶק אֵיפַת צֶדֶק וְהִין צֶדֶק יִהְיֶה לָכֶם אֲנִי יְהוָה אֱלֹהֵיכֶם אֲשֶׁר־הוֹצֵאתִי אֶתְכֶם מֵאֶרֶץ מִצְרָיִם

36[6] Equitable *balances, just weights*[7], *a just ephah, and a just hin*[8], shall you have: I am the LORD your God, who brought you out of the land of Egypt.

וּשְׁמַרְתֶּם אֶת־כָּל־חֻקֹּתַי וְאֶת־כָּל־מִשְׁפָּטַי וַעֲשִׂיתֶם אֹתָם אֲנִי יְהוָה

37[9] And you shall observe all My statutes, and all My ordinances, and do them: I am the LORD.[10]

---

[1] LXX adds *your God*

[2] Leviticus 19:33 - b.Bava Metzia 59b, b.Yevamot 46b 47a, Deuteronomy 10:18-19 24:14, Ein Yaakov Bava Metzia:59b, Ein Yaakov Megillah:17b, Exodus 22:21 23:9, Ezekiel 22:7 22:29, Jeremiah 7:6, Malachi 3:5, Mas.Gerim 3:2, Numbers.R 8:2, Pseudo-Phocylides 39, y.Bikkurim 3:3

[3] Leviticus 19:34 - Deuteronomy 10:19, Exodus 12:48-12:49, Leviticus 19:18, Matthew 5:43, mt.Hilchot Avadim 6:6, Pesikta de R'Kahana 12.17, Pseudo-Phocylides 40, z.Acharei Mot 78b
Leviticus 19:34-37 - 4QLeva

[4] Leviticus 19:35 - Amos 8:5-6, b.Bava Batra [Rashi] 89a, b.Bava Batra 89b, b.Bava Metzia 61b, Commandment #181, Deuteronomy 1:13 1:15, Ein Yaakov Bava Metzia:61b, Ezekiel 22:12-13, Gates of Repentance 3.87, Jastrow 396b 526b 734a 850b 858a 1826a 1502b, Leviticus 19:15, Matthew 7:2, Micah 6:1, mt.Hilchot Geneivah 7:1 8:7, Philo Quis Rerum Divinarum Heres 162, Proverbs 11:1 16:11 20:10, Pseudo-Phocylides 12, Ruth.R 1:2, Siman 62:7, z.BereshitA 387, z.Prologue 148, z.Safra Det'zniuta 70

[5] LXX *measures and weights and scales*

[6] Leviticus 19:36 - b.Avodah Zara [Rashi] 58a, b.Bava Metzia 49a 61b, b.Berachot [Rashi] 12b, b.Sanhedrin 39a, Commandment #182, Deuteronomy 25:13-15, Ein Yaakov Bava Metzia:49a, Ein Yaakov Sanhedrin:39a, Exodus 20:2, Gates of Repentance 3.087, Jastrow 348a 748b, Mesillat Yesharim 11:Nekiyut-in-Oaths, mt.Hilchot Geneivah 7:12 8:1, Numbers.R 15:17, Philo De Specialibus Legibus IV 193, Proverbs 11:1 20:10, Saadia Opinions 10:15, Siman 62:17, t.Bava Batra 5:7, y.Bava Batra 5:5, y.Gittin 6:1, z.Acharei Mot 78b, z.Acharei Mot 312, z.BereshitA 387, z.Pekudei 617 683, z.Trumah 918

[7] 4QLeve *weights*

[8] LXX *There shall be among you just balances and just weights and just liquid measure*

[9] Leviticus 19:37 - 1 John 3:22-23, b.Chullin [Tosefot] 61a, Deuteronomy 4:1-2 4:5-6 5:1 6:1-2 8:1, Leviticus 18:4-5, mt.Hichot Meilah 8:8, Psalms 23:4 23:34, z.Acharei Mot 78b

[10] LXX adds *your God*

Kedoshim – Chapter 20[1]

וַיְדַבֵּר יְהוָה אֶל־מֹשֶׁה לֵּאמֹר	1[2] And the LORD spoke to Moses, saying:
וְאֶל־בְּנֵי יִשְׂרָאֵל תֹּאמַר אִישׁ אִישׁ מִבְּנֵי יִשְׂרָאֵל וּמִן־הַגֵּר׀ הַגֵּר בְּיִשְׂרָאֵל אֲשֶׁר יִתֵּן מִזַּרְעוֹ לַמֹּלֶךְ מוֹת יוּמָת עַם הָאָרֶץ יִרְגְּמֻהוּ בָאָבֶן	2[3] *And*[4], you shall say to the children of Israel: Whoever of the *children*[5] of Israel, or of the strangers who sojourn in Israel, who gives of his offspring to Molech; he shall be put to death, yes death; the people of the land shall stone him with stones.
וַאֲנִי אֶתֵּן אֶת־פָּנַי בָּאִישׁ הַהוּא וְהִכְרַתִּי אֹתוֹ מִקֶּרֶב עַמּוֹ כִּי מִזַּרְעוֹ נָתַן לַמֹּלֶךְ לְמַעַן טַמֵּא אֶת־מִקְדָּשִׁי וּלְחַלֵּל אֶת־שֵׁם קָדְשִׁי	3[6] I also will set My face against that man, and will cut him off from among his people, because he has given of his seed to Molech, *to defile*[7] *My sanctuary, and to profane My holy name*[8].
וְאִם הַעְלֵם יַעְלִימוּ עַם הָאָרֶץ אֶת־עֵינֵיהֶם מִן־הָאִישׁ הַהוּא בְּתִתּוֹ מִזַּרְעוֹ לַמֹּלֶךְ לְבִלְתִּי הָמִית אֹתוֹ	4[9] And if the people of the land hide their eyes from that man at all, when he gives of his seed to Molech, and do not put him to death;
וְשַׂמְתִּי אֲנִי אֶת־פָּנַי בָּאִישׁ הַהוּא וּבְמִשְׁפַּחְתּוֹ וְהִכְרַתִּי אֹתוֹ וְאֵת׀ כָּל־	5[10] Then I will set My face against that man, and *against*[11] his family, and will cut him off, *and all who go astray after*

---

[1] Mesillat Yesharim 5:Factors Detracting from Zehirus

[2] Leviticus 20:1-3 - 4QLeve
Leviticus 20:1-6 - 11QpaleoLeva
Leviticus 20:1-27 - Josephus Antiquities 3.12.1

[3] Leviticus 20:2 - 2 Chronicles 4:3 9:6, 2 Kings 17:17 23:10, Acts 7:43 7:58-59, b.Chagigah 11b, b.Kereitot 2a, b.Sanhedrin 64b, Deuteronomy 12:31 13:11-11 17:5-7 18:10 21:21, Ezekiel 16:20-21 20:26 20:31 23:37 23:39, Isaiah 57:5-57:6, Jeremiah 7:31 8:35, Leviticus 17:8 17:13 17:15 18:21 20:27 24:14 24:23, m.Sanhedrin 7:1, mt.Hilchot Avodat Kochavim vChukkoteihem 6:3, Numbers 15:35-36, Pesikta de R'Kahana 2.7, Psalms 10:38, Sifre Devarim Shoftim 171, y.Sanhedrin 7:10, z.Acharei Mot 302
Leviticus 20:2-5 - Testament of Solomon 26:1

[4] Missing in LXX

[5] 11QpaleoLeva *house*

[6] Leviticus 20:3 - 1 Peter 3:12, 2 Corinthians 6:16, b.Sanhedrin 64b, b.Sheviit 7b, Ein Yaakov Shevuot:39a, Ezekiel 5:11 20:39 23:38-39, Gates of Repentance 3.45, Guide for the Perplexed 1:37 3:37 3:47, Leviticus 15:31 17:10 18:21, mt.Hilchot Avodat Kochavim vChukkoteihem 6:4 11:1, Numbers 19:20, y.Sanhedrin 7:10, y.Sheviit 1:2

[7] 11QpaleoLeva *profane*

[8] LXX *profane the name of them who are consecrated to me*

[9] Leviticus 20:4 - 1 Kings 20:42, 1 Samuel 3:13-14, Acts 17:30, b.Ketubot 30b, Deuteronomy 13:9 17:2-5, Joshua 7:12, Revelation 2:14, Sifre Devarim Shoftim 171, y.Sotah 9:12
Leviticus 20:4-5 - t.Sotah 15:7

[10] Leviticus 20:5 - b.Kereitot 2a, b.Ketubot 30b, b.Sanhedrin [Rashi] 64b, b.Sheviit 39ab, b.Sotah [Rashi] 9a, Ein Yaakov Shevuot:39a, Exodus 20:5, Guide for the Perplexed 3:37 3:46, Hosea 2:5 2:13, Jastrow 1099a, Jeremiah 3:2 32:28-35 8:39, Leviticus 17:7 17:10, mt.Hilchot Yesodei haTorah 5:4, Psalms 10:39

[11] Missing in LXX

הַזֹּנִים אַחֲרָיו לִזְנוֹת אַחֲרֵי הַמֹּלֶךְ
מִקֶּרֶב עַמָּם

וְהַנֶּפֶשׁ אֲשֶׁר תִּפְנֶה אֶל־הָאֹבֹת וְאֶל־
הַיִּדְּעֹנִים לִזְנוֹת אַחֲרֵיהֶם וְנָתַתִּי אֶת־
פָּנַי בַּנֶּפֶשׁ הַהִוא וְהִכְרַתִּי אֹתוֹ מִקֶּרֶב
עַמּוֹ

וְהִתְקַדִּשְׁתֶּם וִהְיִיתֶם קְדֹשִׁים כִּי אֲנִי
יְהוָה אֱלֹהֵיכֶם

וּשְׁמַרְתֶּם אֶת־חֻקֹּתַי וַעֲשִׂיתֶם אֹתָם
אֲנִי יְהוָה מְקַדִּשְׁכֶם

כִּי־אִישׁ אִישׁ אֲשֶׁר יְקַלֵּל אֶת־אָבִיו
וְאֶת־אִמּוֹ מוֹת יוּמָת אָבִיו וְאִמּוֹ קִלֵּל
דָּמָיו בּוֹ

him, to go astray after Molech[1], from among their people.

6[2] And the soul who *turns to the ghosts, and to the familiar spirits, to go astray after them*[3], I will even set My face against that soul, and will cut him off from among his people.

7[4] *Sanctify yourselves, therefore, and*[5] be holy; for *I am*[6] the LORD your God[7].

8[8] And keep My statutes, and do them: *I am the LORD who sanctifies you*[9].

9[10] For whatever man there is who curses his father or his mother shall be put to death, yes, death; he has *cursed*[11] his father or his mother; *his blood shall be on him*[12].

---

[1] LXX *and all who have been of one mind with him, so that he should go a whoring to the princes*
[2] Leviticus 20:6 - 1 Chronicles 10:13-10:14, b.Kereitot [Rashi] 3b, b.Kereitot 2a, b.Megillah [Rashi] 24b, b.Sanhedrin [Tosefot] 65a, Deuteronomy 18:10-18:14, Exodus 34:15-34:16, Ezekiel 6:9, Hosea 4:12, Isaiah 8:19, Leviticus 19:26 19:31 20:27, m.Keritot 1:1, Numbers 15:39, Numbers.R 11:7, Pesikta de R'Kahana 24.16, Psalms 73:27, Sibylline Oracles 3.218
[3] LXX *shall follow those who have in them divining spirits, or enchanters*
[4] Leviticus 20:7 - 1 Peter 1:15-16, 1 Thessalonians 4:3 4:7, b.Berachot 53b, Colossians 3:12, Ephesians 1:4, Guide for the Perplexed 3:33, Hebrews 12:14, Leviticus 11:44 19:2, Leviticus.R 24:8, mt.Hilchot Deot 5:4, Numbers.R 9:7, Philippians 2:12-13, Tanya Likutei Aramim §27, y.Sanhedrin 7:10, z.Acharei Mot 78b, z.Tazria 49b, z.Balak 109 426, z.Kedoshim 117, z.Tazria 138, z.Tzav 104, z.Vayera 327, z.Vayikra 423
[5] Missing in LXX
[6] Missing in LXX
[7] LXX adds *is holy*
[8] Leviticus 20:8 - 1 Corinthians 1:30, 1 Thessalonians 5:23, 2 Thessalonians 2:13, Exodus 7:13, Ezekiel 20:12 13:28, James 1:22, John 13:17, Leviticus 18:4-18:5 19:37 21:8, Matthew 5:19 7:24 12:50, Numbers.R 9:7, Pesikta Rabbati 8:5, Revelation 22:14, z.Acharei Mot 78b
[9] 1PpaleoLeva *for I the LORD who sanctify them, is holy*
[10] Leviticus 20:9 - 1 Kings 2:32, 2 Samuel 1:16, b.Bava Metzia 94b, b.Chullin 78b, b.Menachot [Rashi] 90b 91a, b.Sanhedrin 66a 85b, b.Sheviit 16a, Deuteronomy 3:16, Exodus 21:17, Joshua 2:19, Judges 9:24, Leviticus 20:11-20:13 20:16 20:27, m.Sanhedrin 7:8, Mark 7:10, Matthew 15:4 3:25, Mekhilta de R'Shimon bar Yochai Bachodesh 55:1, Mekhilta de R'Shimon bar Yochai Nezikin 62:3, Mekilta de R'Ishmael Bahodesh 8:4, Mekilta de R'Ishmael Nezikin 5:108, Mekilta de R'Ishmael Nezikin 5:87, Midrash Tanchuma Kedoshim 15, mt.Hilchot Mamrim 5:1 5:4, Numbers.R 9:7, Proverbs 20:20 6:11 6:17, y.Yevamot 11:2 11:7
[11] L:XX *spoken evil of*
[12] LXX *he is guilty*

וְאִישׁ אֲשֶׁר יִנְאַף אֶת־אֵשֶׁת אִישׁ אֲשֶׁר יִנְאַף אֶת־אֵשֶׁת רֵעֵהוּ מוֹת־יוּמַת הַנֹּאֵף וְהַנֹּאָפֶת

10[1] And the man who commits adultery with another man's wife, even he who commits adultery with his neighbor's wife, *both the adulterer and the adulteress shall be put to death, yes, death*[2].

וְאִישׁ אֲשֶׁר יִשְׁכַּב אֶת־אֵשֶׁת אָבִיו עֶרְוַת אָבִיו גִּלָּה מוֹת־יוּמְתוּ שְׁנֵיהֶם דְּמֵיהֶם בָּם

11[3] And the man who lies with his father's wife—he has uncovered his father's nakedness—both of them shall be put to death, yes, death; *their blood shall be upon them*[4].

וְאִישׁ אֲשֶׁר יִשְׁכַּב אֶת־כַּלָּתוֹ מוֹת יוּמְתוּ שְׁנֵיהֶם תֶּבֶל עָשׂוּ דְּמֵיהֶם בָּם

12[5] And if a man lies with his daughter-in-law, both of them shall be put to death, yes, death; they have wrought corruption; *their blood shall be on them*[6].

וְאִישׁ אֲשֶׁר יִשְׁכַּב אֶת־זָכָר מִשְׁכְּבֵי אִשָּׁה תּוֹעֵבָה עָשׂוּ שְׁנֵיהֶם מוֹת יוּמָתוּ דְּמֵיהֶם בָּם

13[7] And if a man lies with mankind, as with a woman, both have committed an abomination: they shall be put to death, yes, death; *their blood shall be on them*[8].

וְאִישׁ אֲשֶׁר יִקַּח אֶת־אִשָּׁה וְאֶת־אִמָּהּ זִמָּה הִוא בָּאֵשׁ יִשְׂרְפוּ אֹתוֹ וְאֶתְהֶן

14[9] And if a man takes with his wife also her mother, it is wickedness: they shall be burnt with fire, both he and they; let

---

[1] Leviticus 20:10 - 2 Samuel 12:13, Avot de R'Natan 16, b.Avodah Zara [Tosefot] 36b, b.Kereitot [Rashi] 2b, b.Kiddushin 19a, b.Sanhedrin [Rashi] 50ab, b.Sanhedrin 51b 52b, b.Sotah [Rashi] 26b, Commandment #286, Deuteronomy 5:18 22:22-24, Deuteronomy.R 1:6, Exodus 20:13, Exodus.R 1:28, Ezekiel 23:45-23:47, John 8:4-8:5, Jubilees 20:4, Leviticus 18:20, Leviticus.R 24:5, Mekhilta de R'Shimon bar Yochai Bachodesh 55:2, Mekilta de R'Ishmael Bahodesh 7:50, Mekilta de R'Ishmael Nezikin 4:26, Midrash Proverbs 6, Midrash Psalms 3:5/6 27:2, Midrash Tanchuma Bamidbar 7, Midrash Tanchuma Ki Tissa 4, mt.Hilchot Issurei Biah 1:6, Numbers.R 1:8 9:2 9:7, Pesikta de R'Kahana 2.1, Pesikta Rabbati 8:5 10:10 21:16 31:2, Sifre Devarim Ki Tetze 235, z.Bereshit 8b, z.Kedoshim 84b, z.Kedoshim 79, z.Prologue 132
[2] LXX *let them die the death, the adulterer and the adulteress*
[3] Leviticus 20:11 - 1 Corinthians 5:1, 4Q251 12, Amos 2:7, b.Kereitot 5a, b.Sanhedrin 54a, Deuteronomy 3:20 3:23, Jubilees 33:10, Leviticus 18:7-8, Mekilta de R'Ishmael Nezikin 5:108, mt.Hilchot Issurei Biah 1:6, Pseudo-Phocylides 179, y.Sanhedrin 7:6
Leviticus 20:11-14 - Jastrow 1357a
[4] LXX [here and elsewhere] *they are guilty*
[5] Leviticus 20:12 - b.Kereitot [Rashi] 5a, Deuteronomy 3:23, Deuteronomy.R 1:6, Ein Yaakov Yoma 87a, Genesis 14:16 14:18, Jastrow 1644a, Jubilees 41:26, Leviticus 18:15 18:23, y.Sanhedrin 7:6
[6] LXX [here and elsewhere] *they are guilty*
[7] Leviticus 20:13 - 1 Corinthians 6:9, 1 Timothy 1:10, b.Gittin 85a, b.Horayot 4a, b.Kereitot [Rashi] 5a, b.Kiddushin [Rashi] 9b, b.Makkot [Tosefot] 6a, b.Nedarim 51a, b.Niddah [Rashi] 13b, b.Sanhedrin [Rashi] 33b, b.Sanhedrin [Tosefot] 45b, b.Sanhedrin 54a, Deuteronomy 23:19, Ein Yaakov Nedarim 51a, Genesis 19:5, Jude 1:7, Judges 19:22, Leviticus 18:22, m.Yevamot 6:1, mt.Hilchot Sanhedrin vHainshin Hameurim Lahem 10:9, Pseudo-Phocylides 4, Romans 1:26-1:27, y.Sanhedrin 7:7
[8] LXX [here and elsewhere] *they are guilty*
[9] Leviticus 20:14 - Amos 2:7, b.Chagigah [Rashi] 11b, b.Kereitot [Rashi] 2b 3b, b.Kereitot 5a, b.Sanhedrin [Rashi] 51a 75b, b.Sanhedrin 75a 76b, b.Yevamot [Rashi] 2b 26a 55b 97a, b.Yevamot 3a 94b 95a, Commandment #287, Deuteronomy 3:23, Jastrow 1357a, Joshua 7:15 7:25, Jubilees 41:26, Leviticus 18:17 21:9, m.Yevamot 11:1, mt.Hilchot Issurei Biah 2:11, mt.Hilchot Sanhedrin vHainshin Hameurim Lahem 14:1, t.Kiddushin 1:4, t.Sanhedrin 12:1, y.Sanhedrin 7:1 9:1, y.Yevamot 2:4 10:6 11:1

וְלֹא־תִהְיֶה זִמָּה בְּתוֹכְכֶם

וְאִישׁ אֲשֶׁר יִתֵּן שְׁכָבְתּוֹ בִּבְהֵמָה מוֹת
יוּמָת וְאֶת־הַבְּהֵמָה תַּהֲרֹגוּ

וְאִשָּׁה אֲשֶׁר תִּקְרַב אֶל־כָּל־בְּהֵמָה
לְרִבְעָה אֹתָהּ וְהָרַגְתָּ אֶת־הָאִשָּׁה
וְאֶת־הַבְּהֵמָה מוֹת יוּמָתוּ דְּמֵיהֶם בָּם

וְאִישׁ אֲשֶׁר־יִקַּח אֶת־אֲחֹתוֹ בַּת־אָבִיו
אוֹ בַת־אִמּוֹ וְרָאָה אֶת־עֶרְוָתָהּ וְהִיא־
תִרְאֶה אֶת־עֶרְוָתוֹ חֶסֶד הוּא וְנִכְרְתוּ
לְעֵינֵי בְּנֵי עַמָּם עֶרְוַת אֲחֹתוֹ גִּלָּה עֲוֹנוֹ
יִשָּׂא

וְאִישׁ אֲשֶׁר־יִשְׁכַּב אֶת־אִשָּׁה דָּוָה
וְגִלָּה אֶת־עֶרְוָתָהּ אֶת־מְקֹרָהּ הֶעֱרָה
וְהִיא גִּלְּתָה אֶת־מְקוֹר דָּמֶיהָ וְנִכְרְתוּ
שְׁנֵיהֶם מִקֶּרֶב עַמָּם

there be no wickedness among you.

15[1] And if a man lies with a beast, he shall be put to death, yes, death; and you shall kill the beast.

16[2] And if a woman approaches to any beast, and lie down with it, you shall kill the woman, and the beast: *they shall be put to death, yes, death*[3]; *their blood shall be on them*[4].

17[5] And if a man shall take his sister, his father's daughter, or his mother's daughter, and sees her nakedness, and she see his nakedness: it is a shameful thing; and they shall be cut off in the sight of the children of their people: he has uncovered his sister's nakedness; he shall bear his iniquity.

18[6] And if a man shall lie with a woman *having her sickness*[7], and shall uncover her nakedness—he has made naked her fountain, and she has uncovered the fountain of her blood—both of them shall be cut off from among their people.

---

[1] Leviticus 20:15 - b.Bava Kamma [Rashi] 40b, b.Bechorot [Rashi] 57a, b.Kiddushin [Rashi] 57b, b.Kiddushin 66a, b.Sanhedrin [Rashi] 15a, b.Sanhedrin [Tosefot] 15b, b.Sanhedrin 54b, b.Temurah 28b, b.Zevachim [Rashi] 27b, Deuteronomy 3:21, Exodus 22:19, Guide for the Perplexed 3:40, Leviticus 18:23, m.Niddah 5:5, m.Sanhedrin 1:4 7:4, Mekilta de R'Ishmael Nezikin 17:72, Midrash Tanchuma Emor 15, mt.Hilchot Nizkei Mammon 11:11, mt.Hilchot Sanhedrin vHainshin Hameurim Lahem 5:2, Pseudo-Phocylides 188, t.Sanhedrin 3:1, y.Sanhedrin 1:2 7:7
[2] Leviticus 20:16 - b.Kereitot [Rashi] 5a, b.Kiddushin [Rashi] 57b, b.Kiddushin 66a, b.Sanhedrin [Rashi] 67b, b.Sanhedrin 2a 15a, b.Zevachim 27b, Exodus 19:13 21:28 21:32, Genesis.R 15:7, Hebrews 12:20, Jastrow 1442b, Leviticus.R 27:3, m.Sanhedrin 1:4 7:4, m.Temurah 6:1, m.Zevachim 8:1 9:3, Mas.Derek Eretz Rabbah 1:7, Mas.Semachot 8:16, Midrash Tanchuma Balak 9, Midrash Tanchuma Emor 8 15, mt.Hilchot Sanhedrin vHainshin Hameurim Lahem 5:2, Numbers.R 20:14, Pesikta de R'Kahana 9.3 20.6, Pesikta Rabbati 42:1, t.Sanhedrin 3:1, y.Sanhedrin 1:2 7:7
[3] LXX *let the die the death*
[4] LXX [here and elsewhere] *they are guilty*
[5] Leviticus 20:17 - 2 Samuel 13:12, 4Q251 12, Avot de R'Natan 34, b.Bechorot [Tosefot] 14b, b.Kereitot [Rashi] 3b, b.Kereitot 2b 3a 15a, b.Kiddushin [Tosefot] 2a, b.Makkot 5b 13b 14a, b.Megillah [Rashi] 7b, b.Sanhedrin [Rashi] 58b, b.Sanhedrin 40b, b.Yevamot 55a 97a, b.Zevachim [Rashi] 16b, Deuteronomy 3:22, Ezekiel 22:11, Genesis 20:12, Jastrow 486a 674b, Leviticus 18:9, mt.Hilchot Shegagot 4:5, mt.Pirkei Avot 5:6, Pirkei de R'Eliezer 21, y.Sanhedrin 5:1 9:1, y.Yevamot 11:1, z.Acharei Mot 357 369 369, z.Vayikra 100
Leviticus 20:17-21 - m.Makkot 3:1
[6] Leviticus 20:18 - b.Horayot 4a, b.Kereitot [Rashi] 16a, b.Makkot 14b, b.Niddah [Rashi] 15a, b.Niddah [Tosefot] 32b, b.Niddah 19a 41b, b.Sanhedrin [Rashi] 55a, b.Yevamot 54a, Ezekiel 18:6 22:10, Jastrow 360b, Leviticus 15:24 18:19, Leviticus.R 19:4, m.Horayot 1:3, m.Keritot 3:10, m.Niddah 2:2, Midrash Tanchuma Metzora 5, mt.Hilchot Issurei Biah 1:10, Numbers.R 9:10, Pesikta de R'Kahana 12.15, Philo De Fuga et Inventione 188, y.Niddah 2:3, y.Sanhedrin 7:5, y.Shabbat 7:2
[7] LXX *who is set apart [for her flux]*

וְעֶרְוַ֞ת אֲח֤וֹת אִמְּךָ֙ וַאֲח֣וֹת אָבִ֔יךָ לֹ֣א
תְגַלֵּ֑ה כִּ֧י אֶת־שְׁאֵר֛וֹ הֶעֱרָ֖ה עֲוֹנָ֥ם
יִשָּֽׂאוּ

19[1] And you shall not uncover the nakedness of your mother's sister, nor of your father's sister; for he has made naked his near kin; they shall bear their iniquity.

וְאִ֗ישׁ אֲשֶׁ֤ר יִשְׁכַּב֙ אֶת־דֹּ֣דָת֔וֹ עֶרְוַ֥ת
דֹּד֖וֹ גִּלָּ֑ה חֶטְאָ֥ם יִשָּׂ֖אוּ עֲרִירִ֥ים יָמֻֽתוּ

20[2] And if a man shall lie with his *uncle's wife*[3]—he has uncovered *his uncle's nakedness*[4]—they shall bear their sin; they shall die childless.

וְאִ֗ישׁ אֲשֶׁ֥ר יִקַּ֛ח אֶת־אֵ֥שֶׁת אָחִ֖יו נִדָּ֣ה
הִ֑וא עֶרְוַ֥ת אָחִ֛יו גִּלָּ֖ה עֲרִירִ֥ים יִהְיֽוּ

21[5] And if a man shall take his brother's wife, it is impurity: he has uncovered his brother's nakedness; they shall be childless.

וּשְׁמַרְתֶּ֤ם אֶת־כָּל־חֻקֹּתַי֙ וְאֶת־כָּל־
מִשְׁפָּטַ֔י וַעֲשִׂיתֶ֖ם אֹתָ֑ם וְלֹא־תָקִ֤יא
אֶתְכֶם֙ הָאָ֔רֶץ אֲשֶׁ֨ר אֲנִ֜י מֵבִ֥יא אֶתְכֶ֛ם
שָׁ֖מָּה לָשֶׁ֥בֶת בָּֽהּ

22[6] You shall, therefore, keep all My statutes, and all My ordinances, and do them, so the land *into which I bring you to dwell, will not vomit you not*[7].

וְלֹ֤א תֵֽלְכוּ֙ בְּחֻקֹּ֣ת הַגּ֔וֹי אֲשֶׁר־אֲנִ֥י
מְשַׁלֵּ֖חַ מִפְּנֵיכֶ֑ם כִּ֤י אֶת־כָּל־אֵ֨לֶּה֙ עָשׂ֔וּ
וָאָקֻ֖ץ בָּֽם

23[8] And you shall not walk in the customs of the nation that I am casting out before you; for they did all these things, so I abhorred them.

וָאֹמַ֣ר לָכֶ֗ם אַתֶּם֮ תִּֽירְשׁ֣וּ אֶת־אַדְמָתָם֒
וַאֲנִ֞י אֶתְּנֶ֤נָּה לָכֶם֙ לָרֶ֣שֶׁת אֹתָ֔הּ אֶ֛רֶץ
זָבַ֥ת חָלָ֖ב וּדְבָ֑שׁ אֲנִי֙ יְהוָ֣ה אֱלֹֽהֵיכֶ֔ם
אֲשֶׁר־הִבְדַּ֥לְתִּי אֶתְכֶ֖ם מִן־הָֽעַמִּֽים

24[9] But I have said to you: 'You shall inherit their land, and I will give it to you to possess it, a land flowing with milk and honey.' I am the LORD your God, who have set you apart from the peoples.

---

[1] Leviticus 20:19 - 4Q251 12, b.Sanhedrin [Rashi] 55a, b.Yevamot 54a, Exodus 6:20, Leviticus 18:6 18:12-18:30, y.Shabbat 7:2

[2] Leviticus 20:20 - b.Chullin [Rashi] 31a, b.Yevamot 54b 55a 97a, Gates of Repentance 3.119, Jastrow 1118a, Jeremiah 22:30, Job 18:19, Leviticus 18:14, Luke 1:7 1:25 23:29, Psalms 13:13, y.Sanhedrin 7:5, y.Shabbat 7:2, z.Vayechi 228a, z.Mishpatim 274, z.Vayechi 388
Leviticus 20:20-24 - 1QpaleoLev

[3] LXX *near kinswoman*

[4] LXX *the nakedness of one near akin to him*

[5] Leviticus 20:21 - b.Ketubot [Rashi] 30b, b.Sanhedrin [Tosefot] 45a, b.Yevamot 54ab 55a, Jastrow 1118a, Leviticus 18:16, m.Bechorot 8:1, Matthew 14:3-4, y.Sanhedrin 7:5 9:1, y.Shabbat 7:2, y.Yevamot 11:1, z.Mishpatim 108b, z.Lech Lecha 320

[6] Leviticus 20:22 - Deuteronomy 4:45 5:1 28:25-28:26, Exodus 21:1, Ezekiel 12:27, Isaiah 26:8-26:9, Leviticus 18:4-18:5 18:25-18:28 19:37 2:33, mt.Hilchot Melachim uMichamoteihem 9:7, Numbers.R 19:5, Psalms 19:9-19:12 9:45 119:106 119:145 119:160 119:164 119:171 119:175 23:20 119:80

[7] LXX *shall not be aggrieved with you, into which I bring you to dwell upon it*

[8] Leviticus 20:23 - b.Bechorot [Rashi] 37b, Commandment #332, Deuteronomy 9:5 12:30-31, Guide for the Perplexed 3:29 3:37, Jastrow 1339a, Jeremiah 10:1-2, Leviticus 18:3 18:24 18:27 18:30, Midrash Proverbs 1, mt.Hilchot Avodat Kochavim vChukkoteihem 11:1, mt.Hilchot Sanhedrin vHainshin Hameurim Lahem 19:4, Psalms 78:59, Siman 3:2, z.Tazria 42b, Zechariah 11:8, z.Balak 426, z.Tazria 4, z.Vayikra 107

[9] Leviticus 20:24 - 1 Kings 8:53, 1 Peter 2:9, 2 Corinthians 6:17, Deuteronomy 7:6 14:2, Exodus 3:8 3:17 6:8 13:5 19:5-6 9:3 9:16, John 15:19, Leviticus 20:26, Numbers 23:9, z.Acharei Mot 78b

וְהִבְדַּלְתֶּ֞ם בֵּֽין־הַבְּהֵמָ֤ה הַטְּהֹרָה֙
לַטְּמֵאָ֔ה וּבֵ֥ין־הָע֛וֹף הַטָּמֵ֖א לַטָּהֹ֑ר
וְלֹֽא־תְשַׁקְּצ֨וּ אֶת־נַפְשֹֽׁתֵיכֶ֜ם בַּבְּהֵמָ֣ה
וּבָע֗וֹף וּבְכֹל֙ אֲשֶׁ֣ר תִּרְמֹ֣שׂ הָֽאֲדָמָ֔ה
אֲשֶׁר־הִבְדַּ֥לְתִּי לָכֶ֖ם לְטַמֵּֽא

25[1]

And you shall separate between the clean beast and the unclean, and between the unclean fowl and the clean; and you shall not make your souls detestable by beast, or by fowl, or by anything from which the ground teems, which I have set apart for you to hold unclean.

וִהְיִ֤יתֶם לִי֙ קְדֹשִׁ֔ים כִּ֥י קָד֖וֹשׁ אֲנִ֣י
יְהוָ֑ה וָאַבְדִּ֥ל אֶתְכֶ֛ם מִן־הָֽעַמִּ֖ים לִהְי֥וֹת
לִֽי

26[2]

And you shall be holy to Me; for I the LORD[3] am holy, and have set you apart from the peoples, that you should be Mine.

וְאִ֣ישׁ אֽוֹ־אִשָּׁ֗ה כִּֽי־יִהְיֶ֨ה בָהֶ֥ם א֛וֹב א֖וֹ
יִדְּעֹנִ֑י מ֣וֹת יוּמָ֔תוּ בָּאֶ֛בֶן יִרְגְּמ֥וּ אֹתָ֖ם
דְּמֵיהֶ֥ם בָּֽם

27[4]

A man also or a woman *who divines by a ghost or a familiar spirit, shall be put to death, yes, death*[5]; *they*[6] shall stone them with stones; *their blood shall be on them.*[7]

---

[1] Leviticus 20:25 - 4Q512 xiv, Acts 10:11-15 10:28, b.Chullin [Rashi] 120b, b.Makkot 16b, b.Meilah 16b 14a, b.Pesachim [Rashi] 24b, b.Zevachim [Rashi] 16b, b.Zevachim [Tosefot] 16b, Deuteronomy 14:3-21, Ephesians 5:7-11, Leviticus 11:1-47, m.Makkot 3:2, m.Nedarim 12:1, m.Parah 9:2, m.Sheviit 3:4, Midrash Tanchuma Chukkat 2, mt.Hilchot Maachalot Assurot 1:1, mt.Hilchot Tefilah 4:10, Siman 4:1, y.Nazir 6:1, z.Shmini 110 116

[2] Leviticus 20:26 - 1 Peter 1:15-16, b.Avodah Zara 76b, b.Chullin [Rashi] 26b, b.Pesachim [Rashi] 14a, Deuteronomy 7:6 14:2 26:18-19, Deuteronomy.R 7:3, Esther.R 7:11, Exodus.R 15:24, Isaiah 6:3 6:11, Leviticus 19:2 20:7 20:24, m.Makkot 3:2, Mekhilta de R'Shimon bar Yochai Bachodesh 49:3, Mekilta de R'Ishmael Pisha 12:21, Midrash Tanchuma Korach 5, mt.Hilchot Avodat Kochavim vChukkoteihem 11:1, Numbers.R 10:1 18:7, Pesikta de R'Kahana 5.5, Pesikta Rabbati 15:5, Pirkei de R'Eliezer 20, Psalms 99:5 99:9, Revelation 3:7 4:8, Shemonah Perachim VI, Siman 3:2, Song of Songs.R 6:5, Tanya Likutei Aramim §46, Titus 2:14, y.Sanhedrin 7:10, z.Balak 190b, z.Tazria 49b, z.Emor 36, z.Tazria 138

[3] LXX adds *your God*

[4] Leviticus 20:27 - 1 Samuel 28:7-9, 4QLeve, b.Kereitot [Tosefot] 3b, b.Kereitot 5a, b.Sanhedrin [Rashi] 53a 65a 67a, b.Sanhedrin 54a 66a, b.Yevamot [Rashi] 4a, Deuteronomy 18:10-12, Exodus 22:18, Jastrow 1b, Leviticus 19:31 20:6, Leviticus.R 26:7, m.Makkot 3:2, m.Sanhedrin 7:1, Mekhilta de R'Shimon bar Yochai Nezikin 62:3 74:4, Mekilta de R'Ishmael Nezikin 17:64, Midrash Tanchuma Emor 2, mt.Hilchot Issurei Biah 1:6, mt.Hilchot Mamrim 5:1, mt.Hilchot Sanhedrin vHainshin Hameurim Lahem 14:1, Sibylline Oracles 3.218, Sifre Devarim Ki Tetze 220 240 242, Sifre Devarim Reeh 90, Sifre Devarim Shoftim 149, z.Emor 88a, m.Makkot 3:2, z.Emor 1 36

[5] LXX *whosoever of them shall have in them a divining spirit, or be an enchanter, let them both die the death*

[6] LXX*you*

[7] LXX [here and elsewhere] *they are guilty*

Emor

Emor[1] – Chapter 21[2]

וַיֹּאמֶר יְהוָה֙ אֶל־מֹשֶׁ֔ה אֱמֹ֥ר אֶל־
הַכֹּהֲנִ֖ים בְּנֵ֣י אַהֲרֹ֑ן וְאָמַרְתָּ֣ אֲלֵהֶ֔ם
לְנֶ֥פֶשׁ לֹֽא־יִטַּמָּ֖א בְּעַמָּֽיו׃

כִּ֚י אִם־לִשְׁאֵר֔וֹ הַקָּרֹ֖ב אֵלָ֑יו לְאִמּ֣וֹ
וּלְאָבִ֔יו וְלִבְנ֥וֹ וּלְבִתּ֖וֹ וּלְאָחִֽיו׃

וְלַאֲחֹת֤וֹ הַבְּתוּלָה֙ הַקְּרוֹבָ֣ה אֵלָ֔יו אֲשֶׁ֥ר
לֹֽא־הָיְתָ֖ה לְאִ֑ישׁ לָ֖הּ יִטַּמָּֽא׃

1[3] And the LORD said to Moses: Speak to the priests, the sons of Aaron, and say to them: No one shall defile himself for the dead among his people;

2[4] except for his kin, who is [5]near to him, for his mother, and for his father, and for his son, and for his daughter, and for his brother;

3[6] and for his sister, a virgin, who is near to him who has had no husband, for her may he defile himself.

---

[1] Emor aliyot: [1] Leviticus 21:1–15, [2] Leviticus 21:16–22:16, [3] Leviticus 22:17–33, [4] Leviticus 23:1–22, [5] Leviticus 23:23–32, [6] Leviticus 23:33–44, [7] Leviticus 24:1–23

[2] Midrash Tanchuma Chukkat 6

[3] Leviticus 21:1 - b.Bava Metzia [Rashi] 18a 30a, b.Bechorot [Rashi] 29a, b.Berachot [Rashi] 19b, b.Ketubot [Rashi] 53a 89b, b.Kiddushin 35b, b.Makkot 21b, b.Nazir 43b, b.Pesachim [Rashi] 47b, b.Rosh Hashanah 16b, b.Sanhedrin [Tosefot] 59a, b.Sanhedrin 5b 47a, b.Sotah 3a 23b, b.Temurah [Rashi] 4b, b.Yevamot 85a 114a, b.Yoma [Rashi] 80b, Ezekiel 20:25, Guide for the Perplexed 3:47, Hosea 5:1, Lamentations.R 1:41, Leviticus 10:6-10:7 19:28 21:11, Leviticus.R 26:1 26:3 26:4 26:7, m.Bava Metzia 2:10, m.Bechorot 7:7, m.Kiddushin 1:7 4:1, m.Menachot 4:3, m.Nazir 6:5 7:1, m.Sotah 3:7, m.Yevamot 11:5, m.Zevachim 12:1, Malachi 2:1 2:4, Midrash Proverbs 9, Midrash Psalms 12:4 19:15, Midrash Tanchuma Emor 1 2 3, mt.Hilchot Avodat Kochavim vChukkoteihem 12:3 12:3, mt.Hilchot Evel 3:1 3:11, mt.Hilchot Sanhedrin vHainshin Hameurim Lahem 19:4, Numbers 19:14 19:16, Numbers.R 10:11 19:4, Pesikta de R'Kahana 4.4, Pesikta Rabbati 14:1, Siman 202:15, t.Bikkurim 2:4, y.Kiddushin 1:7, y.Sotah 3:7, z.Emor 88a 88b, z.Emor 1 9
Leviticus 21:1-3 - Commandment #375
Leviticus 21:1-4 - 4QLeve
Leviticus 21:1-6 - m.Yevamot 10:1
Leviticus 21:1-11 - Josephus Antiquities 4.8.28
Leviticus 21:1-15 - Minchah [Shabbat Monday Thursday Torah reading - Parashah Emor]
Leviticus 21:1-24 - Josephus Antiquities 4.8.23

[4] Leviticus 21:2 - 1 Thessalonians 4:13, b.Bava Batra [Rashi] 18b, b.Bava Metzia [Rashi] 18a, b.Nazir 43b, b.Sanhedrin [Rashi] 28b, b.Shabbat [Rashi] 105b, b.Sotah 3a, b.Yevamot 22b 55b 90b, Jastrow 823b 1509a 1586b, Leviticus 18:6, m.Menachot 4:3, m.Sotah 3:7, m.Yevamot 2:5, m.Zevachim 12:1, Mas.Semachot 4:1 4:4 4:32, Midrash Psalms 12:4, mt.Hilchot Evel 2:1 2:6 2:12 2:15 3:12, mt.Hilchot Kriat Shema 4:3, Numbers.R 10:11, Siman 202:1, z.Emor 16

[5] LXX adds *very*

[6] Leviticus 21:3 - b.Bava Metzia [Rashi] 18a, b.Bava Metzia [Tosefot] 30b, b.Nazir 43b, b.Shabbat [Rashi] 105b, b.Sotah 3a, b.Yevamot 60a, b.Zevachim 1a, Commandment #376 [mourn for them like other Israelites, who must mourn for their relatives], m.Menachot 4:3, m.Sotah 3:7, m.Zevachim 12:1, Mas.Semachot 4:5 4:8, mt.Hilchot Evel 2:1 2:6 2:10 2:12-13 2:15, y.Yevamot 6:4, z.Emor 89a, z.Vayera 112a, z.Emor 16 20, z.Vayera 353

לֹא יִטַּמָּא בַּעַל בְּעַמָּיו לְהֵחַלּוֹ | 4[1] | He shall not defile himself, being a chief man among his people, to profane himself.

"לֹא־יִקְרְחָה׳ "לֹא־יִקְרְחוּ" קָרְחָה בְּרֹאשָׁם וּפְאַת זְקָנָם לֹא יְגַלֵּחוּ וּבִבְשָׂרָם לֹא יִשְׂרְטוּ שָׂרָטֶת | 5[2] | They shall not make baldness on their head, nor shall they shave off the corners of their beard, nor make any cuttings in their flesh.

קְדֹשִׁים יִהְיוּ לֵאלֹהֵיהֶם וְלֹא יְחַלְּלוּ שֵׁם אֱלֹהֵיהֶם כִּי אֶת־אִשֵּׁי יְהוָה לֶחֶם אֱלֹהֵיהֶם הֵם מַקְרִיבִם וְהָיוּ קֹדֶשׁ | 6[3] | They shall be holy to their God, and not profane the name of their God; for the offerings of the LORD made by fire, the bread of their God, they do offer; therefore, they shall be holy.

אִשָּׁה זֹנָה וַחֲלָלָה לֹא יִקָּחוּ וְאִשָּׁה גְּרוּשָׁה מֵאִישָׁהּ לֹא יִקָּחוּ כִּי־קָדֹשׁ הוּא לֵאלֹהָיו | 7[4] | They shall not take a woman who is a *harlot, nor profaned*[5]; nor shall they take a woman put away by her husband; for he is holy to his God.

וְקִדַּשְׁתּוֹ כִּי־אֶת־לֶחֶם אֱלֹהֶיךָ הוּא מַקְרִיב קָדֹשׁ יִהְיֶה־לָּךְ כִּי קָדוֹשׁ אֲנִי | 8[6] | You shall sanctify him; for he offers the bread of your God; he shall be holy to you; for I the LORD, who sanctifies

---

[1] Leviticus 21:4 - b.Bava Metzia [Rashi] 18a, b.Kiddushin 77a, b.Nazir 3a, b.Yevamot 22b 90b, Ezekiel 24:16-24:17, m.Menachot 4:3, m.Sotah 3:7, m.Yevamot 9:1, m.Zevachim 12:1, y.Nazir 3:5 7:1

[2] Leviticus 21:5 - Amos 8:10, b.Kiddushin 35b, b.Makkot 20a 21a, b.Nazir 40b 58ab, b.Sheviit [Tosefot] 3a, b.Yevamot 5a, b.Zevachim [Rashi] 14a, Deuteronomy 14:1, Ezekiel 20:20, Genesis.R 11:6, Isaiah 15:2 22:12, Jeremiah 16:6 24:37, Leviticus 10:6 19:27-19:28, m.Negaim 1:1, Micah 1:16, mt.Hilchot Avodat Kochavim vChukkoteihem 12:12 12:12 12:15 12:15, Numbers.R 10:1, Sifre Devarim Reeh 96, y.Kiddushin 1:7, z.Emor 89a, z.Emor 21 25 25, z.Naso Idra Raba 138
Leviticus 21:5-6 - 4QpaleoExodm

[3] Leviticus 21:6 - 1 Peter 2:9, b.Bava Metzia [Rashi] 30a, b.Sanhedrin 51b 53b 83ab, b.Yevamot 20ab, b.Zevachim 14a, Commandment #377 [shall not serve in the Sanctuary until after sunset], Exodus 4:36 5:44, Ezekiel 20:7, Ezra 8:28, Isaiah 4:11, Jastrow 704a, Leviticus 3:11 10:3 18:21 19:12 21:8, m.Nedarim 1:3, Malachi 1:6-1:7 1:11-12, Midrash Psalms 21:2, mt.Hilchot Biat haMikdash 4:4, mt.Hilchot Gezelah Vaavedah 11:18, mt.Hilchot Sanhedrin vHainshin Hameurim Lahem 19:2, z.Vayishlach 166b, z.Vayishlach 18
Leviticus 21:6 [LXX] - Psalms of Solomon 2:3
Leviticus 21:6-12 - 11Qpaleol.eva

[4] Leviticus 21:7 - 1 Timothy 3:11, 4QMMT B 77-82, b.Bava Batra [Rashi] 127b 160b, b.Bava Batra 32a, b.Bava Metzia [Rashi] 10b, b.Bava Metzia [Tosefot] 30a, b.Gittin 82b, b.Kiddushin [Rashi] 77b, b.Makkot [Rashi] 13a, b.Sanhedrin [Tosefot] 82a, b.Sanhedrin 5b, b.Yevamot [Rashi] 56b, b.Yevamot 24a 137a 52a 55a 92a 94a, Commandment #378 #379 #380, Deuteronomy 24:1-4, Ezekiel 20:22, Guide for the Perplexed 3:49, Isaiah 2:1, Jastrow 382b 388a 470b, Leviticus 21:8 21:13-14, Leviticus.R 24:6, m.Eduyot 8:2, m.Kiddushin 4:1, m.Temurah 6:2, m.Yevamot 1:4 2:4 9:1 10:3, Mas.Semachot 2:14 4:4 4:17, Midrash Tanchuma Ki Tissa 17, Midrash Tanchuma Vayera 8, mt.Hilchot Issurei Biah 17:2, mt.Hilchot Gerusin 10:1, mt.Hilchot Ishut 1:7, mt.Hilchot Nesiat Kapayim 15:6, mt.Hilchot Melachim uMichamoteihem 7:8, mt.Hilchot Sanhedrin vHainshin Hameurim Lahem 16:6 18:3 19:4, y.Kiddushin 3:12, y.Yevamot 9:1 10:5, z.Vayakhel 216b, z.Vayakhel 430
Leviticus 21:7-9 - 4Q251 11

[5] LXX *harlot and profaned*

[6] Leviticus 21:8 - b.Chullin [Tosefot] 87a, b.Gittin 59b, b.Horayot 12b, b.Megillah [Rashi] 28a, b.Menachot [Tosefot] 109a, b.Moed Katan 28b, b.Yevamot 88b, Commandment #381, Ein Yaakov Gittin:59b, Ein Yaakov Nedarim:62a, Exodus 19:10 19:14 4:41 5:1 29:43-44, Hashem, Hashem, Hebrews 7:26 10:29, Jastrow 704a, John 10:36 17:19, Leviticus 11:44-45 19:2 20:7-8 21:6, mt.Hilchot Ishut 24:22, mt.Hilchot Klei haMikdash Vihaovdim Bo 4:1, mt.Hilchot Tumat Ochalin 16:12, Siman 144:9 45:5, t.Sanhedrin 4:1, y.Horayot 3:1, y.Yevamot 2:4, z.Mishpatim 23, z.Naso 85

יְהוָה מְקַדִּשְׁכֶם

וּבַת אִישׁ כֹּהֵן כִּי תֵחֵל לִזְנוֹת אֶת־
אָבִיהָ הִיא מְחַלֶּלֶת בָּאֵשׁ תִּשָּׂרֵף

וְהַכֹּהֵן הַגָּדוֹל מֵאֶחָיו אֲשֶׁר־יוּצַק עַל־
רֹאשׁוֹ שֶׁמֶן הַמִּשְׁחָה וּמִלֵּא אֶת־יָדוֹ
לִלְבֹּשׁ אֶת־הַבְּגָדִים אֶת־רֹאשׁוֹ לֹא
יִפְרָע וּבְגָדָיו לֹא יִפְרֹם

וְעַל כָּל־נַפְשֹׁת מֵת לֹא יָבֹא לְאָבִיו
וּלְאִמּוֹ לֹא יִטַּמָּא

וּמִן־הַמִּקְדָּשׁ לֹא יֵצֵא וְלֹא יְחַלֵּל אֵת
מִקְדַּשׁ אֱלֹהָיו כִּי נֵזֶר שֶׁמֶן מִשְׁחַת
אֱלֹהָיו עָלָיו אֲנִי יְהוָה

you[1], am holy.

9[2] And the daughter of any priest, if she profanes herself by playing the harlot, she profanes[3] her father: she shall be burnt with fire.

10[4] And the priest who is highest among his brethren, upon whose head the anointing oil is poured, and who is consecrated to put on the garments, shall not let the hair of his head go loose, nor rend his clothes;

11[5] Nor shall he go in to any dead body, nor defile himself for his father, or for his mother;

12[6] Nor shall he go out of the sanctuary, nor profane the sanctuary of his God; for the consecration of the anointing oil of his God is upon him: I am the LORD.

---

[1] 11QpaleoLEVa LXX *them*

[2] Leviticus 21:9 - 1 Samuel 2:17 2:34 3:13-14, 1 Timothy 3:4-3:5, Avot de R'Natan 34, b.Makkot [Tosefot] 2a, b.Menachot [Tosefot] 51b, b.Pesachim 75a, b.Sanhedrin [Rashi] 46a 84b, b.Sanhedrin [Tosefot] 14a, b.Sanhedrin 50ab 51ab 52a 66b 76a, Ein Yaakov Sanhedrin:52a, Ezekiel 9:6, Genesis 14:24, Genesis.R 46:11 85:10, Isaiah 9:14, Jastrow 1633b, Joshua 7:15 7:25, Jubilees 20:4, Leviticus 19:29 20:14, m.Sanhedrin 7:2, m.Terumot 7:2, m.Yevamot 9:1, Malachi 2:3, Matthew 11:20-24, mt.Hilchot Issurei Biah 1:6 3:3, mt.Hilchot Sanhedrin vHainshin Hameurim Lahem 15:11, Sifre Devarim Ki Tetze 240, Titus 1:6, y.Sanhedrin 7:1 9:1, y.Terumot 7:2, y.Yevamot 11:1
Leviticus 21:9-12 - 4QLeve

[3] 4QLeve adds *the house of*

[4] Leviticus 21:10 - 2 Samuel 15:30, b.Bava Batra [Rashi] 99b, b.Chullin 134a, b.Horayot 9a 12b, b.Kiddushin 15a, b.Yoma [Rashi] 73a, b.Yoma 18a, Ein Yaakov Horayot:9a, Ein Yaakov Yoma:18a, Esther 6:12, Exodus 28:2-4 29:29-30, Genesis 13:34, Guide for the Perplexed 3:47, Jastrow 213a 1227a 1235a, Job 1:20, Leviticus 8:7-9 8:12 10:6-7 13:45 16:32, Leviticus.R 26:9, m.Horayot 3:4, Mas.Semachot 4:19, Matthew 26:65, Midrash Tanchuma Emor 4, mt.Hilchot Biat haMikdash 1:10, mt.Hilchot Evel 7:6, mt.Hilchot Klei haMikdash Vihaovdim Bo 4:12 5:1 5:6, mt.Hilchot Shegagot 15:6, Numbers 11:25, Psalms 13:2, t.Kippurim 1:6, t.Sanhedrin 4:1, y.Yoma 1:3, z.Emor 89b, z.Emor 13 25
Leviticus 21:10-12 - Midrash Proverbs 1

[5] Leviticus 21:11 - 2 Corinthians 5:16, b.Bava Kamma [Rashi] 11ab, b.Chullin 72a, b.Horayot 12b, b.Nazir 38a 44a 47a 48a 49a, b.Niddah [Tosefot] 15a, b.Sanhedrin [Rashi] 18a 19a 35b, b.Sanhedrin 4ab, b.Shabbat [Rashi] 132a, b.Yoma [Rashi] 13b, b.Zevachim [Rashi] 16a 99a, Commandment #382 #383, Deuteronomy 9:9, Genesis.R 86:3, Leviticus 19:28 21:1-2, Luke 9:59-60 14:26, m.Bechorot 7:7, m.Horayot 3:4-5, m.Nazir 7:1, m.Sanhedrin 2:1, m.Zevachim 2:1, Mas.Semachot 4:4, Matthew 8:21-22 12:46-50, mt.Hilchot Evel 3:6, Numbers 6:7 19:14, Philo De Fuga et Inventione 109, y.Nazir 7:1, z.Ki Tetze 124 125

[6] Leviticus 21:12 - Acts 10:38, b.Bava Kamma [Rashi] 11a, b.Bechorot 47a, b.Horayot 12b, b.Kereitot 7a, b.Nazir 42b, b.Sanhedrin 18a 19a 84a, b.Shabbat [Rashi] 132a, b.Sheviit [Tosefot] 14a, b.Yevamot [Tosefot] 55b, b.Yoma [Rashi] 13b 73a, b.Zevachim [Rashi] 99a, b.Zevachim [Tosefot] 18a, b.Zevachim 16ab, Exodus 4:36 29:6-7, Exodus.R 37:3, Isaiah 13:1, Jastrow 1468b, Leviticus 8:9-12 8:30 10:7, Leviticus.R 10:3 10:3 10:3, m.Sanhedrin 2:1, mt.Hilchot Biat haMikdash 2:5, mt.Hilchot Evel 7:6, mt.Hilchot Klei haMikdash Vihaovdim Bo 5:7, Numbers.R 10:11, Siman 202:1, t.Sanhedrin 4:1, t.Shevuot 1:6, y.Horayot 2:7 3:1 3:3, y.Sanhedrin 2:1, z.Acharei Mot 78b, z.Emor 14 25

וְה֗וּא אִשָּׁ֛ה בִבְתוּלֶ֖יהָ יִקָּֽח	13[1]	And he shall take a wife[2] in her virginity.
אַלְמָנָ֤ה וּגְרוּשָׁה֙ וַחֲלָלָ֣ה זֹנָ֔ה אֶת־אֵ֖לֶּה לֹ֣א יִקָּ֑ח כִּ֛י אִם־בְּתוּלָ֥ה מֵעַמָּ֖יו יִקַּ֥ח אִשָּֽׁה	14[3]	A widow, or one divorced, or a profaned woman, or a harlot, these he shall not take; but a virgin of his own people shall he take to wife.
וְלֹֽא־יְחַלֵּ֥ל זַרְע֖וֹ בְּעַמָּ֑יו כִּ֛י אֲנִ֥י יְהוָ֖ה מְקַדְּשֽׁוֹ	15[4]	And he shall not profane his seed among his people; for I am the LORD who sanctify him.
וַיְדַבֵּ֥ר יְהוָ֖ה אֶל־מֹשֶׁ֥ה לֵּאמֹֽר	16[5]	And the LORD spoke to Moses, saying:
דַּבֵּ֥ר אֶל־אַהֲרֹ֖ן לֵאמֹ֑ר אִ֣ישׁ מִֽזַּרְעֲךָ֞ לְדֹרֹתָ֗ם אֲשֶׁ֨ר יִהְיֶ֥ה בוֹ֙ מ֔וּם לֹ֣א יִקְרַ֔ב לְהַקְרִ֖יב לֶ֥חֶם אֱלֹהָֽיו	17[6]	Speak to Aaron, saying: Whoever of your seed throughout their generations who has a blemish, he shall not approach to offer the bread of his God.
כִּ֥י כָל־אִ֛ישׁ אֲשֶׁר־בּ֥וֹ מ֖וּם לֹ֥א יִקְרָ֑ב	18[7]	For whichever man has a blemish, he shall not approach: a blind man, or a

---

[1] Leviticus 21:13 - 2 Corinthians 11:2, b.Bechorot [Tosefot] 3a, b.Chullin [Tosefot] 88a, b.Horayot 12b, b.Ketubot [Rashi] 30a, b.Ketubot 97b 1b, b.Kiddushin 77a, b.Sanhedrin [Rashi] 18b, b.Yevamot [Rashi] 59b 61a, b.Yevamot 59a, b.Zevachim [Rashi] 13a, Commandment #384, Jastrow 470b, Ezekiel 20:22, Leviticus 21:7, m.Horayot 3:4, m.Yevamot 9:1, mt.Hilchot Ishut 1:8, mt.Hilchot Naarah Betulah 1:6, mt.Hilchot Issurei Biah 17:13, Revelation 14:4, mt.Hilchot Sanhedrin vHainshin Hameurim Lahem 18:2, y.Bikkurim 1:5, y.Horayot 3:2, y.Ketubot 1:3, y.Kiddushin 4:6, y.Yevamot 8:2, z.Emor 29
Leviticus 21:13-14 - 4QpaleoExodm
[2] LXX adds *of his own tribe*
[3] Leviticus 21:14 - 4Q251 11, b.Avodah Zara [Tosefot] 36b, b.Bava Metzia [Tosefot] 30a, b.Chagigah [Rashi] 14b, b.Ketubot 29b, b.Kiddushin [Rashi] 10a, b.Kiddushin 64a 77ab 78a, b.Menachot [Rashi] 58b, b.Pesachim [Tosefot] 41b, b.Sanhedrin [Rashi] 18b, b.Temurah 5b, b.Yevamot 59a 60a 61ab 77b, Commandment #385, Ezekiel 20:22, Guide for the Perplexed 3:49, Leviticus 21:7, Leviticus.R 24:6, m.Horayot 3:4, m.Kiddushin 4:1, m.Sanhedrin 2:1, m.Yevamot 9:1, Mas.Derek Eretz Rabbah 1:6, Mas.Semachot 4:4, mt.Hilchot Ishut 1:7 1:7, mt.Hilchot Melachim uMichamoteihem 7:8, y.Bikkurim 1:5, y.Horayot 2:7, y.Kiddushin 4:6, y.Sanhedrin 9:1, y.Yevamot 6:2 6:4 8:2 11:1, z.Emor 35 398
[4] Leviticus 21:15 - 1 Corinthians 7:14, b.Bechorot 56b, b.Ketubot 14b 29b, b.Kiddushin 64a 68a 77a 78a, b.Niddah [Rashi] 69b, b.Pesachim [Rashi] 72b, b.Sanhedrin [Rashi] 51a, b.Sotah [Rashi] 6a, b.Sotah 23b 26b, b.Temurah 5b 29b, b.Yevamot [Rashi] 15b 44b, b.Yevamot 69a 1b, Commandment #386, Ezra 3:2 9:2, Genesis 18:19, Jastrow 470a, Leviticus 21:8, m.Bikkurim 4:4, m.Orlah 2:16, m.Yevamot 9:1, Malachi 2:11 2:15, mt.Hilchot Sanhedrin vHainshin Hameurim Lahem 19:4, Nehemiah 13:23-13:29, Romans 11:16, y.Kiddushin 4:6, y.Makkot 1:1, y.Sotah 3:7 4:1, y.Yevamot 6:1 6:2 8:3, z.Acharei Mot 78b, z.Emor 90a, z.Emor 33
[5] Leviticus 21:16 - m.Avot 5:6, m.Chullin 1:6
Leviticus 21:16-23 - mt.Hilchot Nesiat Kapayim 15:2, mt.Hilchot Beit HaBechirah 7:20
Leviticus 21:16-24 - mt.Hilchot Beit Habechirah 5:8 5:9 7:20
[6] Leviticus 21:17 - 1 Thessalonians 2:10, 1 Timothy 3:2, b.Chullin 24ab, b.Ketubot 72b, b.Yevamot 1b, b.Zevachim [Rashi] 99a, Commandment #387, Hebrews 7:26, Leviticus 3:11 3:16 10:3 21:6 21:21 22:20-25, m.Avot 5:6, m.Bikkurim 4:4, m.Ketubot 7:7, m.Kiddushin 2:5, m.Middot 2:5, m.Orlah 2:16, mt.Hilchot Biat haMikdash 6:1, mt.Hilchot Sanhedrin vHainshin Hameurim Lahem 19:4, Numbers 16:5, Numbers.R 9:7, Philo De Specialibus Legibus I 117, Psalms 65:5, z.Emor 90b 41, z.Vayishlach 18
Leviticus 21:17-20 - 4QLevb
Leviticus 21:17-23 - 4QMMT B 49-54, m.Megillah 4:7
[7] Leviticus 21:18 - 1 Timothy 3:2-3 3:7, b.Bechorot 43b 44a, b.Yevamot [Tosefot] 32b, Isaiah 8:10, Jastrow 1058a 1594a 1627b, Leviticus 22:19-25, m.Avot 5:6, m.Terumot 8:1, Matthew 23:16-17 23:19, Midrash Psalms 68:9, mt.Hilchot Biat haMikdash 6:2 6:4 7:5 7:9 8:7, t.Bechorot 4:10, Titus 1:7 1:10, z.Pekudei 237a, z.Emor 42 46, z.Pekudei 320, z.Pinchas 630

אִישׁ עִוֵּר אוֹ פִסֵּחַ אוֹ חָרֻם אוֹ שָׂרוּעַ

lame, *or he who has anything maimed, or anything too long*[1],

אוֹ אִישׁ אֲשֶׁר־יִהְיֶה בוֹ שֶׁבֶר רָגֶל אוֹ שֶׁבֶר יָד

19[2] or a man who *is broken-footed, or broken-handed*[3],

אוֹ־גִבֵּן אוֹ־דַק אוֹ תְּבַלֻּל בְּעֵינוֹ אוֹ גָרָב אוֹ יַלֶּפֶת אוֹ מְרוֹחַ אָשֶׁךְ

20[4] or *crook-backed, or a dwarf, or who has his eye overspread, or is scabbed, or scurvy, or has his stones crushed*[5];

כָּל־אִישׁ אֲשֶׁר־בּוֹ מוּם מִזֶּרַע אַהֲרֹן הַכֹּהֵן לֹא יִגַּשׁ לְהַקְרִיב אֶת־אִשֵּׁי יְהוָה מוּם בּוֹ אֵת לֶחֶם אֱלֹהָיו לֹא יִגַּשׁ לְהַקְרִיב

21[6] No man of the seed of Aaron the priest, who has a blemish, shall come near to offer the offerings of the LORD made by fire; he has a blemish; he shall not come near to offer the bread of his God.

לֶחֶם אֱלֹהָיו מִקָּדְשֵׁי הַקֳּדָשִׁים וּמִן־הַקֳּדָשִׁים יֹאכֵל

22[7] He may eat the bread of his God, both of the most holy, and of the holy.

אַךְ אֶל־הַפָּרֹכֶת לֹא יָבֹא וְאֶל־הַמִּזְבֵּחַ לֹא יִגַּשׁ כִּי־מוּם בּוֹ וְלֹא יְחַלֵּל אֶת־מִקְדָּשַׁי כִּי אֲנִי יְהוָה מְקַדְּשָׁם

23[8] Only he shall not go into the veil, nor come near to the altar, because he has a blemish; so he does not profane My holy places; for I am the LORD who sanctifies them.

וַיְדַבֵּר מֹשֶׁה אֶל־אַהֲרֹן וְאֶל־בָּנָיו וְאֶל־כָּל־בְּנֵי יִשְׂרָאֵל

24[9] And Moses spoke to Aaron, and to his sons, and to all *the children of*[10] Israel.

---

[1] LXX *with his nose disfigured, or his ears cut*

[2] Leviticus 21:19 - b.Bechorot 45a, b.Yevamot 1b, Midrash Psalms 68:9, mt.Hilchot Biat haMikdash 6:2 6:4 6:7 7:9 7:10, t.Sanhedrin 12:1

[3] LXX *has a broken hand or a broken foot*

[4] Leviticus 21:20 - b.Bechorot 43a-44b, b.Megillah 29a, b.Pesachim [Rashi] 73a, b.Sanhedrin [Tosefot] 4b, b.Zevachim [Rashi] 35b 85b, Deuteronomy 23:3, Ein Yaakov Megillah:29a, Genesis.R 99 [Excl]:1, Isaiah 8:3, Jastrow 171a 203a 206b 207b 208a 509b 762b 838b 841a 857a 987a 1361a, Josephus Antiquities 4.8.40, m.Bechorot 7:2, Mekhilta de R'Shimon bar Yochai Bachodesh 51:1, Mekilta de R'Ishmael Bahodesh 4:20, Midrash Psalms 68:9, Midrash Tanchuma Bamidbar 7, mt.Hilchot Biat haMikdash 6:4 7:5 7:8 7:10 8:4 8:12, Numbers.R 1:8, t.Bechorot 5:4

[5] LXX *humpbacked, or blear-eyed, or who has lost his eyelashes, or a man who has a malignant ulcer, or tetter, or one who has lost a testicle*

[6] Leviticus 21:21 - b.Bechorot 43a, b.Chullin [Rashi] 24b, b.Eruvin [Rashi] 105a, b.Zevachim [Rashi] 16a, Commandment #388, Leviticus 21:6 21:8 21:17, Mesillat Yesharim 26:Trait of Kedushah, mt.Hilchot Biat haMikdash 6:1 6:4
Leviticus 21:21-24 - 4QLeve

[7] Leviticus 21:22 - 1 Corinthians 9:13, b.Yevamot [Rashi] 33a, b.Zevachim 11b 102a [Rashi] 15b 99a, Leviticus 2:3 2:10 6:16-17 6:29 7:1 22:10-13 24:8-9, mt.Hilchot Biat haMikdash 6:1 6:12, mt.Hilchot Maaseh haKorbanot 10:17, Numbers 18:9-10 18:19, z.Vayishlach 166b, z.Naso 187
Leviticus 21:22-32 - 4QpaleoExodm

[8] Leviticus 21:23 - b.Bechorot 43b, b.Eruvin 105a, b.Kiddushin [Rashi] 66b, b.Sanhedrin 84a [Tosefot] 84a, b.Sheviit [Rashi] 6b, b.Zevachim [Rashi] 15b, Commandment #389, Exodus 30:6-8 40:26-27, Ezekiel 44:9-14, Leviticus 15:31 21:12, mt.Hilchot Biat haMikdash 6:1, mt.Hilchot Sanhedrin vHainshin Hameurim Lahem 19:4, z.Acharei Mot 78b, z.Vayeshev 181a, z.Vayeshev 37

[9] Leviticus 21:24 - 1 Timothy 1:18, 1QpaleoLev, 2 Timothy 2:2, 4QLevb, Colossians 4:17, Malachi 2:1-7, Mekhilta de R'Shimon bar Yochai Pisha 3:2

[10] Missing in 4QLeva; found in 1QpaleoLev, LXX, MT, SP

Emor – Chapter 22

וַיְדַבֵּר יְהוָה אֶל־מֹשֶׁה לֵּאמֹר

דַּבֵּר אֶל־אַהֲרֹן וְאֶל־בָּנָיו וְיִנָּזְרוּ
מִקָּדְשֵׁי בְנֵי־יִשְׂרָאֵל וְלֹא יְחַלְּלוּ אֶת־
שֵׁם קָדְשִׁי אֲשֶׁר הֵם מַקְדִּשִׁים לִי אֲנִי
יְהוָה

אֱמֹר אֲלֵהֶם לְדֹרֹתֵיכֶם כָּל־אִישׁ
אֲשֶׁר־יִקְרַב מִכָּל־זַרְעֲכֶם אֶל־
הַקָּדָשִׁים אֲשֶׁר יַקְדִּישׁוּ בְנֵי־יִשְׂרָאֵל
לַיהוָה וְטֻמְאָתוֹ עָלָיו וְנִכְרְתָה הַנֶּפֶשׁ
הַהִוא מִלְּפָנַי אֲנִי יְהוָה

אִישׁ אִישׁ מִזֶּרַע אַהֲרֹן וְהוּא צָרוּעַ אוֹ
זָב בַּקָּדָשִׁים לֹא יֹאכַל עַד אֲשֶׁר יִטְהָר
וְהַנֹּגֵעַ בְּכָל־טְמֵא־נֶפֶשׁ אוֹ אִישׁ אֲשֶׁר־
תֵּצֵא מִמֶּנּוּ שִׁכְבַת־זָרַע

אוֹ־אִישׁ אֲשֶׁר יִגַּע בְּכָל־שֶׁרֶץ אֲשֶׁר

1[1] And the LORD spoke Moses, saying:

2[2] Speak Aaron and to his sons, who separate themselves from the things of the children of Israel, which they hallow to Me, they shall not profane My holy name: I am the LORD.

3[3] Say to them: Whoever of all your seed throughout your generations, who approaches the holy things, which the children of Israel hallow to the LORD, having his uncleanness on him, that soul shall be cut off from before Me: I am the LORD[4].

4[5] Whomever of the seed of Aaron is a leper, or has an *issue*[6], he shall not eat the holy things, until he is clean. And whomever touches anyone who is unclean by the dead; or from whomever issues a flow of seed;

5[7] or whoever touches any swarming[1]

---

[1] Leviticus 22:1 - Gates of Repentance 3.090
Leviticus 22:1-6 - 1QpaleoLev
[2] Leviticus 22:2 - b.Chullin [Tosefot] 114b, b.Gittin [Tosefot] 60a, b.Meilah [Rashi] 10a, b.Menachot [Rashi] 20a, b.Sanhedrin [Rashi] 83a, b.Shabbat 33a, b.Sheviit [Rashi] 18b, b.Temurah 3a, b.Yevamot [Rashi] 32b, b.Zevachim 15b 16a 14a 44a 45ab [Rashi] 15b 19b 46a 109a 112b [Tosefot] 18a 43a, Deuteronomy 15:19, Ein Yaakov Shabbat 33a, Exodus 13:12 4:38, Gates of Repentance 3.136, Jastrow 891b, Leviticus 15:31 18:21 19:12 20:3 21:6 22:3-6 22:32, Leviticus.R 19:2 19:2, m.Zevachim 1:2, mt.Hilchot Biat haMikdash 4:1, mt.Hilchot Sanhedrin vHainshin Hameurim Lahem 19:2, Numbers 6:3-8 18:32, Numbers.R 10:8, Sifre Numbers 23:3, Song of Songs.R 5:11, z.Acharei Mot 78b
Leviticus 22:2-3 - Commandment #390
Leviticus 22:2-33 - 4QLevb
[3] Leviticus 22:3 - 2 Thessalonians 1:9, b.Bava Batra 120a, b.Kereitot [Rashi] 2ab, b.Meilah 10b, b.Menachot [Tosefot] 25b, b.Sheviit [Rashi] 7a, b.Zevachim 45b [Rashi] 15b 46ab [Tosefot] 43b, Exodus 33:14-15, Leviticus 7:20-21, m.Keritot 1:1, m.Meilah 1:2, m.Zevachim 3:4, Matthew 1:41, Mekilta de R'Ishmael Pisha 8:98, Mekilta de R'Ishmael Pisha 10:46, Numbers 19:13, Psalms 16:11 51:12, Tanya Igeret Hateshuvah §5, y.Sheviit 1:2-3, z.Acharei Mot 78b, z.Terumah 142b 299 820
Leviticus 22:3-4 - Commandment #405
[4] LXX adds *your God*
[5] Leviticus 22:4 - b.Avodah Zara 68b, b.Bava Batra 9b, b.Bava Kamma [Rashi] 25a, b.Bava Kamma 25b, b.Bechorot 3b 40b, b.Chagigah 4b, b.Chullin [Rashi] 113b, b.Eruvin [Rashi] 69b, b.Kereitot [Rashi] 2a, b.Makkot [Rashi] 18b, b.Makkot 14b, b.Menachot [Tosefot] 14b, b.Niddah [Rashi] 32a, b.Niddah 41b 43b, b.Shabbat 64a, b.Sheviit 6b, b.Yevamot [Rashi] 73b, b.Yevamot 70a 71a 72b 74a 75a, b.Zevachim [Rashi] 43b 45b, b.Zevachim [Tosefot] 15b 14a 33b, Guide for the Perplexed 3:46, Leviticus 2:3 2:10 6:25-29 11:24-28 11:39 13:2-3 13:44-46 14:1-32 15:2-3 15:13-16 21:1 21:22, mt.Hilchot Sanhedrin vHainshin Hameurim Lahem 19:2, mt.Hilchot Shaar Avot Hatuman 5:1, mt.Hilchot Terumot 7:1, mt.Hilchot Tumat Ochalin 16:8, Numbers 18:9 18:19 19:11-16, Philo De Specialibus Legibus I 118, y.Yevamot 8:1
Leviticus 22:4-6 - 4QLeV1
[6] LXX *issue of the reins*
[7] Leviticus 22:5 - b.Bava Batra 9b, b.Bava Kamma 25b, b.Niddah 43b 55a, b.Shabbat 64a, b.Zevachim [Rashi] 43b, Leviticus 11:24-11:28 11:43-11:44 15:7 15:19

יִטְמָא־לוֹ אוֹ בְאָדָם אֲשֶׁר יִטְמָא־לוֹ
לְכֹל טֻמְאָתוֹ

נֶפֶשׁ אֲשֶׁר תִּגַּע־בּוֹ וְטָמְאָה עַד־הָעֶרֶב 6²
וְלֹא יֹאכַל מִן־הַקֳּדָשִׁים כִּי אִם־רָחַץ
בְּשָׂרוֹ בַּמָּיִם

וּבָא הַשֶּׁמֶשׁ וְטָהֵר וְאַחַר יֹאכַל מִן־ 7⁴
הַקֳּדָשִׁים כִּי לַחְמוֹ הוּא

נְבֵלָה וּטְרֵפָה לֹא יֹאכַל לְטָמְאָה־בָהּ 8⁶
אֲנִי יְהוָה

וְשָׁמְרוּ אֶת־מִשְׁמַרְתִּי וְלֹא־יִשְׂאוּ עָלָיו 9⁷
חֵטְא וּמֵתוּ בוֹ כִּי יְחַלְּלֻהוּ אֲנִי יְהוָה
מְקַדְּשָׁם

thing, by which he is made unclean, or a man of whom he may take uncleanness, whatever uncleanness he has;

6² ³The soul who touches any such shall be unclean until the evening, and shall not eat of the holy things, unless he bathes his flesh in water.

7⁴ And when the sun is down, he shall be clean; and afterward he may eat of the holy things, because *it*⁵ is his bread.

8⁶ That which dies of itself, or is torn of beasts, he shall not eat to defile himself: I am the LORD.

9⁷ They shall, therefore, keep My charge, lest they bear sin for it, and die, if they profane it: I am the LORD who sanctifies them.

---

[1] 4QLeve adds *unclean*

[2] Leviticus 22:6 - 1 Corinthians 6:11, b.Makkot 19b, b.Niddah [Tosefot] 41b, b.Yevamot 73b 74b, b.Zevachim [Rashi] 43b, Haggai 2:13, Hebrews 10:22, Leviticus 11:24-25 15:5 16:24-28, m.Challah 1:9, Numbers 19:7-19:10, Philo De Somniis I 81
Leviticus 22:6-7 - Ein Yaakov Berachot:2a

[3] 11QpaleoLeva

[4] Leviticus 22:7 - 1 Corinthians 9:4 9:13-14, b.Berachot 2a, b.Chullin [Rashi] 113b, b.Pesachim 46b, b.Sanhedrin [Rashi] 83b, b.Shabbat 14b, b.Sheviit [Rashi] 6b, b.Sotah [Rashi] 29b, b.Yevamot 70a 74b 75a, b.Zevachim [Rashi] 43b, b.Zevachim [Tosefot] 14a, Deuteronomy 18:3-4, Ecclesiastes.R 8:13, Ein Yaakov Berachot:2a, Jastrow 328a 517a 520b 814b, Leviticus 21:22, m.Challah 1:9, m.Negaim 14:3, m.Parah 3:7, m.Zevachim 2:1 12:1, Midrash Tanchuma Emor 9 11, mt.Hilchot Biat haMikdash 4:4, mt.Hilchot Shaar Avot Hatuman 11:3, mt.Hilchot Terumot 7:2, Numbers 18:11-19, y.Berachot 1:1, y.Bikkurim 2:1, y.Orlah 2:1, z.Balak 80, z.Metzora 13, z.Mishpatim 137

[5] LXX *they are*

[6] Leviticus 22:8 - 4Q251 7, b.Bava Kamma [Rashi] 63a, b.Chullin [Rashi] 20b 27b 140a, b.Chullin [Tosefot] 71a 120b, b.Chullin 1b, b.Niddah [Rashi] 42a, b.Niddah 42b, b.Sheviit [Rashi] 7b, b.Yevamot [Rashi] 83b, b.Zevachim [Rashi] 50b, b.Zevachim 69b 70a, Deuteronomy 14:21, Exodus 22:31, Ezekiel 20:31, Leviticus 7:24 11:39-11:40 17:15, z.Acharei Mot 78b

[7] Leviticus 22:9 - b.Chagigah 18b, b.Chullin [Tosefot] 101ab 120b 130b, b.Chullin 113b 136a, b.Kereitot 7a, b.Makkot [Rashi] 13a, b.Meilah [Rashi] 18b, b.Meilah [Tosefot] 20a, b.Menachot [Rashi] 77b, b.Menachot [Tosefot] 62b, b.Niddah [Rashi] 13b, b.Pesachim [Rashi] 32b 33a, b.Sanhedrin [Rashi] 15a 84a, b.Sanhedrin 83ab 90b, b.Shabbat [Rashi] 69b, b.Sheviit [Rashi] 6b 24b, b.Sheviit [Tosefot] 23b 16a, b.Yevamot [Rashi] 73b 75a, b.Yevamot 86a, b.Zevachim [Rashi] 11b 14a 43b, b.Zevachim 45a, Ein Yaakov Sanhedrin:90b, Exodus 4:43, Leviticus 10:1-10:2 16:2 22:16, m.Shevuot 8:3, mt.Hilchot Biat haMikdash 4:1, mt.Hilchot Sanhedrin vHainshin Hameurim Lahem 19:2, mt.Hilchot Terumot 6:6 7:1, Numbers 18:22 18:32, y.Bikkurim 2:1, y.Rosh Hashanah 1:3, y.Sheviit 1:2, z.Acharei Mot 78b

וְכָל־זָר לֹא־יֹאכַל קֹדֶשׁ תּוֹשַׁב כֹּהֵן
וְשָׂכִיר לֹא־יֹאכַל קֹדֶשׁ

וְכֹהֵן כִּי־יִקְנֶה נֶפֶשׁ קִנְיַן כַּסְפּוֹ הוּא
יֹאכַל בּוֹ וִילִיד בֵּיתוֹ הֵם יֹאכְלוּ
בְלַחְמוֹ

וּבַת־כֹּהֵן כִּי תִהְיֶה לְאִישׁ זָר הִוא
בִּתְרוּמַת הַקֳּדָשִׁים לֹא תֹאכֵל

וּבַת־כֹּהֵן כִּי תִהְיֶה אַלְמָנָה וּגְרוּשָׁה
וְזֶרַע אֵין לָהּ וְשָׁבָה אֶל־בֵּית אָבִיהָ
כִּנְעוּרֶיהָ מִלֶּחֶם אָבִיהָ תֹּאכֵל וְכָל־זָר
לֹא־יֹאכַל בּוֹ

10[1] No common man shall eat of the holy thing: a tenant of a priest, or a hired servant, shall not eat of the holy thing.

11[2] But if a priest buys any soul, the purchase of his money, he may eat of it; and *he who is born*[3] in his house, they may eat of his bread.

12[4] And if a priest's daughter is married to a common man, she shall not eat what is set apart from the holy things.

13[5] But if a priest's daughter is a widow, or divorced, and has no child, and returns to her father's house, as in her youth, she may eat of her father's bread; but there shall no common man may eat of it.

[1] Leviticus 22:10 - 1 Samuel 21:6, b.Bava Metzia [Rashi] 53a, b.Chagigah 18b, b.Kereitot 4b, b.Ketubot 25a, b.Kiddushin 69b, b.Makkot [Rashi] 13a 18b, b.Menachot [Rashi] 74a, b.Pesachim [Rashi] 32b 33a 96a, b.Pesachim 23a, b.Sanhedrin 83b, b.Sheviit [Rashi] 24b, b.Yevamot [Rashi] 85b, b.Yevamot 68ab 70ab 71a, b.Zevachim [Tosefot] 33b, b.Zevachim 82b, Commandment #402 [uncircumcised persons may not eat terumah; the law of the korban Pesach applies to other holy things by similarity of phrase; the prohibition against uncircumcised folk eating holy things is an essential principle of the Torah] #406 #407, Exodus 5:33, Jastrow 412a 712a, m.Edoyot 3:2, m.Gittin 3:3, m.Shabbat 9:6, m.Yevamot 7:1, Matthew 12:4, Mekhilta de R'Shimon bar Yochai Pisha 17:3, Midrash Tanchuma Bo 10, mt.Hilchot Eruvin 1:14, mt.Hilchot Maaser Sheni vneta Revai 3:5, mt.Hilchot Sanhedrin vHainshin Hameurim Lahem 19:2, mt.Hilchot Terumot 6:5 7:10, Philo De Specialibus Legibus I 120, y.Ketubot 3:2, y.Shabbat 2:5, y.Terumot 7:1, y.Yevamot 8:1, z.Acharei Mot 73b 305, z.Mishpatim 121b 136 507, z.Ha'azinu 203, z.Ki Tetze 134 Leviticus 22:10-16 - 4QMMT b 24-27
[2] Leviticus 22:11 - b.Bava Batra [Rashbam] 138a 141b, b.Gittin [Rashi] 28b, b.Gittin 42b 43a 85a, b.Ketubot 57b 58a, b.Kiddushin [Rashi] 10b, b.Kiddushin 5a, b.Nedarim [Ran] 73b, b.Niddah [Rashi] 43b, b.Niddah 44a, b.Sanhedrin [Rashi] 55b, b.Yevamot [Rashi] 56a 67a 69b 72a, b.Yevamot 57a 66a 67b, Exodus 12:44, Genesis 17:13, m.Eduyot 3:2 8:2, m.Gittin 1:6 3:3, m.Terumot 8:1 11:9, m.Yevamot 7:1-2 9:5 11:5 11:7, mt.Hilchot Terumot 6:1 7:18 8:5, Numbers 18:11-13, y.Ketubot 5:4, y.Sotah 3:7, y.Terumot 11:4, y.Yevamot 7:1 7:4 9:5
Leviticus 22:11-17 - 4QLev1
[3] 4QLevb LXX *those who are born*
[4] Leviticus 22:12 - b.Avodah Zara [Tosefot] 58b, b.Chullin [Tosefot] 131b, b.Ketubot 25a, b.Kiddushin 69b, b.Niddah [Rashi] 44b, b.Niddah [Tosefot] 69b, b.Pesachim [Rashi] 49a, b.Sanhedrin [Rashi] 55b 69a, b.Sanhedrin 51a, b.Sotah [Rashi] 29a, b.Sotah 26b, b.Yevamot [Tosefot] 15b, b.Yevamot 68ab 69a 87a, Commandment #500, Ein Yaakov Pesachim:49a, Isaiah 16:13, Leviticus 21:3, m.Eduyot 3:2 3:6, m.Gittin 3:3, m.Yevamot 3:10 7:1 7:2 13:2, Mas.Semachot 1:1, Midrash Psalms 137:11, mt.Hilchot Issurei Biah 18:3, mt.Hilchot Sanhedrin vHainshin Hameurim Lahem 19:4, mt.Hilchot Terumot 6:7 10:12, Philo De Specialibus Legibus I 129, Tanya Igeret Hakodesh §12, y.Yevamot 6:3 9:5, z.Mishpatim 95a 21
[5] Leviticus 22:13 - b.Bava Batra [Tosefot] 109a 115a, b.Chullin [Rashi] 41a, b.Kiddushin 4a, b.Kiddushin 75b, b.Niddah [Rashi] 43b, b.Niddah 44a, b.Pesachim [Rashi] 49a, b.Sanhedrin 51a, b.Sotah [Rashi] 28a, b.Sotah 26b, b.Yevamot [Rashi] 86b, b.Yevamot 45a 67b 68ab 70a 87ab, Genesis 14:11, Jastrow 1053b, Leviticus 10:14, m.Edoyot 3:2, m.Gittin 3:3, m.Terumot 7:2, m.Yevamot 7:6 9:6 3:10 7:1, mt.Hilchot Terumot 8:2, Numbers 18:11-18:19, Numbers.R 7:4, Tanya Likutei Aramim §31, y.Sotah 4:1, y.Yevamot 7:4 7:6 9:5 9:8, z.Mishpatim 21 134 101a, z.Vayikra 7a, z.Pinchas 612-614, z.Vayikra 92 96 97

וְאִישׁ כִּי־יֹאכַל קֹדֶשׁ בִּשְׁגָגָה וְיָסַף חֲמִשִׁיתוֹ עָלָיו וְנָתַן לַכֹּהֵן אֶת־הַקֹּדֶשׁ

14[1] And if a man eats of the holy thing through error, then he shall put its fifth part to it, and shall give to the priest the holy thing.

וְלֹא יְחַלְּלוּ אֶת־קָדְשֵׁי בְּנֵי יִשְׂרָאֵל אֵת אֲשֶׁר־יָרִימוּ לַיהוָה

15[2] And they shall not profane the holy things of the children of Israel, which they set apart to the LORD;

וְהִשִּׂיאוּ אוֹתָם עֲוֹן אַשְׁמָה בְּאָכְלָם אֶת־קָדְשֵׁיהֶם כִּי אֲנִי יְהוָה מְקַדְּשָׁם

16[3] And cause them to bear the iniquity that brings guilt, when they eat their holy things; for I am the LORD who sanctifies them.

וַיְדַבֵּר יְהוָה אֶל־מֹשֶׁה לֵּאמֹר

17[4] And the LORD spoke to Moses, saying:

דַּבֵּר אֶל־אַהֲרֹן וְאֶל־בָּנָיו וְאֶל כָּל־בְּנֵי יִשְׂרָאֵל וְאָמַרְתָּ אֲלֵהֶם אִישׁ אִישׁ מִבֵּית יִשְׂרָאֵל וּמִן־הַגֵּר בְּיִשְׂרָאֵל אֲשֶׁר יַקְרִיב קָרְבָּנוֹ לְכָל־נִדְרֵיהֶם וּלְכָל־נִדְבוֹתָם אֲשֶׁר־יַקְרִיבוּ לַיהוָה לְעֹלָה

18[5] Speak to Aaron, and to his sons, and to all the children of Israel, and say to them: Whoever of the house of Israel, or of the strangers[6] in Israel, who brings his offering, whether it is any of their vows, and[7] any of their freewill offerings that are brought to the LORD for a burnt offering;

---

[1] Leviticus 22:14 - b.Bava Kamma [Tosefot] 7a, b.Bava Metzia [Rashi] 52b, b.Bava Metzia [Tosefot] 47a, b.Bava Metzia 54ab 99b, b.Berachot [Rashi] 35b, b.Chagigah [Rashi] 18b, b.Chullin [Tosefot] 13b, b.Chullin 136a, b.Gittin [Rashi] 54a, b.Gittin [Tosefot] 20a, b.Kereitot [Rashi] 7a, b.Kereitot 6b, b.Meilah [Rashi] 15a 18b, b.Meilah 19a, b.Menachot [Rashi] 60a 77b, b.Menachot [Tosefot] 34b, b.Nedarim 34b, b.Pesachim [Rashi] 31b 32b 34b, b.Pesachim 32ab, b.Sanhedrin [Tosefot] 4b, b.Shabbat [Rashi] 25a 69b, b.Yevamot [Rashi] 90a, b.Yoma 80b 81a, Jastrow 755a, Leviticus 5:15-5:19 3:13 3:15, m.Bava Metzia 4:7, m.Bikkurim 1:8, m.Meilah 4:2, m.Terumot 6:6, mt.Hilchot Sanhedrin vHainshin Hameurim Lahem 18:3, mt.Hilchot Terumot 6:6 10:18 10:26, y.Ketubot 3:2, y.Terumot 6:1-3 7:1, z.Ha'azinu 203, z.Mishpatim 507 Leviticus 22:14-16 - z.Mishpatim 121b
[2] Leviticus 22:15 - b.Arachin [Rashi] 5b, b.Chullin [Rashi] 136a, b.Chullin 130b, b.Makkot [Rashi] 13a, b.Niddah 32a, b.Sanhedrin 83a, b.Temurah [Tosefot] 3a, b.Zevachim [Tosefot] 2a 15b, b.Zevachim 3b 11b 45a 46b, Commandment #408, Ezekiel 22:26, Leviticus 19:8 22:9, Leviticus.R 1:9, mt.Hilchot Maachalot Assurot 10:19, mt.Hilchot Sanhedrin vHainshin Hameurim Lahem 19:2, Numbers 18:32, y.Demai 6:2, y.Kiddushin 2:9, y.Maaser Sheni 2:1, y.Nedarim 11:3, y.Shabbat 9:4, y.Taanit 1:6, y.Yoma 8:1
[3] Leviticus 22:16 - 1 Peter 2:24, 1QS 5:14-15, b.Sanhedrin 90b, Ein Yaakov Sanhedrin:90b, Isaiah 53:11-53:12, Leviticus 7:18 20:8 22:9, mt.Hilchot Maachalot Assurot 10:19, Numbers.R 10:17, Psalms 38:5, Sifre Numbers 24:1, z.Acharei Mot 78b
[4] Leviticus 22:17 - b.Pesachim 42a, b.Temurah 7b [Rashi] 6a, Pesikta Rabbati 14:10, y.Nazir 5:1 Leviticus 22:17-20 - Pesikta Rabbati 14:10
[5] Leviticus 22:18 - Acts 18:18, b.Avodah Zara [Tosefot] 5b, b.Bava Batra [Tosefot] 8a, b.Chullin [Rashi] 5a, b.Chullin 13b, b.Kiddushin [Rashi] 24b, b.Menachot [Rashi] 5a 25a 51b, b.Menachot [Tosefot] 14b, b.Menachot 73b 24a, b.Nazir 25a 62a, b.Nedarim [Ran] 78a, b.Shekalim [Taklin Chadatin] 3b, b.Shekalim 12b, b.Temurah [Tosefot] 7a, b.Temurah 2b 3a, b.Yevamot [Tosefot] 32b, b.Zevachim 45a, Deuteronomy 12:6 12:17 16:10, Ecclesiastes 5:5, Jonah 1:16 2:9, Leviticus 1:2 1:10 7:16 17:10 17:13 23:38, mt.Hilchot Issurei Mizbeiach 3:1, mt.Hilchot Maaseh haKorbanot 1:8, Nahum 2:1, Numbers 15:3 15:14-15:16, Psalms 22:26 56:13 61:6 61:9 65:2 66:13 20:14 20:18, Sifre.z Numbers Naso 6:2, y.Nazir 9:1, y.Shekalim 4:4, z.Mishpatim 95a
Leviticus 22:18-20 - t.Makkot 5:4
Leviticus 22:18-21 - Leviticus.R 2:9 2:9
[6] 4QLevb adds who dwell
[7] 4QLevb or

לִרְצֹנְכֶם תָּמִים זָכָר בַּבָּקָר בַּכְּשָׂבִים
וּבָעִזִּים

19[1] That you may be accepted, you shall offer[2] a male without blemish, of the cattle, of the sheep, or of the goats.

כֹּל אֲשֶׁר־בּוֹ מוּם לֹא תַקְרִיבוּ כִּי־לֹא
לְרָצוֹן יִהְיֶה לָכֶם

20[3] But you shall not bring whatever has a blemish; it shall not be acceptable for you.

וְאִישׁ כִּי־יַקְרִיב זֶבַח־שְׁלָמִים לַיהוָה
לְפַלֵּא־נֶדֶר אוֹ לִנְדָבָה בַּבָּקָר אוֹ בַצֹּאן
תָּמִים יִהְיֶה לְרָצוֹן כָּל־מוּם לֹא יִהְיֶה־
בּוֹ

21[4] And whoever brings a sacrifice of peace offerings to the LORD in fulfilment of a clearly uttered vow, or *for*[5] a freewill offering[6], of the herd or of the flock, it shall be perfect to be accepted; it shall have no blemish.

עַוֶּרֶת אוֹ שָׁבוּר אוֹ־חָרוּץ אוֹ־יַבֶּלֶת
אוֹ גָרָב אוֹ יַלֶּפֶת לֹא־תַקְרִיבוּ אֵלֶּה
לַיהוָה וְאִשֶּׁה לֹא־תִתְּנוּ מֵהֶם עַל־
הַמִּזְבֵּחַ לַיהוָה

22[7] Blind, or broken, or maimed, or having *a discharge, or scabbed, or scurvy*[8], [9]you shall not offer *these*[10] to the LORD, nor make an offering by fire of them on the altar to the LORD.

וְשׁוֹר וָשֶׂה שָׂרוּעַ וְקָלוּט נְדָבָה תַּעֲשֶׂה
אֹתוֹ וּלְנֵדֶר לֹא יֵרָצֶה

23[11] Either a bullock or a lamb *that has anything too long or too short*[12], that you may offer for a freewill offering;

---

[1] Leviticus 22:19 - 1 Peter 1:19 2:22-24 3:18, 2 Corinthians 5:21, b.Chullin [Rashi] 23a, b.Shekalim 12b, b.Zevachim [Rashi] 35b 85b, Ephesians 5:27, Exodus 12:5, Hebrews 9:14, John 19:4, Leviticus 1:3 1:10 4:32, Luke 23:14 23:41 23:47, Matthew 3:4 3:19 3:24 3:54, mt.Hilchot Maaseh haKorbanot 1:8, Song of Songs.R 4:12, y.Kiddushin 1:5, y.Shekalim 4:4

[2] LXX *your freewill offering*

[3] Leviticus 22:20 - 1 Peter 1:19, b.Menachot 25a, b.Temurah [Rashi] 7b, b.Temurah 5b 6b 14a, Commandment #508 [such beasts are prohibited from being set apart for sacrifice], Deuteronomy 15:21 17:1, Hebrews 9:14, Leviticus 22:25, Malachi 1:8 1:13-14, mt.Hilchot Issurei Mizbeiach 1:2, mt.Hilchot Sanhedrin vHainshin Hameurim Lahem 19:4, z.Emor 46, z.Noach 131, z.Pekudei 956

[4] Leviticus 22:21 - b.Avodah Zara [Rashi] 13b [Tosefot] 6a, b.Bechorot [Tosefot] 34a, b.Bechorot 33b 39a, b.Beitzah 27b, b.Gittin [Rashi] 56a, b.Menachot [Tosefot] 11b, b.Menachot 56b, b.Moed Katan [Rashi] 13a, b.Temurah [Rashi] 21a, Commandment #509 #510, Deuteronomy 23:23-24, Ecclesiastes 5:5-6, Genesis 4:20 35:1-3, Leviticus 3:1 3:6 7:11-38, mt.Hilchot Issurei Mizbeiach 1:1 1:7, mt.Hilchot Sanhedrin vHainshin Hameurim Lahem 19:4, Numbers 15:3 15:8, Proverbs 7:14, Psalms 50:14, t.Makkot 5:4, t.Temurah 1:10, Tanya Igeret Hateshuvah §2, y.Pesachim 1:8, y.Terumot 8:4
Leviticus 22:21-27 - 11QpaleoLeva

[5] 4QLevb *in the way of*

[6] LXX adds *or an offering in your holidays*

[7] Leviticus 22:22 - b.Bechorot 14b 39a 40b 41a, b.Eruvin [Rashi] 103a, b.Sotah 46a, b.Temurah [Rashi] 7b, b.Temurah [Tosefot] 7a 28a, b.Temurah 6b, b.Yoma 63b, b.Zevachim [Rashi] 73b, Commandment #511, Commandment #512, Jastrow 442b 500a, Leviticus 1:9 1:13 3:3 3:5 21:18-21 22:20, Leviticus.R 7:2, Malachi 1:8, mt.Hilchot Biat haMikdash 7:4 7:10 7:11, mt.Hilchot Issurei Mizbeiach 1:4, mt.Hilchot Sanhedrin vHainshin Hameurim Lahem 19:4, Pesikta de R'Kahana 24.5, Sifre Devarim Reeh 126

[8] 11QpaleoLeva *having scabs, or a rash or a discharge*; LXX *or has its tongue cut out, or is troubled with warts, or has a malignant ulcer, or tetters*

[9] 4QLevb adds *or crushed testicles*

[10] 4QLevb *an offering made by fire*

[11] Leviticus 22:23 - b.Bava Kamma [Rashi] 29a, b.Bechorot 3b, b.Chullin [Rashi] 81a, b.Chullin 80b, b.Menachot 25a, b.Pesachim 42a, b.Temurah 5b 6a 7ab 14a, b.Zevachim [Rashi] 114b, Jastrow 1374a, Leviticus 21:18, mt.Hilchot Arachim Vacharamim 5:6, mt.Hilchot Biat haMikdash 7:9, mt.Hilchot Issurei Mizbeiach 2:5, mt.Hilchot Sanhedrin vHainshin Hameurim Lahem 19:4, Pesikta Rabbati 14:10

[12] LXX *with the ears cut off, or that has lost its tail*

וּמָע֖וּךְ וְכָת֣וּת וְנָת֑וּק וְכָר֛וּת לֹ֥א
תַקְרִ֖יבוּ לַֽיהוָ֑ה וּבְאַרְצְכֶ֖ם לֹ֥א תַעֲשֽׂוּ ׃ 24[1]

וּמִיַּ֣ד בֶּן־נֵכָ֗ר לֹ֥א תַקְרִ֛יבוּ אֶת־לֶ֥חֶם
אֱלֹהֵיכֶ֖ם מִכָּל־אֵ֑לֶּה כִּ֣י מָשְׁחָתָ֤ם בָּהֶם֙
מ֣וּם בָּ֔ם לֹ֥א יֵרָצ֖וּ לָכֶֽם ׃ 25[3]

וַיְדַבֵּ֥ר יְהוָ֖ה אֶל־מֹשֶׁ֥ה לֵּאמֹֽר ׃ 26[5]

שׁ֣וֹר אוֹ־כֶ֤שֶׂב אוֹ־עֵז֙ כִּ֣י יִוָּלֵ֔ד וְהָיָ֛ה
שִׁבְעַ֥ת יָמִ֖ים תַּ֣חַת אִמּ֑וֹ וּמִיּ֣וֹם הַשְּׁמִינִ֗י
וָהָ֔לְאָה יֵרָצֶ֔ה לְקָרְבַּ֥ן אִשֶּׁ֖ה לַֽיהוָֽה ׃ 27[6]

but for a vow it shall not be accepted. Whatever has its stones bruised, or crushed, or torn, or cut, you shall not offer[2] to the LORD; nor shall you do thus in your land.

Nor from the hand of a foreigner shall you offer the bread of your God of any of these, because *their corruption is in them*[4], there is a blemish in them; they shall not be accepted for you.

And the LORD spoke to Moses, saying:

When a bullock, or a sheep, or a goat, is brought forth, then it shall be seven days under the dam; but from the eighth day and thereafter it may be accepted for *an offering*[7] made by fire to the LORD.

---

[1] Leviticus 22:24 - b.Bechorot 33b 39b, b.Chagigah 14b, b.Chullin [Tosefot] 13b 115a, b.Kiddushin 25b, b.Menachot 56b, b.Shabbat 11b 111a, b.Temurah [Rashi] 7b, b.Temurah 7a, Commandment #106 #513, Deuteronomy 23:3, Guide for the Perplexed 3:49, Leviticus 21:20 22:20, mt.Hilchot Issurei Biah 16:10, mt.Hilchot Issurei Mizbeiach 1:4, mt.Hilchot Sanhedrin vHainshin Hameurim Lahem 19:4 19:4, t.Yevamot 10:5, z.Mishpatim 108b, z.Acharei Mot 136, z.Mishpatim 275

[2] 11QpaleoLEva adds *these*

[3] Leviticus 22:25 - 1 John 5:18, b.Avodah Zara 23b, b.Bava Kamma [Tosefot] 40b, b.Bechorot 57a, b.Chullin [Tosefot] 13b 115a, b.Chullin 23a, b.Menachot [Tosefot] 73b, b.Sotah 46a, b.Temurah [Rashi] 7b, b.Temurah 7a 28b, b.Yoma 64a, b.Zevachim [Rashi] 81a 114a, b.Zevachim [Tosefot] 72a 74a, b.Zevachim 77b, Commandment #514, Ephesians 2:12, Exodus.R 10:3, Ezra 6:8-10, Leviticus 21:6 21:8 21:21-22, m.Zevachim 8:1, Malachi 1:7-1:8 1:12-14, Midrash Psalms 78:13 105:9, mt.Hilchot Issurei Mizbeiach 1:6 3:6, mt.Hilchot Sanhedrin vHainshin Hameurim Lahem 19:4, Numbers 15:14-16 17:5, Pesikta Rabbati 48:1, Song of Songs.R 1:39, y.Avodah Zarah 2:1, z.Noach 65a

[4] 11QpaleoLEva *they are corrupt*; LXX *corrupted things are in them*

[5] Leviticus 22:26 - b.Megillah 30b, Jastrow 853b, Pesach first day [Pesikta Rabbati 48], z.Emor 91a
Leviticus 22:26-23:44 - Mas.Soferim 17:6, Torah reading for 16th of Nissan and 1st [and 2nd in Chutz LAretz] days of Sukkot, Torah Reading Pesach Day Two Part One, Torah Reading Sukkot Day One, Torah Reading Sukkot Day Two
Leviticus 22:26-27 - Midrash Tanchuma Emor 5
Leviticus 22:26-23:44 - mt.Hilchot Tefilah 13:8 13:12

[6] Leviticus 22:27 - b.Avodah Zara [Rashi] 8a 23b, b.Bava Batra [Rashbam] 121a, b.Bava Kamma [Rashi] 44a, b.Bava Kamma [Tosefot] 11b 77b, b.Bava Kamma 65b 77b 78a, b.Bechorot 14a 54b 57a [Rashi] 21b [Tosefot] 12a, b.Chullin 78a 81a [Rashi] 51b 60a 74b 75a 83a 115a 130a [Tosefot] 78b, b.Megillah [Rashi] 30b, b.Meilah [Rashi] 2b 13a, b.Menachot 6a 38ab [Rashi] 12a 16b [Tosefot] 25a, b.Niddah 41a [Rashi] 40ab, b.Rosh Hashanah [Rashi] 26a, b.Shabbat 135b 136a, b.Shekalim [Taklin Chadatin] 15a, b.Temurah [Tosefot] 24b, b.Yevamot [Rashi] 84a, b.Yoma 63b, b.Zevachim 12a [Rashi] 27b 71b [Tosefot] 114b, Commandment #515, Deuteronomy.R 6:1, Ecclesiastes.R 3:18 3:21, Esther.R 7:11, Exodus 22:30, Exodus.R 31:9, Guide for the Perplexed 3:49, Jastrow 368b 1410a 1541b, Leviticus 12:2-3 19:23-24 22:25, Leviticus.R 27:1 27:3 27:10, Mekhilta de R'Shimon bar Yochai Kaspa 76:4, Mekilta de R'Ishmael Kaspa 1:110, Midrash Psalms 27:6, Midrash Tanchuma Bo 11, Midrash Tanchuma Emor 6-8 10 12 15-16, mt.Hilchot Issurei Mizbeiach 3:4 3:8, Numbers.R 10:14 20:5, Pesikta de R'Kahana 9-7 9.9-10, Pesikta Rabbati 14:2 25:2 48:1-4, Siman 177:1, t.Shabbat 15:7, y.Yevamot 11:7, z.Emor 52 53 59 60 68, z.Pinchas 769, z.Tazria 26 36
Leviticus 22:27-28 - 4QMMT B 36-38, Pesikta Rabbati 48:3

[7] LXX *a burnt offering*

וְשׁ֖וֹר אוֹ־שֶׂ֑ה אֹת֣וֹ וְאֶת־בְּנ֔וֹ לֹ֥א תִשְׁחֲט֖וּ בְּי֥וֹם אֶחָֽד	28[1]	And whether it is cow or ewe, you shall not kill it and its young both in one day.
וְכִי־תִזְבְּח֥וּ זֶֽבַח־תּוֹדָ֖ה לַיהוָ֑ה לִֽרְצֹנְכֶ֖ם תִּזְבָּֽחוּ	29[2]	And when you sacrifice a sacrifice of thanksgiving to the LORD, you shall sacrifice it that you may be accepted.
בַּיּ֤וֹם הַהוּא֙ יֵֽאָכֵ֔ל לֹֽא־תוֹתִ֥ירוּ מִמֶּ֖נּוּ עַד־בֹּ֑קֶר אֲנִ֖י יְהוָֽה	30[3]	On the same day it shall be eaten; you shall leave none of it until the morning: I am the LORD.
וּשְׁמַרְתֶּם֙ מִצְוֹתַ֔י וַעֲשִׂיתֶ֖ם אֹתָ֑ם אֲנִ֖י יְהוָֽה	31[4]	And you shall keep My commandments and do them: *I am the LORD*[5].
וְלֹ֤א תְחַלְּלוּ֙ אֶת־שֵׁ֣ם קָדְשִׁ֔י וְנִ֨קְדַּשְׁתִּ֔י בְּת֖וֹךְ בְּנֵ֣י יִשְׂרָאֵ֑ל אֲנִ֥י יְהוָ֖ה מְקַדִּשְׁכֶֽם	32[6]	And you shall not profane My holy name; but I will be hallowed among the children of Israel: I am the LORD who hallow you,
הַמּוֹצִ֤יא אֶתְכֶם֙ מֵאֶ֣רֶץ מִצְרַ֔יִם לִהְי֥וֹת לָכֶ֖ם לֵאלֹהִ֑ים אֲנִ֖י יְהוָֽה	33[7]	I who brought you out of the land of the Egyptians, to be your God: I am the LORD.

---

[1] Leviticus 22:28 - b.Avodah Zara [Rashi] 5b, b.Bava Kamma [Tosefot] 71b 76a, b.Bechorot 24a [Rashi] 15a [Tosefot] 3a, b.Chullin 78ab 79b 82a 83a [Rashi] 81a [Tosefot] 38b 79a 80b 115a, b.Kereitot [Tosefot] 9b, b.Yoma 64a, Chibbur Yafeh 6 {24a}, Commandment #159, Deuteronomy 14:21 22:6-7, Deuteronomy.R 6:1, Exodus 23:19 10:26, Genesis.R 75:13 76:6, Guide for the Perplexed 3:48, Jastrow 668a 1468b, Lamentations.R 1:50 1:50 Petichata DChakimei:24, Leviticus.R 27:11, m.Avot 5:6, m.Chullin 4:5 5:1-2 5:5 6:3, m.Zevachim 14:2, Midrash Psalms 22:17 52:4 119:32, Midrash Tanchuma Emor 13, mt.Hilchot Maaseh haKorbanot 3:2, mt.Hilchot Sanhedrin vHainshin Hameurim Lahem 16:5 19:4, mt.Hilchot Shechitah 12:1, mt.Hilchot Shevitat Yom Tov 2:4, Pesikta de R'Kahana 9.11, t.Shechitat Chullin 4[5]:5, z.Emor 92a, z.Emor 71

[2] Leviticus 22:29 - 1 Peter 2:5, Amos 4:5, Hebrews 13:15, Hosea 14:4, Jastrow 36b, Leviticus 7:12-15, Leviticus.R 27:12, Midrash Tanchuma Emor 14, Pesikta de R'Kahana 9.12, Psalms 11:22 20:17
Leviticus 22:29-30 - Mekhilta de R'Shimon bar Yochai Pisha 10:2

[3] Leviticus 22:30 - b.Pesachim 57a, Commandment #516, Exodus 16:19-20, Leviticus 7:15-18 19:7, mt.Hilchot Pesulei haMikdashim 18:9, z.Acharei Mot 78b

[4] Leviticus 22:31 - 1 Thessalonians 4:1-4:2, b.Rosh Hashanah 25a, Deuteronomy 4:40, Leviticus 18:4-5 19:37, Mas.Kallah Rabbati 8:9, Numbers 15:40, z.Acharei Mot 78b, z.Emor 84

[5] Missing in 4QLevb LXX

[6] Leviticus 22:32 - 1 Corinthians 1:2, b.Avodah Zara 27b 54a, b.Berachot 21b, b.Sanhedrin 74ab [Rashi] 75a, b.Megillah 23b, Commandment #4 #5, Ein Yaakov Avodah Zarah 27b, Ein Yaakov Berachot 21b, Exodus 19:5-6, Gates of Repentance 3.61 3.158, Genesis.R 91:3, Isaiah 5:16, John 17:17, Leviticus 10:3 18:21 20:8 21:8 21:15 22:2 22:16, Luke 11:2, Matthew 6:9, Midrash Tanchuma Bereshit 1, mt.Hilchot Tefilah 8:6, mt.Hilchot Melachim uMichamoteihem 10:2, mt.Hilchot Yesodei haTorah 5:1, t.Shabbat 15:17, y.Megillah 4:4, y.Sanhedrin 1:4 3:5, y.Sheviit 4:2, z.Acharei Mot 78b, z.Pekudei 194 231a, z.Terumah 56 119 129b 133a, z.Emor 86 91

[7] Leviticus 22:33 - b.Eruvin 39a, Exodus 6:7 20:2, Leviticus 11:45 19:36 1:38, Numbers 15:41, z.Acharei Mot 78b

Emor – Chapter 23[1]

<table>
<tr>
<td>וַיְדַבֵּר יְהֹוָה אֶל־מֹשֶׁה לֵּאמֹר</td>
<td>1[2]</td>
<td>And the LORD spoke to Moses, saying:</td>
</tr>
<tr>
<td>דַּבֵּר אֶל־בְּנֵי יִשְׂרָאֵל וְאָמַרְתָּ אֲלֵהֶם מוֹעֲדֵי יְהֹוָה אֲשֶׁר־תִּקְרְאוּ אֹתָם מִקְרָאֵי קֹדֶשׁ אֵלֶּה הֵם מוֹעֲדָי</td>
<td>2[3]</td>
<td>Speak to the children of Israel and say to them: The appointed seasons of the LORD, which you shall proclaim to be holy convocations, these are My appointed seasons.</td>
</tr>
<tr>
<td>שֵׁשֶׁת יָמִים תֵּעָשֶׂה מְלָאכָה וּבַיּוֹם הַשְּׁבִיעִי שַׁבַּת שַׁבָּתוֹן מִקְרָא־קֹדֶשׁ כָּל־מְלָאכָה לֹא תַעֲשׂוּ שַׁבָּת הִוא לַיהֹוָה בְּכֹל מוֹשְׁבֹתֵיכֶם</td>
<td>3[4]</td>
<td>Six days shall work be done; but on the seventh day is a sabbath of solemn rest, a holy convocation; you shall do no manner of work; it is a sabbath to the LORD in all your dwellings.</td>
</tr>
<tr>
<td>אֵלֶּה מוֹעֲדֵי יְהֹוָה מִקְרָאֵי קֹדֶשׁ אֲשֶׁר־תִּקְרְאוּ אֹתָם בְּמוֹעֲדָם</td>
<td>4[5]</td>
<td>These are the appointed seasons of the LORD, even holy convocations, which you shall proclaim in their appointed season.</td>
</tr>
</table>

---

[1] z.Tzav 31b

[2] Leviticus 23:1 - HellenisticSynagoguePrayers 5:16, m.Megillah 3:5, m.Pesachim 5:3, Philo De Specialibus Legibus I 112, Saadia Opinions 3:5
Leviticus 23:1-3 - 2QNumd, Philo De Specialibus Legibus II 56-139
Leviticus 23:1-8 - 4QLevb
Leviticus 23:1-44 - Sifre Devarim Reeh 127

[3] Leviticus 23:2 - 2 Chronicles 6:5, 2 Kings 10:20, b.Bava Batra [Rashi] 121a, b.Nedarim [Ran] 78a, b.Rosh Hashanah 24a 25a, Colossians 2:1, Deuteronomy.R 2:14, Exodus 23:14-17 8:5, Hosea 2:11, Isaiah 1:13-14 9:20, Jastrow 103a, Joel 1:14 2:15, John 5:1, Jonah 3:5-9, Lamentations 1:4, Lamentations.R Petichata DChakimei:11, Leviticus 23:4 23:21 23:37 23:44, Mekilta de R'Ishmael Pisha 9:5, Midrash Psalms 4:4, mt.Hilchot Kiddush HaChodesh 1:7 2:10 3:2, mt.Hilchot Matnot Aniyim 4:6, Nahum 2:1, Numbers 10:2-3 10:10 5:39, Numbers.R 21:25, Pesikta Rabbati 15:, Philo De Cherubim 87, Philo De Specialibus Legibus II 51, Psalms 81:4, Saadia Opinions 3:5, y.Nedarim 6:8, y.Rosh Hashanah 1:8 3:1, y.Sanhedrin 1:2, y.Sheviit 10:1, z.Emor 93b, z.Emor 94, z.Ki Tetze 142
Leviticus 23:2-9 - m.Yevamot 7:5

[4] Leviticus 23:3 - Acts 15:21, b.Chullin 11b, b.Pesachim 84a, b.Shabbat 133a, b.Yoma 76a, Deuteronomy 5:13-5:14, Exodus 16:23 16:29 20:8-11 23:12 31:13-17 10:21 35:2-3, Isaiah 8:2 8:6 10:13, Leviticus 19:3, Luke 13:14 23:56, Mekhilta de R'Shimon bar Yochai Shabbata 84:1, Mekilta de R'Ishmael Pisha 9:37, mt.Hilchot Chametz uMatzah 29:2 30:1, Revelation 1:10, y.Bava Kamma 3:4, y.Shabbat 7:1 15:3, z.Emor 94b, z.Emor 98 112

[5] Leviticus 23:4 - b.Chagigah [Rashi] 7b, b.Menachot [Tosefot] 51a, b.Nedarim [Ran] 78ab, b.Rosh Hashanah 21b 22a 24a 25a, b.Sotah [Rashi] 41a, b.Temurah [Rashi] 14a, b.Zevachim [Tosefot] 8b, Ein Yaakov Rosh Hashanah:25a, Exodus 23:14, Exodus.R 15:2, Jastrow 103a, Kiddusha Rabba [Yom Tov morning], Lamentations.R Petichata DChakimei:11, Leviticus 23:2 23:37, m.Rosh Hashanah 1:9 2:9, Mekhilta de R'Shimon bar Yochai Shabbata 84:1, Mekilta de R'Ishmael Bahodesh 7:74, Mekilta de R'Ishmael Shabbata 1:91, Midrash Tanchuma Pinchas 17, mt.Hilchot Tefilah 2:5, Numbers.R 21:25, Pesikta de R'Kahana 5.13, Pesikta Rabbati 15:19 41:1, t.Megillah 3:5, t.Sukkah 3:1, y.Rosh Hashanah 1:3 1:8 2:6, z.Emor 94a, z.Beshalach 71, z.Emor 100, z.Pinchas 786
Leviticus 23:4-8 - 1QpaleoLev, Liber Antiquitatum Biblicarum 13:4, Philo De Specialibus Legibus II 150-161
Leviticus 23:4-14 - Josephus Antiquities 4.10.5
Leviticus 23:4-44 - mt.Hilchot Tefilah 13:8

בַּחֹדֶשׁ הָרִאשׁוֹן בְּאַרְבָּעָה עָשָׂר 5[1]
לַחֹדֶשׁ בֵּין הָעַרְבָּיִם פֶּסַח לַיהוָה

וּבַחֲמִשָּׁה עָשָׂר יוֹם לַחֹדֶשׁ הַזֶּה חַג 6[2]
הַמַּצּוֹת לַיהוָה שִׁבְעַת יָמִים מַצּוֹת
תֹּאכֵלוּ:

בַּיּוֹם הָרִאשׁוֹן מִקְרָא־קֹדֶשׁ יִהְיֶה לָכֶם 7[3]
כָּל־מְלֶאכֶת עֲבֹדָה לֹא תַעֲשׂוּ

וְהִקְרַבְתֶּם אִשֶּׁה לַיהוָה שִׁבְעַת יָמִים 8[4]
בַּיּוֹם הַשְּׁבִיעִי מִקְרָא־קֹדֶשׁ כָּל־
מְלֶאכֶת עֲבֹדָה לֹא תַעֲשׂוּ

וַיְדַבֵּר יְהוָה אֶל־מֹשֶׁה לֵּאמֹר 9[6]

דַּבֵּר אֶל־בְּנֵי יִשְׂרָאֵל וְאָמַרְתָּ אֲלֵהֶם 10[7]
כִּי־תָבֹאוּ אֶל־הָאָרֶץ אֲשֶׁר אֲנִי נֹתֵן
לָכֶם וּקְצַרְתֶּם אֶת־קְצִירָהּ וַהֲבֵאתֶם
אֶת־עֹמֶר רֵאשִׁית קְצִירְכֶם אֶל־הַכֹּהֵן

5[1] In the first month, on the fourteenth day of the month at dusk, is the LORD's Passover.

6[2] And on the fifteenth day of the same month is the festival of unleavened bread to the LORD; seven days you shall eat unleavened bread.

7[3] In the first day you shall have a holy convocation; you shall do no manner of servile work.

8[4] And you shall bring an [5]offering made by fire to the LORD seven days; in the seventh day is a holy convocation; you shall do no manner of servile work.

9[6] And the LORD spoke to Moses saying:

10[7] Speak to the children of Israel and say to them: When you come into the land that I give to you, and shall reap its harvest, then you shall bring the sheaf of the firstfruits of your harvest to the priest.

---

[1] Leviticus 23:5 - 1 Corinthians 5:7-8, 2 Chronicles 35:18-19, Deuteronomy 16:1-8, Exodus 12:2-14 12:18-19 13:3-10 23:15, Joshua 5:10, Luke 22:7, Mark 14:12, Matthew 2:17, Numbers 9:2-7 28:16-17, z.Emor 95a, z.Emor 128

[2] Leviticus 23:6 - Acts 12:3-12:4, b.Succah 16a, Deuteronomy 16:8, Exodus 12:15-16 13:6-7 10:18, Mekilta de R'Ishmael Pisha 2:69, Numbers 28:17-28:18, y.Sukkah 2:7, z.Emor 95b

[3] Leviticus 23:7 - b.Chagigah 18a, b.Moed Katan 20a, b.Pesachim 5a, b.Shabbat 23a, Commandment #116, Exodus.R 15:23, Leviticus 23:8 23:21 23:25 23:35-36, m.Rosh Hashanah 1:9, mt.Hilchot Shevitat Yom Tov 1:1-2, Numbers 28:18-25

[4] Leviticus 23:8 - b.Moed Katan 20a, Commandment #118 #119, mt.Hilcnot Shofar Sukkah vLulav 1:4, Sifre.z Numbers Shelah 14:34, y.Rosh Hashanah 4:3, y.Sukkah 3:11, z.Bo 39b

[5] LXX *whole burnt offering*

[6] Leviticus 23:9 - Ecclesiastes.R 1:4 1:4
Leviticus 23:9-14 - m.Menachot 5:3, mt.Hilchot Kiddush HaChodesh 4:3, mt.Pirkei Avot 5:4, Pesach second day [Pesikta Rabbati 18], Philo De Specialibus Legibus II 176-187, Siman 120:1
Leviticus 23:9-15 - m.Chalah 1:1, m.Rosh Hashanah 1:2, mt.Hilchot Beit HaBechirah 7:12
Leviticus 23:9-20 - mt.Hilchot Beit Habechirah 7:12

[7] Leviticus 23:10 - 1 Corinthians 15:20-23, Avot de R'Natan 35, b.Makkot [Rashi] 8b, b.Menachot 4ab 60b 70b 71a 72a 83b 84a, b.Menachot [Tosefot] 45b 68a, b.Nazir 9b, b.Nedarim 58a, b.Pesachim [Rashi] 11a, b.Pesachim 23a, b.Rosh Hashanah 13a, b.Shabbat 131a, Commandment #517, Deuteronomy 16:9, Esther.R 10:4, Exodus 22:29 23:16 23:19 10:22 10:26, Ezekiel 20:30, James 1:18, Joshua 3:15, Leviticus 2:12-16 14:34 23:17, Leviticus.R 28:1, m.Kelim 1:6, m.Megillah 2:6, m.Menachot 10:1 10:5 8:1, m.Sotah 2:1, m.Sukkah 3:10, m.Zevachim 9:5 14:3, Mekilta de R'Shimon bar Yochai Shabbata 85:2, mt.Hilchot Beit HaBechirah 7:12, mt.Hilchot Issurei Mizbeiach 6:10, mt.Hilchot Temidim Umusafim 7:5 7:13, Numbers 15:2 15:18-21 4:26, Numbers.R 7:8, Pesikta de R'Kahana 8.1-2, Pesikta Rabbati 18:1-6, Philo De Somniis II 75, Proverbs 3:9-10, Revelation 14:4, Romans 11:16, Sifre Devarim Ekev 41, z.Emor 96a
Leviticus 23:10-11 - Pesikta Rabbati 18:6
Leviticus 23:10-12 - Jastrow 358b 427b
Leviticus 23:10-14 - Jastrow 1053b, Pesikta Rabbati 41:2, Sifre Devarim Ekev 44
Leviticus 23:10-21 - Midrash Proverbs 23
Leviticus 23:10-25 - 4QLevb

וְהֵנִיף אֶת־הָעֹמֶר לִפְנֵי יְהוָה לִרְצֹנְכֶם מִמָּחֳרַת הַשַּׁבָּת יְנִיפֶנּוּ הַכֹּהֵן	11[1]	And he shall wave the sheaf before the LORD, to be accepted for you; *on the day after the sabbath the priest shall wave it*[2].
וַעֲשִׂיתֶם בְּיוֹם הֲנִיפְכֶם אֶת־הָעֹמֶר כֶּבֶשׂ תָּמִים בֶּן־שְׁנָתוֹ לְעֹלָה לַיהוָה	12[3]	And in the day when you wave the sheaf, you shall offer a male lamb without blemish of the first year for a [4]burnt offering to the LORD.
וּמִנְחָתוֹ שְׁנֵי עֶשְׂרֹנִים סֹלֶת בְּלוּלָה בַשֶּׁמֶן אִשֶּׁה לַיהוָה רֵיחַ נִיחֹחַ וְנִסְכֹּה יַיִן רְבִיעִת הַהִין:	13[5]	And the meal offering thereof shall be two-tenth parts of an ephah of fine flour mingled with oil, an offering made by fire to the LORD for a sweet savor; and its drink offering shall be of wine, the fourth-part of a hin.
וְלֶחֶם וְקָלִי וְכַרְמֶל לֹא תֹאכְלוּ עַד־עֶצֶם הַיּוֹם הַזֶּה עַד הֲבִיאֲכֶם אֶת־קָרְבַּן אֱלֹהֵיכֶם חֻקַּת עוֹלָם לְדֹרֹתֵיכֶם בְּכֹל מֹשְׁבֹתֵיכֶם	14[6]	And you shall not eat bread, *or*[7] parched corn, *or fresh ears*[8], until this selfsame day, until you have brought the offering of your God; it is a statute forever throughout your generations in all your dwellings.
וּסְפַרְתֶּם לָכֶם מִמָּחֳרַת הַשַּׁבָּת מִיּוֹם	15[9]	And you shall count for you from the morning after the day of rest, from the

[1] Leviticus 23:11 - b.Menachot [Rashi] 59b 61a, b.Nedarim 58a, b.Succah [Rashi] 41a, Exodus 5:24, Jastrow 764a, Kuzari 3.040, Leviticus 9:21 10:14, Leviticus.R 28:5, m.Chagigah 2:4, m.Eduyot 2:10, m.Megillah 2:5-6, m.Menachot 10:1 10:5, m.Sukkah 3:10, mt.Hilchot Shekalim 4:5, mt.Hilchot Temidim Umusafim 7:3 7:11, Pesikta de R'Kahana 8.3, Pesikta Rabbati 18:2 18:4/5, z.Emor 159

[2] LXX *On the morrow of the first day [of the Festival of Matzot] the priest shall lift it up*

[3] Leviticus 23:12 - 1 Peter 1:19, b.Megillah 20b, b.Menachot [Rashi] 4b, b.Nedarim 58a, Hebrews 10:10-12, Leviticus 1:10, m.Menachot 10:1 10:5, z.Emor 183

[4] LXX adds *whole*

[5] Leviticus 23:13 - b.Menachot 89b, b.Nedarim 58a, b.Pesachim [Rashi] 77a, b.Yoma [Rashi] 7a, Exodus 29:40-41 6:9 6:24, Ezekiel 4:11 21:24 22:14, Joel 1:9 1:13 2:14, Leviticus 2:14-16 6:20 14:10, m.Menachot 9:4, Numbers 15:3-12 4:10, z.Emor 183

[6] Leviticus 23:14 - b.Bava Metzia [Tosefot] 115b, b.Kereitot 5a, b.Menachot [Rashi] 5ab, b.Menachot [Tosefot] 58b, b.Menachot 68ab 70b 84a, b.Nedarim 58a, b.Pesachim 23a, b.Rosh Hashanah [Tosefot] 13a, b.Rosh Hashanah 30b, b.Shabbat 105a, b.Sotah [Rashi] 49a, b.Succah [Rashi] 41a, b.Succah 41b, Commandment #518 #519 #520, Deuteronomy 16:12, Ein Yaakov Pesachim:68b, Exodus 10:26, Gates of Repentance 3.105, Genesis 4:4-5, Jastrow 595a, Joshua 5:11-12, Jubilees 2:33, Leviticus 3:17 10:11 19:23-25 25:2-3, m.Chalah 1:1, m.Kiddushin 1:9, m.Orlah 3:9, mt.Hilchot Maachalot Assurot 10:2, mt.Hilchot Sanhedrin vHainshin Hameurim Lahem 19:4, mt.Hilchot Temidim Umusafim 7:9 7:11, mt.Hilchot Yesodei haTorah 9:1, Nehemiah 9:14, Numbers 15:20-21, Psalms 19:9, Ralbag SOS 5, Siman 172:1 45:21, t.Menachot 10:26, y.Challah 1:1 1:3, y.Kiddushin 1:8, y.Orlah 3:1 3:7, y.Pesachim 2:1

[7] Missing in 4QLevb

[8] Missing in LXX

[9] Leviticus 23:15 - b.Megillah [Tosefot] 20b, b.Menachot 65b 66a, b.Rosh Hashanah [Rashi] 5a, Commandment #127, Deuteronomy 16:9-10, Ecclesiastes.R 1:4, Exodus 10:22, Jastrow 600a 1677a, Leviticus 23:10-11 1:8, Leviticus.R 28:3, m.Chagigah 2:4, mt.Hilchot Temidim Umusafim 7:6 7:22, Numbers 4:26, Pesikta de R'Kahana 8.1, Pesikta Rabbati 18:2, Sifre Devarim Reeh 135 136, Siman 120:10-11, z.Emor 97a, z.Tetzaveh 183a, z.Emor 149 162 164 174, z.Pinchas 806, z.Tetzaveh 67

Leviticus 23:15-16 - Seder Sefirat Haomer [counting of the Omer], Sifre Devarim Reeh 136

Leviticus 23:15-20 - Jubilees 15:2

Leviticus 23:15-21 - Liber Antiquitatum Biblicarum 13:5, Philo De Specialibus Legibus II 176-187

הֲבִיאֲכֶ֗ם אֶת־עֹ֙מֶר֙ הַתְּנוּפָ֔ה שֶׁ֖בַע שַׁבָּת֣וֹת תְּמִימֹ֑ת תִּהְיֶֽינָה

day you brought the sheaf of the *waving*[1]; there shall be seven complete weeks;

עַ֣ד מִֽמָּחֳרַ֤ת הַשַּׁבָּת֙ הַשְּׁבִיעִ֔ת תִּסְפְּר֖וּ חֲמִשִּׁ֣ים י֑וֹם וְהִקְרַבְתֶּ֛ם מִנְחָ֥ה חֲדָשָׁ֖ה לַיהוָֽה

16[2] Even to the morning after the seventh week you shall number fifty days; and you shall present a new meal offering to the LORD.

מִמּוֹשְׁבֹ֣תֵיכֶ֗ם תָּבִ֣יאּוּ[3]׀ לֶ֤חֶם תְּנוּפָה֙ שְׁתַּ֔יִם שְׁנֵ֣י עֶשְׂרֹנִ֗ים סֹ֤לֶת תִּהְיֶ֙ינָה֙ חָמֵ֣ץ תֵּאָפֶ֔ינָה בִּכּוּרִ֖ים לַֽיהוָֽה

17[4] You shall bring out of your dwellings two wave loaves of two-tenth parts of an ephah; they shall be of fine flour, they shall be baked with leaven, for firstfruits to the LORD.

וְהִקְרַבְתֶּ֣ם עַל־הַלֶּ֗חֶם שִׁבְעַ֤ת כְּבָשִׂים֙ תְּמִימִם֙ בְּנֵ֣י שָׁנָ֔ה וּפַ֧ר בֶּן־בָּקָ֛ר אֶחָ֖ד וְאֵילִ֣ם שְׁנָ֑יִם יִהְי֤וּ עֹלָה֙ לַֽיהוָ֔ה וּמִנְחָתָם֙ וְנִסְכֵּיהֶ֔ם אִשֵּׁ֥ה רֵֽיחַ־נִיחֹ֖חַ לַיהוָֽה

18[5] And you shall present with the bread seven lambs without blemish of the first year, and one young bullock, and two rams; they shall be a [6]burnt offering to the LORD, with their meal offering, and their drink offerings, an offering made by fire, of a sweet savor unto the LORD.

וַעֲשִׂיתֶ֞ם שְׂעִיר־עִזִּ֥ים אֶחָ֖ד לְחַטָּ֑את וּשְׁנֵ֧י כְבָשִׂ֛ים בְּנֵ֥י שָׁנָ֖ה לְזֶ֥בַח שְׁלָמִֽים

19[7] And you shall offer one male goat for a sin offering, and two male lambs of the first year for a sacrifice of peace offerings.

---

[1] LXX *heave offering*

[2] Leviticus 23:16 - Acts 2:1, b.Chagigah 14b, b.Menachot [Rashi] 68b 77b, b.Menachot [Tosefot] 59a, b.Menachot 65b 66a 83b 84b, b.Rosh Hashanah [Rashi] 5a, b.Succah 37b, b.Taanit 14b, b.Zevachim [Rashi] 57b, m.Chagigah 2:4, mt.Hilchot Issurei Mizbeiach 6:10, mt.Hilchot Temidim Umusafim 8:2, mt.Pirkei Avot 5:4, Numbers 4:26, Sifre Devarim Reeh 135, z.Pinchas 804
Leviticus 23:16-19 - mt.Hilchot Temidim Umusafim 8:1
Leviticus 23:16-20 - mt.Hilchot Beit HaBechirah 7:12

[3] Unexpected Dagesh in א is seen in תָּבִ֣יאּוּ

[4] Leviticus 23:17 - 1 Corinthians 15:20, Avot de R'Natan 35, b.Beitzah 20b, b.Menachot [Rashi] 14b 52b, b.Menachot [Tosefot] 47a 95b, b.Menachot 16a 45b 46b 57b 69b 77b 78a 83b, b.Shabbat 131a, b.Sheviit 15b, b.Zevachim 57b, Deuteronomy 26:1-26:2, Exodus 22:29 23:16 23:19 10:22 10:26, James 1:18, Jastrow 465a 704a, Leviticus 2:12 7:13 23:10, m.Arachin 2:2, m.Avot 5:5, m.Kelim 1:6, m.Menachot 2:2 3:6 8:1 10:6 11:1 11:4 11:9, m.Parah 2:1, m.Pesachim 7:4, m.Sukkah 5:7, m.Zevachim 9:5 14:3, Matthew 13:33, Midrash Tanchuma Pinchas 12, mt.Hilchot Beit HaBechirah 7:12, mt.Hilchot Issurei Mizbeiach 5:10 6:10, mt.Hilchot Kiddush HaChodesh 4:15, mt.Hilchot Maaseh haKorbanot 1:4, mt.Hilchot Shekalim 4:5, mt.Hilchot Temidim Umusafim 8:2 8:9, mt.Pirkei Avot 5:4, Numbers 15:17 15:19-21 4:26, Numbers.R 7:8 12:15, Proverbs 3:9-10, Revelation 14:4, Romans 8:23, Ruth.R 4:2, Sifre Devarim Ekev 41, Sifre Devarim Ki Tavo 297, t.Challah 2:7, t.Demai 1:28, y.Shabbat 19:1, z.Tetzaveh 183a 183b 72 73, z.Emor 157
Leviticus 23:17-20 - Commandment #521

[5] Leviticus 23:18 - b.Meilah [Rashi] 9a, b.Menachot [Rashi] 13b 62a, b.Menachot [Tosefot] 44b, b.Menachot 45ab, b.Sheviit 15b, b.Temurah [Rashi] 14a, b.Yoma [Rashi] 3a, Leviticus 23:12-13, m.Meilah 2:6, m.Menachot 4:3, Malachi 1:13-1:14, Numbers 15:4-12 28:27-31, y.Sanhedrin 7:7, z.Tetzaveh 183a 72

[6] LXX *whole*

[7] Leviticus 23:19 - 2 Corinthians 5:21, b.Bava Kamma [Rashi] 11b, b.Beitzah [Rashi] 20b, b.Chagigah [Rashi] 6a, b.Menachot [Rashi] 13b 45b 48b, b.Menachot [Tosefot] 82b, b.Pesachim [Rashi] 13b, b.Temurah [Rashi] 14a, b.Zevachim [Rashi] 6b, b.Zevachim [Tosefot] 97b, b.Zevachim 55a, Leviticus 3:1-17 4:23-28 7:11-18 16:15, m.Avot 5:5, m.Eduyot 8:6, m.Menachot 2:2 3:6, m.Pesachim 7:4, m.Zevachim 5:5, mt.Hilchot Maaseh haKorbanot 5:3 9:3, Numbers 15:24 4:30, Romans 8:3

וְהֵנִיף הַכֹּהֵן| אֹתָם עַל לֶחֶם הַבִּכּוּרִים תְּנוּפָה לִפְנֵי יְהוָה עַל־שְׁנֵי כְּבָשִׂים קֹדֶשׁ יִהְיוּ לַיהוָה לַכֹּהֵן

20[1]

And the priest shall wave them with the bread of the firstfruits for a wave offering before the LORD, with the two lambs; they shall be holy to the LORD for the priest.

וּקְרָאתֶם בְּעֶצֶם| הַיּוֹם הַזֶּה מִקְרָא־קֹדֶשׁ יִהְיֶה לָכֶם כָּל־מְלֶאכֶת עֲבֹדָה לֹא תַעֲשׂוּ חֻקַּת עוֹלָם בְּכָל־מוֹשְׁבֹתֵיכֶם לְדֹרֹתֵיכֶם

21[2]

And you shall make a proclamation on the selfsame day; there shall be a holy convocation to you; you shall do no manner of servile work; it is a statute forever in all your dwellings throughout your generations.

וּבְקֻצְרְכֶם אֶת־קְצִיר אַרְצְכֶם לֹא־תְכַלֶּה פְּאַת שָׂדְךָ בְּקֻצְרֶךָ וְלֶקֶט קְצִירְךָ לֹא תְלַקֵּט לֶעָנִי וְלַגֵּר תַּעֲזֹב אֹתָם אֲנִי יְהוָה אֱלֹהֵיכֶם

22[3]

And when you reap the harvest of your land, you shall not wholly reap the corner of your field, nor shall you gather the gleaning of your harvest; you shall leave them for the poor, and for the stranger: I am the LORD your God.

וַיְדַבֵּר יְהוָה אֶל־מֹשֶׁה לֵּאמֹר

23[4]

And the LORD spoke to Moses, saying:

דַּבֵּר אֶל־בְּנֵי יִשְׂרָאֵל לֵאמֹר בַּחֹדֶשׁ

24[5]

Speak to the children of Israel, saying:

[1] Leviticus 23:20 - 1 Corinthians 9:11, b.Arachin [Rashi] 11b, b.Arachin 25b, b.Bava Kamma [Rashi] 11b, b.Menachot [Rashi] 15a 46b 59b 61a, b.Menachot [Rashi] 83a, b.Menachot [Tosefot] 44b, b.Menachot 16a 45b 46a 48a 62ab, b.Pesachim [Rashi] 13b, b.Succah [Rashi] 37b, b.Zevachim [Rashi] 55a 98a, b.Zevachim [Tosefot] 44b 97b, Deuteronomy 18:4, Ephesians 2:14, Exodus 5:24, Leviticus 7:29-34 8:29 10:14-15 23:17, Leviticus.R 29:9, Luke 2:14, m.Megillah 2:5, mt.Hilchot Pesulei haMikdashim 17:8, mt.Hilchot Temidim Umusafim 8:11`, Numbers 18:8-12, t.Menachot 7:20
[2] Leviticus 23:21 - b.Chagigah 14b, b.Shabbat [Tosefot] 20a, b.Succah [Rashi] 28b, Bahir 105, Commandment #128 #129, Deuteronomy 16:11, Exodus 12:16-17, Genesis 17:7, Isaiah 11:10, Lamentations.R Petichata DChakimei:11, Leviticus 23:2-4 23:7 23:14, Numbers 18:23, y.Megillah 1:4
[3] Leviticus 23:22 - 2 Corinthians 9:5-12, 4Q284a, Avot de R'Natan 38, b.Bava Kamma [Rashi] 28a, b.Bava Kamma 94a, b.Bava Metzia [Rashi] 9b, b.Chagigah 14b, b.Chullin [Rashi] 134b 137a, b.Chullin 131b, b.Gittin 12a, b.Makkot 16b, b.Nedarim [Ran] 44b 83b, b.Rosh Hashanah 32a, b.Sanhedrin [Rashi] 88a, b.Temurah 6a, Commandment #41, Deuteronomy 16:11-14 24:19-21, Ein Yaakov Rosh Hashanah 31b, Isaiah 58:7-8 10:10, Jastrow 604a, Job 31:16-21, Leviticus 19:9-10, Leviticus.R 29:2, Luke 11:41, m.Peah 1:1, mt.Hilchot Avodat Kochavim vChukkoteihem 10:5 10:5, mt.Hilchot Mamrim 4:2 4:2, mt.Hilchot Tefilah 7:11, mt.Hilchot Matnot Aniyim 1:1 3:1 3:18 4:2, mt.Hilchot Sanhedrin vHainshin Hameurim Lahem 19:4, Numbers.R 5:1, Pesikta de R'Kahana 23.5, Proverbs 11:24-25, Psalms 41:2-4 16:9, Ruth 2:3-7 2:15-23, t.Peah 1:1, y.Peah 4:1, z.Acharei Mot 78b
Leviticus 23:22-29 - 11Qpaleol.eva
[4] Leviticus 23:23 - b.Megillah 30b, Jastrow 896b, m.Megillah 3:5, Mas.Soferim 17:6
Leviticus 23:23-25 - Philo De Specialibus Legibus II 188-192
[5] Leviticus 23:24 - 1 Chronicles 15:28, 1 Corinthians 15:52, 1 Thessalonians 4:16, 2 Chronicles 5:13, b.Eruvin [Rashi] 40a, b.Megillah 30b, b.Rosh Hashanah 11a 28b 29b 32ab 34a, Commandment #130, Ein Yaakov Rosh Hashanah 10b 16a 31b, Ezra 3:6, Isaiah 3:13, Jastrow 596a 1510b 1516a, Jubilees 6:23, Leviticus 1:9, Leviticus.R 29:1 29:7 29:12, m.Megillah 2:5, m.Rosh Hashnah 4:5, Midrash Psalms 9:11, mt.Hilchot Beit Habechirah 1:12, mt.Hilchot Chametz uMatzah 21:12 29:20, mt.Hilchot Shabbat 1:1, mt.Hilchot Tefilah 2:6, mt.Hilcnot Shofar Sukkah vLulav 2:6 3:1 6:15, Numbers 10:9-10:10 29:1-6, Pesikta de R'Kahana 23.1-4 23.6-10 23.12, Pesikta Rabbati 15:0 40:1-7, Psalms 81:2-81:5 98:6, t.Megillah 3:6, t.Rosh Hashanah 2:10 2:13, y.Megillah 3:6, y.Rosh Hashanah 3:5 4:1, z.Emor 100b 98b 187 206, z.Vayakhel 398
Leviticus 23:24-32 - Liber Antiquitatum Biblicarum 13:6

הַשְּׁבִיעִ֜י בְּאֶחָ֣ד לַחֹ֗דֶשׁ יִהְיֶ֤ה לָכֶם֙ שַׁבָּת֔וֹן זִכְר֥וֹן תְּרוּעָ֖ה מִקְרָא־קֹֽדֶשׁ

In the seventh month, in the first day of the month, shall be a solemn rest to you, a memorial proclaimed with the blast of horns, a holy convocation.

25[1] כָּל־מְלֶ֥אכֶת עֲבֹדָ֖ה לֹ֣א תַעֲשֹׂ֑וּ וְהִקְרַבְתֶּ֥ם אִשֶּׁ֖ה לַיהוָֽה

You shall do no manner of servile work; and you shall bring an [2]offering made by fire to the LORD.

26[3] וַיְדַבֵּ֥ר יְהוָ֖ה אֶל־מֹשֶׁ֥ה לֵּאמֹֽר

And the LORD spoke to Moses, saying:

27[4] אַ֡ךְ בֶּעָשׂ֣וֹר לַחֹדֶשׁ֩ הַשְּׁבִיעִ֨י הַזֶּ֜ה י֧וֹם הַכִּפֻּרִ֣ים ה֗וּא מִֽקְרָא־קֹ֙דֶשׁ֙ יִהְיֶ֣ה לָכֶ֔ם וְעִנִּיתֶ֖ם אֶת־נַפְשֹׁתֵיכֶ֑ם וְהִקְרַבְתֶּ֥ם אִשֶּׁ֖ה לַיהוָֽה

Howbeit on the tenth day of this seventh month is the day of atonement; there shall be a holy convocation to you, and you shall *afflict*[5] your souls; and you shall bring an [6]offering made by fire to the LORD.

28[7] וְכָל־מְלָאכָה֙ לֹ֣א תַעֲשׂ֔וּ בְּעֶ֖צֶם הַיּ֣וֹם הַזֶּ֑ה כִּ֣י י֤וֹם כִּפֻּרִים֙ ה֔וּא לְכַפֵּ֣ר עֲלֵיכֶ֔ם לִפְנֵ֖י יְהוָ֥ה אֱלֹהֵיכֶֽם

And you shall do no manner of work in that same day; for it is a day of atonement, to make atonement for you before the LORD your God.

29[8] כִּ֤י כָל־הַנֶּ֙פֶשׁ֙ אֲשֶׁ֣ר לֹֽא־תְעֻנֶּ֔ה בְּעֶ֖צֶם הַיּ֣וֹם הַזֶּ֑ה וְנִכְרְתָ֖ה מֵֽעַמֶּֽיהָ

For whatever soul it is who shall not be *afflicted*[9] in that same day, he shall be cut off[10] from his people.

---

[1] Leviticus 23:25 - b.Rosh Hashanah 32b, b.Shabbat 131b, Commandment #131, Leviticus 23:21, mt.Hilchot Sanhedrin vHainshin Hameurim Lahem 19:1, y.Rosh Hashanah 4:1

[2] LXX adds *whole burnt*

[3] Leviticus 23:26 - m.Sotah 7:7, m.Yoma 7:1, z.Emor 104b
Leviticus 23:26-32 - mt.Hilchot Avodat Yom haKippurim 3:10, Philo De Specialibus Legibus II 193-203
Leviticus 23:26-32 - Josephus Antiquities 4.10.3, mt.Hilchot Tefilah 12:8

[4] Leviticus 23:27 - 2 Corinthians 7:10-7:11, Acts 2:37-2:38, b.Chullin 11b, b.Kereitot 7a, b.Megillah 24a, b.Menachot [Tosefot] 36a, b.Sheviit 13a, b.Sotah 40b, b.Yoma 76a, Commandment #133, Daniel 10:2-10:3, Exodus 6:10, Ezra 8:21, Isaiah 10:5, James 4:9, Leviticus 16:11 16:15 16:24 16:29-16:31 1:9, Mas.Soferim 11:2, Numbers 29:7-29:11, Philo De Congressu Quaerendae Eruditionis Gratia 89, Psalms 35:13, Saadia Opinions 5:8, t.Kippurim 4:9, y.Bava Kamma 3:4, y.Sotah 7:6, y.Yoma 7:1, z.Acharei Mot 69b, z.Bo 39b 40b, z.Emor 101a, Zechariah 12:10, z.Acharei Mot 239, z.Bo 160 176, z.Emor 228, z.Tetzaveh 116 118, z.Vayakhel 398
Leviticus 23:27-32 - Apocalypse of Elijah 1:13

[5] LXX *humble*

[6] LXX adds *whole burnt*

[7] Leviticus 23:28 - 1 John 2:2 4:10 5:6, b.Kereitot [Rashi] 2a, b.Kereitot [Rashi] 2a, b.Sheviit [Rashi] 2a 13b, b.Sheviit 13a, b.Yoma 81a, Cairo Damascus 11:18, Daniel 9:24, Exodus.R 15:23, Hebrews 9:12 9:26 10:10 10:14, Isaiah 5:10, Leviticus 16:34, Midrash Proverbs 10, Pirkei de R'Eliezer 29, Romans 5:10-5:11, Zechariah 3:9, z.Emor 224

[8] Leviticus 23:29 - b.Bava Kamma [Rashi] 11b, b.Bava Kamma [Tosefot] 11a, b.Chullin [Rashi] 120a, b.Kereitot [Rashi] 2a, b.Nedarim [Ran] 80b, b.Succah [Rashi] 6a, b.Yevamot 40a, b.Yoma 80ab 81a, Commandment #134, Ezekiel 7:16, Genesis 17:14, Guide for the Perplexed 3:41, Isaiah 22:12, Jeremiah 7:10, Leviticus 23:27 23:32, m.Keritot 1:1, m.Makkot 3:2, m.Yoma 8:2, mt.Hilchot Sanhedrin vHainshin Hameurim Lahem 19:1, mt.Hilchot Shevitat Esor 1:4, mt.Hilchot Shevitat Asor 1:4 2:5, mt.Hilchot Teshuvah 8:5, Numbers 5:2, y.Yoma 8:3, z.Tetzaveh 118
Leviticus 23:29-30 - mt.Hilchot Teshuvah 8:5

[9] LXX *humbled*

[10] LXX uses *cut off* as well

וְכָל־הַנֶּפֶשׁ אֲשֶׁר תַּעֲשֶׂה כָּל־מְלָאכָה בְּעֶצֶם הַיּוֹם הַזֶּה וְהַאֲבַדְתִּי אֶת־הַנֶּפֶשׁ הַהִוא מִקֶּרֶב עַמָּהּ	30[1]	And whatever soul it be who does any manner of work in that same day, that soul will I destroy from among his people.
כָּל־מְלָאכָה לֹא תַעֲשׂוּ חֻקַּת עוֹלָם לְדֹרֹתֵיכֶם בְּכֹל מֹשְׁבֹתֵיכֶם	31[2]	You shall do no manner of work; it is a statute forever throughout your generations in all your dwellings.
שַׁבַּת שַׁבָּתוֹן הוּא לָכֶם וְעִנִּיתֶם אֶת־נַפְשֹׁתֵיכֶם בְּתִשְׁעָה לַחֹדֶשׁ בָּעֶרֶב מֵעֶרֶב עַד־עֶרֶב תִּשְׁבְּתוּ שַׁבַּתְּכֶם	32[3]	It shall be *to you a sabbath of solemn rest*[4], and you shall *afflict*[5] your souls; in the ninth day of the month at evening, from evening to evening, shall you keep your sabbath[6].
וַיְדַבֵּר יְהוָה אֶל־מֹשֶׁה לֵּאמֹר	33[7]	And the LORD spoke to Moses, saying:
דַּבֵּר אֶל־בְּנֵי יִשְׂרָאֵל לֵאמֹר בַּחֲמִשָּׁה עָשָׂר יוֹם לַחֹדֶשׁ הַשְּׁבִיעִי הַזֶּה חַג הַסֻּכּוֹת שִׁבְעַת יָמִים לַיהוָה	34[8]	Speak to the children of Israel, saying: On the fifteenth day of this seventh month is the festival of tabernacles for seven days to the LORD.
בַּיּוֹם הָרִאשׁוֹן מִקְרָא־קֹדֶשׁ כָּל־מְלֶאכֶת עֲבֹדָה לֹא תַעֲשׂוּ	35[9]	On the first day shall be a holy convocation; you shall do no manner of servile work.
שִׁבְעַת יָמִים תַּקְרִיבוּ אִשֶּׁה לַיהוָה בַּיּוֹם הַשְּׁמִינִי מִקְרָא־קֹדֶשׁ יִהְיֶה לָכֶם וְהִקְרַבְתֶּם אִשֶּׁה לַיהוָה עֲצֶרֶת הִוא	36[10]	Seven days you shall bring an offering made by fire unto the LORD; on the eighth day shall be a holy convocation to you; and you shall bring an [11]offering made by fire to the LORD; *it*

---

[1] Leviticus 23:30 - 1 Corinthians 3:17, b.Yoma 74b 81a, Ezekiel 14:9, Gates of Repentance 3.159, Genesis 17:14, Guide for the Perplexed 3:17, Jastrow 1073b, Jeremiah 15:7, Leviticus 20:3 20:5-20:6, m.Keritot 1:1, m.Makkot 3:2, m.Megillah I:5, m.Parah 2:1, m.Pesachim 7:4, mt.Hilchot Teshuvah 8:5, y.Yoma 8:3, zephaniah 2:5, z.Acharei Mot 43

[2] Leviticus 23:31 - Commandment #135, m.Makkot 3:2, y.Yoma 8:3

[3] Leviticus 23:32 - 1 Corinthians 11:31, b.Berachot 8b, b.Pesachim 68b, b.Rosh Hashanah 9a 20b, b.Yoma 81b, Commandment #136, Derech Hashem Part IV 6§08, Hebrews 4:3 4:11, Isaiah 9:15 57:18-19 58:3-7 13:3, Jastrow 1093b, Kuzari 2.020, Leviticus 16:31 23:27, Leviticus.R 32:3, Matthew 5:4 11:28-30, Mekhilta de R'Shimon bar Yochai Bachodesh 54:2, mt.Hilchot Shevitat Esor 1:6, Psalms 35:13 51:18 69:11-12 126:5-6, mt.Hilchot Shevitat Asor 1:6, z.Acharei Mot 67a, z.Acharei Mot 239

[4] LXX *a holy sammath of rest for you*

[5] LXX *humble*

[6] LXX plural

[7] Leviticus 23:33-36 - Philo De Specialibus Legibus II 204-213

[8] Leviticus 23:34 - b.Beitzah 30b, b.Moed Katan 20a, b.Succah 9a, b.Zevachim [Tosefot] 37b, Deuteronomy 16:13-15, Exodus 23:16 10:22, Ezra 3:4, Hebrews 11:9 11:13, John 1:14 7:2, m.Sheviit 3:8, Nehemiah 8:14, Numbers 5:12, Sifre Devarim Reeh 140 142, Siman 134:12, t.Megillah 3:8, y.Sukkah 2:7, z.Emor 102b, Zechariah 14:16-19, z.Emor 257 260

Leviticus 23:34-44 - Jubilees 32:4

[9] Leviticus 23:35 - b.Moed Katan 20a, b.Shabbat 23a, Commandment #137 #138, Leviticus 23:7-8 23:24-25, m.Sheviit 3:8

[10] Leviticus 23:36 - 2 Chronicles 7:8-7:11, b.Chagigah 6a, b.Menachot [Tosefot] 44b, Commandment #139 #140 #522, Deuteronomy 16:8, Joel 1:14 2:15, John 7:37, m.Sheviit 3:8, Nehemiah 8:18, Numbers 29:12-38, Sifre Devarim Reeh 135, y.Chagigah 2:4

[11] LXX adds *whole burnt*

כָּל־מְלֶאכֶת עֲבֹדָה לֹא תַעֲשׂוּ

אֵלֶּה מוֹעֲדֵי יְהוָה אֲשֶׁר־תִּקְרְאוּ אֹתָם
מִקְרָאֵי קֹדֶשׁ לְהַקְרִיב אִשֶּׁה לַיהוָה
עֹלָה וּמִנְחָה זֶבַח וּנְסָכִים דְּבַר־יוֹם
בְּיוֹמוֹ

מִלְּבַד שַׁבְּתֹת יְהוָה וּמִלְּבַד מַתְּנוֹתֵיכֶם
וּמִלְּבַד כָּל־נִדְרֵיכֶם וּמִלְּבַד כָּל־
נִדְבוֹתֵיכֶם אֲשֶׁר תִּתְּנוּ לַיהוָה

אַךְ בַּחֲמִשָּׁה עָשָׂר יוֹם לַחֹדֶשׁ הַשְּׁבִיעִי
בְּאָסְפְּכֶם אֶת־תְּבוּאַת הָאָרֶץ תָּחֹגּוּ
אֶת־חַג־יְהוָה שִׁבְעַת יָמִים בַּיּוֹם
הָרִאשׁוֹן שַׁבָּתוֹן וּבַיּוֹם הַשְּׁמִינִי
שַׁבָּתוֹן

is a day of solemn assembly[1]; you shall do no manner of servile work.

37[2] These are the appointed seasons of the LORD, which you shall proclaim to be holy convocations, to bring an [3]offering made by fire to the LORD, a [4]burnt offering, and a meal offering, *a sacrifice*[5], and drink offerings, each on its own day;

38[6] Besides the sabbaths of the LORD, and beside your gifts, and beside all your vows, and beside all your freewill offerings, which you give to the LORD.

39[7] However, on the fifteenth day of the seventh month, when you have [8]gathered in the fruits of the land, you shall keep the festival of the LORD seven days; the first day shall be a solemn rest, and the eighth day shall be a solemn rest.

---

[1] LXX *it is a time of release*
[2] Leviticus 23:37 - b.Bechorot 14a, b.Chagigah 18a, b.Megillah 20b, b.Menachot [Tosefot] 49a, b.Menachot 44b 79a, b.Temurah 14a, b.Yoma [Rashi] 34a, Bahir 105, Deuteronomy 16:16-17, Ecclesiastes 3:1, Jastrow 103a, Leviticus 23:2 23:4, mt.Hilchot Issurei Mizbeiach 6:10, Sifre Devarim Reeh 63, z.Emor 303, z.Korach 9
[3] LXX adds *burnt*
[4] LXX adds *whole*
[5] Missing in LXX
[6] Leviticus 23:38 - 1 Chronicles 29:3-8, 2 Chronicles 35:7-8, 4Q270 frag 6 5.21, 4Q271 frag 5 1.12, b.Menachot [Tosefot] 44b, b.Temurah 14a, Cairo Damascus 11.17-18, Cairo Damascus 11.18, Deuteronomy 12:6, Exodus 20:8-11, Ezra 2:68-69, Genesis 2:2-3, Lamentations.R 2:10, Leviticus 19:3 23:3, Numbers 5:39, Sifre Devarim Reeh 63, y.Avodah Zarah 1:1, y.Rosh Hashanah 1:1
[7] Leviticus 23:39 - b.Beitzah [Rashi] 8b, b.Chagigah [Rashi] 5a, b.Chagigah 18a, b.Menachot [Rashi] 65b, b.Pesachim 5a, b.Rosh Hashanah 7a, b.Shabbat 24b, b.Succah 16a, Deuteronomy 16:13, Exodus 23:16, Gates of Repentance 3.146, Leviticus 23:24 23:34 23:36, Mekilta de R'Ishmael Pisha 9:108, mt.Hilchot Beit Habechirah 1:12 1:12, Pesikta de R'Kahana 27.7, Pesikta Rabbati 51:8
Leviticus 23:39-43 - m.Sheviit 3:8, Philo De Specialibus Legibus II 204-213
[8] LXX adds *completely*

וּלְקַחְתֶּ֨ם לָכֶ֜ם בַּיּ֣וֹם הָרִאשׁ֗וֹן פְּרִ֨י עֵ֤ץ הָדָר֙ כַּפֹּ֣ת תְּמָרִ֔ים וַעֲנַ֥ף עֵץ־עָבֹ֖ת וְעַרְבֵי־נָ֑חַל וּשְׂמַחְתֶּ֗ם לִפְנֵ֛י יְהוָ֥ה אֱלֹהֵיכֶ֖ם שִׁבְעַ֥ת יָמִֽים

40[1] And you shall take on the first day the fruit of goodly [2]trees, branches of palm trees, and boughs of thick trees, and willows[3] of the brook, and you shall rejoice before the LORD your God seven days[4].

וְחַגֹּתֶ֤ם אֹתוֹ֙ חַ֣ג לַֽיהוָ֔ה שִׁבְעַ֥ת יָמִ֖ים בַּשָּׁנָ֑ה חֻקַּ֤ת עוֹלָם֙ לְדֹרֹ֣תֵיכֶ֔ם בַּחֹ֧דֶשׁ הַשְּׁבִיעִ֛י תָּחֹ֖גּוּ אֹתֽוֹ

41[5] *And you shall keep it a festival to the LORD seven days in the year[6]*; it is a statute forever in your generations; you shall keep it in the seventh month.

בַּסֻּכֹּ֥ת תֵּשְׁב֖וּ שִׁבְעַ֣ת יָמִ֑ים כָּל־הָֽאֶזְרָח֙ בְּיִשְׂרָאֵ֔ל יֵשְׁב֖וּ בַּסֻּכֹּֽת

42[7] You shall dwell in booths seven days; all who are homeborn in Israel shall dwell in booths;

לְמַ֘עַן֮ יֵדְע֣וּ דֹרֹֽתֵיכֶם֒ כִּ֣י בַסֻּכּ֗וֹת

43[8] That your generations may know I made the children of Israel to dwell in

---

[1] Leviticus 23:40 - 1 Peter 1:8, 4QLevb, b.Bava Batra [Rashi] 137ab, b.Beitzah 20b, b.Berachot 57a, b.Megillah 20b, b.Menachot [Tosefot] 38a, b.Menachot 16a, b.Niddah [Tosefot] 15a, b.Pesachim 5a 38a, b.Rosh Hashanah [Rashi] 30a, b.Sanhedrin [Tosefot] 4a, b.Shabbat 36a 131b, b.Succah [Rashi] 36b 41a, b.Succah 11b 27b 29b 31a 32a-34b 35a 41b 43a 44a 45b, b.Taanit [Tosefot] 2b, Bahir 176, Bahir 98 172, Chibbur Yafeh 30 {135a}, Commandment #141, Deuteronomy 16:14-15, Ein Yaakov Sukkah 30a, Esther.R 7:11 9:2, Exodus.R 2:5 15:23, Genesis.R 63:8, Isaiah 11:10 18:10, Jastrow 134a 288b 334a 343b 349b 624b 657a 663a 698b 699a 719a 1037a 1096a 1104b 1112a 1298a 1674b, John 12:13 16:22, Leviticus.R 29:8 30:1 30:2 30:5 30:8, Liber Antiquitatum Biblicarum 13:7, m.Menachot 3:6, m.Sotah 3:6 4:2, Matthew 21:8, Mekhilta de R'Shimon bar Yochai Pisha 13:1, Mesillat Yesharim 19:Chassidut-Man-and-Hashem, Midrash Psalms 17:5 26:5 98:2, Midrash Tanchuma Emor 17-22, Midrash Tanchuma Pinchas 14, mt.Hilcnot Shofar Sukkah vLulav 1:3 7:1 7:7 8:10 8:12, Nehemiah 8:14-17, Numbers.R 14:4 21:22, Pesikta de R'Kahana 27.1-3 27.6-9, Pesikta Rabbati 42:1 51:1-8, Philippians 3:3 4:4, Psalms 92:13, Revelation 7:9, Romans 5:11, Sefer Yetzirah 1:13, Sifre Devarim Reeh 140, Sifre Devarim Reeh 140, Siman 136 136:5 137 137:8, Song of Songs.R 2:11, Sukkot first day [Pesikta Rabbati 51], t.Sukkah 2:7, Tanya Kuntress Acharon §4, y.Megillah 2:6, y.Orlah 1:1, y.Rosh Hashanah 4:3, y.Sheviit 1:5, y.Sukkah 3:1-5 3:7 3:11 4:1, y.Yevamot 12:2, z.Emor 104a 283, z.Ha'azinu 113, z.Mishpatim 498, z.Tetzaveh 124 130 132, z.Vayechi 213 214, z.Vayikra 412 420
Leviticus 23:40-42 - Derech Hashem Part IV 8§02, Jubilees 16:29
[2] LXX adds *fruit of*
[3] LXX adds *and branches of osiers*
[4] LXX adds *in the year*
[5] Leviticus 23:41 - b.Beitzah 19a 20b, b.Chagigah 9a, b.Pesachim 70b, Mekhilta de R'Shimon bar Yochai Pisha 9:5, Nehemiah 8:18, Numbers 5:12, Sifre Devarim Reeh 142, y.Chagigah 1:5
[6] Missing in LXX
[7] Leviticus 23:42 - 2 Corinthians 5:1, b.Arachin 3b, b.Avodah Zara 3a, b.Kiddushin 34a, b.Menachot [Tosefot] 56b, b.Sanhedrin [Tosefot] 3b, b.Sanhedrin 4a, b.Sheviit [Tosefot] 20b, b.Succah 2a 6b 9b 16a 27b 28ab 36b 43ab, b.Zevachim [Tosefot] 40a, b.Zevachim 37b, Commandment #117 #142, Deuteronomy.R 7:5, Ecclesiastes.R 11:1, Exodus.R 15:23, Genesis 9:17, Genesis.R 41:1 48:10, Hebrews 11:13-11:16, Jastrow 38a 587b 805a, Jeremiah 11:10, m.Sotah 1:1, mt.Hilcnot Shofar Sukkah vLulav 5:25 6:2 6:5, Nehemiah 8:14-8:17, Numbers 24:2 24:5, Pesikta de R'Kahana 28.a S2.6, Sifre Devarim Reeh 140, Siman 134:14 135:1, y.Pesachim 2:1, y.Sukkah 1:1 2:7 2:10, y.Yevamot 12:1, z.Emor 103b, z.Emor 264 268 271 276 277, z.Tetzaveh 134
Leviticus 23:42-24:2 - 4Q365 23 1-3, 4Q365 frag 23 ll.1-4
Leviticus 23:42-43 - Midrash Tanchuma Emor 22, Ushpizin [Sukkot]
[8] Leviticus 23:43 - b.Eruvin 3a, b.Sanhedrin [Tosefot] 3b, b.Sanhedrin 4a, b.Succah 2a 6b 11b, b.Zevachim [Tosefot] 40a, b.Zevachim 37b, Deuteronomy 31:10-13, Exodus 13:14, Guide for the Perplexed 1:21, Numbers.R 14:2, Pesikta de R'Kahana S2.6, Pesikta Rabbati 14:3, Psalms 78:5-6, Siman 135:1, y.Sukkah 1:1, z.Acharei Mot 78b, z.Pinchas 815

הוֹשַׁבְתִּי אֶת־בְּנֵי יִשְׂרָאֵל בְּהוֹצִיאִי אוֹתָם מֵאֶרֶץ מִצְרָיִם אֲנִי יְהוָה אֱלֹהֵיכֶם

booths[1], when I brought them out of the land of Egypt: I am the LORD your God.

וַיְדַבֵּר מֹשֶׁה אֶת־מֹעֲדֵי יְהוָה אֶל־בְּנֵי יִשְׂרָאֵל

44[2] And Moses declared to the children of Israel the appointed seasons of the LORD.

Emor – Chapter 24

וַיְדַבֵּר יְהוָה אֶל־מֹשֶׁה לֵּאמֹר

1[3] And the LORD spoke to Moses, saying:

צַו אֶת־בְּנֵי יִשְׂרָאֵל וְיִקְחוּ אֵלֶיךָ שֶׁמֶן זַיִת זָךְ כָּתִית לַמָּאוֹר לְהַעֲלֹת נֵר תָּמִיד

2[4] Command the children of Israel, that they bring you pure olive oil beaten for the light, to cause a lamp to burn continually.

מִחוּץ לְפָרֹכֶת הָעֵדֻת בְּאֹהֶל מוֹעֵד יַעֲרֹךְ אֹתוֹ אַהֲרֹן מֵעֶרֶב עַד־בֹּקֶר לִפְנֵי יְהוָה תָּמִיד חֻקַּת עוֹלָם לְדֹרֹתֵיכֶם

3[5] Outside the veil of the testimony, in the tent of meeting, shall Aaron order it from evening to morning before the LORD continually; it shall be a statute forever throughout your generations.

עַל הַמְּנֹרָה הַטְּהֹרָה יַעֲרֹךְ אֶת־הַנֵּרוֹת לִפְנֵי יְהוָה תָּמִיד

4[6] *He shall order the lamps on the pure candlestick before the LORD continually[7].*

---

[1] LXX *tents*

[2] Leviticus 23:44 - b.Bava Batra 120b, b.Megillah 31a 32a, b.Menachot [Tosefot] 72a, b.Menachot 72b, b.Nedarim [Rashi] 78b, b.Nedarim 78a, b.Pesachim 77a, b.Rosh Hashanah 24a, b.Yoma [Tosefot] 51a, Ein Yaakov Megillah:32a, Kiddusha Rabba [Yom Tov morning], Leviticus 21:24 23:1-2, m.Megillah 3:6, Maariv Yom Tov, Mas.Soferim 10:2 17:8, Matthew 18:20, Midrash Tanchuma Pinchas 17, Numbers.R 21:25, y.Megillah 3:7 4:1, y.Nedarim 6:8, y.Pesachim 7:4, z.BereshitA 466, z.Emor 290

[3] Leviticus 24:1-23 - m.Menachot.04:3

[4] Leviticus 24:2 - 1 Samuel 3:3-4, 2 Chronicles 13:11, 2 Corinthians 4:6, Acts 2:18, b.Menachot 86b, Ein Yaakov Menachot:86b, Ephesians 1:17-18 5:8-14, Exodus 27:20-21 15:37 16:24, Genesis.R 19:9, Isaiah 8:20 11:2, John 1:4 1:9 5:35 8:12, Lamentations.R Petichata DChakimei 4, Leviticus.R 2:4 31:1 31:4 31:7 31:9, Luke 2:19 12:35, Matthew 4:16 5:16 25:1-8, Midrash Tanchuma Tetzaveh 1, mt.Hilchot Avodat Kochavim vChukkoteihem 8, Numbers 8:2-4, Numbers.R 7:6, Pesikta de R'Kahana 2.7 15.1, Philippians 2:15-16, Philo De Specialibus Legibus I 296, Proverbs 6:23, Psalms 119:105 119:130, Sifre Numbers 1:2-3, Song of Songs.R 7:12, z.Emor 104b, z.Trumah 579
Leviticus 24:2-4 - Midrash Tanchuma Behaalotcha 1
Leviticus 24:2-23 - 4QLevb

[5] Leviticus 24:3 - b.Megillah 21a, b.Menachot 86b 98b, b.Shabbat 22b, Ein Yaakov Menachot 86b, Ein Yaakov Shabbat 22b, Jastrow 1043b, Leviticus.R 31:11, Midrash Tanchuma Tetzaveh 2, mt.Hilchot Beit Habechirah 3:8

[6] Leviticus 24:4 - 1 Chronicles 4:15, 1 Kings 7:49, b.Menachot [Tosefot] 34b, b.Menachot 29a, Exodus 25:31-39 7:8 37:17-24 15:37, Hebrews 9:2, Jeremiah 4:19, Midrash Tanchuma Bechukkotai 4, Midrash Tanchuma Emor 15, Numbers 3:31 4:9, Numbers.R 15:1, Revelation 1:20-2:1 2:5 11:4, t.Menachot 7:7, Zechariah 4:2-3 4:11-14

[7] LXX *You shall burn the lamps on the pure lampstand before the Lord until the morrow*

וְלָקַחְתָּ סֹלֶת וְאָפִיתָ אֹתָהּ שְׁתֵּים
עֶשְׂרֵה חַלּוֹת שְׁנֵי עֶשְׂרֹנִים יִהְיֶה
הַחַלָּה הָאֶחָת

5^1 And you shall take fine flour, and bake twelve cakes from it: two-tenth parts *of an ephah*[2] shall be in one cake.

וְשַׂמְתָּ אוֹתָם שְׁתַּיִם מַעֲרָכוֹת שֵׁשׁ
הַמַּעֲרָכֶת עַל הַשֻּׁלְחָן הַטָּהֹר לִפְנֵי
יְהוָה

6^3 And you shall set them in two rows, six in a row, on the pure table before the LORD.

וְנָתַתָּ עַל־הַמַּעֲרֶכֶת לְבֹנָה זַכָּה וְהָיְתָה
לַלֶּחֶם לְאַזְכָּרָה אִשֶּׁה לַיהוָה

7^4 And you shall put pure frankincense[5] with each row, that it may be to the bread for a memorial part, even an offering made by fire to the LORD.

בְּיוֹם הַשַּׁבָּת בְּיוֹם הַשַּׁבָּת יַעַרְכֶנּוּ
לִפְנֵי יְהוָה תָּמִיד מֵאֵת בְּנֵי־יִשְׂרָאֵל
בְּרִית עוֹלָם

8^6 Every sabbath day he shall set it in order before the LORD continually; it is from the children of Israel, an everlasting covenant.

וְהָיְתָה לְאַהֲרֹן וּלְבָנָיו וַאֲכָלֻהוּ בְּמָקוֹם
קָדֹשׁ כִּי קֹדֶשׁ קָדָשִׁים הוּא לוֹ מֵאִשֵּׁי
יְהוָה חָק־עוֹלָם

9^7 And it shall be for Aaron and his sons; and they shall eat it in *a*[8] holy place; for it is most holy to him of the offerings of the LORD made by fire, a perpetual *due*[9].'

---

[1] Leviticus 24:5 - 1 Kings 18:31, 1 Samuel 21:4-5, Acts 2:7, Avot de R'Natan 35, b.Menachot [Rashi] 59a, b.Menachot 76ab 94b 98a, Ecclesiastes.R 7:16, Exodus 1:30 16:23, James 1:1, Leviticus.R 32:3, m.Meilah 2:7, m.Menachot 3:6 5:3, m.Menachot 6:6 11:1 11:4, m.Tamid 2:5, m.Zevachim 14:3, Matthew 12:4, Midrash Tanchuma Emor 23, Midrash Tanchuma Tzav 1, mt.Hilchot Beit HaBechirah 3:13, mt.Hilchot Temidim Umusafim 5:1 5:7
Leviticus 24:5-8 - mt.Pirkei Avot 5:4
Leviticus 24:5-9 - Ein Yaakov Pesachim:3b, m.Avot 5:5, m.Pesachim 7:4, m.Sukkah 5:7, m.Zevachim 9:5, Midrash Proverbs 23, Siman 29:9, z.Terumah 136a
[2] Missing in LXX
[3] Leviticus 24:6 - 1 Corinthians 14:40, 1 Kings 7:48, 2 Chronicles 4:19 13:11, b.Chagigah 26b, b.Menachot 29a 94a 96b 98a, b.Pesachim [Rashi] 109b, b.Yoma 21a, Exodus 25:23-24 37:10-16 15:36 40:22-23, Hebrews 9:2, mt.Hilchot Beit HaBechirah 3:13
[4] Leviticus 24:7 - 1 Corinthians 11:23-25, Acts 10:4 10:31, b.Menachot [Rashi] 7b 94b, b.Menachot 62a 77b 96a 98a, b.Pesachim [Rashi] 78a, b.Shabbat [Rashi] 133b, b.Shekalim 18b, b.Sotah 37a, b.Yoma [Rashi] 24b, b.Zevachim [Rashi] 63a 11a, Ephesians 1:6, Exodus 12:14 13:9 17:14, Genesis 9:16, Hebrews 7:25, John 6:35 6:51, Leviticus 2:2, m.Menachot 2:2 3:6 11:5, m.Yoma 2:5, mt.Hilchot Beit Habechirah 3:14, mt.Hilchot Temidim Umusafim 5:2, Numbers.R 4:14, Ralbag SOS 1, Ralbag Wars 6part2:5, Revelation 8:3-4, t.Menachot 11:15
[5] LXX adds *and salt*
[6] Leviticus 24:8 - 1 Chronicles 9:32 23:29, 2 Chronicles 2:3, b.Menachot 21b, b.Yoma [Rashi] 34a, m.Yoma 2:5, Matthew 12:3-5, Midrash Tanchuma Bechukkotai 4, Midrash Tanchuma Emor 15, Midrash Tanchuma Tzav 1, Nehemiah 10:34, Numbers 4:7, t.Menachot 7:7, z.Terumah 153b
[7] Leviticus 24:9 - 1 Samuel 21:6, b.Avodah Zara 10b, b.Bava Batra [Rashbam] 114b, b.Bava Batra 143a, b.Menachot [Rashi] 8a 19a 46a 95a, b.Menachot [Tosefot] 76b, b.Menachot 12b 16a 76a, b.Sanhedrin 21a, b.Yoma [Rashi] 34a, b.Yoma 14b, Ein Yaakov Avodah Zarah:10b, Exodus 29:32-33, Leviticus 6:16 8:3 8:31 10:17 21:22, Luke 6:4, Malachi 1:12, Mark 2:26, Matthew 12:4, Midrash Tanchuma Bechukkotai 4, mt.Hilchot Temidim Umusafim 4:14, mt.Hilchot Zechiyah Umatanah 11:5, y.Yoma 1:2
Leviticus 24:9-14 - 11Qpaleol.eva
[8] LXX *the*
[9] LXX *statute*

וַיֵּצֵא בֶּן־אִשָּׁה יִשְׂרְאֵלִית וְהוּא בֶּן־
אִישׁ מִצְרִי בְּתוֹךְ בְּנֵי יִשְׂרָאֵל וַיִּנָּצוּ
בַּמַּחֲנֶה בֶּן הַיִּשְׂרְאֵלִית וְאִישׁ
הַיִּשְׂרְאֵלִי

10[1] And the son of an Israelite woman, whose father was an Egyptian, went out among the children of Israel; and the son of the Israelite woman and a man of Israel fought together in the camp.

וַיִּקֹּב בֶּן־הָאִשָּׁה הַיִּשְׂרְאֵלִית אֶת־
הַשֵּׁם וַיְקַלֵּל וַיָּבִיאוּ אֹתוֹ אֶל־מֹשֶׁה
וְשֵׁם אִמּוֹ שְׁלֹמִית בַּת־דִּבְרִי לְמַטֵּה־
דָן:

11[2] And the son of the Israelitish woman *blasphemed the Name*[3], and cursed; and they brought him to Moses. And his mother's name was Shelomit, the daughter of Dibri, of the tribe of Dan.

וַיַּנִּיחֻהוּ בַּמִּשְׁמָר לִפְרֹשׁ לָהֶם עַל־פִּי
יְהוָה

12[4] And they put him in ward, that it might be declared to them at the mouth of the LORD.

וַיְדַבֵּר יְהוָה אֶל־מֹשֶׁה לֵּאמֹר

13 And the LORD spoke to Moses, saying:

הוֹצֵא אֶת־הַמְקַלֵּל אֶל־מִחוּץ לַמַּחֲנֶה
וְסָמְכוּ כָל־הַשֹּׁמְעִים אֶת־יְדֵיהֶם עַל־
רֹאשׁוֹ וְרָגְמוּ אֹתוֹ כָּל־הָעֵדָה

14[5] 'Bring forth he who has cursed outside the camp; and let all who heard him press their hands on his head, and let all the congregation stone him.

וְאֶל־בְּנֵי יִשְׂרָאֵל תְּדַבֵּר לֵאמֹר אִישׁ
אִישׁ כִּי־יְקַלֵּל אֱלֹהָיו וְנָשָׂא חֶטְאוֹ

15[6] And you shall speak to the children of Israel, saying: Whoever curses his God shall bear his sin.

---

[1] z.Emor 306, z.Shemot 35

[2] Leviticus 24:11 - 1 Kings 21:10 21:13, 1 Timothy 1:13, 2 Chronicles 32:14-17, 2 Kings 18:30 18:35 18:37-19:3 19:6 19:10 19:22, 2 Samuel 12:14, Acts 6:11-13, b.Sanhedrin 56a, Exodus 3:15 18:22 18:26 20:7, Exodus.R 1:28 48:2, Isaiah 8:21, Jastrow 1154b, Job 1:5 1:11 1:22 2:5 2:9-10, Leviticus 24:15-16, Leviticus.R 32:5, Matthew 26:65, Midrash Psalms 114:4, Midrash Tanchuma Shemot 9, Midrash Tanchuma Vayakhel 4, Numbers 15:33-35, Pesikta de R'Kahana 11.6, Pirkei de R'Eliezer 48, Psalms 74:18 74:22, Revelation 16:11 16:21, Romans 2:24, Sifre.z Numbers Pinchas 27:1, z.Emor 310 106a, z.Balak 123, z.Bechukotai 19, z.BereshitA 466, z.Shemot 35
Leviticus 24:11-12 - 4QLev-Numa

[3] LXX *named THE NAME*

[4] Leviticus 24:12 - b.Sanhedrin 78b, Exodus 18:15-16 18:23, Numbers 15:34 3:5 36:5-6, z.Emor 106a, z.Emor 319

[5] Leviticus 24:14 - Acts 7:58-59, b.Sanhedrin [Rashi] 44b 49b, b.Sanhedrin 42b 43a 56a, b.Sotah 23b, Deuteronomy 13:10 17:7 21:21 22:21, Jastrow 126a, John 8:59 10:31-33, Joshua 7:25, Leviticus 13:46 20:2 20:27, Leviticus.R 32:1, m.Sanhedrin 6:1, Mas.Soferim 4:9, mt.Hilchot Avodat Kochavim vChukkoteihem 2:10, mt.Hilchot Sanhedrin vHainshin Hameurim Lahem 12:3, Numbers 5:2-4 15:35-36, y.Ketubot 4:5, y.Sanhedrin 5:1 6:1, y.Sotah 3:8, z.Emor 106a, z.Emor 314

[6] Leviticus 24:15 - b.Bava Kamma [Tosefot] 15a, b.Chagigah 11b, b.Kereitot 7ab, b.Kiddushin 30b, b.Menachot [Tosefot] 14b, b.Pesachim 93b, b.Sanhedrin 56a, b.Sheviit 36a, b.Sotah [Tosefot] 24b, b.Yevamot [Rashi] 101a, Ein Yaakov Kiddushin:30b, Exodus 22:28, Jastrow 1544b, Leviticus 5:1 20:16-17, Mekhilta de R'Shimon bar Yochai Nezikin 62:3, Mekhilta de R'Ishmael Bahodesh 8:20, Numbers 9:13, Pesikta Rabbati 23/24:2, Philo De Vita Mosis II 203, Saadia Opinions 3:1 5:1, y.Kiddushin 1:7, y.Peah 1:1, y.Sanhedrin 7:8, z.Emor 315 320, z.Yitro 378

וְנֹקֵב שֵׁם־יְהוָה֙ מ֣וֹת יוּמָ֔ת רָג֥וֹם יִרְגְּמוּ־ב֖וֹ כָּל־הָעֵדָ֑ה כַּגֵּר֙ כָּֽאֶזְרָ֔ח בְּנָקְבוֹ־שֵׁ֖ם יוּמָֽת׃

16[1] And he who blasphemes the name[2] of the LORD, *he shall be put to death, yes, death*[3]; all the congregation shall certainly stone him[4]; the stranger, as well as the homeborn, *when he blasphemes the Name, he shall be put to death*[5].

וְאִ֕ישׁ כִּ֥י יַכֶּ֖ה כָּל־נֶ֣פֶשׁ אָדָ֑ם מ֖וֹת יוּמָֽת׃

17[6] And he who smites any man mortally *shall be put to death, yes, death*[7].

וּמַכֵּ֥ה נֶֽפֶשׁ־בְּהֵמָ֖ה יְשַׁלְּמֶ֑נָּה נֶ֖פֶשׁ תַּ֥חַת נָֽפֶשׁ׃

18[8] And he who smites a beast mortally *shall make it good:*[9] life for life.

וְאִ֕ישׁ כִּֽי־יִתֵּ֥ן מ֖וּם בַּעֲמִית֑וֹ כַּאֲשֶׁ֣ר עָשָׂ֔ה כֵּ֖ן יֵעָ֥שֶׂה לּֽוֹ׃

19[10] And if a man *maims his neighbor; as he has done, so shall it be done to him*[11]:

שֶׁ֚בֶר תַּ֣חַת שֶׁ֔בֶר עַ֚יִן תַּ֣חַת עַ֔יִן שֵׁ֖ן תַּ֣חַת שֵׁ֑ן כַּאֲשֶׁ֨ר יִתֵּ֥ן מוּם֙ בָּֽאָדָ֔ם כֵּ֖ן יִנָּ֥תֶן בּֽוֹ׃

20[12] *Breach for breach*[13], eye for eye, tooth for tooth; as he has maimed a man, so shall it be rendered to him.

---

[1] Leviticus 24:16 - 1 Kings 21:10-21:13, 1 Timothy 1:13, Acts 2:11, b.Sanhedrin 56ab 66a, b.Sheviit 36a, b.Temurah [Rashi] 4a, Deuteronomy.R 2:25, Ein Yaakov Sanhedrin:56b, Exodus 20:7, Genesis.R 16:6 100 [Excl]:2, Guide for the Perplexed 1:64, James 2:7, Jastrow 438a 930b, John 8:58-59 10:33-136, Joseph and Aseneth 11:15, m.Sotah 3:8, Mark 3:28-29, Matthew 12:31 26:66, Mekhilta de R'Shimon bar Yochai Bachodesh 55:1, Mekilta de R'Ishmael Kaspa 1:61, Mekilta de R'Ishmael Nezikin 4:28 5:100, Midrash Tanchuma Balak 5, Midrash Tanchuma Vayikra 7, mt.Hilchot Avodat Kochavim vChukkoteihem 2:7 2:7, mt.Hilchot Melachim uMichamoteihem 9:1, Pesikta de R'Kahana 12.1 22.5a, Psalms 74:10 74:18 19:20, Seder Olam 5:Marah, Song of Songs.R 1:16, y.Sanhedrin 7:8, z.Emor 321 326, z.Korach 11

[2] LXX *names the name*

[3] LXX *let him die the death*

[4] LXX adds *with stones*

[5] LXX *let him die for naming the name of the Lord*

[6] Leviticus 24:17 - b.Arachin [Tosefot] 26a, b.Bava Kamma [Rashi] 10b 16a 43b, b.Bava Kamma [Tosefot] 35a, b.Bava Kamma 83b, b.Bechorot [Tosefot] 3a, b.Chullin [Tosefot] 88a, b.Niddah 44b, b.Sanhedrin [Tosefot] 84b, b.Sanhedrin 78a, Deuteronomy 19:11-12 3:24, Exodus 21:12-14, Genesis 9:5-6, Mekhilta de R'Shimon bar Yochai Nezikin 61:1, Mekilta de R'Ishmael Nezikin 4:2 4:59 5:13 8:16, mt.Hilchot Rotzeach Ushmirat Nefesh 4:6, Numbers 35:30-31, y.Bava Kamma 4:6
Leviticus 24:17-18 - Mekhilta de R'Shimon bar Yochai Nezikin 65:1

[7] LXX *let him die the death*

[8] Leviticus 24:18 - b.Bava Kamma [Rashi] 4b, b.Bava Kamma 10b 83b, b.Beitzah 21a, b.Nazir 48a, Exodus 21:34-36, Kuzari 3.047, Leviticus 24:21, Mekhilta de R'Shimon bar Yochai Pisha 11:1
Leviticus 24:18-21 - mt.Hilchot Naarah Betulah 1:13

[9] LXX *and it shall die, let him render*

[10] Leviticus 24:19 - b.Bava Kamma [Rashi] 4a 26b 34b 53b 87a, b.Bava Kamma [Tosefot] 42a, b.Bava Kamma 26a 33a 83b 84a, b.Gittin [Rashi] 42b, b.Ketubot 32b, b.Sanhedrin [Rashi] 2a, Deut 19:21, Josephus Antiquities 4.8.35, m.Bava Kamma 3:10 8:2, Matthew 5:38 7:2, Mekhilta de R'Ishmael Nezikin 8:79, mt.Hilchot Nizkei Mammon 7:3, mt.Hilchot Sanhedrin vHainshin Hameurim Lahem 16:12

[11] LXX *shall inflict a blemish on his neighbor, as he has done to him, so shall it be done to himself in return*

[12] Leviticus 24:20 - b.Bava Kamma [Rashi] 5a, b.Bava Kamma 83b 84a, b.Ketubot 32b, Deuteronomy 19:21, Exodus 21:23-25, Guide for the Perplexed 3:41, Josephus Antiquities 4.8.35, Kuzari 3.46-47, Matthew 5:38, Mekhilta de R'Ishmael Nezikin 6:2, mt.Hilchot Chovel Umazik 1:3

[13] LXX *bruise for bruise*

וּמַכֵּה בְהֵמָה יְשַׁלְּמֶנָּה וּמַכֵּה אָדָם יוּמָת

מִשְׁפַּט אֶחָד יִהְיֶה לָכֶם כַּגֵּר כָּאֶזְרָח יִהְיֶה כִּי אֲנִי יְהוָה אֱלֹהֵיכֶם

וַיְדַבֵּר מֹשֶׁה אֶל־בְּנֵי יִשְׂרָאֵל וַיּוֹצִיאוּ אֶת־הַמְקַלֵּל אֶל־מִחוּץ לַמַּחֲנֶה וַיִּרְגְּמוּ אֹתוֹ אָבֶן וּבְנֵי־יִשְׂרָאֵל עָשׂוּ כַּאֲשֶׁר צִוָּה יְהוָה אֶת־מֹשֶׁה

21[1] *And he who kills a beast shall make it good; and*[2] he who kills a man shall be put to death.

22[3] You shall have one *manner of law*[4], as for the stranger, so for the home-born; for I am the LORD your God.'

23[5] And Moses spoke to the children of Israel, and they brought forth he who cursed out of the camp, and stoned him with stones. And the children of Israel did as the LORD commanded Moses.

[1] Leviticus 24:21 - b.Bava Kamma [Tos] 2a 86b, b.Bava Kamma 35a 83b 84a, b.Ketubot 35ab, b.Niddah [Tos] 18a, b.Menachot [Tos] 2b, b.Sanhedrin [Tos.] 2b, b.Sanhedrin 79b 84b, Exodus 21:33, Exodus.R 1:28, Jastrow 1349a 1704a, Leviticus 24:17-18, Mekhilta de R'Shimon bar Yochai Nezikin 62:1, Mekilta de R'Ishmael Nezikin 5:13 7:2 8:69, mt.Hilchot Chovel Umazik 6:1, mt.Hilchot Geneivah 3:1, Numbers.R 10:11, y.Bava Kamma 1:1, y.Ketubot 3:2 3:4, y.Shabbat 2:5, y.Terumot 7:1
[2] Missing in LXX
[3] Leviticus 24:22 - b.Bava Batra [Rashbam] 171a, b.Bava Kamma 83b 84a, b.Ketubot 33a, b.Kiddushin 62b, b.Makkot [Tosefot] 6ab, b.Sanhedrin [Tosefot] 2b 6a, b.Sanhedrin 3a 28a 32a, Exodus 12:49, Leviticus 17:10 19:34, mt.Hilchot Edut 3:1, Numbers 9:14 15:15-16 15:29, Pseudo-Phocylides 39, t.Shevuot 3:8, y.Sanhedrin 4:1, z.Acharei Mot 78b
[4] LXX *judgment* [i.e., what qualifies as a death penalty to the Jew, so too the convert]
[5] Leviticus 24:23 - b.Sanhedrin 42b 43a 45a, Hebrews 2:2-3 10:28-29, Leviticus 24:14-16, Numbers 15:35-36, z.Vayakhel 215a

Behar Sinai

Behar[1] – Chapter 25[2]

וַיְדַבֵּר יְהוָה אֶל־מֹשֶׁה בְּהַר סִינַי לֵאמֹר

1[3] And the LORD spoke to Moses in mount Sinai, saying:

דַּבֵּר אֶל־בְּנֵי יִשְׂרָאֵל וְאָמַרְתָּ אֲלֵהֶם כִּי תָבֹאוּ אֶל־הָאָרֶץ אֲשֶׁר אֲנִי נֹתֵן לָכֶם וְשָׁבְתָה הָאָרֶץ שַׁבָּת לַיהוָה

2[4] Speak to the children of Israel and say to them: When you enter the land that I give you, then the land shall keep a sabbath to the LORD.

שֵׁשׁ שָׁנִים תִּזְרַע שָׂדֶךָ וְשֵׁשׁ שָׁנִים תִּזְמֹר כַּרְמֶךָ וְאָסַפְתָּ אֶת־תְּבוּאָתָהּ

3[5] Six years you shall sow your field, and six years you shall prune your vineyard, and gather in the produce.

וּבַשָּׁנָה הַשְּׁבִיעִת שַׁבַּת שַׁבָּתוֹן יִהְיֶה לָאָרֶץ שַׁבָּת לַיהוָה שָׂדְךָ לֹא תִזְרָע וְכַרְמְךָ לֹא תִזְמֹר

4[6] But the seventh year shall be a sabbath of solemn rest for the land, a sabbath to the LORD; you shall neither sow your field, nor[7] prune your vineyard.

---

[1] Behar aliyot: [1] Leviticus 25:1–13, [2] Leviticus 25:14–18, [3] Leviticus 25:19–24, [4] Leviticus 25:25–28, [5] Leviticus 25:29–38, [6] Leviticus 25:39–46, [7] Leviticus 25:47–26:2
Behar and Bechukkotai are combined when there are only 50 available reading days in the year.
[2] Ein Yaakov Shabbat 32b
[3] Leviticus 25:1 - Exodus 19:1, Galatians 4:24-25, Hellenistic Synagogal Prayers 5:17, Leviticus.R 33:1, m.Sanhedrin 3:3, Numbers 1:1 10:11-12, Numbers.R 1:3, Sifre Devarim Ekev 41, z.Behar 107b 1 8
Leviticus 25:1-2 - Midrash Tanchuma Behar 1
Leviticus 25:1-7 - m.Avot 5:8, m.Bava Metzia 9:10, m.Beitzah 4:7, m.Rosh Hashanah 1:1, mt.Pirkei Avot 5:7
Leviticus 25:1-13 - Minchah [Shabbat Monday Thursday Torah reading - Parashah Behar Sinai]
Leviticus 25:1-55 - Josephus Antiquities 3.12.3
[4] Leviticus 25:2 - 2 Chronicles 12:21, b.Nedarim [Rashi] 58b, Commandment #210, Deuteronomy 8:8 8:49 10:4, Exodus 23:10, Isaiah 8:8, Jeremiah 3:5, Kuzari 2.018, Leviticus 14:34 23:32 26:34-35, Leviticus.R 1:1, Midrash Tanchuma Bamidbar 17, Midrash Tanchuma Behar 1, mt.Hilchot Shemitah vYovel 1:1 4:25, Numbers.R 3:8, Psalms 24:1-2 19:16, y.Kilayim 8:1, y.Orlah 1:2, y.Peah 7:7, y.Pesachim 4:9, y.Sanhedrin 7:5, y.Shabbat 7:2, z.Behar 1 5 14
Leviticus 25:2-3 - Mekilta de R'Ishmael Bahodesh 3:19-20
Leviticus 25:2-7 - Deuteronomy.R 2:6, Jubilees 7:37
Leviticus 25:2-8 - Genesis.R 10:4
[5] Leviticus 25:3 - b.Nedarim 61a, Exodus 23:10, m.Avot 5:9, Mekhilta de R'Shimon bar Yochai Kaspa 78:3, mt.Hilchot Shemitah vYovel 10:2, Numbers.R 3:8, y.Kilayim 8:1 8:1, y.Sanhedrin 7:5, y.Shabbat 7:2, y.Sheviit 1:1 2:5, z.Behar 15, z.Pinchas 747
[6] Leviticus 25:4 - 2 Chronicles 12:21, b.Bava Batra [Rashbam] 80b, b.Makkot 8b 21b, b.Menachot [Tosefot] 84a, b.Moed Katan 3ab, b.Pesachim [Rashi] 47b, b.Rosh Hashanah 8b 9a [Tosefot] 10b, b.Shabbat [Rashi] 68b, Commandment #212 #213, Exodus 23:10-11, Kuzari 2.018, Lamentations.R 1:34, Leviticus 25:20-23 26:34-35 2:43, m.Bechorot 4:8, m.Makkot 3:9, m.Yadayim 4:3, mt.Hilchot Sanhedrin vHainshin Hameurim Lahem 19:4, mt.Hilchot Shemitah vYovel 1:1, Philo De Specialibus Legibus II 86, y.Kilayim 8:1, y.Orlah 1:2, y.Sanhedrin 7:5, y.Shabbat 7:2, z.Behar 15 16, z.Vayelech 17
[7] LXX adds *shall you*

אֵת סְפִיחַ קְצִירְךָ לֹא תִקְצוֹר וְאֶת־ עִנְּבֵי נְזִירֶךָ לֹא תִבְצֹר שְׁנַת שַׁבָּתוֹן יִהְיֶה לָאָרֶץ	5[1]	Whatever grows of itself of your harvest you shall not reap, and *the grapes of your undressed vine you shall not gather*[2]; it shall be a year of solemn rest for the land.
וְהָיְתָה שַׁבַּת הָאָרֶץ לָכֶם לְאָכְלָה לְךָ וּלְעַבְדְּךָ וְלַאֲמָתֶךָ וְלִשְׂכִירְךָ וּלְתוֹשָׁבְךָ הַגָּרִים עִמָּךְ	6[3]	And the Sabbath produce of the land shall be food *for you*[4]: for you, and for your servant and for your maid, and for your hired servant and for the settler by your side who sojourns with you;
וְלִבְהֶמְתְּךָ וְלַחַיָּה אֲשֶׁר בְּאַרְצֶךָ תִּהְיֶה כָל־תְּבוּאָתָהּ לֶאֱכֹל	7[5]	And for your cattle, and for the beasts that are in your land, shall all its increase shall be for food.
וְסָפַרְתָּ לְךָ שֶׁבַע שַׁבְּתֹת שָׁנִים שֶׁבַע שָׁנִים שֶׁבַע פְּעָמִים וְהָיוּ לְךָ יְמֵי שֶׁבַע שַׁבְּתֹת הַשָּׁנִים תֵּשַׁע וְאַרְבָּעִים שָׁנָה	8[6]	And you shall number seven sabbaths of years, seven times seven years; and there shall be the days of seven sabbaths of years, even forty-nine years.
וְהַעֲבַרְתָּ שׁוֹפַר תְּרוּעָה בַּחֹדֶשׁ הַשְּׁבִעִי בֶּעָשׂוֹר לַחֹדֶשׁ בְּיוֹם הַכִּפֻּרִים	9[7]	Then shall you make a proclamation with the blast of the horn on the tenth

---

[1] Leviticus 25:5 - 2 Kings 19:29, b.Avodah Zara [Rashi] 15b, b.Bava Metzia [Tosefot] 58a, b.Ketubot [Rashi] 112a, b.Makkot [Tosefot] 8b, b.Menachot [Tosefot] 84a, b.Shabbat [Rashi] 68b, Commandment #214, Commandment #215, Ecclesiastes.R 10:10, Isaiah 13:30, Jastrow 891b 1013b, mt.Hilchot Beit Habechirah 3:13, mt.Hilchot Sanhedrin vHainshin Hameurim Lahem 19:4, mt.Hilchot Shemitah vYovel 1:2 1:3 4:2, Numbers.R 10:8, y.Sheviit 8:6 8:6

[2] LXX *you shall not gather fully the grapes of your dedication*

[3] Leviticus 25:6 - Acts 2:44 4:32 4:34-4:35, b.Arachin [Rashi] 30b, b.Avodah Zara 62a, b.Bava Kamma 11b 102a, b.Bechorot 12b, b.Eruvin [Rashi] 82a, b.Kiddushin [Rashi] 20a, b.Menachot 84a, b.Pesachim 52b, b.Rosh Hashanah [Rashi] 22a, b.Sanhedrin [Rashi] 26a, b.Succah [Rashi] 39a, b.Succah 40a, b.Taanit 19b, b.Zevachim [Rashi] 76a, Exodus 23:11, Jastrow 3943 786b 858a 1520a, Leviticus 1:20, m.Kiddushin 2:7, m.Sheviit 8:1, Mekhilta de R'Shimon bar Yochai Kaspa 78:3, Mekilta de R'Ishmael Kaspa 3:101, mt.Hilchot Beit Habechirah 3:13, mt.Hilchot Shemitah vYovel 4:1 5:13 5:17, y.Demai 3:1, y.Sheviit 8:1
Leviticus 25:6-7 - Mekilta de R'Ishmael Kaspa 3:103

[4] Missing in LXX

[5] Leviticus 25:7 - b.Bava Kamma [Rashi] 11b, b.Bava Kamma 101a, b.Chullin [Tosefot] 120b, b.Menachot [Tosefot] 5b 14b, b.Niddah 51b, b.Pesachim 52b, b.Rosh Hashanah [Rashi] 15a, b.Sanhedrin 26a, b.Shabbat [Rashi] 68b, b.Taanit 6b, b.Zevachim [Tosefot] 31a, m.Nidah 6:7, m.Sheviit 8:1, mt.Hilchot Shemitah vYovel 5:5 7:1, t.Sheviit 2:20 5:1, y.Sheviit 4:6 6:4 9:2
Leviticus 25:7-10 - mt.Hilchot Shevitat Yom Tov 7:12

[6] Leviticus 25:8 - b.Arachin [Tosefot] 32b, b.Beitzah 37b, b.Menachot [Tosefot] 65b, Commandment #221, Genesis 2:2, Jubilees 50:2, Leviticus 23:15, Mas.Abadim 1:1, Midrash Tanchuma Behar 1, mt.Hilchot Shemitah vYovel 10:1, mt.Hilchot Tefilah 2:8, Philo De Virtutibus 99, Sefer Yetzirah 4:15, y.Rosh Hashanah 1:2, z.Vayetze 154a, z.Behar 16, z.Vayetze 141
Leviticus 25:8-16 - Jastrow 567a, m.Bechorot 8:10
Leviticus 25:8-55 - z.Yitro 85b

[7] Leviticus 25:9 - 1 Thessalonians 1:8, 11Q13 2.25, 2 Corinthians 5:19-21, Acts 13:38-39, b.Arachin 2b 28b, b.Rosh Hashanah [Rashi] 26a, b.Rosh Hashanah [Tosefot] 26b 16a, b.Rosh Hashanah 27b 30a 33b 34a, b.Shabbat 96b 131b, Commandment #216, Jastrow 359b, Leviticus 16:20 16:30 23:24 23:27 25:10-12 3:17 3:24, m.Megillah 2:5, m.Rosh Hashanah 3:2, Mas.Abadim 1:1, mt.Hilchot Shemitah vYovel 10:1 10:10, mt.Hilchot Shofar Sukkah vLulav 1:1 1:6 3:1, Numbers 10:10 12:4, Pesikta Rabbati 39:1, Philo De Congressu Quaerendae Eruditionis Gratia 89, Psalms 89:16, Romans 10:18 15:19, Siman 133:25, y.Rosh Hashanah 1:2 3:5 4:1, z.Yitro 81b, z.Emor 82, z.Yitro 301

תַּעֲבִירוּ שׁוֹפָר בְּכָל־אַרְצְכֶם

day of the seventh month; in the day of atonement you shall make proclamation with the horn throughout all your land.

וְקִדַּשְׁתֶּם אֵת שְׁנַת הַחֲמִשִּׁים שָׁנָה
וּקְרָאתֶם דְּרוֹר בָּאָרֶץ לְכָל־יֹשְׁבֶיהָ
יוֹבֵל הִוא תִּהְיֶה לָכֶם וְשַׁבְתֶּם אִישׁ
אֶל־אֲחֻזָּתוֹ וְאִישׁ אֶל־מִשְׁפַּחְתּוֹ תָּשֻׁבוּ

10[1] And you shall hallow the fiftieth year, and proclaim liberty throughout the land to all its inhabitants; it shall be a jubilee for you; you shall let every man return to his possession, and every man shall return to his family.

יוֹבֵל הִוא שְׁנַת הַחֲמִשִּׁים שָׁנָה תִּהְיֶה
לָכֶם לֹא תִזְרָעוּ וְלֹא תִקְצְרוּ אֶת־
סְפִיחֶיהָ וְלֹא תִבְצְרוּ אֶת־נְזִרֶיהָ

11[2] That fiftieth year shall be a jubilee to you; you shall not sow, neither reap what grows of itself, *nor gather the grapes of the undressed vines*[3].

כִּי יוֹבֵל הִוא קֹדֶשׁ תִּהְיֶה לָכֶם מִן־
הַשָּׂדֶה תֹּאכְלוּ אֶת־תְּבוּאָתָהּ

12[4] For it is a jubilee; it shall be holy to you; you shall eat its increase out of the field.

בִּשְׁנַת הַיּוֹבֵל הַזֹּאת תָּשֻׁבוּ אִישׁ אֶל־
אֲחֻזָּתוֹ

13[5] *In this year of jubilee*[6] you shall return every man to his possession.

---

[1] Leviticus 25:10 - 1 Peter 2:16, 2 Corinthians 3:17, 2 Peter 2:19-20, b.Arachin 32b, b.Bechorot 52b, b.Gittin [Rashi] 65a, b.Kiddushin 38b, b.Megillah [Rashi] 14b, b.Nedarim 61a, b.Rosh Hashanah 9b 24a, b.Sanhedrin 10b, b.Yoma [Rashi] 86b, Commandment #222, Esther.R 2:9, Exodus 20:2, Exodus.R 15:23, Ezra 1:3, Galatians 4:25-5:1 5:13, Isaiah 1:9 49:24-25 61:1-3 15:4, Jastrow 289a 1052a 1319b, Jeremiah 10:8 34:13-17, John 8:32-36, Leviticus 1:13 25:26-28 25:33-34 27:17-24, Leviticus.R 29:11, Luke 2:14 4:16-21, m.Rosh Hashanah 2:7, Mekhilta de R'Shimon bar Yochai Kaspa 78:3, Mekhilta de R'Shimon bar Yochai Nezikin 59:3, Mekilta de R'Ishmael Nezikin 2:87, Midrash Tanchuma Bamidbar 17, mt.Hilchot Shemitah vYovel 10:1, Numbers 36:2-9, Numbers.R 3:8, Pesikta de R'Kahana 23.1, Psalms 2:7, Romans 6:17-18, Sefer Yetzirah 4:15, y.Gittin 4:3, y.Rosh Hashanah 2:5, y.Sanhedrin 1:2, y.Sheviit 10:2, z.Tetzaveh 183a, z.Vayakhel 211a 220a, z.Yitro 83b, Zechariah 9:11-12, z.Behar 17 21, z.Ha'azinu 86, z.Safra Det'zniuta 73, z.Tetzaveh 70 71, z.Vayakhel 318 495, z.Yitro 353
[2] Leviticus 25:11 - b.Rosh Hashanah 9b, Commandment #223 #224 #225, Leviticus 25:4-5 3:17, mt.Hilchot Sanhedrin vHainshin Hameurim Lahem 19:4, y.Rosh Hashanah 3:5
[3] LXX *neither shall ye gather its dedicated fruits*
[4] Leviticus 25:12 - b.Avodah Zara 54b, b.Kiddushin 53a 58a, b.Pesachim [Tosefot] 52a, b.Succah 40b, b.Zevachim [Rashi] 16b, Exodus.R 15:23, Jastrow 338b, Leviticus 25:6-25:7, mt.Hilchot Shemitah vYovel 5:15 6:6, y.Sheviit 4:6 4:7 7:1 9:3, z.Lech Lecha 447, z.Mishpatim 501 510, z.Yitro 396
[5] Leviticus 25:13 - 11Q13 2.2, b.Arachin 30b 31b, b.Bava Batra 112a, b.Kiddushin 20a, b.Succah 40b, Leviticus 1:10 27:17-24, mt.Hilchot Shemitah vYovel 11:19, Numbers 12:4, Sifre Devarim Reeh 112, z.Behar 20, z.Toldot 68
Leviticus 25:13-14 - t.Arachin 5:9
[6] LXX *In the year of the release [even] the jubilee of it*

וְכִי־תִמְכְּרוּ מִמְכָּר לַעֲמִיתֶךָ אוֹ קָנֹה מִיַּד עֲמִיתֶךָ אַל־תּוֹנוּ אִישׁ אֶת־אָחִיו

14[1] And if you sell[2] to your neighbor, or buy of your neighbor's hand, you shall not wrong one another.

בְּמִסְפַּר שָׁנִים אַחַר הַיּוֹבֵל תִּקְנֶה מֵאֵת עֲמִיתֶךָ בְּמִסְפַּר שְׁנֵי־תְבוּאֹת יִמְכָּר־לָךְ

15[3] According to the number of years after the jubilee you shall buy of your neighbor, and according to the number of years of the crops he shall sell to you.

לְפִי רֹב הַשָּׁנִים תַּרְבֶּה מִקְנָתוֹ וּלְפִי מְעֹט הַשָּׁנִים תַּמְעִיט מִקְנָתוֹ כִּי מִסְפַּר תְּבוּאֹת הוּא מֹכֵר לָךְ

16[4] According to the multitude of the years you shall increase its price, and according to the fewness of the years you shall diminish its price; for he sells the number of crops to you.

וְלֹא תוֹנוּ אִישׁ אֶת־עֲמִיתוֹ וְיָרֵאתָ מֵאֱלֹהֶיךָ כִּי אֲנִי יְהֹוָה אֱלֹהֵיכֶם

17[5] And you shall not wrong one another; but you shall fear [6]your God; for I am the LORD your God.

וַעֲשִׂיתֶם אֶת־חֻקֹּתַי וְאֶת־מִשְׁפָּטַי תִּשְׁמְרוּ וַעֲשִׂיתֶם אֹתָם וִישַׁבְתֶּם עַל־הָאָרֶץ לָבֶטַח

18[7] You shall do My statutes and keep My ordinances and do them; and you shall dwell in the land in safety.

---

[1] Leviticus 25:14 - 1 Corinthians 6:8, 1 Samuel 12:3-4, 2 Chronicles 16:10, 4Q271 1 i 5, 4Q271 frag 3 ll.4-5, Amos 5:11-12 8:4-7, b.Arachin 30b, b.Avodah Zara [Rashi] 63a, b.Avodah Zara [Tosefot] 15a 71a, b.Bava Batra [Rashbam] 83b, b.Bava Batra [Tosefot] 54b, b.Bava Kamma [Tosefot] 88a 57a, b.Bava Metzia [Rashi] 48a, b.Bava Metzia 47b 51a 56b 58b, b.Bechorot [Tosefot] 3b, b.Bechorot 13ab, b.Ketubot [Rashi] 84a, b.Kiddushin [Rashi] 11b 14b, b.Kiddushin 20a 26a, b.Makkot [Tosefot] 3b, b.Menachot [Tosefot] 67a, b.Succah 40b, b.Temurah [Rashi] 16a, Commandment #170 #229, Deuteronomy 16:19-20, Ecclesiastes 5:9, Ein Yaakov Bava Metzia:58b, Ezekiel 22:7 22:12-13, Gates of Repentance 3.24 3.178, Isaiah 1:17 3:12-15 5:7 9:15 10:6, James 5:1-5, Jastrow 1391b, Jeremiah 22:17, Job 20:19-20, Judges 4:3, Leviticus 19:13 1:17, Leviticus.R 33:1, Luke 3:14, m.Bava Metzia 4:3 4:9, Mesillat Yesharim 11:Traits-of-Nekuyut, Micah 2:2-3 6:10-12 7:3, Midrash Tanchuma Behar 1, mt.Hilchot Avadim 8:11, mt.Hilchot Mechirah 12:1 13:8, Nehemiah 9:36-37, Proverbs 14:31 21:13 22:16 4:3 4:8 4:16, Psalms 10:19, Siman 62:1, t.Bava Metzia 3:25, y.Bava Metzia 4:2, z.Yitro 211
Leviticus 25:14-18 - Midrash Tanchuma Behar 1
[2] i.e., *land*
[3] Leviticus 25:15 - b.Arachin [Rashi] 3b, b.Arachin [Tosefot] 4a, b.Arachin 14b 18b 29b 30a 33b, b.Bava Metzia 16a, b.Gittin 48a, b.Kiddushin [Rashi] 20b [Tosefot] 21a, b.Niddah 47a, b.Rosh Hashanah [Rashi] 29a, Leviticus 27:18-23, mt.Hilchot Shemitah vYovel 11:5-6 11:9, Philippians 4:5, t.Arachin 5:1
[4] Leviticus 25:16 - b.Arachin 14b 29b, b.Kiddushin [Rashi] 20b, b.Yevamot 46a, Leviticus 1:27 1:51
Leviticus 25:16-17 - t.Bava Metzia 3:25
[5] Leviticus 25:17 - 1 Samuel 12:24, 1 Thessalonians 4:6, 2 Chronicles 19:7, Acts 9:31 10:2 10:35, b.Bava Batra [Rashi] 78a, b.Bava Metzia [Tosefot] 61a, b.Bava Metzia 58b 59ab, b.Shabbat [Tosefot] 81b, b.Yoma [Rashi] 71b, Commandment #28, Deuteronomy 1:18, Ein Yaakov Bava Metzia:58b 59b, Exodus 20:17, Gates of Repentance 3.24 3.49 3.165 3.214 3.219, Genesis 20:11 22:12 15:9 18:18, Jeremiah 7:5-6 22:16, Leviticus 19:14 19:32 1:14 1:43, Luke 12:5, Malachi 3:5, Mesillat Yesharim 11:Nekiyut-in-Hurtful-Speech 11:Traits-of-Nekuyut, mt.Hilchot Mechirah 14:12 14:18, mt.Hilchot Teshuvah 7:8, Nehemiah 5:9 5:15, Proverbs 1:7 22:22, Psalms 19:10, Romans 3:18 11:20, Siman 29:17 63:1, z.Acharei Mot 78b, z.Chukat 17, z.Ha'azinu 135, z.Vayakhel 81
[6] LXX adds *the LORD*
[7] Leviticus 25:18 - b.Sanhedrin [Tosefot] 60a, Deuteronomy 12:10 28:1-14 9:12 9:28, Ezekiel 33:24-26 9:29 34:25-28 36:24-28, Jeremiah 7:3-7 23:6 1:5 9:16, Leviticus 19:37 26:3-12, Midrash Tanchuma Ki Tavo 1, Proverbs 1:33, Psalms 4:9 7:18, z.Bechukotai 16

וְנָתְנָה הָאָרֶץ פִּרְיָהּ וַאֲכַלְתֶּם לָשֹׂבַע וִישַׁבְתֶּם לָבֶטַח עָלֶיהָ

19[1] And the land shall yield her *fruit*[2], and you shall eat until you have enough, and dwell there in safety.

וְכִי תֹאמְרוּ מַה־נֹּאכַל בַּשָּׁנָה הַשְּׁבִיעִת הֵן לֹא נִזְרָע וְלֹא נֶאֱסֹף אֶת־תְּבוּאָתֵנוּ

20[3] And if you shall say: 'What shall we eat the seventh year? Behold, we may not sow, nor gather in our increase;'

וְצִוִּיתִי אֶת־בִּרְכָתִי לָכֶם בַּשָּׁנָה הַשִּׁשִּׁית וְעָשָׂת אֶת־הַתְּבוּאָה לִשְׁלֹשׁ הַשָּׁנִים

21[4] Then I will command My blessing on you in the sixth year, and it shall bring forth produce for the three years.

וּזְרַעְתֶּם אֵת הַשָּׁנָה הַשְּׁמִינִת וַאֲכַלְתֶּם מִן־הַתְּבוּאָה יָשָׁן עַד הַשָּׁנָה הַתְּשִׁיעִת עַד־בּוֹא תְּבוּאָתָהּ תֹּאכְלוּ יָשָׁן

22[5] And you shall sow the eighth year, and eat of the produce, the old store; until the ninth year; until her produce comes in, you shall eat the old store.

וְהָאָרֶץ לֹא תִמָּכֵר לִצְמִתֻת כִּי־לִי הָאָרֶץ כִּי־גֵרִים וְתוֹשָׁבִים אַתֶּם עִמָּדִי

23[6] And the land shall not be sold in perpetuity; for the land is Mine; for you are strangers and settlers with Me.

וּבְכֹל אֶרֶץ אֲחֻזַּתְכֶם גְּאֻלָּה תִּתְּנוּ לָאָרֶץ

24[7] And in all the land of your possession you shall grant a redemption for the land.

כִּי־יָמוּךְ אָחִיךָ וּמָכַר מֵאֲחֻזָּתוֹ וּבָא גֹאֲלוֹ הַקָּרֹב אֵלָיו וְגָאַל אֵת מִמְכַּר אָחִיו

25[8] If your brother becomes poor, and sells some of his possession, then his kinsman who is next to him shall come and shall redeem what his brother has sold.

---

[1] Leviticus 25:19 - Ezekiel 34:25-28 12:30, Isaiah 6:23 65:21-22, Jastrow 224b 1151a, Joel 2:24 2:26, Leviticus 2:5, Philo De Specialibus Legibus II 117, Psalms 67:7 85:13, Saadia Opinions 10:5

[2] LXX *increase*

[3] Leviticus 25:20 - 2 Chronicles 1:9, 2 Kings 6:15-6:17 7:2, b.Menachot [Rashi] 5b, b.Pesachim 51b, b.Rosh Hashanah [Rashi] 3a, Hebrews 13:5-13:6, Isaiah 1:2, Leviticus 1:4, Luke 12:29, Matthew 6:25-6:34 8:26, Numbers 11:4 11:13, Philippians 4:6, Psalms 78:19-78:20, z.Behar 110b, z.Behar 52 57

[4] Leviticus 25:21 - 2 Corinthians 9:10, b.Nedarim 61a, b.Rosh Hashanah 13a, Deuteronomy 4:3 4:8, Exodus 16:29, Exodus.R 15:23, Genesis 2:12 17:47, Leviticus 1:4 25:8-11, Mekilta de R'Ishmael Bahodesh 1:98, Proverbs 10:22, Psalms 13:3

[5] Leviticus 25:22 - 2 Kings 19:29, b.Bava Batra [Rashi] 92a, b.Rosh Hashanah 13b, Ein Yaakov Bava Batra:91b, Isaiah 13:30, Jastrow 995b, Joshua 5:11-5:12, Leviticus 2:10, y.Sukkah 1:1

[6] Leviticus 25:23 - 1 Chronicles 5:15, 1 Kings 21:3, 1 Peter 2:11, 2 Chronicles 7:20, b.Arachin 15b, b.Bava Metzia [Rashi] 109a, b.Bava Metzia 79a, b.Gittin 47a, b.Sanhedrin 16b, Commandment #267, Deuteronomy 8:43, Exodus 19:5, Exodus.R 3:13, Ezekiel 24:14, Genesis 23:4 23:9, Guide for the Perplexed 3:39, Hebrews 11:9-13, Hosea 9:3, Isaiah 8:8, Jastrow 567a 855a, Joel 2:18 4:2, Kuzari 2.18, Leviticus 1:10, Leviticus.R 2:2, Midrash Psalms 18:32, Midrash Tanchuma Behar 1, Midrash Tanchuma Terumah 3, mt.Hilchot Shemitah vYovel 11:1, mt.Hilchot Terumot 1:10, Numbers.R 15:17 23:11, Philo De Cherubim 108, Psalms 24:1 39:13 85:2 23:19, y.Demai 5:9, y.Gittin 4:9, z.Mishpatim 94b, z.Ki Tisa 36, z.Mishpatim 9
Leviticus 25:23-28 - mt.Hilchot Shemitah vYovel 10:16

[7] Leviticus 25:24 - 1 Corinthians 1:30, b.Kiddushin 21a, b.Yevamot 54a, Commandment #226, Ephesians 1:7 1:14 4:30, Jastrow 567a, Leviticus 1:27 1:31 25:51-53, mt.Hilchot Shemitah vYovel 10:16, Romans 8:23

[8] Leviticus 25:25 - 2 Corinthians 8:9, b.Arachin 30b, b.Kiddushin 9a 20a 21a, Hebrews 2:13-14, Jastrow 216b, Jeremiah 32:7-8, Leviticus.R 34:1, Midrash Psalms 9:12, Midrash Tanchuma Behar 1 2 3 4, mt.Hilchot Avadim 1:1, mt.Hilchot Shemitah vYovel 11:3 11:18, Revelation 5:9, Ruth 2:20 3:2 3:9 3:12 4:4-6, t.Arachin 5:9, z.Pinchas 54

וְאִישׁ כִּי לֹא יִהְיֶה־לּוֹ גֹּאֵל וְהִשִּׂיגָה
יָדוֹ וּמָצָא כְּדֵי גְאֻלָּתוֹ

וְחִשַּׁב אֶת־שְׁנֵי מִמְכָּרוֹ וְהֵשִׁיב אֶת־
הָעֹדֵף לָאִישׁ אֲשֶׁר מָכַר־לוֹ וְשָׁב
לַאֲחֻזָּתוֹ

וְאִם לֹא־מָצְאָה יָדוֹ דֵּי הָשִׁיב לוֹ וְהָיָה
מִמְכָּרוֹ בְּיַד הַקֹּנֶה אֹתוֹ עַד שְׁנַת
הַיּוֹבֵל וְיָצָא בַּיֹּבֵל וְשָׁב לַאֲחֻזָּתוֹ

וְאִישׁ כִּי־יִמְכֹּר בֵּית־מוֹשַׁב עִיר חוֹמָה
וְהָיְתָה גְּאֻלָּתוֹ עַד־תֹּם שְׁנַת מִמְכָּרוֹ
יָמִים תִּהְיֶה גְאֻלָּתוֹ

וְאִם לֹא־יִגָּאֵל עַד־מְלֹאת לוֹ שָׁנָה
תְמִימָה וְקָם הַבַּיִת אֲשֶׁר־בָּעִיר
אֲשֶׁר־לֹא ״אֲשֶׁר־לוֹ״ חֹמָה לַצְּמִיתֻת
לַקֹּנֶה אֹתוֹ לְדֹרֹתָיו לֹא יֵצֵא בַּיֹּבֵל:

וּבָתֵּי הַחֲצֵרִים אֲשֶׁר אֵין־לָהֶם חֹמָה
סָבִיב עַל־שְׂדֵה הָאָרֶץ יֵחָשֵׁב גְּאֻלָּה

26[1] And if a man has no one to redeem it, and he becomes rich and finds sufficient means to redeem it;

27[2] Then let him count the years of its sale and restore the overplus to the man to whom he sold it; and he shall return to his possession.

28[3] But if he does not have sufficient means to get it back for himself, then what he has sold shall remain in the hand of he who bought it until the year of jubilee; and in the jubilee it shall go out, and he shall return to his possession.

29[4] And if a man sells a dwelling house in a walled city, then he may redeem it within a whole year after it is sold; for a full year he shall have the right of redemption.

30[5] And if it is not redeemed within the space of a full year, then the house that is in the walled city shall be made sure in perpetuity to he who bought it, throughout his generations; it shall not go out in the jubilee.

31[6] But the houses of the villages that have no walls around them shall be reckoned with the fields of the country; they may

[1] Leviticus 25:26 - b.Arachin 30a 30b, b.Kiddushin [Rashi] 21a, b.Kiddushin 21a, b.Makkot 8a, b.Sanhedrin [Tosefot] 86a, Jastrow 369b 825a, Leviticus 5:7, mt.Hilchot Shemitah vYovel 11:17

[2] Leviticus 25:27 - b.Arachin [Rashi] 29b 33a, b.Arachin [Tosefot] 31a, b.Arachin 14b 30a, Jastrow 343a, m.Arachin 9:2 9:7, Mekhilta de R'Shimon bar Yochai Nezikin 60:1, mt.Hilchot Shemitah vYovel 11:14 11:16, t.Arachin 5:2

[3] Leviticus 25:28 - 1 Corinthians 15:52-54, 1 Peter 1:4-5, 1 Thessalonians 4:13-18, b.Arachin [Rashi] 26a, b.Arachin 14b 28b 29a, Isaiah 35:9-10, Jeremiah 8:15, Leviticus 1:10 1:13, y.Gittin 4:9
Leviticus 25:28-29 - 4QLevb
Leviticus 25:28-36 - 11QpaleoLeva

[4] Leviticus 25:29 - b.Arachin [Rashi] 29a 33a, b.Arachin [Tosefot] 32b, b.Arachin 18b 30b 31a 31b 32a 33b, b.Ketubot 57b, b.Kiddushin 20ab, b.Megillah 3b, b.Menachot [Tosefot] 43a, b.Nazir 5a, b.Niddah 47a, b.Succah [Rashi] 3b, Commandment #269, m.Arachin 9:3 9:5 9:7, Mekhilta de R'Shimon bar Yochai Pisha 3:1, Mekhilta de R'Ishmael Pisha 17:211, Midrash Tanchuma Behar 1 3, Midrash Tanchuma Bo 14, mt.Hilchot Beit HaBechirah 7:14, mt.Hilchot Shemitah vYovel 12:1, Numbers.R 9:24 10:17, Saadia Opinions 8:3, t.Arachin 5:9, t.Maaser Sheni 2:15, y.Megillah 1:1

[5] Leviticus 25:30 - b.Arachin [Tosefot] 4a, b.Arachin 15b 29a 31a-33b, b.Bava Kamma 82b, b.Chullin [Tosefot] 65a, b.Gittin [Rashi] 74b, b.Megillah 3b 5b 10b, b.Rosh Hashanah [Rashi] 29a, b.Rosh Hashanah 6b, b.Sheviit 16a, b.Yoma 65b, b.Zevachim [Tosefot] 73a, Ein Yaakov Arachin 15b, Guide for the Perplexed 1:12, Jastrow 467a 1288a 1290a, Leviticus.R 7:6, m.Arachin 9:4, Mas.Soferim 6:5, mt.Hilchot Beit HaBechirah 7:14, mt.Hilchot Shemitah vYovel 12:5 12:8 12:9, Numbers.R 9:24, Pesikta Rabbati 41:3, Saadia Opinions 8:3, t.Bava Metzia 4:2, y.Maasrot 3:4, z.Ki Tissa 189b

[6] Leviticus 25:31 - b.Arachin 32a 33a 33b, b.Kiddushin 21ab, b.Megillah 5b, mt.Hilchot Shemitah vYovel 12:10, Philo De Specialibus Legibus II 116, Psalms 49:8-9, z.Behar 22

תִּהְיֶה־לֹּו וּבַיֹּבֵל יֵצֵא

וְעָרֵי הַלְוִיִּם בָּתֵּי עָרֵי אֲחֻזָּתָם גְּאֻלַּת
עֹולָם תִּהְיֶה לַלְוִיִּם

וַאֲשֶׁר יִגְאַל מִן־הַלְוִיִּם וְיָצָא מִמְכַּר־
בַּיִת וְעִיר אֲחֻזָּתֹו בַּיֹּבֵל כִּי בָתֵּי עָרֵי
הַלְוִיִּם הִוא אֲחֻזָּתָם בְּתֹוךְ בְּנֵי יִשְׂרָאֵל

וּשְׂדֵה מִגְרַשׁ עָרֵיהֶם לֹא יִמָּכֵר כִּי־
אֲחֻזַּת עֹולָם הוּא לָהֶם

וְכִי־יָמוּךְ אָחִיךָ וּמָטָה יָדֹו עִמָּךְ
וְהֶחֱזַקְתָּ בֹּו גֵּר וְתֹושָׁב וָחַי עִמָּךְ

אַל־תִּקַּח מֵאִתֹּו נֶשֶׁךְ וְתַרְבִּית וְיָרֵאתָ
מֵאֱלֹהֶיךָ וְחֵי אָחִיךָ עִמָּךְ

be redeemed, and they shall go out in the jubilee.

32¹ But as for the cities of the Levites, the houses of the cities of their possession, the Levites shall have a perpetual right of redemption.

33² And if a man purchases of the Levites, then the house that was sold in the city of his possession shall go out in the jubilee; for the houses of the cities of the Levites are their possession among the children of Israel.

34³ But the fields of the open land around their cities may not be sold; for that is their perpetual possession.

35⁴ And if your brother becomes poor, and his means fail with you; then you shall uphold him: he shall liver with you as a stranger and a settler.

36⁵ You shall take no interest from him or increase; but fear your God⁶; so your brother may live with you.

---

¹ Leviticus 25:32 - b.Arachin 33b [Rashi] 26b 32a 33b [Tosefot] 4a, Joshua 21:1-45, m.Arachin 9:8, mt.Hilchot Arachim Vacharamim 4:21, mt.Hilchot Shemitah vYovel 13:7, Numbers 35:1-8

² Leviticus 25:33 - b.Arachin [Rashi] 3b, b.Arachin [Tosefot] 3b, b.Arachin 33a 33b, b.Bava Metzia 109a, b.Rosh Hashanah [Rashi] 29a, Deuteronomy 18:1-18:2, m.Arachin 9:8, mt.Hilchot Shemitah vYovel 11:8, Numbers 18:20-24

³ Leviticus 25:34 - Acts 4:36-37, b.Arachin 28a 33b 34a [Tosefot] 28b 31b, Commandment #268, Leviticus 1:23, m.Arachin 8:5, mt.Hilchot Shemitah vYovel 13:4, Numbers 35:2-5, t.Arachin 4:33

⁴ Leviticus 25:35 - 1 John 3:17, 2 Corinthians 8:9 9:1 9:12-15, Acts 11:29, b.Arachin 30b, b.Avodah Zara [Rashi] 20a, b.Avodah Zara 64b, b.Bava Metzia [Tosefot] 111b, b.Bava Metzia 71a 114a, b.Kiddushin [Rashi] 14a, b.Kiddushin 20a, b.Pesachim [Rashi] 21b, b.Yevamot [Rashi] 47a, Deuteronomy 10:18-19 15:7-8 24:14-15, Exodus 23:9, Galatians 2:10, Hebrews 13:2, James 2:5-6, Jastrow 7733 1659a, John 12:8, Josephus Antiquities 4.8.25, Leviticus 19:34 1:25, Luke 6:35, Mark 14:7, Matthew 1:35, Midrash Tanchuma Behar 1 2, mt.Hilchot Avodat Kochavim vChukkoteihem 10:2, mt.Hilchot Matnot Aniyim 7:1 10:7, mt.Hilchot Melachim uMichamoteihem 10:10 10:12, mt.Hilchot Shevuot 6:11, mt.Hilchot Shabbat 2:12, mt.Hilchot Zechiyah Umatanah 3:11, Proverbs 14:20-21 14:31 17:5 19:17, Psalms 37:26 41:2 16:5 16:9, Romans 12:13 12:18 12:20, Siman 34:12
Leviticus 25:35-36 - t.Arachin 5:9

⁵ Leviticus 25:36 - Avot de R'Natan 26, b.Arachin 30b, b.Avodah Zara [Tosefot] 6a 26b, b.Bava Kamma 102a, b.Bava Metzia [Rashi] 60b, b.Bava Metzia [Tosefot] 111b, b.Bava Metzia 61b 62a 71a 75b 88b, b.Berachot [Rashi] 12b, b.Ketubot [Rashi] 15b, b.Kiddushin [Rashi] 33b, b.Nedarim 65b, b.Temurah 6b, Deuteronomy 23:21-21, Ein Yaakov Bava Metzia:62a, Exodus 22:25, Ezekiel 18:8 18:13 18:17 22:12, Gates of Repentance 3.25, Jastrow 748b, Leviticus 1:17, m.Bava Metzia 5:1 5:11, Mas.Gerim 1:10, Mekilta de R'Ishmael Beshallah 1:150, Mekilta de R'Ishmael Kaspa 1:28, Midrash Tanchuma Mishpatim 9, mt.Hilchot Malveh VLoveh 4:2, mt.Hilchot Matnot Aniyim 7:1, mt.Hilchot Shevuot 6:11, Nehemiah 5:7-10 5:15, Numbers.R 15:17, Proverbs 4:8, Psalms 15:5, Pseudo-Phocylides 83, Sifre Devarim Ki Tetze 235 262, Sifre Devarim Shoftim 186-187, Siman 34:1, t.Sotah 5:11, Tanya Igeret Hakodesh §16, y.Bava Metzia 5:1 5:8, y.Nedarim 9:4
Leviticus 25:36-53 - 4 Maccabees 2:9

⁶ LXX adds I am the LORD

אֶת־כַּסְפְּךָ לֹא־תִתֵּן לוֹ בְּנֶשֶׁךְ וּבְמַרְבִּית לֹא־תִתֵּן אָכְלֶךָ

37[1] You shall not lend him your money with interest, *nor give him your victuals for increase*[2].

אֲנִי יְהוָה אֱלֹהֵיכֶם אֲשֶׁר־הוֹצֵאתִי אֶתְכֶם מֵאֶרֶץ מִצְרָיִם לָתֵת לָכֶם אֶת־אֶרֶץ כְּנַעַן לִהְיוֹת לָכֶם לֵאלֹהִים

38[3] I am the LORD your God, who brought you forth out of the land of Egypt, to give you the land of Canaan, to be your God.

וְכִי־יָמוּךְ אָחִיךָ עִמָּךְ וְנִמְכַּר־לָךְ לֹא־תַעֲבֹד בּוֹ עֲבֹדַת עָבֶד

39[4] And if your brother with you becomes poor, and sells himself to you, you shall not make him to serve *as a bondservant*[5].

כְּשָׂכִיר כְּתוֹשָׁב יִהְיֶה עִמָּךְ עַד־שְׁנַת הַיֹּבֵל יַעֲבֹד עִמָּךְ

40[6] He shall be as a hired servant, and as a settler with you; he shall serve with you until the year of jubilee.

וְיָצָא מֵעִמָּךְ הוּא וּבָנָיו עִמּוֹ וְשָׁב אֶל־מִשְׁפַּחְתּוֹ וְאֶל־אֲחֻזַּת אֲבֹתָיו יָשׁוּב

41[7] Then he shall go out from you, he and his children with him, and shall return to his own family, and he shall return to the possession of his fathers.

כִּי־עֲבָדַי הֵם אֲשֶׁר־הוֹצֵאתִי אֹתָם מֵאֶרֶץ מִצְרָיִם לֹא יִמָּכְרוּ מִמְכֶּרֶת עָבֶד

42[8] For they are My servants, whom I brought forth out of the land of Egypt; they shall not be sold as bondmen.

---

[1] Leviticus 25:37 - b.Avodah Zara [Tosefot] 20a, b.Bava Metzia 60b 61a 75b, b.Yoma [Tosefot] 52b, Commandment #171, m.Bava Metzia 5:1 5:11, Mekilta de R'Ishmael Kiaspa 1:25, Midrash Tanchuma Mishpatim 9, mt.Hilchot Malveh vLoveh 4:1, Sifre Devarim Ki Tetze 262, Siman 65:1, y.Bava Metzia 5:1 5:8

[2] LXX *you shall not lend your meat to him to be returned with increase*

[3] Leviticus 25:38 - b.Bava Metzia 61b, b.Ketubot 11b, b.Temurah 6b, Ein Yaakov Ketubot:110b, Exodus 20:2, Exodus.R 15:23, Genesis 17:7, Hebrews 11:16, Jeremiah 7:2 7:34 8:38, Leviticus 11:45 22:32-33, Numbers 15:41, t.Avodah Zarah 4:5, z.Acharei Mot 78b

[4] Leviticus 25:39 - 1 Kings 9:22, 2 Kings 4:1, b.Arachin 30b, b.Bava Kamma [Rashi] 113b, b.Bava Metzia 71a, b.Kiddushin [Rashi] 14b, b.Kiddushin 20a, Commandment #190, Deuteronomy 15:12-15:14, Exodus 1:14 21:2 22:3, Jeremiah 1:14 3:7 6:8 10:14, Leviticus 1:46, m.Bava Kamma 8:3, m.Bava Metzia 1:5, m.Kiddushin 1:2, Mekhilta de R'Shimon bar Yochai Nezikin 58:2 60:1, Mekilta de R'Ishmael Nezikin 1:27, Mekilta de R'Ishmael Nezikin 1:57, Midrash Tanchuma Behar 1 3, mt.Hilchot Avadim 1:1 1:7, Nehemiah 5:5, Sifre Devarim Reeh 118, z.Mishpatim 5

[5] LXX *with the servitude of a slave*

[6] Leviticus 25:40 - b.Arachin [Rashi] 30b, b.Arachin 29a, b.Bava Kamma [Tosefot] 87b, b.Kiddushin [Tosefot] 15a, b.Kiddushin 14b, Exodus 21:2-21:3, Mas.Abadim 1:2, Mekilta de R'Ishmael Nezikin 1:65, Mekilta de R'Ishmael Nezikin 1:71, Mekilta de R'Ishmael Nezikin 2:89, mt.Hilchot Avadim 1:7 1:10 2:2 2:5, mt.Hilchot Shemitah vYovel 10:13, Sifre Devarim Reeh 123, y.Kiddushin 1:2

[7] Leviticus 25:41 - b.Bava Metzia 71a, b.Chagigah 2b, b.Kiddushin 15a 21b 22a, b.Makkot 13a, Exodus 21:3, Jastrow 1556b, John 8:32, Leviticus 1:10 1:28, Mekhilta de R'Shimon bar Yochai Nezikin 58:3, Mekilta de R'Ishmael Nezikin 1:119, Midrash Tanchuma Behar 1, mt.Hilchot Avadim 1:2 1:9 3:8, Romans 6:14, Titus 2:14, y.Kiddushin 1:2

[8] Leviticus 25:42 - 1 Corinthians 7:21-7:23, b.Bava Metzia [Rashi] 77a, b.Bava Metzia [Tosefot] 48a, b.Kiddushin 15a, b.Sanhedrin 86a, Commandment #191, Jastrow 981a, Leviticus 1:55, Mekilta de R'Ishmael Nezikin 1:95, Mekilta de R'Ishmael Nezikin 3:62, mt.Hilchot Avadim 1:5, mt.Hilchot Geneivah 9:1, Romans 6:22, z.Balak 205

לֹא־תִרְדֶּה בוֹ בְּפָרֶךְ וְיָרֵאתָ מֵאֱלֹהֶיךָ | 43[1]

You shall not rule over him with rigor; but shall fear [2]your God.

וְעַבְדְּךָ וַאֲמָתְךָ אֲשֶׁר יִהְיוּ־לָךְ מֵאֵת הַגּוֹיִם אֲשֶׁר סְבִיבֹתֵיכֶם מֵהֶם תִּקְנוּ עֶבֶד וְאָמָה | 44[3]

And as for your bondmen and your bondmaids whom you may have, of the nations who are around you, of those you can buy bondmen and bondmaids.

וְגַם מִבְּנֵי הַתּוֹשָׁבִים הַגָּרִים עִמָּכֶם מֵהֶם תִּקְנוּ וּמִמִּשְׁפַּחְתָּם אֲשֶׁר עִמָּכֶם אֲשֶׁר הוֹלִידוּ בְּאַרְצְכֶם וְהָיוּ לָכֶם לַאֲחֻזָּה | 45[4]

Moreover, of the children of the strangers who sojourn among you, of those you may buy, and of their families who are with you, whom they have fathered in your land; and they may be your possession.

וְהִתְנַחַלְתֶּם אֹתָם לִבְנֵיכֶם אַחֲרֵיכֶם לָרֶשֶׁת אֲחֻזָּה לְעֹלָם בָּהֶם תַּעֲבֹדוּ וּבְאַחֵיכֶם בְּנֵי־יִשְׂרָאֵל אִישׁ בְּאָחִיו לֹא־תִרְדֶּה בוֹ בְּפָרֶךְ | 46[5]

And you may make them an inheritance for your children after you, to hold for a possession: of those you may take as your bondmen forever; but over your brethren the children of Israel you shall not rule, one over another, with rigor.

וְכִי תַשִּׂיג יַד גֵּר וְתוֹשָׁב עִמָּךְ וּמָךְ אָחִיךָ עִמּוֹ וְנִמְכַּר לְגֵר תּוֹשָׁב עִמָּךְ אוֹ לְעֵקֶר מִשְׁפַּחַת גֵּר | 47[6]

And if a stranger who is a settler with you becomes rich, and your brother become poor beside him, and sells himself to the stranger who is a settler with you, or to the *children of the sojourner's family*[7],

---

[1] Leviticus 25:43 - Colossians 4:1, Commandment #192, Deuteronomy 1:18, Ephesians 6:9, Exodus 1:13-14 1:17 1:21 2:23 3:7 3:9 5:14, Ezekiel 10:4, Isaiah 23:6 10:3, Leviticus 1:17 1:46 1:53, Malachi 3:5, mt.Hilchot Avadim 1:6

[2] LXX adds *the LORD*

[3] Leviticus 25:44 - Exodus 12:44, Isaiah 14:1-2, m.Bava Kamma 8:3, m.Bava Metzia 1:5, m.Megillah 3:6, m.Rosh Hashanah 2:7, m.Shekalim 4:1, Mekilta de R'Ishmael Nezikin 2:24, Mekilta de R'Ishmael Nezikin 7:12, Psalms 2:8-9, Revelation 2:26-27

[4] Leviticus 25:45 - b.Gittin 37b, b.Kiddushin [Rashi] 6b, b.Kiddushin 67b, b.Sotah 3b, b.Yevamot 46a 78b, Esther.R Petichata:3, Isaiah 56:3-56:6, Jastrow 1391b 1392b, m.Kiddushin 1:3, mt.Hilchot Avadim 9:2, y.Yevamot 8:3
Leviticus 25:45-49 - 4QLevb

[5] Leviticus 25:46 - b.Bava Batra [Rashbam] 68a 128a 137a 149b 150a, b.Bava Batra [Tosefot] 119b, b.Bava Batra 11b, b.Bava Kamma [Rashi] 62b, b.Bava Kamma [Tosefot] 62b, b.Bava Metzia [Rashi] 12ab 56b, b.Bava Metzia 73b, b.Bechorot [Rashi] 51a, b.Bechorot 13a, b.Berachot [Rashi] 47b, b.Gittin [Rashi] 38a, b.Gittin 38b 39a, b.Ketubot 43ab, b.Kiddushin [Rashi] 7a, b.Kiddushin 16ab 22b, b.Megillah 23b, b.Nazir 61b, b.Nedarim [Ran] 70b 80b, b.Niddah 47a, b.Sanhedrin [Rashi] 15a, b.Sheviit [Rashi] 4b 37b, b.Sotah 3ab, Commandment #199, Gates of Repentance 3.060, Isaiah 14:2, Leviticus 1:43, Mekhilta de R'Shimon bar Yochai Nezikin 58:2, Mekilta de R'Ishmael Nezikin 1:33 1:62 9:2 9:60, mt.Hilchot Arachim Vacharamim 8:2, mt.Hilchot Avadim 9:6, mt.Hilchot Geneivah 2:2, mt.Hilchot Gezelah Vaavedah 8:14, mt.Hilchot Mechirah 2:1, y.Demai 5:9, y.Gittin 4:9, y.Ketubot 4:1-2, y.Kiddushin 1:1 1:3, z.Behar 63 74

[6] Leviticus 25:47 - 1 Samuel 2:7-2:8, b.Arachin [Rashi] 29a 30a, b.Arachin 30b, b.Bava Kamma 113b, b.Bava Metzia 71a, b.Gittin [Rashi] 38a, b.Kiddushin 14b 20a, b.Yevamot 46a 47a, Esther.R 10:13, James 2:5, Jastrow 202a, Leviticus 1:26, Midrash Tanchuma Behar 1, mt.Hilchot Avadim 1:3, t.Arachin 5:9, y.Bava Metzia 5:5
Leviticus 25:47-55 - 4Q159 2-4 1-3

[7] LXX *proselyte by extraction*

אַחֲרֵי נִמְכַּר גְּאֻלָּה תִּהְיֶה־לּוֹ אֶחָד מֵאֶחָיו יִגְאָלֶנּוּ

48[1] After he is sold he may be redeemed; one of his brethren may redeem him;

אוֹ־דֹדוֹ אוֹ בֶן־דֹּדוֹ יִגְאָלֶנּוּ אוֹ־מִשְּׁאֵר בְּשָׂרוֹ מִמִּשְׁפַּחְתּוֹ יִגְאָלֶנּוּ אוֹ־הִשִּׂיגָה יָדוֹ וְנִגְאָל

49[2] Or his uncle, or his uncle's son, may redeem him, or anyone who is a near kin to him of his family may redeem him; or if he becomes rich, he may redeem himself.

וְחִשַּׁב עִם־קֹנֵהוּ מִשְּׁנַת הִמָּכְרוֹ לוֹ עַד שְׁנַת הַיֹּבֵל וְהָיָה כֶּסֶף מִמְכָּרוֹ בְּמִסְפַּר שָׁנִים כִּימֵי שָׂכִיר יִהְיֶה עִמּוֹ

50[3] And he shall reckon with he who bought him from the year he sold himself to him to the year of jubilee; and the price of his sale shall be according to the number of years; according to the time of a hired servant he shall be with him[4].

אִם־עוֹד רַבּוֹת בַּשָּׁנִים לְפִיהֶן יָשִׁיב גְּאֻלָּתוֹ מִכֶּסֶף מִקְנָתוֹ

51[5] If there are yet many years, according to them he shall give back the price of his redemption out of the money for which he was bought.

וְאִם־מְעַט נִשְׁאַר בַּשָּׁנִים עַד־שְׁנַת הַיֹּבֵל וְחִשַּׁב־לוֹ כְּפִי שָׁנָיו יָשִׁיב אֶת־גְּאֻלָּתוֹ

52[6] And if but a few years remain until the year of jubilee, then he shall reckon with him; according to his years shall he give back the price of his redemption.

כִּשְׂכִיר שָׁנָה בְּשָׁנָה יִהְיֶה עִמּוֹ לֹא־יִרְדֶּנּוּ בְּפֶרֶךְ לְעֵינֶיךָ

53[7] As a servant hired year by year he shall be with him; he shall not rule with rigor over him in your sight.

וְאִם־לֹא יִגָּאֵל בְּאֵלֶּה וְיָצָא בִּשְׁנַת הַיֹּבֵל הוּא וּבָנָיו עִמּוֹ

54[8] And if he is not redeemed by any of these means, then he shall go out in the year of Jubilee, he, and his children with him.

---

[1] Leviticus 25:48 - b.Arachin 30ab, b.Bava Kamma [Rashi] 113b, b.Bava Kamma 113a, b.Kiddushin 20b 21b, Galatians 4:4-5, Hebrews 2:11-13, Leviticus 1:25 1:35, Mas.Abadim 2:8, mt.Hilchot Avadim 1:4, Nehemiah 5:5 5:8

[2] Leviticus 25:49 - b.Kiddushin [Rashi] 20b, b.Kiddushin 15b 21a, b.Yevamot 54b, Esther.R 10:13, Leviticus 1:26, mt.Hilchot Avadim 2:7, Song of Songs.R 1:18, y.Sanhedrin 7:5, y.Shabbat 7:2, z.Ki Tetze 103, z.Mishpatim 395

[3] Leviticus 25:50 - b.Arachin 30a, b.Bava Kamma 113b, b.Bava Metzia [Tosefot] 87b, b.Bechorot [Tosefot] 13b, b.Kiddushin [Rashi] 14b, b.Kiddushin 16a 14a 18a, Deuteronomy 15:18, Isaiah 16:14 21:16, Job 7:1-7:2 14:6, Leviticus 1:40 1:53, mt.Hilchot Avadim 2:8, mt.Hilchot Deot 5:13, mt.Hilchot Nachalot 6:9, y.Kiddushin 1:2

[4] LXX *from year to year*

[5] Leviticus 25:51 - b.Arachin 30a 30b, b.Bava Batra [Tosefot] 54b, b.Bechorot 13ab, b.Gittin [Rashi] 38a, b.Kiddushin [Rashi] 4b, b.Kiddushin [Tosefot] 2b, b.Kiddushin 8a 14b 16a 20ab, y.Kiddushin 1:2 Leviticus 25:51-52 - 4QLevb

[6] Leviticus 25:52 - b.Arachin 30a 30b, b.Kiddushin 20ab, y.Kiddushin 1:2

[7] Leviticus 25:53 - b.Bava Kamma [Tosefot] 99a, b.Bava Metzia 65a, b.Bechorot [Tosefot] 27b, b.Kiddushin [Rashi] 15b, b.Kiddushin [Tosefot] 14b, Commandment #193, Leviticus 1:43 1:46, mt.Hilchot Avadim 1:6, mt.Hilchot Matnot Aniyim 8:10, y.Kiddushin 1:2

[8] Leviticus 25:54 - b.Kiddushin 15b, Exodus 21:2-21:3, Isaiah 1:9 1:25 4:3, Jastrow 202b, Leviticus 25:40-25:41, mt.Hilchot Avadim 2:6, y.Kiddushin 1:2

כִּי־לִי בְנֵי־יִשְׂרָאֵל עֲבָדִים עֲבָדַי הֵם
אֲשֶׁר־הוֹצֵאתִי אוֹתָם מֵאֶרֶץ מִצְרָיִם
אֲנִי יְהוָה אֱלֹהֵיכֶם

55[1] For to Me the children of Israel are servants; they are My servants whom I brought forth out of the land of Egypt: I am the LORD your God.

Behar – Chapter 26[2]

לֹא־תַעֲשׂוּ לָכֶם אֱלִילִם וּפֶסֶל וּמַצֵּבָה
לֹא־תָקִימוּ לָכֶם וְאֶבֶן מַשְׂכִּית לֹא
תִתְּנוּ בְּאַרְצְכֶם לְהִשְׁתַּחֲוֹת עָלֶיהָ כִּי
אֲנִי יְהוָה אֱלֹהֵיכֶם

1[3] *You shall not make idols for yourselves, nor shall you rear up a graven image, or a pillar, nor shall you place any figured stone in your land, to bow down unto it; for I am the LORD your God.[4]*

אֶת־שַׁבְּתֹתַי תִּשְׁמֹרוּ וּמִקְדָּשִׁי תִּירָאוּ
אֲנִי יְהוָה

2[5] You shall keep My sabbaths and reverence My sanctuary: I am the LORD.

---

[1] Leviticus 25:55 - 1 Corinthians 7:22-23 9:19 9:21, b.Bava Batra [Tosefot] 13a, b.Bava Batra 10a, b.Bava Kamma 116b, b.Bava Metzia 10a, b.Kiddushin 22b, Ein Yaakov Bava Batra:10a, Ein Yaakov Bava Metzia:10a, Ein Yaakov Kiddushin:22b, Exodus 13:3 20:2, Exodus.R 30:1 33:5, Galatians 5:13, Gates of Repentance 3.167, Isaiah 19:3, Jastrow 1035b, Leviticus 1:42, Leviticus.R 2:2, Luke 1:74-75, Mas.Abadim 2:7, Mas.Gerim 4:3, Mekilta de R'Ishmael Nezikin 18:18, Midrash Psalms 113:2 119:40, Midrash Tanchuma Behaalotcha 11, Midrash Tanchuma Massei 10, Numbers.R 8:2 15:17 16:27 23:11, Pesikta Rabbati 21:22, Psalms 20:16, Romans 6:14 6:17-18 6:22, Song of Songs.R 1:38, t.Bava Kamma 7:5, y.Bava Metzia 6:2, y.Kiddushin 1:2, z.Bo 40a, z.Vayikra 99 7b, z.Balak 205, z.Behar 75 76, z.Bo 165, z.Ki Tisa 74, z.Pinchas 181, z.Tzav 59, z.Yitro 378
[2] mt.Hilchot Teshuvah 9:1 9:1, t.Megillah 3:31
[3] Leviticus 26:1 - 1 Corinthians 10:19-20, Acts 17:29, b.Megillah 22b, Exodus 20:4-5 20:20 23:24 10:17, Commandment #25, Deuteronomy 4:16-19 5:8-9 16:21-22 3:15, Exodus.R 15:23, Gates of Repentance 3.92, Guide for the Perplexed 3:45, Isaiah 2:20 44:9-20 48:5-8, Jastrow 478a 1125b 1362a 1495a, Jeremiah 10:3-8, Leviticus 19:4, m.Megillah 3:3, Mekhilta de R'Shimon bar Yochai Bachodesh 53:2, Mekhilta de R'Ishmael Bahodesh 6:63, mt.Hilchot Avodat Kochavim vChukkoteihem 6:6-7, mt.Hilchot Beit Habechirah 1:10, mt.Hilchot Sanhedrin vHainshin Hameurim Lahem 19:4, mt.Hilchot Tefilah 5:13, Numbers 9:52, Pesikta de R'Kahana 12.4, Psalms 97:7 115:4-8, Revelation 13:14-15 22:15, Romans 2:22-23, y.Avodah Zarah 4:1 4:4, z.Acharei Mot 78b, z.Bechukkotai 112a 113a, z.Ki Tetze 74
[4] LXX *I am the LORD your God: you shall not make to yourselves gods made with hands, or graven; neither shall you rear up a pillar for yourselves, neither shall you set up a stone for an object in your land to worship it: I am the LORD your God.*
[5] Leviticus 26:2 - Leviticus 19:30, Midrash Tanchuma Behar 1, Song of Songs.R 4:8, z.Acharei Mot 78b, z.Ekev 56, z.Kedoshim 30
Leviticus 26:2-5 - Liber Antiquitatum Biblicarum 13:10
Leviticus 26:2-16 - 4QLXXLeva

Bechukkotai

Bechukkotai[1] – Chapter 26

אִם־בְּחֻקֹּתַי תֵּלֵכוּ וְאֶת־מִצְוֹתַי
תִּשְׁמְרוּ וַעֲשִׂיתֶם אֹתָם

3[2]   If you walk in My statutes, and keep My commandments, and do them;

וְנָתַתִּי גִשְׁמֵיכֶם בְּעִתָּם וְנָתְנָה הָאָרֶץ
יְבוּלָהּ וְעֵץ הַשָּׂדֶה יִתֵּן פִּרְיוֹ

4[3]   Then, I will give your rains[4] in their season, and the land shall yield her produce, and the [5]trees of the field shall yield their fruit.

וְהִשִּׂיג לָכֶם דַּיִשׁ אֶת־בָּצִיר וּבָצִיר
יַשִּׂיג אֶת־זָרַע וַאֲכַלְתֶּם לַחְמְכֶם
לָשֹׂבַע וִישַׁבְתֶּם לָבֶטַח בְּאַרְצְכֶם

5[6]   And your threshing shall reach to the vintage, and the vintage shall reach to the sowing time; and you shall eat your bread until you have enough, and dwell in your land safely[7].

---

[1] Bechukkotai aliyot: [1] Leviticus 26:3–5, [2] Leviticus 26:6–9, [3] Leviticus 26:10–46, [4] Leviticus 27:1–15, [5] Leviticus 27:16–21, [6] Leviticus 27:22–28, [7] Leviticus 27:29–34
Behar and Bechukkotai are combined when there are only 50 available reading days in the year.
[2] Leviticus 26:3 - b.Avodah Zara 5a, b.Bava Batra 88b, b.Kiddushin 61b, b.Megillah [Rashi] 31a, b.Sheviit [Tosefot] 36b, Deuteronomy 7:12 11:13-15 28:1-14, Ecclesiastes.R 8:7, Isaiah 1:19 48:18-19, Jastrow 1378a 1662a, Joshua 23:14-15, Judges 2:1-2, Leviticus 18:4-5, Leviticus.R 35:1 35:7, m.Megillah 3:6, Matthew 7:24-25, Midrash Psalms 18:28 72:3, Midrash Tanchuma Bechukkotai 1-3, Midrash Tanchuma Bereshit 1, Midrash Tanchuma Reeh 4, Numbers.R 3:12 11:7, Philo De Praemiis et Poenis 101, Psalms 81:13-17, Revelation 22:14, Romans 2:7-10, Saadia Opinions 5:1 9:2 9:2, t.Rosh Hashanah 2:2, Tanya Kuntress Acharon §5, z.Bechukotai 1 16 18 24, z.Kedoshim 43, z.Naso 18, z.Trumah 663
Leviticus 26:3-4 - Exodus.R 2:4, Midrash Tanchuma Bechukkotai 2 3, Sifre Devarim Ekev 42
Leviticus 26:3-13 - Minchah [Shabbat Monday Thursday Torah reading - Parashah Bechukosai]
Leviticus 26:3-46 - Mas.Soferim 12:1 17:7
[3] Leviticus 26:4 - 1 Kings 17:1, Acts 14:17, Amos 4:7-4:8, b.Rosh Hashanah 26a, b.Taanit 22b, Deuteronomy 11:14 4:12, Ein Yaakov Taanit:22b, Exodus.R 41:2, Ezekiel 34:26-27 12:30, Genesis.R 6:5, Haggai 2:18-19, Isaiah 5:6 6:23, James 5:7 5:17-18, Jastrow 1434b, Jeremiah 14:22, Job 5:10 37:11-13 38:25-28, Joel 2:23-24, Leviticus 1:21, Leviticus.R 35:8, Matthew 5:45, Midrash Psalms 72:3, Psalms 65:10-14 67:7 68:10 85:13 8:13, Revelation 11:6, Saadia Opinions 9:2, Zechariah 8:12, z.Bechukotai 20, z.Vayera 434
[4] 4QLXXLeva adds *in your land*
[5] 4QLXXLeva adds *fruit*
[6] Leviticus 26:5 - 1 Peter 1:5, 1 Timothy 6:17, Acts 14:17, Amos 9:13, Deuteronomy 11:15, Exodus 16:8, Ezekiel 34:25-28, Jeremiah 23:6, Job 11:18-19, Joel 2:19 2:26, John 4:35-36, Lamentations.R Petichata DChakimei 11, Leviticus 25:18-19, Midrash Tanchuma Bechukkotai 2, Proverbs 1:33 18:10, Psalms 46:2-8 90:1 91:1-14, Matthew 9:37-38 23:37, Saadia Opinions 9:2, Sifre Devarim Ekev 42, z.Toldot 45 46
[7] LXX adds *and war shall not go through your land*

וְנָתַתִּי שָׁלוֹם בָּאָרֶץ וּשְׁכַבְתֶּם וְאֵין מַחֲרִיד וְהִשְׁבַּתִּי חַיָּה רָעָה מִן־הָאָרֶץ וְחֶרֶב לֹא־תַעֲבֹר בְּאַרְצְכֶם

וּרְדַפְתֶּם אֶת־אֹיְבֵיכֶם וְנָפְלוּ לִפְנֵיכֶם לֶחָרֶב

וְרָדְפוּ מִכֶּם חֲמִשָּׁה מֵאָה וּמֵאָה מִכֶּם רְבָבָה יִרְדֹּפוּ וְנָפְלוּ אֹיְבֵיכֶם לִפְנֵיכֶם לֶחָרֶב

וּפָנִיתִי אֲלֵיכֶם וְהִפְרֵיתִי אֶתְכֶם וְהִרְבֵּיתִי אֶתְכֶם וַהֲקִימֹתִי אֶת־בְּרִיתִי אִתְּכֶם

וַאֲכַלְתֶּם יָשָׁן נוֹשָׁן וְיָשָׁן מִפְּנֵי חָדָשׁ תּוֹצִיאוּ

וְנָתַתִּי מִשְׁכָּנִי בְּתוֹכְכֶם וְלֹא־תִגְעַל נַפְשִׁי אֶתְכֶם

6[8] And I will give peace in the land, and you shall lie down, and no one shall make you afraid; and I will cause evil beasts to cease out of the land, *nor shall the sword go through your land*[9].

7[10] And you shall chase your enemies, and they shall fall before you by the sword.

8[11] And five of you shall chase one hundred, and one hundred of you shall chase *ten thousand*[12]; and your enemies shall fall before you by the sword.

9[13] And I will *have respect to*[14] you, and make you fruitful, and multiply you; and will establish My covenant with you.

10[15] And you shall eat *old store long kept, and you shall bring forth the old from before the new*[16].

11[17] And I will set My tabernacle among you, and My soul shall not abhor you.

---

[8] Leviticus 26:6 - 1 Chronicles 22:9, 2 Kings 2:24 17:25-26, Acts 12:6, b.Taanit 22b, Ein Yaakov Taanit 22b, Exodus 23:29, Exodus.R 41:2, Ezekiel 5:17 14:15 14:17 14:21 10:25, Genesis.R 6:5 66:2, Haggai 2:9, Hosea 2:18, Isaiah 9:8 11:9 21:7, Jeremiah 6:10 7:27, Job 5:23 11:19, John 14:27, Lamentations.R 1:53, Leviticus 2:22, Leviticus.R 35:1 35:8, Mas.Perek Hashalom 1:1, Mekilta de R'Ishmael Pisha 12:37, Mekilta de R'Ishmael Pisha 12:51, Micah 4:4, Midrash Psalms 18:28 120:6, mt.Hilchot Taaniot 2:4, Numbers.R 11:7, Philippians 4:7-9, Proverbs 3:24 6:22, Psalms 3:6 4:9 29:11 85:9 127:1-2 3:14, Romans 5:1, Saadia Opinions 9:2, z.Bechukkotai 25-26 55 113b, Zechariah 9:10, Zephaniah 3:13
[9] Missing in LXX
[10] Leviticus 26:7 - b.Kiddushin 66a
[11] Leviticus 26:8 - 1 Chronicles 11:11 11:20, 1 Samuel 14:6-16 17:45-52, b.Sotah [Tosefot] 11a, Deuteronomy 4:7 8:30, Joshua 23:10, Judges 7:19-21, Midrash Tanchuma Shoftim 16, Numbers 14:9, Philo De Praemiis et Poenis 94, Psalms 81:15-16, Tanna Devei Eliyahu 3 11, z.Bechukotai 45 46
[12] LXX *tens of thousands*
[13] Leviticus 26:9 - 2 Kings 13:23, Birchat HaChammah.Ana Bekoach, Deuteronomy 4:4 4:11, Exodus 1:7 2:25 6:4, Ezekiel 17:2, Genesis 6:18 17:6-7 17:20 2:4 4:3 4:14, Hebrews 8:9, Isaiah 7:3, Jeremiah 9:3, Lamentations.R 3:7, Luke 2:12, m.Avot 5:8, Midrash Psalms 119:63, Nehemiah 2:20 9:23, Numbers.R 11:7, Pesikta de R'Kahana 19.4, Pesikta Rabbati 21:15, Psalms 89:4 11:38 138:6-7, Saadia Opinions 9:2 Leviticus 26:9-13 - Lamentations.R 3:7 Petichata DChakimei:11
[14] LXX *look upon*
[15] Leviticus 26:10 - 2 Kings 19:29, b.Bava Batra [Rashbam] 92a, Ein Yaakov Bava Batra:91b, Jastrow 601a, Joshua 5:11, Leviticus 1:22, Luke 12:17, Midrash Psalms 145:1, Philo De Sacrificiis Abelis et Cain 79, Philo Quis Rerum Divinarum Heres 279, Saadia Opinions 9:2
[16] LXX *that which is old and very old, and bring forth the old to make way for the new*
[17] Leviticus 26:11 - 1 Kings 8:13 8:27, b.Arachin 2a, b.Sheviit 16b, Deuteronomy 8:19, Ein Yaakov Eruvin:2a, Ephesians 2:22, Exodus 1:8 5:45, Exodus.R 31:10, Ezekiel 37:26-28, Jastrow 854a, Jeremiah 14:21, Joshua 22:19, Lamentations 2:7, Leviticus 20:23, Leviticus.R 6:5, Midrash Tanchuma Bechukkotai 3, Midrash Tanchuma Mishpatim 11, Pesikta Rabbati 21:15, Psalms 76:3 78:59 78:68-69 10:40 132:13-14, Revelation 21:3, z.Bechukkotai 114a, Zechariah 11:8, z.Bechukotai 30 32, z.Pekudei 396, z.Trumah 263

וְהִתְהַלַּכְתִּי֙ בְּתֽוֹכְכֶ֔ם וְהָיִ֥יתִי לָכֶ֖ם
לֵֽאלֹהִ֑ים וְאַתֶּ֖ם תִּהְיוּ־לִ֥י לְעָֽם

12[18] And I will *walk among you, and will*[19] be your God, and you shall be My people.

אֲנִ֞י יְהוָ֣ה אֱלֹֽהֵיכֶ֗ם אֲשֶׁ֨ר הוֹצֵ֤אתִי
אֶתְכֶם֙ מֵאֶ֣רֶץ מִצְרַ֔יִם מִֽהְיֹ֥ת לָהֶ֖ם
עֲבָדִ֑ים וָֽאֶשְׁבֹּר֙ מֹטֹ֣ת עֻלְּכֶ֔ם וָאוֹלֵ֥ךְ
אֶתְכֶ֖ם קֽוֹמְמִיּֽוּת

13[20] I am the LORD your God, who brought you forth out of the land of the Egyptians, *that you should not be their bondmen*[21]; and I have broken the *bars of your yoke*[22], and *made you go upright*[23].

וְאִם־לֹ֥א תִשְׁמְע֖וּ לִ֑י וְלֹ֣א תַעֲשׂ֔וּ אֵ֥ת
כָּל־הַמִּצְוֺ֖ת הָאֵֽלֶּה

14[24] But if you will not listen to Me, and will not do all *these*[25] commandments;

וְאִם־בְּחֻקֹּתַ֣י תִּמְאָ֔סוּ וְאִ֥ם אֶת־מִשְׁפָּטַ֖י
תִּגְעַ֣ל נַפְשְׁכֶ֑ם לְבִלְתִּ֤י עֲשׂוֹת֙ אֶת־כָּל־
מִצְוֺתַ֔י לְהַפְרְכֶ֖ם אֶת־בְּרִיתִֽי

15[26] And if you shall reject My statutes, and if your soul abhors My ordinances, so you will not do all My commandments, but break My covenant;

אַף־אֲנִ֞י אֶֽעֱשֶׂה־זֹּ֣את לָכֶ֗ם וְהִפְקַדְתִּ֨י
עֲלֵיכֶ֤ם בֶּֽהָלָה֙ אֶת־הַשַּׁחֶ֣פֶת וְאֶת־

16[27] I also will do this to you: I will *appoint terror over you, even consumption and fever, that shall make the eyes fail, and*

---

[18] Leviticus 26:12 - 2 Corinthians 6:16, Deuteronomy 23:16, Exodus 3:6 6:7 19:5-19:6, Ezekiel 11:20 12:38, Genesis 3:8 5:22 5:24 6:9 17:7, Guide for the Perplexed 3:32, Hebrews 11:16, Isaiah 12:2 17:10, Jeremiah 7:23 11:4 6:22 7:34 8:38, Joel 2:27, Jubilees 1:17, Kuzari 1.109, Lamentations.R 2:17 Petichata DChakimei:11, Matthew 22:32, Midrash Tanchuma Tzav 12, Pesikta Rabbati 33:12, Philo De Mutatione Nominum 266, Philo De Somniis I 148, Philo De Somniis II 248, Philo De Virtutibus 184, Philo Fragment Preserved by Antonius Ser. LXXXII 184, Psalms 50:7 68:19-68:21, Revelation 2:1 21:7, z.Bechukkotai 114a, Zechariah 13:9

[19] Missing in 4QLXXLeva

[20] Leviticus 26:13 - 1 Corinthians 6:19-20, b.Bava Batra 75a 88b, b.Sanhedrin 1a, Exodus 20:2, Exodus.R 25:8, Ezekiel 10:27, Genesis.R 12:6, Isaiah 3:23, Jastrow 771b 1378a, Jeremiah 2:20, Lamentations.R Petichata DChakimei:11, Leviticus 1:38 1:42 1:55, Mekhilta de R'Shimon bar Yochai Pisha 18:2, Midrash Psalms 129:1, Midrash Tanchuma Bereshit 6, Midrash Tanchuma Ekev 7, Midrash Tanchuma Reeh 4, Numbers.R 8:2 13:12, Pesikta de R'Kahana 12.17, Psalms 81:7-11 20:16, Song of Songs.R 1:37, z.Acharei Mot 78b

[21] LXX *where you were slaves*

[22] 4QLXXLeva *the yoke of your bars*

[23] LXX *brought you forth openly*

[24] Leviticus 26:14 - Acts 3:23, b.Megillah 31b, Deuteronomy 28:15-28:68, Hebrews 12:25, Jeremiah 17:27, Lamentations 1:18 2:17, Leviticus 2:18, Leviticus.R 6:5 35:1, Malachi 2:2, Mas.Soferim 12:1, Midrash Tanchuma Bechukkotai 3, Midrash Tanchuma Reeh 4, Numbers.R 9:47, Ralbag Wars 6part02:13, t.Megillah 3:9, Tanna Devei Eliyahu 5
Leviticus 26:14-15 - Mesillat Yesharim 5:Factors Detracting from Zehirus
Leviticus 26:14-44 - Jastrow 1200a 1378a
Leviticus 26:14-46 - mt.Hilchot Tefilah 13:2 13:18

[25] 4QLXXLeva LXX *my*

[26] Leviticus 26:15 - 1 Thessalonians 4:8, 2 Chronicles 12:16, 2 Kings 17:15, 2 Samuel 12:9-10, Acts 13:41, b.Bava Batra 88b, Deuteronomy 7:16, Exodus 19:5 24:7, Ezekiel 16:59, Genesis 17:14, Hebrews 8:9, Isaiah 24:5, Jeremiah 6:19 11:10 7:33, Leviticus 2:43, Numbers 15:31, Numbers.R 3:12, Proverbs 1:7 1:30 5:12, Psalms 50:17, Romans 8:7, Siman 144:4, z.Bechukkotai 114b, Zechariah 7:11-13, z.Bechukotai 42

[27] Leviticus 26:16 - 1 Samuel 2:33, b.Shabbat 32b, Deuteronomy 28:21-22 28:32-35 4:51 28:65-67 8:25, Ein Yaakov Shabbat:32b, Exodus 15:26, Ezekiel 9:10, Guide for the Perplexed 3:17, Haggai 1:6, Hebrews 10:31, Isaiah 7:2 10:4 65:22-24, Jastrow 752a 1549b, Jeremiah 5:17 12:13 15:8 20:4, Job 15:20-21 18:11 20:25 7:8, Judges 6:3-6 6:11, Leviticus.R 6:5 6:5, Micah 6:15, mt.Hilchot Talmud Torah 6:11, Pesikta de R'Kahana 16.11, Psalms 73:19 78:33 13:6, Sifre Devarim Ekev 43, Zechariah 14:12

הַקֻּדֵּחַת מְכַלֵּוֹת עֵינַיִם וּמְדִיבָת נָפֶשׁ
וּזְרַעְתֶּם לָרִיק זַרְעֲכֶם וַאֲכָלֻהוּ
אֹיְבֵיכֶם

וְנָתַתִּי פָנַי בָּכֶם וְנִגַּפְתֶּם לִפְנֵי אֹיְבֵיכֶם
וְרָדוּ בָכֶם שֹׂנְאֵיכֶם וְנַסְתֶּם וְאֵין־רֹדֵף
אֶתְכֶם

וְאִם־עַד־אֵלֶּה לֹא תִשְׁמְעוּ לֵי וְיָסַפְתִּי
לְיַסְּרָה אֶתְכֶם שֶׁבַע עַל־חַטֹּאתֵיכֶם

וְשָׁבַרְתִּי אֶת־גְּאוֹן עֻזְּכֶם וְנָתַתִּי אֶת־
שְׁמֵיכֶם כַּבַּרְזֶל וְאֶת־אַרְצְכֶם כַּנְּחֻשָׁה

וְתַם לָרִיק כֹּחֲכֶם וְלֹא־תִתֵּן אַרְצְכֶם
אֶת־יְבוּלָהּ וְעֵץ הָאָרֶץ לֹא יִתֵּן פִּרְיוֹ

וְאִם־תֵּלְכוּ עִמִּי קֶרִי וְלֹא תֹאבוּ
לִשְׁמֹעַ לֵי וְיָסַפְתִּי עֲלֵיכֶם מַכָּה שֶׁבַע
כְּחַטֹּאתֵיכֶם

וְהִשְׁלַחְתִּי בָכֶם אֶת־חַיַּת הַשָּׂדֶה
וְשִׁכְּלָה אֶתְכֶם וְהִכְרִיתָה אֶת־
בְּהֶמְתְּכֶם וְהִמְעִיטָה אֶתְכֶם וְנָשַׁמּוּ
דַּרְכֵיכֶם

the soul to languish[28]; and you shall sow your seed in vain, for your enemies shall eat it.

17[29] And I will set My face against you, and you shall be smitten before your enemies; those who hate you shall rule over you; and you shall flee when no one pursues you.

18[30] And if for these things you will not yet listen to Me, I will chastise you seven times more for your sins.

19[31] And I will break the pride of your power; and I will make your heaven as iron, and your earth as brass.

20[32] And your strength shall be spent in vain; for your land shall not yield her produce, nor shall the trees of the land yield their fruit.

21[33] And if you walk contrary to Me, and will not listen to Me; I will bring seven times more plagues on you according to your sins.

22[34] And I will send the beast of the field among you, *that shall rob you of your children*[35], and destroy your cattle, and make you few in number; *and your ways shall become desolate*[36].

---

[28] LXX *even bring upon you perplexity and the itch, and the fever that causes your eyes to waste away, and disease that consumes your life*

[29] Leviticus 26:17 - 1 Samuel 4:10 7:1, Deuteronomy 4:25, Hellenistic Synagogal Prayers 10:10, Jeremiah 19:7, Judges 2:14, Lamentations 1:5, Leviticus 17:10 20:5-6 26:36-37, Nehemiah 9:27-30, Proverbs 4:1, Psalms 53:6 68:2-3 106:41-42
Leviticus 26:17-26 - 11Qpaleol.eva

[30] Leviticus 26:18 - 1 Samuel 2:5, Daniel 3:19, Gates of Repentance 2.002, Lamentations.R 2:21 Petichata DChakimei:27, Leviticus 2:21 2:24 2:28, Leviticus.R 6:5 35:1, Numbers.R 2:9, Proverbs 24:16, Psalms 119:164, Ralbag Wars 4:6, z.Bechukkotai 115a, z.Metzorah 54a, z.Bechukotai 44, z.Metzora 30

[31] Leviticus 26:19 - 1 Kings 17:1, 1 Samuel 4:3 4:11, b.Gittin 37a, Daniel 4:34, Deuteronomy 4:23, Ecclesiastes.R 10:11, Ezekiel 7:24 6:6, Isaiah 2:12 1:11 2:5, Jastrow 601a 699a 1434b, Jeremiah 13:9 14:1-14:6, Luke 4:25, Midrash Psalms 21:2, Midrash Tanchuma Bechukkotai 2 3, Numbers.R 3:12, Sifre Devarim Ekev 43, zephaniah 3:11, z.Shmini 15

[32] Leviticus 26:20 - 1 Corinthians 3:6, Deuteronomy 11:17 4:18 28:38-40 4:42, Galatians 4:11, Habakkuk 2:13, Haggai 1:9-11 2:16, Isaiah 17:11 1:4, Job 7:40, Leviticus 2:4, Psalms 11:34 7:1, Sifre Devarim Ekev 43

[33] Leviticus 26:21 - Gates of Repentance 2.002, Guide for the Perplexed 3:36, Leviticus 2:18 2:27, Numbers.R 10:2, Ralbag Wars 4:6, z.Trumah 66, z.Vayechi 22

[34] Leviticus 26:22 - 2 Chronicles 15:5, 2 Kings 2:24 17:25, b.Shabbat 33a, Deuteronomy 8:24, Ein Yaakov Shabbat:33a, Ezekiel 5:17 14:15 14:21 9:28, Guide for the Perplexed 3:37, Isaiah 24:6 9:8, Jeremiah 15:3, Judges 5:6, Lamentations 1:4, Leviticus 2:6, Micah 3:12, Zechariah 7:14

[35] LXX *and they shall devour you*

[36] Missing in LXX

Hebrew	Verse	English
וְאִם־בְּאֵלֶּה לֹא תִוָּסְרוּ לִי וַהֲלַכְתֶּם עִמִּי קֶרִי	23[37]	And if in spite of these things you will not be corrected to Me, but will walk contrary to Me;
וְהָלַכְתִּי אַף־אֲנִי עִמָּכֶם בְּקֶרִי וְהִכֵּיתִי אֶתְכֶם גַּם־אָנִי שֶׁבַע עַל־חַטֹּאתֵיכֶם	24[38]	then I will indeed walk contrary to you[39]; and I, even I will smite you, seven times for your sins.
וְהֵבֵאתִי עֲלֵיכֶם חֶרֶב נֹקֶמֶת נְקַם־בְּרִית וְנֶאֱסַפְתֶּם אֶל־עָרֵיכֶם וְשִׁלַּחְתִּי דֶבֶר בְּתוֹכְכֶם וְנִתַּתֶּם בְּיַד־אוֹיֵב	25[40]	And I will bring a sword upon you, that shall execute the vengeance of the covenant; and you shall be gathered together in your cities; and I will send *the pestilence among*[41] you; and you shall be delivered into the hand of the enemy.
בְּשִׁבְרִי לָכֶם מַטֵּה־לֶחֶם וְאָפוּ עֶשֶׂר נָשִׁים לַחְמְכֶם בְּתַנּוּר אֶחָד וְהֵשִׁיבוּ לַחְמְכֶם בַּמִּשְׁקָל וַאֲכַלְתֶּם וְלֹא תִשְׂבָּעוּ	26[42]	When I *break your staff*[43] of bread, ten women shall bake your bread in one oven, and they shall ration your bread by weight; and you shall eat, and not be satisfied.
וְאִם־בְּזֹאת לֹא תִשְׁמְעוּ לִי וַהֲלַכְתֶּם עִמִּי בְּקֶרִי	27[44]	And if for all this you will not listen to Me, but walk contrary to Me;
וְהָלַכְתִּי עִמָּכֶם בַּחֲמַת־קֶרִי וְיִסַּרְתִּי אֶתְכֶם אַף־אָנִי שֶׁבַע עַל־חַטֹּאתֵיכֶם	28[45]	Then I will walk contrary to you in fury; and I also will chastise you seven times for your sins
וַאֲכַלְתֶּם בְּשַׂר בְּנֵיכֶם וּבְשַׂר בְּנֹתֵיכֶם תֹּאכֵלוּ	29[46]	And you shall eat the flesh of your sons, and the flesh of your daughters

---

[37] Leviticus 26:23 - Amos 4:6-12, b.Rosh Hashanah 26a, b.Shabbat 33a, Ein Yaakov Shabbat:33a, Ezekiel 24:13-14, Isaiah 1:16-1:20, Jastrow 1109b, Jeremiah 2:30 5:3, Leviticus 2:21
Leviticus 26:23-24 - Gates of Repentance 2.2

[38] Leviticus 26:24 - 2 Samuel 22:27, Guide for the Perplexed 3:36, Isaiah 15:10, Job 9:4, Lamentations.R 2:21, Psalms 18:27

[39] 11QpaleoLeva adds *in hostile wrath*

[40] Leviticus 26:25 - 2 Samuel 24:15, Amos 4:10, b.Sanhedrin [Tosefot] 45a, b.Sanhedrin 52b, b.Shabbat 33a, Cairo Damascus 1.17-18, Commandment #285, Deuteronomy 4:21 8:25 8:35 8:41, Ein Yaakov Shabbat:33a, Ezekiel 5:17 6:3 14:17 20:37 21:9-22 5:8 9:2, Hebrews 10:28-30, Isaiah 34:5-6, Jeremiah 9:17 14:12-13 15:2-4 24:10 29:17-18, Judges 2:14-2:16, Lamentations 2:21, Leviticus.R 6:5, Luke 21:11, Mekhilta de R'Shimon bar Yochai Nezikin 61:1 64:1, Mekilta de R'Ishmael Nezikin 7:60, Mekilta de R'Ishmael Pisha 12:28, Numbers 14:12 17:14, Psalms 78:62-64 94:1, y.Sanhedrin 7:1 7:3, z.Beshallach 66a, z.Noach 66b, z.Vaera 26a, z.Beshalach 464, z.Noach 162, z.Vaera 77, z.Vayikra 326

[41] LXX *out death against*

[42] Leviticus 26:26 - b.Menachot [Rashi] 87b, b.Pesachim [Rashi] 37ab, b.Shabbat 33a, Ein Yaakov Shabbat:33a, Ezekiel 4:10 4:16 5:16 14:13, Haggai 1:6, Hosea 4:10, Isaiah 3:1 9:21, Jastrow 1009b, Jeremiah 14:12, Lamentations 4:3-9, Micah 6:14, Psalms 9:16, Sifre Devarim Ekev 40, z.Toldot 45
Leviticus 26:26-33 - 4QLev-Numa

[43] LXX *afflict you with famine*

[44] Leviticus 26:27 - Guide for the Perplexed 3:36, Leviticus 2:21 2:24, Ralbag Wars 4:6
Leviticus 26:27-28 - Gates of Repentance 2.002, mt.Hilchot Taaniot 1:3

[45] Leviticus 26:28 - Bahir 65-67, Ezekiel 5:13 5:15 8:18, Isaiah 3:4 11:18 15:3 18:15, Jeremiah 21:5, Nahum 1:2 1:6, Ralbag Wars 4:6, z.Bechukotai 48 55 56, z.Shoftim 18, z.Trumah 66

[46] Leviticus 26:29 - 2 Kings 6:28-29, Deuteronomy 28:53-57, Ezekiel 5:10, Jeremiah 19:9, Lamentations 2:20 4:10, Luke 23:29, Matthew 24:19

you shall eat.

וְהִשְׁמַדְתִּ֞י אֶת־בָּמֹֽתֵיכֶ֗ם וְהִכְרַתִּי֙ אֶת־ **30**[47]
חַמָּנֵיכֶ֔ם וְנָֽתַתִּי֙ אֶת־פִּגְרֵיכֶ֔ם עַל־פִּגְרֵ֖י
גִּלּֽוּלֵיכֶ֑ם וְגָעֲלָ֥ה נַפְשִׁ֖י אֶתְכֶֽם

And I *will* destroy *your high places, and cut down your sun pillars*[48], and cast your carcasses on the carcasses of your idols; and My soul shall abhor you.

וְנָֽתַתִּ֤י אֶת־עָֽרֵיכֶם֙ חָרְבָּ֔ה וַֽהֲשִׁמּוֹתִ֖י **31**[49]
אֶת־מִקְדְּשֵׁיכֶ֑ם וְלֹ֣א אָרִ֔יחַ בְּרֵ֖יחַ
נִֽיחֹֽחֲכֶֽם

And I will make your cities a waste, and will bring your sanctuaries to desolation, and I will not smell the savor of your *sweet odors*[50].

וַֽהֲשִׁמֹּתִ֥י אֲנִ֖י אֶת־הָאָ֑רֶץ וְשָֽׁמְמ֤וּ עָלֶ֨יהָ֙ **32**[51]
אֹֽיְבֵיכֶ֔ם הַיֹּֽשְׁבִ֖ים בָּֽהּ

And I will bring *the*[52] land into desolation; and your enemies who dwell there shall be astonished at it.

וְאֶתְכֶם֙ אֱזָרֶ֣ה בַגּוֹיִ֔ם וַהֲרִֽיקֹתִ֥י **33**[53]
אַֽחֲרֵיכֶ֖ם חָ֑רֶב וְהָֽיְתָ֤ה אַרְצְכֶם֙ שְׁמָמָ֔ה
וְעָֽרֵיכֶ֖ם יִֽהְי֥וּ חָרְבָּֽה

And I will scatter you among the nations, and I will draw out the sword after you; and your land shall be desolate, and your cities shall be a waste.

אָ֣ז תִּרְצֶ֤ה הָאָ֨רֶץ֙ אֶת־שַׁבְּתֹתֶ֔יהָ כֹּ֚ל **34**[54]
יְמֵ֣י הָשַּׁמָּ֔ה וְאַתֶּ֖ם בְּאֶ֣רֶץ אֹֽיְבֵיכֶ֑ם אָ֚ז
תִּשְׁבַּ֣ת הָאָ֔רֶץ וְהִרְצָ֖ת אֶת־שַׁבְּתֹתֶֽיהָ

Then the land shall be paid her sabbaths, while it lies desolate and you are in your enemies' land; then the land shall rest and be repaid her sabbaths.

כָּל־יְמֵ֥י הָשַּׁמָּ֖ה תִּשְׁבֹּ֑ת אֵ֣ת אֲשֶׁ֧ר לֹֽא־ **35**[55]
שָֽׁבְתָ֛ה בְּשַׁבְּתֹֽתֵיכֶ֖ם בְּשִׁבְתְּכֶ֥ם עָלֶֽיהָ

As long as it lies desolate it shall have rest; that rest it did not receive in your sabbaths, when you lived on it.

---

[47] Leviticus 26:30 - 1 Kings 13:2, 2 Chronicles 14:2-4 23:17 7:1 34:3-7, 2 Kings 23:8 23:16 23:20, Avot de R'Natan 38, b.Sanhedrin 63b 64a, b.Shabbat 33a, Ein Yaakov Shabbat:33a, Ezekiel 6:3-6 6:13, Isaiah 3:9, Jeremiah 8:1-3 14:19, Leviticus 20:23 2:11 2:15, Leviticus.R 10:7, Mekhilta de R'Shimon bar Yochai Pisha 9:3, Midrash Psalms 18:32, mt.Hilchot Maaser 2:3, mt.Hilchot Maaser Sheni vneta Revai 3:4, Numbers.R 7:10, Psalms 78:58-59 89:39, Song of Songs.R 4:8

[48] LXX *will render your pillars desolate, and will utterly destroy your wooden images made with hands*

[49] Leviticus 26:31 - 2 Chronicles 12:19, 2 Kings 25:4-10, 4Q266 8 v 3-4, 4Q266 frag 11 ll.3-4, 4Q270 frag 7 1.18, Acts 6:14, Amos 5:21-23, b.Megillah 28a, b.Shabbat 33a, Ein Yaakov Shabbat:33a, Ezekiel 6:6 9:6 21:12 21:20 24:21, Genesis 8:21, Hebrews 10:26, Isaiah 1:7 1:11-14 24:10-12 18:3, Jastrow 210b 1597a, Jeremiah 4:7 9:12 22:5 2:6 2:9 4:13, Lamentations 1:1 1:10 2:7, Luke 21:5-6 21:24, Matthew 24:1-2, Micah 3:12, Midrash Tanchuma Bechukkotai 3, mt.Hilchot Beit Habechirah 6:16, mt.Hilchot Tefilah 11:11, Nehemiah 2:3 2:17, Psalms 74:3-8, y.Megillah 3:3, z.Pekudei 360, z.Tzav 14

[50] LXX *sacrifices*

[51] Leviticus 26:32 - 1 Kings 9:8, b.Shabbat [Rashi] 33a, Daniel 9:2 9:18, Deuteronomy 4:37 29:22-27, Ezekiel 5:15 33:28-29, Habakkuk 3:17, Isaiah 1:7-1:8 5:6 5:9 6:11 24:1 32:13-14 16:11, Jeremiah 9:12 18:16 19:8 1:11 1:18 1:38 20:2 20:22, Lamentations 4:12 5:18, Luke 21:20

[52] LXX *your*

[53] Leviticus 26:33 - Avot de R'Natan 38, b.Shabbat 33a, Deuteronomy 4:27 28:64-66, Ezekiel 12:14-16 20:23 22:15, Ein Yaakov Shabbat 33a, James 1:1, Jeremiah 9:17, Lamentations 1:3 4:15, Numbers.R 7:10, Lamentations.R Petichata DChakimei:13, Luke 21:24, Psalms 44:12, Zechariah 7:14

[54] Leviticus 26:34 - 2 Chronicles 12:21, Avot de R'Natan 38, b.Shabbat 33a, Ein Yaakov Shabbat:33a, Jastrow 1493b, Jubilees 50:3, Leviticus 25:2-4 1:10 2:43, m.Avot 5:9, Midrash Psalms 85:1, z.Vayera 117b, z.Vayera 451

[55] Leviticus 26:35 - Avot de R'Natan 38, b.Shabbat 33a, Ein Yaakov Shabbat:33a, Isaiah 24:5-24:6, Romans 8:22

וְהַנִּשְׁאָרִ֣ים בָּכֶ֗ם וְהֵבֵ֤אתִי מֹ֙רֶךְ֙ 36[56]
בִּלְבָבָ֔ם בְּאַרְצֹ֖ת אֹיְבֵיהֶ֑ם וְרָדַ֣ף אֹתָ֗ם
ק֚וֹל עָלֶ֣ה נִדָּ֔ף וְנָ֗סוּ מְנֻֽסַת־חֶ֙רֶב֙ וְנָפְל֖וּ
וְאֵ֥ין רֹדֵֽף

וְכָשְׁל֧וּ אִישׁ־בְּאָחִ֛יו כְּמִפְּנֵי־חֶ֖רֶב 37[59]
וְרֹדֵ֣ף אָ֑יִן וְלֹא־תִֽהְיֶ֤ה לָכֶם֙ תְּקוּמָ֔ה
לִפְנֵ֖י אֹיְבֵיכֶֽם

וַאֲבַדְתֶּ֖ם בַּגּוֹיִ֑ם וְאָכְלָ֣ה אֶתְכֶ֔ם אֶ֖רֶץ 38[61]
אֹיְבֵיכֶֽם

וְהַנִּשְׁאָרִ֣ים בָּכֶ֗ם יִמַּ֙קּוּ֙ בַּֽעֲוֺנָ֔ם בְּאַרְצֹ֖ת 39[62]
אֹיְבֵיכֶ֑ם וְאַ֛ף בַּעֲוֺנֹ֥ת אֲבֹתָ֖ם אִתָּ֥ם
יִמָּֽקּוּ

וְהִתְוַדּ֤וּ אֶת־עֲוֺנָם֙ וְאֶת־עֲוֺ֣ן אֲבֹתָ֔ם 40[63]
בְּמַעֲלָ֖ם אֲשֶׁ֣ר מָֽעֲלוּ־בִ֑י וְאַ֕ף אֲשֶׁר־
הָלְכ֥וּ עִמִּ֖י בְּקֶֽרִי

36[56] And as for those of you who are left, I will send *a faintness*[57] into their heart in the lands of their enemies; and the sound of a *driven*[58] leaf shall chase them; and they shall flee, as one flees from the sword; and they shall fall when no one pursues.

37[59] *And they shall stumble upon each another, as if before the sword when no one pursues; and you shall have no power to stand before*[60] your enemies.

38[61] And you shall perish among the nations, and the land of your enemies shall consume you.

39[62] And those of you who are left shall pine away in their iniquity in your enemies' lands; and they shall pine away in the iniquities of their fathers with them.

40[63] And they shall confess their iniquity, and the iniquity of their fathers, in their treachery they committed against Me, and also because they have walked contrary to Me.

---

[56] Leviticus 26:36 - 1 Samuel 17:24, 2 Chronicles 14:13, 2 Kings 7:6-7, b.Avodah Zara [Rashi] 28b, b.Chullin [Rashi] 126a, b.Niddah 4b, Deuteronomy 1:44 28:65-67, Ezekiel 21:12 21:17 21:20, Genesis 11:5, Isaiah 7:2 7:4 6:17, Jastrow 750b, Job 15:21-22, Joshua 2:9-11 5:1, Leviticus 26:7-8 2:17, mt.Hilchot Metamei Mishkav Umoshav 1:1 6:3, mt.Hilchot Parah Adumah 13:9, Philo De Praemiis et Poenis 148, Proverbs 4:1

[57] LXX *bondage*

[58] LXX *shaken*

[59] Leviticus 26:37 - 1 Samuel 14:15-16, b.Sanhedrin 27b, b.Sheviit 39a, Ein Yaakov Sanhedrin:27b, Ein Yaakov Shevuot:39a, Gates of Repentance 3.195, Isaiah 10:4, Jastrow 1111a, Jeremiah 13:10, Joshua 7:12-13, Judges 2:14 7:22, Numbers 14:42, Numbers.R 10:5, Song of Songs.R 7:14

[60] LXX *And brother shall disregard brother as in war, when none pursues; and ye shall not be able to withstand*

[61] Leviticus 26:38 - b.Makkot 24a, Deuteronomy 4:26-27 4:48 28:68, Ein Yaakov Makkot:24a, Guide for the Perplexed 1:30, Isaiah 3:13, Jeremiah 42:17-18 18:22 44:12-14 44:27-28

[62] Leviticus 26:39 - b.Sanhedrin 27b, Deuteronomy 5:9 28:65 6:1, Exodus 20:5 10:7, Ezekiel 4:17 6:9 18:2-3 18:19 20:43 24:23 9:10 12:31, Hosea 5:15, Jastrow 832a, Jeremiah 3:25 5:12 7:30, Lamentations 4:9, Matthew 23:35-36, Nehemiah 1:9, Numbers 14:18, Numbers.R 8:5, Psalms 32:3-4, Ralbag Wars 4:6, Romans 11:8-11:10, Zechariah 10:9

[63] Leviticus 26:40 - 1 John 1:8-10, 1 Kings 8:33-36 8:47, Daniel 9:3-20, Deuteronomy 4:29-4:31 30:1-30:3, Ezekiel 12:31, Gates of Repentance 1.040, Hosea 5:15-6:2, Jeremiah 3:12-3:15 31:19-31:21, Job 33:27-33:28, Joshua 7:19, Jubilees 1:22, Leviticus 2:21 2:24 26:27-26:28, Luke 15:18-15:19, mt.Hilchot Taaniot 5:1, Nehemiah 9:2-9:5, Numbers 5:7, Numbers.R 8:5, Proverbs 4:13, Psalms 32:5, Siman 121:1

אַף־אֲנִי אֵלֵךְ עִמָּם בְּקֶרִי וְהֵבֵאתִי
אֹתָם בְּאֶרֶץ אֹיְבֵיהֶם אוֹ־אָז יִכָּנַע
לְבָבָם הֶעָרֵל וְאָז יִרְצוּ אֶת־עֲוֺנָם

41[1] I also will walk contrary to them, and bring them into the land of their enemies; if by chance their uncircumcised hearts are humbled, and they paid the punishment of their iniquity;

וְזָכַרְתִּי אֶת־בְּרִיתִי יַעֲקוֹב וְאַף אֶת־
בְּרִיתִי יִצְחָק וְאַף אֶת־בְּרִיתִי אַבְרָהָם
אֶזְכֹּר וְהָאָרֶץ אֶזְכֹּר

42[2] Then I will remember My covenant with Jacob, and also My covenant with Isaac, and I will remember also My covenant with Abraham; and I will remember the land.

וְהָאָרֶץ תֵּעָזֵב מֵהֶם וְתִרֶץ אֶת־
שַׁבְּתֹתֶיהָ בָּהְשַׁמָּה מֵהֶם וְהֵם יִרְצוּ
אֶת־עֲוֺנָם יַעַן וּבְיַעַן בְּמִשְׁפָּטַי מָאָסוּ
וְאֶת־חֻקֹּתַי גָּעֲלָה נַפְשָׁם

43[3] For the land shall lie forsaken without them, and shall be repaid her sabbaths while she lies desolate without them; and they shall be paid the punishment for their iniquity; because, even because they rejected My ordinances, and their souls repelled My statutes.

וְאַף־גַּם־זֹאת בִּהְיוֹתָם בְּאֶרֶץ אֹיְבֵיהֶם
לֹא־מְאַסְתִּים וְלֹא־גְעַלְתִּים לְכַלֹּתָם
לְהָפֵר בְּרִיתִי אִתָּם כִּי אֲנִי יְהוָה
אֱלֹהֵיהֶם

44[4] And yet for all that, when they are in the land of their enemies, I will not reject them, nor will I abhor them to utterly destroy them, and to break My covenant with them; for I am the LORD their God.

---

[1] Leviticus 26:41 - 1 Kings 21:29, 1 Peter 5:5-6, 2 Chronicles 12:6-7 12:12 8:26 33:12-13 9:19 9:23, Acts 7:51, Colossians 2:11, Daniel 9:7-14 9:18-19, Deuteronomy 6:6, Ecclesiastes.R 1:36, Exodus 10:3, Ezekiel 6:9 20:43 20:7 20:9, Ezra 9:13 9:15, Galatians 5:6, James 4:6-9, Jeremiah 4:4 6:10 9:26-27, Lamentations.R 1:57, Luke 14:11 18:14, Matthew 23:12, mt.Hilchot Teshuvah 2:4 2:5, Nehemiah 9:33, Philippians 3:3, Psalms 39:10 51:4-5, Romans 2:28-29

[2] Leviticus 26:42 - b.Shabbat [Tosefot] 55a, Deuteronomy 4:31, Exodus 2:24 6:5, Exodus.R 44:9, Ezekiel 36:1-15 36:33-34, Genesis 9:16 22:15-18 2:5 4:15, Genesis.R 1:15, Guide for the Perplexed 3:51, Joel 2:18, Leviticus.R 36:1 36:5, Luke 2:12, Mas.Derek Eretz Zutta 1:16, Mas.Kallah Rabbati 3:25, Mekilta de R'Ishmael Pisha 1:26, Midrash Psalms 117:2, mt.Hilcnot Shofar Sukkah vLulav 3:9, Mussaf Rosh Hashanah, Psalms 85:2-3 10:45 16:23, Selichot, Siman 78:4, t.Kereitot 4:15, y.Sanhedrin 10:1, z.Acharei Mot 66b, z.Beshallach 53a, z.Shemot 9b, z.Vayera 117b 119a, z.Vayishlach 168a, z.Beshalach 200, z.Acharei Mot 182 183, z.Shemot 149 150 150, z.Vayechi 74, z.Vayera 22 476, z.Vayishlach 50

[3] Leviticus 26:43 - 1 Kings 8:46-48, 2 Chronicles 9:12 36:14-16, 2 Kings 17:7-17, Amos 5:10, b.Bava Batra 88b, b.Shabbat 33a, Daniel 9:7-9 9:14, Ein Yaakov Shabbat:33a, Hebrews 12:5-11, Isaiah 2:16, Jastrow 5853 732a 1054b 1378a 1437a, Jeremiah 7:20, Job 5:17 34:31-32, John 7:7 15:23-24, Lamentations.R Petichata DChakimei:21, Leviticus 2:15 2:30 26:34-35 2:41, Leviticus.R 34:9, Mekhilta de R'Shimon bar Yochai Bachodesh 48:1, Mekhilta de R'Ishmael Bahodesh 10:55, Midrash Psalms 94:2, Midrash Tanchuma Yitro 16, Psalms 50:15 50:17 119:67 119:71 119:75, Romans 8:7, Ruth.R 5:9, Sifre Devarim Vaetchanan 32, Zechariah 11:8

[4] Leviticus 26:44 - 2 Kings 13:23, 3 Maccabees 6:15, b.Megillah 11a, Chibbur Yafeh 19 {85a}, Deuteronomy 4:29-31, Ein Yaakov Megillah:11a, Esther.R 8:7 Petichata:4, Exodus.R 23:5, Ezekiel 14:22-123, Jastrow 723b, Jeremiah 14:21 6:11 33:20-21 9:26, Lamentations.R 1:57 5:20, Mas.Semachot 8:14, Midrash Psalms 53:2, Nehemiah 9:31, Pesikta de R'Kahana 16.11, Pesikta Rabbati 31:3, Psalms 89:34 94:14, Romans 11:2 11:26, Siman 78:4, z.Acharei Mot 78b, z.Bechukkotai 112a 115b, z.Haazinu 297b, z.Shemot 14a, z.Vayera 116a, z.Acharei Mot 64 179, z.Bechukotai 4 56 57, z.Ha'azinu 215 221, z.Korach 45, z.Shemot 236, z.Trumah 586
Leviticus 26:44-45 - Selichot

וְזָכַרְתִּי לָהֶם בְּרִית רִאשֹׁנִים אֲשֶׁר
הוֹצֵאתִי־אֹתָם מֵאֶרֶץ מִצְרַיִם לְעֵינֵי
הַגּוֹיִם לִהְיֹת לָהֶם לֵאלֹהִים אֲנִי יְהוָה

45[1] But for their sakes I will remember the covenant of their ancestors, whom I brought forth out of the land of the Egyptians in the sight of the nations, that I might be their God: I am the LORD.

אֵלֶּה הַחֻקִּים וְהַמִּשְׁפָּטִים וְהַתּוֹרֹת
אֲשֶׁר נָתַן יְהוָה בֵּינוֹ וּבֵין בְּנֵי יִשְׂרָאֵל
בְּהַר סִינַי בְּיַד־מֹשֶׁה

46[2] These are the statutes and ordinances and laws, which the LORD made between Him and the children of Israel in mount Sinai by the hand of Moses.

Bechukkotai – Chapter 27[3]

וַיְדַבֵּר יְהוָה אֶל־מֹשֶׁה לֵּאמֹר

1[4] And the LORD spoke to Moses, saying:

דַּבֵּר אֶל־בְּנֵי יִשְׂרָאֵל וְאָמַרְתָּ אֲלֵהֶם
אִישׁ כִּי יַפְלִא נֶדֶר בְּעֶרְכְּךָ נְפָשֹׁת
לַיהוָה

2[5] Speak to the children of Israel, and say to them: When a man shall clearly utter a vow of persons to the LORD, according to your valuation,

וְהָיָה עֶרְכְּךָ הַזָּכָר מִבֶּן עֶשְׂרִים שָׁנָה
וְעַד בֶּן־שִׁשִּׁים שָׁנָה וְהָיָה עֶרְכְּךָ
חֲמִשִּׁים שֶׁקֶל כֶּסֶף בְּשֶׁקֶל הַקֹּדֶשׁ

3[6] Then your valuation shall be for the male from twenty years old to sixty years old, even your valuation shall be fifty *shekels*[7] of silver, after the *shekel*[8] of the sanctuary.

---

[1] Leviticus 26:45 - 2 Corinthians 3:15-16, Exodus 2:24 6:8 19:5-6 20:2, Exodus.R 44:9, Ezekiel 20:9 20:14 20:22, Genesis 12:2 15:18 17:7-8, Kuzari 3.017, Leviticus 22:33 1:38, Luke 1:72-73, mt.Hilcnot Shofar Sukkah vLulav 3:9, Mussaf Rosh Hashanah, Psalms 98:2-3, Romans 11:12 11:23-26 11:28-29, z.Acharei Mot 78b, z.Vayetze 160a 278

[2] Leviticus 26:46 - Avot de R'Natan 1, Deuteronomy 6:1 12:1 13:5, Exodus.R 30:24, Genesis.R 12:2, Jastrow 427b, John 1:17, Leviticus 7:38 8:36 1:1 3:34, Mekilta de R'Ishmael Bahodesh 3:21, Numbers 4:37, Pesikta Rabbati 4:3, Psalms 77:21, Sifre.z Numbers Naso 6:23

[3] Midrash Proverbs 10, mt.Hilchot Arachim Vacharamim 1:2 8:2, mt.Hilchot Mamrim 4:2, mt.Hilchot Temurah 1:6

[4] Leviticus 27:1 - b.Ketubot 54a, b.Nedarim 20a
Leviticus 27:1-8 - mt.Hilchot Shevitat Yom Tov 7:11
Leviticus 27:1-9 - m.Beitzah 5:2
Leviticus 27:1-27 - mt.Hilchot Chametz uMatzah 23:14

[5] Leviticus 27:2 - 1 Samuel 1:11 1:28, b.Arachin [Rashi] 18a, b.Arachin [Rashi] 5ab, b.Arachin 2a 4ab 20a, b.Bava Metzia [Rashi] 71b 114a, b.Chagigah 10a, b.Ketubot [Rashi] 46a, b.Nazir 61ab 62a, b.Nedarim [Ran] 19b, b.Nedarim 20a, b.Pesachim 66b, b.Sanhedrin [Rashi] 25a, b.Temurah [Rashi] 2b, b.Temurah 3a, b.Zevachim [Tosefot] 45a, Deuteronomy 23:23-24, Ecclesiastes 5:5-6, Genesis 28:20-22, Jastrow 362a 746a, Judges 11:30-31 11:39, Leviticus.R 37:1, m.Arachin 1:1 1:3 5:3, m.Bikkurim 4:4, m.Sanhedrin 1:3, Mas.Soferim 10:7, Midrash Tanchuma Bechukkotai 4-6, mt.Hilchot Arachim Vacharamim 1:1 1:6 2:21, mt.Hilchot Nedarim 11:1, Numbers 6:2 21:2 6:5, y.Nazir 4:1
Leviticus 27:2-4 - Midrash Tanchuma Bechukkotai 5
Leviticus 27:2-8 - Commandment #523
Leviticus 27:2-13 - Jastrow 1118b
Leviticus 27:2-29 - m.Megillah 4:3

[6] Leviticus 27:3 - 2 Kings 12:5, b.Arachin [Rashi] 18b, b.Arachin 4b 7b 8a 19a, b.Bechorot 42a, b.Chullin [Tosefot] 22b, b.Nedarim 20a, b.Niddah 28b, b.Shabbat 136b, Esther.R 7:14, Exodus 6:13, Leviticus 5:15 6:6 3:14 3:25, Numbers 3:47 18:16, Philo De Specialibus Legibus II 33

[7] LXX *didrachms*
[8] LXX *standard*

וְאִם־נְקֵבָה הִוא וְהָיָה עֶרְכְּךָ שְׁלֹשִׁים שָׁקֶל

4[1] And if it is a female, then your valuation shall be thirty *shekels*[2].

וְאִם מִבֶּן־חָמֵשׁ שָׁנִים וְעַד בֶּן־עֶשְׂרִים שָׁנָה וְהָיָה עֶרְכְּךָ הַזָּכָר עֶשְׂרִים שְׁקָלִים וְלַנְּקֵבָה עֲשֶׂרֶת שְׁקָלִים

5[3] And if it is from five years old to twenty years old, then your valuation shall be for the male twenty *shekels*[4], and for the female ten *shekels*[5].

וְאִם מִבֶּן־חֹדֶשׁ וְעַד בֶּן־חָמֵשׁ שָׁנִים וְהָיָה עֶרְכְּךָ הַזָּכָר חֲמִשָּׁה שְׁקָלִים כָּסֶף וְלַנְּקֵבָה עֶרְכְּךָ שְׁלֹשֶׁת שְׁקָלִים כָּסֶף

6[6] And if it is from a month old to five years old, then your valuation shall be for the male five *shekels*[7]of silver, and for the female your valuation shall be three *shekels*[8]of silver.

וְאִם מִבֶּן־שִׁשִּׁים שָׁנָה וָמַעְלָה אִם־זָכָר וְהָיָה עֶרְכְּךָ חֲמִשָּׁה עָשָׂר שָׁקֶל וְלַנְּקֵבָה עֲשָׂרָה שְׁקָלִים

7[9] And if it be from sixty years old and upward: if it be a male, then your valuation shall be fifteen *shekels*[10], and for the female ten *shekels*[11].

וְאִם־מָךְ הוּא מֵעֶרְכֶּךָ וְהֶעֱמִידוֹ לִפְנֵי הַכֹּהֵן וְהֶעֱרִיךְ אֹתוֹ הַכֹּהֵן עַל־פִּי אֲשֶׁר תַּשִּׂיג יַד הַנֹּדֵר יַעֲרִיכֶנּוּ הַכֹּהֵן

8[12] But if he is too poor for your valuation, then he shall be set before the priest, and the priest shall value him; the priest shall value him according to the means of he who vowed.

וְאִם־בְּהֵמָה אֲשֶׁר יַקְרִיבוּ מִמֶּנָּה קָרְבָּן לַיהוָה כֹּל אֲשֶׁר יִתֵּן מִמֶּנּוּ לַיהוָה יִהְיֶה־קֹּדֶשׁ

9[13] And if it is a *beast*[14], from which men bring an offering to the LORD, all that any man gives of such to the LORD shall be holy.

---

[1] Leviticus 27:4 - b.Arachin 4b 19a, b.Chullin [Tosefot] 22b, b.Nedarim 20a, b.Niddah 28b, b.Shabbat 136b, Matthew 2:15 27:9-10, Zechariah 11:12-13

[2] LXX *didrachms*

[3] Leviticus 27:5 - b.Arachin 18ab [Rashi] 18a, b.Nedarim 20a, b.Niddah [Rashi] 48a, m.Arachin 4:4 Leviticus 27:5-22 - 4QLev-Numa

[4] LXX *didrachms*

[5] LXX *didrachms*

[6] Leviticus 27:6 - .Arachin 18b [Rashi] 5a, b.Chullin [Rashi] 2a, b.Nedarim 20a, b.Sanhedrin [Rashi] 88a, Jastrow 1119a, Numbers 3:40-43 18:14-16

[7] LXX *didrachms*

[8] LXX *didrachms*

[9] Leviticus 27:7 - b.Arachin [Rashi] 4b, b.Arachin 18ab, b.Bava Batra 121b, b.Nedarim 20a, b.Niddah [Rashi] 48a, Jastrow 1119a, m.Arachin 4:4, Psalms 90:10

[10] LXX *didrachms*

[11] LXX here and after *didrachms*

[12] Leviticus 27:8 - 2 Corinthians 8:12, b.Arachin 4ab 7b 14ab 24a [Tosefot] 20a, b.Bava Metzia [Rashi] 113b, b.Bava Metzia 114a, b.Bechorot [Rashi] 11a, b.Kiddushin [Rashi] 14a, b.Megillah 11a, b.Nedarim 20a, b.Sanhedrin [Rashi] 2a 14b, b.Taanit 7b, Ein Yaakov Megillah 11a, Ein Yaakov Taanit 7b, Jastrow 369b 773a 782a 9583, Jeremiah 5:7, Leviticus 5:7 5:11 12:8 14:21-22, Luke 21:1-4, m.Arachin 4:1, Mark 14:7, mt.Hilchot Arachim Vacharamim 2:21 3:2-3, t.Arachin 2:15

[13] Leviticus 27:9 - b.Arachin 5a, b.Chullin [Rashi] 69b, b.Chullin 69b, b.Temurah 10b 13a 32b, b.Yoma [Tosefot] 50b, Guide for the Perplexed 3:46, mt.Hilchot Arachim Vacharamim 5:7, mt.Hilchot Maaseh haKorbanot 15:2, z.Pinchas 761

Leviticus 27:9-10 - mt.Hilchot Temurah 1:11

Leviticus 27:9-11 - Pesikta Rabbati 14:10

[14] LXX *cattle*

לֹא יַחֲלִיפֶ֫נּוּ וְלֹא־יָמִיר אֹת֛וֹ ט֥וֹב בְּרָ֖ע אוֹ־רַ֣ע בְּט֑וֹב וְאִם־הָמֵ֨ר יָמִ֤יר בְּהֵמָה֙ בִּבְהֵמָ֔ה וְהָיָה־ה֥וּא וּתְמוּרָת֖וֹ יִֽהְיֶה־קֹּֽדֶשׁ

וְאִם֙ כָּל־בְּהֵמָ֣ה טְמֵאָ֔ה אֲשֶׁ֡ר לֹא־יַקְרִ֙יבוּ מִמֶּ֥נָּה קָרְבָּ֖ן לַֽיהוָ֑ה וְהֶֽעֱמִ֥יד אֶת־הַבְּהֵמָ֖ה לִפְנֵ֥י הַכֹּהֵֽן

וְהֶעֱרִ֤יךְ הַכֹּהֵן֙ אֹתָ֔הּ בֵּ֥ין ט֖וֹב וּבֵ֣ין רָ֑ע כְּעֶרְכְּךָ֥ הַכֹּהֵ֖ן כֵּ֥ן יִהְיֶֽה

וְאִם־גָּאֹ֖ל יִגְאָלֶ֑נָּה וְיָסַ֥ף חֲמִישִׁת֖וֹ עַל־עֶרְכֶּֽךָ

וְאִ֗ישׁ כִּֽי־יַקְדִּ֨שׁ אֶת־בֵּית֥וֹ קֹ֨דֶשׁ֙ לַֽיהוָ֔ה וְהֶעֱרִיכוֹ֙ הַכֹּהֵ֔ן בֵּ֥ין ט֖וֹב וּבֵ֣ין רָ֑ע כַּאֲשֶׁ֨ר יַעֲרִ֥יךְ אֹת֛וֹ הַכֹּהֵ֖ן כֵּ֥ן יָקֽוּם

10[1] He shall not alter it, nor change it, a good for a bad, or a bad for a good; and if he shall change any beast for beast, then both it and the one for which it is changed shall be holy.

11[2] And if it is an unclean beast, of which they may not bring as an offering to the LORD, then he shall set the beast before the priest.

12[3] And the priest shall value it, whether it is good or bad; as you, the priest, values it, so shall it be.

13[4] But if he will indeed redeem it, then he shall add its fifth part to your valuation.

14[5] And when a man shall sanctify his house to be holy to the LORD, then the priest shall value it, whether it is good or bad; as the priest shall value it, so shall it stand.

---

[1] Leviticus 27:10 - b.Arachin 2ab, b.Bava Metzia 47a [Rashi] 91a [Tosefot] 55a, b.Bechorot 14b 60a, b.Chullin 2a 69a [Rashi] 130a [Tosefot] 81a, b.Horayot [Rashi] 6b, b.Makkot [Tosefot] 10a, b.Meilah [Rashi] 10b, b.Menachot 93a [Rashi] 77b 81a [Tosefot] 51b, b.Sanhedrin [Tosefot] 14a, b.Temurah 2ab 3a 5b 7b 9a 13a [Rashi] 4b 7a 10b 16b 14a 20b 16a, b.Yevamot [Rashi] 84a, b.Yoma [Rashi] 50ab, b.Zevachim 9a 37b [Rashi] 6a 49a, Commandment #524 #525, Guide for the Perplexed 3:41, James 1:8, Jastrow 1676a, Leviticus 27:15-33, m.Bechorot 2:2 9:8, m.Chullin 2:10, m.Nazir 5:1, m.Temurah 1:2, mt.Hilchot Sanhedrin vHainshin Hameurim Lahem 19:4, mt.Hilchot Temurah 1:1 1:14-15 1:19 2:1 3:5 4:13, Pesikta Rabbati 29/30B:4 40:6, t.Makkot 5:5 5:10, z.Bo 33a, z.Bo 13
[2] Leviticus 27:11 - 4Q251 9 1-2a, b.Arachin [Rashi] 6b, b.Bechorot [Rashi] 14a 15a 31b, b.Bechorot 37b, b.Chullin [Rashi] 30a 84a 130a, b.Menachot 1b 101a, b.Sanhedrin [Rashi] 14b, b.Shekalim [Taklin Chadatin] 12b, b.Shekalim 13a, b.Sheviit [Rashi] 10b 11b, b.Temurah [Rashi] 16a, b.Temurah 33a, Deuteronomy 23:20, Jastrow 360b, Malachi 1:14, mt.Hilchot Arachim Vacharamim 5:1 5:9, mt.Hilchot Issurei Mizbeiach 1:10 6:4, mt.Hilchot Kilayim 9:11, y.Shekalim 4:4, z.Bo 33a
Leviticus 27:11-13 - Commandment #526, Commandment #527
Leviticus 27:11-19 - 11Qpaleol.eva
[3] Leviticus 27:12 - b.Arachin [Rashi] 6b, b.Bechorot [Rashi] 14a 15a 31b, b.Bechorot 14b, b.Chullin [Rashi] 30a 84a, b.Sanhedrin [Rashi] 14b, b.Shekalim [Taklin Chadatin] 12b, b.Shekalim 13a, b.Temurah 33ab, mt.Hilchot Arachim Vacharamim 5:9, mt.Hilchot Issurei Mizbeiach 6:4, y.Shekalim 4:4, z.Bo 33a
[4] Leviticus 27:13 - b.Arachin 14b, b.Sanhedrin [Rashi] 14b, b.Zevachim 6a, Guide for the Perplexed 3:46, Jastrow 1137a, Leviticus 5:16 6:4-5 22:14 3:10 3:15 3:19, m.Maaser Sheni 4:3, mt.Hilchot Arachim Vacharamim 7:4, mt.Hilchot Issurei Mizbeiach 6:5, t.Arachin 4:28
[5] Leviticus 27:14 - b.Arachin [Tosefot] 15a, b.Arachin 21a 25b, b.Avodah Zara 63a, b.Bava Batra [Rashi] 88a 133b, b.Bava Kamma 68b 69b, b.Bava Metzia [Rashi] 71b, b.Bava Metzia 6a, b.Bechorot [Rashi] 50b, b.Bechorot 50b, b.Chullin 139a, b.Pesachim [Rashi] 30b, b.Sanhedrin [Rashi] 14a, b.Shekalim 12a, b.Temurah 9a 29b, Josephus Antiquities 4.8.32, Leviticus 25:29-25:31 3:21, m.Sanhedrin 1:3 10:6, mt.Hilchot Arachim Vacharamim 6:21, Numbers 18:14, Psalms 101:2-101:7, y.Shekalim 4:4
Leviticus 27:14-24 - Jastrow 320b

וְאִם־הַמַּקְדִּישׁ יִגְאַל אֶת־בֵּיתוֹ וְיָסַף
חֲמִישִׁית כֶּסֶף־עֶרְכְּךָ עָלָיו וְהָיָה לוֹ

15[1] And if he who sanctified it will redeem his house, then he shall add the fifth part of the money of your valuation to it, and it shall be his.

וְאִם ׀ מִשְּׂדֵה אֲחֻזָּתוֹ יַקְדִּישׁ אִישׁ
לַיהוָֹה וְהָיָה עֶרְכְּךָ לְפִי זַרְעוֹ זֶרַע
חֹמֶר שְׂעֹרִים בַּחֲמִשִּׁים שֶׁקֶל כָּסֶף

16[2] And if a man shall sanctify to the LORD part of the field of his possession, then your valuation shall be according to its sowing; the sowing of a chomer of barley shall be valued at fifty *shekels*[3] of silver.

אִם־מִשְּׁנַת הַיֹּבֵל יַקְדִּישׁ שָׂדֵהוּ
כְּעֶרְכְּךָ יָקוּם

17[4] If he sanctifies his field from the year of jubilee, according to your valuation it shall stand.

וְאִם־אַחַר הַיֹּבֵל יַקְדִּישׁ שָׂדֵהוּ וְחִשַּׁב־
לוֹ הַכֹּהֵן אֶת־הַכֶּסֶף עַל־פִּי הַשָּׁנִים
הַנּוֹתָרֹת עַד שְׁנַת הַיֹּבֵל וְנִגְרַע
מֵעֶרְכֶּךָ

18[5] But if he should sanctify his field after the jubilee, then the priest shall reckon to him the money according to the years that remain until the year of jubilee, and *an abatement shall be made from your valuation*[6].

וְאִם־גָּאֹל יִגְאַל אֶת־הַשָּׂדֶה הַמַּקְדִּישׁ
אֹתוֹ וְיָסַף חֲמִשִׁית כֶּסֶף־עֶרְכְּךָ עָלָיו
וְקָם לוֹ

19[7] And if he who sanctified the field will indeed redeem it, then he shall add the fifth part of the money of your valuation to it, and it shall be given to him.

---

[1] Leviticus 27:15 - b.Arachin 16a, b.Bava Metzia [Tosefot] 54a, b.Bava Metzia 54b, b.Bechorot [Rashi] 4b 11a 32b, b.Bechorot 41b, b.Menachot [Rashi] 82a, b.Menachot [Tosefot] 34b, b.Nedarim [Rashi] 36b, b.Shekalim 12a, b.Temurah 2b 9b 10a, b.Yoma [Rashi] 50b, b.Zevachim [Rashi] 6a, Guide for the Perplexed 3:46, Leviticus 3:13, mt.Hilchot Arachim Vacharamim 7:4, mt.Hilchot Temurah 4:13, y.Shekalim 4:4

[2] Leviticus 27:16 - Acts 4:34-37 5:4, b.Arachin [Rashi] 16a, b.Arachin 14ab 25a, b.Bava Batra [Rashi] 72ab 102b, b.Bava Batra 71a 103a, b.Bava Metzia [Rashi] 16a, b.Kiddushin 61a, Ezekiel 45:11-14, Hosea 3:2, Isaiah 5:10, Jastrow 1524a, m.Arachin 3:1-2 7:1 7:5, Mas.Soferim 10:7, mt.Hilchot Arachim Vacharamim 4:3

Leviticus 27:16-21 - Mas.Abadim 1:1, Mas.Kallah Rabbati 8:9

Leviticus 27:16-24 - Commandment #528

[3] LXX here and after *didrachms*

[4] Leviticus 27:17 - b.Arachin [Rashi] 24a, b.Arachin 18a 24b, b.Bava Batra [Rashi] 103a, b.Bava Batra [Tosefot] 102b, b.Bava Metzia [Rashi] 16a, mt.Hilchot Arachim Vacharamim 3:1 4:10

Leviticus 27:17-24 - z.Yitro 85b

[5] Leviticus 27:18 - b.Arachin [Rashi] 24a, b.Arachin 14b 24b 25ab, b.Bava Batra [Rashbam] 103a, b.Bava Metzia [Rashi] 16a, b.Sanhedrin [Rashi] 14b, b.Shabbat 77b, Genesis.R 4:5 13:15, Jastrow 242b 271b, Leviticus 25:15-16 1:27 25:51-52, Leviticus.R 15:1, Mas.Kallah Rabbati 8:9, mt.Hilchot Arachim Vacharamim 4:7, mt.Hilchot Shemitah vYovel 11:6, t.Arachin 4:8-9, y.Berachot 9:2, y.Kiddushin 1:2, y.Taanit 1:3

[6] LXX *it shall be deducted as an equivalent from his full valuation*

[7] Leviticus 27:19 - b.Arachin [Rashi] 14a 25a, b.Arachin 30b 33a, b.Bava Batra 103a, b.Bava Metzia [Rashi] 55b 16a, b.Bava Metzia 54a, b.Bechorot [Rashi] 13b, b.Bechorot 11a 50b, b.Berachot 47b, b.Eruvin [Rashi] 31b, b.Gittin [Rashi] 52a, b.Kiddushin 5a 11b 20b 29a, b.Menachot [Rashi] 90a 83a, b.Menachot [Tosefot] 14b, b.Pesachim 35b, b.Sanhedrin [Rashi] 14b, b.Shabbat [Tosefot] 128a, b.Zevachim [Rashi] 6a, Leviticus 3:13, m.Arachin 3:2, m.Bava Metzia 4:8, mt.Hilchot Arachim Vacharamim 4:5 7:1, mt.Hilchot Maaser Sheni vneta Revai 8:7, mt.Hilchot Mechirah 9:2, y.Kiddushin 1:6

וְאִם־גָּאֹל יִגְאַל אִישׁ מִמַּעַשְׂרוֹ חֲמִשִׁיתוֹ יֹסֵף עָלָיו

31[1] And if a man will redeem something of his tithe, he shall add to it its fifth part[2].

וְכָל־מַעְשַׂר בָּקָר וָצֹאן כֹּל אֲשֶׁר־יַעֲבֹר תַּחַת הַשָּׁבֶט הָעֲשִׂירִי יִהְיֶה־קֹּדֶשׁ לַיהוָה

32[3] And all the tithe of the herd or the flock, whatever passes under the rod, the tenth shall be holy to the LORD.

לֹא יְבַקֵּר בֵּין־טוֹב לָרַע וְלֹא יְמִירֶנּוּ וְאִם־הָמֵר יְמִירֶנּוּ וְהָיָה־הוּא וּתְמוּרָתוֹ יִהְיֶה־קֹּדֶשׁ לֹא יִגָּאֵל

33[4] He shall not inquire whether it is good or bad, nor shall he change it; and if he changes it at all, then both it and that for which it is changed shall be holy; it shall not be redeemed.

אֵלֶּה הַמִּצְוֹת אֲשֶׁר צִוָּה יְהוָה אֶת־מֹשֶׁה אֶל־בְּנֵי יִשְׂרָאֵל בְּהַר סִינָי

34[5] These are the commandments the LORD commanded Moses for the children of Israel in mount Sinai.

Hazak! Hazak, venit'chazek!
Be strong! Be strong and let us be strengthened!

---

[1] Leviticus 27:31 - 4Q270 9 ii 10, 4Q270 frag 2 2.10, b.Arachin [Rashi] 27b, b.Bava Kamma 69b, b.Bava Metzia [Rashi] 45b 46a 52b 54b 55b, b.Bava Metzia 53b, b.Kiddushin [Rashi] 54b, b.Menachot [Rashi] 82a, m.Demai 1:2, mt.Hilchot Beit HaBechirah 4:1, mt.Hilchot Maaser Sheni vneta Revai 5:1 5:4, mt.Hilchot Matnot Aniyim 6:3, t.Sheviit 7:7, y.Bava Metzia 4:5, y.Maaser Sheni 4:6 5:2, y.Peah 7:5

[2] LXX adds *and it shall be his*

[3] Leviticus 27:32 - 4QMMT B 62-64, b.Bava Kamma 78a, b.Bava Metzia [Rashi] 6b, b.Bava Metzia 7a, b.Bechorot 12a 14b 21b 32a 53a-54b 57a 58b-60b, b.Chullin [Rashi] 69b 114a 130a 133b, b.Chullin 136b, b.Horayot [Rashi] 13b, b.Meilah [Rashi] 13a, b.Menachot [Tosefot] 55a, b.Menachot 6a, b.Niddah [Tosefot] 28a 40a, b.Temurah [Rashi] 5b 13b, b.Temurah 5b 18b 21a 29a, b.Zevachim [Tosefot] 56b 114b, b.Zevachim 9a 37b, Bahir 103, Commandment #410, Ezekiel 20:37, Jastrow 860a, Jeremiah 9:13, Jubilees 32:15, Liber Antiquitatum Biblicarum 5:4, m.Bechorot 2:2 9:1, m.Chagigah 1:4, m.Chullin 1:7 2:10, m.Maaser Sheni 1:2, m.Meilah 3:6, m.Nazir 5:3, m.Nedarim 2:4, m.Rosh Hashanah 1:1, m.Shekalim 8:8, m.Zevachim 1:2 5:8, Mekhilta de R'Shimon bar Yochai Pisha 19:2, Mekilta de R'Ishmael Nezikin 7:52, Mekilta de R'Ishmael Pisha 18:23, Micah 7:14, Midrash Tanchuma Bo 12, mt.Hilchot Bechorot 6:1 7:1 7:4, mt.Hilchot Chametz uMatzah 23:14, mt.Hilchot Melachim uMichamoteihem 4:7, mt.Hilchot Nedarim 1:13, Philo De Congressu Quaerendae Eruditionis Gratia 94, Philo De Posteritate Caini 95, Pirkei de R'Eliezer 37, Sifre Devarim Ekev 41, Sifre Devarim Reeh 105, Tanya Kuntress Acharon §05, y.Nazir 5:2 Leviticus 27:32-33 - Commandment #411

[4] Leviticus 27:33 - b.Bava Kamma 13a, b.Bava Metzia [Tosefot] 47a, b.Bava Metzia 47a, b.Bechorot [Rashi] 14a 21b 31a 32b 58b, b.Bechorot 14b 31b 32ab 36b, b.Bechorot 53b 57a, b.Chullin [Rashi] 69b 133b 137a, b.Nedarim 69b, b.Temurah [Tosefot] 14b, b.Temurah 5b 13a 14a, b.Yoma [Rashi] 51a, b.Zevachim [Rashi] 45a 71b, b.Zevachim 6a 9a, Ecclesiastes.R 8:4, Guide for the Perplexed 3:46, Jastrow 748a, Leviticus 3:10, m.Temurah 1:6, mt.Hilchot Bechorot 6:5, mt.Hilchot Pesulei haMikdashim 6:10, mt.Hilchot Temurah 1:1 1:12, Philo Legum Allegoriae III 110, y.Kiddushin 2:1, y.Maaser Sheni 1:1, y.Nazir 2:1, y.Rosh Hashanah 1:1

[5] Leviticus 27:34 - b.Megillah 2b, b.Menachot [Rashi] 30a, b.Sanhedrin [Rashi] 53b, b.Shabbat 41a, b.Sheviit [Rashi] 35a, b.Yevamot [Tosefot] 71b, b.Yevamot 20a, b.Yoma 80a, Deuteronomy 4:5 4:45, Ein Yaakov Megillah:2b, Ein Yaakov Temurah 16a, Galatians 4:24-25, Hebrews 12:18-25, Jastrow 824a, John 1:17, Leviticus 2:46, Midrash Tanchuma Shelach 14, mt.Hilchot Arachim Vacharamim 6:7, Numbers 1:1, Ruth.R 4:5, y.Megillah 1:5, y.Shabbat 13:3, y.Yevamot 2:4, z.Pekudei 236b, z.Pekudei 310, z.Vayechi 382